THE SOCIAL WORK SKILLS WORKBOOK

Seventh Edition

Barry R. Cournoyer
Emeritus Professor of Social Work
Indiana University

BROOKS/COLE
CENGAGE Learning·

Australia • Brazil • Japan • Korea • Mexico • Singapore • Spain • United Kingdom • United States

The Social Work Skills Workbook,
Seventh Edition
Barry R. Cournoyer

Executive Editor: Mark Kerr

Senior Acquiring Sponsoring Editor:
Seth Dobrin

Assistant Editor: Naomi Dreyer

Editorial Assistant: Coco Bator

Managing Development Editor:
Elizabeth Momb

Senior Brand Manager: Elisabeth Rhoden

Senior Market Development Manager:
Kara Kindstrom

Manufacturing Planner: Judy Inouye

Rights Acquisitions Specialist:
Thomas McDonough

Design, Production Services, and Composition:
PreMediaGlobal

Cover Image: © Thinkstock, © DVARG

For product information and technology assistance, contact us at
Cengage Learning Customer & Sales Support, 1-800-354-9706.
For permission to use material from this text or product,
submit all requests online at **www.cengage.com/permissions.**
Further permissions questions can be e-mailed to
permissionrequest@cengage.com

Library of Congress Control Number: 2013930603

ISBN-13: 978-1-285-17719-9

ISBN-10: 1-285-17719-3

Brooks/Cole
20 Davis Drive
Belmont, CA 94002-3098
USA

Cengage Learning is a leading provider of customized learning solutions with office locations around the globe, including Singapore, the United Kingdom, Australia, Mexico, Brazil, and Japan. Locate your local office at **www.cengage.com/global.**

Cengage Learning products are represented in Canada by Nelson Education, Ltd.

To learn more about Brooks/Cole, visit **www.cengage.com/brookscole**

Purchase any of our products at your local college store or at our preferred online store **www.cengagebrain.com.**

Printed in the United States of America
2 3 4 5 6 7 17 16 15 14 13

TABLE OF CONTENTS

Part I Professionalism

CHAPTER 1   Introduction   3

CHAPTER 2   Introduction to Professionalism   27

CHAPTER 3   Critical Thinking, Scientific Inquiry, and Career-Long Learning   55

CHAPTER 4   Valuing Diversity, Advancing Human Rights and Social Justice, and Promoting Social Well-Being through Policy Practice   107

CHAPTER 5   Ethical Decision Making   143

CHAPTER 6 Talking and Listening—The Basic Interpersonal Skills   181

CHAPTER 7 Preparing   221

CHAPTER 8 Beginning   245

CHAPTER 11 Contracting 389

CHAPTER 12 Working and Evaluating 425

CHAPTER 13 Ending 477

PREFACE

The original impetus for creating *The Social Work Skills Workbook* began with observations and, yes, complaints from students that social work professors and their textbooks tend to "talk about practice rather than help us learn what to do and how to do it." This was a typical comment: "In the classroom, the professors talk at such abstract levels that when I'm with clients, I don't really know what I'm supposed to do." Clearly, we needed more practical and applied learning materials.

The seventh edition of *The Social Work Skills Workbook* continues to address these needs and provides opportunities for learners to gain proficiency in the essential social work skills. This edition maintains the general organizational structure of earlier versions. However, several changes enhance its congruence with the mission of the profession and the nature and scope of contemporary social work practice; current and anticipated socioeconomic and cultural conditions; and emerging research findings. This edition continues to reflect an integration of the social work skills and the competencies[1] identified in the current Educational Policy and Accreditation Standards (EPAS) of the Council on Social Work Education (CSWE). Many of the skills and abilities tested in the social work licensing examinations[2] sponsored by the Association of Social Work Boards (ASWB) are also addressed. The skills workbook, however, is not designed as a study guide for either the CSWE endorsed EPAS competencies or the ASWB sponsored licensing examinations. Rather, the skills are consistent with the purposes of the social work profession, its core values and ethics, and findings from empirical research studies.

Each social work skill (see Appendix 16) is associated with one or more of the core competencies, the practice knowledge, and the practice behaviors[3] identified in the EPAS (see Appendix 17). In addition, the Social Work Skills Test (see Appendix 2) may be used to advance individual student learning or for social work program evaluation. Students may complete the skills test at the beginning of a course or program of study and then again at the end to provide a direct indication of learning progress. Professors may find students' responses to the first test helpful in determining which skills to emphasize or reinforce during the learning experience.

The perspective adopted in this edition is also influenced by additional factors that profoundly affect individuals, families, and communities throughout North America and the world. These include the devastating consequences of "the Great Recession" (Peck, 2011) and continued

---

[1] Appendix 17 contains a table of social work skills that support the core EPAS competencies. Appendix 18 contains an instrument titled "Self-Appraisal of Proficiency in the EPAS Core Competencies, Practice Knowledge, and Practice Behaviors."

2 Appendices 19 and 20 contain instruments titled "Self-Appraisal of Proficiency in the ASWB Knowledge, Skills, and Abilities" for the Bachelor's and Master's level examinations, respectively.

3 Note: In addition to the 41 practice behaviors identified in the 2008 EPAS, several of the 28 aspects of practice knowledge also involve application and, in effect, constitute practice behaviors. For ease of identification, we classify the 41 practice behaviors (PBs) as PB01 through PB41 and the 28 aspects of practice knowledge (PK) as PK01 through PK28.

high levels of unemployment (Shierholz, 2012, Feb. 3), underemployment, and homelessness—including families and children who lack housing (Homelessness Research Institute, 2012, January); rising income and wealth inequality, diminished opportunity, and decreasing socioeconomic mobility (Organisation for Economic Co-operation and Development, 2011); rising health care costs (Klein, 2012, March 2); increased expense and decreased value of some forms of higher education (Arum & Roksa, 2011); apparently increasing self-admiration, narcissism, and materialism (Campbell, Bush, Brunell, & Shelton, 2005; Twenge, 2006; Twenge & Campbell, 2009); pervasive incivility toward and intolerance of "others" (Bey, 2012, March 2); high and disproportionate rates of incarceration—especially among racial and ethnic minority groups (Alexander, 2010; Henrichson & Delaney, 2012, January); extensive and growing medicalization of personal and social problems (Szasz, 2007; Whitaker, 2010); deleterious effects of increasing rates of climate and oceanic change (Hönisch et al., 2012); continued adoption of ideological dogma, violence, and oppression as "acceptable" means to control and dominate people—especially women and children; widespread distribution of political and commercial propaganda that distort or oversimplify complex issues (Larsen, 2006; Postman, 1985); and an apparent willingness among many to accept superstitious or opinionated statements and logically irrational arguments as if they were true and factually correct (Jacoby, 2008).

More hopeful phenomena include nonviolent, democratic movements against oppressive regimes and social action against other forms of injustice; evidence of general trends toward gradually decreasing levels of worldwide violence (Pinker, 2011); potential for greater earthly "abundance" in the future (Diamandis & Kotler, 2012); and a growing body of research findings that confirm and illuminate the powerful influence of situational and contextual factors in motivating human behavior and understanding human experience (DeSteno & Valdesolo, 2011; Sommers, 2011). Consistent with social work's "person-in-environment" perspective, studies that highlight the "power of context" serve to inform the selection of case examples and exercises included in this edition.

This edition reflects increased emphasis on social advocacy and political action; and maintains its focus upon scientific inquiry, critical thought, and the role of nomothetic[4] and ideographic[5] research-based knowledge in collaborative decision making with clients. Such emphases reflect current socioeconomic conditions as well as contemporary views of evidence-based and outcome-informed practice. They also reflect expectations outlined in the EPAS and the profession's codes of ethics. Clearly, social workers must be guided by practice-relevant, nomothetic research findings. However, we must also engage in ideographic evaluation of our own work with individuals, families, groups, organizations, communities, and societies. Interventions and activities that help many or even most people sometimes prove to be ineffective with a particular client system. Therefore, we have to evaluate client outcomes throughout the course of our efforts to determine the impact of our collaborative efforts with client systems. Indeed, systematic evaluation of service impact represents a hallmark of professionalism and, when evaluative feedback is shared and discussed with clients, powerfully contributes to favorable outcomes (Anker, Duncan, & Sparks, 2009; Lambert, 2010b; Miller et al., 2006).

---

[4] The term "nomothetic" refers to research studies that relate to or contribute to general scientific knowledge. In our context, the term applies to research studies that involve groups of participants, often randomly selected and sometimes compared with members of control groups, so that the results or findings may be generalized to a larger population.
[5] The term "ideographic" (or idiographic) refers to studies that pertain to scientific knowledge of a particular or specific kind. In our context, ideographic studies often involve the systematic evaluation of a client system's progress toward problem resolution or goal attainment. In social work, the most common forms of ideographic research are single-system or N-1 studies.

Especially when combined with lack of critical thought, insufficient knowledge about safe and effective services can result in damage to individuals, families, groups, organizations, communities, and societies. Social workers who think in a naïve, thoughtless, ignorant, egocentric, ethnocentric, xenophobic, or superstitious manner are frequently ineffective and sometimes harmful to others. During an era when personal opinions, popular myths, and "truthiness" are commonly confused with facts, truth, and validity; and ideology is frequently presented as "knowledge," scientific inquiry and critical thought are vitally important. We desperately need scholarly, rational, reflective, and indeed skeptical people in contemporary society to recognize unsubstantiated claims, falsehoods, shams, scams, cons, and quackery—many of which are inflicted upon desperate and highly vulnerable populations. As professional helpers who often serve people and groups on the margins of society, social workers must be adept at scientific inquiry, critical thinking, and career-long learning—not only for our own welfare but also for the well-being of our clients and communities. Given their importance for contemporary practice, many of the end-of-chapter summary exercises involve scientific inquiry, critical thinking, and career-long learning activities.

This edition of *The Social Work Skills Workbook* may be used (1) as the primary text for social work practice and social work skills laboratory courses (which might be titled "interviewing skills," "interpersonal skills," "professional skills," "interactional skills," "interpersonal communication skills," "microskills," "practice skills," or "helping skills" labs); (2) as a text for introductory, "immersion" or socialization seminars or modules; (3) as a workbook for social work practice courses; (4) by social work students and field instructors during practicum experiences; and (5) by professional social workers seeking to enhance their professionalism and their proficiency in the essential social work skills.

Social work programs may use the skills workbook in two courses or over two terms in their BSW or MSW foundation curriculums. This approach allows students additional time to complete and reflect upon the numerous skill-building exercises, and to refine materials included within their Social Work Skills Learning Portfolios (see Appendix 1) that result from completion of chapter exercises. To facilitate such an option, this edition is organized into two major parts. *Part I: Professionalism* introduces students to the values, culture, and context of social work. It contains an introduction and four chapters that address the dimensions and characteristics of professionalism: (1) integrity, knowledge and self-efficacy, self-understanding and self-control, and social support; (2) critical thinking, scientific inquiry, and career-long learning; (3) valuing diversity and difference, advancing human rights and social justice, and promoting social well-being through policy practice; and (4) ethical decision making. The exercises contained in Part I emphasize these aspects of professionalism and involve scientific inquiry, critical thought and reflection, independent learning, and preparation of several written documents.

Part II: Social Work Skills emphasizes skills needed for contemporary practice. Part II begins with a review of the basic skills of talking and listening followed by chapters that address social work skills associated with the seven phases of practice: (1) preparing, (2) beginning, (3) exploring, (4) assessing, (5) contracting, (6) working and evaluating, and (7) ending. The exercises in Part II are competency-based and focus on the development of proficiency in the social work skills.

Numerous appendices appear at the conclusion of the book. Some relate to specific learning exercises and others complement content addressed in the chapters. Several, such as the Social Work Skills Test, encourage assessment as a means to promote learning.

Bachelor of Social Work (BSW) or Master of Social Work (MSW) programs may use individual students' or student cohorts' responses to Social Work Skills Test items as evidence of growth in learning. When students' results on skills test items are aggregated in pre- and posttest form, they may be used to help meet CSWE accreditation standards. The EPAS require programs to assess students' progress toward the achievement of each core competency.

Furthermore, programs must use the results of such assessments to improve program quality and educational outcomes. Typically, social work programs expect their students to demonstrate proficiency in most or all of the social work skills reflected in this book. Indeed, the skills presented here support student learning in the core EPAS competencies, the 28 practice knowledge (PK) areas, and the 41 practice behaviors (PB) required for BSW or MSW program accreditation. Because each of the social work skills supports one or more of the core EPAS competencies, Social Work Skills Test items—especially when used in "before" and "after" fashion—can contribute much relevant data for student learning outcome assessment of individual learners, student cohorts, and the program as a whole. Furthermore, because many of the exercises result in word-processed documents for inclusion in their Social Work Skills Learning Portfolios, learners naturally create additional relevant information for potential use in outcome assessment by the learners themselves, by their professors or advisers, and by the organizations or units that sponsor the educational program. Indeed, when collated and aggregated, responses to Social Work Skills Test items and to the numerous self-appraisal exercises contained in *The Social Work Skills Workbook*, and documents produced for the Social Work Skills Learning Portfolio can help social work programs evaluate progress toward the achievement of their educational goals, objectives, and core competencies as part of their effort to improve outcomes and meet CSWE accreditation standards.

As described in Appendix 1, the Social Work Skills Learning Portfolio is essentially a collection of selected products prepared during the completion of *The Social Work Skills Workbook*. The documents are stored in a designated portion of an electronic storage medium such as a computer hard drive or removable disk. Prepared in word-processed format, the learning portfolio provides ready access to documentary evidence of progress in developing proficiency in the social work skills. The Social Work Skills Learning Portfolio may be used for self-assessment purposes or by professors to evaluate individual student learning. Social work schools and departments may use the portfolios of student cohorts (or samples thereof) to evaluate the general effectiveness of a course or educational program. Educators may use the assessments and evaluations *formatively* to identify additional individual or group learning needs, or *summatively* to determine a rank, status, or grade.

Some skill-building exercises involve resources available through the Internet whereas others require personal reflection, self-analysis, or some form of critical thinking and scholarly inquiry. Certain exercises may provoke discomfort as learners question or challenge strongly held personal beliefs, attitudes, and ideologies. Indeed, I hope that you do feel some discomfort—enough to stimulate you to think skeptically and critically about your own ideas and those of others; and, perhaps, to change your mind about some things you once assumed to be true. As social workers, we routinely face extraordinarily difficult and highly stressful situations that challenge our personal views, values, and expectations. We must learn to cope with and manage considerable individual, interpersonal, social, and intellectual discomfort so that we can maintain primary focus on our clients' needs and goals, and on our own professional responsibilities.

I encourage you to use the exercises in this book to explore and indeed question your assumptions about humans and human behavior, about fairness, and about life and living. I suggest that you "don't believe everything you think." Appreciate that social work commonly involves complex "deep thinking" about personal and social phenomena that trigger powerful emotions and attitudes. As you use this book, I hope you learn to examine and analyze the underlying assumptions and the nature, source, and quality of the evidence, if any, used to support the values and ideas that guide your approach to others and the world around you.

The individuals, families, groups, organizations, and communities that social workers serve are diverse in multiple ways. Therefore, problems, issues, and scenarios that involve diversity, human rights and social justice, and policy practice are represented in the book. Many of the end-of-chapter summary exercises address aspects of culture, status, and difference as they relate to policies and practices that affect human rights and social justice.

The exploring, assessing, and contracting chapters are enhanced so that the relationships among the client-and-worker collaboratively generated assessment, the agreed-upon goals for work, and the strategies, interventions, and action steps selected to pursue those goals are more clear, coherent, and transparent. These changes should help you and your clients develop a coherent case formulation that incorporates change-oriented hypotheses and a contract or service agreement. Not surprisingly, these professional activities involve critical thinking and scientific inquiry, and attention to diversity and difference.

I have attempted to update this edition to reflect new and emerging scientific knowledge, including findings from systematic reviews of the research literature and meta-analytic studies concerning the significance, safety, and effectiveness of the processes and skills presented here. For example, based on several outcome studies, the processes of assessment, evaluation, and solicitation of feedback from clients and others affected by our services gain a prominent place in all phases of practice: from preparing all the way through ending and, when possible, after that as well.

Professionalism continues to receive attention. Integrity, professional knowledge and self-efficacy, self-understanding and self-control, social support, and, as discussed above, critical thinking and scientific inquiry, and career-long learning as well as valuing diversity and difference, advancing human rights and social justice, ethical decision making, and promoting social well-being through policies and practices are interrelated as fundamental aspects of professionalism. They are essential for developing and maintaining competence as a social worker. Ecological factors such as social support receive attention, as do strengths, resources, resiliencies, and assets within person-in-environment contexts. Recognizing that most people, groups, organizations, and communities seek out helping professionals because they are experiencing personal and social problems, goals intended to address, resolve, eliminate, or ameliorate those problems serve as the guiding focus for social work practice.

This edition of the skills book is arranged in the following manner:

Part I: Professionalism begins with an introductory chapter that provides an introduction to and overall perspective about the nature of social work practice, populations served, social problems addressed, and settings where social service occurs. Chapter 1 contains a definition of social work skills and discussion of their relationship to the mission and purposes of the profession. In this chapter, you learn about the conceptual framework used to select skills addressed in the book, and become familiar with the common factors and essential facilitative qualities and the characteristics of professionalism that ethical, effective social workers consistently reflect in our work with and on behalf of clients.

Chapter 2 explores the topic of professionalism in greater depth. In this chapter, you examine aspects of integrity and complete instruments to stimulate further consideration of the issue in relation to professional practice. You consider the dimensions of the contemporary social work knowledge base. Several exercises yield self-assessment information related to the characteristics of social work professionalism. For example, you complete activities designed to further your learning about the professional social work knowledge base and your own self-efficacy. You engage in exercises to expand your understanding of contextual factors such as family of origin, the social and environmental ecology, critical events, and social support as well as the more individually oriented dimension of personality.

In Chapter 3 you explore skills associated with critical thinking, scientific inquiry, and career-long learning. You become acquainted with the universal intellectual standards and learn to recognize logical fallacies, identify threats to validity and reliability in research designs, and review research studies. In Chapter 4 you learn about valuing diversity and difference, accepting others and respecting autonomy, advancing human rights and social justice, and promoting social well-being through policy practice. In Chapter 5 you review the processes of ethical decision making in social work practice. In that chapter, you learn about fundamental legal duties and obligations that apply to all helping professionals and review the core values and ethical principles that apply specifically to social workers. You consider the issue of malpractice, the implications of recent court decisions, and the passage of relevant laws. You explore analytic and decision-making processes by which to address ethical conflicts and dilemmas and apply scientific inquiry and critical thinking skills to their resolution. Finally, you complete several exercises to strengthen your proficiency in the ethical decision-making skills.

Part II: Social Work Skills begins with Chapter 6. In that chapter, you learn about the fundamental interpersonal skills of talking and listening and communicating in a culturally sensitive manner. Included in the chapter are talking skills associated with voice, speech, and language; nonverbal body language; and listening skills related to hearing, observing, encouraging, and remembering. You also practice writing skills needed to prepare professional quality documents. Then, you combine talking and listening skills in the form of active listening. Active listening helps social workers invite, listen, remember, and reflect what other people express. Because of the rich racial, ethnic, and cultural diversity throughout North America, we pay considerable attention to the significance of language, choice of words, and nonverbal behavior within the context of cultural diversity and difference. As in previous chapters, you also complete several exercises designed to promote skill development in these basic talking and listening skills and to continue to strengthen your critical thinking and lifelong learning abilities in this area.

Chapters 7 through 13 address the skills associated with the following phases or processes of social work practice: (1) preparing, (2) beginning, (3) exploring, (4) assessing, (5) contracting, (6) working and evaluating, and (7) ending. Each chapter includes a general introduction to the purpose and tasks associated with that particular phase. Following the introduction, the social work skills commonly used during the phase are identified and illustrated. After each section and toward the conclusion of each chapter, you complete exercises designed to help you learn to apply the skills in a proficient manner and to further your abilities to engage diversity and difference, think critically, inquire scientifically, and pursue career-long learning.

Completion of the learning exercises leads to the preparation of two "case records." Based on self-understanding gained through earlier exercises, you prepare the description and assessment sections of your own "Personal Case Record." In addition, you produce a more complete "Practice Case Record" in the course of conducting five interviews with a colleague who agrees to serve as a "practice client." The five interviews provide an opportunity for you to simulate all phases of the working relationship (preparing, beginning, exploring, assessing, contracting, working and evaluating, and ending). In addition to the description, assessment, and contract sections, you also prepare progress notes and a closing summary as you engage your colleague in this intensive practice exercise. Both "case records" represent important written products for inclusion in the Social Work Skills Learning Portfolio.

The cases and situations used as illustrative examples and incorporated with learning exercises come from a variety of service settings and circumstances. Although many of the case vignettes involve interaction with individuals, families, and groups, several relate to work with organizations and communities. The significance of social and environmental factors is consistently reflected as are the interrelationships between people and the environment. Several examples of extra-client systems (for example, referral sources, community resources, or related social systems) are incorporated, and case vignettes are chosen with a view toward diversity of age, gender, sexual orientation, and racial, ethnic, cultural, and socioeconomic status.

Professors who employ the workbook in their social work courses may use the exercises in a variety of ways. As part of a homework or in-class assignment, they could ask students to respond to only some rather than all exercises. Professors may then call on class members to share their responses and discuss the characteristics that account for proficient applications of the skills. Alternately, professors may assign certain exercises as written homework for evaluation. Numerous self-assessment opportunities stimulate evaluation processes of various kinds, including self- and peer assessment, as well as evaluation by instructors. Indeed, professors may use aggregated assessment data to highlight skill areas that need further collective attention or to move more quickly through those where proficiency is already high. Similarly, students and professors may periodically review the Social Work Skills Learning Portfolios for formative or summative assessment purposes and perhaps as a part of program evaluation.

During classroom meetings, professors may ask students to form pairs, triads, or small groups to carry out selected learning exercises. Role plays in which learners alternately assume the part of client and social worker can be especially effective learning experiences—particularly when there is timely and constructive feedback from the professor. In general, professors should recognize that, ultimately, we use the social work skills in the context of helping people. Therefore learning processes that approximate the actual doing with opportunities for evaluative feedback are preferred. "Talking about" topics can lead to considerable insight. However, when skills and competencies are involved, doing, applying, and practicing tend to yield a much greater return on our educational investment.

This edition contains several appendices to support learning. Appendix 1 introduces the Social Work Skills Learning Portfolio and contains a checklist of products that may be included. Appendix 2 contains the Social Work Skills Test. Students and professors may use test items for pretest and posttest purposes. The skills test may also serve as an overall gauge of knowledge and proficiency in a wide range of social work skills. Appendix 3 presents the Social Work Skills Self-Appraisal Questionnaire, another tool for assessing proficiency in the skills addressed in the workbook. Relevant portions (that is, subscales) of the questionnaire appear at the conclusion of each chapter to enable students to track changes in their perceived proficiency over time.

Appendices 4–10 include scales to facilitate students' self-assessment and professional development in the areas of self-efficacy, self-control, social support, critical thinking, lifelong learning, acceptance of others, and social well-being. Appendix 11 contains "The Interview Rating Forms—Client Version" and Appendix 12 contains guidelines and forms needed for the multiweek experiential interviewing exercise. Appendix 13 contains an alphabetized vocabulary of English "feeling words" that learners may find useful for developing their empathic reflection skills. Appendix 14 includes an example of the description, assessment, and contract (DAC) portions of a case record. Appendix 15 consists of a Social Work Skills Interview Rating Form for assessing skills performance during interviews with simulated or actual clients. Appendix 16 contains a table of social work skills. Appendix 17 contains a table of social work skills that support each of the core EPAS competencies. Appendix 18 contains a self-rating instrument to appraise your proficiency in the EPAS competencies, practice knowledge dimensions, and practice behaviors. Appendices 19 and 20 include tools to assess your proficiency in the knowledge, skills, and abilities addressed in the ASWB Bachelor- and Masters-level licensure examinations. Finally, Appendix 21 contains blank answer sheets that students may use to complete the true-false and multiple-choice portions of the Social Work Skills Test.

In addition to the appendices, ancillary learning resources are available through the book's companion website—accessible via the Cengage Learning portal at www.cengage.com. The author also sponsors a website dedicated to the practice of social work, professionalism, and the teaching and learning of social work skills. You may access that site at www.thesocialworkskills.com.

Preliminary Assessment

Before proceeding to Chapter 1 of *The Social Work Skills Workbook*, some students may complete[6] one or more of the skills-related assessment and self-appraisal instruments contained in the Appendices: The Social Work Skills Test (Appendix 2), the Social Work Skills Self-Appraisal Questionnaire (Appendix 3), the Self-Appraisal of Proficiency in the EPAS Core Competencies, Practice Knowledge, and Practice Behaviors (Appendix 18), and the Self-Appraisal of Proficiency in the ASWB Knowledge, Skills, and Abilities (Appendix 19: Bachelor's or Appendix 20: Master's). If you complete one or more of these tools before reading and undertaking the exercises contained in Chapters 1 through 13, you obtain natural baseline data upon which to gauge your learning progress. If or when you take the same instruments later on—after completing the exercises and assignments—you can then compare your initial responses and scores with subsequent ones to provide an indication of the scope and growth in learning.

Acknowledgments

The seventh edition of *The Social Work Skills Workbook* reflects the experience of some 40 years of social work practice and more than 35 years of university teaching. Over the years, clients and students have consistently been my most important teachers. I am most appreciative of my physically challenged students and clients. Time and time again, they forgave my mistakes and guided me toward awe and reverence.

I am especially indebted to those clients and students who allowed me a glimpse into their worlds. Their life stories are remarkable. I feel privileged to participate with them in their heroic journeys. Indeed, students in my social work courses have been my most gifted teachers. If they have learned half of what I have learned from them, I will feel satisfied. I also appreciate the letters and e-mail messages I have received from social work students and professors. I treasure their suggestions for improving the book.

I would also like to recognize those social workers whose teachings and writings have affected me professionally and contributed to the approach taken in this workbook. Dr. Eldon Marshall, my former professor and current friend and colleague, was the first to introduce me to the interpersonal helping skills. I shall never forget his class or the impact of my first videotaped interview. Dr. Dean Hepworth, through both his teaching and writing, furthered the skills emphasis begun during my master's education. My former colleague, the late Dr. Beulah Compton, also deserves much credit. Her clear conception of fundamental social work processes has served me well indeed. I shall long remember our sometimes heated but always stimulating conversations about social work practice.

I am also grateful to my colleagues at the Indiana University School of Social Work. An extraordinary group of professionals, your dedication to student learning continues to inspire.

---

[6] Some students may be assigned to complete instruments contained in the Appendices while others may voluntarily choose to experiment with them.

I wish to express my appreciation to the reviewers whose suggestions led to improvements in this and earlier editions:

Scott Boyle, College of Social Work, University of Utah

Tracy Carpenter-Aeby, East Carolina University

Robert Evans, Vincennes University

Dr. Pearl Fisk, Fordham University Graduate School of Social Service

Dexter Freeman, Fayetteville State University

Tim Hanshaw, Limestone College

Dr. Mary Lewis, North Carolina AT&T State University

Bethany Lighthart, Southewestern Michigan College

Craig Mosher, Luther College

Caroline Reid, Eastern Kentucky University

Deb Aden Ripperda, University of Sioux Falls

Sherrill A. C. Robinson, Kansas State University

Jan A. Rodgers, Dominican University

Cindy West, University of Tennessee at Martin

Patricia Wilson, Vincennes University

Finally, I want to thank my mother, Marjorie Murphy Cournoyer, for her love and compassion for others; my late father, Armand Cournoyer, for his courage, determination, and resilience; and Grant and Karma Hughes, my wife's parents, for their unflagging support. And, most importantly, to my loving partner, Catherine Hughes Cournoyer, and our children, John Paul and Michael, I can express only enormous gratitude. Catherine is the most generous person I have ever met and without question the best social worker. Each day, she and the boys continue to make me more and better than I could possibly be without them.

Barry R. Cournoyer
Emeritus Professor of Social Work
Indiana University

BOX P1.1

Other Books Authored or Coauthored by Barry R. Cournoyer

◆ Cournoyer, Barry R., & Stanley, Mary J. (2002). *The Social Work Portfolio: Planning, Assessing and Documenting Lifelong Learning in a Dynamic Profession.* Pacific Grove, CA: Brooks/Cole.

◆ Cournoyer, Barry R. (2004). *The Evidence-Based Social Work Skills Book.* Boston: Allyn & Bacon.

◆ Compton, Beulah R., Galaway, Burt, & Cournoyer, Barry R. (2005). *Social Work Processes* (7th ed.). Pacific Grove, CA: Brooks/Cole.

PART I
PROFESSIONALISM

INTRODUCTION

Welcome to the exciting and challenging world of social work! As a social worker, you may serve individuals, families, groups, organizations, and communities in all kinds of situations. You may do so directly or indirectly through the development and implementation of policies and programs; organization of groups and communities; leadership of organizations; or the design and conduct of socially relevant research studies and evaluation projects. The range of settings in which you might function is wide and varied. The contexts for social work practice are often complex, usually demanding, and always challenging. Despite the extraordinary demands, service as a social worker remains one of the most satisfying and personally rewarding endeavors. Indeed, findings from surveys reveal that social work is among the eight most satisfying careers. Social workers often attribute their satisfaction to the following: (1) intellectual stimulation, (2) job security, (3) professional autonomy, and (4) extensive direct contact with clients (CareerJournal.com editors, 2006, July 11a, 2006, July 11b).

The demands, challenges, and responsibilities of social work service are sometimes daunting. To serve competently in such circumstances, social workers today need to be knowledgeable, thoughtful, ethical, accountable, and proficient. In this chapter, we review the purpose and goals of the book (see Box 1.1); introduce you to the mission of the social work profession and; introduce you to the mission of the social work profession and to a conception of social work skills; outline the phases of practice; and briefly describe the qualities and characteristics of professionalism needed for ethical, effective social work practice in our complex, ever-changing, contemporary society (see Box 1.2).

BOX 1.1

The Social Work Skills Workbook: Learning Goals

Following completion of *The Social Work Skills Workbook*, learners should be able to:

◆ Apply the characteristics of professionalism in all aspects of social work practice.
◆ Think critically in professional contexts and throughout the phases of practice.
◆ Inquire scientifically to seek, discover, evaluate, and apply relevant knowledge in professional practice.
◆ Engage diversity and difference, and accept others in a culturally sensitive and respectful manner.
◆ Apply core social work values, ethics, and relevant legal obligations in ethical decision making and professional practice.
◆ Demonstrate oral and written communication skills in working with individuals, families, groups, organizations, communities, and colleagues.
◆ Advocate for human rights and social justice, and engage in policy practice to promote social well-being.
◆ Prepare, begin, explore, assess, contract, work and evaluate, and end with individuals, families, groups, organizations, and communities.
◆ Assess and evaluate one's proficiency in the social work skills.
◆ Integrate, synthesize, and plan career-long learning through the preparation of a Social Work Skills Learning Portfolio.

Purpose

The overall purpose of *The Social Work Skills Workbook* is to help learners develop a strong sense of professionalism and gain proficiency in skills needed for effective social work practice. These skills are consistent with the mission, purpose, and scope of the social work profession and its values and ethics.

The Social Work Skills Workbook provides opportunities for you to learn to apply the characteristics of professionalism, and to understand and practice the essential social work skills. All of the various skills that might potentially have relevance for some social workers on certain occasions in some situations are not included. Rather, the book addresses those skills that are (1) most applicable to the mission, purposes, and scope of the social work profession, (2) compatible with and supportive of the phases or processes of contemporary social work practice, (3) representative of the characteristics of professionalism, (4) consistent with social work values, ethics, and obligations, (5) supported by research-based knowledge, (6) reflective of the common factors and essential facilitative qualities associated with effective helping, and (7) consistent with the core competencies, practice knowledge, and practice behaviors[1] identified in the Educational Policy and Accreditation Standards (EPAS) (Council on Social Work Education, 2008) as well as knowledge, skills, and abilities addressed in social work licensing examinations.

---

[1] The letters *EP* (Educational Policy) and their associated numbers are used to identify each of the EPAS core competencies (for example, EP2.1.1 or EP2.1.4) while the letters PB (Practice Behavior) and PK (Practice Knowledge) and associated numbers are used to identify each of the 41 practice behaviors (for example, PB03 or PB 39) and the 28 aspects of practice knowledge (for example, PK07 or PK23).

BOX 1.2
Chapter Purpose

The purpose of this chapter is to introduce learners to the social work profession and the skills, common factors, facilitative qualities, and professional characteristics needed for ethical, effective social work practice in contemporary society.

Goals

Following completion of this chapter, learners should be able to:

◆ Describe the mission and purposes of the social work profession.
◆ Identify the characteristics of professionalism.
◆ Define the concepts of social work skills and competencies.
◆ Identify the phases or processes of social work practice.
◆ Discuss the three essential facilitative qualities of empathy, respect, and authenticity.
◆ Identify the nine aspects of professionalism addressed in *The Social Work Skills Workbook*.
◆ Describe the five common factors associated with effective helping relationships.
◆ Describe the purposes and functions of *The Social Work Skills Learning Portfolio*.

Core EPAS Competencies

The skills addressed in this chapter support the following core EPAS competencies:

◆ Identify as a professional social worker and conduct oneself accordingly (EP2.1.1).
◆ Apply critical thinking to inform and communicate professional judgments (EP2.1.3).
◆ Engage diversity and difference in practice (EP2.1.4).
◆ Apply knowledge of human behavior and the social environment (EP2.1.7).
◆ Respond to contexts that shape practice (EP2.1.9).
◆ Engage, assess, intervene, and evaluate with individuals, families, groups, organizations, and communities (EP2.1.10[a–d]).

The social work skills are organized and presented to coincide with the phases or processes of contemporary social work practice. Of course, any phase-to-phase or stage-to-stage approach runs the risk of suggesting that service to all client systems follows the same linear sequence and that the characteristics and skills relevant to one phase are distinctly different from those of another. This is not the case. Sometimes work usually undertaken in one phase emerges in another, or the sequence must change to address urgent circumstances. Indeed, many of the dynamics, tasks, functions, and skills applicable to one phase are, in work with a particular client system, evident in other phases as well. We typically use certain skills (for example, empathic reflection, questioning, and seeking feedback) repeatedly throughout the course of our efforts with and for the people we serve. Many skills may be applied in similar fashion in work with individuals, dyads, families, groups, organizations, and communities. Others must be adapted somewhat to accommodate the size and composition of the client system, or when engaged in policy practice and advocacy. Indeed, reflective thought and sound judgment are vital in the selection and application of skills throughout all phases of practice.

Box 1.1 contains the learning goals of *The Social Work Skills Workbook*. Table 1.1 displays the relationship between them and the 10 core EPAS competencies.

Professionalism is essential precisely because the social work skills cannot and should not be applied mechanically without careful consideration of the people and contexts involved. Aspects of professionalism, such as integrity, knowledge, critical thinking, ethical decision making, and recognition of human rights processes such as basic fairness and inclusiveness so integral to the advancement of social justice and the promotion of social well-being, serve as the basic foundation and context within which the social work skills emerge (see Figure 1.1). Absent such a professional foundation, the skills could easily be implemented in an insensitive, shallow, inappropriate, untimely, and ultimately damaging manner.

At some point in your career as a social worker, you might serve in a child-protection capacity, responding to indications that a child may be at risk of abuse or neglect. You may help families improve their child-caring capabilities or serve in the emergency room of a hospital, intervening with people and families in crises. You might lead groups for sexually victimized children or provide education and counseling to abusive or incarcerated adults. You could aid couples in strained relationships or help single parents who seek guidance and support in rearing their children. You may serve people who abuse alcohol and drugs or help family members affected by the substance abuse of a parent, child, spouse, or sibling. You might work in a residential setting for youthful offenders, a prison for adults, or a psychiatric institution.

You might serve in a university counseling center, working with college students, faculty members, and other campus employees. You could help people challenged in some way—perhaps physically or mentally, or both. You might serve in a school system or perhaps as a consultant to a local police department or a state or national agency or bureau. You might serve as a member of the armed services—helping soldiers, sailors, marines, airmen, or members of the coast guard and their families. You could work in a mayor's office, serve on the staff of a state legislator, or perhaps even become a member of Congress yourself.

You may function in a crisis intervention capacity for a suicide prevention service. You could work for a health maintenance organization (HMO), a managed health care system, or an employee assistance program (EAP). As a social worker, you might act as an advocate for people who have experienced discrimination, oppression, or exploitation, perhaps because of racism, sexism, or ageism. You might take action to prevent human sex trafficking—one of the contemporary forms of slavery. You might organize groups or communities, or perhaps help workers to form or participate in a labor union. You might engage in social entrepreneurship and create social programs designed to aid people or groups in need. You might analyze policies, conduct research related to various social problems, or evaluate the effectiveness and outcomes of intervention programs and practices. You might work with homeless people, runaway youth, or street people struggling to survive through panhandling or prostitution. You might work with people victimized by crime or perhaps with those who previously engaged in criminal activity. You might serve in a domestic violence program, providing social services to people affected by child abuse, spouse abuse, or elder abuse. You could provide psychosocial services to people dealing with a physical illness, such as cancer, kidney failure, Alzheimer's disease, or HIV/AIDS, and help their families cope with the myriad psychosocial effects of such conditions. You might work in a hospice, helping people with a terminal illness prepare for their own death or that of a family member. You could help unemployed and underemployed people find employment or locate needed services and resources by providing information and arranging referrals. You might serve documented or undocumented immigrants, refugees, transients, or migrant workers. You might counsel individuals suffering from a serious mental illness, such as schizophrenia or bipolar disorder, and provide support and education to their families. You could work in an assisted care

T A B L E 1.1
Relationship of *The Social Work Skills Workbook* Learning Goals and the Core EPAS Competencies

The Social Work Skills Workbook	Core EPAS Competencies (2008)
Upon completion of the skills book, learners should be able to:	*Graduates of CSWE-accredited BSW and MSW programs should be able to:*
◆ LG01: Apply the characteristics of professionalism in all aspects of social work practice.	◆ EP2.1.1: Identify as a professional social worker and conduct oneself accordingly.
◆ LG02: Think critically in professional contexts and throughout the phases of practice.	◆ EP2.1.3: Apply critical thinking to inform and communicate professional judgments. ◆ EP2.1.9: Respond to contexts that shape practice.
◆ LG03: Inquire scientifically to seek, discover, evaluate, and apply relevant knowledge in professional practice.	◆ EP2.1.6: Engage in research-informed practice and practice-informed research. ◆ EP2.1.7: Apply knowledge of human behavior and the social environment.
◆ LG04: Engage diversity and difference, and accept others in a culturally sensitive and respectful manner.	◆ EP2.1.4: Engage diversity and difference in practice.
◆ LG05: Apply core social work values, ethics, and relevant legal obligations in ethical decision making and professional practice.	◆ EP2.1.2: Apply social work ethical principles to guide professional practice.
◆ LG06: Demonstrate oral and written communication skills in working with individuals, families, groups, organizations, communities, and colleagues.	◆ EP2.1.3: Apply critical thinking to inform and communicate professional judgments.
◆ LG07: Advocate for human rights and social justice, and engage in policy practice to promote social well-being.	◆ EP2.1.5: Advance human rights and social and economic justice. ◆ EP2.1.8: Engage in policy practice to advance social and economic well-being and to deliver effective social work services.
◆ LG08: Prepare, begin, explore, assess, contract, work and evaluate, and end with individuals, families, groups, organizations, and communities.	◆ EP2.1.10(a–d): Engage, assess, intervene, and evaluate with individuals, families, groups, organizations, and communities.
◆ LG09: Assess and evaluate one's proficiency in the social work skills and competencies.	◆ EP2.1.1: Identify as a professional social worker and conduct oneself accordingly.
◆ LG10: Integrate, synthesize, and plan career-long learning through the preparation of a Social Work Skills Learning Portfolio.	◆ EP2.1.1: Identify as a professional social worker and conduct oneself accordingly. ◆ EP2.1.9: Respond to contexts that shape practice.

Note: "LG" refers to Learning Goal and "EP" to Educational Policy

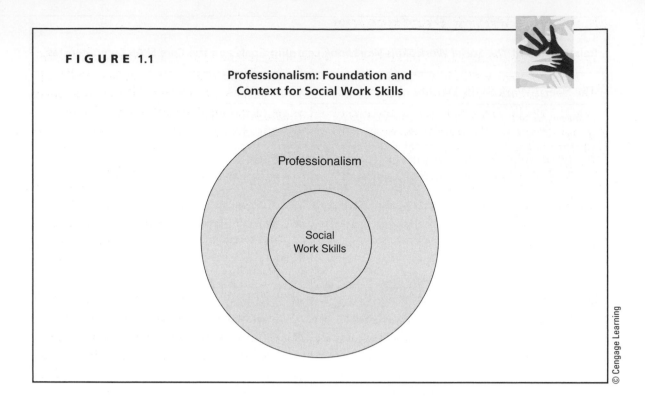

FIGURE 1.1

Professionalism: Foundation and Context for Social Work Skills

Professionalism

Social Work Skills

© Cengage Learning

facility for aged people, leading groups for residents or counseling family members. You might serve in a halfway house, work with foster parents, or perhaps provide information and support to teenage parents. You might serve active or retired military personnel and their families or work in industry, consulting with employers and employees about problems and issues that affect their well-being during times of economic instability.

In conjunction with affected individuals and groups, you might engage in the design, development, and establishment of organizations that promote social well-being among vulnerable populations and struggling communities. You might consult with or help to facilitate the creation of social or political advocacy groups that promote social and economic justice; or participate in those that need additional support.

The range of settings where you might work and the variety of functions that you could fulfill are mind-boggling. Such breadth, diversity, and complexity can be overwhelming. You may ask yourself, "Can I possibly learn what I need to so that I can serve competently as a social worker in all those places, serving such different people, and helping them to address such complex issues?" The answer to that question is certainly NO!

You and I could never become truly competent in all the arenas where social workers practice because it would require a greater breadth and depth of knowledge and expertise than any one person could ever acquire. Indeed, social workers need a specialized body of knowledge and skill for each practice setting, each special population group, and each social problem. You cannot know everything, do everything, or be competent in helping people struggling with every one of the enormous array of psychosocial issues. However, you can acquire expertise in those skills that are common to social work practice with all population groups and all problems in all settings. These common social work skills bring coherence to the profession, despite its extraordinary variety and complexity.

A Social Work Profession

In addition to applying a common set of skills, social workers tend to approach clients from a similar perspective—one that is reflected in a set of core values and a distinctive language, and epitomized in the name of our profession. Our profession is "social work" and we call ourselves "social workers." We do not attach "ist" to the end of our name, as do our sister helping professionals in psychology and psychiatry. Rather, we proudly identify ourselves as "workers." In so doing, we establish a view of ourselves as equal rather than superior to others; that we work with and on behalf of people; and that we do much more than think, study, and advise—we also take action.

In this context, the terms "profession," "professional," and "professionalism" warrant some clarification. A profession is a "vocation or calling, especially one that involves some branch of advanced learning or science" as, for example, the medical profession (*The Oxford American Dictionary of Current English* [Online], 1999). For many of us, social work is both a vocation and a calling. We sincerely want to help others and are motivated by more than money and status to do so. Although the term "professional" as used, for example, in the sentence, "She is a professional," connotes a relatively high social status—as would befit those with advanced learning—many social workers use the term to refer to qualities such as integrity, competence, and conscientiousness rather than as a sign of rank or privilege. In this sense, we distinguish those who have earned a college diploma or advanced degree, or possess a license to practice a profession from those who both possess the relevant educational and legal credentials *and* regularly perform in a respectful, caring, competent, and ethical manner. The former may be members of a profession while the latter are professional indeed.

Social workers tend to be less interested in social status and more interested in the characteristics, qualities, and practice behaviors reflected by ethical and effective social workers. We refer to these as aspects of professionalism.

Social workers usually refer to the people we serve as *clients, people,* or *consumers* rather than *patients, subjects,* or *cases.* Social workers also favor the word *assessment* rather than *diagnosis, study, examination,* or *investigation.* Furthermore, we tend to look for *strengths, assets, resources, resiliencies, competencies,* and *abilities* rather than attending exclusively to *problems, obstacles, deficiencies,* or *pathologies.* We also commonly adopt helping processes that involve *cooperation, collaboration, mutuality, shared decision making,* and often *joint action* rather than *prescription, direction,* or *coercion.* In addition, we use language that is easily understood by all. Eschewing esoteric terminology, such as is often associated with the legal, medical, and psychology professions, we attempt to speak the "language of the people." In so doing, we may downplay our special, advanced knowledge and expertise; and slightly diminish our perceived social status in order to promote a sense of collaboration, equal participation, and mutual respect with clients. The active encouragement of equal status with others, reflected in our identity as social workers and our use of the people's language, is characteristic of most contemporary social workers regardless of our particular practice settings.

Professional social workers have earned a baccalaureate, master's, or doctoral degree in social work and, usually, we are licensed or certified to practice social work in our locale. We adopt certain common values that pervade all aspects of our helping activities, pledge adherence to a social work code of ethics, and tend to view social work in a manner similar to that reflected in the International Federation of Social Workers' (IFSW) definition (2000):

> The social work profession promotes social change, problem solving in human relationships and the empowerment and liberation of people to enhance well-being. Utilising theories of human behaviour and social systems, social work intervenes at the points where people interact with their environments. Principles of human rights and social justice are fundamental to social work. (para. 1)

While our specialized education, subscription to a code of ethics, and public endorsement in the form of legal certification or licensure are similar to that of medical doctors or lawyers, the mission of the social work profession is radical and perhaps even revolutionary in nature. Rather than promoting a status quo, social workers seek to "promote social change," contribute to the "the empowerment and liberation of people," and pursue "human rights and social justice" (International Federation of Social Workers, 2000, para. 1). In pursuing such a radical mission, we social workers sometimes risk our jobs and social status.

Regardless of our practice setting or position, social workers tend to view person-in-environment, person-and-environment, or person-in-context[2] as the basic unit of attention. This too is a radical notion, especially in North America where the individual is commonly viewed iconically as an autonomous, independent, and completely free-willed creature who can readily choose to become whatever and whomever he or she wishes to become, regardless of current or past circumstances. Social workers recognize that the physical and social environments profoundly affect people and influence their development and behavior as well as their subjective experience. We understand that hurricanes or tsunamis, tornadoes, earthquakes, floods or droughts; war, civil conflict, acts of terror, or crimes of violence; political, cultural, and economic conditions; access to food, clean air, water, and opportunities for training and education impact humans and their thoughts, emotions, and actions. In addition, social workers realize that many communities are predisposed to react favorably or unfavorably to characteristics clearly beyond an individual's control (for example, one's gender, skin color, height, physical ability, intellect, attractiveness, nationality or ethnicity, religious affiliation, political or philosophical beliefs, and language, dialect, or accent). While we celebrate individuals' resilience and capacity to overcome obstacles and transcend limitations, we recognize that resource-rich environments containing wide-ranging opportunities enable individuals to more readily maximize their potential and fulfill their aspirations than do resource-scarce settings. Social workers resist temptations to blame people for circumstances beyond their control.

Recognizing the power of context, social workers consider the enhancement of social functioning and the promotion or restoration of "a mutually beneficial interaction between individuals and society to improve the quality of life for everyone" (Minahan, 1981, p. 6) as an overriding purpose of practice. This consistent dual focus on people and environment leads social workers to consider multiple systems—even when an individual person or family is formally the "client." Indeed, social workers always consider and usually involve other people or other social systems in the helping process.

In the Preamble to its Code of Ethics, the National Association of Social Workers (NASW) states that:

A historic and defining feature of social work is the profession's focus on individual well-being in a social context and the well-being of society. Fundamental to social work is attention to the environmental forces that create, contribute to, and address problems in living.

Social workers promote social justice and social change with and on behalf of clients…. Social workers are sensitive to cultural and ethnic diversity and strive to end discrimination, oppression, poverty, and other forms of social injustice. (2008)

---

[2] In this book, we use the term *person* or *persons* in the same manner we use the term *client* or *clients*. We recognize that a *client* may be an individual person, dyad, family, group, organization, community, or even a society with which a social worker has an agreement to provide services. Similarly, the word *person* or *persons* in terms such as *person(s)-in-environment*, *person(s)-and-situation*, *person(s)-in-context*, or *person(s)-problem-situation* could mean an individual person or several people according to the time and circumstances.

In its Educational Policy and Accreditation Standards, the Council of Social Work Education indicates that:

> The purpose of the social work profession is to promote human and community well-being. Guided by a person and environment construct, a global perspective, respect for human diversity, and knowledge based on scientific inquiry, social work's purpose is actualized through its quest for social and economic justice, the prevention of conditions that limit human rights, the elimination of poverty, and the enhancement of the quality of life for all persons. (2008, para. 1).

Notice that the NASW and the Council on Social Work Education (CSWE), like the IFSW, endorse a radical conception of the profession. These organizations suggest that social work's mission involves the promotion of social and economic justice; the enhancement of social well-being and quality of life; and the elimination of "discrimination, oppression, poverty, and other forms of social injustice" (National Association of Social Workers, 2008, Preamble). Such aspirations do not appear in the mission statements or ethical codes of other professions. Social work alone dares to endorse publicly such potentially controversial ideas and to establish them as central to its professional identity, purpose, and *raison d'être*.

Given our focus on social change, social workers tend to conceive of people and situations as dynamic and as having the potential for planned change. We view professional practice as predominantly for clients: the individuals, families, groups, organizations, communities, and societies that we serve. Whatever personal benefit we might gain is secondary; the notion of service to others is primary. The primacy of service in social work is reflected through a special sensitivity to those living in poverty; unemployed or underemployed people; vulnerable populations and at-risk individuals; and oppressed peoples. Indeed, people with the lowest status, the fewest resources, and the least power constitute social work's most cherished constituency.

Social workers recognize that professional service to others often involves powerful interpersonal and social processes that have considerable potential for harm as well as for good. We realize that competent practice requires exceptional personal and professional integrity, a highly developed understanding of ourselves, and extraordinary personal discipline and self-control. In particular, social workers must be expert critical thinkers and energetic lifelong learners to make sense of the ever-increasing glut of information—much of it false, misleading, and nonsensical.

A great deal more than good intentions, admirable personal qualities, and compassionate feelings are required. As social workers, we must base our words and actions on professional knowledge; critical thought; social work values, ethics, and obligations; and, of course, the analogous knowledge, thoughts, values, and aspirations of the people with whom we are so fortunate to work.

Social Work Skills

The terms *skill* and *competency* have become extremely popular in social work and other helping professions during the past half century. In addition to the emphasis on competencies suggested by the EPAS (Council on Social Work Education, 2008), numerous social work textbooks incorporate the words *skill or skills*, *competence*, *competency*, or *competencies* in their titles (Bogo, 2010; Corcoran, 2011; Cummins, Sevel, & Pedrick, 2006; Hennessey, 2011; Hepworth, Rooney, Rooney, Strom-Gottfried, & Larsen, 2006; Ragg, 2011; Shulman, 2009; Sidell & Smiley, 2008).

Johnson (1995) describes skill as "the practice component that brings knowledge and values together and converts them to action as a response to concern and need" (p. 55) and "a complex organization of behavior directed toward a particular goal or activity" (p. 431). Smalley (1967) views skill as a "social worker's capacity to use a method in order to further a process directed toward the accomplishment of a social work purpose as that purpose finds expression in a specific program or service" (p. 17). Skill also has been described as "the production of specific behaviors under the precise conditions designated for their use" (Middleman & Goldberg, 1990, p. 12).

Henry (1981) suggests that skills are "finite and discrete sets of behaviors or tasks employed by a worker at a given time, for a given purpose, in a given manner" (p. vii). She (Henry, 1992) also cites Phillips (1957), who characterizes skill as "knowledge in action" (p. 20).

These various descriptions and definitions are extremely useful. They provide context for the way we approach skills in this book. For our purposes, we will use the definition of *social work skill* presented in Box 1.3.

This definition of *skill* approximates the definition of *competency* as used by the CSWE. In the EPAS, competencies are "measurable practice behaviors that are comprised of knowledge, values, and skills" (Council on Social Work Education, 2008, p. 3, EP2.1). In the context of professional education, social work skills are competencies and competencies are skills. As cognitive and interpersonal practice behaviors, the skills addressed in this book reflect social work values and require professional knowledge and expertise in their application. Skills must be implemented at or above a satisfactory level of proficiency.

Although they are usually associated with particular phases or processes of practice, professional skills should never be viewed as technical activities to complete, robot-like, at exactly the same relative time and in precisely the same way with all clients and all situations. Rather, we select, combine, and adapt specific social work skills to suit the particular needs and characteristics of the person-in-environment. Social workers think carefully about timing and context as they make judgments about which skills to use and when and how to use them.

The range and scope of skills that social workers might use in the context of service are wide and varied. A "social worker's skills include being proficient in communication, assessing problems and client workability, matching needs with resources, developing resources, and changing social structures" (Barker, 2003, p. 399). More than 30 years ago, the National Association of Social Workers (1981) outlined 12 skills:

1. Listen to others with understanding and purpose.
2. Elicit information and assemble relevant facts to prepare a social history, assessment, and report.
3. Create and maintain professional helping relationships.
4. Observe and interpret verbal and nonverbal behavior and use knowledge of personality theory and diagnostic methods.

BOX 1.3
Definition: Social Work Skill

A social work skill is a circumscribed set of discrete cognitive and behavioral actions that are consistent and congruent with (1) research-based knowledge; (2) social work values, ethics, and obligations; (3) the essential facilitative qualities or the "core conditions"; (4) the characteristics of professionalism; and (5) a legitimate social work purpose within the context of a phase or process of practice.

5. Engage clients (including individuals, families, groups, and communities) in efforts to resolve their own problems and to gain trust.
6. Discuss sensitive emotional subjects supportively and without being threatening.
7. Create innovative solutions to clients' needs.
8. Determine the need to terminate the therapeutic relationship.
9. Conduct research, or interpret the findings of research and professional literature.
10. Mediate and negotiate between conflicting parties.
11. Provide interorganizational liaison services.
12. Interpret and communicate social needs to funding sources, the public, or legislators. (pp. 17–18)

Notice how the 12 skills refer to specific behavioral actions. The Council on Social Work Education adopted a similar approach when they identified 10 core competencies needed by professional social workers. Incorporated in the EPAS (Council on Social Work Education, 2008, pp. 3–7), graduates of accredited social work programs should be able to:

1. Identify as a professional social worker and conduct oneself accordingly (EP2.1.1).
2. Apply social work ethical principles to guide professional practice (EP2.1.2).
3. Apply critical thinking to inform and communicate professional judgments (EP2.1.3).
4. Engage diversity and difference in practice (EP2.1.4).
5. Advance human rights and social and economic justice (EP2.1.5).
6. Engage in research-informed practice and practice-informed research (EP2.1.6).
7. Apply knowledge of human behavior and the social environment (EP2.1.7).
8. Engage in policy practice to advance social and economic well-being and to deliver effective social work services (EP2.1.8).
9. Respond to contexts that shape practice (EP2.1.9).
10. Engage, assess, intervene, and evaluate with individuals, families, groups, organizations, and communities (EP2.1.10[a–d]).

Box 1.4 contains a "word cloud" of key terms contained in the EPAS competencies.

BOX 1.4

Key Terms Contained in the Core EPAS Competencies

The skills addressed in this book support the core competencies and the practice knowledge dimensions and practice behaviors contained in the EPAS (Council on Social Work Education, 2008). Interestingly, they are also consistent with the most important qualities that employers of college graduates seek in their prospective employees. These include the abilities to: "work in a team structure," "verbally communicate with persons inside and outside the organization," "make decisions and solve problems," "obtain and process information, plan, organize, and prioritize work," "analyze quantitative data," "create and/or edit written reports," and "influence others." Employers also prefer candidates who possess "technical knowledge related to the job" and are proficient "with computer software" (National Association of Colleges and Employers, 2011).

More specifically, however, the skills addressed in this book serve the tasks associated with commonly identified phases or processes of social work practice, the common factors and essential facilitative qualities exhibited by most effective professional helpers, and the fundamental characteristics of professionalism. In this context, we identify seven phases of social work practice (see Figure 1.2).

These seven phases extend the four outlined in the EPAS (Council on Social Work Education, 2008). The EPAS state that graduates of CSWE-accredited social work programs can "engage, assess, intervene, and evaluate with individuals, families, groups, organizations, and communities" (EP2.1.10[a–d]).

The preparing, beginning, and exploring skills support the *engagement* and some of the *assessment* competencies; the assessing and contracting skills support the *assessment* competency; and the working and evaluating, and the ending skills support the *intervention* and *evaluation* competencies (see Figure 1.3) identified in sections EP2.1.10(a–d) of the EPAS (Council on Social Work Education, 2008).

We separate the discrete behaviors associated with each phase or process into small, manageable units of thought and action that are consistent with the common factors and essential facilitative qualities and compatible with the central characteristics of professionalism. Integrated and synthesized in this fashion, they form the social work skills. As illustrated in Table 1.2, we organize the social work skills according to the seven phases of practice reflected in *The Social Work Skills Workbook* or the four phases outlined in the Educational Policy and Accreditation Standards

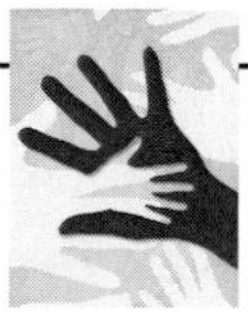

FIGURE 1.2

Phases of Practice

- Preparing
- Beginning
- Exploring
- Assessing
- Contracting
- Working & Evaluating
- Ending

© Cengage Learning

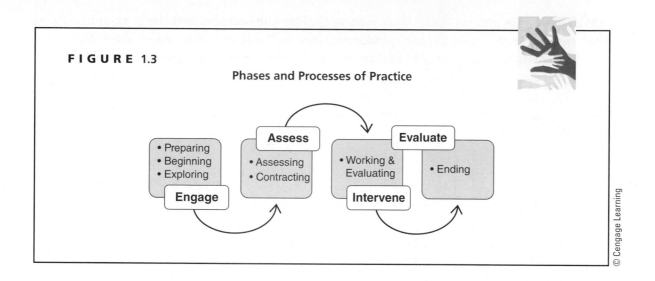

FIGURE 1.3

Phases and Processes of Practice

TABLE 1.2
Phases of Practice and Client System Size: Framework for Organizing Phase-Related Social Work Skills

Seven Phases of Social Work Practice (Cournoyer)	Four Phases of Social Work Practice: EPAS Competency EP2.10(a–d)	EP2.1.10 (a–d-1) Individuals	EP2.1.10 (a–d-2) Families	EP2.1.10 (a–d-3) Groups	EP2.1.10 (a–d-4) Organizations	EP2.1.10 (a–d-5) Communities
SW1.0 Preparing	EP2.1.10(a) Engage	✓	✓	✓	✓	✓
SW2.0 Beginning	EP2.1.10(a) Engage	✓	✓	✓	✓	✓
SW3.0 Exploring	EP2.1.10(a) Engage	✓	✓	✓	✓	✓
SW4.0 Assessing	EP2.1.10(b) Assess	✓	✓	✓	✓	✓
SW5.0 Contracting	EP2.1.10(b) Assess	✓	✓	✓	✓	✓
SW6.0 Working & Evaluating	EP2.1.10(c) Intervene EP2.1.10(d) Evaluate	✓	✓	✓	✓	✓
SW7.0 Ending	EP2.1.10(c) Intervene EP2.1.10(d) Evaluate	✓	✓	✓	✓	✓

(EPAS) of the Council on Social Work Education. The skills included in this text are applicable to work with individuals, families, groups, organizations, and communities (see EP2.1.10[a–d]).

In demonstrating these skills and competencies in work with client systems of different sizes at various phases or stages of practice, social workers consistently demonstrate the following essential facilitative qualities:

- Empathy
- Respect
- Authenticity

We also integrate the following characteristics of professionalism throughout all aspects of our service to and with others:

- Integrity
- Professional knowledge and self-efficacy
- Self-understanding and self-control
- Social support
- Critical thinking, scientific inquiry, and career-long learning
- Valuing diversity and difference
- Advancing human rights and social justice
- Promoting social well-being
- Ethical decision making

Each of these characteristics requires integrated knowledge of the values, ethics, and legal obligations that inform our professional thoughts and actions. Indeed, the values of the social work profession permeate all aspects of our service to and work with others.

Common Factors and the Working Relationship

Findings from numerous research studies suggest that certain common factors present in helping relationships account for many of the beneficial outcomes (Asay & Lambert, 1999; Barth et al., 2012; Hoffart, Borge, Sexton, & Clark, 2008; Murphy, 1999; Scovern, 1999; Sparks & Duncan, 2010; Wampold, 2010). These common factors are separate from the effects of specific intervention approaches and techniques. In other words, they are common to most, if not all, helping endeavors and are not specific to any particular approach.

As early as the 1930s, helping professionals (Rosenzweig, 1936) discussed the presence of implicit common factors in diverse therapeutic approaches. Subsequent analyses of the research yielded several general categories of factors associated with client outcomes in counseling and psychotherapy (Lambert, 1992; Lambert & Bergin, 1994; Lambert & Cattani-Thompson, 1996; Sprenkle, Blow, & Dickey, 1999). Not specific to any particular practice model or approach, these factors are associated with favorable outcomes:

Client Factors and Situational Factors: The strengths, assets, resources, challenges, and limitations within the client, the client's social situation, and the physical/ecological environment are strongly associated with service outcomes. Clients' stage of change and degree of motivation are also relevant (Prochaska, 1999; Prochaska & Norcross, 2007; Prochaska, Norcross, & DiClemente, 1994). Indeed, the internal and external aspects that clients bring to the relationship with a helping professional generally have more of an influence than any other single element (Asay & Lambert, 1999; Bohart & Tallman, 2010; Lambert, 1992; Miller, Wampold, & Varhely, 2008; Tallman & Bohart,

1999; Wampold, 2001, 2010). For example, within the context of counseling and psychotherapy, as much as 87 percent (Wampold, 2001) of the variability in therapeutic outcomes is associated with client and external or situational factors. Social work's emphasis on "starting where the client is" and our focus on the person-in-environment correspond to this finding. By incorporating client strengths and ecosystem assets in our service to others, social workers can supplement our own relatively modest impact—about 13 percent—on client outcomes.

Helper and Relationship Factors: The personal characteristics of the helping professional and the relationship between the client and helper also influence client outcomes (Asay & Lambert, 1999; Lambert, 1992). Social workers have long recognized the importance of the helper's personal qualities and the relationship between the client and worker (Perlman, 1979). Your dedication, integrity, and concern for others and your proficiency in the social work skills can help you establish and maintain positive working relationships with clients and others with whom you interact as part of your professional activities.

Hope and Expectancy Factors: Hopefulness, optimism, and expectations that the helping encounter will be beneficial significantly affect client outcomes (Lambert, 1992). Social workers commonly encourage hope and serve as examples to others through our positive attitudes, energy, and enthusiasm. However, we do so in an honest, open, realistic, and honorable fashion. We eschew false promises and excessive bravado as we recognize and celebrate the power of hope, anticipation, and positive expectations (Perlman, 1969).

Model/Technique and Allegiance Factors: The theoretical approaches or models, change strategies, intervention techniques, and practice protocols adopted in the process of helping affect client outcomes. Helpers' allegiance to the approaches adopted or interventions undertaken also contribute. By allegiance, we mean the degree to which helpers believe in the value and effectiveness of what they do and how they do it. When combined, the hope and expectancy, and the model/technique and allegiance factors account for about the same amount of client outcome impact as do relationship factors (Asay & Lambert, 1999; Lambert, 1992).

Other scholars have reached similar conclusions about common factors. In addition to the quality of the working relationship and client expectancies, Weinberger (1993, 1995, 2003) emphasizes the importance of (1) exposure to and exploration of problem issues, (2) practice in coping with or mastering aspects of the problematic issues, and (3) development of a conceptual means[3] or framework to understand and explain why and how the problems occur and how they can be managed.

Evaluative Feedback Factor: Previously underappreciated, systematic evaluative feedback from clients has gained increasing recognition as a powerful factor associated with better outcomes. Indeed, the quality and the effectiveness of the helping process tends to improve when clients provide regular, formalized evaluative feedback about the helper, the helping relationship, the service approach, and progress toward desired goals; and the helper regularly inquires about and tabulates results, and uses findings to make adjustments in approach or style (Crits-Christoph et al., 2012; Hawkins, Lambert, Vermeersch, Slade, & Tuttle, 2004; Lambert, 2010a; Lambert & Shimokawa, 2011; Lambert, Whipple, Vermeersch, Smart, & Hawkins, 2002; Slade, Lambert, Harmon, Smart, & Bailey, 2008; Whipple & Lambert, 2011). Regardless of intervention approach or model, the routine use of brief evaluation instruments (Campbell & Hemsley, 2009; Duncan et al., 2003; Luborsky, 1996) tends to increase the probability of service success and decrease the likelihood of failure

---

[3] In a later chapter, we consider the topic of "conceptual means" in our discussion of the explanatory and change-oriented hypotheses that clients and workers adopt during the course of their work together.

(Anker, Duncan, & Sparks, 2009; Lambert, 2010a, 2010b; Miller, Duncan, Sorrell, & Brown, 2005; Miller et al., 2006). Regular use of evaluative tools also facilitates client satisfaction and, importantly, enhances the quality of the worker–client relationship.

Recognition of the significance of relationship factors and helper characteristics has encouraged researchers to explore personal qualities that might be associated with better client outcomes. Qualities such as empathy, caring, noncontrolling warmth, acceptance, affirmation, sincerity, and encouragement are frequently included among the characteristics of effective helpers (Duncan, Miller, Wampold, & Hubble, 2010; Hubble, Duncan, & Miller, 1999). When professionals reflect these facilitative qualities, we tend to foster

> a cooperative working endeavor in which the client's increased sense of trust, security, and safety, along with decreases in tension, threat, and anxiety, lead to changes in conceptualizing his or her problems and ultimately in acting differently by reframing fears, taking risks, and working through problems in interpersonal relationships (i.e., clients confront and cope with reality in more effective ways). (Lambert & Cattani-Thompson, 1996, p. 603)

Identifying and measuring all the potential factors that affect the outcome of helping processes are enormously complicated undertakings. The picture is especially complex for social workers who fulfill disparate professional functions in extremely varied settings with a wide range of populations confronting extremely challenging social issues. Different social workers in different contexts assume quite different roles and responsibilities. Indeed, a single social worker may emphasize certain characteristics at various times. The social worker serving parents and siblings of babies in the neonatal care unit of a children's hospital emphasizes different qualities than does the worker who serves people addicted to heroin or crack cocaine. Similarly, the social worker "engaged in advocacy may need a more aggressive, directive, dominant approach" (Kadushin, 1983, p. 84). However, even while advocating in a straightforward, assertive manner, social workers remain empathic, respectful, and authentic. Indeed, when these dimensions accompany them, direct assertive expressions are likely to be especially impactful.

Despite the breadth and diversity inherent in social work and the evolutionary nature of relevant research findings, certain aspects of the worker–client experience appear related to client satisfaction and effective outcomes. Krill (1986) suggests that the relationship between a social worker and a client is more likely to be productive if:

- The participants like and respect each other.
- The client is clearly told what to expect and how to contribute to the helping process.
- The worker is warm, genuine, and sincere and regularly expresses empathy about the client's experience.
- The worker and client engage in goal-directed activities such as practice, in-session tasks, or between-session action steps.
- The social worker actively seeks to involve significant people in the client's life in the helping process. (p. xi)

The characteristics of effective helpers are often called the facilitative qualities or the core conditions (Carkhuff & Truax, 1965; Rogers, 1951, 1957, 1961; Truax & Carkhuff, 1967). When consistently demonstrated by helping professionals, the qualities of empathy, respect, and authenticity contribute to the development and maintenance of a special rapport with our clients. Various authors refer to this special relationship rapport as the helping relationship, the working relationship, the therapeutic alliance, professional rapport, or the working alliance. Perlman (1979) suggested that we could distinguish the professional working relationship between social worker and client from other relationships by the following characteristics:

- It is formed for a recognized and agreed-upon purpose.
- It is time-bound.
- It is *for* the client.
- It carries authority.
- It is a controlled relationship. (pp. 48–77)

The nature and quality of the working relationship are affected by the common factors and by the degree of agreement about what to do and how to do it. When social workers and clients agree on the problems or issues they will address in their work together; the goals they will pursue, the methods by which they plan to achieve those goals; and the means by which they will evaluate progress, the likelihood of success improves. Disagreements on one or more of these aspects can strain, damage, or even rupture the working alliance, leading to diminished hope and motivation, and decreased goal-oriented activity. In many instances, disagreements about problems, goals, and plans emerge in first meetings and become so troublesome that clients do not return for a subsequent visit.

Obviously, the quality of the working relationship is powerfully affected by workers' attitudes toward and behavior with clients. Consensus about problems, goals, and plans is more easily reached when social workers consistently reflect the essential facilitative qualities. Under such conditions, the risk of harm tends to decrease and the likelihood of benefit tends to increase. Indeed, a positive working alliance is clearly associated with favorable outcomes in work with individuals, couples, families, groups, and organizations (Anker, Owen, Duncan, & Sparks, 2010; Escudero, Heatherington, & Friedlander, 2010; Horvath & Bedi, 2002; Horvath, Symonds, & Tapia, 2010; Martin, Garske, & Davis, 2000; Meier, Barrowclough, & Donmall, 2005; Muran & Barber, 2010; Owen, Rhoades, Stanley, & Markman, 2011; Piper & Ogrodniczuk, 2010; Safran & Muran, 2000; Watson & Kalogerakos, 2010). However, demonstrating these qualities alone is rarely enough to enable clients to reach agreed-upon goals. Social workers nearly always need to add expert knowledge and skills to help clients progress toward goal attainment; and, together with our clients, we often seek situational, social, or environmental change as well. Furthermore, social workers must apply the facilitative qualities differentially according to the individual and cultural characteristics of each client. Some clients feel quite uneasy when the worker is frequently and intensively empathic. They might prefer a formal encounter in which the worker provides direct advice and guidance in a businesslike fashion. Others seem to benefit from an emotionally close and intimate relationship where both the client and the worker share personal thoughts and feelings. Obviously, client characteristics play a powerful role in both the process and outcomes of the working relationship. Motivated clients who participate actively in the process and anticipate favorable results tend to benefit from competent, relevant services. Clients who are ambivalent or pessimistic and those who passively or reluctantly engage in the process tend to experience less favorable outcomes. Of course, both social workers and clients may change, sometimes from moment to moment, during an encounter. Indeed, many clients seem to follow certain stages of change (Prochaska, 1999; Prochaska et al., 1994). Indeed, some people first contact social workers well before they are ready or motivated to engage actively in plans for change. A caring, involved, and encouraging worker may help to increase a client's hope and optimism and thus help the client to proceed to a more active stage of change. Conversely, a motivated, energetic, hard-working client may encourage a social worker to become more understanding and supportive.

Regardless of theoretical orientation and choice of intervention approach, effective helpers tend to reflect certain facilitative qualities in our service to others. Helping professionals express these conditions differentially according to the individual client, the unique circumstances of the person-in-environment, the nature of the social worker's role, and the phase of service. Nonetheless, as a general guide, social workers should consistently reflect the following essential facilitative qualities in relationships with others: (1) empathy, (2) respect, and (3) authenticity.

Empathy

The term *empathy* (Altmann, 1973; Bohart & Greenberg, 1997a, 1997b; Bozarth, 1997; Keefe, 1976; Pinderhughes, 1979; Rogers, 1975) is widely used in social work and other helping professions. Derived from the Greek word *empatheia*, empathy may be described as a process of joining in the feelings of another, of feeling how and what another person experiences, of feeling with someone, or of "suffering with" another.

Scholars in the areas of neuroscience, social psychology, philosophy, and anthropology have approached the study of empathy from different perspectives. Batson (2009), for example, notes that some researchers focus on "how" people come to understand what others are thinking, feeling, or experiencing while others study those factors that lead people to respond to others' distress with care, compassion, and understanding. Among the various research uses of the empathy concept include those that involve: recognizing the thoughts, feelings, and internal subjective experience of someone else; feeling personally distressed when observing another person's distress or feeling the emotions that another person feels; adopting another's perspective and imagining how she or he might be thinking and feeling; matching the body position, movements, and mannerisms of someone; imagining oneself in another person's place or circumstances and identifying what one would think and feel; and feeling sympathy for a distressed other (Batson, 2009).

Empathy may indeed appear in several forms. For example, when we interact with someone who feels distress and we both feel her or his distress and show our concern, we engage in *proximal empathy*. When we become concerned about people outside our immediate vicinity—perhaps those in another part of our community or in a distant corner of the world—we reflect *altruistic empathy*. When we say or do something that contributes to others' discomfort and then, upon noticing their reaction, express our awareness and show our concern—perhaps by acknowledging the impact of our own actions—we engage in *self-corrective empathy* (Quann & Wien, 2006, July).

Not surprisingly, a capacity and willingness to take on others' perspectives, imagine being in their circumstances, or feel what they feel, is fundamental to most moral philosophies. Stotland (2001) concludes that "the key antecedent condition for empathy appears to be the empathizer's imagining himself or herself as having the same experience as the other—thus imaginatively taking the role of the other" (Empathy section, para 6). In effect, empathy involves the proverbial "putting oneself in another's shoes." Indeed, empathic imagination is reflected in both the Golden and Silver Rules which hold, respectively, that we should (1) treat others as we would like to be treated and (2) not treat others in ways that we would not like to be treated.

Along with several other species, *Homo sapiens* seem to possess an innate capacity for empathy. Among human children, empathic reactions first become apparent in the one-to-two-year age range; overlapping with the period known as the "terrible twos." In social contexts, toddlers readily display empathic responses to others' expressions of distress or discomfort. In effect, they are empathic "mind-readers" (Ickes, 2003) who routinely perceive and experience what others are experiencing (Iacoboni, 2008).

Frans de Waal (2009) suggests that empathy is multilayered and involves three core elements along with multiple subordinate capacities. The core three include: (a) the ability to adopt another's perspective or point of view; (b) concern for others—often manifested through expressions and acts of consolation, that is, seeking to comfort or console another; and (c) feeling what the other is feeling or matching the emotional state or expression of the other.

Unless socialized out of us, most humans possess an ability to transcend our selfish tendencies and recognize that we are part of a larger community; a larger whole or "hive" (Haidt, Seder, & Kesebir, 2008) and connect empathically with other members (de Waal, 2009; Trout, 2009). Roman Krznaric uses the term "outrospection" (2012) in an attempt to encourage humans to focus less on our own and more on others' thoughts, feelings, and circumstances. He concludes that, individually and collectively, many of us are becoming so self-oriented and self-centered that our empathic abilities are beginning to atrophy.

Considerable scholarship suggests that a key foundation for human morality involves this extraordinary capacity for empathy (Carter, Harris, & Porges, 2009). If so, individuals and groups that highly value empathy would likely be more kind, "moral," and altruistic than those that devalue and discourage empathic involvement with others. Indeed, tolerance, acceptance, compassion, and generosity toward others—especially others who are "different" in some way—require considerable levels of empathy.

Perhaps especially in social contexts that place great importance on the individual; value self-interest; emphasize adversarial conflict and competition; and promote extreme notions of personal autonomy and individual responsibility, empathic interest in the experiences of others is likely to diminish as children grow into adulthood. Indeed, some cultures tend to emphasize the "self" much more than the "other"; and the "I" and "me" much more than the "you," "we," or "us." In such contexts, individuals may focus primarily on themselves; their own thoughts, feelings, and experiences; and their own appearance, possessions, status, and wealth. Conversely, they may ignore or discount people outside their primary social circle and especially those who differ from themselves. In some sociopolitical and economic contexts, self-centeredness and self-admiration may be promoted as a high moral value. Indeed, greed and the accumulation and display of material wealth may be equated with goodness.

The Latin phrase *caveat emptor* (let the buyer beware) captures an ethos in which benefitting oneself at the expense of another is viewed as legitimate and, indeed, desirable. The burden of responsibility is placed upon consumers to be knowledgeable, vigilant, and self-disciplined in their resistance to sellers' deception, distortion, pressure, and manipulation. Sellers who intentionally disregard predictable negative consequences to consumers and profit greatly from such exchanges tend to increase their wealth and status, and enhance their reputation as valued members of a community. Empathic feelings for exploited consumers are suppressed while the benefits to oneself are emphasized.

Obviously, greed and selfishness are hardly limited to the economic sphere. Self-centeredness and self-admiration, perhaps to the extent of narcissism, may be endemic in some societies and some cultures (Campbell, Bush, Brunell, & Shelton, 2005; Twenge & Campbell, 2009; Twenge, Konrath, Foster, Campbell, & Bushman, 2008). Interestingly, a preoccupation with oneself may run counter to humans' evolution as highly social animals (Aronson & Aronson, 2012; Brooks, 2011). Despite a prevailing view that humans are basically selfish creatures, much evidence suggests that we are also cooperative and collaborative in nature. Humans actually tend to be extraordinarily "groupish" (Christakis & Fowler, 2009; Haidt et al., 2008; McTaggart, 2011; Montagu & Matson, 1979) in their social behavior. Somewhat like bees in a hive, we tend to thrive in most social contexts and decline in solitary environments. Is it any wonder that severe punishments often involve banishment from one's community or imprisonment in long-term solitary confinement?

Social workers in particular tend to recognize the importance of the social dimensions of human experience. We seek to transcend the powerful cultural and economic forces that promote excessive egocentricity by developing strength and skill in empathic understanding, communication, and connectedness. We recognize that our efforts to help others address problems and pursue goals become more effective when we genuinely experience and express authentic empathy. Simply stated, helpers who sincerely experience and accurately demonstrate empathy in their helping activities tend to be more effective than those who do not (Bohart & Greenberg, 1997a; Breggin, 1997; Patterson, 1984).

In social work, however, we make a distinction between empathy and several related emotional responses. Social workers tend to view empathy as a conscious and intentional joining with others in their subjective experience. It involves being intellectually and emotionally present, attentive, and responsive in relationships. However, empathy is not an expression of *feeling for* or *feeling toward* as we might if we pity another person. Nor is it a diagnostic or evaluative appraisal (Hammond, Hepworth, & Smith, 1977, p. 3). Rather, empathy involves thinking and feeling *as and with another*.

Naturally, there are limits to anyone's ability and willingness to feel with and feel as another does. In fact, as a professional social worker, you must always retain a portion of yourself for your professional responsibilities. Be careful not to overidentify with clients. Clients retain ownership of their thoughts and feelings. They are not yours to keep. Indeed, if you were to "take" or assume clients' feelings as your own, you might well become controlling or perhaps paternalistic or maternalistic in your approach to them.

Empathy helps us gain an understanding of, appreciation for, and sensitivity to the people we serve. Through empathic connection with your clients, you increase the probability of developing rapport and maintaining productive working relationships; and, partly as a result, improve the chances for an effective outcome.

Respect

Integrally related to empathy is the facilitative quality of *respect* (Hammond et al., 1977, pp. 170–203). Respect suggests an attitude of noncontrolling, warm, caring, and nonpossessive acceptance of other people. Involving aspects of awe or reference, wonder, and curiosity, respect includes the demonstration of unconditional positive regard (Rogers, 1957, 1961) and recognition of the unique experience of each individual person. In intercultural contexts, respect also includes the genuine acceptance of difference and, indeed, the celebration of diversity. Respect of this nature goes far beyond basic tolerance to include appreciation for the value of diversity and difference in human communities and throughout the biological and ecological environment as well.

We humans tend to spend most of our time with people like ourselves, who live and work in similar circumstances, who have comparable incomes and social status, who hold views that resemble our own, and who express interest in and affection toward us. Conversely, we tend to spend less time with people unlike ourselves, who live and work in different circumstances, who have much higher or lower incomes and social status, who espouse views that differ from our own, and are unfriendly or disinterested in us. Very few of us actively seek out and engage people who differ from ourselves and even fewer of us seem willing to consider the relevance, utility, or reasonableness of points of view that conflict with our own.

Some of us frequently engage in a "let's blame them" form of thinking in which selected problems in the world or in our own lives are viewed as caused by various others—people we call *them* as distinguished from people we call *us*. This kind of thinking is often linked to scapegoating and sometimes to hatred, discrimination, persecution, and conflict. There are numerous examples throughout the course of human history. What often happens is that a particular group, usually one having greater numbers or possessing greater wealth or status and power, holds another group—usually one that is smaller in size or possessing less wealth, status or power—responsible for past or current social or economic problems. In recent and contemporary history, humans have blamed members of other religious faiths or nonbelievers, other racial or ethnic groups, and people in different circumstances or statuses. For example, immigrants, welfare recipients, women, union members, and persons who are gay or lesbian have been blamed for a myriad of social and economic problems. Obviously, views that certain others are lesser than we are and the cause of our problems contributes to an "us" versus "them" form of thinking which, in turn, fosters various forms of prejudice, discrimination, segregation, and oppression. Such thinking is apparent in all spheres of society— from the international and societal levels to the family, neighborhood, and organizational levels. Indeed, individuals and groups within school communities commonly engage in various kinds of bullying—sometimes by students toward other students; sometimes by students toward adults; sometimes by adults toward students, and sometimes by adults toward other adults.

Despite these human tendencies to judge, divide, and separate, we social workers routinely work with people who differ from ourselves—and often differ in multiple ways. Before long, you will undoubtedly begin to serve people who are very much unlike yourself in personal, familial, philosophical, religious, or political views. And, sometimes, you will serve clients who are extremely similar to yourself. At times, you may find that you do not personally like some clients; and some clients will dislike you. You may disagree with the beliefs, attitudes, and actions of many others. Nonetheless, as a social worker, you maintain respect for and caring acceptance of the people you serve or engage.

Social workers aspire to view each person as unique and inherently valuable, and as an important member of the human community. We convey our respect and regard by prizing and cherishing the personhood of all clients, regardless of the nature of their racial or ethnic backgrounds, gender, sexual orientation, age, ability, appearance, status, views, actions, or circumstances. Although we may personally disapprove of some clients' words or deeds, we continue to care about and accept them as unique people of dignity and worth. Furthermore, we recognize the fundamental right of clients to make their own decisions. This ability to respect clients neither because of nor in spite of their views, attributes, behaviors, or circumstances is an essential facilitative condition in social work practice.

Caring for clients as valuable human beings, however, does not preclude you from formulating professional assessments or prevent you from offering suggestions and advice. You need not turn off your brain to demonstrate positive regard for others. Nor does respect for clients mean that you neglect other people, groups, or communities in the process. Indeed, a person-in-environment perspective suggests that you always consider people and social systems affecting and affected by the clients you serve.

Authenticity

Authenticity refers to the genuineness and sincerity of a person's manner of relating. Reflecting fundamental honesty, an authentic social worker is natural, real, and personable. The presentation is congruent, so that verbal, nonverbal, and behavioral expressions reflect synchronicity. Words and deeds match. The genuine social worker is nondefensive; open to others' ideas, suggestions, and feedback; and forthright in sharing thoughts and feelings. "An authentic person relates to others personally, so that expressions do not seem rehearsed or contrived" (Hammond et al., 1977, p. 7).

Earlier, we discussed the significance of regularly and systematically seeking evaluative feedback from clients. Such processes involve aspects of authenticity in that social workers strive to transcend preconceived notions and biases, and use client feedback to reduce the likelihood that our service might be ineffective or harmful, and increase the probability that it might actually help.

Certainly, various psychological and social services have the capacity to and often do benefit consumers. Indeed, our professional efforts often dramatically enhance the lives of the individuals, families, groups, organizations, and communities we serve. Unfortunately, however, we can also do much damage. Studies suggest that between 9 and 14 percent of clients are detrimentally affected by counseling and psychotherapy services. In other words, a substantial number of clients are worse off than they were before they sought professional help. At least as disturbing as these figures, and perhaps more so, is the fact that many and perhaps most helping professionals cannot accurately identify which of their clients are deteriorating (Lambert & Shimokawa, 2011). We social workers, like most other humans, reflect a tendency to ignore information that challenges our view of ourselves as "good people, doing good work." We tend to believe that we would certainly recognize it if any of our clients failed to benefit or worsened during our service to them. However, Lambert and his colleagues' research studies (Crits-Christoph et al., 2012; Hawkins et al., 2004; Lambert, 2010a, 2010b; Lambert & Shimokawa, 2011; Lambert et al., 2002; Slade et al., 2008) suggest that unless our clients provide us with regular, formal, and systematic evaluative feedback, and unless we use that feedback to improve the quality of our services, we will probably also fail to notice when our clients fail to progress or begin to worsen. Authentic social workers actively attempt to seek evaluative feedback from clients.

Genuineness, congruence, transparency, or authenticity (Rogers, 1961) may sometimes seem contrary to the notion of the professional social worker as cool, calm, and collected. However, professionalism in social work does not mean adopting a stiffly formal or overly controlled attitude. As a social worker, you need not and should not present yourself as an unfeeling, detached, computer-like technician. People seeking social services almost always prefer to talk with a knowledgeable and competent professional who comes across as a living, breathing, feeling human being—not as someone playing a canned role, spouting clichés, or repeating the same phrases again and again.

This emphasis on authenticity or genuineness in the working relationship, however, does not grant us license to say or do whatever we think or feel in that moment. Remember that the helping relationship is fundamentally *for* the client. It is not primarily for us social workers. Expression of our own thoughts and feelings for any purpose other than serving the client and working toward mutually agreed-upon goals is, at best, inefficient and, at worst, harmful.

Professionalism

Integral to the values and ethics of social work and inherent in several aspects of the essential facilitative qualities, *professionalism* is so important to social workers individually and collectively that it requires special attention. Professionalism includes several characteristics: (1) integrity, (2) professional knowledge and self-efficacy, (3) self-understanding and self-control, (4) social support, (5) critical thinking, scientific inquiry, and career-long learning, (6) valuing diversity and difference, (7) advancing human rights and social justice, (8) promoting social well-being, and, of course, (9) ethical decision making. We explore these characteristics in the next few chapters.

Summary

Social work has a radical mission that includes promoting social and economic justice, enhancing social well-being and quality of life, and eliminating discrimination, oppression, and poverty. In pursuit of these aspirations, effective social workers regularly demonstrate empathy, respect, authenticity, and professionalism in our work with others. These characteristics and qualities are reflected throughout the entire helping process—from preparing for and beginning with clients through the conclusion of work. They are also apparent in our exchanges with other members of client systems, referral sources, various stakeholders, and members of the general public.

CHAPTER 1: SUMMARY EXERCISE

1. Reflect upon the content addressed in this introductory chapter. Then, use your own thoughts and ideas to word-process brief essay responses to the items listed below. Do not refer to reference materials or consult other people.

    a. What do the terms *social and economic justice*, and *social well-being* mean to you?

    b. What do the terms *human rights*, *discrimination*, *oppression*, and *poverty* mean to you?

    c. How do you think the concepts of *equality* and *inequality* relate to social and economic justice, social well-being, and to human rights, discrimination, oppression, and poverty?

    d. Identify a group of people affected by a social problem with whom you would find it easy to experience and demonstrate *empathy*, *respect*, *authenticity*, and *professionalism*. Then, identify a group of people with whom you would currently find it extremely difficult to experience and demonstrate empathy, respect, authenticity, and professionalism. Discuss how and why you currently think the former would be easy and the latter so difficult.

    e. Finally, discuss your thoughts about and reactions to social work's mission and purpose, and to its conception as a radical profession.

    Organize your short essay responses in accord with the items. Label the document "Introduction to Social Work: Preliminary Thoughts and Ideas" and include it within your electronic Social Work Skills Learning Portfolio (see Appendix 1).

CHAPTER 1: SELF-APPRAISAL

As you finish this chapter, please reflect on your learning by completing the following self-appraisal exercise.

SELF-APPRAISAL: INTRODUCTION

Please respond to the following items by carefully reading each statement. Then use the following 4-point rating scale to indicate the degree to which you agree or disagree with each statement. Record your numerical response in the space provided:

4 = Strongly agree   2 = Disagree

3 = Agree   1 = Strongly disagree

4	3	2	1	Rating Statement
				At this point in time, I can
☐	☐	☐	☐	1. Describe the mission and purposes of the social work profession.
☐	☐	☐	☐	2. Identify the characteristics of professionalism.
☐	☐	☐	☐	3. Define the concepts of social work skills and competencies.
☐	☐	☐	☐	4. Identify the phases or processes of social work practice.
☐	☐	☐	☐	5. Describe the essential facilitative qualities or conditions of empathy, respect, and authenticity.
☐	☐	☐	☐	6. Identify the nine aspects of professionalism addressed in *The Social Work Skills Workbook*.
☐	☐	☐	☐	7. Describe the five common factors associated with effective helping relationships.
☐	☐	☐	☐	8. Describe the purposes and functions of *The Social Work Skills Learning Portfolio*.
				Subtotal

Note: These items are identical to those contained in the Introduction section of the Social Work Skills Self-Appraisal Questionnaire presented in Appendix 3. If you completed that self-appraisal before beginning Chapter 1, you have already responded to these items once before. You may now compare the responses you made on that occasion with those you made this time. Also, compare the two subtotals. If you believe that you have progressed in terms of your proficiency, the more recent subtotal should be higher than the earlier one.

CHAPTER 2

INTRODUCTION TO PROFESSIONALISM

Society entrusts the profession of social work and social workers with the status, authority, and responsibility for providing social services to vulnerable people. In this chapter, we begin to explore several fundamental aspects of professionalism (see Box 2.1). We examine the concept of professionalism and consider the following dimensions: integrity, professional knowledge and self-efficacy, self-understanding and self-control, and social support. In Chapter 3, we explore the processes of scientific inquiry, critical thinking, and career-long or lifelong learning. In Chapter 4, we consider diversity and difference, human rights and social and economic justice, social well-being, and policy practice. In Chapter 5, we address the complex and ever-demanding challenges of ethical decision making—one of the most crucial aspects of professionalism.

Each of the four chapters contains learning exercises to help you explore these interrelated aspects. Here in Chapter 2, you also learn to prepare a family genogram, an eco-map, and a critical events timeline; and you become familiar with a contemporary approach to personality assessment. These tools should enhance your self-understanding and help some clients better understand themselves and their social environments as well. In addition, you create more materials for your Social Work Skills Learning Portfolio.

Professionalism: A Working Definition and Conceptual Framework

Membership in the community of professional helpers involves considerable status, power, and prestige. A professional is one who "has or displays . . . skill, knowledge, experience, standards, or expertise . . . [and is] . . . competent, efficient" (*The Oxford English Dictionary* [OED] *Online*, 2009). In the case of social work, however, professionalism goes well beyond knowledge, competence, and expertise to incorporate qualities of honesty, honor, and humility; dedication, commitment, and altruism; and, importantly, adherence to a core set of values and a code of ethics. Our conception of professionalism in social work includes the dimensions of: (1) sophisticated knowledge, competence, self-efficacy, and expertise in the provision of social work services; (2) respect for and adherence to the values of the social work profession and its code of ethics; (3) personal and professional integrity, self-understanding and self-control, and social support; (4) critical thinking, scientific inquiry, and career-long learning; (5) engagement in diversity and respect for difference; (6) advancement of human rights and social justice; and (7) promotion of social well-being.

Figure 2.1 depicts this working definition in the form of a conceptual framework. Notice that the terms "status" and "licensed" do not appear in the conceptual framework. Although social workers certainly do benefit from their status and authority as licensed or certified professionals, the fundamental aspects of professionalism involve our knowledge, attitudes, ideals, expertise, and actions rather than our social position, educational achievements, or prestige. Indeed, sometimes our privileged status as professionals may leave us hesitant to take action against discrimination, oppression, inequality, and other forms of social injustice. Perhaps because we have worked so long and hard to become professionals, we may fear the loss of our social status—and perhaps our employment—if we were to actively advocate against certain aspects of injustice. Such ambivalence is hardly surprising. In general, professionals have greater access to power and prestige than do nonprofessionals. Risk of diminished status or threat of job loss tends to promote an establishmentarian orientation that favors the social, political, and economic status quo and may interfere with our mission as a radical profession.

Although social work's mission clearly involves advocacy for human rights, elimination of discrimination and oppression, an end to poverty, promotion of social and economic justice, and the

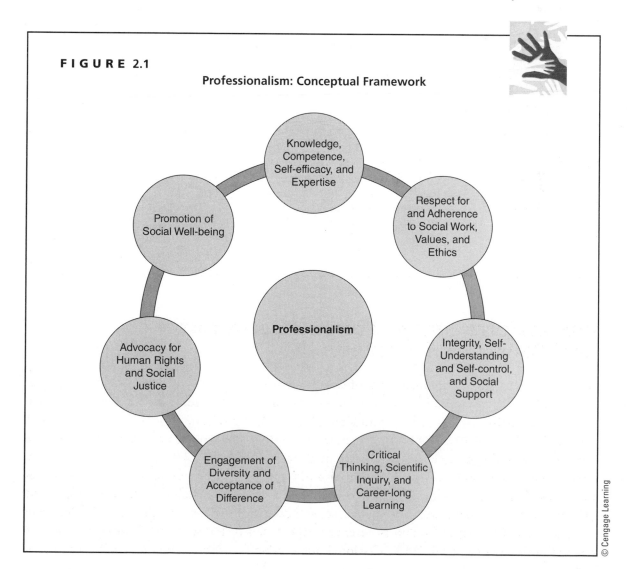

FIGURE 2.1

Professionalism: Conceptual Framework

Knowledge, Competence, Self-efficacy, and Expertise

Respect for and Adherence to Social Work, Values, and Ethics

Promotion of Social Well-being

Professionalism

Integrity, Self-Understanding and Self-control, and Social Support

Advocacy for Human Rights and Social Justice

Critical Thinking, Scientific Inquiry, and Career-long Learning

Engagement of Diversity and Acceptance of Difference

© Cengage Learning

enhancement of all persons' quality of life, we social workers sometimes reflect cautious and conservative tendencies—even when current conditions reflect obvious and pervasive social injustice. Despite our understandable hesitation and inertia, however, let's be courageous. Let's engage in active, conscientious attempts to transcend our own self-interest and safety as we learn how to pursue social work's mission and help clients address issues, achieve their goals, and enhance the quality of their lives while also working to eliminate poverty and promote social and economic justice.

Individuals, families, groups, organizations, communities, and the society as a whole depend on the social work profession to fulfill vital psychosocial functions and address pressing social problems. Each year, people invest enormous amounts of public and private monies into health and human services of all kinds. Several millions receive services from the approximately 700,000 social workers in the United States alone.

In the 2012–2013 Occupational Outlook Handbook, the U.S. Bureau of Labor Statistics (BLS) reported that about 650,500 social workers were employed in the United States during 2010. The job outlook appears favorable for the next decade as employment opportunities for more than 160,000 additional social workers are anticipated by 2020. That should bring the total number of employed social workers to more than 810,000 (2012, March 29). Table 2.1 illustrates the number of employed social workers by type of setting in 2010.

The actual number of social workers employed in the United States is probably considerably higher than the official figures indicate, as many social workers appear within other occupational categories (for example, substance abuse and behavioral disorder counselors; educational, vocational, and school counselors; marriage and family therapists; probation officers). Furthermore, the BLS figures do not include self-employed social workers. There are indeed a lot of us!

Social workers affect people in profound ways—usually for better, but sometimes for worse. Given the large number of social workers and the nature and scope of the services we provide, the importance of professionalism cannot be overemphasized. When social workers are competent and trustworthy, our clients feel satisfied and society as a whole benefits. The overall reputation of social workers and our profession improves. However, when social workers lack professionalism, many people suffer. Clients or others affected by our policies, programs, and practices may be harmed. Indeed, some clients may lose their lives due to social workers' negligence or incompetence. Because a few social workers lack professionalism, employers may become reluctant to hire others. The stature of the profession may decline, and funding sources may become less inclined to support social services in general.

TABLE 2.1
Number of Employed Social Workers in the United States by Setting in 2010

Social Work Employment Setting	Number
Child, family, and school social workers	295,700
Health care social workers	152,700
Mental health and substance abuse social workers	126,100
Social workers, all others	76,000
TOTAL	650,500
Source: U.S. Bureau of Labor Statistics, Employment Projections Program (2012, March 29)	

Because the stakes are so high, social workers are obligated—personally, morally, ethically, and legally—to reflect high standards of professionalism in all aspects of our service activities. Fortunately, most of us are committed to providing ethical and effective services to our clients and promoting a better quality of life for all people. Most social workers are knowledgeable in their areas of practice and honest and trustworthy in their relations with others. Most social workers sincerely try to demonstrate understanding, respect, compassion, and competence in their efforts to provide high-quality services. Most of us try to keep current with advances in professional knowledge. We also recognize that personal behavior in our private lives may affect both our professional reputation and the quality of our professional performance. Indeed, most social workers fully realize that a positive professional reputation among colleagues and constituents results primarily from conscientious attention and consistent adherence to high standards of professionalism.

Integrity

Fundamental to the facilitative qualities of authenticity and respect, integrity is an essential aspect of professionalism. Within the context of social work service, integrity suggests honesty, truthfulness, sincerity, humility, and trustworthiness. In its Code of Ethics, the National Association of Social Workers (NASW, 2008) states that "Social workers should not participate in, condone, or be associated with dishonesty, fraud, or deception" (Section 4.04). However, professional integrity goes well beyond the absence of misbehavior. Rather, it involves the active engagement in ethical behavior.

As a social worker, you demonstrate integrity when you share information that is supported by valid and reliable evidence, and, conversely, when you refrain from repeating invalid and unreliable information. You reflect integrity when you publicly acknowledge others' contributions and credit sources of information used to support your statements and positions. You demonstrate integrity when you openly state that you are sharing a personal opinion rather than a professional recommendation or admit ignorance when you do not know the answer to a particular question. You exemplify integrity when you resist temptations to cheat, lie, or misrepresent facts and when you recognize that your immediate thoughts and emotional reactions may not always serve as a valid basis for professional action. You reflect integrity when you keep your promises and fulfill your commitments. You display integrity when you willingly acknowledge mistakes and errors in your own thoughts, words, and deeds; and change your mind when credible evidence challenges your previously held beliefs.

You manifest integrity when you report to a colleague who exploited a client, cheated on an exam, or plagiarized a report; or, when you admit that you have done so. You reflect integrity when you reveal that your organization intentionally defrauded its funding sources by billing for services it did not provide; and perhaps lose your job when you do so. Despite laws intended to protect honest whistleblowers from retaliation, we recognize that the consequences of trying to right wrongs and combat injustice can be painful indeed (Devine & Maassarani, 2011; Kohn, 2011; Press, 2012). Unfortunately, direct or indirect punishment sometimes results from "doing the right thing."

The Code of Ethics of the NASW includes integrity as one of its core values and describes the related ethical principle as follows:

Value: Integrity

Ethical Principle: Social workers behave in a trustworthy manner.

Social workers are continually aware of the profession's mission, values, ethical principles, and ethical standards and practice in a manner consistent with them. Social workers act honestly and responsibly and promote ethical practices on the part of the organizations with which they are affiliated. (2008, Ethical Principles section, para. 6)

As you consider various aspects of professionalism, none will be more essential than integrity. Adherence to the values and ethics of the profession and to fundamental moral principles such as sincerity, fairness, truthfulness, reliability, dedication, and loyalty is central to professional integrity. However, integrity goes beyond the sum of these virtues to include a general sense of coherence, wholeness, and harmony with social work roles, responsibilities, and expectations. Involving the essential facilitative quality of authenticity as well as personal honor, professional integrity relates to virtually all facets of professional social work. Consider, for example, the notions of trust and credibility. Clients tend to seek the services of social workers and other helping professionals because they assume they will receive honest, fair, responsible, and competent treatment. Indeed, first meetings often reflect an initial trust that may continue throughout the entire course of the relationship. However, clients tend to notice when a professional's words or actions suggest insincerity, irresponsibility, unfairness, incompetence, or dishonesty. Lapses of integrity jeopardize the assumption of goodwill and may leave disappointed clients and their friends and family members unwilling to trust other social workers in the future.

In some instances, these losses may be permanent as a client concludes "I'll never go back to that place" or "I'll never go to another social worker again" or even "I guess it's hopeless." Relationships with colleagues, employers, and community members are similar in this regard. Lapses in integrity can, in short order, damage or destroy personal, family, friendship, and professional relationships.

Perhaps because integrity is so often associated with honesty, trustworthiness, and personal character, one's reputation is extremely difficult to recover once it is damaged. Several years ago, the prestigious *New York Times* discovered that one of its reporters had committed journalistic fraud through numerous instances of falsification, fabrication, and plagiarism. Recognizing the potential impact on its reputation for accuracy and integrity, the *Times* assigned an investigative team to study the trail of deceptive reporting. The investigators summarized their findings in lengthy reports prominently published in the *Times* itself (*The New York Times* staff, 2003, May 11a, 2003, May 11b).

The reporter will probably never work in journalism again. Publishers and editors simply cannot trust him. He is no longer credible. The damage to his personal and professional reputation is so severe that association with any newspaper or magazine would tarnish its image as well. However, the effects go well beyond the individual reporter and even the *Times*. His actions raise questions about the profession of journalism itself. After all, he managed to falsify and plagiarize dozens of reports. How many other reporters are doing the same? Can readers trust any reporters or any newspapers to be honest and accurate?

Some social workers and some social service organizations also violate basic principles of integrity. A few have neglected to fulfill fundamental responsibilities such as regularly checking on the welfare of abused or neglected children under their supervision (Associated Press, 2009, June 9; "Danieal Kelly," 2009; Kaufman & Jones, 2003; Wynn, 2012, May 23). When violations such as these occur, the consequences may be profound. Trust in social workers erodes and regard for the child welfare system declines. Relatives, neighbors, and other citizens may fail to report suspicions of child neglect or abuse out of fear that children will be worse off in the care of the system than they would be if left alone. As a result, children may go without needed protective services and some may suffer severe injuries or die (Associated Press, 2009, June 9).

Some organizations and some social workers have systematically defrauded public and private insurance services by assigning medical or psychiatric diagnoses that do not actually apply to their clients (Reamer, 2008). Others have falsified documents to suggest that they completed work or provided services they did not actually perform (Snider, 2012, April 19; Spears, 2012, July 24; Ujifusa, 2008, July 30). When questioned about such practices, some have obstructed judicial process—perhaps by rewriting or destroying client records (Reuters News Service, 2009, April 21; Wynn, 2012, May 23).

In addition, some social workers have exploited clients for their own personal or financial benefit (Clarridge, 2009, May 9; Shifrel, 2009, June 25). Indeed, sexual relations with clients—expressly forbidden by social work ethical codes—remain a common form of client exploitation (Berkman, Turner, Cooper, Polnerow, & Swartz, 2000). Some social workers have enriched their own bank accounts by embezzling funds from their agencies; by billing clients or third-party insurers for unnecessary services; or by stealing money from foster children (The Associated Press, 2000) or from elderly or disabled clients (WSLS-TV Staff Reports, 2010, October 27). Violations such as these affect many lives. Clients and their loved ones are often directly injured and, of course, the offending social workers often lose their jobs, their licenses, and careers. Some are heavily fined and some go to jail. In addition, the reputations of social workers in general and the profession as a whole are damaged.

In contemporary life, social workers' reputations may also be affected—often quite unfairly—by the incredible memory capacity of our digital devices and the insidious presence of the Internet. Once recorded—whether via a cell phone or laptop camera, an audio or video recorder, or in computer memory—a more or less permanent artifact remains available, perhaps forever. Indeed, we should probably presume that most things that are transmitted or posted electronically remain somewhere in cyberspace. Messages sent via e-mail, instant message, or Twitter; postings on Facebook, MySpace, or other social-networking websites; or statements made in blogs or electronic forums can become quite embarrassing at points in our careers. Those pictures taken during a spring break vacation can come back to haunt us!

Many employers now regularly search the Internet for information about and digital artifacts related to job applicants (de la Llama, Trueba, Voges, Barreto, & Park, 2012). As part of the application process, some now ask prospective employees to permit them access to their personal Facebook pages. Even when the reality is entirely understandable and quite innocent, the appearance of personal impropriety can negatively affect our professional reputation, our ability to obtain or maintain a position, and our opportunity to help people in need.

Helping professionals tend to benefit from a presumption of integrity. What an extraordinary gift! Involving exceptional power and influence, it carries enormous moral responsibility. Cherish it and consider your personal and professional integrity and reputation among your most valuable assets. Keep your promises. Maintain a sense of humility. Sincerely acknowledge your mistakes. Be forthcoming about your level of knowledge, skills, and areas of competence. Tell your clients and colleagues the truth. Be transparent about your work. Furthermore, and perhaps most importantly, be brutally honest with yourself. Adopt an extreme attitude in this regard. Among helping professionals, self-deception is a most dangerous conceit.

Knowledge and Self-Efficacy

Advanced professional knowledge is, of course, essential for ethical and effective social work practice. In social work, the particular knowledge required varies considerably according to the characteristics of the setting, the issues for work, the populations served, and the roles assumed. However, a common base of knowledge exists for all social workers. For instance, educational programs accredited by the Council on Social Work Education (2008) offer curriculums that include knowledge about:

◆ The social work profession—including its history, mission, and core values, ethics and relevant laws and regulations
◆ Human rights, civil rights, and social and economic justice

- ◆ Research and the principles of logic, scientific inquiry, and reasoned discernment
- ◆ Effective oral and written communication
- ◆ Human behavior and the social environment—including human development across the life span, social systems, and theories and knowledge that further understanding of biological, social, cultural, psychological, and spiritual aspects of human activity and development
- ◆ Diversity, difference, and culture; poverty, oppression, discrimination, marginalization, and alienation; and privilege, power, and acclaim
- ◆ The history and current structures of social policies and services; the role of policy in service delivery; and the role of practice in policy development
- ◆ The dynamic organizational, community, and societal contexts, which influence social work practice and the profession
- ◆ Social work practice—including theoretical and research-based models relevant for engaging, assessing, preventing, intervening, and evaluating in service with individuals, families, groups, organizations, and communities (pp. 3–7)

In addition, the CSWE indicates that graduates of accredited programs should be able to demonstrate specific competencies, which "are measurable practice behaviors that are comprised of knowledge, values, and skills" (2008, p. 3). A large array of competencies, knowledge dimensions, and related practice behaviors are identified—many of which are demonstrable in field practicum experiences. In addition to classroom and laboratory courses, the field practicum enables students to apply professional knowledge in supervised practice contexts. In such settings, students learn through doing, and refine skills and competencies that would be difficult to develop in any other way.

Although they may vary in specific information and emphasis, all CSWE accredited social work programs address these common knowledge areas and help students develop proficiency in specific competencies. The CSWE expectations are consistent with those suggested by the NASW (1981, p. 17). They are also congruent with the content areas addressed in the nationally standardized social work licensing examinations used throughout most of the 50 states, the District of Columbia, Puerto Rico, the U.S. Virgin Islands, and several Canadian provinces.

The major content areas addressed in nationally standardized Bachelor's and Master's level examinations sponsored by the Association of Social Work Boards (ASWB) (2011)[1] include those contained in Table 2.2. The ASWB also sponsors Advanced Generalist and Clinical Examinations. These nationally standardized social work examinations ensure that reasonably equivalent standards exist throughout most of the United States and Canada. They, along with the policies of NASW and CSWE, help to establish a common social work knowledge base.

In addition to sophisticated knowledge and skill, social workers must *believe* that they can make a difference. Just as clients benefit when they believe in the goodwill, integrity, and competence of social workers, social workers benefit from self-confidence as well. Supported by knowledge and expertise, we need attitudes of hope, optimism, and self-efficacy.

For social workers, self-efficacy involves the "confidence in their ability to execute specific skills in a particular set of circumstances and thereby achieve a successful outcome" (Holden, Meenaghan, Anastas, & Metrey, 2001, p. 116). Without knowledge-based self-efficacy, social workers would likely be relatively inactive, passive observers rather than energetic, collaborative agents of change. Gary Holden, in particular, has contributed greatly to the development of specialized

---

[1] You may access the Association of Social Work Boards at www.aswb.org, the Council on Social Work Education at www.cswe.org, and the National Association of Social Workers at www.socialworkers.org.

TABLE 2.2
Content Areas: ASWB Sponsored Bachelor's and Master's Examinations

	Bachelor's Examination	Proportion of Exam Items	Master's Examination	Proportion of Exam Items
I.	Human development, diversity, and behavior in the environment	27%	Human development, diversity, and behavior in the environment	28%
II.	Assessment	28%	Assessment and intervention planning	24%
III.	Direct and indirect practice	26%	Direct and indirect practice	21%
IV.	Professional relationships, values, and ethics	19%	Professional relationships, values, and ethics	27%
		100.00%		100.00%

Adapted from Association of Social Work Boards, 2011.

self-efficacy assessment instruments for use in social work practice and education (Holden, 1991; Holden, Barker, Rosenberg, & Onghena, 2008; Holden, Cuzzi, Rutter, Chernack, & Rosenberg, 1997; Holden, Cuzzi, Rutter, Rosenberg, & Chernack, 1996; Holden, Cuzzi, Spitzer, et al., 1997; Holden, Meenaghan, & Anastas, 2003). In addition to specific forms of self-efficacy, people tend to benefit from a generalized belief in their own competence to effect change in themselves and their lives (Bandura, 1977, 1992, 1995a, 1997, 1995b).

> People make causal contributions to their own psychosocial functioning through mechanisms of personal agency. Among the mechanisms of agency, none is more central or pervasive than people's beliefs of personal efficacy. Perceived self-efficacy refers to beliefs in one's capabilities to organize and execute the courses of action required to manage prospective situations. Efficacy beliefs influence how people think, feel, motivate themselves, and act. (Bandura, 1995a, p. 2)

As the 21st century unfolds, social workers and the social work profession face extraordinary, and probably unprecedented, challenges (Austin, 1997). A broad and deep base of current, valid, and reliable knowledge and a correspondingly strong sense of self-efficacy are required for ethical and effective social work practice in the often unpredictable, contemporary world.

In addition to the Council on Social Work Education (2008), the National Association of Social Workers (1981), and the Association of Social Work Boards (2011), eminent social workers (Bartlett, 1958, 1970; Minahan, 1981) have also helped to clarify the general parameters of a common social work knowledge base. In actual practice, however, social workers also require a great deal of specialized knowledge that applies to the unique characteristics of the clientele and communities we serve. Suppose, for example, that you provide social work services to women physically abused in domestic violence circumstances. Just imagine how much you would need to know to serve your clients and community effectively!

You would need to be well acquainted with the current theoretical and research literature concerning the nature and outcome of social services for domestically abused women; and those for abusive men and children exposed to such violence as well. You would need to know the factors that contribute to domestic violence, as well as those that tend to reduce its likelihood. You would have to understand the range of risks facing women in such circumstances and know how to assess the risk of injury or death. You would need to know what to do when risk is high, moderate, or low; and how to help clients consider the risk–benefit ratio of various courses of action.

In approaching service from a person-in-environment perspective, you would need to know how to identify, assess, and intervene in primary and secondary social systems. Knowledge about the racial and ethnic cultures of your community would help. Knowledge about and skill in determining the biopsychosocial needs of children affected by domestic violence could apply in many circumstances. Expertise in assessing the strengths and potentials of all members of the primary social system—including people suspected of initiating violence—could help to deepen understanding and identify possible solutions. You would need to know the laws and regulations of the locale where you serve and the professional values and ethics that might apply. You would have to be familiar with the actual and potential resources—locally, nationally, and, sometimes, internationally—that might become needed at various times in the process. In sum, competent social work service in such a setting would require a truly sophisticated level of both general and specialized professional knowledge and expertise.

This book focuses on social work skills. It does not address the entire common social work knowledge base or the specific expertise needed in particular service contexts. There are several extremely rich sources of information in these areas. Recently published textbooks in human behavior and social environment, social policy, research, and social work practice cover the common base extraordinarily well. In addition, numerous high-quality professional journals that address specific aspects, dimensions, approaches, and areas of social service can also help to inform social workers.

In this book, you explore an important part of the common social work knowledge base. However, it is only a part. We focus here on the qualities of professionalism and the skills needed for ethical, effective social work practice throughout the preparing, beginning, exploring, assessing, contracting, working and evaluating, and ending phases of practice.

Self-Understanding and Self-Control

In addition to integrity, knowledge, and self-efficacy, professionalism also involves a sophisticated level of self-understanding and self-control. Because social work practice involves the conscious and deliberate use of various facets of yourself, you become the medium through which to convey knowledge, attitudes, and skill. Therefore, you need a truly extraordinary depth of self-awareness and a well-developed ability to access different aspects of yourself in your efforts to serve others. Without self-understanding, you could, and indeed most likely would, repeat your own personal patterns of thinking, feeling, and behavior with clients or colleagues. You might sometimes act out unresolved personal issues in professional settings or behave inappropriately without understanding why. Despite the most noble and idealistic of motives, and a determined intention to help others, if you lack self-awareness or self-control you may unwittingly enact ideological, emotional, or behavioral patterns that damage the very people you hope to help (Caplan & Caplan, 2001; Keith-Lucas, 1972).

Self-understanding and self-control are not products or outcomes that can be completed and then set aside. Rather, they reflect ongoing processes through which we grow personally and professionally. Self-understanding and self-control tend to reduce the risk of harm to others, which can occur if you are unaware of or unable to manage your own thoughts, feelings, and behavior. Effective service requires that you know how you tend to think about things, how you react to stress or conflict, how you address problems and obstacles, how you present yourself, how you appear to others, and what mannerisms you commonly exhibit. Acknowledge your ideological preferences and recognize which issues cause you anxiety or uneasiness; which topics trigger emotional reactivity; what kinds of people, problems, or events elicit fear or anger; and which patterns of personal interaction you prefer or dislike. Of course, such a level of self-understanding does not occur through a single set of exercises, a course, or a complete program of university study. It certainly does not accompany a bachelor's (BSW), master's (MSW), or doctoral degree in social work (DSW or PhD). Rather, sophisticated self-understanding is an ongoing endeavor that continues throughout life.

At a minimum, social workers must understand how their personal beliefs, attitudes, and ideologies might influence or interfere with their professional activities. Appreciate how your family and cultural background and orientation affect your personal views as well as your psychosocial functioning and relationship patterns (Kondrat, 1999). Recognize the impact of significant life events, and identify your personality characteristics. Learn about your preferred relational styles including how you typically seek, receive, and give social support. Become aware of your own biases, stereotypes, prejudices, and tendencies to discriminate for or against others, as well as the ways in which you might express genuine acceptance of others. Identify how different situations and contexts affect you, your mood, attitudes, and actions. Examine how you respond to uncertainty and frustration. Then, based on your increased self-understanding, develop ways and means to calm or center yourself and manage maladaptive patterns of thought, feeling, and behavior that can interfere with your ability to provide high-quality social work services.

As is the case with most worthwhile endeavors, engaging in self-awareness activities involves certain risks. You may discover aspects of yourself that you have not previously recognized or considered. For example, you may learn that you have a strong need for power, control, and predictability in relationships. You may crave certainty and become uneasy in novel or chaotic situations. You may find that you relate to women with less interest, energy, or attention than you do to men; or to low-income people with less enthusiasm than to those of high economic status. You could realize that your personal belief systems (that is, religious, spiritual, or philosophical) prevent you from gaining a scientific understanding of various phenomena. You may realize that you have not fully examined the potential implications of a physical challenge that you personally face (for example, vision or hearing loss) for clients you serve. You may become aware of fixed racial or ethnic stereotypes that interfere with engagement and objective assessment of individual members of certain groups. You might become aware of unmet childhood needs for acceptance and approval that lead you to avoid confrontation or withdraw from conflict. You may find that you experience heightened anxiety when you are in the presence of authority figures. You may discover that you have problems with alcohol or drugs; that you suffer from occasional periods of depression or carry substantial unresolved rage; or that you are unsuited for a career in the profession of social work.

The processes of self-exploration and self-discovery may give rise to disturbing thoughts, feelings, or sensations. You may even find yourself reconsidering significant life choices. Indeed, numerous dangers are inherent in any serious process of self-examination. However, as a social worker, the pursuit of self-understanding is usually well worth the costs. Failure to grow in self-awareness may put you and the people you serve at considerable risk.

As you increase your self-understanding, you may recognize a parallel need for self-control and self-discipline. As professional social workers, we manage our thoughts, feelings, words, gestures, and behavior. We regulate our reactions. Under conditions where other people might well be overwhelmed by powerful emotions and impulses, we maturely choose our words and actions in accord with our professional purpose, knowledge, values, ethics, and the agreed-upon goals for service.

As professional social workers, we manage our emotions and "restrict impulses or behaviors to appropriate circumstances in the environment" (Barker, 2003, p. 387). In work with and on behalf of clients, we carefully select our verbal as well as our nonverbal expressions. Manage both your overt and covert behavior by skillfully choosing the words you say; adjusting your body movements, gestures, and facial expressions; and modulating your voice and speech. Of course, doing all these things simultaneously requires an extraordinary degree of self-control.

At times, it may even be necessary to control your inner thoughts and feelings to better serve clients and advocate on their behalf. Self-control is one of the true hallmarks of professionalism. It distinguishes a professional social worker from a friendly person with good intentions.

Furthermore, social workers manage patterns of personal behavior that might affect our professional judgment and performance. Suppose you happen to be a highly extroverted, talkative, or even garrulous person. You would have to recognize and manage how much you talk so that clients have a genuine opportunity to share information about themselves, their concerns, and their situations. Conversely, if you are shy, introverted, and reluctant to express yourself, challenge the pattern so that clients and members of the public can benefit from your professional knowledge and expertise.

Address your fears, anxieties, and compulsive habits that might negatively influence your professional performance. Excessive eating, dieting, exercising, television-watching, or computer use may indirectly interfere with effective social work practice. Substance misuse can easily impair judgment. Procrastination may be a problem, as might issues with authority, a quick temper, or impulsivity. Narrow, fixed beliefs and ideologies, and strong needs for certainty can impede our helpfulness. Similarly, some interpersonal or interactional social patterns may become compulsive and interfere with professional functioning. For example, some people may use sex in a compulsive manner while others may be excessively dependent upon others' approval and acceptance.

Unnecessarily adopting the social role of "rescuer" may be problematic. Rescuing may be evident when a social worker views clients as victims in need of rescue or salvation. The "social worker-as-savior" may assume disproportionate control over and responsibility for clients. Rather than enhancing competence, rescuing behavior often weakens others' sense of autonomy and self-efficacy, and can diminish their sense of empowerment. Of course, sometimes people actually need rescuing. A child in danger of freezing to death because she lives under a bridge in winter should receive warm shelter. This would not be rescuing in the compulsive sense, as it would be if you took responsibility for the decisions of fully competent adults.

Self-understanding and self-control are continuous processes that you may advance through personal counseling, individual or group psychotherapy, consultation or supervision by experienced social workers, and participation in professional workshops and training institutes. If you are open to it, self-awareness and self-discipline may also improve as a natural outgrowth of interaction with peers, clients, friends, and family members.

The Family: Context for Development

Social workers have long recognized that families powerfully influence the course of social, psychological, and even biological development (see, for example, Hartman & Laird, 1983). Family and childhood experiences significantly affect people's attitudes, beliefs, values, personality characteristics, and behavioral patterns. Families tend to be the primary means of cultural socialization. Unless you are keenly aware of the influence of your family experiences, you may inadvertently or unconsciously play out a family role or pattern in your work with clients and colleagues. Among the common family roles that many social workers seem to assume include rescuer, peacemaker, hero, and parental child (Satir, 1972; Wegscheider-Cruse, 1985). Of course, sometimes it is entirely proper to use a part of your family-based self in social work practice. In all such cases, however, it should be consciously planned and adopted for a clearly identified social work purpose.

The intergenerational family genogram is one way to become more aware of how our families[2] influence us. A genogram[3] is a graphic representation of one's family tree or pedigree[4] (Wattendorf & Hadley, 2005). It provides a picture of the parties involved and a chronology of significant events or themes. In addition, a genogram may be used as "a subjective interpretive tool" (McGoldrick & Gerson, 1985, p. 2) to develop hypotheses about a person's psychosocial characteristics or a family's interactional patterns.

We commonly use certain symbols to prepare family genograms (McGoldrick, Gerson, & Shellenberger, 1999). For instance, we usually use squares to represent males and circles to identify females. Bracket lines represent spousal relationships. A solid bracket line (|_____|) reflects a committed couple (for example, marriage or its equivalent). A dashed bracket line (|_ _ _|) indicates a relationship of somewhat lesser commitment. A dotted bracket line (| . . . . |) suggests a relatively uncommitted relationship (for example, a short-term affair). A line extended downward from a relationship bracket line indicates a pregnancy, biological child, or adopted child from that relationship. Separations and breakups or divorces are indicated by one and two slash marks (/ and //) respectively, cutting across the relationship bracket line. We place pregnancies and children from each relationship in order from the earliest to latest, proceeding from left to right. We indicate deaths by an X symbol placed within the pertinent circle or square. If known, we provide names of people and dates of birth, adoption, marriage, separation, divorce, and death alongside the symbols. For example, we might note just above or beneath a bracket line indicating a marriage relationship "mar. 3/18/1997." This indicates that the couple married on March 18, 1997. If this relationship leads to a birth or adoption, such events might be recorded by "dob. 4/21/1999" or "adop. 4/21/1999." If the couple later separates, we could indicate that event by "sep. 4/23/2004." A subsequent divorce could be shown by "div. 5/7/2005."

You may add descriptions of individual people and relationships with brief notations. For example, one family member may have served in the military during a war, and perhaps another suffered from diabetes. Indeed, circumstances may warrant a genetic family history (Bernhardt & Rauch, 1993) to trace biological and physiological phenomena across generations. We may also record significant events such as major accidents, injuries, crimes, and changes of residence or occupation. Additional symbols or notations may be used to characterize the nature of selected relationships (McGoldrick & Gerson, 1985; McGoldrick et al., 1999). Very close relationships, those that are emotionally cool, those that are strained, and those that involve conflict may be identified. You may place the sources of information at the bottom of the genogram along with the date and name of the person who prepared the genogram.

A family genogram may be as brief or as extensive as the person or people organizing the information want it to be. Some people pursue its creation with great zeal, spending hours interviewing parents, aunts and uncles, and grandparents. They may even contact distant relatives and former neighbors. Others base their genograms solely on information they personally recall. Usually, the intended purpose for the genogram affects the amount of energy expended in data collection and preparation. Genograms may be prepared in the present—the family as it is now—or

---

[2]Not all people have biological or adopted families of origin. Many children grow up in foster-care settings, children's institutions, or hospitals. In such circumstances, some adaptation of the genogram may be necessary to identify significant persons in the individual's life. Sometimes, creation of an eco-map (see the next section) may be more applicable than a genogram.

[3]For an example of a genogram created with the program Relativity,™ go to http://www.interpersonaluniverse.net /genogram.html.

[4]Medical physicians and geneticists often use the term *family pedigree* to describe a graphic representation of illnesses and diseases that occur within three or more generations of a family.

the past tense—how it existed at some earlier point. It is even possible to prepare a genogram based on predictions of the future—how the family may appear 5 or 10 years hence. Many people find it useful to take "genogrammatic" snapshots of the family as they remember it at significant points in their development (for example, beginning grammar school, graduating from high school, leaving home, entering military service or college, marrying, or giving birth to or adopting children).

As an illustrative example, consider the case of Mrs. Lynn Chase. Later, we will learn more about her and her situation. At this point, however, we are primarily concerned with displaying a typical genogram, as shown in Figure 2.2. Susan Holder, the social worker who

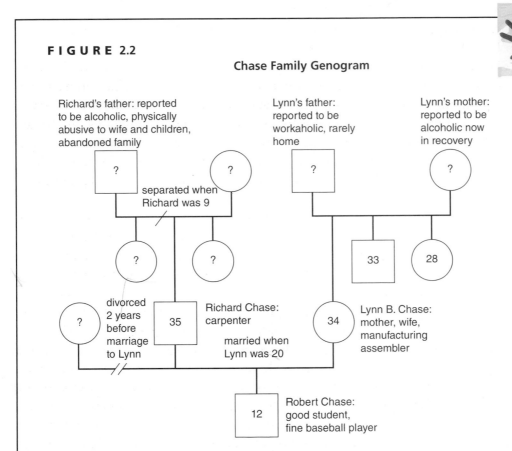

FIGURE 2.2

Chase Family Genogram

Richard's father: reported to be alcoholic, physically abusive to wife and children, abandoned family

Lynn's father: reported to be workaholic, rarely home

Lynn's mother: reported to be alcoholic now in recovery

separated when Richard was 9

divorced 2 years before marriage to Lynn

Richard Chase: carpenter

married when Lynn was 20

Lynn B. Chase: mother, wife, manufacturing assembler

Robert Chase: good student, fine baseball player

Notes: *Richard's father is reported to have left the family when Richard was approximately 9 years old. Lynn says that Richard, his siblings, and his mother were physically and emotionally abused by his father, who apparently was also alcoholic.*

Lynn was the eldest child in a family where she remembers that her father was rarely at home and generally uninvolved in family matters. Her mother is reported to have been alcoholic and was often intoxicated during Lynn's childhood years. Lynn apparently assumed many adult responsibilities at an early age. As a result, she may exhibit some of the characteristics of a "parental child" of an alcoholic family system.

There are noticeable family themes of alcoholism and possibly workaholism. Richard may have been physically and emotionally abused as a child. Both Lynn and Richard may tend to assume great amounts of personal responsibility.

Robert is a good student and a fine baseball player.

Prepared by_____
Susan Holder, MSW
Social Worker

From the perspective of: Lynn B. Chase
Date: January 13

prepared the genogram from Mrs. Chase's perspective, pulled together a considerable amount of information in readily accessible form. There are concise notes regarding some major intergenerational family themes and patterns. This genogram could be an important reference in Susan's service to Mrs. Chase.

Although many social workers are quite familiar with family genograms, there are other forms of genograms as well. For example, you may sometimes find it useful to collaborate with clients in the preparation of cultural genograms (Congress, 1994; Hardy & Laszloffy, 1995; Keiley et al., 2002) or spiritual genograms (Frame, 2000; Hodge, 2001a, 2001b, 2005). In child welfare service, creation of household or placement genograms may be especially helpful (Altshuler, 1999; McMillen & Groze, 1994; McMillen & Rideout, 1996).

Ecological Assessment

In addition to family experiences, the broader ecological contexts in which people live also affect us. We are influenced by past and present social and environmental circumstances as well as by expectations for our future. In effect, situations matter; and, they do so in powerful ways (Sommers, 2011). Circumstances influence our thoughts, emotional feelings, bodily sensations, and behavioral actions. As human beings, social workers are, of course, affected by situational factors as well. Ecological factors influence various aspects of both our personal and professional lives. Indeed, our past and current social ecologies are quite likely to affect our professional experience and performance as social workers.

Eco-maps (Hartman, 1978; Hartman & Laird, 1983) serve as an extremely useful tool for portraying situational contexts because they provide a diagrammatic representation of clients' social worlds. In addition to presenting an overview of a person, family, or household in context, eco-maps readily highlight the energy-enhancing and energy-depleting relationships between members of a primary social system (for example, a family or household) and the outside world (Mattaini, 1993a, 1993b, 1995). The graphic nature of the eco-map highlights social strengths and deficiencies, and helps to identify areas of conflict and compatibility. Eco-maps may serve multiple purposes. For example, they may reveal areas where resources may be accessed or changes could occur (Fieldhouse & Bunkowsky, 2002; Hodge, 2000, 2005). They naturally complement genograms (Mattaini, 1990).

Squares or circles are used to represent members of the primary social system (for example, the household). We draw these in the middle of a sheet of paper and place them within a large circle. Other significant social systems with which the person, family, or household members interact are also identified and encircled. Lines characterize the interactions and relationships among the identified social systems. A solid line (———) reflects a strong and generally positive relationship; a dotted line (·········) reflects a tenuous relationship; and a hatched line (+++++) reflects a stressful or conflicted relationship. Arrows ($\rightarrow$) may indicate the direction of the flow of energy or resources between systems and subsystems. These relationship lines may characterize the exchange of energy among family members. Plus (+), minus (–), and plus-minus (±) signs may be placed adjacent to relationship lines as supplements, indicating that a relationship is energy enhancing, energy depleting, or evenly balanced in terms of energy investment and return.

As an illustrative example, Figure 2.3 contains an eco-map of the Chase family. Using information provided by Mrs. Chase, the social worker depicted important social systems with which the Chase family members interact, illustrating and characterizing the relationships among the systems. When used in the context of providing social work services, the eco-map gives both the worker and client a great deal of information in graphic form. As you can easily observe, Mrs. Chase appears to expend much more energy than she receives from most interactions with other people and social systems.

FIGURE 2.3

Chase Family Eco-Map

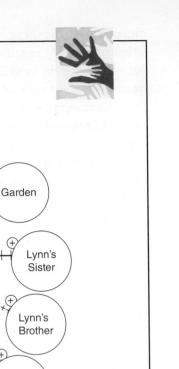

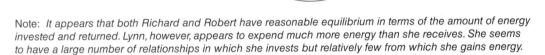

Note: *It appears that both Richard and Robert have reasonable equilibrium in terms of the amount of energy invested and returned. Lynn, however, appears to expend much more energy than she receives. She seems to have a large number of relationships in which she invests but relatively few from which she gains energy.*

Prepared by————————————
Susan Holder, MSW
Social Worker

From the perspective of: Lynn B. Chase

Timelines

Events and experiences in both the past and the present may affect human beings in profound and often unexpected ways. Expectations concerning the future also influence our current thoughts, feelings, and actions. One way to organize information in the temporal dimension is through timelines. A timeline is a simple table that reflects, in shorthand fashion, important events or experiences in chronological order during a designated period. At least two kinds of timelines may be especially useful. A "Critical Events Timeline" provides an opportunity to outline significant or meaningful experiences in a person's life. A "Problem Timeline" provides a means to trace the origin and development of a particular issue or problem. Other timelines may be helpful as well. For example, a "Relationship Timeline" can provide a graphic temporal representation of key moments in a personal, family, or professional relationship. A "Successes Timeline" can facilitate the process of looking for strengths by recording dates of accomplishments, achievements, and other successful experiences. All sorts of timelines are conceivable. You can even extend timelines into the future by imagining or forecasting significant events, moments, or experiences that might occur and could have an impact later on in life.

Creating your own timelines tends to produce considerable self-understanding—because you must actively reflect on important lifetime events. Clients may also benefit from the experience of constructing their own timelines. At times, however, someone else may need to help. For example, a parent might generate a timeline for a child, or a social worker might create a timeline to record critical events in the life of a support group.

The guidelines for creating timelines are quite simple and highly flexible. Feel free to be creative. The basic components are (1) a fairly long, continuous, horizontal, or vertical line representing a period of time, (2) several perpendicular, intersecting, or angled lines of shorter length to indicate the dates of selected events, and (3) short descriptions of the events or experiences adjacent to the shorter lines. You may use additional codes or symbols for other purposes as well. For example, events of a positive nature may be indicated with a plus sign (+), whereas those of a negative nature could be accompanied by a minus (–) sign. You could serve the same purpose by placing positive events above a horizontal timeline (or to the left of a vertical timeline) and those of a negative nature below (or to the right of) the timeline.

Figure 2.4 contains Lynn Chase's "Critical Events Timeline." In this instance, the social worker prepared a preliminary timeline based on information provided by Mrs. Chase. Later, she gave the working draft to Mrs. Chase, who edited the timeline and returned a copy of the updated version.

As you notice, the Critical Events Timeline yields a temporal outline of important experiences in Mrs. Chase's life. When used in the context of serving clients, timelines give both parties ready access to significant information. Both Mrs. Chase and her social worker may use the timeline for easy reference throughout the course of their work together.

Personality Assessment

Helping professionals frequently use the term *personality*. However, they may attribute quite diverse meanings to the concept. Indeed, one of the most challenging questions that behavioral scientists ask is, "What is personality?" In addressing that question, Magill (1998) suggests that "most theorists agree that people have an internal 'essence' that determines who they are and that guides their behavior, but the nature of that essence differs from theory to theory" (p. 453). Personality theorists vary in terms of the relative emphasis they place upon particular aspects of this personal essence. Some focus upon instinctual urges, others highlight motivational factors, and still others emphasize internal conflicts. Some reflect their strong interest in human developmental processes, others in internal or external expectations, and still others in enduring types, characteristics, or traits. These diverse theoretical approaches to personality may be categorized into (1) type, (2) trait, (3) psychodynamic/psychoanalytic, (4) behavioral, (5) social learning/social cognitive, and (6) humanistic theories (Roeckelein, 1998, pp. 374–375).

Because of our core professional values and our emphasis on person-in-environment as a focal point, social workers recognize that situations and circumstances strongly influence human experience and action. Indeed, social workers recognize that situational factors may override personality characteristics so that even strongly moral and conscientious people sometimes take immoral or unethical action (Zimbardo, 2007) and, conversely, those who routinely engage in morally reprehensible behavior occasionally behave in incredibly generous and

FIGURE 2.4

Lynn Chase–Critical Events Timeline

35 years ago	Lynn Shaughnessy is born
Age 5–12	Unhappy childhood
	Father often away; mother drinks heavily
	Lynn is a good student
Age 12	Boy calls Lynn "fat"; very upsetting
Age 13	Maternal uncle makes sexual approach
Age 15	Feels intense shame during confession to priest
Age 18	First dates; first sexual experiences as high school senior
Age 19	Drinks heavily; parties often; has multiple sex partners
	Meets Richard
Age 20	Marries Richard; stops heavy drinking
Age 22	Robert is born
Age 26	Cyst is discovered and removed; Lynn unable to have more children
Age 34	In July Lynn goes to work at Fox manufacturing; begins to experience headaches, loses weight, frequently feels irritable, starts smoking again
Age 35	In January, Lynn makes her first visit to the agency

honorable ways. Through our recognition of the power of social and environmental factors—external to the person—social workers may be better suited to counter the prevailing popular tendency to over-estimate psychological factors in attempting to explain or understand human phenomena. The overvaluing of personal (internal) and the undervaluing of social and environmental (external) factors is known as the "fundamental attribution error" (Ross, 1977). Interestingly, when people attempt to explain their own lapses of judgment or their own misbehavior, they often mention external factors such as other people or circumstances. For example: "I was late because my alarm clock didn't go off." Or, "I lost my temper because he behaved so despicably." Conversely, when explaining the misbehavior of others—perhaps especially those who differ in some way—people often refer to individual traits, dispositions, or personality characteristics. For example: "He got into the auto accident because he's an alcoholic." Or, "He steals because he's a sociopath."[5]

As you consider individual characteristics or traits, temperament, or personality, keep the fundamental attribution error in mind. Situations strongly influence our thoughts, feelings, sensations, and behavior. Even personality characteristics—such as introversion and extraversion—are influenced by circumstances. The shy introvert may become the life of the party when she is with her closest friends while the gregarious extrovert may become the quiet wallflower in the company of experts outside his field. In sum, personality helps us understand some human phenomena at certain times in some circumstances. However, personality-based explanations that fail to consider and include contextual factors often convey an incomplete picture at best.

As you might imagine, various personality researchers have developed assessment instruments that correspond to different theoretical perspectives. Currently, one of the most popular trait approaches to personality assessment involves attention to the following "big five" or OCEAN personality factors: *openness, conscientiousness, extraversion, agreeableness,* and *neuroticism* (Benet-Martinez & John, 1998; Digman, 1990; John, 2007–2009; John, Donahue, & Kentle, 1991; John, Naumann, & Soto, 2008; John & Srivastava, 1999; Srivastava, 2006; Srivastava, John, Gosling, & Potter, 2003).

Most of the "big five" dimensions are self-explanatory. However, the following brief descriptions may provide greater clarity:

- *Extraversion* implies an energetic approach toward the social and material world and includes traits such as sociability, activity, assertiveness, and positive emotionality.
- *Agreeableness* contrasts a prosocial and communal orientation toward others with antagonism and includes traits such as altruism, tender-mindedness, trust, and modesty.
- *Conscientiousness* describes socially prescribed impulse control that facilitates task- and goal-directed behavior, such as thinking before acting, delaying gratification, following norms and rules, and planning, organizing, and prioritizing tasks.
- *Neuroticism* contrasts emotional stability and even-temperedness with negative emotionality such as feeling anxious, nervous, sad, and tense.
- *Openness to Experience* (vs. closed-mindedness) describes the breadth, depth, originality, and complexity of an individual's mental and experiential life. (John & Srivastava, 1999, p. 30)

Social Support

Social work is not a solitary endeavor. Rather, it is social profession dedicated to the resolution of social problems and the enhancement of social well-being through the provision of social services. Grounded in a person-in-environment perspective and motivated by a mission to serve individuals, families, groups, organizations, communities, and societies, social workers are deeply involved with others. The nature of the work requires regular collaboration and cooperation, ongoing supervision or consultation, and a great deal of social support. In the absence of energy-enhancing and reality-testing support, social workers would quickly deplete

---

[5] The "ultimate attribution error" involves a tendency to view misbehavior on the part of low-status or "undesirable" people as a result of their character or personality; and to explain their positive behavior by reference to contextual or situational factors and special circumstances. In other words, "they" (as opposed to "we") are considered personally responsible for mistakes and failures but not personally responsible for successes and achievements.

their personal resources and increase the likelihood of improperly meeting some of their own psychosocial needs and personal wants through their relationships with clients. Indeed, isolated social workers who lack strong, positive personal and professional social networks are quite vulnerable to numerous temptations.

Genograms and eco-maps graphically represent family and social relationships. Timelines illustrate the temporal dimension. Scales regarding self-control and acceptance of others provide information about personal beliefs, behaviors, and attitudes. All these exercises promote self-understanding. They may also reveal something about the contexts within which social support is given and accepted or withheld and rejected.

Social support is probably essential for human well-being (Lang, 2002; Lincoln, 2000; Sinha, Nayyar, & Sinha, 2002; Turner & Marino, 1994; Whitfield & Wiggins, 2003). In terms of human evolution, dependable social relationships were associated with a greater chance of individual and species survival (Lumsden & Wilson, 1981; Wright, 1995). Our brains are undoubtedly affected by our relationships (Siegel, 2012a, 2012b) and the human drive for social connection may be genetically hard-wired and reflected in our biochemistry. Because of its importance, social relationships and social support represent especially relevant themes for social workers—personally as well as professionally. Social support includes those "formal and informal activities and relationships that provide for the needs of humans in their efforts to live in society. These needs include . . . a network of other individuals and groups who offer encouragement, access, empathy, role models, and social identity" (Barker, 2003, p. 407).

The genogram and eco-map you prepare (see Exercises 2-4 and 2-5 later in the chapter) should provide excellent graphic representations of the primary and secondary social systems with which you interact. Maps such as these help people identify key relationships and social systems. They may not, however, fully reflect the nature of the feelings and experiences of social support that occur within various systems and interactions. For this purpose, another kind of assessment may be needed.

Recognize that social support involves several dimensions. As a social worker, you and your clients sometimes identify sources of social support that are satisfying or energizing—because they represent strengths within their social world. You might help clients take steps to increase the size or enhance the quality of their social networks and relationships. Sometimes a client's family members and friends might join you and your client in meetings intended to further such goals. At other times, you and a client may determine that certain people or groups are unlikely to become sources of support. In such contexts, your client may decide to reconfigure or restructure selected social networks. Efforts such as these may help clients enhance their social functioning and improve the overall quality of their lives.

Of course, social relationships and social networks also influence social workers. Indeed, the nature and extent of your own social supports are likely to affect the quality of your professional work, as well as the satisfaction you experience in providing service. The interpersonal and emotional demands of professional social work practice can be substantial. Social workers who feel personally and professionally supported in their networks and personal relationships are better prepared to cope effectively with the inevitable stress and the numerous temptations that accompany professional practice. For example, suppose you are a social worker who does not feel supported in your relationships with family members and friends. Might you be tempted to seek such support from some of your clients? Conversely, might your attitude toward clients who do not appear supportive of their families be affected?

Especially when faced with multiple demands of a highly stressful nature, social workers can indeed be influenced by their own social circumstances. As social workers steeped in the person-in-environment perspective, we recognize the importance of the social world for our clients' well-being. Let's not underestimate its importance for our own.

Summary

Social workers come from all sorts of backgrounds. We exhibit a wide range of personality profiles and social lifestyles. We are attracted to the profession for many different reasons. Our motivations for service vary. Some of us have a strong sense of altruism—a desire to give of ourselves to others. Others have a philosophical commitment to social justice or a better world. Some are motivated by religious conviction, and some of us are proponents of a particular cause that we hope to promote through a career in social work. Others follow in the footsteps of a relative or other significant person who served as a social worker. Some see social work as a way to continue in a family role, such as caretaker, with which we are personally familiar, whereas others see social work as a way to become a counselor or psychotherapist.

Some of us choose educational programs in social work because we think admission requirements are lower, course work less challenging, and professors less rigorous than in certain other schools or departments. Still others have personal or social problems that we believe might be resolved through social work education and through service to others, or perhaps we have been clients ourselves and identified with the social workers who served us.

In this chapter, you considered several characteristics of professionalism. At this point, you can probably recognize the significance of integrity, advanced knowledge and self-efficacy, self-understanding and self-control, and social support as they pertain to professionalism in social work practice. You also understand how to prepare genograms, eco-maps, and timelines, and can appreciate multiple dimensions of personality.

As you completed this chapter, you learned to adopt a person-in-environment perspective. You recognized that there are powerful, ongoing, and often invisible, interactions between personal aspects of individual people and the social and environmental contexts in which they function. We hope that you have gained some awareness of the relationships among various personal attributes and social circumstances as well as becoming familiar with the professional characteristics needed for effective service as a social worker in contemporary society.

CHAPTER 2: SUMMARY EXERCISE

1. Go to the "psychtests TestYourself" website at http://testyourself.psychtests.com /testid/3090 to find a brief online test of integrity and work ethics. Complete the 30-item questionnaire. Your responses will be calculated and a score and brief report generated. Use your web browser to copy and save the "Snapshot Report." You may be given an opportunity to purchase a full report. However, you are under no obligation to do. Since your responses help establish the test's psychometric properties, the researchers benefit every time you or someone else completes the instrument. Use Table 2.3 to date and record your score.[6] Once completed, take a few minutes to reflect on the implications of your responses by addressing the following questions: In what life areas have you exhibited strong integrity? In what areas would you like to develop greater integrity? What social work practice situations will challenge you the most to maintain a strong sense of personal and professional integrity? Make a mental (or, if you wish, a written) note of your responses.

---

[6] At some point in the future, you may choose to retake this or other scales to determine if your growth and development or changes in your situation have influenced your scores.

TABLE 2.3
Integrity and Work Ethics Test

Date	Integrity and Work Ethics Score

2. Go to Appendix 4 and complete the General Self-Efficacy (GSE) Scale. Reflect upon the items and your rating for each. Also consider your total score. Date and record your GSE Scale score in Table 2.4. Once completed, take a few minutes to reflect on the implications of your responses by addressing the following questions: In what life areas have you exhibited strong self-efficacy? In what areas would you like to develop greater self-efficacy? What social work practice situations will challenge you the most to maintain a strong sense of personal and professional self-efficacy? In what circumstances could a disproportionate sense of self-efficacy be counterproductive? Make a mental (or, if you wish, a written) note of your responses.

TABLE 2.4
General Self-Efficacy

Date	General Self-Efficacy Scale Score

3. Go to Appendix 5 and complete the Self-Control Schedule. Use the questions and your answers to assess your current level of self-control. Date and record your scores in Table 2.5. Then, reflect on the implications of your responses by addressing the following questions: In what life areas have you exhibited strong self-control? In what areas would you like to develop greater self-control? What social work practice situations will challenge you the most to maintain personal and professional self-control? Make a mental (or, if you wish, a written) note of your responses.

TABLE 2.5
Self-Control Schedule Score

Date	Self-Control Schedule Score

© Cengage Learning 2014

4. As part of an effort to enhance your self-understanding, prepare a genogram of three generations of your family. Use paper and pencil or word-processing or drawing software to create the genogram. Several word-processing packages allow for the creation of squares, circles, triangles, and lines to link them. You could also use one of the "family genogram" programs available commercially or as shareware.[7] Sometimes, however, it is quicker and easier to draw a genogram by hand and then, if needed, scan it as an image to in a word-processed document. In creating the genogram, include your grandparents and parents, if possible, as well as your siblings and yourself. If you have children or grandchildren, you may include them as the fourth and fifth generations, respectively. For this exercise, rely on your own memory rather than seeking information from other family members. Try to include the approximate dates and categories of significant family events

---

[7] You may download a trial copy of GenoPro® at http://www.genopro.com.

such as births, deaths, marriages, divorces, separations, graduations, military service, hospitalizations, relocations, injuries, and traumatic experiences. Include pleasant as well as unpleasant events. If you do not remember details, enter question marks instead of facts.

When you have completed the genogram, reflect on your childhood and family experiences by addressing the following questions: As a child, what role or roles (for example, family hero, scapegoat, peacemaker, rescuer, or parental child) did you play in your family? What role or roles do you currently tend to play in family or family-like relationships? When you were young, how did adults and children express affection in your family? How do you tend to express affection now? How did adults and children in your family express feelings such as anger, fear, and joy? At this point in your life, how do you express these feelings? How were children and others educated, guided, and disciplined in your family? Who performed these socialization functions? Today, how do you attempt to educate, influence, correct, or control others? How did your family reflect its ethnic and cultural identity and heritage? How do you? What is your conception of the ideal family? How does it compare with your actual family experience? Make a mental (or, if you wish, a written) note of your responses.

5. As a part of the ongoing effort to enhance your self-understanding, use paper and pencil or word-processing or drawing software to prepare an eco-map of your current social ecology. Several word-processing packages allow for the creation of assorted graphic symbols and means to draw lines to link them. You could also use a specialized eco-map computer program.[8] Sometimes, however, it is quicker and easier to draw an eco-map (or a genogram) by hand and then, if needed, electronically scan it so that you may paste the image into a word-processed document. As you prepare the eco-map, identify sources of stress or conflict as well as sources of support and nurturance. Use arrows ($\rightarrow$) to indicate the direction of energy or resource flow between yourself and other people and systems; use plus (+), minus (–), or plus-minus (±) signs to reflect energy use.

Once completed, reflect upon the eco-map and its preparation. Consider what it might suggest about your current social situation. Then address the following questions: Which relationships in your current situation enhance your energy level? Which deplete energy? How does your social situation affect the physical, intellectual, and emotional energy you have available for use in critical thinking and lifelong learning activities, service to clients, and other aspects of your social work roles? What would you consider

---

[8] You may view an eco-map created with the Ecotivity™ program at http://www.interpersonaluniverse.net/ecomap.html.

the ideal social situation? How does it compare with your current situation? Given the nature of your present social situation, what kinds of clients and what issues would be likely to elicit strong emotional reactions? What changes in your current social situation might enhance the psychological, emotional, physical, cultural, and social resources needed to provide high-quality social work services to clients? Make a mental (or, if you wish, a written) note of your responses.

6. Prepare a personal critical events timeline. Use paper and pencil or a word-processing or drawing software program to create a simple linear table. Use the basic guidelines described earlier in the chapter to identify the approximate dates of events and experiences that you believe have significantly affected your life. Once completed, reflect upon the timeline and its preparation by reflecting on the following questions: What events or experiences in your life were "turning" or "tipping points" that led you to change directions or alter the course of your life direction? What events stimulated you to change your mind about something? Also consider your critical events timeline in relation to the roles and responsibilities of social workers. What do you see as the implications of various critical events for you and your professional career? Make a mental (or, if you wish, a written) note of your responses.

7. Use a search engine such as Google, Bing, or Yahoo to find an online copy of the Big Five Personality Test located on the www.outofservice.com/bigfive/ website (Potter, 1996–2009).[9] The instrument is a free, 45-item, online version of a big five inventory (John et al., 1991; John et al., 2008; Srivastava et al., 2003). Once there, click on the "Learn more about the Big Five" and the "Read our consent form" links to familiarize yourself with this approach to personality assessment, and learn about the conditions and your rights regarding use of this online instrument.

---

[9] A similar 41-item, five-factor personality test is available at http://www.personalitytest.org.uk/.

If you understand and consent to the guidelines, complete the Big Five Personality Test and receive your results in the form of a summary report that includes percentile scores. Recognize that your scores may change somewhat over time or in different circumstances. Please date and record your scores in Table 2.6. Once completed, take a few minutes to reflect on the implications of your responses by addressing the following questions: On which dimensions do you think the scores accurately reflect your personality? Which seem inaccurate? How would your closest friends react to the personality profile suggested by the scores? Where would they agree or disagree?

TABLE 2.6
"Big Five" Scores Worksheet

	Date	Date	Date
Dimension	Percentile Scores	Percentile Scores	Percentile Scores
O (Openness to Experience)			
C (Conscientiousness)			
E (Extraversion)			
A (Agreeableness)			
N (Neuroticism)			

© Cengage Learning

Let's assume that a "perfect" or "ideal" personality profile does not exist. Indeed, we might readily imagine situations where extreme strength or weakness on any of the five dimensions might be adaptive or maladaptive; and other situations where moderate strength, as reflected by mid-range scores, might be so. For example, extreme extraversion may, in certain circumstances, interfere with our capacity to listen quietly to another or limit our ability to be content in a solitary environment. On the other hand, extreme introversion might inhibit our ability to express ourselves assertively in public contexts or to advocate strongly on behalf of a client or an important cause. Recognizing the inherent limitations of any personality-only assessment approach and the importance of contextual factors, reflect for a few minutes and then identify which scores on the big five dimensions, if any, you might change in order to (a) feel more whole, balanced, and personally satisfied with yourself; and (b) perform more effectively as a professional social worker. Make a mental (or, if you wish, a written) note of your responses.

8. As a supplement to the genogram and eco-map, complete the Social Support Appraisals Scale (SS-A) in Appendix 6. This questionnaire helps you to assess your personal experience of social support. Use Table 2.7 to date and record your Family Subscale, Friends Subscale, and Overall Social Support Appraisal scores. Once completed, reflect upon your responses and their implications by addressing the following questions: Where and from whom do you experience the greatest social support? Where and from whom do you experience the least? What kinds or forms of social support do you most like to give? What kinds or forms do you most like to receive? In what ways would you like to change your current social support systems? Why? What steps could you take to make those changes? What would indicate, demonstrate, or "prove" that you had successfully made those changes? Make a mental (or, if you wish, a written) note of your responses.

T A B L E 2.7
Social Support Appraisals Scale

Date	Family Subscale Score	Friends Subscale Score	Overall Social Support Appraisals Score

© Cengage Learning 2014

9. Reflect on and integrate the results of this chapter's content and the learning exercises through a brief discussion of the implications of integrity, knowledge and self-efficacy, self-understanding (of family, eco-systems, timelines, and personality) and self-control, and social support as aspects of professionalism in social work practice. Prepare your discussion in the form of a two- to three-page word-processed report (500–750 words) titled "Implications of Integrity, Professional Knowledge and Self-Efficacy, Self-Understanding and Self-Control, and Social Support for Social Work Practice." When you have finished, include the report in your Social Work Skills Learning Portfolio.

As you finish this chapter, please reflect on your learning by completing the following self-appraisal exercise.

SELF-APPRAISAL: PROFESSIONALISM

Please respond to the following items to help you reflect upon professionalism as presented in this chapter. Read each statement carefully. Then use the following 4-point rating scale to indicate the degree to which you agree or disagree with each statement. Record your numerical response in the space provided:

4 = Strongly agree   2 = Disagree

3 = Agree   1 = Strongly disagree

4	3	2	1	Rating Statement
				At this point in time, I can
☐	☐	☐	☐	1. Discuss the significance of professionalism for effective social work practice.
☐	☐	☐	☐	2. Discuss integrity as an integral aspect of professionalism.
☐	☐	☐	☐	3. Discuss the relationship of professional knowledge and self-efficacy, and self-understanding and self-control to effective social work practice.
☐	☐	☐	☐	4. Prepare a family genogram.
☐	☐	☐	☐	5. Prepare an eco-map.
☐	☐	☐	☐	6. Prepare a critical events timeline.
☐	☐	☐	☐	7. Discuss the dimensions of a personality assessment and recognize limitations in person-only forms of understanding and explanation.
☐	☐	☐	☐	8. Discuss the relationship of social support to effective social work practice.
☐	☐	☐	☐	9. Discuss the implications of selected aspects of professionalism for social work practice.
				Subtotal

Note: These items are identical to those contained in the Professionalism section of the Social Work Skills Self-Appraisal Questionnaire presented in Appendix 3. If you completed that self-appraisal before beginning Chapter 1, you have already responded to these items once before. You may now compare the responses you made on that occasion with those you made this time. Also, compare the two subtotals. If you believe that you have progressed in terms of your proficiency, the more recent subtotal should be higher than the earlier one.

CRITICAL THINKING, SCIENTIFIC INQUIRY, AND CAREER-LONG LEARNING

Social workers must possess an extraordinary breadth and depth of knowledge, have access to even more, and be able to understand and analyze a massive amount of emerging information to provide effective, up-to-date services to people facing difficult challenges. The intellectual demands faced by social workers in contemporary practice are daunting. To meet them, we need highly developed skills for critical thinking, scientific inquiry, and lifelong learning. Indeed, the Council on Social Work Education (2008) expects graduates of both undergraduate and master's programs to "apply critical thinking to inform and communicate professional judgments" (p. 4), understand and apply the "principles of logic, scientific inquiry, and reasoned discernment" (p. 4), and "engage in career-long learning" (p. 3).

In this chapter, we explore additional aspects of professionalism to complement those addressed in Chapter 2. These include critical thinking, scientific inquiry, and career-long learning.

Critical Thinking and Scientific Inquiry

Critical thinking involves "the propensity and skill to use reflective skepticism when engaged in some specific activity" (McPeck, 1990, p. 3). Involving "the careful examination and evaluation of beliefs and actions" (Gibbs & Gambrill, 1996, p. 3), critical thinking is "the art of thinking about your thinking while you are thinking in order to make your thinking better: more clear, more accurate, or more defensible" (Paul, 1993, p. 462). Scientific inquiry

> involves making observations; posing questions; examining books and other sources of information to see what is already known; planning investigations; reviewing what is already known in light of experimental evidence; using tools to gather, analyze, and interpret data; proposing answers, explanations, and predictions; and communicating the results. Inquiry requires identification of assumptions, use of critical and logical thinking, and consideration of alternative explanations. (National Research Council, 1996, p. 23)

Obviously, scientific inquiry and critical thinking are inseparable—perhaps especially as applied in social work practice. Membership in a profession requires advanced, specialized "knowledge of some subject, field, or science . . . [gained through] . . . prolonged training and a formal qualification" (*Oxford American Dictionary of Current English* [Online], 1999). In its definition of social work, the International Federation of Social Workers states that "social work bases its methodology on a systematic body of evidence-based knowledge derived from research and practice evaluation, including local and indigenous knowledge specific to its context" (2000, Theory section, para. 1).

The National Science Teachers Association (NSTA) recognizes the importance of science and scientific inquiry in the complex and ever-changing world of the 21st century. The NSTA board of directors (2004, October) suggests that students should understand:

- That science involves asking questions about the world and then developing scientific investigations to answer their questions.
- That there is no fixed sequence of steps that all scientific investigations follow. Different kinds of questions suggest different kinds of scientific investigations.
- That scientific inquiry is central to the learning of science and reflects how science is done.
- The importance of gathering empirical data using appropriate tools and instruments.
- That the evidence they collect can change their perceptions about the world and increase their scientific knowledge.
- The importance of being skeptical when they assess their own work and the work of others.
- That the scientific community, in the end, seeks explanations that are empirically based and logically consistent. (pp. 2–3)

The NTSA board further indicates that students should:

- Learn how to identify and ask appropriate questions that can be answered through scientific investigations.
- Design and conduct investigations to collect the evidence needed to answer a variety of questions.
- Use appropriate equipment and tools to interpret and analyze data.
- Learn how to draw conclusions and think critically and logically to create explanations based on their evidence.
- Communicate and defend their results to their peers and others. (p. 2)

Genuinely professional social workers engage in scientific inquiry and critical thought about all aspects of their work—including the selection and application of theories and research findings that inform our knowledge base and guide our decisions and actions. Furthermore, in our collaborative work with clients, we regularly monitor, assess, and evaluate progress toward goal achievement and use those findings to make adjustments in plans and actions steps.

As helping professionals, we have, in effect, agreed to a "social contract" with society and the people we serve. Our knowledge and expertise must be based on more than good intentions or on the opinions of colleagues, supervisors, professors, or textbook authors. As professionals, we must be rational and thoughtful in our pursuit, discovery, analysis, and application of knowledge for use in service to others. The evidence we select cannot derive from personal or ideological bias, prejudice, or superstition. Rather, our evidence base is built upon and supported by findings from research studies, sophisticated logical analysis, traditional intellectual standards (Paul & Elder, 1996), empirical results from our work with clients and, of course, direct feedback from clients themselves. We must be scientifically minded and critically thinking because the validity and relevance of our knowledge base, the quality of our analyses, and the nature of our judgments profoundly affect people's lives.

The Council on Social Work Education (2008) recognizes that knowledge alone does not necessarily lead to good decisions. Social workers must ask questions about the validity, reliability, and relevance of information that might guide the nature and quality of our service. We realize that our ideas, beliefs, or judgments are subject to error. Therefore, we conscientiously remain open to credible evidence that calls them into question. We think deeply (LeGault, 2006) and remain open to the possibility of changing our minds (Brockman, 2009) as we carefully consider factors such as risk of harm, efficiency, probability of success, and sometimes cost-effectiveness. We also consider legal and ethical dimensions and consciously reflect upon the cultural implications of the words we might use and the actions we could take.

In considering the value of information, critical thinkers tend to be adept at:

- Distinguishing between verifiable facts and value claims.
- Distinguishing relevant from irrelevant information, claims, or reasons.
- Determining the factual accuracy of a statement.
- Determining the credibility of a source.
- Identifying ambiguous claims or arguments.
- Identifying unstated assumptions.
- Detecting bias.
- Identifying logical fallacies.
- Recognizing logical inconsistencies in a line of reasoning.
- Determining the strength of an argument or claim (Beyer, 1988).

Thoughtful reflection and analysis are necessary throughout all phases, aspects, and forms of professional social work. Particularly because social workers commonly address unstructured issues that do not have easy "right" or "wrong," "true" or "false," or "multiple-choice" solutions, we generally engage in complex rather than dichotomous thinking (Berlin, 1990). In particular, we apply several critical thinking and scientific inquiry skills, including the abilities to:

- Identify and frame the nature of issues accurately.
- Formulate useful, relevant, and appropriate questions to guide data collection.
- Collect relevant, valid, reliable, and useful information.
- Select or formulate relevant, valid, reliable, and useful thinking processes by which to reach decisions or make judgments based on relevant, valid, reliable, and useful information.
- Use relevant, valid, reliable, and useful thinking processes to reach and support professional decisions and judgments.
- Base actions on sound professional decisions and judgments.
- Evaluate the effects of decisions, judgments, and actions.
- Reconsider and revise judgments and actions based on relevant, valid, reliable, and useful information.

Proficiency in these abilities requires considerable intellectual prowess. Social workers must think clearly, logically, complexly, and creatively to adapt effectively to the wide range of people, issues, and contexts we face. The stakes are extremely high. Social work practice is complex, multidimensional, multisystemic, and certainly challenging. There are few simple issues and fewer easy solutions. Social workers proficient in critical thinking skills are better able to address complicated issues and more likely to benefit others. Those of us who do not think critically represent a genuine risk of harm to our clients, our colleagues, and ourselves.

Especially when we feel frustrated, overwhelmed, and ineffective in the face of obstacles, we may be tempted to just "try something." We might take some action—perhaps any action—to reduce feelings of stress, confusion, and powerlessness; and we may do without seriously considering the consequences on others. At other times, we might feel an impulse to respond to a client in a certain way because of our own strongly held personal beliefs, our own passion, or our own individual experiences. Occasionally, we might be tempted to react to a client as we might to one of our own family members—perhaps as a parent might react to a child or sometimes as a child to a parent. Critical thinking skills provide balance, rationality, and sometimes restraint in such contexts.

Similarly, we may find ourselves attracted to information presented on television, in popular magazines, or on the Internet. We might think, "I could try this with my clients." Be extremely careful. Think critically and inquire scientifically before taking action based on such information. Although some popular information may be accurate, pertinent, and useful, much is untested, unexamined, or even false. Critical thinking skills are essential to determine the relative validity, reliability, and relevance of information for professional social work service.

Although all human beings engage in various "thinking" activities, it appears that relatively few of us are highly skilled in critical thinking; and fewer still regularly engage in "thinking practice" in an effort to improve. Elder and Paul (1996; Paul & Elder, 2002, p. 47) describe six stages of critical thinking development:

◆ *The Unreflective Thinker* (remains unaware of significant problems in her or his thinking)
◆ *The Challenged Thinker* (becomes aware of problems in thinking)
◆ *The Beginning Thinker* (tries to improve quality of thinking, but does so without regular practice)
◆ *The Practicing Thinker* (recognizes the necessity of and engages in regular practice to improve thinking proficiency)
◆ *The Advanced Thinker* (improves quality of thinking in accordance with nature and extent of practice)
◆ *The Master Thinker* (skilled and insightful thinking becomes second nature)

Paul and Elder's critical thinking stages reflect some similarities to Perry's model of intellectual development. Perry (1970) suggests that during their educational experience, college students tend to adopt positions within four categories of intellectual development: (1) dualism, (2) multiplicity, (3) contextual relativism, and (4) committed relativism (Battaglini & Schenkat, 1987; Belenky, Clinchy, Goldberger, & Tarule, 1986; Moore, 2003, October; Perry, 1970, 1981).

College students often begin their education as dualistic thinkers, whose thinking occurs in simplistic and dichotomous fashion. Things are either "good or bad," "correct or incorrect," "right or wrong," or "true or false." *Dualistic thinkers* often assume that absolute truth exists; there is a valid source (for example, a supernatural being or force, a sacred or authoritative text, or a superior authority) for that knowledge; and someone (for example, a professor, parent, employer, or a political or religious leader) has legitimate access to that valid source. Dualistic thinkers often make claims without providing evidence or arguments to substantiate them, or by referring to authorities or authoritative sources as if they were infallible.

Unfortunately, life does not present in a true–false, right–wrong, or good–bad fashion. Many issues and situations are complex and dynamic. When we approach life's challenges in simplistic, dualistic fashion, we usually overlook potentially useful perspectives and fail to consider innovative solutions. Furthermore, such a lens seriously interferes with our ability to appreciate, understand, and empathize with others.

During their college experience, students often begin to realize that there are, indeed, many different points of view and frames of reference. Dualistic thinking may give way to an open appreciation of multiple perspectives because "anything could be true" or "your opinion is just as good as anybody else's." *Multiplistic thinkers* often make claims based upon an assumption that perspectives cannot, and perhaps should not, be judged by others or by external standards. Furthermore, "everyone has a right to his or her point of view." When making claims, multiplistic thinkers may provide support in the form of statements such as, "That's my view. I have a right to my opinion—just as you have a right to yours."

A major problem with multiplistic thinking is that opinions, positions, and claims are not all equally valid, reasonable, or relevant. Some claims have such a low probability of validity that we professionals can dismiss them as erroneous, irrational, unreasonable, unlikely, or invalid. Indeed, some views (for example, notions of racial, religious, or national superiority) routinely contribute to much human suffering. By accepting all ideas as valid and legitimate, multiplistic thinkers could easily tolerate ludicrous, superstitious, dangerous, or even genocidal positions.

Whereas dualistic thinkers believe they know absolutely what is right and wrong and can readily take action based upon such certainty, multiplistic thinkers may be unable to assess various positions from a rational or scientific perspective and, as a result, may become indecisive and passive. Dualistic thinking (for example, national, racial, or religious bigotry and hatred) can lead to attempts to eliminate undesired peoples from existence (for example, the Holocaust and the genocides in Armenia, Cambodia, Darfur, East Timor, Rwanda and Burundi, Kosovo, Macedonia, and Sierra Leone). Multiplistic thinking can lead to passivity and indecision in the face of complex and competing viewpoints. As Edmund Burke reputedly said, "All that is necessary for the triumph of evil is that good people do nothing." Inaction may contribute to rather than ameliorate danger when human beings are at risk.

In contrast to multiplistic thinkers, *contextually relativistic thinkers* realize that different points of view or frames of reference vary in terms of their value or utility vis-à-vis the situation or circumstance. The context influences the relativistic thinker's perspective and judgment. As social workers, we often engage in this kind of thinking when we attempt to understand clients from a person-in-environment perspective. Seeking to understand and empathize, we often find value in the experiences and viewpoints of people from various cultures and circumstances. The combination of attention to context and empathic understanding without judgment often contributes greatly to our ability to develop strong working relationships and alliances with people confronting challenging issues as well as those who differ from us in some way. Contextual considerations are crucial to genuine respect and understanding. However, if we remain exclusively focused on the particular people and the immediate situation, we may fail to consider transcendent factors (for example, human rights, social justice, the safety and well-being of children, the rights of minorities, and the ecological health of planet earth) and the long-term consequences of our actions.

As you might infer, one problem with situational or contextually relativistic thinking is its inconsistent and amorphous quality. If we consider ideas and phenomena in only personal and situational terms, others find it difficult to trust us because we seem to change so much. Indeed, interactions with a situational thinker often lead to a sense of uncertainty about that person's identity. The person seems to change in accord with changing circumstances. In the extreme, there is a chameleon-like quality. We cannot know whether the situational thinker will keep a promise or maintain a position in the face of challenge or during times of stress and change. He or she might readily neglect a commitment, alter a position, or reverse a decision because of changing circumstances. The situational thinker often lacks a general sense of continuity and congruence in the form of a personal or professional identity and a philosophical perspective from which to address the inevitable tensions associated with multiple viewpoints, various and dynamic circumstances, and changing demands. Situational thinkers often find it extremely difficult and sometimes quite frightening to make final decisions and firm commitments, or to take strong intellectual positions. After all, circumstances might change.

In contrast to situational thinkers, *committed relativistic thinkers* develop a general philosophy with a set of values or guiding principles through which to approach life and consider various points of view. Committed thinkers reflect a coherent identity and a tangible sense of "self." Well-conceived values and principles complement multiplistic and situational thinking and contribute to the development of logically coherent positions on complex issues. By applying transcendent values and principles (such as conceptions of human rights or social and economic justice) to ideas, positions, proposals, and intellectual dilemmas, committed thinkers can prioritize, reach conclusions, make decisions, and take action. In committed thinking, value-based principles, the particulars of the situation, and various perspectives are all considered. When conflicts among these aspects arise, committed thinkers apply their philosophically based values and guiding principles along with their understanding of the facts of the situation to reach a resolution. Rather than simply accumulating evidence to support preconceived positions, the committed relativist engages in a sophisticated thinking process that takes into account multiple perspectives, situational differences, and relevant values. This complex, principled thinking process leads to intellectually defensible positions.

On occasion, committed thinkers reconsider their own philosophical frames of reference and may revise certain value-based principles in light of emerging knowledge, experience, evidence, and analysis. When such adaptations occur, it is usually because a higher-level principle supersedes one of lower value. For example, a committed thinker might assign greater value to the principles of honor, integrity, human rights, and social justice than to those of personal security and safety. As a result, she might publicly advocate for the release of women who were incarcerated solely because they left abusive husbands or girls who ran away from adult men whom they had been forced to marry (Human Rights Watch, 2012). She might protest against the use of the death penalty by the state. She might advocate on behalf of hate crimes legislation. Or, she might "tell the truth" about a colleague's fraudulent behavior despite threats that she "will lose her job" if she does so.

As you might imagine, when pressured, stressed, or challenged, humans often experience a diminished capacity for complex thinking. Under pressure, dualistic thinkers tend to become more fervent in their right–wrong views and multiplistic thinkers become more ambivalent and indecisive. When distressed, situational thinkers often lose their ability to process complex ideas, consider diverse perspectives, or adapt to changing circumstances in a rational manner. Committed thinkers, on the other hand, may be more capable of considering various points of view and situational factors, as well as their philosophically based values and principles in reaching rational decisions—despite the feelings of distress associated with challenge, disagreement, and conflict. A coherent sense of identity and a willingness to reconsider positions based upon emerging evidence may enhance their ability to cope with unexpected demands in a thoughtful manner.

Development of critical thinking and scientific inquiry skills requires familiarity with concepts such as claim, argument, assertion, premise, assumption, and conclusion. Whether a friendly neighbor shares a story during a backyard conversation or a scientist publishes an article in a professional journal, humans commonly express information in the form of an argument. In this context, the term *argument* does not mean a disagreement between two or more people. Rather, "to argue is to produce considerations designed to support a conclusion. An argument is either the process of doing this . . . or the product, i.e. the set of propositions adduced (the premises), the pattern of inference and the conclusion reached" (Blackburn, 1996, Argument section, para. 1).

In philosophical usage, an argument is one or more statements (called "premises"; singular "premise" or "premiss") advanced in order to support another statement (the conclusion). . . . Premises actually support a conclusion only when there is the appropriate sort of logical connection between the premises and the conclusion. In deductive arguments, the conclusion must be true given the truth of the premises; in an inductive argument, the truth of the premises makes the conclusion more probable. Any deductive argument in which the premises really do have the appropriate logical connection with the conclusion is called a "valid" argument; in invalid arguments, this connection is lacking. A valid argument may, however, fail to support its conclusion because one or more of its premises is false—for example:

◆ All pigs fly.
◆ All flying things are lighter than air.
◆ Therefore, all pigs are lighter than air.

This argument is valid, but it fails to convince because both of its premises are false. Most of us realize that few, if any, pigs can fly and most things that can and do fly are substantially heavier than air. An argument with at least one false premise is called "unsound"; a sound argument is a valid argument all of whose premises are true. (Martin, 1994, pp. 24–25)

In effect, an argument represents an attempt to establish the truth or validity of an idea through a series of statements. Arguments contain two major parts. One part, the claim or conclusion, is the proposed idea or position. Other terms for claims and conclusions are *propositions, thesis statements, assertions,* or *central arguments*. In research studies, claims and conclusions are often called hypotheses and conclusions, respectively.

The second part of an argument is the premise. Premises are the grounds or foundations that support claims and conclusions. Alternate terms for premises are *data, support, findings,* or *evidence*. Solid data (for example, facts, results from scientific studies, empirical findings) represent strong evidence to support a claim or conclusion. If the data are weak, they may, in effect, merely represent another claim rather than serve as genuine support for the original claim. An unsubstantiated claim supported by another unsubstantiated claim is not much of an argument.

Recognizing Logical Fallacies

Social workers' abilities to examine an argument, assess the legitimacy and relevance of claims and conclusions, and evaluate the credibility of evidence are becoming increasingly significant because we are in the midst of an extraordinary and continuously expanding information explosion. Information of all kinds and quality is widely disseminated through the popular media, and especially via the Internet. Much of this information is of dubious quality. Most of us realize that opinions are not facts, beliefs are not truths, and information is not knowledge. Many statements—even those expressed by professionals, professors, and other authorities—reflect flawed logic or faulty reasoning and contain readily identifiable logical fallacies. Moore and Parker (1995) suggest that a logical fallacy is a "bad argument, one in which the reasons advanced for a claim fail to warrant its acceptance" (p. 125). Pine (1996) states that a

logical fallacy is an argument that is usually psychologically persuasive but logically weak. By this definition we mean that fallacious arguments work in getting many people to accept conclusions, that they make bad arguments appear good even though a little commonsense reflection will reveal that people ought not to accept the conclusions of these arguments as strongly supported. . . . [W]e can think of these fallacies as "informal" because they are most often found in the everyday exchanges of ideas, such as newspaper editorials, letters to the editor, political speeches, advertisements, disagreements between people, and so on. (pp. 113–114)

If you are alert for them, you can find logical fallacies in journal articles, textbooks, formal talks, papers, and presentations. We can certainly recognize them in our own thoughts and in the words we speak or write. Indeed, logical fallacies appear in every facet of life and from every imaginable source. Although advertisers, politicians, and sales representatives are widely recognized as purveyors of false information through persuasive but logically fallacious arguments, helping professionals also engage in such practices—sometimes intentionally but often unwittingly. Indeed, we suspect that a majority of human beings may be considered "unreflective thinkers" who typically do not recognize logical fallacies in their own or others' arguments. Indeed, humans seem to be quite susceptible to quackery (Barrett & Jarvis, 1993) of all kinds, and we commonly accept as "true" all sorts of superstitious beliefs. Shermer (1997) uses the term *pseudoscience* to reflect aspects of these phenomena. Social work professors and students are certainly not exempt.

Scholars in the field of logic and communication have identified hundreds of informal fallacies. In the paragraphs that follow, please find a summary of several of the more common. Notice the two-letter "codes." You may use them to annotate fallacies that appear in various written and oral statements. By regularly using the codes, you can strengthen the ability to assess the credibility of your own and others' claims, assertions, and arguments. Some of the more common logical fallacies include the following (Cournoyer, 2004):

Ad Hominem (AH): Someone claims that the evidence or information should not be considered because the person or organization presenting it is somehow flawed or unworthy. For example, a social work student might claim that information presented by a professor should be rejected because "the professor is a feminist." Obviously, "she's a feminist" is an unsupported assertion. If it is accurate, we do not understand why that would be a flaw or how it would mean that all information provided by someone who espouses feminist views would necessarily be inaccurate or invalid.

Anecdotal Evidence (AE): As "grounds" to support a claim, someone describes one or a few circumstances where the claim applies. For example, a social work professor might claim that college students today cheat more that students did a decade earlier. To support the claim, the professor might say, "Just last semester, one student copied five pages of materials straight from the Internet and thought I wouldn't catch it." Citing one or a few examples does not mean a claim is true or, for that matter, false. It is simply poor evidence. Most of us could identify examples to support almost any claim. Those examples, however, may not be representative of the group or phenomenon in question.

Appeal to Pity (AP): Someone attempts to support a claim by suggesting that failure to accept it would lead to loss or hardship. For example, a client might argue, "If my spouse leaves me, I'll have no reason to live." Pity for the client might lead the spouse to remain in the relationship or the social worker to encourage the client's spouse to do so. In logical terms, however, the client has not provided grounds to support the claim that his reason for living is, has been, will be, or should be in any way related to his spouse's presence. As may be the case in this example, appeals to pity often reflect an element of "emotional blackmail."

Begging the Question (BQ): Someone seeks to support a claim by restating the claim or by proposing one that is essentially similar. In effect, the basic claim remains unsubstantiated by data or evidence. For example, a social worker might assert that "my client is angry and uncooperative" and support the claim by saying, "She's really hostile."

Biased Sample (BS): Someone makes a claim about a group, population, or phenomenon and uses data drawn from an unrepresentative sample as grounds. This logical fallacy is similar to anecdotal evidence in that both reflect an invalid attempt at generalization.

Burden of Proof (BP): Someone makes a claim and places the burden of supporting or proving it upon others. This is a common trick in sales, as when the sales representative asks a potential customer to provide reasons why he or she should not want a particular product or service.

Confirmation Bias (CB): Someone seeks, finds, or perceives only those reasons or evidence to support a currently held belief and fails to look for, notice, comprehend, or integrate reasons and evidence that challenge the validity of that belief. Indeed, confirmation bias is commonly reflected in many college papers as students conduct literature reviews limited to books and articles that support their theses while ignoring resources that refute them. Manifestations of confirmation bias are apparent throughout contemporary society and, perhaps especially, in the political arena where simplistic ideology dominates public discussion.

Despite their advanced education, professional people are not exempt from the insidious temptations of confirmation bias. For example, a social worker who serves in a psychiatric facility and specializes in the psychological treatment of individual patients tends to "discover" that the "causes" of most clients' troubles are psychiatric or psychological in origin; and that the solutions involve either psychotropic medications or some form of psychotherapy. Conversely, the social worker who helps vulnerable communities organize themselves to seek and petition for greater and fairer police protection, improved schools, and increased employment opportunities tends to recognize causes and solutions that are political, legal, sociocultural, or economic in nature. The psychologically oriented social worker is less likely to search for or discover social, environmental, economic, or political causes and solutions just as the community-oriented social worker is less likely to find psychological or psychiatric factors.

False Dilemma (FD): Someone makes a claim and suggests that only two options apply. For example, an advocate for a certain political position might frame the issue in dichotomous, "either/ or" fashion such as, "Do you prefer the patriotic or unpatriotic approach?" Dichotomization can overly simplify complex phenomena or issues and lead people to overlook data and perspectives that are not included among the limited positions presented.

Personal Experience (PE): Someone asserts that all opinions, conclusions, and approaches to a phenomenon or issue are ultimately based on personal beliefs and experience. Therefore, all are equally legitimate and none should be considered superior. Relativistic thinking of this kind would be consistent with Perry's "multiplicity" stage. Of course, some claimants intentionally use this fallacious argument in an attempt to persuade or dissuade others. Some social workers are susceptible to PE reasoning in their effort to be empathic and respectful of others. You may notice this in your classes when a fellow student or the professor makes unsupported, unreasonable, irrelevant, or outrageous comments that go unchallenged.

Popular Belief (PB) *and Popular Practice* (PP): Someone attempts to support a claim because "others believe it's true" or "everybody does it." For example, a claimant might argue that a large proportion of the general population believe in psychic phenomena (see, for example, Shermer, 1997). Therefore, "we should believe in them too." Or a student who plagiarized might claim that she should not receive a failing grade because survey findings indicate that a large percentage of students do so as well (Scanlon & Neumann, 2002). Obviously, because something is widely believed does not make it true; and misbehavior does not become right simply because it is commonly practiced.

Post Hoc (PH) *or Post Hoc Ergo Propter Hoc*: Someone claims that because something followed something else in time, the earlier caused the later. "Our team scored the touchdown (B) because I crossed my fingers, closed my eyes, and sat on my hands (A)." Therefore, A caused B. The Latin phrase *post hoc ergo propter hoc* means, "after this, therefore because of this." In part, this reflects a common misconception about correlation. Events that precede other events do not necessarily cause them. The same holds true for events that accompany other events. The latter is called the *Cum Hoc* (CH) fallacy. The Latin phrase *cum hoc ergo propter hoc* means, "with this, therefore because of this."

A seemingly endless array of superstitious beliefs and behaviors result from *post hoc* and *cum hoc* reasoning. For example, suppose a social work student forgets that an examination is scheduled for the next day. She stays up late, drinks a lot of beer, and does not study the textbooks or review any of her class-based notes. She arrives to the class still recovering from the previous night's activities, learns that an exam is scheduled, and somehow completes the test during the time allowed. To her surprise and delight, she later learns that she received the highest exam grade in the class. She tells a classmate that she plans to repeat the process before the next exam because it "worked so well the last time." She concludes that "beer-drinking but not studying leads to good grades in that social work class." Imagine the actual consequences of such an approach. Despite the obvious flaws in such reasoning, similar processes routinely occur at the family, group, organization, community, and societal levels. As a result of fallacious *post hoc* and *cum hoc* reasoning, numerous highly costly but profoundly ineffective laws, regulations, policies, and practices are proposed and implemented.

Red Herring (RH), *Smokescreen, or Diversion*: Someone presents irrelevant information as part of a claim or argument. A common debating trick, use of a red herring distracts others from the original claim—which may well go unexamined as the participants explore the unrelated topic instead. You may well be familiar with "bait and switch" tactics in sales, where one item is advertised but another is presented when customers visit the store.

Same Cause (SC): Someone argues that because two or more events or phenomena occur simultaneously, one must "cause" the other or they must result from the same cause. Sometimes intentional, the SC fallacy often results from a basic misunderstanding about correlational or associational data. Although high correlations may lead us to formulate useful hypotheses about causal factors, they cannot establish causation. Suppose, for example, a social worker serves a family where a child experiences symptoms of anxiety and the child's mother frequently expresses herself in a loud manner. We cannot reasonably infer that the child's anxiety and the mother's loud expression result from the same cause, nor can we firmly establish either that the mother's manner of expression causes the child's anxiety or that the child's anxiety causes the mother's loud expression.

Slippery Slope (SS): Someone asserts that one event will inevitably lead to other, more serious events. Typically, the SS argument does not include data to establish a strong relationship between the one and the others. Advocates of various kinds, perhaps especially politicians, commonly use the "slippery slope" argument to justify severe legal, social, and military actions on grounds that "failure to do so will lead to something far worse." Like the AP argument, use of the SS tactic often triggers an emotional reaction. Rather than pity, however, others tend to experience fear as they conclude that dire consequences are virtually inevitable. Thus engaged, many fail to examine carefully the evidence regarding the relative probability that catastrophic events will indeed follow the event in question.

Straw Man (SM): Someone "substitutes an inaccurate, incomplete, or distorted characterization of another person's position and then proceeds to challenge the validity of the substitution (or straw man)" (Cournoyer, 2004, p. 145). Like that of the red herring, the straw man strategy may divert others so that the original argument remains unexamined.

Unsubstantiated Assertion (UA): This is a claim or assertion that lacks supporting grounds, data, or evidence. For example, a social worker might claim, "My boss is sexist." However, because the social worker fails to provide criteria for sexism or evidence to support the claim that the boss meets those criteria, it remains an incomplete argument that cannot be validated.

Wishful Thinking (WT): Someone asserts that something is true because he or she wishes it were true and would feel uncomfortable concluding that it is false. For example, a social worker might assert that his close friend and colleague Joe could not have embezzled money from the agency because "Joe would never do such a thing." Of course, good friends sometimes do bad things—despite our favorable view of them.

There are dozens, perhaps hundreds, of logical fallacies and thousands of variations. As social workers, we must think critically about all aspects of our professional work—including the sources used and the thinking processes adopted to guide our judgments, decisions, and actions. Logical fallacies represent genuine threats to the quality and validity of our conclusions. If we recognize our fallacious thinking, then we may take steps to control, manage, or counteract it in order to improve the quality of our decisions and behavior. In this regard, social work professionals are similar to scientists in that every research project involves numerous threats to validity. Scientists, therefore, must be alert both to flaws in their own logic and reasoning and also to the risks and threats associated with the phases and processes of their research endeavors. Researchers recognize the various threats to the validity of their studies and seek to control or manage those threats to increase the likelihood of valid results. In so doing, however, scientifically minded researchers recognize that even the very best studies seldom yield definitive findings. Rather, they think in terms of probabilities. That is, they recognize that their findings—even when threats to validity are controlled—reflect a certain probability of being true or false. Indeed, when researchers publish the results of their studies, they commonly report the statistical probability that their findings might be due to unknown factors or "chance." Researchers understand that determining that a claim or hypothesis reflects a high probability of validity (or a low probability of error) is usually the best result possible. Absolute certainty is rare.

Scientific Inquiry

In pursuit of valid conclusions, scientific researchers attempt to control for or manage the numerous threats to internal and external validity and reduce the probability of false positives and false negatives while increasing the likelihood of true positives and true negatives. As Table 3.1 shows, when someone holds a belief, asserts a claim, or proposes a hypothesis that something is true, and it actually is true or valid, we call that a *true positive*. When someone believes, claims, or hypothesizes that something is false or invalid, and it actually is false or invalid, we call that a *true negative*. A *false positive* occurs when someone asserts that something is true or valid, but it actually is false or invalid. A *false negative* results when someone suggests that something is false or invalid, but it actually is true or valid.

TABLE 3.1
True and False Positives and Negatives

	The Claim, Conclusion, Assessment, or Hypothesis Is Actually True	The Claim, Conclusion, Assessment, or Hypothesis Is Actually False
Belief that the Claim, Conclusion, Assessment, or Hypothesis Is True	*True Positive (Valid)*	*False Positive (Invalid)*
Belief that the Claim, Conclusion, Assessment, or Hypothesis Is False	*False Negative (Invalid)*	*True Negative (Valid)*

© Cengage Learning

We often use these terms in reference to medical laboratory tests. When we provide some blood or urine for testing, laboratory personnel analyze the sample, and submit a report containing the results. We might learn, for instance, that a test shows signs of elevated cholesterol levels in our blood. If accurate, the results would represent a true positive. That is, the test indicates that we have high cholesterol and we actually do. If the test shows that we do not have high levels of blood cholesterol when we in fact do not, then the results would represent a true negative. Occasionally, however, the results of medical lab tests are inaccurate. That is, a test might indicate we have high cholesterol when we actually do not. This would be a false positive. A false negative would occur when a test fails to show we have high cholesterol when we actually do.

These same processes occur in social work. For example, suppose a social worker, her supervisor, and a parent all believe that Susie, a 14-year-old, uses marijuana and amphetamines. They base their beliefs (that is, their claims or conclusions) on changes in Susie's behavior, her performance in school, and her social network. However, Susie says that she is not using those or any other drugs. After several random blood and urine samples are taken and tested by a reliable laboratory, the results confirm that she is telling the truth. The adults' beliefs represent a false positive. They believed that their conclusions were accurate when they were actually false. Susie's statement represents a true negative. She denied that she was taking drugs and indeed she really was not using them.

Another example of a false positive includes a child-protection worker's conclusion that a child's parents are abusive and neglectful when they are actually engaged, caring, and protective. Of course, such invalid claims and conclusions can have devastating effects. Parents wrongfully accused of child abuse—especially sexual abuse can experience a lifetime of pain and suffering because of the after effects of false allegations. Like false positives, however, false negatives can also have disastrous and sometimes life-ending consequences. Suppose, for example, a social worker concludes that her depressed client Jesse is not suicidal when he actually does plan to end his life within a few days. When Jesse does commit suicide, the social worker realizes that her conclusion was mistaken. Had the social worker reached a different conclusion, she might have taken assertive action to protect Jesse from his own suicidal motives and plans.

Other examples of false negatives include claims or conclusions that a person is not homicidal when he actually is, that a parent is not abusive of her child when she is, that a man did not rape a woman when he did, that a spouse was not violent toward her partner when she was, that a social service program is ineffective in helping its clients when it is effective, that human activity does not contribute to global climate change when it truly does, that human slavery no longer exists when it does, or that the genocide of approximately 6 million Jewish people and another 5 million Gypsies, homosexual people, and other minorities during the Holocaust did not occur when it actually did.

In our efforts to increase the likelihood of true positives and true negatives and reduce the likelihood of false positives and false negatives, we must think critically and scientifically about our hypotheses, judgments, and actions. Failure to do so may have serious consequences for clients as well as for social workers.

Indeed, social workers engage in scientific inquiry to: (1) reduce the likelihood of harm to clients and others affected by our ideas and actions; (2) increase the probability of positive outcomes for people—especially those affected by our services; (3) improve the ongoing quality of policies, programs, and practices in general; and (4) increase the effectiveness of programs and practices that affect our own current clients.

The Council on Social Work Education (2008) expects graduates of accredited programs to "comprehend quantitative and qualitative research and understand scientific and ethical approaches to building knowledge . . . [and] . . . employ evidence-based interventions, evaluate their own practice, and use research findings to improve practice, policy, and social service delivery" (p. 5). Although a single, approach to scientific investigation probably does not exist, the various "scientific methods" do tend to following a relatively similar several-stage process (see Figure 3.1). Most scientific endeavors include the following steps:

1. Recognize a problem or phenomenon for investigation.

2. Review the relevant research literature to learn what others have discovered and to determine if someone else has already investigated the phenomenon or solved the problem.

3. Formulate a specific question or hypothesis that captures what you hope to test or investigate. Typically, the question is phrased in an "if A, will B?" or an "if C, then D" fashion. For example, as social workers we hope to resolve social problems such as hunger, poverty, unemployment, oppression, discrimination, or exploitation. We might, therefore, formulate a question such as, "If a government implements a proposed social policy intended to reduce the incidence of a particular social problem, will the incidence among the population actually decrease?" Or, we might prepare a hypothesis such as, "If we provide people affected by the social problem a particular kind of social work service, they will experience a reduction in the frequency, intensity or severity, extent, or duration of that social problem." At one time, hypotheses were typically phrased in a "null" manner. That is, researchers would hypothesize that they would find "no difference" in average outcome among members of a group that received the service or experienced the phenomenon and a group that experienced something else. For example, we might prepare a null hypothesis such as, "There will be no (statistically significant) difference between the average severity and duration of the social problem among members of a group who receive professional social work services and the average severity and duration of the social problem among group members who receive peer support."

4. Design a research protocol to answer the question or test the hypothesis. Identify relevant independent variables and determine the dependent variable or variables that will be used to measure the incidence, frequency, severity, or duration of the problem or phenomenon. Control for or manage threats to internal and external validity.

5. Implement the research design, make and record observations, take measurements, and collect data.

6. Summarize the observations, measurements, and data. Conduct statistical or other analyses.

7. Disseminate findings and conclusions in the form of a report or research paper. Provide descriptive information about the problem, the population or sample, the variables, and the research design so that other researchers may replicate the investigation.

Contemporary scientists and researchers fully recognize that there has never been a single "scientific method." There are several. Indeed, the National Science Teachers Association board of directors (2000, July) endorsed a position statement about the nature of science. A portion of that statement reads as follows:

Although no single universal step-by-step scientific method captures the complexity of doing science, a number of shared values and perspectives characterize a scientific approach to understanding nature. Among these are a demand for naturalistic explanations supported by empirical evidence that are, at least in principle, testable against the natural world. Other shared elements include observations, rational argument, inference, skepticism, peer review and replicability of work. (para. 3)

Although some social workers conduct large-scale scientific research studies on a full-time basis, most of us regularly use skills of scientific inquiry for two main purposes: (1) to search for

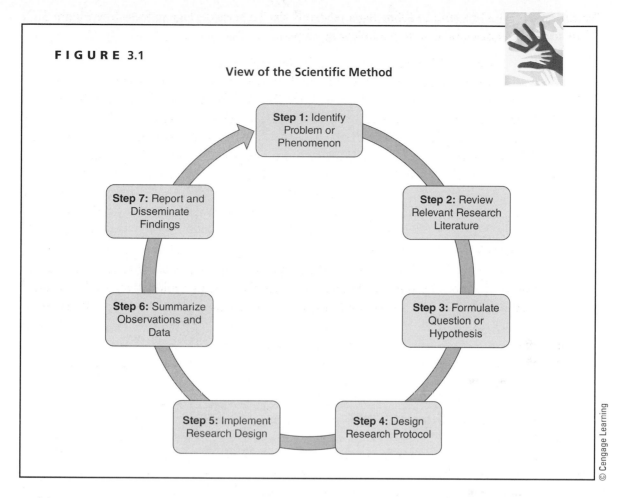

FIGURE 3.1

View of the Scientific Method

Step 1: Identify Problem or Phenomenon

Step 2: Review Relevant Research Literature

Step 3: Formulate Question or Hypothesis

Step 4: Design Research Protocol

Step 5: Implement Research Design

Step 6: Summarize Observations and Data

Step 7: Report and Disseminate Findings

and locate practice-related research studies, analyze them for their quality and relevance, and translate credible findings for use in our professional activities; and (2) to evaluate the effectiveness of our service to clients. We may refer to these two forms of scientific inquiry as nomothetic and ideographic research, respectively (Cournoyer, 2004; Cournoyer & Powers, 2002). When combined and integrated, they constitute the essential elements of evidence-based social work.

Evidence-based social work involves the mindful and systematic identification, analysis, and synthesis of nomothetic and ideographic evidence of practice effectiveness as a primary part of an integrative and collaborative process concerning the selection, application, and evaluation of service to members of target client groups. The evidence-based decision-making process includes consideration of professional ethics and experience as well as the cultural values and personal judgments of consumers. (Cournoyer, 2004, p. 4)

Evidence-based practice involves several steps[1] (see Figure 3.2). The first involves the identification or creation of a question that propels the process. The *practice-relevant question* should be formulated in a precise manner so that it includes (1) a social problem, issue, or goal; (2) a client or other target population; (3) at least one practice or policy approach or intervention, or an assessment tool or instrument; and (4) an effect or outcome.

The *search* involves (1) identification of keywords and their synonyms derived from the question; (2) preparation of a specific, keyword-based plan about where and how to conduct

---

[1] For a more comprehensive examination and review of these processes, see Cournoyer (2004).

the search; (3) formulation of guidelines for analyzing and criteria for including and excluding materials located through the search; (4) implementation of the search plan; and (5) discovery and storage of located resources.

The *analysis* involves (1) a careful review of the located resources to determine their relative credibility; (2) exclusion of resources that fail to meet guidelines and inclusion criteria, and selection of those that do; (3) organization, synthesis, and translation of the selected resources into meaningful practice or policy principles and guidelines; and (4) consultation with prospective clients or others potentially affected by the implementation of a policy or plan.

The *application*[2] involves (1) collaborative decision making with clients or affected others about the goodness-of-fit between the evidence-based practice or policy and their personal and cultural values, traditions, capacities, and preferences; (2) adaptations based upon the professional's practice experience and the unique characteristics of the individual, family, group, organization, or community; and (3) implementation of the agreed-upon plans.

The *evaluation*[3] involves (1) collaborative measurement or assessment of the outcomes and effects of the practice or policy (for example, progress toward problem resolution or goal achievement as well as client satisfaction); (2) incorporation of findings to adapt, revise, or change the practice or policy to improve the quality of the process and the effectiveness of the outcomes; and (3) application of the new or revised plans and continued evaluation of outcomes and effects (Cournoyer, 2004).

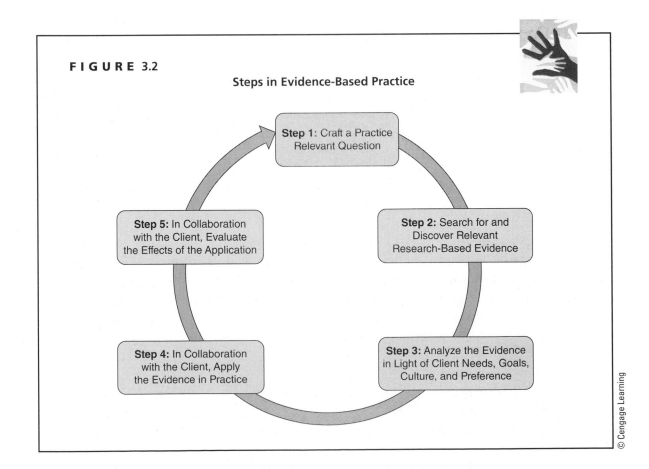

FIGURE 3.2

Steps in Evidence-Based Practice

Step 1: Craft a Practice Relevant Question

Step 2: Search for and Discover Relevant Research-Based Evidence

Step 3: Analyze the Evidence in Light of Client Needs, Goals, Culture, and Preference

Step 4: In Collaboration with the Client, Apply the Evidence in Practice

Step 5: In Collaboration with the Client, Evaluate the Effects of the Application

© Cengage Learning

---

[2] See the contracting as well as the working and evaluating skills in later chapters.

[3] See the working and evaluating skills in a later chapter.

As social workers search for research-based evidence of policy, program, or practice effectiveness, we typically use keywords derived from well-crafted, practice-relevant questions to guide our investigation. We also identify sources likely to contain descriptive reports of relevant research studies. In contemporary practice, many social workers can readily access online bibliographic databases of journal articles, books, reports, and dissertations. Of course, colleges and universities, and many health and social agencies purchase access to fee-based, commercial databases where the full-text of research articles and entire books may be viewed. In addition, many public libraries now include such access for their subscribers.

Some organizations conduct systematic reviews of the research literature that pertains to particular topics. For example, the Cochrane Collaboration conducts rigorous analyses of the research literature in health and medicine, including some psychosocial and psychiatric topics (2012a). The Campbell Collaboration (C2) conducts systematic reviews of the pertinent research literature in the areas of education, social welfare, and criminal justice (2012a). The Department for International Development (DFID) prepares systematic reviews on topics related to international development (2012). The Collaboration for Environmental Evidence (CEE) hosts a library of systematic reviews that pertain to environmental issues (2012). The International Initiative for Impact Evaluation (3ie) sponsors a database of systematic reviews related to the impact of social and economic development activities (2012). The Evidence for Policy and Practice Information and Coordinating Centre (EPPI) undertakes systematic reviews in the areas of "education and social policy, health promotion and public health, international health systems and development, (and) participative research and policy" (2012). Such organizations carefully "filter" those research studies that meet or exceed certain selection criteria, and synthesize their findings for use by helping professionals and policy makers.

In our efforts to appraise relevant research studies, we first consider the question of their likely credibility or validity. There are several kinds of validity. For example, *construct validity* involves the strength of the relationship between the way the phenomenon under investigation is conceptualized and measured and the actual phenomenon itself. *Conclusion validity* refers to the strength of a relationship of some kind—causal or correlational—between the activity under investigation and the outcome.

Two other types of validity are especially relevant for social work. These are *internal* and *external validity*. We use the term *internal validity* to refer to a research design's capacity to determine that an independent variable caused change in a dependent variable. For example, in the helping professions, researchers and practitioners are interested in whether or not a particular policy, program, practice approach, or intervention strategy actually works—that is, accomplishes the goal of helping the people it is designed to help. *External validity* refers to the research design's capacity to permit findings to be generalized, or externalized, to a larger population. In other words, can we reasonably extend the findings beyond the relatively small sample of participants to the population from which they were drawn (Roth & Fonagy, 1996)?

A research study seeking to determine the effectiveness of a teenage violence prevention program in Indianapolis, Indiana, would reflect internal validity if it could accurately determine whether or not (and, ideally, to what degree) the program caused a reduction in teenage violence in that city. The study would reflect external validity if the findings could be generalized beyond Indianapolis to other cities and towns in the United States or throughout the world.

Researchers generally attempt to avoid or minimize threats to validity. Just as critical thinkers seek to avoid logical fallacies, scientific researchers try to control or manage threats to internal and external validity.

Recognizing Threats to Internal and External Validity

Earlier, we reviewed an abbreviated list of several logical fallacies. We now do the same for the various threats to internal and external validity in the conduct of scientific research (Campbell, Cook, & Cook, 1979; Campbell & Stanley, 1966; Cook & Campbell, 1979; Grinnell, 1997; Grinnell & Unrau, 2008; Isaac & Michael, 1971; Rubin & Babbie, 2007; Yegidis & Weinbach, 2002). Some of the threats to internal validity in research studies include:

Selection and Assignment: Participants in research studies understandably vary from one another in certain respects. Some may be taller, heavier, darker, or older than others. Some may have less education or less income; some may be introverted whereas others may be extraverted in social relations. These variations could potentially affect the outcomes of the study. For this reason, experimental (for example, intervention or treatment) groups are usually paired with control or comparison groups. When the selection and assignment from the population to the experimental and control groups are random, there is a good chance that the average characteristics of each group will be about the same. When randomization is not feasible, sometimes pertinent characteristics of participants are "matched" so that each group reflects a similar composition. However, when the average characteristics of the groups differ from one another, the researchers cannot determine if the intervention actually caused the effects. The differing characteristics of the groups, rather than the intervention, could have led to the results.

History: Even during research studies, "things happen." When a significant event (for example, a natural disaster, a political or social upheaval, a military engagement, or a terrorist attack) occurs sometime between the onset and the conclusion of the study (for example, between pretest and posttest), researchers cannot determine that the intervention actually caused the effects. Indeed, the effects may result from participants' reaction to the unexpected, external event.

Maturation: In addition to "things happening" during the course of a research study, participants change for other, more expected reasons as well. For example, as children age, they develop more complex cognitive abilities and social skills. During adolescence, young people change in numerous ways: physiologically, hormonally, emotionally, and socially. Indeed, their brains continue to develop throughout the teen years. During old age, people also change in many ways—some for the better, some for the worse. In general, however, we can expect that human beings of all ages will mature and change in some ways over time. Participants in research studies are no exception. Especially in long-term studies, scientifically minded researchers anticipate that time and aging will affect participants—which can influence outcomes and make it difficult to determine if the intervention or the maturation of the participants caused the effects.

Attrition: During the course of a research study, some participants may discontinue. They may dropout for various reasons—some within and some outside their personal control. Participants sometimes die or become ill, or move to a new location because of a change in employment or life circumstances. Some participants choose to leave the study because they have benefited in some way or perhaps because they lose interest.

Attrition threatens the validity of the study because the people who dropout may differ from those who remain. As a result, the groups (for example, intervention and control or comparison) may become dissimilar and nonequivalent or "mismatched." Furthermore, the resulting "sample" may become unrepresentative of the population from which it is drawn.

Repeated Testing Effects: When participants complete a test or measure two or more times, they may be affected by the testing experience in some way. Participants may improve their scores on a posttest because they remember some of the items or otherwise retain relevant knowledge from the pretest. Or, participants may become more or less relaxed, complacent, or motivated after repeated testings.

Instrumentation Effects: In addition to testing effects, the tests or measures themselves may be invalid, unreliable, or irrelevant to the participants. They may be presented or administered in an improper manner, and errors may be made in scoring. Obviously, if an instrument does not accurately measure what the researchers hope to test, or if it does so unreliably, the validity of the study becomes questionable indeed.

Statistical Regression toward the Mean: Researchers understand that participants' test scores tend to moderate in second, third, and subsequent administrations. In other words, participants who score unusually high or unusually low in a first test tend to move toward the group average during subsequent tests. This general statistical tendency may account for some of the change in participants' pretest and posttest scores. As with other threats, regression toward the mean may make it difficult for researchers to determine how much of the effect was due to the intervention and how much was the result of this powerful statistical tendency.

Reactivity: Participants in research studies are usually fully aware that they are being studied. Awareness of participation may trigger reactions of various kinds. Some participants may become motivated to "try harder" or perhaps distort their responses to tests and measures (for example, through "Hawthorne effects"). Others may anticipate improvement and, based on positive expectations and placebo effects, progress accordingly. In addition, participants from an experimental group sometimes interact with those from a comparison group so that participants' responses are affected (for example, comparison group members might learn about the treatment or intervention from members of the experimental group and try out some of the ideas or techniques). Like participants, researchers themselves sometimes react to the research experience. Occasionally, they inadvertently compensate members of control or comparison groups for the lack of treatment by providing special or unusual care, sympathy, or interest; or, they might pay extra attention to participants of the experimental condition. These various reactive effects can complicate determination of the actual causes of intervention outcomes.

Causal Ambiguity: Sometimes researchers cannot determine whether the independent variable (for example, a treatment or intervention) causes changes in the dependent variable (for example, scores on measures) or vice versa. For example, suppose a researcher discovers that early dropouts from a substance abuse treatment program are more likely to misuse drugs or alcohol than those participants who complete the entire program. Researchers might infer that program completion results in decreased substance abuse (that is, the independent variable affected the dependent variable). However, as Rubin and Babbie (2001, pp. 299–300) discuss, these findings could also be interpreted to suggest that decreased substance misuse leads to program completion (that is, the dependent variable affected the independent variable).

In addition to numerous threats to internal validity, research studies are also subject to threats to external validity as well (Campbell & Stanley, 1966; Grinnell, 1997; Royse, 1995; Rubin & Babbie, 2001; Yegidis, Weinbach, & Morrison-Rodriquez, 1999). Some threats to external validity include:

Pretest Intervention Interaction: Earlier we discussed the effects of repeated testing as a threat to internal validity. In addition, the pretest may influence participants' reaction to and behavior vis-à-vis the research experience. If the participants change as a result of the pretest, they may become a nonrepresentative sample of the population. If they are no longer representative of the larger population, then the findings of the research study cannot reasonably be generalized beyond the experimental sample. To do so would raise questions about the study's external validity.

Selection Intervention Interaction: Earlier we discussed the effects of selection and assignment as a threat to internal validity. Selection can also affect external validity as well. Unless randomized selection or carefully matched assignment occurs, we cannot be certain that the sample is truly representative of the population from which it is drawn. Sometimes research studies may involve such a narrowly defined and specific group of participants that the findings cannot reasonably be generalized to many, if any, other people.

Reactivity: As discussed earlier, the research experience may trigger various reactions among participants. Such reactive effects may threaten external as well as internal validity as participants change in such a way that they no longer can be considered a truly representative sample of the larger population. As a result, the findings cannot validly be generalized beyond the study's participants themselves.

Researcher and Confirmation Bias: Most human beings are subject to confirmation bias. That is, we tend to see what we hope or expect to see. Researchers are not exempt from this general human tendency. Researchers also tend to find what they expect to find and, usually inadvertently and unconsciously, they may subtly encourage or reward participants in the intervention group to change in the expected direction and, thereby, confirm their hypotheses. This threat to internal validity may become an external threat if researchers know which participants are in an intervention group and which are in a comparison group. Researchers' actions to confirm their bias may cause changes among participants such that they lose their status as a representative sample of the larger population.

Understanding Research Designs

Awareness and understanding of the threats to internal and external validity aid us in our review and analysis of research studies. Knowledge of various research designs and their comparative strengths and weaknesses helps as well. For example, many excellent studies are qualitative or nonexperimental in nature. They often contribute extraordinarily useful information about particular problems and specific population groups, and especially how people are affected by various circumstances. They are, however, usually less useful for determining cause-and-effect relationships (for example, establishing that a practice intervention contributes to achievement of clients' goals). Experimental, quasi-experimental, and single-system research designs are usually better for that purpose.

In our search for evidence of policy, program, or practice effectiveness, social workers generally prefer to use findings from research studies that manage threats to internal and external validity, and can reasonably establish a causal relationship between intervention and outcome. Indeed, some proponents of evidence-based practice have proposed hierarchies of preferred research approaches. For example, Nathan and Gorman (2007) rank research studies into six general types:

Type 1 Studies: These are the most rigorous and involve a randomized, prospective clinical trial. Such studies also must involve comparison groups with random assignment, blinded assessments, clear presentation of exclusion and inclusion criteria, state-of-the-art diagnostic methods, adequate sample size to offer statistical power, and clearly described statistical methods.

Type 2 Studies: These are clinical trials in which an intervention is made, but some aspect of the Type 1 study requirement is missing—for example, a trial in which a double blind cannot be maintained, a trial in which two treatments are compared but the assignment is not randomized, and a trial in which there is a clear but not fatal flaw such as a period of observation that is felt to be too short to make full judgments on treatment efficacy. Such studies clearly do not merit the same consideration as Type 1 studies, but often make important contributions and generally should not be ignored.

Type 3 Studies: These are clearly methodologically limited. Generally, Type 3 studies are open-treatment studies aiming at obtaining pilot data. They are highly subject to observer bias and can usually do little more than indicate if a treatment is worth pursuing in a more rigorous design. Also included in this category are case control studies in which patients are identified and then information about treatment is obtained from them retrospectively. Such studies can, of course, provide a great deal of naturalistic information but are prone to all of the problems of uncontrolled data collection and retrospective recall error.

Type 4 Studies: Reviews with secondary data analysis can be useful, especially if the data analytic techniques are sophisticated. Modern methods of meta-analysis attempt to account for the fact that, for example, negative studies tend to be reported at a substantially lower rate than positive outcome studies.

Type 5 Studies: Reviews without secondary data analysis are helpful to give an impression of the literature but are clearly subject to the writer's opinion and sometimes are highly biased.

Type 6 Studies: This encompasses a variety of reports that have marginal value, such as case studies, essays, and opinion papers. (pp. xii–xiii)

In recognition of the increasingly sophisticated nature of contemporary systematic reviews and meta-analyses of the research literature, and their special value in regard to evaluating practice effectiveness, Guyatt, Sackett, and Sinclair (1995) propose a somewhat different classification approach:

- ◆ Level 1: High-Quality Systematic Reviews and Meta-Analyses
- ◆ Level 2: Randomized Controlled Studies with Clear Results
- ◆ Level 3: Randomized Controlled Studies with Unclear Results
- ◆ Level 4: Cohort Studies
- ◆ Level 5: Case Controlled Studies
- ◆ Level 6: Cross-Sectional Surveys
- ◆ Level 7: Case Reports (Greenhalgh, 1997b)

Contemporary social workers must be proficient in accessing and assessing current research related to social problems they address, the clients they serve, and the services they provide. Typically, this means that we must locate and carefully read and reflect upon recent research studies in our fields of practice. Technological advances over the course of the last few decades now enable researchers to conduct sophisticated "systematic reviews" (Akobeng, 2005; Cook, Greengold, Ellrodt, & Weingarten, 1997; Greenhalgh, 1997a, 1997b; Grimshaw et al., 2001; Helmer, Savoie, Green, & Kazanjian, 2001; Hunt & McKibbon, 1997; Jones & Evans, 2000; Pai et al., 2004) and "meta-analyses" (Akobeng, 2005; Cook et al., 1992; Glass, 1976; Hunt, 1997; Rudner, Glass, Evartt, & Emery, 2000; Sutton, Abrams, Jones, Sheldon, & Song, 2000; Videka-Sherman, 1988, 1995; Wierzbicki & Pekarik, 1993) of relevant research studies. Especially popular as a tool for determining evidence-based and "best" practices in medicine, systematic reviews and meta-analyses are becoming more common among other helping professions and disciplines as well (Cournoyer, 2004; Cournoyer & Powers, 2002; Hunt, 1997).

Unlike modern systematic reviews and meta-analyses, traditional literature reviews can easily be influenced by researchers' intentional or unintentional confirmation biases and may not be truly systematic, objective, comprehensive, or rigorous. Influenced by their preconceived beliefs and predictions, traditional reviewers expect to find and often do indeed locate studies and sources that support their own ideas. Resources that challenge, contradict, or refute their ideas somehow remain undiscovered, ignored, or dismissed. As a "study of studies," truly systematic reviews and meta-analyses of the research literature better manage such threats to validity and, because the methodology is clearly described, others researchers may replicate the review and meta-analysis to determine if equivalent findings result.

One limitation in both the Nathan and Gorman (2007) and the Guyatt et al. (1995) schemas may be the relatively low-level placement of single-system design research. The external-validity limitations of single-system research are obvious. Social workers recognize that we cannot generalize to larger populations the results of single-system evaluations of our work with individuals, families, groups, organizations, and communities. Random selection from larger populations and random assignment to experimental or control groups are generally impossible in the context of day-to-day social work practice. Therefore, the particular clients that we serve may not be representative of one or more larger populations. Nonetheless, single-system evaluation is enormously meaningful to service recipients and others affected by the work we do. Perhaps more importantly, single-system evaluation can readily be incorporated as a regular, routine aspect of all of our professional activities, and its use can directly enhance the quality and effectiveness of our services. When combined with systematic examination of the research-based practice literature, professional experience, collaboration with clients, and critical thinking, single-system evaluation completes the notion of evidence-based social work.[4]

Adopting Universal Intellectual Standards

In our examination of practice-relevant research, social workers attempt to maintain a truly professional and scientific perspective. We recognize threats to validity, identify logical fallacies in our own and others' claims and conclusions, engage in sophisticated analysis, and adopt rigorous standards of scholarship. Elder and Paul (1996; Paul & Elder, 1996, 1997) propose an array of universal intellectual standards and valuable intellectual traits that may guide social workers and other scholars as we engage in critical thinking, scientific inquiry, and career-long learning. The following represents a slightly adapted version of their universal standards:[5]

- ◆ Humility
- ◆ Empathy
- ◆ Fairness
- ◆ Courage
- ◆ Honesty and Integrity
- ◆ Clarity, Precision, and Accuracy
- ◆ Relevance
- ◆ Intellectual Sophistication
- ◆ Logic

The intellectual standards apply to the way we think and learn, and speak and write about practice, policy, and professional issues. Perhaps most importantly, they affect the people we serve. If we consider that the essential common element of both critical thinking and scientific inquiry is *learning*, then these principles apply to formal learning (for example, academic courses, seminars, workshops, conferences, training institutes) as well as informal learning (for example, self-directed reading of research studies and systematic reviews of the literature; consultation and conversations with colleagues and community members; and work and evaluation with our individual, family, group, organization, and community clients). If we apply both the code of ethics and these

---

[4] See Chapter 12 for specific information about single-system evaluation.
[5] For a more specific application of these standards to social work situations, see Cournoyer and Stanley (2002).

intellectual standards to our professional activities and especially to our career-long learning, our clients and colleagues and the members of our community will almost certain benefit.

Humility: We reflect humility in our professional activities and career-long learning experiences when we recognize and publicly acknowledge our own knowledge and skill deficits. Intellectual humility is consistent with the Code of Ethics of the National Association of Social Workers (2008), which states that "Social workers should provide services and represent themselves as competent only within the boundaries of their education, training, license, certification, consultation received, supervised experience, or other relevant professional experience" (1.04[a] Competence).

Humility also involves considerable open-mindedness and a readiness to transcend our human tendency toward confirmation bias. We must be able to change our minds about things we strongly believe (Brockman, 2009). For instance, suppose you are a social worker who believes drug addiction is a disease that, in many ways, resembles other conditions such as diabetes or cancer. Some of your clients have a similar view or, perhaps due to your influence or the influence of your agency's culture, soon adopt such a view. Other clients, however, believe that their use of drugs is primarily the result of their own choices. Rather than victims of a disease which they contracted, they prefer to view drug usage as a learned behavior for which they and those who introduced them to the substances are responsible.

Let's say that through your use of client-satisfaction and goal-centered measures with clients treated from both perspectives, you gather strong evidence that a larger proportion of clients whose nondisease view of addiction is respected by you and the agency achieve their goals than do those who are encouraged to adopt a disease perspective. Let's say you also conduct a systematic review of the research literature and find that when professional helpers and clients adopt similar hypotheses about the causes and solutions to problems, outcomes tend to be superior (Caspar et al., 2012). Given this new information, you change your mind about addiction. You might conclude that, "For some people drug misuse is the result of a disease, for others it is learned behavior, for others it is a combination; and for others it is something else altogether. At this time, I cannot conclude that one view is more correct than another; nor am I certain that it is in our clients' best interest that my agency or I expect all clients to adopt the same "agency-approved" view. It seems quite possible that many views are valid—especially when those views fit the facts of the situation and the knowledge and perspectives of the people involved."

Empathy: We reflect empathy in our professional activities and career-long learning experiences when we respect the views and experience of others, and genuinely consider the potential implications of ideas and actions on those likely to be affected by them. If we limit ourselves to our own views and our own experience, we are likely to learn less than if we include those of others—especially those who differ from ourselves.

As social workers, we routinely reflect, analyze, and synthesize information and points-of-view from multiple sources. A person-in-environment perspective requires that we consider the experience and views of others—including those who are not, technically speaking, clients. This involves the extremely difficult process of intellectual empathy—the willingness and ability to understand the perspectives of many other people, groups, and communities; including some that are only potentially or indirectly affected.

Fairness: We reflect fairness in our professional activities and career-long learning experiences when we exercise intellectual self-discipline and control our tendencies toward bias of various kinds. Humans are often prejudiced, egocentric, ethnocentric, and superstitious in our approach to learning. We commonly accept information that confirms and supports our beliefs, opinions, and expectations and ignore that which contradicts or refutes them. Intellectual fairness requires that we transcend our tendencies toward confirmation bias and genuinely seek out and seriously consider all relevant credible information that pertains to our learning focus.

Courage: We reflect intellectual courage in our professional activities and career-long learning experiences when we change our preconceived beliefs and opinions on the basis of more credible evidence or more complete and sophisticated analyses. Courage is most apparent when our revised, evidence-based views are unpopular with others—perhaps especially people or groups in positions of power and authority. We manifest courage when we publicly argue on behalf of ideas that are thoughtfully constructed and supported by valid research findings, and argue against ideas that lack an evidence base and are associated with biased ideology, superstition, suspect assumptions, and false conclusions.

Many social workers take extraordinary personal risks on behalf of clients and other vulnerable populations. Sometimes, they are supported by friends, colleagues, and their professional associations in their courageous efforts. Unfortunately, some social workers are scapegoated, abused, imprisoned, or killed when they speak out about and act to publicize or prevent violations of human rights and other forms of social injustice. As members of a radical profession, social workers often challenge the authority of powerful people and institutions and question the validity of dominant views and practices. Whenever we engage in such advocacy, we can anticipate strong and forceful reactions to us as individuals and to our profession as a whole. All social workers but especially those who serve in child welfare; those who work in violent communities or in areas of political or military conflict; those who organize vulnerable groups; and those who seek to reduce poverty, discrimination, and oppression and advance social and economic justice require a very high courage quotient (Biswas-Diener, 2012) indeed.

Honesty and Integrity: We reflect honesty and integrity in our professional activities and career-long learning experiences when we adopt rigorous standards of thought and behavior; sincerely search for, discover, and share genuinely credible information; publicly distinguish facts from opinions and our personal views from our professional judgments; revise our thinking on the basis of better evidence or more sophisticated reasoning; acknowledge and credit the contributions of others, and identify our sources of information; and readily admit to and accept responsibility for our own mistakes.

Clarity, Precision, and Accuracy: We reflect intellectual clarity, precision, and accuracy when we express ourselves so that others can comprehend the true meaning of our words. We keep our audience in mind as we communicate in a sincere effort to increase understanding and avoid misunderstanding. In our oral and written communication, we express ourselves in simple and direct language, and avoid professional jargon that can confuse or diminish others. Frequently, we provide examples, discuss and provide supporting evidence, display graphic illustrations, and sometimes use metaphors or analogies to convey our message clearly, precisely, and accurately so that others can more easily understand.

Relevance: We reflect relevance when we engage in activities that pertain directly to our professional goals and objectives and those of our clients. We keep our focus on what we seek to discover and resist our human tendency to attend to familiar, or to distracting and irrelevant material.

Intellectual Sophistication: We reflect intellectual sophistication when we approach professional topics and issues in a manner that adequately addresses their relative complexity. We resist both the temptation to approach complicated matters in an overly simplistic or dichotomous way as well as the tendency to make straightforward topics excessively complex.

Logic: We reflect logic in our professional activities and career-long learning experiences when we think and express ourselves in the form of complete arguments that contain evidence or credible rationales for our claims or conclusions. We resist the human tendency to engage in fallacious, superstitious, incomplete, and biased thinking. We avoid logical fallacies so that our ideas and statements are both well-reasoned and reasonable.

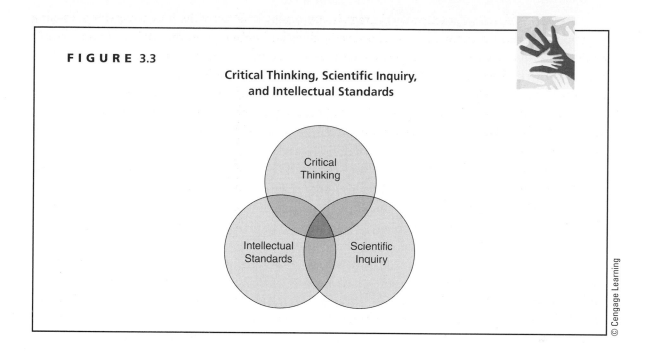

FIGURE 3.3

Critical Thinking, Scientific Inquiry,
and Intellectual Standards

Critical
Thinking

Intellectual
Standards

Scientific
Inquiry

© Cengage Learning

As you consider these universal intellectual standards in conjunction with the logical fallacies and the threats to internal and external validity, you probably recognize numerous similarities and areas of commonality (see Figure 3.3). Without scientific evidence, logic alone can lead us to reasonable—but false—conclusions based on invalid premises. Without critical thought, scientific evidence alone can lead to unwarranted implications and generalizations, and inappropriate applications. Without intellectual standards, we can easily lose perspective and, perhaps most important of all, neglect the primacy of the people we serve.

Reviewing Research Studies

When social workers become familiar with the numerous forms of logical fallacies, the fundamentals of scientific inquiry, the basics of research designs, and the various threats to internal and external validity, we can usually quickly recognize credible from incredible arguments. When we hear commercials and infomercials or read advertisements about magical pills for weight loss or increased sexual prowess, and magnets or special crystals to reduce pain or cure disease, we view them with great skepticism. When we read Web-based materials that lack authors' names or affiliations and provide facts and statistical findings without citing original sources or providing references, we dismiss them as unsubstantiated claims. When we receive an e-mail message from an unknown "legal representative" who announces that a million dollars in our name has been discovered in the bank of a distant country, we do not reply to the message. Rather, we immediately deposit the message in our spam folder. When we hear spokespeople from one political campaign berate an opposing candidate, we remain properly skeptical of the assertions. Claims such as these are easy to appraise—and easy to dismiss.

On the other hand, assessing the credibility of articles that appear in professional journals can be quite difficult. Many articles are theoretical in nature while others reflect the opinions of their authors. Some contain summaries or discussions of studies conducted by other researchers. We might refer to these as authority-based(Gambrill, 1999, 2001) as opposed to research-based. Authority-based articles reflect the thoughts and suggestions of people who have some status vis-à-vis the topic. For example, a senior social worker who, for 25 years, has served adult men who have molested children may be ascribed some degree of expert status. If he publishes an article that contains his experience-based opinions about how best to help this particular client population, we would consider it authority-based. Similarly, when a client who recovered from years of childhood sexual abuse writes an article about the best and worst psychosocial services she received, she does so as an authority. She experienced the events and is an expert about her own life. Authority-based articles are often extremely helpful to social workers—providing us with perspective, ideas to consider, and often useful anecdotal material. However, they do not carry the same degree of credibility as research-based articles.

Research-based articles are generally even more challenging to understand and evaluate than those that are authority based. Authors of research articles often use unusual terminology and commonly apply statistics in describing the significance of their findings. Members of the general public are typically ill-equipped to comprehend the various facets of research studies and appraise the credibility of results. As professional social workers, however, we need to review and evaluate research studies that relate to the profession's mission as well as our own particular service roles and functions, the social problems we address, and the clients we serve. Certainly, many vulnerable populations groups and communities might benefit if more social workers actually conducted research studies—especially those about the outcomes of social policies and intervention practices. However, we must, at a minimum, be able to read, understand, and appraise research articles. Because social work adopts a person-in-environment perspective, we must be able to read research articles that appear in medical, sociological, psychological, economics, anthropological, policy and political, administration, cultural, and epidemiological journals as well as those that emanate from our own profession.

Genuine research articles can be distinguished from others by the clear specification of research questions or hypotheses, definition of core terms and concepts, detailed description of the research methods and measures, systematic analysis of the data, presentation of findings that logically derive from the analysis, and discussion of those findings. A central feature of credible research is its potential for replication. If the study cannot be repeated by other researchers, its findings must be viewed with caution. When studies are replicated and similar results obtained, the conclusions achieve increased credibility.

Most research articles reflect an organizational structure that includes some or all of the sections outlined below. These sections are not mutually exclusive. Some researchers merge two or more, or use additional sections to increase clarity and ease of reading.

- Abstract
- Introduction
- Method
- Analysis
- Findings/Results
- Discussion
- References

Before you begin to review a research article, first ask yourself why you intend to read it. Is it about a topic that interests you personally or professionally? Has it been assigned to you by a professor? What is your level of motivation to read and understand the contents? At this point in time, are you able to focus your attention, concentrate, and critically consider the material? If your purpose is unclear and your interest level, motivation, and concentration levels are low, take steps to "get your head together." Sometimes, you can dramatically alter your mental state by taking a few moments to relax your body, perhaps through a short-meditation exercise or several deep breaths, and clear the clutter from your mind. In particular, replace any preconceived conceptions, assumptions, or biases with genuine open-mindedness. Remember the logical fallacies and the universal intellectual standards. Social workers need mental discipline in many aspects of our professional lives: before meeting with a client, a supervisor, a group of potential funders, or perhaps a legislative committee. By comparison, preparing to review a research article—even a complicated one—should be quite manageable.

When you are ready to begin, recognize that understanding and evaluating research articles take time and patience (Greenhalgh, 2001). Many studies require several readings to comprehend the contents and recognize their strengths and weaknesses. Keshav (2007) recommends a three-pass approach. However, as busy social work students and practicing professionals, two readings may be all we can manage.

First Reading: First, read the title, abstract, and information about the author. Make note of the author's discipline, organizational affiliation, and contact information. Notice if any conflicts of interest are mentioned. For example, a researcher may be funded by a company, foundation, or governmental agency; or may be employed by or receive funds from a source that could be affected by the results of the study. In addition to financial and status conflicts, all of us also have implicit conflicts of interest. For example, a medical researcher benefits when a new diagnostic entity—for which a prescription drug or a clinical procedure may be applied—is "discovered." Similarly, social workers benefit when a social problem—for which social services may be needed—is publicized. In both instances, demand increases and "markets" for their respective professional services tend to expand, providing opportunities for themselves and their colleagues.

Abstracts involve brief summaries of the research. They are sometimes prepared quickly and may not have been as carefully or as precisely crafted as the contents of the article itself. Recognizing that the abstract may not be fully accurate, we generally refrain from paraphrasing or quoting passages from them and refer to the actual text of articles instead.

Next read the introduction to identify the focus of the article and clarify the research questions or hypotheses. The purpose of the study should be clearly specified so that readers can determine if the questions are addressed and answered, and the objectives achieved. The introductory section should also contain some mention of the type of research study. Determine if the research study is qualitative, quantitative, or perhaps of a mixed nature containing both quantitative and qualitative aspects. Identify the context for the study. Are earlier research studies in the field mentioned? Is there discussion of some theoretical basis for the goals and questions pursued through the study? Does the study represent a continuation and extension of previous research? Is it a replication study? Does the study make a genuine contribution to the knowledge base in this particular area? Are key terms or concepts defined and assumptions explicitly stated? What is the quality of the writing?

After reading the introduction, scan the remaining section and subsection headings to gain a sense of the organizational structure. Then, read the section that contains a summary of the findings and a discussion of their possible meaning and implications. This section may be titled "discussion" or perhaps "conclusions."

Determine if the conclusions section fulfills the stated purpose of the study and contains answers to each of the research questions. There should be a logical and coherent flow from the introduction, through the section headings, and on to the conclusions. If the structure is disorganized, lacks coherence, or if the conclusions fail to address the identified purpose of the study, become a bit skeptical. Prepare yourself for some critical thinking.

Finally, examine the references section. Notice the names of the cited authors, the sources, and the kinds of publications. Do the references come from credible (for example, refereed published journals) or more questionable sources (for example, popular magazines, newspapers, or websites)? What is the proportion of research-based to authority-based references? Do the authors cite the work of other researchers in addition to their own publications?

Second Reading: Now that you are familiar with the purpose, research questions, and conclusions of the study, read the article more carefully. Refer to Nathan and Gorman's (2007) six general types or Guyatt et al.'s (1995) seven categories (outlined earlier in this chapter) to classify the research approach. Research studies may occur in many forms and may involve experiments, surveys, interviews, or several other forms of data collection. Once classified, decide if the research design described in the article could reasonably yield valid, reliable, and relevant answers to the stated research questions. Also, identify any potential threats to internal and external validity inherent in the research method and determine if the author addresses those threats. If the design does not fit the stated purpose (for example, a descriptive case study cannot determine that a policy, program, or intervention caused a positive outcome) or if the design and its implementation contain several uncontrolled threats to internal or external validity, become more skeptical.

Many research studies incorporate control or comparison groups, often randomly assigned, as a means to manage various validity threats. Control groups serve valuable functions and may help to identify powerful placebo[6] effects. Many participants make substantial progress toward problem resolution, symptom reduction, or goal achievement when provided a placebo treatment (for example, a sugar pill or friendly listening). Therefore, before a program or practice can be considered effective, experimental group participants must, at a minimum, reflect considerably better outcomes than control group participants who receive a placebo (Brody & Brody, 2000; Specter, 2011, Dec. 12; Womack, 2001). Under such conditions and especially if there is a large sample size, significant differences at the $p < 0.01$ and especially at the $p < 0.05$ level are fairly easy to obtain. A drug that is only modestly better than a sugar pill may not actually be especially effective. If participants in a social program or service progress only slightly more than people in a waitlisted control group who receive periodic phone calls from a concerned volunteer, we might raise serious questions about its impact—even if the differences reflect significance at, say, a $p = 0.49$ level.

Control groups that involve an established, proven intervention, rather than a placebo, represent a more rigorous comparison. Their use results in a fairer competition. As social workers, we look for psychosocial programs, practices, and policies that are both superior to placebo and, whenever possible, better than at least one strong alternative intervention.

Although they lack control group comparisons, single-participant ($N = 1$, single-case, or single-subject) studies are extremely useful for individual social workers who genuinely want evaluative feedback from and about the clients they serve. Clients are more likely to improve when professional helpers formally and systematically seek such feedback (Anker, Duncan, & Sparks, 2009; Crits-Christoph et al., 2012; Lambert & Shimokawa, 2011). When a social worker aggregates the results of several of her own $N = 1$ studies, she may be able to distinguish the characteristics of those clients who reflect favorable outcomes and service satisfaction from those whose goals are not achieved and are less satisfied with the quality of service. Recognize, however, that the findings from your $N = 1$ studies, even when aggregated, cannot reasonably be generalized to larger populations of either clients or social workers. Clients are not usually randomly assigned to particular social workers offering discrete services; and, social workers who conduct

---

[6] *Placebo* refers to a positive effect that follows provision of an inert or neutral intervention. On the other hand, *nocebo* refers to a negative effect following such a provision.

such single-system studies are probably not representative of "average" social workers. As such, $N = 1$ studies are not generalizable, despite their utility to our clients and to ourselves. Their external validity must be questioned.

As you continue to read the article, consider the study's participants: Who are they? How were they selected? Where did they come from? What are they like? Are they truly representative of a particular population so that we might reasonably extrapolate findings to that larger group? For example, some studies involve only male adults who have been assigned a particular classification or diagnosis. Whatever findings emerge from such studies cannot legitimately be applied to children, to women, or to other men that have not been so classified. Recognize that the identification and selection of participants may be based upon invalid or unreliable criteria. For example, many psychiatric diagnoses are of questionable validity. Furthermore, the process by which people are diagnosed may be unreliable. In addition, participants classified according to a particular psychiatric diagnosis may vary widely in terms of the symptoms experienced, their severity, or their duration. As a result, generalization from the study sample to the larger population of people assigned the same diagnosis may be unwarranted.

As you proceed to review the article, examine the embedded charts, tables, figures, and diagrams. Compare them to the narratives contained in the analysis, results, or findings sections. Identify any discrepancies between the graphic and narrative material. Check the arithmetic. Mathematical errors are not uncommon and tables and charts sometimes contain obvious errors.

Look carefully to determine how participants who dropout or otherwise fail to complete the study are addressed. Some researchers fail to incorporate noncompleters in their analyses. A few occasionally, and fraudulently, encourage certain participants—those who are not scoring in a desired direction—to discontinue. If such discontinued participants are excluded from the analysis, a study's result can appear a great deal more positive that it actually is. For example, if researchers only publish data about those who complete a program designed to reduce or eliminate substance misuse, it is quite likely that their findings would be at least somewhat inflated. A greater proportion of participants who continue to misuse substances would probably leave the study early while a greater proportion of those who are making progress would probably remain until the end. Authors of credible research articles discuss explicitly how they deal with the issue of discontinuation and noncompletion.

Another example: suppose a researcher is studying the effectiveness of a particular practice or program in helping clients address intimate relationship problems. Let's say 100 couples are included in the study. Fifty are randomly assigned to a program specifically designed to help couples improve the quality of their relationship by enhancing their communication and problem-solving skills. The other 50 are assigned to meet with a person who listens carefully and empathically but does not identify a focus or purpose for the meetings, does not offer any advice, and does not teach any communication or problem-solving skills. In other words, these couples receive a placebo in the form of friendly and supportive listening. All couples have the same number of 1-hour meetings, at the same 1-week intervals, and over the same 6-week period. They also receive the same before and after measures of relationship satisfaction, and communications and problem-solving ability. The researcher concludes that the "after" scores on all measures indicate that the couples provided with communications and problem-solving skills services made significantly greater gains in terms of relationship satisfaction and communications and problem-solving ability than did the couples who were provided with a good listener. However, as you examine a table containing the before and after scores of the two groups of couples, you notice that fewer than 100 couples are included. You also observe that 45 of the original 50 couples who received "good listening" but only 34 of the original 50 couples who received skills training had both before and after scores. What happened to the 21 missing couples? Did they dropout before completing the 6-week study so that they could not complete the "after" measures? If so, why did they discontinue? Might a larger proportion of the skills group have discontinued because they were dissatisfied with the nature or quality of the service? What are the implications of the greater number and proportion of missing data about the experimental group participations? How does the researcher address the absence of data from 21 percent of the couples? Does the researcher compare only the scores of completers from the two groups? If so, is it possible that the finding of significant improvement of the skills-focused couples over the listening-only couples represents a distortion of the evidence? Could it be that some of those who discontinued early were not benefitting from the service? Might some have experienced relationship deterioration and dropped out to forestall more problems? What if the noncompleters were included in the data analysis? Would the results be essentially the same or might they differ from the published findings? Is it conceivable that the good-listening service might have been as effective or perhaps even more effective than the skills-focused service, and may have been more satisfying to participants?

Authors of credible research articles explicitly discuss the strengths and weaknesses of all aspects of the study, and highlight the limitations of the findings. They describe how they deal with incomplete data and take steps to ensure that the analysis and the findings are indeed based upon all the evidence. As you read research articles that include favorable but exclude unfavorable data, question their legitimacy and credibility. Identify logical fallacies that appear in the narrative and graphic contents of research articles. You may use the two-letter, logical fallacy codes that we discussed earlier in this chapter to note relevant passages. Also, apply the universal intellectual standards to the material. Some articles—even a few that appear in professional journals—reflect lapses in humility, fairness, integrity, precision, logic, or other intellectual standards. Indeed, a few are, quite simply, irrelevant to the field of study or fail to contribute to the knowledge base.

Annotating: As you complete your second reading, prepare a summary annotation of each research article in word-processed form for entry into a reference management database[7] or spreadsheet. If you enter summary notations into a database, you may easily search for, find, and refer to them later as needed. Suppose, for example, you decide to submit a proposal to your state legislature. You think the state should develop and implement a program intended to facilitate foster children's access to college or technical education. In addition to anecdotal and local demographic information, you would also need research-based evidence to support your written proposal and, perhaps later, your oral testimony to a legislative committee.

In preparing annotated summaries, write concisely and avoid duplication. You may include the following information in your annotated reference database of research articles:

1. Bibliographic Information:

   a. Author(s)
   b. Date of Publication
   c. Article Title
   d. Journal Name
   e. Volume Number
   f. Issue Number
   g. Page Numbers

2. Date of (Your) Access and Review:
3. Author's Abstract:

---

[7] You may create a bibliographic database or spreadsheet with an open source office suite such as those available at www.openoffice.org or www.libreoffice.org, or commercial products such as Microsoft Office. Specific reference management software products are commercially available. A few of the more recognizable are Citavi, EndNote, ProCite, and Reference Manager.

4. Your Notes about the Research Study:

   a. Type of Research Study (see Nathan and Gorman [2007] or Guyatt et al. [1995]):
   b. Key Terms and Concepts:
   c. Characteristics and Number of Participants in the Study:
   d. Participants Selection Process:
   e. Research Questions or Hypotheses:
   f. Measures Used:
   g. Threats to Internal and External Validity:
   h. Results (Brief Narrative Summary):
   i. Statistical Findings:
   j. Strengths and Weaknesses of Study:
   k. Quoted Passages and Page Numbers:

A database containing annotated entries of relevant research articles may be searched, sorted, and cross-referenced for use in preparing program proposals, formatting in-text citations, and finalizing references or bibliography sections. Of course, such a database is extremely helpful for numerous professional social work functions such as creating grant and research proposals, annual reports, position papers, and, obviously, writing papers for a university assignment.

About the "New" Statistics

Researchers usually present findings in statistical as well as narrative and graphical form. Some social workers, often unnecessarily but perhaps understandably, hesitate to examine statistics contained in research articles because they involve strange symbols and often many numbers. Although you should refer to research and statistics textbooks for more detailed information, be aware that the probable accuracy of a statistical finding is affected by the "power" associated with its application. Statistical power may be described as the probability that a particular statistical procedure will correctly detect a difference in a sample when such a difference actually exists in the larger population. For example, in the context of social work–related research, low power increases the likelihood of discovering and reporting false negative and sometimes false positive findings (see Table 3.1 earlier in this chapter). In other words, if the size of a sample is small, a statistical procedure may indicate a greater difference that actually exists or, more commonly, fail to identify a significant difference despite the fact that there is one. For instance, a researcher may compare the outcomes of two types of social work interventions designed to help unemployed people obtain employment. Within 3 months of the conclusion of the study, it appears that an almost identical proportion of participants in each group had become gainfully employed. The researchers concluded that the interventions were essentially equivalent in terms of effectiveness—because they detected no significant difference between average employment outcomes of the two groups of participants. Unfortunately, the size of the sample was small and the statistical power low. A later study involving a much larger number of participants, subsequently determined that one intervention produced much better employment gains than the other. Social workers who rely on the results of the earlier, low-power study might wrongly conclude that either intervention might legitimately be considered for use with unemployed clients. Those who read the high-power, larger study recognize that one approach clearly represents a superior option.

In order to decrease the chances of false findings, researchers often conduct power analyses as part of the planning process to determine an optimum sample size. If we neglect such analyses, we run the risk of finding and reporting erroneous results because a sample size is too small or, sometimes, too large. Just as low-power studies can fail to detect a substantial difference between groups, high-power studies can sometimes exaggerate the significance of a trivial difference. Given a large enough sample, you can usually find something that appears statistically significant—if you run enough statistical procedures on different aspects of the data. Remember, at the $p = 0.05$ and $p = 0.10$ levels, about 5 and 10 times out of 100, respectively, we may expect to obtain significance as a result of random chance alone.

Furthermore, some peer-reviewers may not be sufficiently knowledgeable about statistical power to recognize the dangers. As a result, articles are sometimes published in refereed journals despite the presence of false negative and false positive findings. If social workers are unaware of these issues, we may overestimate the credibility of some research articles.

In addition, certain statistical procedures are designed for use with particular types of data, others for application to small or large sample sizes but not both, and some are only appropriate for particular research designs. In other words, statistical procedures may occasionally be used in an improper manner so that any findings can reasonably be questioned. For example, various t-tests can legitimately be used with continuous data but not with dichotomous or categorical data. Similarly, the Chi Square, Fisher's Exact, and McNemar tests may be applied to categorical but not continuous or interval level data.

Most of us have heard the frequently quoted phrase, "Lies . . . damned lies . . . and statistics." Indeed, discovery of a significant difference between groups or variables does not necessarily suggest that the difference is truly meaningful. As Cameron suggests: "not everything that can be counted counts, and not everything that counts can be counted" (1963). Furthermore, perhaps inadvertently as a result of naiveté or unconscious bias, some researchers may use statistics inappropriately to produce favorable results. Greenhalgh (2001) identified the following "10 Ways To Cheat On Statistical Tests When Writing Up Results":

1. Throw all your data into a computer and report as significant any relation where $p < 0.05$.
2. If baseline differences between the groups favour the intervention group, remember not to adjust for them.
3. Do not test your data to see if they are normally distributed. If you do, you might get stuck with non-parametric tests, which aren't as much fun.
4. Ignore all withdrawals (dropouts) and non-responders, so the analysis only concerns subjects who fully complied with treatment.
5. Always assume that you can plot one set of data against another and calculate an "r value" (Pearson correlation coefficient), and that a "significant" r value proves causation.
6. If outliers (points that lie a long way from the others on your graph) are messing up your calculations, just rub them out. But if outliers are helping your case, even if they seem to be spurious results, leave them in.
7. If the confidence intervals of your result overlap zero difference between the groups, leave them out of your report. Better still, mention them briefly in the text but don't draw them in on the graph and ignore them when drawing your conclusions.
8. If the difference between two groups becomes significant four and a half months into a six month trial, stop the trial and start writing up. Alternatively, if at six months the results are "nearly significant," extend the trial for another three weeks.
9. If your results prove uninteresting, ask the computer to go back and see if any particular subgroups behaved differently. You might find that your intervention worked after all in Chinese women aged 52–61.

10. If analysing your data the way you plan to does not give the result you wanted, run the figures through a selection of other tests. (Greenhalgh, 2001, p. 77)

In addition, some differences may be statistically significant but may not represent a practical difference. For example, let's consider a hypothetical study of men who engaged in domestic violence with their intimate partners. Suppose that researchers discover a significant, favorable difference between the average rates of violence of a small number of men who completed a 30-day jail diversion program when compared to an equivalent number of men who spent 30 days in jail. They also report that the probability that the observed difference results from chance alone is less than 5 percent ($p = 0.048$). The findings seem to indicate that the diversion program yields a substantially better outcome, in terms of reduced domestic violence, than a month in jail. However, before we fully endorse the diversion program, let's consider the meaning of the p-statistic. The $p = 0.048$ statistic indicates that an average difference in domestic violence level between the participants in the diversion and jail experiences would be incorrectly detected (when there actually is no difference) almost 5 times out of every 100. In terms of significance testing, lower p-values are better than higher ones: $p = 0.01$ reflects a lower risk of a false finding than $p = 0.05$ which, in turn, reflects less risk than $p = 0.10$, and so on. However, because the null hypothesis serves as the basis for most statistical procedures (that is, we seek to find that there is "no difference" between two groups or two variables), discovering a difference at a given p-value may not mean much at all.

The hypothetical study mentioned above reveals a significant difference at the $p = 0.048$ level in the average rate of partner abuse when men who completed a jail diversion program are compared to those who served 30-day jail terms. Suppose that the majority of men in both groups discontinued violence altogether. However, two of the men who completed the jail diversion program continued a pattern of intimate partner violence at an average of once per week and two of the men who fulfilled their 30-day sentence in jail engaged in violence at a twice-weekly average rate. As a result, the average rate of violence appears considerably lower for participants in the diversion program. Does that mean that the jail diversion program is clearly superior to a 30-day jail sentence in reducing subsequent partner violence? Perhaps not; the same number and percentage of men from each group continued to engage in weekly violence.

Although research and statistical procedures can sometimes lead to questionable results, the proper use of statistics in the right context with appropriate data tends to increase precision and illuminate findings. Indeed, statistics generally serve to moderate threats to validity and increase the likelihood of obtaining accurate findings. However, significance testing alone does not directly indicate the size of the difference between groups or variables. Therefore, editors of professional journals such as those sponsored by the American Psychological Association (2009b) now require researchers to complement significance testing and the resulting p-values with effect size (ES) statistics.[8] The ES statistics reveal the amount of difference and the direction of that difference between two groups, or the magnitude of relationship between two variables (for example, before and after, or baseline and intervention phase scores). In other words, they reveal the size of the effect. Effect size statistics are especially useful when attempting to determine the effectiveness of an intentional intervention such as a psychosocial program or practice, or a drug or medical procedure. Therefore, social workers and others in the helping disciplines find

---

[8] We anticipate that in the near future, more professional journals will require researchers to publish confidence intervals (CIs) to further complement effect sizes and significance levels. As an estimate of both the precision and the stability of numerical finding, confidence intervals indicate the probability (usually 95 percent) that an outcome obtained in a sample-based study also occurs within a given range in the larger population (for example, plus or minus 3 points).

them more meaningful, informative, and practical than statistical significance tests alone. Effect size statistics can, for example, indicate how much better or worse are the outcomes for participants in one program compared to those in another. They reveal the size and direction of the difference. Extremely useful for outcome evaluation, they can be applied to studies of the effectiveness of policies, practice approaches, and many other factors associated with change-related efforts. Importantly, they may also be used in single-case studies ($N = 1$) of direct service to individuals, dyads, families, groups, organizations, and communities. You may recall that the use of formal, systematic evaluative feedback as routine part of service is associated with markedly enhanced outcomes (Anker et al., 2009; Crits-Christoph et al., 2012; Lambert, 2010a; Slade, Lambert, Harmon, Smart, & Bailey, 2008).

Effect size may be calculated in several different ways depending, in part, upon the nature of the research question, the type of data, and the chosen statistical test.[9] They may be derived from score averages on a standardized measurement, percentages (for example, the percentage of clients who achieve their goals), or correlations. Calculations differ for ANOVAs, t-tests, correlations, and regressions. To illustrate, let's assume that we want to determine the size of the difference between a group of people participating in an 8-week Type-2 diabetes prevention program (experimental group) and a group of people who are waiting to start the program (waitlisted control group). All participants are pre-diabetic and at high risk of developing diabetes in the near future. Blood sugar levels serve as the effectiveness measure (dependent variable). In other words, we seek to determine if the prevention program is more effective at lowering blood sugar levels than being waitlisted. To calculate an effect size, you could subtract the average blood level of the waitlisted control group from the average level of the experimental group at the end of the 8-week program and then divide the result by the standard deviation (SD) of the control group. That formula is:

$$\text{Effect size} = \frac{[\text{Experimental Group Mean}] - [\text{Control Group Mean}]}{[\text{Control Group Standard Deviation}]}$$

As a direct social worker, you may also calculate an effect size for each client system you serve if you use before and after (pre-, post-, or follow-up) measures that relate to the agreed-upon problem or goal. For example, suppose a new client comes to you and says, "I'm too judgmental about others. I immediately think critical and negative thoughts about the people I'm with—no matter who they are." After some exploration with you, she decides that she is even more judgmental about herself. She adds that dimension as a problem for work. Together, you hypothesize that if she can first become more self-compassionate, she might find it easier behave more empathically and more generously toward others. She agrees to collect data about her daily level of self-compassion on the basis of a 10-point subjective rating scale where *1 = Little or No Daily Self-Compassion* and *10 = Maximum Daily Self-Compassion*. Together, you decide that the self-compassion ratings for the 7 days following the first meeting will serve as the baseline. Following that 7-day period, you will meet again and begin the intervention phase. She agrees to continue to record daily self-compassion ratings throughout the course of your work together and will share them during your weekly meetings (see Table 3.2).

These daily self-compassion ratings may also be displayed in graphic form. Clients seem to understand and value visual presentations of numerical data such as depicted in Figure 3.4.

You may obtain a no assumption effect size (NAES) for $N = 1$ data such as those related to daily self-compassion presented above by applying the formula displayed below. You simply

---

[9] A Web-based effect size calculator (Wilson, 2012) may be found on The Campbell Collaboration website at http://www.campbellcollaboration.org/resources/effect_size_input.php.

TABLE 3.2
Example of a Daily Subjective Rating Record

Date	Daily Self-Compassion Rating (1–10 Scale)
Baseline Phase	
4/2/2012	4.0
4/3/2012	3.5
4/4/2012	4.0
4/5/2012	4.5
4/6/2012	3.5
4/7/2012	4.5
4/8/2012	4.0
Intervention Phase: Week 1	
4/10/2012	7.0
4/11/2012	7.5
4/12/2012	7.0
4/13/2012	8.0
4/14/2012	8.0
4/15/2012	7.0
4/16/2012	7.5
Intervention Phase: Week 2	
4/17/2012	8.0
4/18/2012	8.5
4/19/2012	8.0
4/20/2012	8.5
4/21/2012	9.0
4/22/2012	8.5
4/23/2012	9.0
Follow-Up Phase	
6/4/2012	6.5
6/5/2012	7.0
6/6/2012	7.5
6/7/2012	7.0
6/8/2012	8.0
6/9/2012	7.5
6/10/2012	7.0

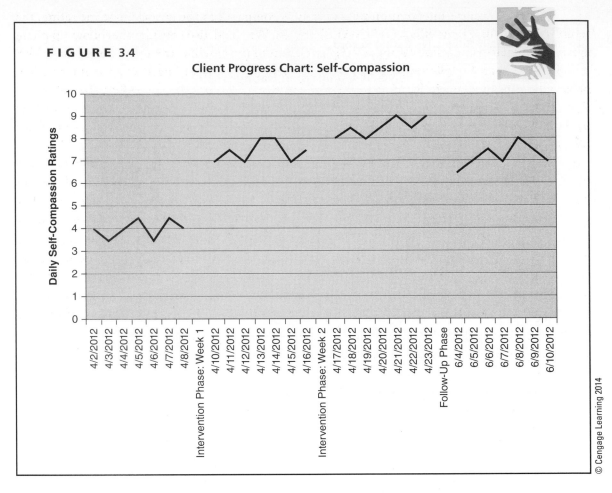

FIGURE 3.4

Client Progress Chart: Self-Compassion

calculate the average of the baseline ratings; subtract the average of either the intervention phase or the follow-up phase, and divide by the standard deviation of the baseline ratings.

$$\text{No Assumption Effect Size} = \frac{[\text{Intervention or Follow-Up Mean}] - [\text{Baseline Mean}]}{[\text{Baseline Standard Deviation}]}$$

Let's apply the formula to the self-compassion example described above. During the baseline phase, the client's average daily self-compassion rating was 4.0; her average during the 2-week intervention phase was 7.96; and the follow-up average was 7.21. The standard deviation of the baseline data was 0.41. We enter the average daily self-compassion rating for the intervention and baseline phases, and the baseline SD into the formula as follows[10]:

$$\text{NAES} = \frac{[7.96] - [4.0]}{[.41]} = 9.66^{11}$$

---

[10] A Web-based tool for managing and displaying N = 1 outcome data, and for calculating no assumption effect sizes is available at http://www.interventioncentral.org/tools/chart_dog_graph_maker. The users' manual may be found at http://www.interventioncentral.org/sites/default/files/pdfs/pdfs_tools/Priscilla_Jones_ChartDog_GraphMaker_Manual_13_April_2012.pdf.

[11] This unusually high effect size is the result of the small number of data points, the small range and limited variation in ratings, and especially the small standard deviation in the baseline phase. In general, you may expect effect sizes to fall in the 0 to 3.0 range.

When the average intervention phase rating is compared to the average baseline rating, the result is a "no assumptions effect size" (NAES) of 9.66. We could also consider the follow-up phase average daily self-compassion rating of 7.21 in relation to the baseline average to obtain an NAES of 7.83. Note that the follow-up ratings were, on average, somewhat lower than the intervention phase ratings but remained higher than the baseline ratings. Nonetheless, the effect sizes obtained when baseline data are compared to both intervention and follow-up data reflect extraordinarily large changes in the positive direction. The fact that none of the intervention or follow-up phase ratings overlap with any of the baseline ratings indicates an unusually strong effect.

There are several different ES statistics. A simple and straightforward approach is to report the size of the effect in percentage terms. Suppose, for example, you serve as a social worker in an inner-city high school. Fewer than half of the students graduate. You plan and implement a pilot study intervention to increase the graduation rates of at-risk students. You identify 50 of the most at-risk students and randomly assign half to an innovative program while the other half receives the usual services.[12] As illustrated in Table 3.3, 19 of the 25 students (76 percent) in the experimental program graduate while 8 of the others (32 percent) do. We can conclude that the experimental program reflects a 44 percent effect size (76 percent minus 32 percent). In other words, the experimental program yielded a 44 percent higher graduation rate than did the usual services afforded to at-risk students—a substantial effect indeed!

TABLE 3.3
Illustrative Example of Effect Size in Percentage Terms (Simulated Data)

	Graduates
Innovative Program	19 (76%)
Usual Services	8 (32%)
Effect Size	44%

© Cengage Learning 2014

The most widely used ES statistics do not directly involve percentages. Cohen's d, Hedges g, and Glass's Δ derive from averages and standard deviations. A Cohen's d of 0.0 suggests that there is no difference. Cohen cautions that the meaning of d should be viewed in relation to the particular context of a study and argues against rigid interpretative rules. Nonetheless, he offers these general guidelines for effect sizes based upon mean differences: $d = 0.2$ suggests a small effect equivalent to a difference of about one-fifth of one standard deviation; $d = 0.5$ indicates a moderate effect equivalent to a difference in the range of one-half a SD; and $d = 0.8$ represents a large effect equivalent to a difference of about four-fifths of a SD (Cohen, 1988).

Suppose, for example, we conduct a study comparing the outcomes of clients served by social workers who adopt a strengths-based practice model (the experimental condition) with those served by social workers who adopt a problem-focused model (the comparison condition). Let's assume that we apply Cohen's effect size procedure to these hypothetical outcome data and obtain an effect size of $d = 2.0$. If the study is credible, we would have to conclude that the former approach is considerably more effective than the latter (at least for clients in the study). Indeed, $d = 2.0$ indicates that the average outcome score of the strengths-based group is two standard deviations above that of the problem-focused group. If valid, that would represent a very large difference indeed!

---

[12] In intervention research, "usual services" may be called "treatment as usual" or TAU.

Several other effect size–related statistics are beginning to appear in journals that publish research articles about the impact or effectiveness of various events, conditions, or interventions. One is the number needed to treat (NNT). The NNT statistic indicates the number of people (for example, clients or residents of a community) that would need to participate for one of them to benefit from the intervention (for example, a medical procedure, a psychosocial program or practice, or a social policy). An NNT of 1.0 indicates that every single individual who participates has a positive outcome. An NNT of 1.1 suggests that 10 of every 11 people receiving a particular service or included in a program benefit. On the other hand, an NNT of 15 suggests that 1 person of every 15 people served exhibits a desired benefit. Yes, a lower NNT score reflects a better outcome.

Relative risk (RR) refers to (a) the probability that a person exposed to or vulnerable to a problem or condition will actually experience that problem or develop that condition divided by (b) the probability that a nonexposed or nonvulnerable person will do so. For example, the relative risk of problems and symptoms associated with posttraumatic stress is greater for people who experience rape, violence, war, and natural disasters than for people who do not experience such events. An RR of 1 indicates that the association between the exposure or vulnerability and the problematic condition probably does not exist. An RR that is greater than 1 reflects an increased risk for members of the exposed group while an RR of less than 1 indicates that exposure is associated with a decreased risk.

Suppose, for example, that we conduct a study of 250 children to determine if there is a relationship between the experience of childhood sexual abuse and symptoms of posttraumatic stress. Assume that we obtain the following hypothetical results (illustrated in Table 3.4): 15 of 150 children who had not experienced sexual abuse manifest symptoms of posttraumatic stress while 35 of 100 who had been sexually abused reflect them. The probability that a child in our study who had not been sexually abused experiences posttraumatic stress symptoms is 15/150 or $p = 0.1$. On the other hand, a child in our study who had been abused reflects a probability of 35/100 or $p = 0.35$ of experiencing posttraumatic stress symptoms. The relative risk is 0.35/0.1 or RR = 3.5. Considerably higher than 1, an RR of 3.5 indicates that children in our study who had been sexually abused are considerably more likely to experience posttraumatic symptoms than children who had not been abused.

An odds ratio (OR) is similar to relative risk in that it involves the likelihood that a specified outcome (such as a problem or condition) will occur if a particular factor (such as an event or situation) is present. However, odds rather than probabilities are used in the calculation of ORs. Odds ratios can be used in some studies where RRs cannot.

Odds are often associated with various forms of gambling, perhaps especially horse racing. Simply stated, the odds of a particular event happening (for example, the occurrence a problem or

TABLE 3.4
Relationship between Childhood Sexual Abuse and Posttraumatic Symptoms (Illustrative Example Based on Simulated Data)

		Posttraumatic Stress Symptoms		
		Yes	No	Total
Sexually Abused	Yes	35	65	100
	No	15	135	150
	Total	50	200	250

condition, or perhaps a solution or achievement) are calculated by dividing the probability that it will occur by the probability that it will not.

The odds concept may be illustrated through a series of coin tosses. The probability that a tossed coin will land on either one side or the other is 50 percent. There are only two sides. If the coin is balanced and the toss fair, the probability of a "heads" is always 50 percent, even when "heads" has previously come up five times in a row. In other words, the chance that the coin will land on the heads side is 1 of 2; the chance of it landing on tails is also 1 of 2. Therefore, the odds of the coin landing on heads (or on tails) are 1-to-1. There is an even chance that the coin will land on heads or on tails. In horse racing, odds are described in a similar way (although arrived at through much different means). Suppose you bet two dollars on a horse that reflects 1-to-2 (1:2) odds. Such a horse would be a strong favorite. If the horse won, you would collect $3: that is one-half the original $2 bet plus the original amount wagered. If the odds were 1-to-1 (1:1), you would collect $4: that is, $2 plus the original wager. On the other hand, a $2 bet on a horse with 2-to-1 (or 2:1) odds would return $6. A $2 bet on a horse reflecting 20-to-1 (or 20:1) odds would yield a payoff of $42. That is 20 times the $2 wager plus the original $2 bet. Of course, in horse racing, odds do not reflect the actual likelihood that horses will win. Rather, they result from complex calculations based on the amount and distribution of money wagered on different horses.

As social workers, however, we are less concerned with coin tosses and horse racing than we are with people, social problems, and solutions. Let's reconsider our hypothetical study of the relationship between the experience of childhood sexual abuse and the presence of symptoms associated with posttraumatic stress. We may calculate odds in this fashion: Divide the number of abused children who experience symptoms (35) by the number of abused children who do not (65). The odds of an abused child having posttraumatic symptoms are (35/65) or 0.538. However, the odds of a nonabused child doing so are (15/135) or 0.111. Notice that odds are similar to but not identical to probabilities. As mentioned above, the probability that an abused child in our hypothetical study experiences symptoms of posttraumatic stress is 0.35 (35/100) and the probability for a nonabused child is 0.10 (15/150).

An *odds ratio* may be calculated on the basis of the odds of a problem or condition occurring among exposed people divided by the odds of that problem or condition in a nonexposed population. It is truly a "ratio of odds." As reflected in our hypothetical study, the odds of an abused child experiencing posttraumatic symptoms are 0.538. We take that figure and divide it by the odds of a nonabused child experiencing the symptoms (.111). The calculation (0.538/0.111) results in an odds ratio (OR) of 4.846. Cohen (1988) provides guidelines for interpreting odds ratios as follows: *1.50 = small; 2.50 = medium; and 4.30 = large.* Given the OR of 4.846 in our fictitious study, we conclude that children who have been subjected to sexual abuse are considerably more likely to experience posttraumatic symptoms than those who have not been sexually abused.

Effect size, number needed to treat, relative risk, and odds ratio all reflect, in somewhat different ways, the size and direction of difference. Such statistical estimates are extremely useful for the purposes of providing clients with information about the likelihood of a positive outcome from a particular treatment or service. In addition, they can help decision makers distinguish more effective from less effective policies and programs. However, there is also another, extremely important benefit. When incorporated in systematic reviews of the research literature, effect size statistics enable researchers to combine the statistical findings of multiple studies through a process called meta-analysis (Glass, 1976).

When researchers conduct a genuine systematic review, they collate all empirical evidence that fits pre-specified eligibility criteria in order to answer a specific research question. It uses explicit, systematic methods that are selected with a view to minimizing bias, thus providing more reliable findings from which conclusions can be drawn and decisions made (Antman, Lau,

Kupelnick, Mosteller, & Chalmers, 1992; Oxman & Guyatt, 1993). The key characteristics of a systematic review are:

- A clearly stated set of objectives with pre-defined eligibility criteria for studies.
- An explicit, reproducible methodology.
- A systematic search that attempts to identify all studies that would meet the eligibility criteria.
- An assessment of the validity of the findings of the included studies, for example through the assessment of risk of bias.
- A systematic presentation, and synthesis, of the characteristics and findings of the included studies. (Higgins & Green, 2011, Section 1.2.2 What is a systematic review?)

Once all the research studies that meet the quality criteria are included in the systematic review of the literature, statistical methods are used to combine and summarize the findings. "**Meta-analysis** is the use of statistical methods to combine results of individual studies. . . . By statistically combining the results of similar studies we can improve the precision of our estimates of treatment effect, and assess whether treatment effects are similar in similar situations" (The Cochrane Collaboration, 2002).

Meta-analyses use the figures and statistics presented in multiple research studies to calculate effect sizes. Suppose, for example, that your systematic review of the research literature yields several high-quality studies that meet your inclusion criteria. If the studies contain group means, d statistics, means t-scores, Z-scores, F-statistics, r-correlations, or p-values, along with standard deviations and the number of participants in the treatment and control or comparison groups, then those values may be converted to a common statistic for combination and meta-analysis (Hunt, 1997).

Rather than simply assuming that each high-quality study is equivalent in credibility and value, meta-analytic procedures incorporate a weighting process. Larger studies are weighted proportionately higher than smaller studies to compensate for the error risks associated with low-power research investigations. Additional processes account for variability in the reliability of measures and other factors. The resulting meta-analytic statistical procedures yield weighted mean correlations, weighted standardized means, or other overall effect size estimates.

For example, Cabral and Smith (2011) completed a meta-analytic study of research studies about the matching of clients and professional helpers in terms of race or ethnicity. In particular, they investigated clients' preferences about helpers' race or ethnicity, perceptions about helpers' of their own versus another race or ethnicity, and service outcomes. Fifty-two studies met their inclusion criteria for the meta-analysis about racial preference. Using Cohen's procedure, they found an average effect size of $d = 0.63$. The results suggest that clients, in general, tend to reflect a moderately strong preference for helpers of their own race or ethnicity. Cabral and Smith also included 81 studies of clients' perceptions about their professional helpers. That meta-analysis yielded an average effect size of $d = 0.32$—suggesting a modest tendency of clients, on average, to perceive professional helpers of their own race or ethnicity slightly more positively than others. Interestingly, in terms of service effectiveness, their meta-analysis of 53 studies of client outcomes produced an average effect size of $d = 0.09$. This suggests that, in general, the mental health outcomes of clients who received services from professional helpers of their own race or ethnicity were not noticeably superior to those who received services from other helpers. However, the researchers observed that the consequences of matching clients and professional helpers on racial or ethnic dimensions were highly variable. For instance, the average effect sizes for all three dimensions (client preference for race or ethnicity of helper, client perception of helper, and mental health services outcomes) among those studies involving African Americans were considerably higher than those studies involving participants from other racial and ethnic groups. These findings highlight the importance of context in understanding human behavior. We can readily understand how some African-Americans might, at least initially, be somewhat suspicious about the motives of majority-status professionals.

Career-Long Learning

Knowledge is expanding and changing at a speed never before known in human history. Some of what we considered true 10 years ago we now know to be false. Other "accepted truths" rapidly become obsolete as researchers continue their studies and advance the professional knowledge base. Given the pace of growth in research-based knowledge, social workers are pressed to stay abreast of the most recent studies. At the same time, we yearn for additional knowledge to help us better help others. In our efforts to serve, most social workers recognize that personally and collectively, we always need to know a great deal more than we currently do—despite the ever-expanding knowledge explosion.

Much of the world and most of North American society are well into the "third wave" (Toffler, 1983), when knowledge and learning attain extraordinary value. As a form of wealth, access to good-quality, relevant knowledge is distributed unevenly among societies and populations. Constituting another kind of inequality, "haves" can be distinguished from "have nots" by the ease and extent to which they can access current, relevant, and accurate knowledge, and the facility with which they can adapt and improve based on it. As Toffler suggests, "The illiterate of the 21st century will not be those who cannot read and write, but those who cannot learn, unlearn, and relearn."

Stan Davis and Jim Botkin (1994) suggest that the total knowledge in the world, on average, doubles about every 7 years. In some subject areas, the doubling of knowledge occurs even more rapidly. As many social workers realize from the rapid obsolescence of their personal computers and cell phones, the rate of change in the technological sciences is simply astonishing. However, the information explosion is hardly limited to high technology (Gleick, 2011). It affects the helping professions as well. As a social worker, you might wonder how much of what you now believe to be true is actually false. You might ask how much of what you learned 1 or 2 years ago is now obsolete. We may reasonably anticipate that more and more of what you now "know" will become less and less relevant, valid, and applicable with each passing year.

Unless social workers continuously and aggressively pursue additional learning and think critically about the information we access, we will inexorably fall further and further behind the knowledge curve. If we do not continue to learn throughout our social work careers, clients could suffer because of our ignorance. We simply must find ways and means to keep current during this never-ending, always expanding knowledge explosion. If we are to serve our clients effectively, up-to-date, valid, and reliable knowledge is vital. We must become "critically thinking, learning people" within the context of "learning organizations," "learning communities," and "learning societies" (Cantle, 2000; Gould & Baldwin, 2004; Senge, 1992). One way to emphasize and track our growth and development is through the preparation and maintenance of a learning portfolio for use throughout our professional careers (Cournoyer & Stanley, 2002). As Hoffer (1973) suggests, "In a time of drastic change, it is the learners who inherit the future. The learned usually find themselves equipped to live in a world that no longer exists" (p. 22).

In addition to the many personal benefits that result from lifelong learning and the maintenance of an associated professional learning portfolio, social workers are ethically obligated to improve their knowledge and skills throughout their careers. Indeed, the Code of Ethics of the

National Association of Social Workers (2008) includes several pertinent ethical principles that reference this responsibility. Consider these excerpts:

◆ Social workers should provide services and represent themselves as competent only within the boundaries of their education, training, license, certification, consultation received, supervised experience, or other relevant professional experience (Section 1.04.a).

◆ Social workers should provide services in substantive areas or use intervention techniques or approaches that are new to them only after engaging in appropriate study, training, consultation, and supervision from people who are competent in those interventions or techniques (Section 1.04.b).

◆ When generally recognized standards do not exist with respect to an emerging area of practice, social workers should exercise careful judgment and take responsible steps (including appropriate education, research, training, consultation, and supervision) to ensure the competence of their work and to protect clients from harm (Section 1.04.c).

◆ Social workers should accept responsibility or employment only on the basis of existing competence or the intention to acquire the necessary competence (Section 4.01.a).

◆ Social workers should strive to become and remain proficient in professional practice and the performance of professional functions. Social workers should critically examine and keep current with emerging knowledge relevant to social work. Social workers should routinely review the professional literature and participate in continuing education relevant to social work practice and social work ethics (Section 4.01.b).

◆ Social workers should base practice on recognized knowledge, including empirically based knowledge, relevant to social work and social work ethics (Section 4.01.c).

The ongoing knowledge explosion and the related changes in information and technology are dramatically affecting social workers and our clients as well as societies throughout the world. Combined with scientific inquiry and critical thinking, career-long learning helps us to grow continuously, develop, and improve so that we may respond effectively and serve clients competently throughout our professional careers. The most effective social workers engage in an ongoing search for valid and relevant knowledge to inform and guide our helping efforts. In effect, we dedicate ourselves to continuous, career-long learning in formal and informal, professional and nonprofessional, and planned and unplanned contexts.

Preparing and Implementing Learning Goals and Plans

Following graduation and licensure, social workers routinely participate in continuing professional development and related educational activities. Indeed, our social work ethics obligate us to engage in ongoing professional development to maintain or enhance our knowledge and skills. In locales where social workers are licensed, regular continuing professional education is legally required.

Much career-long learning can occur through professional workshops, conferences, institutes, and seminars. Some social workers take relevant college or university courses to enhance their professional development and, of course, many engage in active, independent learning based on their own goals and plans.

Specifying your own learning goals represents a first step in the process of developing and then implementing a learning plan. We identify learning goals based upon an assessment of our learning wants and needs. A common impetus involves the professional roles and functions we fulfill, or aspire to fulfill, in our service as social workers. For example, a social worker might be assigned to supervise four or five other professionals. Inexperienced in supervision, she might establish a goal to learn about contemporary supervision theories and practices. Another typical motivation involves our practice experiences. For example, based upon measures of both outcome and client satisfaction, a social worker might recognize that he is quite ineffective in his efforts to help a certain category of clients (for example, members of a particular age, racial, or ethnic group or those affected by a particular problem). Wanting to better help clients, he decides to learn about evidence-based practices for service to that particular group of clients.

Careful preparation of learning goals according to certain educational standards tends to improve the quality of our plans as well as increase the likelihood of goal accomplishment. When we write learning goals that are descriptive and contain within them a clear action verb and a tangible outcome indicator, we increase the probability of both pursuing and achieving those goals. Furthermore, we become better able to demonstrate or "prove" that we have indeed accomplished them—as documented by our outcome indicators and incorporated in our professional learning portfolios.

For instance, suppose I say, "I want to learn about human trafficking" and establish that as my learning goal. It is a very timely and important topic indeed. Even a brief review of the research literature yields shocking information about the buying and selling of human beings throughout the world. Yes, slavery is widely present in the 21st century.

Once I identify the topic, I might search for some materials and do some reading about human trafficking. However, I might do so in a casual or perhaps haphazard way that raises questions about the nature and credibility of the resources I find. My efforts might not produce tangible evidence of learning or I might gradually lose interest in my learning goal.

On the other hand, suppose I establish this as my learning goal: *Within 30 days from today's date, I will complete a systematic search of the professional journals for credible research articles about the characteristics, needs, problems, and issues faced by trafficked humans from at least one region of the world; review, analyze, and synthesize the high quality, relevant research literature; and prepare and distribute a 10-page summary report of my learning.*

This version of an individualized learning goal is more specific and descriptive, and contains precise action verbs such as *search, review, analyze, synthesize, prepare,* and *distribute*. It also contains both a time frame and a tangible outcome indicator in the form of the 10-page report. The report documents the nature, extent, and quality of the learning. We can refer to the document in the future to refresh our memories or, importantly, to serve as a basis for additional learning; and for inclusion in our professional portfolios. For instance, based upon accomplishment of this initial learning goal, I might subsequently want to learn how best to provide culturally sensitive and effective social work services to trafficked humans; or to learn about policy and program initiatives that reflect evidence of effectiveness in reducing the extent of human trafficking.

Careful preparation of learning objectives that contain precise, descriptive action verbs tend to promote learning and advance its evaluation. In academic settings, Bloom's Taxonomy of Cognitive Learning Objectives (see Table 3.5) is widely used as a guide for the formulation of learning objectives (Bloom & Krathwohl, 1956).[13] If you examine the learning objectives contained in the required course syllabi of most accredited BSW or MSW curriculums, you would probably observe a progression toward higher levels of Bloom's Taxonomy over time. Early courses (for example, first semester or year) often place greater emphasis on *recollection, comprehension,* and some *application* whereas later courses tend to emphasize *application* and the critical thinking dimensions of *analysis, synthesis,* and *evaluation*.

In addition, the test items contained in the nationally standardized social work licensing exams sponsored by the Association of Social Work Boards (ASWB) are selected according to Bloom's taxonomy. Because of its nature as a high-stakes examination, most of the items correspond to the application, analysis, evaluation, or synthesis levels of cognitive learning. Few items require applicants to recall or comprehend relevant knowledge without also applying, analyzing, synthesizing, or evaluating it for social work practice.

---

[13]Anderson and Krathwohl (2001) have published a revised version of the taxonomy that elaborates upon and clarifies the original. For a summary of the revised model, go to the website of the Iowa State University Center for Excellence in Learning and Teaching at http://www.celt.iastate.edu/teaching/RevisedBlooms1.html.

TABLE 3.5
Brief Descriptions of Bloom's Taxonomy of Cognitive Learning Objectives

1. *Recollection.* The ability to recall is the basic level of learning and refers simply to the ability to remember material such as facts and basic theoretical terms and concepts.

2. *Comprehension.* The ability to comprehend refers to an understanding of the material. This is often demonstrated by providing an explanation, summary, or interpretation of the material. Comprehension implies recognition or recollection. Therefore, when we pursue comprehension-level learning, we presume that recollection-level learning either is a part of that process or has previously occurred.

3. *Application.* The ability to apply knowledge refers to use of the material in a particular situation. In social work, this might be demonstrated through the use of rules, methods, and principles in applying a skill in service to or for a client. Application implies comprehension (and recollection). Therefore, when we pursue application-level learning, we presume that comprehension-level learning either is a part of the process or has previously occurred. In other words, we cannot apply something that we cannot recollect and do not understand.

4. *Analysis.* The ability to analyze involves the careful identification and examination of the various elements of the material. Relationships among and between components are carefully considered in terms of organizational structure and internal coherence. Although we might argue that application sometimes involves deep thought, analysis represents the first substantive critical thinking dimension contained within Bloom's taxonomy. Like application, analysis cannot occur without recollection and understanding. That is, we cannot analyze something that we do not remember and do not understand. In addition, analysis often requires understanding of how knowledge has been applied. For example, we might analyze how a policy, program, service, or practice has been implemented with an individual, family, group, organization, or community.

5. *Synthesis.* The ability to synthesize includes pulling together elements in a new way to form an innovative structure. The creation of a new conceptual model could be a form of synthesis. Synthesis represents the second critical thinking dimension contained within Bloom's taxonomy. Synthesis typically involves analysis. In the cognitive sense, synthesis could proceed until or unless an analysis was complete. Therefore, when we aspire to synthesis-level learning, we presume that analysis-level learning is part of the process or has previously occurred. For example, we could not reasonably propose changes (a form of synthesis) to a current policy, program, service, or practice without a careful, systematic analysis.

6. *Evaluation.* The ability to evaluate involves the determination of the relative value of knowledge for a defined purpose. Typically, this would include the creation, adoption, or adaptation of evaluative criteria as an application tool followed by its use in measuring or evaluating phenomena. Evaluation represents the third critical thinking dimension contained within Bloom's taxonomy. Evaluation, then, involves analysis and often synthesis. In the cognitive sense, evaluation could not proceed until or unless an analysis was complete. A new or adapted evaluation tool could not be created without synthesis. Therefore, when we pursue evaluation-level learning, we presume that analysis and synthesis have or will occur. It is difficult to imagine a situation where a valid, reliable, and relevant evaluation process could proceed before or without careful analysis and synthesis.

© Cengage Learning

Although commonly used for academic or test-development purposes, we can also use Bloom's taxonomy to help us formulate our own, individualized personal and professional learning goals. You might phrase your learning goals to include a clear action verb that corresponds to a desired level of Bloom's taxonomy, a time frame, and a product that documents your learning. Table 3.6[14] contains a list of several action verbs that you might consider.

---

[14]Adapted from Cournoyer and Stanley (2002).

TABLE 3.6
Selected Action Verbs Corresponding to Bloom's Taxonomy

Recollection	Comprehension	Application	Analysis	Synthesis	Evaluation
Duplicate	Classify	Adapt	<u>Analyze</u>	Arrange	Appraise
Highlight	<u>Comprehend</u>	Adopt	Appraise	Assemble	Arbitrate
Indicate	Construe	<u>Apply</u>	Audit	Build	Argue
Identify	Define	Choose	Break down	Collect	Assay
Label	Describe	Conduct	Calculate	Combine	Assess
List	Discuss	Demonstrate	Categorize	Compile	Criticize
Locate	Explain	Dramatize	Chart	Compose	Defend
Match	Express	Employ	Compare	Constitute	Determine
Memorize	Interpret	Exercise	Contrast	Construct	Estimate
Name	Report	Exploit	Criticize	Create	<u>Evaluate</u>
Order	Restate	Illustrate	Diagram	Design	Grade
Point out	State	Implement	Differentiate	Develop	Judge
Recall	Translate	Operate	Discriminate	Formulate	Rank
Recognize		Practice	Dissect	Generate	Rate
<u>Recollect</u>		Schedule	Distinguish	Hypothesize	Support
Remember		Select	Examine	Organize	Value
Repeat		Sketch	Experiment	Originate	
Reproduce		Solve	Inventory	Plan	
Underline		Use	Question	Predict	
			Study	Prepare	
			Test	Propose	
				<u>Synthesize</u>	

Source: Adapted from Cournoyer and Stanley (2002).

By formulating learning goals in a precise manner that includes an action verb, a time frame, and a tangible product or performance, planning for goal achievement becomes quite straightforward. An early step involves identifying and scheduling tasks associated with acquiring information needed to learn what you seek to learn and produce what you have specified as your outcome indicator. Once you have all the needed resources in hand, proceed to read, review, analyze, and synthesize the information so that you may fully understand and apply it to your goal. Incidentally, if you analyze and synthesize what you read and review, and write about it in your own words (and perhaps incorporate it into a database), you dramatically increase the likelihood of retaining that information in long-term memory. If one of your learning goals involves application—that is, the development of skill or competence in a practice-relevant behavior—then you should probably schedule regular practice sessions. In both learning about and learning to do, incorporate self-evaluation and, if possible, evaluative feedback from others. For example, after you have written a draft version of a document related to your learning goal, ask a couple of competent and trusted colleagues to review it and provide feedback about its quality vis-à-vis the universal intellectual standards. Ask them to identify any logical fallacies and highlight areas that are difficult to understand. Also, be sure to ask them to mention the strengths of the paper and provide you with social support. If you are learning a skill or refining a practice behavior, ask a colleague to observe you demonstrating it. When possible videotape your practice sessions to make it easier for you to self-evaluate and for others to provide constructive feedback. Request that your reviewers identify areas of strength as well as weakness, and welcome their positive social support for your efforts.

Consider your colleagues' feedback and, if it seems reasonably accurate and useful, make changes in your written product or in the way you are practicing the skill or practice behavior. After making the revisions, conduct another self-evaluation before completing the final version of the document or implementing the skill or practice behavior in your professional work.

Documenting Learning

When you have implemented your plans and, ideally, reached your learning goals, store relevant materials and especially your final products or outcomes in a Professional Lifelong Learning Portfolio—similar to the Social Work Skills Learning Portfolio that you create as you complete this book. In today's world, an electronic portfolio is usually superior to a paper version in that you may include a range of products that result from your career-long learning projects. For instance, you may include digitized photos and drawings, or audio- or video-recording demonstrations of your practice competencies.

When electronic versions of your learning outcomes are not available or cannot be digitized, you may simply store them in folders or boxes in a file cabinet. Whether in paper or digital form, however, such documentation serves many purposes. For example, you may (1) review material to refresh your memory about something you have learned before, (2) use a document as a foundation for more advanced learning in the same or a similar area, (3) distribute documents to colleagues to advance their learning, or (4) share selected items in interviews for employment. Indeed, some employers now request samples of professional writing as a part of the application process. If you have ready access to a few examples of your best written work, you can easily respond to such requests. If you have a video-recording of your competent demonstration of various practice skills, you may offer to provide that as well.

In career-long learning, social workers seek to remain scientifically minded, logical in our critical thinking, and faithful to our code of ethics and to the universal intellectual standards. When we reflect these principles in our own efforts to learn, we increase the likelihood that the individuals, families, groups, organizations, and communities we serve will also subsequently benefit from our learning as they receive higher-quality care. Failure to keep abreast of findings from emerging research studies and reluctance to engage in relevant professional development activities may constitute a breach of ethics or a violation of social work licensing regulations, and may contribute to allegations of malpractice. Indeed, continuous career-long learning has become an essential aspect of contemporary professionalism. Clients and the community at large have every right to expect that social workers are up-to-date. In addition, most of us accrue great personal, as well as professional, satisfaction when we routinely think critically, engage in scholarly inquiries, and pursue opportunities to learn and grow throughout our lives.

Summary

Critical thinking, scientific inquiry, and career-long learning have become especially important for social workers during the 21st century. The popular media and the ever-expanding Internet regularly and increasingly disseminate misleading, superstitious, pseudoscientific, and false information. We may anticipate that many people are susceptible to unsubstantiated claims and statements of all kinds. In the United States alone, millions of dollars are spent each year on ineffective diet pills and plans, longevity potions and supposed cancer cures, male and female sexual enhancement products, and a host of other "quick cures" promoted by "doctors" and "experts" of one kind or another. Many cite pseudoscientific research studies and anecdotal endorsements, and virtually all contain obvious logical fallacies in their advertisements and marketing materials.

Although the general public may easily be duped by incredible claims, anecdotal stories, and pseudoscientific articles that appear in popular media and on the Web, as professionals we must remain scientifically minded, critically thoughtful, logical, and alert to unsubstantiated and poorly supported assertions. We need to rely upon findings from credible research studies—rather than easily accessed but suspect popular material. In addition, where and when appropriate, we help our clients and members of our communities become more sophisticated thinkers and active learners in their own right. Otherwise, they can remain susceptible to the powerful misleading and manipulative propaganda and the pseudoscientific messages that are increasing exponentially throughout the world.

CHAPTER 3: SUMMARY EXERCISES

1. Go to Appendix 7 and complete the Critical Thinking Questionnaire. This instrument will help you assess selected aspects of critical thinking. It is not a graded test. You cannot pass or fail. Furthermore, the validity and reliability of the instrument have not yet been established. It is not a precise tool. Therefore, please view the instrument and your results as a catalyst for you to consider how you conceptualize and approach critical thinking.

    When you have completed the questionnaire and calculated the results, record your score in Table 3.7. Consider the implications of your responses by reflecting on the following questions: (a) What do your responses suggest about your approach to critical thinking? (b) Why might critical thinking be especially important for social workers during the 21st century? (c) What steps might you take to become a more proficient, critical thinker?

    You might choose to word-process a few summary notations about your reflective responses to these questions. They might come in handy for a later exercise.

TABLE 3.7 Critical Thinking Questionnaire	
Date	CTQ Score

© Cengage Learning 2014

2. Access the Internet and use the keywords "Distinguishing Science Pseudoscience Coker" in a search engine to locate an article titled "Distinguishing Science and Pseudoscience" (Coker, 2001) on the Quackwatch website at www.quackwatch.com. Download the article and then read and reflect upon its contents. You might scan other titles on the website. Several are quite interesting.

   Following that, conduct an Internet search to find Michael Shermer's discussion of 10 science-minded questions to consider in evaluating the credibility of claims. Originally presented as "Baloney Detection: How to draw boundaries between science and pseudoscience, Part I" and "More Baloney Detection: How to draw boundaries between science and pseudoscience, Part II" in the November and December issues, respectively, of the journal Scientific American (Shermer, 2001, Dec., 2001, Nov.), you may also use the keywords "Shermer baloney detection" to locate his YouTube video on the topic (Shermer, 2009). The questions are based, in part, on Carl Sagan's famous "baloney detection kit" as contained in *The Demon Haunted World* (Sagan, 1995).

   You might record the 10 questions in a word-processed document. They might be useful in a later exercise.

3. Please go to Appendix 8 to complete the Lifelong Learning Questionnaire. This instrument will help you assess selected aspects of lifelong learning. Like the Critical Thinking Questionnaire, the validity and reliability have not yet been established. Therefore, please view the instrument and your results as a catalyst for you to consider how you think about and approach career- or lifelong learning.

   When you have completed the questionnaire and calculated the results, record your score in Table 3.8. Reflect on the implications of your responses by addressing the following questions: (a) What do your responses suggest about you as a lifelong learner? (b) Why might continuous, career-long learning be especially important for social workers during the 21st century? (c) What steps might you take to become a more proficient career-long learner?

   You might choose to word-process a few summary notations about your reflective responses to these questions. They might come in handy for a later exercise.

TABLE 3.8
Lifelong Learning Questionnaire

Date	LLQ Score

© Cengage Learning 2014

4. Conduct a scholarly search to locate a copy of a genuine systematic review that contains a meta-analysis. You might use the keywords "systematic review" or "meta-analysis" along with a term that reflects a social problem or issue of your choice. You might use any of the scientific bibliographic database services available through your college or university, or through your public library. You could also access www.pubmed.gov[15] to find a citation

---

[15] Although the PubMed resource includes links to some full-text articles, most citations contain only bibliographic details and an abstract. Once you locate the citation, you may have to go to your library, another online source, or request the article through interlibrary loan.

and then secure the article from another source as needed. If you need help, consult your research librarian—who can, if you are authentic, empathic, and respectful—be an absolutely incredible resource! Once you find an article that meets your criteria, read it carefully to become familiar with an example of a systematic review and meta-analysis. It should be distinctly different from more general reviews of the literature with which you are probably quite familiar. Use the space provided below to record the citation in APA style format. Also identify how you obtained a copy of the article itself.

5. Assume that you have completed your formal social work education and now serve as a professional social worker in some part of the world. You have recently taken a new position that requires you to work with members of a specific ethnic minority group about which you know almost nothing and with whom you have no experience. Use a word-processing program to create a table similar to that shown in Table 3.9. Then, use that table to record a specific learning goal that relates to an ethnic minority group about which you actually do know little and have had limited experience. Outline plans to pursue that goal. Be sure to identify some tangible means to evaluate and document progress toward the achievement of your specific learning goal.

TABLE 3.9 Learning Goal and Plans for Learning and Evaluation	
Learning Goal	
Learning Plan	
Evaluation and Documentation Plan	

© Cengage Learning 2014

6. Identify one social problem or issue with which you are unfamiliar. Prepare a clearly stated practice-relevant research question to guide your search for knowledge about the chosen topic and ways to reduce its incidence or impact. For example, if you choose a topic such as "domestic violence," you might formulate a question such as, "What does the research evidence suggest about the effectiveness of family-oriented social services in reducing or eliminating domestic violence among intimate adult partners?" Follow the example provided in Table 3.10 (A Sample Table of Synonyms and Keywords)[16] to

TABLE 3.10
Sample Table of Synonyms and Keywords Related to Intimate Partner Violence

"What does the research evidence suggest about the effectiveness of family-oriented social services in reducing or eliminating domestic violence among intimate adult partners?"

	Population	Social Problem	Social Service	Research-Based Evidence of Effectiveness
1	Adult(s)	Batter; Battering	Approach	Best Practice
2	Couple	Domestic violence	Counseling	Consensus Statement
3	Domestic partner	Intimate Partner Violence	Family	Effects, Effective, Effectiveness
4	Intimate partner(s)	Partner Violence	Guideline	Efficacy
5	Marriage; Marital	Relationship conflict	Intervention	Empirical
6	Partner(s)	Spouse abuse	Manual	Evaluation
7	Spouse, Spousal		Model	Evidence
8			Policy	Meta-Analysis
9			Program	Outcome
10			Protocol	Promising
11			Psychotherapy	Research
12			Social work	Standard
13			Strategy	Study
14			Technique	Trial
15			Therapy	
16			Treatment	

---

[16] Adapted from Table 2.2 of Cournoyer (2004), p. 34.

create subject terms, phrases, or keywords that capture the central components of your research question. Use a word-processing program to create a similar table in which to record your question and the relevant synonyms and keywords. Title the table so that it is easily identifiable; perhaps in a fashion such as "Table of Synonyms and Keywords Related to (insert your social problem topic)." When complete, include the table in your Social Work Skills Learning Portfolio.

7. Reflect on and integrate the results of this chapter's content and the learning exercises through a brief discussion of the implications of critical thinking and scientific inquiry and career-long learning as aspects of professionalism in social work practice. Include a copy of the table that contrasts some of the characteristics of science and pseudoscience presented by Dr. Rory Coker in his "Distinguishing Science and Pseudoscience" article. Also, include a list of Shermer's 10 baloney-detection questions. Be sure to properly cite the sources of these materials to avoid plagiarism and to reflect high ethical and intellectual standards. Recognize that Coker's table and Shermer's questions constitute quoted material and should be cited accordingly. Prepare your discussion in the form of a two- to three-page word-processed report (500–750 words) titled "Implications of Critical Thinking and Scientific Inquiry, and Career-Long Learning for Social Work Practice." When you have finished, include the report in your Social Work Skills Learning Portfolio.

CHAPTER 3: SELF-APPRAISAL

As you finish this chapter, please reflect on your learning by completing the following self-appraisal exercise.

SELF-APPRAISAL: CRITICAL THINKING, SCIENTIFIC INQUIRY, AND CAREER-LONG LEARNING SKILLS

Please respond to the following items. Your answers should help you assess your proficiency in the critical thinking skills. Read each statement carefully. Then, use the following 4-point rating scale to indicate the degree to which you agree or disagree with each statement. Record your numerical response in the space provided.

4 = Strongly agree; 2 = Disagree;

3 = Agree; 1 = Strongly disagree

4	3	2	1	Rating Statement
				At this point in time, I can
☐	☐	☐	☐	1. Discuss critical thinking and scientific inquiry, and career-long learning and their implications for social work practice.
☐	☐	☐	☐	2. Use critical thinking skills to assess the credibility of a claim, conclusion, or argument; and to evaluate the quality of a research study.
☐	☐	☐	☐	3. Recognize logical fallacies in my own and in others' written and verbal communications.
☐	☐	☐	☐	4. Use scientific inquiry skills to formulate a precise question and search for, discover, and analyze one or more research studies related to a practice or policy-relevant topic.
☐	☐	☐	☐	5. Adopt universal intellectual standards in my scholarly and professional activities.
☐	☐	☐	☐	6. Assess my career-learning needs, establish learning goals, prepare learning plans, and document learning progress.
☐	☐	☐	☐	7. Assess proficiency in the skills of critical thinking and scientific inquiry, and career-long learning.
				Subtotal

Note: These items are identical to those contained in the Critical Thinking, Scientific Inquiry, and Career-Long Learning section of the Social Work Skills Self-Appraisal Questionnaire presented in Appendix 3. If you completed that self-appraisal before beginning Chapter 1, you have already responded to these items once before. You may now compare the responses you made on that occasion with those you made this time. Also, compare the two subtotals. If you believe that you have progressed in terms of your proficiency, the more recent subtotal should be higher than the earlier one.

VALUING DIVERSITY, ADVANCING HUMAN RIGHTS AND SOCIAL JUSTICE, AND PROMOTING SOCIAL WELL-BEING THROUGH POLICY PRACTICE

As social workers, we encounter and serve an incredibly wide and varied array of individuals, families, groups, organizations, and communities. We constantly engage diversity and difference and often recognize extraordinary acts of courage, determination, resilience, generosity, sacrifice, and heroism. Unfortunately, we also frequently observe profound assaults on human dignity, flagrant disregard for basic human rights, and pervasive and insidious forms of social and economic injustice. As social workers act to secure and protect human dignity and individual rights, advance social justice, and promote social well-being, we rely upon our capacities to engage, respect, accept, and advocate for diverse others who differ, at least in some ways, from ourselves.

Continuing the processes begun in Chapters 2 and 3, in this chapter (see Box 4.1) we explore the following dimensions of professionalism: (1) valuing diversity and difference, (2) advancing human rights and social justice, and (3) promoting social well-being through policy practice.

The Council on Social Work Education (2008) requires social work graduates to "engage diversity and difference in practice" (p. 4), "advance human rights and social justice" (p. 5), and "engage in policy practice to advance social and economic well-being" (p. 6). However, the concepts of "diversity," "human rights," "social justice," and "social and economic well-being" are ambiguous, complex, and often quite controversial. Nonetheless, they represent major target domains for social work practice in general and for advocacy and policy practice in particular (see Figure 4.1).

BOX 4.1
Chapter Purpose

The purpose of this chapter is to help learners acquire the knowledge and skills needed to value diversity and difference, advance human rights and social justice, and promote social well-being through policy practice.

Goals

Following completion of this chapter, learners should be able to:

◆ Value diversity and difference in service to others.
◆ Accept others and respect their autonomy.
◆ Discuss the characteristics of human rights and concepts associated with social and economic justice.
◆ Advance human rights and social and economic justice.
◆ Discuss concepts and factors associated with social and economic well-being.
◆ Engage in policy practice to promote social and economic well-being.
◆ Assess proficiency in the knowledge and skills associated with valuing diversity and difference, advancing human rights and social and economic justice, and engaging in policy practice to promote social and economic well-being.

Core EPAS Competencies

The skills addressed in this chapter support the following core EPAS competencies:

◆ Engage diversity and difference in practice (EP2.1.4).
◆ Advance human rights and social and economic justice (EP2.1.5).
◆ Engage in policy practice to advance social and economic well-being and to deliver effective social work services (EP2.1.8).
◆ Respond to contexts that shape practice (EP2.1.9).

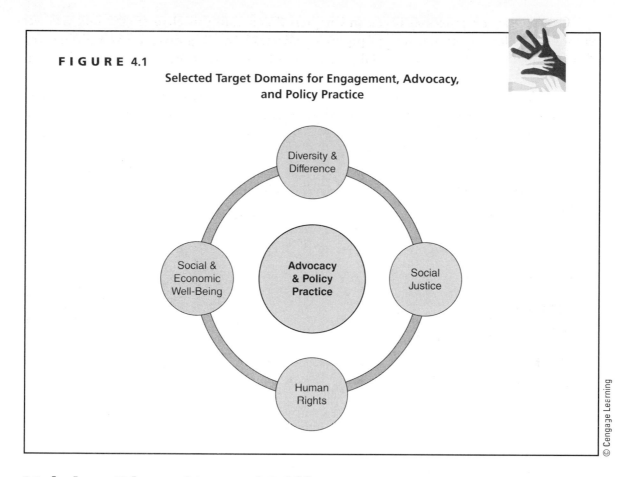

FIGURE 4.1

Selected Target Domains for Engagement, Advocacy, and Policy Practice

Diversity & Difference

Social & Economic Well-Being

Advocacy & Policy Practice

Social Justice

Human Rights

© Cengage Learning

Valuing Diversity and Difference

In *The Social Work Dictionary*, the term *diversity* is defined as "variety, or the opposite of homogeneity. In social organizations the terms usually refers to the range of personnel who more accurately represent minority populations and people from varied backgrounds, cultures, ethnicities, and viewpoints" (Barker, 2003, p. 126). The Council on Social Work Education (2008) indicates that the "dimensions of diversity are understood as the intersectionality of multiple factors including age, class, color, culture, disability, ethnicity, gender, gender identity and expression, immigration status, political ideology, race, religion, sex, and sexual orientation" (p. 5).

The notion of intersectionality adds sophistication to the topic of diversity. Rather than approaching diversity as a unidimensional phenomenon (for example, age or race or sex), an intersectionality perspective (Jaramillo, 2010) views diversity in terms of multiple, interacting factors, identities, or perceived characteristics (for example, age-and-race-and-sex-and-economic status-and-occupation-and-religious or philosophical view-and-sexual orientation-and-political views). Such a multidimensional perspective recognizes that people often view themselves in different and more nuanced ways than others view them. If we consider only the 15 dimensions included in the EPAS (and, of course, there are many more), the complexity becomes apparent (see Table 4.1). For example, Kim could self-identify on any one or more of these 15 dimensions (and numerous others) and do so in various ways at different times and in different contexts (Mehrotra, 2010). In addition, other people might assign quite different diversity dimensions to Kim than she identifies

TABLE 4.1
Intersectionality: 15 Diversity Dimensions

	Age	Class	Color	Culture	Disability	Ethnicity	Gender	Gender Identity	Gender Expression	Immigration Status	Political Ideology	Race	Religion	Sex	Sexual Orientation
Age	▓														
Class		▓													
Color			▓												
Culture				▓											
Disability					▓										
Ethnicity						▓									
Gender							▓								
Gender Identity								▓							
Gender Expression									▓						
Immigration Status										▓					
Political Ideology											▓				
Race												▓			
Religion													▓		
Sex														▓	
Sexual Orientation															▓

for herself. They too might emphasize certain dimensions at various times and circumstances. Furthermore, Kim might be subject to discrimination due to some form of interlocking oppression (Hulko, 2009). Interlocking oppression is a form of subjugation that is based upon multiple, interacting factors (for example, a disabled female child of minority racial and minority religious status may be subject to discrimination and abuse in school and playground settings). Of course, in some contexts, Kim may experience privilege due to another constellation of factors (for example, youth and beauty).

starts from the premise that **people live multiple, layered identities** derived from social relations, history and the operation of structures of power. People are members of more than one community at the same time, and can simultaneously experience oppression and privilege (e.g. a woman may be a respected medical professional yet suffer domestic violence in her home). **Intersectional analysis aims to reveal multiple identities, exposing the different types of discrimination and disadvantage that occur as a consequence of the combination of identities.** (Association for Women's Rights in Development, 2004, August, p. 2)

In her private life, Sue Choi views herself as a young, lesbian woman of Korean ancestry, and a member of the Unitarian faith. In her work life, she sees herself as a lawyer. Others, of course, emphasize different dimensions as they observe or interact with her. Indeed, Sue has been subject to various forms of prejudice, discrimination, and oppression because of others' perception of her as "different." Nonetheless, she maintains a strong and coherent sense of identity and self-respect. Generous toward and accepting of others, she also feels a great deal of self-compassion (Neff, 2011).

Mr. Hussein Ali is a 50-year-old individual who has unambiguous male physical characteristics. He views himself as masculine, male, and heterosexual. Originally from the country of Uganda, he legally immigrated more than 25 years ago and is now a naturalized citizen. He has dark brown skin color and believes in Allah, the God of the prophet Mohammed. He speaks five languages. Although some people consider him disabled, Hussein does not—despite the fact that at age 8, his left leg was amputated after he stepped on a landmine. He wears a state-of-the-art artificial leg that enables him to walk, run, ride bicycles, and snow ski. He regularly plays tennis and golf. He is a graduate of Harvard University with a PhD in economics. He works as an investment banker and earns an annual income of approximately $575,000. His net worth is more than $12 million. He is a father, husband, and grandfather. In political terms, he views himself as socially progressive and fiscally conservative. And, that represents only a few of the hundreds of ways Dr. Ali is "unique," "different" or "diverse." The multidimensional aspects and the complexity associated with this one person are staggering. Imagine the extent of diversity within groups and communities when we recognize that people tend to view themselves and others in various ways at different times and in different circumstances.

When a number of individuals are grouped in some way (for example, into a community, an organization, a household, or an interest group), they differ according to multiple intersectional dimensions of diversity (for example, skin color, height, weight, age, gender, political views, religious affiliation, language, physical or mental ability, status of some kind, appearance, or attractiveness). When their individual characteristics reflect heterogeneity, we may call that group "diverse." The wider the range and type of differences among the members of the group, the greater is the degree or extent of diversity. Substantial diversity is highly valued in some contexts and strongly devalued in others.

Bankers such as Dr. Ali, stockbrokers, and other financial experts recognize the value of diversity in investments. Indeed, the term a *diversified stock portfolio* is commonly used to suggest that someone has invested in a wide range of different kinds of companies or industries so that if one suffers a downturn, others are there to compensate. Diversified investments provide much greater financial security than, say, investment in a single business or even several companies in the same industry (for example, auto corporations such as General Motors, Ford, and Chrysler).

Mayors of cities and towns prefer to have a diversified base of businesses, industries, and other employment opportunities for their constituents. Similarly, employers prefer to have access to a diversified population who can meet the staffing and production needs of their companies and organizations. A diversified workforce and a wide range of employment opportunities tend to maintain social and economic stability—even when circumstances are uncertain and challenging. Contrast that with a "one-company town" where most people work for a single employer. If that company fails or relocates to a different state or nation, the consequences for the community and its people can be disastrous.

The scientific disciplines of biology and ecology also view diversity as a hallmark of health. In general, ecosystems that contain a large and wide variety of plant and animal life at different ages or stages of development tend to be healthier and better able to withstand challenges and threats than those which reflect fewer varieties. Recognition of the importance of biodiversity for the planet earth and, indeed, for the future of humans, led to a United Nations–sponsored international treaty at the Rio de Janeiro Earth Summit in June 1992. Titled The Convention on Biological Diversity, the treaty has three main goals: (1) to conserve biological diversity, (2) to use biological diversity in a sustainable fashion, and (3) to share the benefits of biological diversity fairly and equitably (1992).

Biodiversity is integrally related to the issue of economic development. Urban, technological, and industrial growth can diminish biodiversity and challenge the earth's capacity for sustainability. The idea of sustainable development incorporates recognition of the importance of biodiversity and environmental health. Concern about the slow pace and direction of international agreements regarding the health of the earth led to a global gathering of about 30,000 individuals, activists, and representatives of both governmental and nongovernmental organizations (NGOs) in Cochabamba, Bolivia, on April 22, 2010.

The conference led to the approval of two documents that question the motivation and capacity of current national governments and the United Nations to address environmental issues and climate change. The documents are: (1) The Universal Declaration of the Rights of Mother Earth and (2) People's Agreement (World People's Conference on Climate Change and the Rights of Mother Earth, 2010a, 2010b).

Twenty years after the first Rio summit, a second UN-sponsored conference (Rio+20) was held in Rio de Janeiro. The United Nations Conference on Sustainable Development resulted in a number of voluntary commitments and a report titled "The Future We Want" (United Nations, 2012). Although these aspirations of these UN initiatives relate to the general topic of biodiversity, we can readily apply them to human diversity as well. Over the long term, diverse and heterogeneous human social systems are usually considerably more healthy, vibrant, and resilient than those reflecting extreme homogeneity. Recognizing that greater diversity generally tends to benefit humankind, social workers tend to celebrate individual and cultural differences, in addition to biological diversity, as valuable forms of social capital (Coleman, 1988; Lin, 2001). Even when human diversity is highly regarded, however, engaging those who differ from ourselves requires considerable sensitivity and especially acceptance. In subsequent chapters, we explore skills associated with culturally sensitive communication for engaging diversity and difference. At this point, we focus on acceptance of others as a vital element of both valuing and engaging diversity and difference in social work practice.

Accepting Others and Respecting Autonomy

Acceptance of others involves processes of self-awareness, cross-cultural understanding, and valuing and joining with people regardless of their degree of similarity or difference. As social workers providing needed services to often highly vulnerable people and to widely diverse communities, we hope to transcend the powerful psychological and social forces that maintain patterns of prejudice, privilege, ethnocentrism, xenophobia, rankism (Fuller, 2002), and discrimination.

Social workers require a capacity to accept all people—those who differ from as well as those who resemble us in appearance, background, attitudes, abilities, and behavior (Armstrong, 2010; Berlin, 2005). All people, families, groups, communities, and societies deserve genuine acceptance from social workers. Such acceptance involves respect for the autonomy and self-determination of those we encounter—a form of respect that is probably easier to apply to "people of similarity" than it is to "people of difference." We humans seem ready to view those most like ourselves as fully equal, capable, and entitled to make their own decisions; and to see those who differ as less equal, less able, and less entitled to autonomy and self-determination.

In the context of diversity and acceptance of others, the term *reverence* seems especially meaningful (Woodruff, 2001). Reverence involves an attitude of deep respect or awe and humility in the presence of another. Although reflecting a religious or spiritual connotation, the concept of reverence aptly captures the special attitude social workers reflect as we express cultural sensitivity and acceptance of others. In service to others, reverence is crucial (Berlin, 2005).

However, in highly competitive and pluralistic societies such as our own, it is exceedingly difficult to develop genuine reverence for others. Our prejudices and sense of privilege may limit our capacity to do so. *Prejudice* is "an opinion about an individual, group, or phenomenon that is developed without proof or systematic evidence. This prejudgment may be favorable but is more often unfavorable and may become institutionalized in the form of a society's laws or customs" (Barker, 2003, p. 336). *Privilege* is "a special right, advantage, or immunity granted or available only to a particular person or group of people" (*New Oxford American Dictionary* [Online], 2010). Such advantages include extraordinary access, opportunities, benefits, and resources that are usually unavailable to nonprivileged others; and, exemptions from certain obligations, duties, or liabilities to which nonprivileged others are commonly subject.

Some privileges are obvious. For example, wealthy individuals who donate large sums of money to support the campaigns of political candidates are virtually guaranteed face-to-face access to those politicians if and when elected. Similarly, in the context of admissions to prestigious colleges and universities, legacy students (children of alumni) are typically viewed more favorably than equally well-qualified, nonlegacy applicants.

Many privileges, however, go unnoticed by both privileged and nonprivileged people alike. Assumptions such as "anything is possible if you are talented and are willing to work long and hard enough" may interfere with our ability to notice our own or others' privileged status and may leave us more susceptible to both "blaming victims" and accepting extreme levels of economic inequality and social injustice (Markman, 2012, July 27; Savani & Rattan, 2012; Savani, Stephens, & Markus, 2011; Valor-Segura, Exposito, & Moya, 2011; van Prooijen & van den Bos, 2009).

Privilege is the often,

> invisible advantage and resultant unearned benefits afforded to dominant groups of people because of a variety of sociodemographic traits. Privilege provides economic and social boosts to dominant groups while supporting the structural barriers to other groups imposed by prejudice. (Franks & Riedel, 2008, para. 1)

Obviously, prejudice and privilege are closely related to each other and to overt discrimination. Discrimination involves the "treatment of people based on identifiable characteristics such as race, gender, religion, or ethnicity" (Barker, 2003, p. 123). Like prejudice, discrimination may be positive or negative (for example, favoring or disfavoring members of a particular group). Predictably, people in historical or contemporary positions of power and privilege may be especially likely to engage in both forms of discrimination; and do so without realizing it. Indeed, privileged peoples may lack conscious awareness of and fail to recognize the discriminatory nature of their own words and actions (Benjamin, 2009; Halley, Amy Eshleman, & Vijaya, 2011; Kivel, 2002; Potapchuk, Leiderman, Bivens, & Major, 2005; Rothenberg, 2002; Saucier, Miller, & Doucet, 2005). As social workers, however, we seek to transcend the powerful psychological and social forces that maintain privileged and prejudicial attitudes and discriminatory behaviors. We try to recognize our own privileged perspectives, embrace the value of diversity, and genuinely accept those who differ from us in appearance, background, beliefs, abilities, and behavior; and to accept others on their own terms. Such a profound level of acceptance involves recognition and respect for others' power and autonomy—something that can be difficult when we intentionally or unintentionally dominate the helping relationship with our status and expertise. Berlin (2005) recognizes this dimension by suggesting that "acceptance of another combines a recognition and endorsement of the other's autonomy (his or her own separate views, goals, feelings, experiences, and capacity to act) with a feeling of affiliation with or connection to him or her" (p. 484).

Acceptance and respect for autonomy do not come easily in a heterogeneous society in which people vary widely in power, status, economic resources, race and ethnicity, religion, culture, education, opportunity, and ideology. If you are similar to most North Americans who aspire to become professional social workers, you have observed prejudicial attitudes and both covert and overt forms of discrimination. In all likelihood, you have also experienced prejudicial thoughts and have personally discriminated for or against others. You have also probably been affected by others' prejudicial attitudes and discriminatory behaviors. Finally, you have probably had experiences where others have attempted to limit or deny your right to make your own decisions and determine your own life course. You have probably also done the same to others—perhaps out of a sense of kindness, concern, and a desire to protect them from risk and danger. Indeed, as policy makers, program leaders, and social workers in practice quickly come to realize, we may unwittingly manipulate, overprotect, and control others in our efforts to help. As we do so, others' autonomy and sense of personal power may be lost or diminished. Recognizing such well-intentioned tendencies, social workers take extra care to encourage, facilitate, and celebrate clients' autonomy—including the right to make independent decisions about matters affecting themselves and their lives.

Occasionally, some members of "out" groups, especially those who have experienced prolonged oppression, judge themselves negatively and critically on the basis of a perceived majority standard. Some may feel ashamed of being who they are, limiting their personal power and self-expression. In contrast, some members of "in" groups reflect attitudes of privilege. They may consider themselves deserving or entitled simply because of their group's traditional status and power. Some may be unable to conceive of limits to their freedom and autonomy. This "tendency to consider one's own group, usually national or ethnic, superior to other groups using one's own group or groups as the frame of reference against which other groups are judged" (Wolman, 1973, p. 129) is called *ethnocentrism*. Occasionally, such ethnocentristic prejudices occur in reverse. For example, some majority-group members hold negatively prejudiced attitudes about themselves, and some minority-group members view themselves as specially entitled or privileged. The forms and manifestations of prejudice and discrimination and privilege are myriad and insidious. As a member of North American society, you have probably adopted some prejudicial attitudes and discriminatory behaviors in your own life. In some ways, you may view yourself as special or entitled to special treatment. As social workers, however, we try to transcend these common cultural patterns in order to better accept, respect, value, and embrace other human beings with special sensitivity to the many multidimensional ways that they differ from ourselves.

Advancing Human Rights and Social and Economic Justice

The concepts of human rights and social and economic justice are at least as complex as the topics of diversity and difference. Our perspective, position, status, roles, and responsibilities powerfully influence our views of human rights and justice. For example, a mother whose daughter was raped and murdered might be less concerned with the human rights of the perpetrator than with ensuring that he is caught and punished. Similarly, military and security officials might be more concerned with protecting their nation from a terrorist attack than with the human rights of potential attackers. Soldiers in battle would understandably be less concerned with the human rights of enemy combatants firing bullets and missiles at them than they would be with eliminating the immediate threat to their own survival. A parent and home owner confronted by an armed burglar would probably be more concerned with the protection of her family and home than with the human rights of the trespasser.

On the other hand, the mother of someone accused of a major crime might be highly concerned with the human rights of the accused; as would the parent of a starving child, the mother of a teenage girl stoned by a group of men because she kissed a boy, or the parent of a political prisoner. A civil rights lawyer might well focus on the violation of individual human rights in the case of an abused and tortured prisoner, an enslaved girl of 14 forced into prostitution, a mentally retarded adolescent convicted of murder and sentenced to death by execution, or families denied an opportunity to rent apartments because they "are" homosexual, racially mixed, of "that religion," or old and disabled.

Social workers are, understandably, also concerned with human rights of various kinds: the rights of children to adequate food, nutrition, and safety; the rights of women to equal protection under the law and to opportunities in society; and the rights of disabled people to equal access to education and other public services. We are also concerned about human rights in regard to the protection of children, women, disabled people, elderly people, and members of minority groups from abuse, exploitation, and oppression. However, our clients include people viewed as "perpetrators" as well as people considered "victims." Furthermore, through our person-in-environment perspective, we emphasize the rights and well-being of both individuals and the communities and societies in which people live. Such a multidimensional view may lead to various intellectual dilemmas. We may be forced to address questions such as, "On this occasion in this situation, should we focus on the rights and wants of the individual or the needs and well-being of the family, group, organization, or community?" Indeed, the tension between private interest and public good, inevitable in many contexts, seems especially pertinent as we consider human rights. And, this tension becomes more pronounced when we consider that some cultures emphasize one aspect more than the other (for example, private interest more than public good; or, vice versa). Furthermore, some cultures place considerable value on respect for and obedience to authority whereas others value individual, independent thought and action. For instance, people in many Western cultures—including the United States—often highly regard individual rights and responsibilities and view established authority with considerable suspicion. In many Eastern cultures, people tend to value strongly the well-being of the group, the community, and society and generally view authority with considerable respect and deference. Finally, people in some regions of the world engage in a continuous struggle to survive because of inadequate food and water supplies, long-term drought, few economic opportunities, or civil war. Under such conditions, consideration of individual human rights may seem less urgent than finding a source of clean water, a loaf of bread, or a refuge from gunfire, grenades, and landmines. Yes, the topic of human rights is quite confusing and extremely complex indeed!

Human Rights

Edmundson suggests that "Human rights recognize *extraordinarily* special, basic interests, and this sets them apart from rights, even moral rights, generally" (2004, p. 191). We can trace aspects of the concept of human rights from the Babylonian Code of Hammurabi to Thomas Spence's *The Real Rights of Man* (1775) and Thomas Paine's *The Rights of Man* (1791). However, the end of World War II, widespread dissemination of information about the Holocaust, and the formation of the United Nations led the newly created General Assembly of the United Nations to approve the Universal Declaration of Human Rights (UDHR) in 1948.

The UDHR contains an array of 30 universal human rights (General Assembly of the United Nations, 1948). Some of the 30 require governments to restrain their power vis-à-vis individuals' human rights. For example, the UDHR states that governments may not infringe upon individuals' rights to freedom of opinion, expression, and movement; freedom of thought, conscience, and religion; freedom from torture; freedom from slavery; and the right to a fair trial. Others require governments to take positive action to provide individuals with access to particular opportunities and resources. Under the UDHR, for example, individuals have rights to education, to work and equitable compensation, to rest and leisure from work, and to an adequate standard of living, including food, clothing, housing, and medical care. In addition to the rights of individual humans, the UDHR also refers to the rights of families, groups, and communities of people. For example, families have a right to privacy and are entitled to protection from unnecessary state intrusion. Furthermore, people, collectively as well as individually, have a right to engage in cultural activities and share knowledge gained from scientific enterprise.

The rights described in the UDHR are "intended to be universal and indivisible—that is, all humans have the right to them regardless of culture, political system, ethnicity, or any other characteristic (universal), and a country cannot select which rights it should grant; all humans should have all rights (indivisible)" (Mapp, 2008, p. 17).

Since 1948, other human rights–related documents have been endorsed by much of the international community. Together with the UDHR, the International Covenant on Civil and Political Rights (General Assembly of the United Nations, 1966a) and the International Covenant on Economic, Social, and Cultural Rights (General Assembly of the United Nations, 1966b) along with their optional protocols are considered the "International Bill of Human Rights" (United Nations Office of the High Commissioner for Human Rights, 1996). We might add to these central documents, the Convention on the Elimination of All Forms of Discrimination against Women (United Nations, 1979), the Convention on the Rights of the Child (United Nations, 1989, December 12), and the Convention on the Rights of Persons with Disabilities (United Nations, 2006, December 13). Collectively, they help us comprehend the nature and meaning of "human rights." As Amnesty International (1997) states:

> Human rights can be defined as those basic standards without which people cannot live in dignity as human beings. Human rights are the foundation of freedom, justice and peace. Their respect allows the individual and the community to fully develop.
>
> The development of human rights has its roots in the struggle for freedom and equality everywhere in the world. The basis of human rights—such as respect for human life and human dignity—can be found in most religions and philosophies.
>
> They are proclaimed in the Universal Declaration of Human Rights. Also, documents such as the International Covenants on Human Rights set out what governments must do and also what they must not do to respect the rights of their citizens.

Characteristics of human rights

- Human rights do not have to be bought, earned or inherited, they belong to people simply because they are human—**human rights are "inherent"** to each individual.
- Human rights are the same for all human beings regardless of race, sex, religion, political or other opinion, national or social origin. We are all born free and equal in dignity and rights—**human rights are "universal."**
- Human rights cannot be taken away; no one has the right to deprive another person of them for any reason. People still have human rights even when the laws of their countries do not recognize them, or when they violate them—for example, when slavery is practiced, slaves still have rights even though these rights are being violated—**human rights are "inalienable."**
- People live in dignity, all human rights are entitled to freedom, security and decent standards of living concurrently—**human rights are "indivisible."** (Amnesty International, 1997, What are human rights?, paras. 1–4)

The Bill of International Human Rights covers a wide range of both rights and responsibilities. The rights fall into three categories:

1. Civil and political rights (also called first generation rights). These are "liberty-orientated" and include the rights to: life, liberty and security of the individual; freedom from torture and slavery; political participation; freedom of opinion, expression, thought, conscience and religion; freedom of association and assembly.
2. Economic and social rights (also called second generation rights). These are "security-orientated" rights, for example the rights to: work; education; a reasonable standard of living; food; shelter and health care.
3. Environmental, cultural and developmental rights (also called third generation rights). These include the rights to live in an environment that is clean and protected from destruction, and rights to cultural, political and economic development.

When we say that each person has human rights, we are also saying that each person has responsibilities to respect the human rights of others. (Amnesty International, 1997, Categories of Rights, paras. 1–4)

Although many social workers readily concur with the principles contained in the International Bill of Human Rights, several nations have signed but not ratified all of the covenants and conventions. Nonetheless, social workers benefit from familiarity with these internationally supported human rights because they represent a vital dimension of social and economic justice.

Social and Economic Justice

Like human rights, social justice[1] involves many forms and dimensions. As Van Soest and Garcia (2003) observe, "The term 'social justice' is widely used in social work without a clearly articulated and shared definition or understanding of it" (p. 44). They encourage us to ask these questions: "What is justice? What is fairness? Is life fair or just? What kind of justice can be expected?" (p. 44).

As a starting point, we can view social justice as a condition in which human rights are cherished as inviolate and indivisible. In a just world, individual rights would be respected by people and social

---

[1] Within the context of this section, we view "legal justice" and "economic justice" as elements of "social justice."

systems wherever humans live, work, or play. Of course, there are different kinds or aspects of social justice. For instance, *distributive justice* involves the allocation or distribution of opportunities, costs, and benefits within social systems. Distributive justice is commonly associated with economic justice—how resources and wealth are distributed within and among groups, communities, and societies—and with society's responsibility for and accountability to the individual person for ensuring fundamental human rights. *Procedural* or *processual justice* refers to the ways and means of interaction and decision making between individuals or within a group, organization, community, or society. Procedural justice involves the fairness of processes involved in, for instance, negotiations of agreements or contracts, selection of authorities (for example, governing officials, judges), and the development and implementation of policies and programs. *Retributive justice* refers to punishment, rehabilitation, compensation, or restitution for harm done by or to one or more members of the social group. *Restorative justice* involves attempts to repair damage done to those negatively affected by offenses. Whereas retribution tends to be associated with revenge upon and punishment of offenders, restoration is associated with efforts, as far as humanly possible, to repair damage or recompense those negatively affected by damaging offenses. Sometimes, efforts by offenders to recompense victims result in transformative experiences for the offenders, the victims, or both. *Intergenerational justice* involves the opportunities, resources, and burdens one generation leaves to others. When previous generations, for example, capture, transport, and enslave millions of human beings, amass an enormous public debt, or create a toxic global ecology, questions of intergenerational justice arise. Subsequent generations are affected by the actions and inactions of earlier generations. *Environmental justice* refers to the distribution of risks and benefits associated with environmental conditions. When, for instance, one group of people is routinely exposed to toxins in the earth, water, or air whereas another group has ready and plentiful access to fresh water, clean air, and rich soil, we may reasonably raise questions about environmental justice.

Over the centuries, many philosophers and social scientists have explored the topic of justice. To determine whether a society is just, Sandel (2009) suggests that we "ask how it distributes the things we prize—income and wealth, duties and rights, powers and opportunities, offices and honors. A just society distributes these goods in the right way; it gives each person his or her due. The hard questions begin when we ask what people are due, and why" (p. 19).

Sandel (2009) identifies three major aspects of justice: "welfare, freedom, and virtue" (p. 19). As depicted in Figure 4.2, these elements sometimes complement each other (or overlap) and sometimes

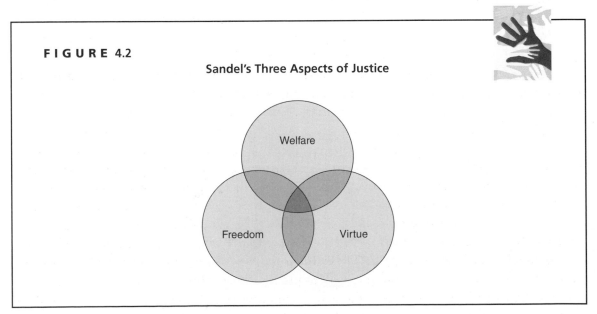

FIGURE 4.2

Sandel's Three Aspects of Justice

Adapted from Sandel's conceptualization.

conflict (or separate). Promotion of the general welfare may conflict with some features of individual freedom or virtue. For instance, a society may engage in the torture or murder of a suspected terrorist (presumably nonvirtuous behavior that violates the freedom and human rights of suspects) in an attempt to safeguard its residents from violent attack (maintain the general welfare). Or, a society may prize the opportunity to accumulate enormous personal wealth (individual freedom) despite its likely promotion of greed and an increase in economic inequality. Excessive selfishness and greed conflict with views about virtue; and severe economic inequality tends to impact the general welfare. On the other hand, efforts to distribute wealth more evenly or to promote universal access to education, employment, or health care (despite their virtuous intent and the benefit to a large proportion of residents) would usually be unsuccessful in a society where individual freedom is valued more highly than virtue and the general welfare.

During the mid- to late 20th and the early 21st centuries, the late John Rawls has been an influential figure in the intellectual exploration of the topic of social justice. Author of *A Theory of Justice* (1971, 1999) and *Justice as Fairness* (1958; Rawls & Kelly, 2001), Rawls' ideas can be controversial and some have indeed been criticized (Sandel, 1982). Nonetheless, his works serve as a useful introduction to the topic of social justice. His approach involves several key concepts and principles.

The idea of the *original position* (Rawls, 1971) involves the assumption of a hypothetical "veil of ignorance." In other words, participants to a negotiation or discussion operate as if they are unaware of their own and others' sex, age, class, race, and status or place in the social structure. Through this hypothetical veil of ignorance, participants may be able to transcend narrow, individual self-interest to devise and agree upon contracts or policies that benefit all participants and nonparticipants alike. Based upon reason rather than narrow self-interest or prejudice, decisions reached when stakeholders adopt the original position likely lead to fair and reasonable distribution of the costs, risks, and benefits associated with an endeavor.

Once we assume the original position, we can more easily understand concepts of justice and fairness, and envision the consequences of laws and principles that discriminate against certain people in terms of opportunity or outcome. Absent the original position, self-interest tends to win out. For instance, if I am male and own a farm or a business and a slave, and consider my wife and children as forms of quasi-property, then I might well propose a process of decision making (for example, voting processes) that includes only male property owners and excludes women, children, and slaves from participation. However, if I adopt the original position, I might well ask questions such as, "What might be the implications of such a decision-making process on me—if I were ignorant about my status now or in the future? I might or might not own property. I might or might not be a man, a woman, a child, or a slave? What would I consider fair and just if I did not know in advance what status I might hold and therefore could not determine how a policy or procedure would personally affect me?"

In some ways, Rawls' original position represents a form of "golden-rule" thinking through which we anticipate the effects of our actions on anybody and everybody affected by those actions. The "golden rule" suggests, in effect, that we "do to others what we would have them do to us." In Confucian philosophy, the concept of *Jen* involves virtues of goodness and benevolence (for example, interest, concern, and care for others—regardless of their station or circumstances). Confucius captures the essence of Jen through the passage "Do not do to others what you would not like them to do to you." This is sometimes referred to as the "silver rule," which naturally serves to complement and complete the "golden rule."

By adopting Rawls' original position, we become more able to consider the implications of our own or others' actions on people who differ from ourselves and to be more fair to others in our words and deeds. We might even become less egocentric, less ethnocentric, less xenophobic, and perhaps even less anthropocentric in our thoughts and actions. Rawls suggests that when we adopt the original position we become more likely to propose reasonable ideas and to think carefully about the ideas of others. If we were to do so, we would engage in discussions until everyone—each adopting the original position—reached a decision that everyone considers fair.

Compare such a perspective and approach with those common in today's financial, political, and industrial circles. In contemporary life, status, privilege, wealth, and power—including access to power—tend to dominate processes of decision making and their outcomes. Unless organized into groups, less powerful people, members of minority communities, immigrants, refugees, prisoners and other people with criminal records, unemployed individuals and families, persons assigned a severe psychiatric diagnosis, less educated or less able people, and homeless people rarely have genuine input into decision-making processes—even though they are often significantly impacted by the results.

Rawls suggests that, in essence, justice is fairness. If people were, somehow, able to adopt the original position in their consensual pursuit of fairness and social justice, they would likely agree on two fundamental principles. The first principle holds that all people have an absolute, inviolate right to certain fundamental liberties—including the right to free speech and participation in decision-making processes that affect us, others, and the community or society as a whole. The second principle suggests that we, collectively, as a community or society of equals—each of us possessing these fundamental liberties—might agree that in certain areas, under certain circumstances, and at certain times, some degree of inequality (in terms of distribution of wealth, power, or opportunity) serves to benefit the community or society as a whole substantially more than does equal distribution under the same conditions. However, we might also decide that the collective benefits of such defined and limited unequal distribution must clearly outweigh its negative effects. Finally, in order to ensure justice as fairness, we would likely adopt the *difference principle*. That principle holds that we might decide to accept some forms of inequality if, but only if, that inequality is directed toward and benefits the least powerful and least advantaged among us. If we adopt the original position, most of us would consider forms of inequality that benefit the powerful and advantaged at the expense of the powerless and disadvantaged to be unfair and unjust.

When certain groups of people are disproportionately incarcerated in jails and prisons, we may appropriately raise questions about the fairness of the *retributive justice* system (Western, 2006). In 2007–2008, approximately 756 of every 100,000 people in the United States were in prison. China (not included in the International Centre for Prison Studies' figures), Russia, and Rwanda had the next-highest prison populations. In contrast, France imprisoned about 96, Canada about 116, Turkey about 142, and Japan about 63 per 100,000 people (Walmsley, 2009).

According to the U.S. Justice Department, 1,612,395 people were imprisoned[2] in state and federal prisons throughout the United States at the end of 2010. This represents an incarceration rate of 943 per 100,000 males and 67 per 100,000 females during that year. As Table 4.2

TABLE 4.2
Estimated Number of State and Federal Prisoners in the United States by Gender, Race, and Hispanic Origin in December 2010

	White	Black	Hispanic	Totals
Males	451,600	561,400	327,200	1,446,000
Females	48,000	26,600	18,700	104,600

Note: Data extracted from Guerino et al. (2012, February 9). Total males and females includes American Indians, Alaska Natives, Asians, Native Hawaiians, and other Pacific Islanders, and people identifying two or more races as well as people under age 18.

---

[2] Does not include local jail populations or those who have been sentenced to less than one year.

illustrates, the total number of state and federally imprisoned African American (black) males exceeds that of white males and the numbers of African American and Hispanic prisoners are disproportionately higher than the percentage of people of African American and of Hispanic origin in the general population (Guerino, Harrison, & Sabo, 2012, Feb. 9). In 2010, approximately 12.6 percent and 16.3 percent of the U.S. population were of African and Hispanic origin, respectively. Some 63.7 percent were of non-Hispanic white origin (Humes, Jones, & Ramirez, 2011, March).

As Table 4.3 reveals, in 2010 the incarceration rates for males and females of African and Hispanic origin were much higher than comparable rates for whites. African and Hispanic Americans were severely overrepresented among the incarcerated population while, conversely, white males and females were substantially underrepresented. For males, the disparity is even greater than for females. The chances that an African American or Hispanic male is, has been, or will become a state or federal prisoner in the United States are much greater than those for a comparable white male.

When there are major differences in the amount and extent of wealth in different areas or populations within a country, or differences between nations, we may ask questions about the fairness of *distributive justice* systems (Edelman, 2012; Smiley & West, 2012). For example, a common way to estimate average per capita income in a nation is to take the annual gross national product (GNP) of a country in U.S. dollars and divide it by the country's population. However, this fails to account for variations in the cost of living in different parts of the world. A dollar in one nation may purchase a great deal more, or less, than in another. Therefore, a more realistic way to estimate annual income for the purposes of comparison is to adjust for cost of living variations. The result of such an adjustment is called Purchasing Power Parity (PPP).

In PPP terms, Luxembourg reflected an average annual per capita income of $63,850 in 2010[3]. The United States per capita average was $47,020. At the other extreme, the average annual per capita incomes in the Democratic Republic of Congo and Liberia were $310 and $330, respectively (World Bank, 2011, July).

The differences between nations are enormous. It takes an average Congolese a full year to accumulate $310 while the average[4] American earns more, about $356, in 2 days. Such disparities, however, exist within nations as well as between them. For example, in 2011, the top 1 percent of

---

TABLE 4.3
Estimated Incarceration Rates of State and Federal Prisoners in the United States by Gender, Race, and Hispanic Origin (Per 100,000 Population)

	White	Black	Hispanic	Total U.S. Population
Males	459 per 100,000	3,074 per 100,000	1,258 per 100,000	943 per 100,000
Females	47 per 100,000	133 per 100,000	77 per 100,000	67 per 100,000

Note: Data extracted from Guerino et al. (2012, February 9).

---

[3] 2010 data for certain nations were not available. We presume that Qatar, United Arab Emirates, and some other nations would reflect high per capita annual incomes.
[4] Recognize that "averages" can be quite misleading. For example, suppose you reside in a nation of 10 people. As a whole, your national income is $10,000. The average is $1,000. However, that average could be obtained as a result of one person having income of $10,000 while the other nine are unemployed; or, through all 10 residents earning $1,000 each.

TABLE 4.4
Poverty Rate in the United States by Gender, Race, and Hispanic Origin: 2010

	White	Black	Hispanic	Asian	Totals
Percent in Poverty	9.9%	27.4%	26.6%	12.1%	15.1%

Note: Data extracted from DeNavas-Walt et al. (2011).

United States households reflected an average wage of approximately $736 per hour ($12.27 per minute) while the bottom 20 percent earned an hourly wage of about $6.20 (10.3 cents per minute).[5]

In 2010, 46,180,000 or 15.1 percent of United States residents were in poverty—up from 12.5 percent in 2007 (DeNavas-Walt, Proctor, & Smith, 2011). As shown in Table 4.4, the poverty rates in 2010 varied greatly according to race and ethnicity.

In 2010, approximately 15,750,000 children (21.6 percent) were in poverty in the United States (Macartney, 2011, Nov.). The rates of children in poverty by race and ethnicity are displayed in Table 4.5.

In addition, some states reflect substantially higher poverty rates than the national average. In 2009–2010, at 22.9 percent and 19.9 percent, respectively, Mississippi and Arizona experienced much higher than average poverty rates, and substantially more so than, for example, New Hampshire at 7.2 percent or Connecticut at 8.4 percent (DeNavas-Walt et al., 2011; U.S. Census Bureau Current Population Survey, 2008).

Average annual income also varies by sex. In 2010, the median annual income was $36,931 for full-time, year-round working women and $47,715 for full-time, year-round working men. In other words, a full-time female employee earned about 77.4 percent of what a full-time male employee did (DeNavas-Walt et al., 2011).

As you might imagine, income differences are not limited to geographical location and gender. Concern about the overall size and the rate of increase in the income and wealth gap between the "rich" and the "poor" and a concurrent decrease in the size of the "middle-class" has grown exponentially over the course of the last several years. Especially since the "Great Recession" that began in 2008, income inequality has become a topic of widespread popular

TABLE 4.5
Children's Poverty Rate in the United States by Race and Ethnicity: 2010

	White	Black	Hispanic	Asian	Totals
Number of Children in Poverty	8,400,000	4,000,000	5,500,000	419,000	15,750,000*
Percent of Children in Poverty	17.0%	38.2%	32.3%	13.0%	21.6%*

Note: Data extracted from Macartney, S. (2011, Nov.). Totals are greater than the sum of column entries because they include additional race groups.

---

[5] Hourly rates based on annual family/household incomes in 2012 as divided by 2080 work hours per year. In 2011, the top 1 percent of U.S. households earned an average of $1,530,773; the bottom 20 percent earned an average of $9,187 (Khimm, 2011, Oct. 6).

discussion (Galbraith, 2012; Pizzigati, 2004; Stiglitz, 2012). Emergence of the "Occupy Wall Street" movement was motivated in large part by the disparity between the economic status of ordinary people and the extraordinary salaries, bonuses, and overall wealth of bankers, fund managers, brokers, and financiers. Especially in light of the pervasive fraud and corruption, greed, and failure in the financial markets along with subsequent tax-supported "bailouts," some people of modest means began to protest the unfairness and injustice inherent in severe income inequality. They argued that massive accumulation of wealth by a few (the "one percent") negatively affects the many (the "99 percent") and diminishes the general welfare. In opposition to the "occupy" movements, other people and groups suggested that individual autonomy and freedom from governmental regulations are, in effect, more important than other values—including the general welfare. They claimed that any individual person or family should be free to accumulate as much personal wealth as possible; that it represented a fundamental human right.

Ideological thinking tends to reflect confirmation bias; and strongly held, dogmatic beliefs usually overpower rationality. Critical thinking is relatively rare in the popular media and in political contexts. As social work professionals, however, we pursue our mission of ending poverty and promoting social and economic justice despite popular beliefs. Furthermore, we do so from a scientific and critical thinking perspective that includes the active participation of people affected by poverty and by social and economic injustice.

In a study of income distribution during the 30 years between 1979 and 2007 (see Figure 4.3), the nonpartisan Congressional Budget Office (CBO) found that after-tax income grew by 277.5 percent for the top 1 percent of U.S. households; 65 percent for the next 19 percent of households; by slightly less than 40 percent for the next 60 percent of households, and by 18 percent for the bottom 20 percent of households (Congressional Budget Office, 2011).

The percentage or share of after-tax income also changed over the course of the 30-year period (Figure 4.4). The share of all annual income of the top 20 percent of U.S. households, after

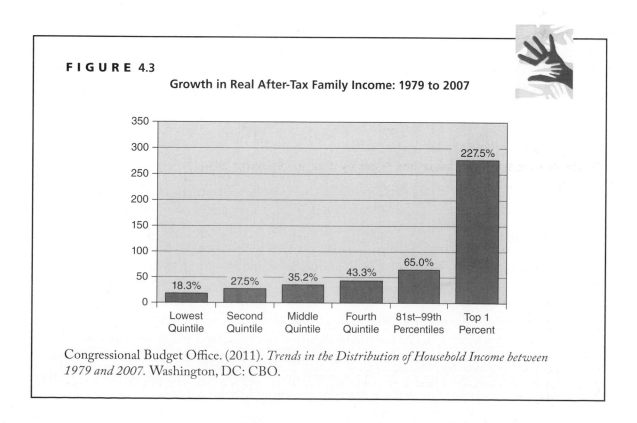

FIGURE 4.3

Growth in Real After-Tax Family Income: 1979 to 2007

Congressional Budget Office. (2011). *Trends in the Distribution of Household Income between 1979 and 2007*. Washington, DC: CBO.

FIGURE 4.4

Shares of Income after Transfers and Federal Taxes, 1979 and 2007

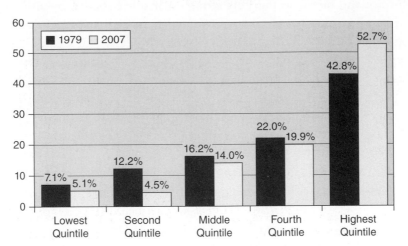

Congressional Budget Office. (2011). *Trends in the Distribution of Household Income between 1979 and 2007.* Washington, DC: CBO.

tax and transfers, grew by about 10 percent during the 1979–2007 time period. However, almost all of that growth occurred within the top 1 percent of U.S. households. The income share of the next 19 percent grew by only one-half of 1 percent while the share of the remaining 80 percent of U.S. households decreased.

> As a result of . . . uneven income growth, the distribution of after-tax household income in the United States was substantially more unequal in 2007 than in 1979: The share of income accruing to higher-income households increased, whereas the share accruing to other households declined. In fact, between 2005 and 2007, the after-tax income received by the 20 percent of the population with the highest income exceeded the after-tax income of the remaining 80 percent. (Congressional Budget Office, 2011, p. ix)

Figure 4.5 illustrates the distribution of average annual family income in dollar amounts in the United States in 2010 (Bricker, Kennickell, Moore, & Sabelhaus, 2012). Table 4.6 illustrates the distribution of average annual family income in 2006 as classified into five income groups: the top .01 percent, the next .09 percent, the remaining portion of the top 1 percent, the next 9 percent, and the remaining 90 percent of families (Fessenden & McLean, 2011, Oct. 28).

Although most households in the United States lost income and wealth as the result of the 2008 Great Recession, by 2011 the top 1 percent regained many of those losses. Figure 4.6 depicts the average income of the bottom 20 percent and the top 1 percent of U.S. households in that year. At $9,187 annual income, the average household in the lowest quintile earned less than the 2012 poverty guideline of $11,170 for single-person households and much less than the guideline for multiple-person family households (Table 4.7). In 2011, the top 1 percent of U.S. households earned an average of $1,530,773.00 per year (Khimm, 2011, Oct. 6). That is about 167 times greater than the average income of the bottom 20 percent of U.S. households.

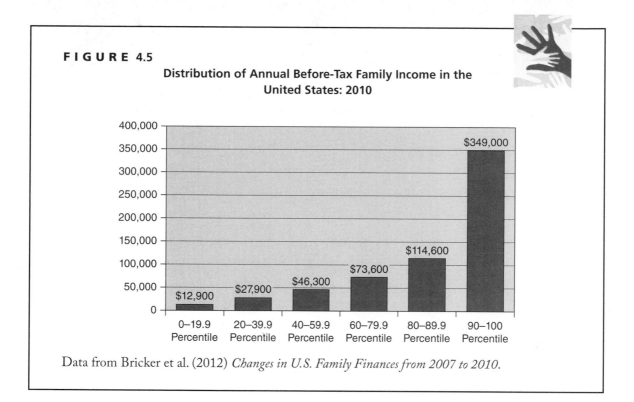

FIGURE 4.5

Distribution of Annual Before-Tax Family Income in the United States: 2010

Data from Bricker et al. (2012) *Changes in U.S. Family Finances from 2007 to 2010.*

TABLE 4.6
Distribution of Average Annual After-Tax Family Income in the United States: 2006

		Number of Families	Average Annual After-Tax Family Income
Top 1%	Top .01%	14,000	$31,000,000
	99.9–99.99% (Next .09%)	135,000	$3,900,000
	99.0–99.9% (Next .90%)	1,350,000	$717,000
Next 9%	90.0–99.0%	13,200,000	$167,000
Bottom 90%	0–90%	132,000,000	$36,000

Note: Based on 2006 U.S. Tax Return data analyzed by Emmanuel Saez (Fessenden & McLean, 2011, Oct. 28)

Discussions on the topic of income inequality, poverty, and distribution of wealth involve questions of measurement as people quite properly ask, "How do we measure that?" Perhaps the most widely known and used measure of income inequality is the Gini index. Also known as the Gini ratio or Gini Coefficient, the index is based (Gini, 1921) upon a relatively simple and straightforward assumption. That is, an equal distribution of income or wealth (or anything else for that matter) is one in which each participant has an equal and proportionate share of the whole. Deviation from that equal distribution reflects some degree of inequality. For example, a nation in which every person (or, every household) enjoyed an equal share of that nation's income (or wealth)

FIGURE 4.6

**Average Annual Household Income in the United States:
2011 Bottom 20 Percent and Top 1 Percent**

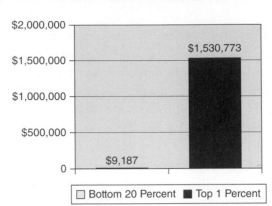

Khimm, S. (2011, Oct. 6). Who are the 1 percent? (updated), *The Washington Post*.

would reflect a Gini index of zero (0). In other words, no person (or household) would reflect any more or any less than anyone else. On the other hand, a Gini index of 1.0 would indicate that the entire nation's income or wealth was possessed by one person or household while the remainder of the population possessed nothing at all. Perfect equality is represented by a zero index or coefficient and the most extreme inequality is represented by 1.

Progress toward greater equality or regress toward greater income inequality can be reflected by changes in the Gini index over time. For example, from 1993 to 2010, the Gini index of United States family household incomes grew from about 0.454 to 0.469. During that time period, the lowest Gini index (the least unequal) occurred in 1995 (0.450) and the highest in 2006 (0.470). The general upward trend, however, reflects gradually increasing inequality (Johnson, 2011, Sep. 15).

Increasing economic inequality, however, is not limited to the United States. During the period from the mid-1980s and the late 2000s, all but five of 22 members[6] of the Organisation for Economic Co-operation and Development (OECD) reflected increasing inequality. Little or no change was evident in France, Hungary, and Belgium; while Turkey and Greece became much more unequal.[7] During the late 2000s, Slovenia, Denmark, Norway, the Czech Republic, the Slovak Republic, Belgium, Finland, and Sweden reflected Gini coefficients of between 0.236 and 0.259. These lower figures indicate that these nations were among the least unequal of 34 OECD countries. Israel, the United States, Turkey, Mexico, and Chile were among the most unequal with Gini coefficients between 0.371 and 0.494. Using the Gini Index, toward the end of the first decade of the 21st century, the United States reflected greater income inequality than all but three of 34 industrialized countries[8] (OECD, 2011).

In addition to the Gini Index, there are other ways to estimate the extent of inequality[9] within or between nations, or according to various factors such as location, education level, family

---

[6] This data set included information from 22 of 34 OECD countries. Data from the other 12 nations were incomplete or unavailable.
[7] Greece and especially Turkey continue to reflect higher than average Gini coefficients when compared to other European nations.
[8] This data set included information from 34 OECD nations.
[9] See, for example, the Theil Index.

size, or other demographic variables. For example, a four-person family living in Spencer, Indiana, and one living in New York City might earn exactly the same income. However, the Hoosier family might live comfortably while the New York family might struggle mightily to house and feed themselves. Similarly, a family in Liberia might manage quite well on an annual income of $2,000 and, compared to the average annual household income of about $330, they might consider themselves extremely well-off.

The concept of "relative poverty" captures the dimension of social context—so important to social workers who adopt a person-in-environment perspective. A common way to determine relative poverty involves calculating how far away a family's annual income is from a nation's (or state or city's) median annual income. In 2010, for example, the median household income in the United States was approximately $50,046 (U.S. Census Bureau, 2012). As you remember from your research or statistics courses, the median is the point at which 50 percent of the population falls above and 50 percent falls below; it is similar but not the same as the mean or average.

If 60 percent of the median annual household income is selected as the relative poverty line in a country (or city or state), then any family household that earns or receives less than that amount would be considered poor—within the context of that locale. Let's use the median household income in the United States in 2010 to illustrate. Sixty percent of $50,046 is about $30,027. Households earning that amount or less would be considered poor—in relative terms. Of course, adjustments can be made for family or household size and geographic location.

Economic mobility is another dimension to consider within the context of poverty and inequality. In general terms, mobility refers to the number or proportion of people in a lower economic category that move to a higher category during a specified period of time. Although people move back and forth from higher to lower and from lower to higher categories, we social workers are primarily interested in upward mobility—especially for those at the lowest levels. That is, we are concerned about people in poverty increasing their annual income and overall security so that they might have more to live on and be less vulnerable to changing socioeconomic circumstances. This aspect of security represents a vital element in social well-being. People who live, literally, paycheck to paycheck, lack the resources necessary to respond to emergencies and sudden changes in social or economic circumstances. Those who have substantial investments, savings accounts, retirement funds, property, and other forms of wealth are in a much better position to survive the inevitable ups and downs of life.

Social workers also focus on generational mobility—that is, the number and proportion of children born to parents in poverty rising to a higher economic status in adulthood. We might ask, "What percentage of children born in poverty escape that poverty?" Although "pulling oneself up by one's bootstraps" or "movin' on up" represents a central motif of the American Dream, the United States reflects less generational mobility than several other highly developed countries such as Canada, Norway, Finland, and Denmark. During the early to mid-2000s in the United States, about 50 percent of "children born to low income parents become low income adults" (Corak, 2006, p. 1).

A single statistic or dimension can never capture the complexity of a large data set or a complex issue such as poverty or inequality. The Gini Index, relative poverty, and mobility indicators are far from perfect measures of income or wealth inequality. Nonetheless, they represent useful attempts to gauge the extent of and, perhaps, progress toward the elimination of poverty and the advancement of some aspects of social and economic justice.

Within the United States, poverty guidelines are used to determine eligibility for various social programs such as Head Start, school breakfast and school lunch programs, legal services, and for securing federal community block grants. For example, the federally sponsored Supplemental Nutrition Assistance Program (SNAP), previously known as food stamps, uses federal poverty guidelines to determine eligibility. In 2012, eligibility was limited to families or households that have a net income no greater than 100 percent of the poverty guideline. Depending upon various other factors, a single-parent with one child who has a net income of about $1,226 per month might have been eligible to receive some food assistance in 2012. The maximum possible allocation was $347 per month in "food stamps" (U.S. Department of Agriculture Food and Nutrition Services, 2012, Apr. 11).

The 2012 U.S. poverty guidelines (U.S. Department of Labor, 2012, Jan. 1) are shown in Table 4.7. If a single female parent with one child earned after-tax income of $15,130, the annual amount suggested by the poverty guideline for 2012, she would have $1,260.83 each month to provide for herself and her child. She might also be eligible for one or more social programs.

Poverty, poverty guidelines, and income inequality are related to the "minimum wage." As it had for the preceding 2 years, the federal minimum wage for 2012 remained at $7.25 per hour. However, each state has a choice about whether or not to establish a minimum wage. For example, in 2012, (1) five states (Alabama, Louisiana, Mississippi, South Carolina, and Tennessee) did not endorse any minimum; (2) four states adopted minimums lower than the federal standard; (3) 17 states had higher levels; and (4) the remaining states accepted the federal wage level as their own (U.S. Department of Labor, 2012, Jan. 1). In 2012, a person who worked 40 hours per week at the federal minimum wage of $7.25 per hour earned a total of $15,080 in pre-tax income over the course of 52 weeks. That's $3,910 more than that year's poverty guideline for a single-person household; $50 less than the guideline for a two-person household; and $7,970 less than that for a family of four.

TABLE 4.7
2012 United States Poverty Guidelines for the 48 Contiguous States and the District of Columbia

Persons in family/ household	Poverty guideline
1	$11,170.00
2	$15,130.00
3	$19,090.00
4	$23,050.00
5	$27,010.00
6	$30,970.00
7	$34,930.00
8	$38,890.00

*For families/households with more than 8 persons, add $3,960 for each additional person.
**Dollar amounts are slightly higher for Hawaii and Alaska.
***The Census Bureau does not use these poverty guidelines to calculate the number of poor people. The Census Bureau uses "poverty thresholds" for that purpose.

U.S. Department of Health and Human Services. (2012). 2012 HHS Poverty Guidelines.

Families with a minimum wage income are likely to remain in poverty even when working full-time, 52 weeks per year. Budgeting for housing, utilities, food, clothing, transportation, costs associated with medical and dental care, and unanticipated expenses on a poverty-level income is incredibly challenging. Under such circumstances, saving for an emergency fund, college, or retirement is virtually impossible.

In the United States, the idea of distributing wealth through governmental action such as minimum wage has traditionally received only modest legislative support. A "maximum wage" (Pizzigati, 1992) or some other limit to the size of individual or family income or wealth has never been seriously considered. In the last several decades, proposals to tax the top income groups at higher rates have not been embraced by a majority of legislators. Investment income has been taxed at considerably lower rates than income earned through individual labor, and sophisticated—but legal—means to defer or avoid taxes have been available to those with sufficient resources to employ tax consultants. In addition, the amount of wealth that may be passed on tax-free to heirs has increased. Despite the fact that most Americans do not inherit money and only a small percentage inherit more than $100,000 (Gokhale & Kotlikoff, 2000, Oct. 1), in 2012 up to $5,120,000 of an estate were not subject to federal inheritance tax. Exemption of $5,120,000 from the "death tax," as inheritance taxes are commonly called, represents a major benefit to the top 1 or 2 percent of households but has little or no relevance to the vast majority of families who have only modest wealth, if any, to pass on to their heirs. If $5,120,000 were taxed at a 35 percent rate, approximately $1,792,000 in federal tax monies would become available, at least potentially, to reduce inequality or fund initiatives for the common good.

Extreme income and wealth inequality within and between nations raise significant questions about distributive justice—much as do high and disproportionate rates of incarceration, and family and childhood poverty. The issue of distributive justice may also arise when allocations of costs, opportunities, and resources vary according to one or more aspects of diversity and difference. Consider, for example, the aspect of gender. The United Nations Development Programme recently introduced a new measure, the Gender Inequality Index (GII). The GII

> reflects women's disadvantage in three dimensions—reproductive health, empowerment and the labour market—for as many countries as data of reasonable quality allow. The index shows the loss in human development due to inequality between female and male achievements in these dimensions. It ranges from 0, which indicates that women and men fare equally, to 1, which indicates that women fare as poorly as possible in all measured dimensions. The health dimension is measured by two indicators: maternal mortality ratio and the adolescent fertility rate. The empowerment dimension is also measured by two indicators: the share of parliamentary seats held by each sex and by secondary and higher education attainment levels. The labour dimension is measured by women's participation in the work force. The Gender Inequality Index is designed to reveal the extent to which national achievements in these aspects of human development are eroded by gender inequality, and to provide empirical foundations for policy analysis and advocacy efforts. (United Nations Human Development Programme, 2011)

In 2011, nations reflecting the lowest GII ratios (lesser gender inequality) included Sweden, Netherlands, Denmark, Switzerland, Finland, Norway, and Germany. The highest GII countries (reflecting greater gender inequality) included Yemen, Chad, Niger, Mali, Congo, and Afghanistan. At that time, the United States ranked 46th among the 146 included nations. Neighbors Canada and Mexico ranked 20th and 79th, respectively (United Nations Human Development Programme, 2011).

Environmental conditions also have significant distributive justice, as well as human rights and well-being, implications. Clean air, access to pure and plentiful water supplies, and the status of the climate represent resources that profoundly affect the quality and duration of human life. Sponsored by the Yale (University) Center for Environmental Law and Policy and the Center for International Earth Science Information Network at Columbia University, the Environmental Performance Index (EPI) is calculated on the basis of 22 snapshot and trend indicators within and across policy categories such as environmental burden of disease, water and water resources, air pollution, biodiversity and habitat, forestry, fisheries, agriculture, and climate change. "These policy categories track performance and progress on two broad policy objectives: Environmental Health and Ecosystem Vitality" (Yale Center for Environmental Law and Policy, 2012, p. 1).

As of 2012, Switzerland, Sweden, Latvia, Norway, Luxembourg, and Costa Rica reflected the most environmentally friendly EPI scores whereas Iraq, Turkmenistan, Uzbekistan, Kazakhstan, and South Africa reflected the least. At that time, the United States ranked 49th[10] of the 132 included nations. Neighbors Canada and Mexico reflected ranks of 37 and 84, respectively, in terms of environmental performance (Yale Center for Environmental Law and Policy, 2012)

Promoting Social Well-Being through Policy Practice

Valuing diversity and difference, and accepting others, are basic to undertaking professional action to advance human rights and social justice, and to eliminate poverty. In our everyday work with individuals, families, groups, organizations, and communities, social workers routinely advocate for the rights of clients, collaboratively pursue social and economic justice for and with them, and seek to promote their social well-being. The social work skills associated with these activities appear in subsequent chapters. However, social workers also recognize that the personal problems, issues, and challenges that clients face frequently relate to social policies, programs, and practices extant in organizations, communities, and societies. Almost all social workers sometimes engage in the analysis, development, and promotion of policies, programs, and practices to help clients address problems and pursue goals. Indeed, Iatridis (2008) states that all social workers "should understand and analyze the effects of social policy decisions on clients. Consequently, they should participate in the formulation and modification of social policy, being active at multiple social policy levels, including the personal, the organizational, the community, and the legislative" (para. 2). We refer to this aspect of social work as policy practice.

Social Well-Being

The concept of social well-being reflects an emphasis on human development—including the realization of potential, quality of life, life satisfaction, and the happiness or contentment of individuals, families, groups, communities, and societies. Diversity, human rights, and social justice relate to and overlap with social well-being. Indeed, we cannot envision how social well-being could emerge unless diversity and difference are valued, human rights respected, and social and economic justice reflected in our social systems. However, quality of life and happiness do not necessarily result from these factors alone. They certainly do not occur as an inevitable consequence of

---

[10] A rank of 1 reflects the most environmentally friendly nation; 132 reflects the least.

the acquisition of wealth or power. Indeed, the United Nations Development Programme (UNDP) recognizes that social well-being is only partly a result of economic security.

In 2011, the UNDP incorporated several related indicators in their Human Development Index (HDI). The HDI is a composite index of three dimensions and four indicators associated with human development. The dimensions include: (1) Health—as indicated or measured by life expectancy at birth; (2) Education—as indicated by expected years of schooling and the average years of schooling; and (3) Living standards—as measured by the gross national income per capita (United Nations Development Programme, 2011a). The Human Development Report (United Nations Development Programme, 2011b) of 2011 indicated that the United States ranked 4th among the 187 included nations on the Human Development Index, neighboring Canada 6th, and Mexico 57th. In 2011, all 10 of the lowest ranked nations were located in Africa.

Social well-being, of course, involves health and longevity, knowledge and education, and decent living standards. However, other, less tangible dimensions are also relevant. For example, quality of life, life satisfaction, subjective well-being, and happiness involve genetic, physiological, psychological, and social aspects. Interest in these interrelated topics has grown enormously—especially within the field of economics—over the past half century. Several scholars and organizations are engaged in ongoing research related to these factors. At this point, there seems to be emerging consensus around several points. For example, it seems clear that genetics and biology play a powerful role in individual and family happiness. Both serotonin and dopamine levels in the brain are associated with experience of subjective well-being (Canli et al., 2005; Ebstein, Novick, Umansky, Priel, & Osher, 1996; Fox, Ridgewell, & Ashwin, 2009). Numerous twin-studies suggest that a great deal of individual happiness is genetically transmitted from one generation to the next (Lykken & Tellegen, 1996; Lyubomirsky, Sheldon, & Schkade, 2005)—perhaps in the form of temperamental characteristics or traits. Indeed, recognition that individual happiness tends to remain moderately stable over time leads to the hypothesis that each person has a kind of a "happiness set-point." Based on their studies (Lyubomirsky, 2006; Lyubomirsky et al., 2005) Lyubomirsky et al. propose a pie chart similar to the one displayed in Figure 4.7.

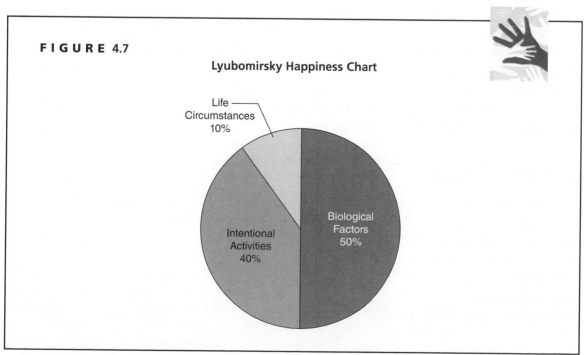

FIGURE 4.7

Lyubomirsky Happiness Chart

Life Circumstances 10%

Intentional Activities 40%

Biological Factors 50%

Adapted from Lyubormirsky's conceptualization.

Lyubomirsky (2006) suggests that about one half of the "differences among people's happiness levels are explained by their immutable genetically-determined set points . . . like genes for intelligence or cholesterol, the set point that a person inherits has a substantial influence on how happy he or she will be" (p. 54). Other research findings, however, raise questions about the strength of the happiness set point notion—for both individuals and populations. Although genetics certainly play a part, it is now clear that many people can and do become substantially happier and remain so on a long-lasting basis (Diener, Lucas, & Scollon, 2006a; Fujita & Diener, 2005; Inglehart, Foa, Peterson, & Welzel, 2008).

According to Lyubomirsky (2006), life circumstances play about a 10 percent role (for example, health, wealth, marriage, death of loved ones, injury and disability, natural and human-made disasters, war, civil conflict). However, she suggests that most people show remarkable resilience and, in time, return to or close to their previous happiness levels. This phenomenon is commonly referred to as the "adaptation theory of well-being" (Brickman & Campbell, 1971). That is, through habituation, people tend to adapt to their circumstances and regain a sense of equilibrium. In addition, people tend to adjust their aspirations to current conditions. For example, following a winnings windfall in a lottery, within a few years many winners, at least those who do not spend everything, adapt to their newfound lifestyle and adjust their aspirations upward—so that the "gap" between what is and what they aspire to (that is, their happiness) remains about the same. Commonly called "keeping up with the Joneses," scholars refer to this as the "hedonic treadmill."

Like the happiness set point, however, the notion of a hedonic treadmill has also been scientifically questioned. It appears that some people, in fact, are able to step off the treadmill and maintain higher levels of life-satisfaction for many years thereafter (Diener et al., 2006a).

The remaining portion of Lyubomirsky's happiness pie involves our intentional activities—that is, how people choose to think and act. According to her, about 40 percent of our happiness, almost as much as the biological factors, results from our cognitions and behavior. This suggests that, like many other facets of life, we can take action to become much happier than the concepts of "happiness set-point" and "hedonic treadmill" would suggest. Indeed, Diener, Lucas, and Scollon (2006b) demonstrate that people can and do influence their own happiness and sense of well-being. Furthermore, it appears that skills associated with optimism and resilience can be taught and learned (American Psychological Association, 2009a).

Despite the relatively large size of the biological and intentional activities portions of Lyubomirsky's proposed happiness pie chart, logic and empirical data suggest that life circumstances—including social and political freedom and economic security—do, after all, play a significant role in the social well-being of both individuals and societies. For example, Inglehart (Inglehart et al., 2008) found that a positive rate of economic development, an increase in per capita gross domestic product (GDP), greater freedom of choice and more opportunities for self-expression, and increasing tolerance toward outgroups were strongly associated with growth in social well-being.

It appears that when societies develop economically, tensions between survival and self-expression values emerge. When a large "share of the population has grown up taking survival for granted . . . [priorities shift] . . . from an overwhelming emphasis on economic and physical security toward an increasing emphasis on subjective well-being, self-expression and quality of life" (Inglehart, 2006, para. 4).

Inglehart and colleagues' findings (Inglehart, 2004, 2006; Inglehart et al., 2008; Inglehart & Welzel, 2005) may help social workers in our efforts to promote social well-being among the individuals, families, groups, organizations, and communities we serve. It seems reasonable to hypothesize, as Abraham Maslow (1943; 1968) did in his "hierarchy of needs," that satisfaction of basic survival needs (that is, physiological, safety, social) generally takes precedence over higher order needs such as self-esteem and self-actualization (see Figure 4.8)[11] or, to use Inglehart and Welzel's terms, self-expression.

If this general thesis of the primacy of survival needs is reasonable, then we can expect higher average levels of subjective well-being among peoples who are economically, politically, and socially secure than among those who lack security in these areas. The evidence generally supports such a thesis. However, even among the developed or rich nations, there is considerable variation in levels of social well-being. For instance, during 2005–2007, the European nations of Germany (especially eastern Germany), France, Spain, and Italy reflected somewhat lesser (but still very positive) levels of social well-being than did the Netherlands, Switzerland, Great Britain, Norway, Finland, or Sweden. By way of contrast, Russia, Ukraine, Serbia, Romania, and Bulgaria reflected much lower levels of social well-being.

Countries in the Western hemisphere generally reported positive social well-being scores during the 2005–2007 period. Indeed, the United States and Canada have consistently reported very positive social well-being for 20 or more years. However, during the mid-2000s, Mexico and Columbia reflected higher scores than their neighbors to the north (Inglehart et al., 2008).

Seligman suggests that "people who are impoverished, depressed, or suicidal care about much more than just the relief of their suffering. These persons care—sometimes desperately—about virtue, about purpose, about integrity, and about meaning" (2002, pp. xi–xii). In addition to satisfaction of survival needs, other factors clearly contribute to life satisfaction, happiness, and social well-being.

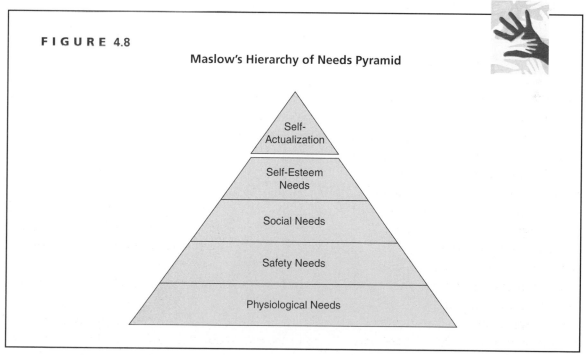

FIGURE 4.8

Maslow's Hierarchy of Needs Pyramid

Self-Actualization

Self-Esteem Needs

Social Needs

Safety Needs

Physiological Needs

Adapted from Maslow's conceptualization.

---

[11] Kenrick et al. (2010) propose a renovation of Maslow's hierarchy of needs in the form of a "Pyramid of Human Motives." Drawing upon knowledge emerging from the fields of evolutionary biology, anthropology, and psychology, their model proceeds hierarchically as follows: Physiological Needs, Self-Protection, Affiliation, Status/Esteem, Mate Acquisition, Mate Retention, and Parenting. Notice the comparatively greater emphasis on the social and relationship aspects of human life and lesser emphasis on the "self." Parenting (teaching, socializing, guiding, mentoring, supporting others) is placed at the highest level of human motives.

A leader in the positive psychology movement, Seligman suggests that happiness involves three different dimensions (see Figure 4.9): (1) a more or less pleasant life that includes considerably more positive than negative emotional experiences, (2) an engaged life in which one becomes challenged by and invested in activities such as work, recreation, and love, and (3) a meaningful life in which one uses her or his assets, talents, and strengths with others in purposeful endeavors that contribute to something greater than oneself. For Seligman, happiness involves much more than pleasurable experience alone. Active engagement and meaningful pursuits contribute as well. Indeed, as Maslow recognized long ago, the power of hedonic pleasure to satisfy and to motivate diminishes over time.

Lyubomirsky et al. (2005) also recognize the limits of hedonism in their proposed architecture of sustainable happiness. They include acts of kindness, generosity, and gratitude among their array of possible intentional activities that contribute to lasting happiness. Seligman (2002) translates Lyubomirsky's conceptual architecture into a human "happiness formula" $H = S + C + V$ where lasting, sustainable happiness (H) results from a combination of our biogenetically set (S) happiness range, life circumstances (C), and intentional or voluntary (V) actions within our control.

Social workers may find the happiness formula useful as we work with individuals, families, groups, organizations, and communities. It may be especially applicable as we engage clients in goal setting and intervention planning, in social and program development activities, and especially in policy practice intended to promote social well-being. In our efforts, however, let's continue to recognize the power of circumstances and situations by maintaining our person-in-environment perspective. Social well-being and individual happiness are more likely among people who are relatively safe from violence, possess some economic security, and live in societies where human rights are highly valued.

Policy Practice

Although the term *policy practice* has been described in various ways, virtually all incorporate the notion of political or community action intended to change the policies or practices of some system. For example, Rocha (2007) defines policy practice "as a change approach that uses advocacy and community practice techniques to change programs and policies at multiple systems levels,

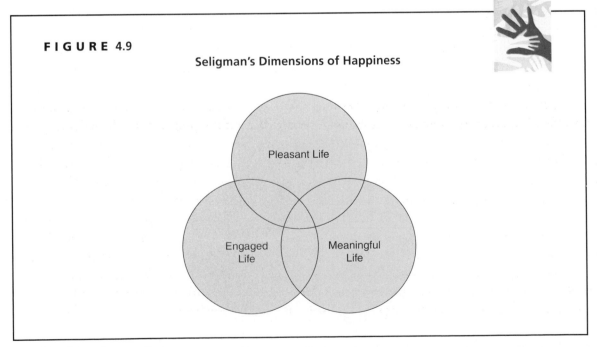

FIGURE 4.9

Seligman's Dimensions of Happiness

Pleasant Life

Engaged Life

Meaningful Life

Adapted from Seligman's conceptualization.

targeted communities, local, state, and federal governments, agencies, bureaucracies, and the courts" (p. 1). In the context of the social work skills, we view policy practice as a natural extension of the advocacy efforts we undertake with and on behalf of individuals, families, groups, and communities. Schneider and Lester (2001) suggest that "social work advocacy is the exclusive and mutual representation of a client(s) or a cause in a forum, attempting to systematically influence decision-making in an unjust or unresponsive system(s)" (p. 64).

Advocacy can involve work on behalf of a particular client (for example, individual, family, group, organization, or community). This is sometimes called case advocacy. In addition, we may advocate with or on behalf of a group of people or a community confronting a similar issue. For example, members of an ethnic minority group may observe that a state or federal program or policy, or local programmatic practice appears discriminatory. This is sometimes called class advocacy, community action, or political or legislative advocacy—depending upon the focus and target of the effort. Finally, we might advocate in pursuit of a particular cause or purpose. For example, we might act to fight discrimination, promote equal access and opportunity, confront injustice, advance human rights and social justice, encourage social development, or enhance social well-being. This form of advocacy may involve aspects of case and class advocacy as well as community and political action, and judicial advocacy; and all are elements of policy practice.

As you might expect, several aspects of professionalism and most of the skills and competencies needed in general social work practice are needed in policy practice as well. As in all social work practice, we must reflect integrity, knowledge, competence, self-understanding, and self-control in our policy practice and advocacy efforts. And, because the demands are so challenging, we need considerable social support to carry on.

Critical thinking, scientific inquiry, and career-long learning are especially significant in policy practice because data collection, aggregation, and analysis are essential, as are review and synthesis of relevant research literature. We often engage groups, organizations, and communities in collaborative advocacy efforts, or encourage them to engage in self-advocacy. Periodically, we analyze current or proposed social policies and programs, develop program plans, or draft policies for possible legislative action. In addition, we often provide expert testimony to legislative committees or in courtroom proceedings.

All of these functions require that we use sophisticated and culturally sensitive talking and listening skills as well as the skills associated with preparing, beginning, exploring, assessing, contracting, working and evaluating, and ending. In policy practice, we often use these skills in work with both clients as well as other individuals, groups, organizations, communities, and with various decision makers (for example, legislators, executives, boards of directors). In addition, we frequently focus as much on policy- and program-relevant documents as we do on the human beings affected by them.

Indeed, the focus on policies involves a double edge. A national or local policy or program may affect hundreds, thousands, or millions of people. If carefully prepared, the benefits may be far-reaching indeed. On the other hand, policies and programs can also produce unintended and unexpected consequences that can be positive for some people and negative for others. Furthermore, unless a policy is determined by direct, universal vote, each individual person in the population affected by that policy is likely to have little and sometimes zero say in its design or implementation.

Suppose, for example, a vocal segment of a community advocated for the enactment of legislation to require all convicted felons, upon completion of their criminal sentence and release from prison and parole, to wear electronic monitoring devices for the remainder of their lives. In certain areas, such legislation could easily become law—over the objections of the former prisoners, their families, and others concerned about the fairness of continuous, lifelong punishment for those who have already completed the terms of their criminal sentence.[12] Members of the general public

---

[12] Such laws might subsequently be overturned by the U.S. Supreme Court.

who are concerned about their personal safety and those who prefer more severe and lengthy punishment for offenders would support its passage. So would people, businesses, and corporations that would benefit economically from such legislation. Companies that manufacture the devices and individuals who would be employed to monitor their electronic activity would certainly lobby for its passage in energetic ways. Indeed, many might well contribute to the reelection campaigns of pro-passage legislators.

Consider another example. Suppose a number of large, well-financed companies in either the U.S. health insurance or the banking industry sought to maintain their large share of the economic market, prevent the introduction of additional competition, and minimize regulatory oversight. Those companies might form associations and employ lobbyists to influence legislators. The associations might prepare and distribute position papers and proposed pieces of legislation. They might advertise widely in the popular media. They might fund academics and researchers to prepare scholarly papers. Employees of the companies might make large donations to legislators' reelection campaigns. Some companies might offer to open branch offices in legislators' districts—if the legislators supported the companies' position. Given their financial resources, their easy access to decision makers, and the effectiveness of their lobbyists, it is quite likely that the health insurance companies or the banks would secure legislative policies they want regardless of the consequences to millions of individuals and families affected by those laws and regulations.

Advocates for social and economic justice engage in some of the same activities as do political lobbyists. Indeed, lobbying and advocating share many common activities—although social work advocates typically have access to fewer funds and resources; and profit motives usually play a smaller part. For example, assume that you are a social worker who works with émigrés seeking asylum and refuge in North America. They are trying to escape the violence and deprivation so common in several parts of the world. The refugees vary in terms of language, religion, ethnic community, culture, dress, and customs. However, they share needs for housing, employment, education, health and mental health care, assistance with immigration processes and procedures, and help with the complexities of making the transition to a different nation and culture. Over the course of more than 10 years, you have assisted and advocated for refugees, usually on a case-by-case basis. At this point, you hope to expand your small program by securing additional funding through private and public sources. You would also like to see changes in state, local, and federal policies and practices to reduce obstacles and facilitate immigration and resettlement of asylum-seeking refugees. In effect, you plan to engage in class advocacy and policy practice with and on behalf of current and future refugees.

In pursuing these goals, you might prepare a policy practice plan that includes the following steps:

1. Based upon your experience with asylum-seeking refugees, prepare a clear statement of the (a) problems facing refugees and (b) the problems with current policies, programs, or practices. Include information about the human impact of current policies and practices as well as their implications in regard to diversity, human rights, social justice, and social well-being. As you draft a problem statement, seek input about the problems with current policies from refugees as well as other service providers.

2. As you continue to refine your problem statement, conduct a scholarly and systematic review of the research literature related to (a) the nature, origin, development, incidence, and extent of the problems refugees confront, (b) the past, present, and potential policies, programs, and practices intended to address those problems, and (c) the positive and negative impact of current policies. Also examine the legislative record associated with the introduction, debate, and passage of current policies. Finally, review state or federal judicial actions and decisions that relate to the problem and the policies.

3. If feasible, complement your review of the research literature and the legislative and judicial records through surveys, focus groups, and other data collection efforts with refugees affected by current policies. Also correspond directly with researchers, policy makers, and policy analysts in the field.

4. Based upon the knowledge gained from the earlier processes, finalize your statement of the problem and generate an array of plausible and, if possible, evidence-based approaches to problem resolution. Typically, this involves preparation of a range of potential changes to current policies, programs, or practices. Sometimes, however, new and innovative proposals are included. Once you generate a list of plausible solutions, seek feedback about the list from refugees, other service providers, and, if possible, researchers and policy makers.

5. In collaboration with refugees and other stakeholders, review the list of proposals. Consider their likely positive and negative effects and implications, anticipate costs and benefits, and estimate potential risks and rewards for both asylum-seeking refugees as well as those likely to be affected by proposed solutions. Identify potential sources of support and opposition. Rank each proposal in terms of (a) likely effectiveness, (b) relative advantages and disadvantages, and (c) probability of adoption and implementation. Choose the optimum proposal.

6. In consultation with refugees and other stakeholders, prepare a specific strategy and plan to secure adoption of the chosen proposal for change (for example, revisions in current policies, programs, or practices or something innovative). Be sure to identify ways to include and involve stakeholders throughout the process. Identify needed resources and relevant stakeholders, formulate short- and long-term goals and associated action steps, establish time frames, and choose means and measures to assess progress and evaluate outcomes.

7. In collaboration with people affected by the problem and other stakeholders, recruit and mobilize supporters, and implement the plans. Anticipate the actions and reactions of opponents and develop plans to counter them. Use contemporary communication technology to coordinate activities and maintain and accelerate momentum. Evaluate progress and make adjustments to the plans based upon assessment data. Continue efforts until your proposal is approved and implemented.

8. Once implemented, evaluate the outcomes of the new or revised policy, program, or practice. Collect and analyze data related to negative as well positive outcomes, and remain alert for unintended favorable and unfavorable consequences. Based upon ongoing assessment and evaluation data, and feedback from consumers and other stakeholders, prepare recommendations for improvements to the now current policy, program, or practice. Develop plans to secure approval of these suggestions.

As you review these eight steps, you may be reminded of other processes that we have explored. Notice the similarities between these steps and the seven stages of practice, the processes included in scientific methodology, the steps in evidence-based practice, and the activities associated with career-long learning. Consider how many aspects of professionalism are involved in these processes. Integrity, knowledge and self-efficacy, critical thinking, scientific inquiry, and lifelong learning are all essential elements of advocacy and policy practice. Recognize the significance of diversity and difference as well as human rights and social and economic justice for the promotion of social well-being through policy practice. Finally, remember that your advocacy work takes time and energy. You, personally, need substantial social and emotional support to maintain your motivation and continue your professional efforts as an advocate for those with little power and limited resources in a social and economic environment that is always challenging and often hostile.

Summary

In this chapter, we explored the following dimensions of professionalism: (1) valuing diversity and difference, (2) advancing human rights and social justice, and (3) promoting social well-being through policy practice. These aspects complement those addressed in earlier chapters. Indeed, all three dimensions incorporate elements of integrity, knowledge and self-efficacy, self-understanding and self-control, social support, critical thinking, scientific inquiry, and career-long learning.

Genuine acceptance of others, including respect for autonomy and self-determination are especially vital when engaging diversity and difference, advancing human rights and social justice, and seeking to eliminate poverty. Policy practice and other forms of class advocacy have the potential to benefit large numbers of people but can also involve risks associated with limited participation by members of the population and by unintended consequences.

CHAPTER 4: SUMMARY EXERCISE

Following completion of this chapter, respond to these summary exercises:

1. Go to Appendix 9 and complete the Acceptance of Others Scale. When you have completed the scale and calculated the results, record your score in Table 4. 8. Consider the implications of your responses by reflecting on the following questions: (a) What do your responses suggest about your current ability to accept others? (b) Why might acceptance of others be especially important for social workers during the 21st century? (c) What steps might you take to become more accepting of others? (d) What steps might you take to become more accepting of yourself?

   You might choose to word-process a few summary notations about your reflective responses to these questions. They might come in handy for a later exercise.

TABLE 4.8
Acceptance of Others Scale Score

Date	Acceptance of Others Scale Score

© Cengage Learning 2014

2. Reflect upon the information about rates of incarceration, human poverty, income and wealth distribution, gender inequality, environmental performance, and social well-being discussed in this chapter. Use a word-processing program to make note of those facts that most surprise, shock, or disturb your views about human rights and social justice. Also, consider how concern for individual human rights and for social and economic justice sometimes conflict. Finally, use the space below to generate two hypotheses about

the roles that culture (including ethnic heritage and religious beliefs) sometimes play in relation to both human rights and social justice.

3. Access the Internet and use a search engine to locate and download descriptions of (a) the 30 human rights included within the United Nations Universal Declaration of Human Rights; and (b) the Bill of Rights and other amendments to the U.S. Constitution. Use the space below to highlight the major differences between the two sets.

4. Go to Appendix 10 and complete the Satisfaction with Life Scale (SWLS). Calculate your score and refer to the guidelines to understand its meaning. Record your

score in Table 4.9. Then, reflect upon your responses to the items as they relate to your own social well-being. Consider how your own well-being might relate to your performance as a social worker. Use the space provided to outline, how you might approach your social work roles during those times when you reflect a strong sense of social well-being; and how you might do so when your sense of well-being is weak or fragile. Also, identify a few things could you do to improve your social well-being and maintain that improvement for an extended period of time.

T A B L E 4.9
Satisfaction with Life Scale Score

Date	SWLS Score

5. Access the Internet and use a search engine to locate the main portal for the Federal Statistics of the United States (http://fedstats.gov). Once there, search for and locate the most recent current population report on the topic: "Income, Poverty, and Health Insurance Coverage in the United States." Scan the report and examine some of the tables and graphs. Use a word-processing program to record the complete citation of the report and to make note of those findings you find most interesting or perhaps disturbing.

6. Access the Internet and use a search engine to locate the most recent National Scorecard on U.S. Health System Performance as published by the Commonwealth Fund (www.comonwealthfund.org). As you review the report, be sure to click on any interactive Web features that summarize the rating criteria and the rankings. Once you have read and understood the report, use a word-processing program to: (a) offer one

or two plausible reasons that the U.S. system ranks where it does; and (b) propose at least one policy action that might lead to improvements in the overall quality of the U.S. health care system.

7. Suppose you are a social worker who knows that increasing the percentage of mothers who breastfeed could save the lives of millions of children (U.S. Department of Health and Human Services' Office on Women's Health & General Services Administration's Federal Citizen Information Center, 2012). Currently, slightly fewer than 35 percent of infants worldwide "are exclusively breastfed for the first 6 months of life, the majority receiving some other food or fluid in the early months . . . infants who are not breastfed are 6 to 10 times more likely to die in the first few months than infants who are breastfed" (World Health Organization, 2009, p. 4). Breastfeeding provides children with all the nutrients needed to grow and develop and protects children from diarrhea and respiratory and other infections. "If every baby were exclusively breastfed from birth for 6 months, an estimated 1.5 million lives would be saved each year. Not just saved but enhanced, because breast milk is the perfect food for a baby's first six months of life—no manufactured product can equal it" (UNICEF, 2009, Why Breastfeed? section, para. 1).

   Using word-processing software, record one or two elements of a policy or program that might lead to an increase in the number and percentage of young mothers who breastfeed in your local community.

8. Reflect on and integrate the results of this chapter's content and the preceding learning exercises through a brief discussion of the implications of valuing diversity and difference, accepting others and respecting autonomy, advancing human rights and social justice, and promoting social well-being through policy practice. As part of the discussion, explore how and why so many well-intentioned people tolerate, justify, and sometimes even celebrate extreme levels of social and economic inequality in their communities and throughout the world. Prepare your document in the form of a two- to three-page word-processed report (500–750 words) titled "Implications of Valuing Diversity and Difference, Accepting Others and Respecting Autonomy, Advancing Human Rights and Social Justice, and Promoting Social Well-Being through Policy Practice." When you have finished, include the report in your Social Work Skills Learning Portfolio.

As you finish this chapter, please reflect on your learning by completing the following self-appraisal exercise.

SELF-APPRAISAL: VALUING DIVERSITY; ADVANCING HUMAN RIGHTS AND SOCIAL JUSTICE; AND PROMOTING SOCIAL WELL-BEING THROUGH POLICY PRACTICE

Please respond to the following items. Your answers should help you assess your proficiency in the skills associated with engaging diversity and accepting others; advancing human rights and social justice; and promoting social well-being through policy practice. Read each statement carefully. Then, use the following 4-point rating scale to indicate the degree to which you agree or disagree with each statement. Record your numerical response in the space provided.

4 = Strongly agree   2 = Disagree

3 = Agree   1 = Strongly disagree

4	3	2	1	Rating Statement
				At this point in time, I can
☐	☐	☐	☐	1. Value diversity and difference in service to others.
☐	☐	☐	☐	2. Accept others and respect their autonomy.
☐	☐	☐	☐	3. Discuss the characteristics of human rights and concepts associated with social and economic justice.
☐	☐	☐	☐	4. Engage in activities to advance human rights and social and economic justice.
☐	☐	☐	☐	5. Discuss concepts and factors associated with social and economic well-being.
☐	☐	☐	☐	6. Engage in policy practice to promote social and economic well-being.
☐	☐	☐	☐	7. Assess proficiency in the knowledge and skills associated with valuing diversity and difference, advancing human rights and social and economic justice, and engaging in policy practice to promote social and economic well-being.
				Subtotal

Note: These items are identical to those contained in the Valuing Diversity, Advancing Human Rights and Social Justice, and Promoting Social Well-Being through Policy Practice Skills section of the Social Work Skills Self-Appraisal Questionnaire presented in Appendix 3. If you completed that self-appraisal before beginning Chapter 1, you have already responded to these items once before. You may now compare the responses you made on that occasion with those you made this time. Also, compare the two subtotals. If you believe that you have progressed in terms of your proficiency, the more recent subtotal should be higher than the earlier one.

ETHICAL DECISION MAKING

The topic of laws, values, and ethics in social work practice is extraordinarily complex. As social workers, our professional values pervade all aspects of our working lives. In some way, each decision we make and every action we take involve legal and ethical considerations. As a result, ethical decision making is a crucial aspect of professionalism in social work practice.

In this chapter, we conclude the exploration of professionalism with the topic of ethical decision making (see Box 5.1). You complete several learning exercises and, as the final element in social work professionalism, integrate them with those completed earlier in the form of an overall assessment of your current readiness for the profession of social work.

Social workers routinely consider the legal, ethical, and sometimes moral implications of professional situations and reach ethical decisions concerning our responsibilities. We confront complex ethical dilemmas daily as we attempt to serve others, advance human rights, and promote social and economic justice. To address these challenging issues, we need a thorough understanding of social work values and ethics (Reamer, 1997, 1998) and those legal obligations that affect and inform our work. Such understanding involves a great deal more than familiarity with legal statutes, case law, and ethical codes. We require a solid grasp of the underlying values. You should know your social work code of ethics and be able to identify the legal and ethical principles that apply in specific situations. When principles conflict, you need the capacity to address and resolve the dilemma. Specifically, you must think critically to determine which ethical principles or legal obligations should take precedence over others in situations where several competing responsibilities apply.[1]

---

[1] The National Association of Social Workers (NASW) Code of Ethics may also be found at http://www.socialworkers .org. Publications about social work ethics from an international perspective may be obtained through the International Federation of Social Workers (IFSW) at http://www.ifsw.org. Information about the Code of Ethics of the Canadian Association of Social Workers (CASW) may be found at http://www.casw-acts.ca. The Code of Ethics for Social Work of the British Association of Social Workers may be accessed at http://www.basw.co.uk and those of the Australian Association of Social Workers at http://www.aasw.asn.au.

BOX 5.1
Chapter Purpose

The purpose of this chapter is to contribute to growth in professionalism by helping learners gain the knowledge, appreciate the values, and implement the skills necessary for ethical decision making within the context of contemporary social work practice. Integration of the topics addressed in Part 1 (Chapters 1–5) occurs through completion of an overall assessment of readiness for the profession of social work.

Goals

Following completion of this chapter, learners should be able to:

◆ Discuss the purposes and functions of ethical decision making.
◆ Identify and discuss the legal duties that apply to helping professionals.
◆ Access the laws that regulate the practice of social work in your locale.
◆ Identify and discuss the fundamental values of the social work profession.
◆ Discuss the ethical principles and standards that guide social work practice.
◆ Identify the relevant legal duties and ethical principles that might apply in various professional contexts and situations.
◆ Analyze and determine the relative priority of competing legal and ethical obligations through the development and use of a case-specific values hierarchy.
◆ Use critical thinking skills to reach ethical decisions and plan appropriate action.
◆ Assess proficiency in the ethical decision-making skills.
◆ Assess your readiness for the profession of social work.

Core EPAS Competencies

The skills addressed in this chapter support the following core EPAS competencies:

◆ Identify as a professional social worker and conduct oneself accordingly (EP2.1.1).
◆ Apply social work ethical principles to guide professional practice (EP2.1.2).
◆ Apply critical thinking to inform and communicate professional judgments (EP2.1.3).
◆ Respond to contexts that shape practice (EP2.1.9).

In our service to clients, social workers use information from a variety of sources: theoretical knowledge, knowledge from research studies, wisdom gained from life experience and service to clients, the expertise of colleagues and supervisors, and agency policies and procedures. One source of information, however, serves as a screen for all others. The values, ethics, and obligations of the profession are preeminent. We must consider every aspect of practice, every decision, every assessment, every intervention, and virtually every action we undertake as social workers from the perspective of our professional ethics and obligations. This dimension supersedes all others. Ethical responsibilities take precedence over theoretical knowledge, research findings, practice wisdom, agency policies, and, of course, our own personal values, preferences, and beliefs. Ethical decision making is a central component of professionalism and should be included along with other dimensions addressed in earlier chapters. This chapter focuses exclusively on this topic by providing you with opportunities to develop proficiency in the ethical decision-making skills (see Box 5.1).

Service as a professional social worker entails considerable personal sacrifice, enormous intellectual effort, and extraordinary self-discipline. Because we affect, for better or worse, the lives of our clients, we bear a substantial burden of personal and professional responsibility. Numerous obligations derive from our commitment to a professional code of ethics and the laws that regulate the practice of social work in our locales. In carrying out our responsibilities, we routinely confront complex ethical issues. To be effective and professionally responsible, we must be able to identify, address, analyze, and resolve ethical issues and dilemmas.

Ethical decision making involves consideration of several dimensions and, of course, a great deal of careful thought. First, recognize those legal duties that apply to all professional helpers. Second, maintain familiarity with state, local, and federal laws and regulations that affect the profession and practice of social work in your locale. Third, thoroughly comprehend the core social work values and have ready access to the social work code of ethics. Fourth, identify those ethical principles and legal duties that pertain to specific social work practice situations. Fifth, when several competing obligations apply, decide which take precedence. Adopt a decision-making approach that reflects a logical and coherent thinking process that includes reference to relevant laws, regulations, and ethics. Sixth, maintain professional-quality records about your ethical decision-making processes and, of course, other aspects of your service to clients. In your records, include a description of and a rationale for actions taken on a legal or ethical basis. Seventh, implement your ethical decision. On occasion, you may decide to take action and, sometimes, you conclude that the most ethical course is to take no action. Eighth, monitor and evaluate the effects and outcomes of your decision and the actions you take. Include the results in your records and, if necessary, revise your action plans and take additional steps as needed.

All of the processes involved in ethical decision making are demanding. However, addressing competing legal and ethical duties represents the greatest challenge of all and requires the most advanced critical thinking skills. Unless there is a conflict among the ethical and legal responsibilities relevant to a particular situation, you should easily be able to make a decision and take appropriate action. You merely conform to the appropriate legal and ethical obligations. In other words, you simply "do the right thing." Unfortunately, the relevant principles and duties may sometimes conflict with one another so that adherence to one obligation involves violation of another. Deciding what to do in such circumstances involves judgment of the highest order.

Understanding Our Legal Obligations

Along with counselors, nurses, psychiatrists, and psychologists, social workers are members of the professional helping community. As a helping professional, you are subject to certain legally determined obligations or duties. These derive from common law, legislation, regulations, and various court decisions. Some legal obligations coincide with the responsibilities suggested by social work values and the code of ethics; others do not. You are responsible for understanding both the legal duties applicable to all professional helpers, and those obligations that apply specifically to social workers. In particular, you need information about the laws and regulations that govern the profession and practice of social work in your locale. In the United States, all 50 states, the District of Columbia, Puerto Rico, and the U.S. Virgin Islands have enacted laws regulating social work. Obtain a copy of the licensing law and accompanying regulations that apply to you. Many are available through the Internet. For example, Title 25 Article 23.6 of the Indiana State Code governs the licensure and practice of social work in the state (Indiana General Assembly, 2012). You may find that article of law by searching the State of Indiana government website. The Association of Social Work Boards (Association of Social Work Boards, 2012) website also contains links to statutes and regulations throughout the United States and to the Canadian provinces of Alberta, British Columbia, Ontario, and Saskatchewan.

Despite the plethora of laws and regulations, the legal duties of professional helpers are not always clear. They are certainly not permanent. Various professional and governmental bodies regularly promulgate new and modify old policies. Courts process thousands of cases each year. Many are precedent setting and lead to regulatory changes. As new laws and policies emerge, they influence the legal duties of professional helpers, including social workers. Obviously, you are subject to these evolving legal responsibilities.

Consider, for example, the topic of malpractice. Malpractice is defined as "a form of negligence that occurs when a practitioner acts in a manner inconsistent with the profession's standard of care—the way an ordinary, reasonable, and prudent professional would act under the same or similar circumstances" (Reamer, 1994, p. 9). Malpractice is

> willful or negligent behavior by a professional person that violates the relevant code of ethics and professional standards of care and that proves harmful to the client. Among a social worker's actions most likely to result in malpractice are inappropriately divulging confidential information, unnecessarily prolonged services, improper termination of needed services, misrepresentation of one's knowledge or skills, providing social work treatment as a replacement for needed medical treatment, the provision of information to others that is libelous or that results in improper incarceration, financial exploitation of the client, sexual activity with a client, and physical injury to the client that may occur in the course of certain treatments (such as group encounters). (Barker, 2003, p. 259)

In legal terms, malpractice, or *mal praxis,* by professional social workers is a form of tort. A tort involves wrongdoing for which damages may be sought through legal action. A person or group may file a lawsuit in civil court because of injury or suffering resulting from the "wrongful actions or inactions" (Saltzman & Proch, 1990, p. 412) of the professional person. The plaintiff, often a client or a member of a client's family, typically seeks monetary damages to compensate for injuries or suffering. Occasionally, courts impose additional damages to punish the professional person guilty of malpractice.

Malpractice involves poor or substandard professional service that results in harm. Failure to meet an accepted standard of care and damage to a client are the two usual criteria on which malpractice cases are determined. There are three common forms of malpractice: (1) malfeasance—where the professional intentionally engages in a practice known to be harmful, (2) misfeasance—where the professional makes a mistake in the application of an acceptable practice, and (3) nonfeasance—where the professional fails to apply a standard, acceptable practice when the circumstances warrant such practice. The first form of malpractice involves intent to harm, or malice, and may constitute criminal behavior, whereas the other two entail negligence or carelessness. The first two forms of malpractice consist of acts of commission and the third involves acts of omission (Kitchener, 2000; Reamer, 1995b).

Malpractice lawsuits may be filed against helping professionals for a wide range of behaviors. For example, in California, following treatment by a psychiatrist and a family therapist, a woman accused her father of childhood sexual abuse. Based on his daughter's allegations that he had molested her when she was a child, the man was fired from his high-paying job and his wife divorced him. Since the time of the allegations, both his daughter and his former spouse refused to have contact with him (Ewing & McCann, 2006; Johnston, 1997).

The man initiated a malpractice lawsuit against the helping professionals. The court concluded that the helping professionals involved had acted improperly by suggesting that the client's emerging recollections of previously repressed memories were necessarily true and valid. In this case, the court did not assert that the daughter's memories were false—only that the validity of the retrieved memories could not be determined because the helping professionals' words and actions were leading and suggestive. The client, in this case, did not originally remember experiences of childhood abuse. Rather, the memories emerged following the words and actions of the professionals who, in effect, suggested to the client that she had probably been the victim of sexual abuse during childhood. The court awarded the accused father several hundred thousand dollars as compensation for the damage caused by the helping professionals' malpractice (Ewing & McCann, 2006; Johnston, 1997).

The topic of repressed, recovered, and false memories has become extraordinarily controversial in recent years—both in and out of courtrooms. Research studies suggest that human memories are quite unlike audio or video recordings. Rather, "memories are records of people's experiences of events and are not a record of the events themselves" (The British Psychological Society, 2008, p. 2). The poor reliability of eyewitness testimony in criminal justice proceedings highlights this phenomenon. Indeed, as initially reported by Borchard (1932) and confirmed by numerous studies since then, "the most common cause of wrongful convictions is eyewitness misidentification" (Gross, Jacoby, Matheson, Montgomery, & Patil, 2004, p. 18). In their study of the U.S. criminal justice system, Gross et al. found that 64 percent of those wrongfully convicted but subsequently exonerated involved mistaken eyewitness identification of the defendant.

Several researchers have demonstrated that false memories can easily be produced—at least within the context of experimental research (Brainerd & Reyna, 2005; Lindsay, Hagen, Read, Wade, & Garry, 2004; Loftus, 1997, 2003). Indeed, the creation of memories that make narrative and contextual sense could well be a human trait that serves many useful functions:

> Remembering is an active, inferential process guided by a person's general knowledge and intuitions about the world and by cues in the present environment. When you hear a story or experience an event, your mind encodes into long-term memory only some parts of the available information. Later, when you try to recount the story or event, you retrieve the encoded fragments and fill in the gaps through your logic and knowledge, which tell you what must have happened even if you can't quite remember it. With repeated, retelling, it becomes harder to distinguish what was present in the original encoding from what was added later. Thus, memory of the story or experience is not a simple readout of the original information but a construction built and rebuilt from various sources. Our ability to construct the past is adaptive because it allows us to make logical and useful sense of our incompletely encoded experiences. But the process can also lead to distortions. (Gray, 2007, p. 329)

Helping professionals can reduce, but not entirely eliminate, their role in promoting and reinforcing inaccurate recollections by avoiding leading questions, suggestive comments, and speculative interpretations about past events. Recognizing that child abuse remains a major social problem and the possibility that traumatic experiences might be forgotten or "repressed," the associations of social work, psychology, and psychiatry have nonetheless published cautionary statements about professionals' approach to the recovery of childhood memories (Alpert et al., 1996; American Psychiatric Association, 2000b; National Association of Social Workers, 1998, June; The British Psychological Society, 2008). These are intended to protect clients from unnecessary pain and suffering, and manage the risk of legal action against their professional membership. During the 1990s, a large number of malpractice lawsuits were filed against practitioners who facilitated "recovery of repressed memories" (Wakefield & Underwager, 1992).

The precise number of lawsuits filed against social workers is difficult to determine. Different authorities (Besharov & Besharov, 1987; Reamer, 1994) provide estimates that range from a few hundred to several thousand. Reamer (1995b) reviewed the malpractice claims against social workers covered by the National Association of Social Workers (NASW) Insurance Trust from 1969 through 1990. He found that "only 1 claim was filed in 1970; 40 claims, however, were filed in 1980, and 126 claims were filed in 1990" (p. 596). In total, some 634 claims were filed during that 20-year period. This represents a relatively small number of the more than 70,000 NASW members insured through the trust (NASW Assurance Services, 2012). However, the rate and frequency of claims against social workers have increased as the years passed and undoubtedly will continue to grow in the future. Of course, should a lawsuit ever be filed against you, it would not necessarily mean that you have, in fact, engaged in malpractice. Some lawsuits are unwarranted, harassing, and even frivolous. You could be the best social worker in the country and still be sued. Nothing you do can guarantee immunity from legal action. However, if someone does sue you, the best defense is undoubtedly ethical, competent, and well-documented service solidly grounded in current practice-related research (Bogie & Coleman, 2002).

Although the increasing frequency of litigation against helping professionals is cause for concern, do not become unduly frightened. The probability of a lawsuit, especially for social workers, remains quite low. Social work is a personally and professionally satisfying career. The litigious nature of contemporary life, however, underscores the importance of understanding the current legal milieu as well as those duties that apply to all social workers and other helping professionals.

Several categorical themes emerge from reviews of lawsuits filed against social workers and other helping professionals (Besharov & Besharov, 1987; Corey, Corey, & Callanan, 2003; Kitchener, 2000; Myers, 1992; Reamer, 1995b; Saltzman & Proch, 1990; VandeCreek & Knapp, 1993). In sum, litigation may result from the following kinds of professional misbehavior:

◆ *Treatment without consent.* A client may allege that professional treatment procedures were undertaken without informed consent; the parents of a minor child may assert that their child was treated without their awareness or consent.

◆ *Professional incompetence, incorrect treatment, or failure to treat.* A client may assert that a social worker did not provide competent professional services, as indicated by the use of inappropriate, inadequate, or unconventional assessment procedures or interventions, or by the failure to provide service when needed.

◆ *Failure to diagnose or incorrect diagnosis or assessment.* A client may assert that a social worker failed to recognize signs of a problem or disorder, assigned an incorrect diagnosis, or formulated an erroneous assessment.

◆ *Failure to report suspected abuse or neglect.* A client, a client's family, or a state agency may assert that a social worker who had information of possible child endangerment failed to report suspicions that a child was being abused or neglected.

◆ *Reporting suspected abuse or neglect.* A client or a client's family may assert that a social worker who reported to state authorities suspicions that a child was being abused or neglected did so without adequate evidence and, as a result, caused severe and irreparable damage to the affected parties.

◆ *Failure to consult or refer to other professionals or specialists.* A client or client's family may allege that a social worker should have consulted a medical doctor when it became apparent that the problems and symptoms revealed by the client suggested the real possibility of a medical condition.

◆ *Failure to prevent a client's suicide.* The family of a client who committed suicide may assert that a social worker knew or should have known that the client was suicidal yet failed to take action necessary to protect the client from his or her own suicidal impulses.

◆ *Causing a client's suicide.* The family of a client who committed suicide may allege that a social worker's words or actions provoked the client to take his or her own life.

- *Failure to warn or protect third parties.* A person injured by a client may assert that a social worker knew or should have known that the client was potentially dangerous and intended to harm the person in question yet failed to take action to notify the targeted individual and protect her or him from the client's violent actions.
- *Inappropriate release of a client.* A client or a client's family may allege that the social worker and other professionals were negligent in permitting a client to leave a facility while the client was in a state of acute distress or incapacity.
- *False imprisonment or arrest.* A client may claim that his or her commitment to a facility, such as a psychiatric institution or drug treatment center, or police arrest constituted wrongful detention or incarceration.
- *Failure to provide adequate care or supervision for a client in residential settings.* A client or a client's family may assert that the client was injured because of the neglectful and inadequate care provided by a social worker and other staff members in a hospital or other facility.
- *Assault or battery.* A client may allege that a social worker was threatening or engaged in improper or inappropriate physical contact.
- *Intentional infliction of emotional distress.* A client may assert that a social worker's actions, such as a counseling procedure or perhaps the removal of a child from the home of a biological parent, so traumatized the client as to cause significant mental or emotional distress.
- *Sexual impropriety.* A client may allege that a social worker used professional authority and expertise for the purposes of sexual seduction and exploitation.
- *Breach of confidentiality.* A client may allege that a social worker inappropriately communicated confidential information to an unauthorized party.
- *Breach of contract, poor results, or failure to cure.* A client may believe that a social worker indicated that his or her marriage would be saved through the process of relationship counseling—in effect, providing a guarantee; because the marriage ended in divorce, the client may assert that the social worker did not fulfill the terms of the agreement.
- *Invasion of privacy.* A client may assert that a child abuse investigation was overreaching or harassing in nature.
- *Defamation of character, libel, or slander.* A client may believe that a social worker, orally or in writing, made an untrue and derogatory statement that harmed the client's reputation.
- *Violation of a client's civil rights.* A client in a residential facility may allege that his or her civil rights were violated when personal property was confiscated by a social worker.
- *Failure to be available when needed.* A client may assert that a social worker was inaccessible or unavailable when he or she was in urgent need of service.
- *Inappropriate termination of treatment or abandonment.* A client may allege that a social worker concluded treatment abruptly or unprofessionally.
- *Malicious prosecution or abuse of process.* A client may allege that a legal action initiated by a social worker, for instance in a child-protection case, was undertaken with full knowledge that the case would be dismissed by the court and therefore was maliciously intended.
- *Inappropriate bill collection methods.* A client may assert that the social worker used invasive and improper means in an attempt to collect on bills that were outstanding.
- *Statutory violations.* A social worker might be sued for violating requirements of the state law under which social workers are legally certified or licensed.
- *Inadequately protecting a child.* A client, the client's family, or a state agency may assert that a child was injured because of the neglectful and inadequate care provided by a social worker.

- *Violating parental rights.* The parents of a child may assert that their rights were violated by a social worker who provided professional services to their child without their informed consent.
- *Inadequate foster care services.* A client, the biological parents of a child, or a state agency may assert that a social worker placed a child in a foster-care setting that provided inadequate or injurious care.

In a review of 634 malpractice claims filed against social workers covered for liability through the NASW Insurance Trust, Reamer (1995b) found examples of malfeasance and misfeasance that included

> flawed treatment of a client (incorrect treatment), sexual impropriety, breach of confidentiality or privacy, improper referral to another service provider, defamation of a client's character (as a result of slander or libel), breach of contract for services, violations of a client's civil rights, improper civil commitment of a client (false imprisonment or arrest), wrongful removal of a child from a home (loss of child custody), assault and battery, improper termination of service (abandonment), improper licensing of staff, and improper peer review. (p. 596)

Examples of nonfeasance included "failure to diagnose properly, failure to protect third parties from harm, failure to treat a client successfully (failure to cure or poor results) or at all, and failure to refer a client for consultation or treatment" (p. 596). The most common allegations involved incorrect treatment (18.6 percent), sexual impropriety (18.45 percent), breaches of confidentiality or privacy (8.68 percent), failure to assess or diagnose or misdiagnosis (5.21 percent), and client suicide (4.42 percent). Although several of these allegations lacked substance, their array and distribution are revealing.

Certain forms of practice and certain settings constitute a greater risk for litigation against social workers. For example, because child welfare work often involves the provision of involuntary services, there is a greater likelihood of both civil and criminal legal action against social workers employed in such settings. As alluded to earlier, practice that involves the exploration or "recovery" of "repressed memories" has led to numerous malpractice lawsuits. Some of these resulted in multimillion-dollar judgments against the helping professionals involved. In June 1996, the National Association of Social Workers issued a Practice Update urging that "social workers who practice in the area of recovered memories should be mindful that this is a high-risk area of practice in an environment of intense controversy" (Summary section, para.1).

Although most malpractice litigation occurs in civil court, social workers may occasionally be subject to criminal action related to the nature and extent of their professional services.

> In Colorado, for example, a caseworker and her supervisor were criminally prosecuted when a child with whom the caseworker was working was killed by her parents. The parents had been reported to the worker as abusive but the worker had chosen to keep the child in the home. The worker and her supervisor were convicted. (Saltzman & Proch, 1990, p. 428)

In the Colorado case, an appellate court later overturned the criminal convictions on technical grounds. Nonetheless, the case illustrates the enormous responsibilities associated with professional social work practice, as well as the litigious nature of contemporary society.

Carefully review the laws and regulations that affect the practice of social work in your locale and those that may relate to your service areas. Laws related to child abuse and neglect, elder abuse, domestic violence, civil rights, sexual harassment, psychological testing, psychotherapy and counseling, child custody, marriage and divorce, and adoption probably pertain in some way to most social workers. Social workers in the United States should be familiar with the Americans with Disabilities Act (ADA) of 1990, Public Law 101-336 (U.S. Department of Justice, 2009); Child Abuse Prevention and Treatment Act (CAPTA), Public Law 93-247, and the Keeping Children and Families Safe Act of 2003, Public Law 108-36 (U.S. Department of Justice, 2009); the Health Insurance Portability and Accountability Act of 1996 (HIPAA), Public Law 104-191, and the Patient Safety and Quality Improvement Act of 2005 (PSQIA), Public Law 104-41 (U.S. Department of Health and Human Services, 2009); the Standards for Privacy of Individually Identifiable Health Information: the "Privacy Rule" (U.S. Department of Health and Human Services, 2001); the federal confidentiality regulations (CFR, Part 2) regarding the privacy rights of people receiving alcohol or drug abuse (substance abuse) treatment services (U.S. Department of Health and Human Services, 2005); the Family Educational Rights and Privacy Act (FERPA) of 1974 (U.S. Department of Education National Center for Education Statistics, 1997, 1998); and other laws and regulations that directly affect social workers and their service to others. Undoubtedly, as time passes, there will be changes in the nature and extent of the legal responsibilities that apply to social workers, but the general legal duties or obligations presented in Box 5.2 and discussed below are likely to remain in effect for many years to come (Everstine & Everstine, 1983, pp. 227–251).

Legal duties tend to parallel those human rights and obligations that are highly valued by a society. In the United States, many fundamental rights are evident in the Constitution, the Bill of Rights and other amendments, and in decisions of the federal courts. As we explored in Chapter 4, the Universal Declaration of Human Rights (General Assembly of the United Nations, 1948) describes the protections afforded, in theory at least, to all people in all countries throughout the world. Article 1 of the declaration begins with the phrase, "All human beings are born free and equal in dignity and rights." Most legal duties that pertain to helping professionals' obligations involve aspects of one or more fundamental human rights.

Duty of Care

As a professional social worker, you are legally obligated to provide a reasonable standard of care in delivering social work services. Clients have a right to expect that you will discharge your professional responsibilities in a competent manner. There is an implied contract to that effect. Services provided should meet at least an adequate standard of care—as determined in part by the social work profession and in part by common expectations of helping professionals. Social workers

BOX 5.2
Legal Obligations of Helping Professionals

- Duty of Care
- Duty to Respect Privacy
- Duty to Maintain Confidentiality
- Duty to Inform
- Duty to Report
- Duty to Warn and Protect

provide services to a diverse clientele in a wide range of settings. As a result, social workers must reflect competence not only in the fundamentals of social work practice but also in helping clients address specific problems and goals. Indeed, all social workers must be able to access, critically review, and incorporate into their service results from scientific research that relate to the people we serve and the problems we help them address. In addition, we also must engage our clients in the systematic evaluation of progress toward goals. For example, social workers who work with families addressing child abuse and neglect issues must be competent in both social work and child welfare practice, and engage in routine evaluation of client safety as well as goal attainment. Those who serve diverse population groups must reflect cultural sensitivity as well. Social workers attempting to help Buddhist immigrants from Laos must know a good deal about Laotian culture, Buddhist beliefs, and, of course, the problems and processes associated with transitions into a new society. Social workers who engage in policy practice and advocacy must know a great deal about policy and program design, development, and implementation; about the outcomes or likely outcomes of current or proposed policies and programs; about political processes and decision making; about the social issue or problem for which the policies and programs refer; and, of course, about the people affected or potentially affected by those current or proposed policies and programs. Obviously, as professionals, social workers must know a great deal about a lot of things, and we must be able to quickly and efficiently learn a great deal more.

In terms of duty of care expectations, the NASW publishes standards of social work practice in, for example, school social work services, health care settings, clinical social work, child welfare, palliative and end of life care, and long-term care facilities as well as work with adolescents, family caregivers of older adults, and clients with substance use problems. Other standards include those related to genetics, technology and social work practice, continuing education, and cultural competence (National Association of Social Workers, 2012a). The Association also prepares policy statements and other publications intended to inform and guide social workers in their professional service (National Association of Social Workers, 2012b).

Spurred on by demands for increased accountability and higher expectations, social work educators have begun to publish textbooks that emphasize a scientific foundation (Bronson & Davis, 2012; Drisko & Grady, 2012; Egan, 2010b; Evans & Hardy, 2010; Fortune, McCallion, & Briar-Lawson, 2010; Glisson, Dulmus, & Sowers, 2012; Grinnell, 2011; Grinnell, Gabor, Unrau, & Gabor, 2010; Kelly, 2010; Markward & Yegidis, 2011; Mathews & Crawford, 2011; Palinkas & Soydan, 2012; Pollio & Macgowan, 2011; Rzepnicki, McCracken, & Briggs, 2012; Sands & Gellis, 2012; Wodarski & Hopson, 2012). Recognizing that an evidence-based perspective includes systematic evaluative feedback from clients as well as findings from high-quality research studies, contemporary social workers are familiar with assessments, services, and interventions that reflect strong theoretical and empirical support.

Professional, governmental, and nongovernmental organizations have begun to publish practice guidelines based on comprehensive reviews and systematic analyses of the relevant research literature. For example, the United States Department of Health and Human Services' Agency for Healthcare Research and Quality sponsors the National Guideline Clearinghouse—a public resource for evidence-based clinical practice guidelines (2012). Although focused on health and mental health care, some guidelines relate to topics of direct interest to many social workers (see, for example, guidelines that involve "abuse," "homeless," or "suicide"). The Substance Abuse and Mental Health Services Administration (SAMHSA) also provides open access to a wealth of information of use to both professionals and the general public. In addition to publications about patient rights, cultural competence, ethics and values, health disparities, prejudice and discrimination, program evaluation, protection and advocacy, and service coordination among many others, SAMHSA also publishes numerous practice guidelines (2012b).

The National Registry of Evidence-based Programs and Practices (NREPP), also sponsored by SAMHSA, includes more than 240 interventions that reflect evidence of practice or program effectiveness. We hope the social work profession follows suit by approving and publishing social work practice guidelines based on systematic reviews and comprehensive analyses of research-based evidence.

If your social work activities are congruent with generally accepted theories and empirical research, and current practice guidelines, you probably meet the reasonable standard of care expectation. Unusual interventions, activities, or procedures that do not have a sound professional rationale and credible evidence to support their safety and effectiveness could place you at increased risk of liability. Social workers who reflect genuine competency in their professional work and maintain records that document their activities and their outcomes typically exceed the reasonable standard of care.

Several additional responsibilities may be included under the general duty of care. For example, as a professional social worker you must be available and accessible to the clients you serve. Clients should be educated about whom to contact and what to do in case of an emergency. Similarly, before going on vacation, you should inform clients well in advance and arrange for equivalent, substitute professional coverage. You must also take action to ensure the physical protection of clients you determine to be (1) imminently dangerous to other persons, (2) imminently dangerous to themselves, or (3) so gravely disabled as to be unable to provide minimal self-care (Everstine & Everstine, 1983, p. 232). You might have to arrange for the supervision or hospitalization of such clients.

Professional record keeping also relates to the "standard of care" obligation. Complete, accurate, timely documentation of the nature, scope, provision, cost, progress, and outcomes of your service serves as evidence of reasonable professional behavior. At a minimum, you should include information concerning the identity of the people you serve, relevant consent forms, dates and kinds of services, assessments and plans, reports of meetings and service-related activities, evaluation of progress toward goals, and closing summaries. Of course, records are primarily for the client in that they help you, the social worker, remember relevant information and maintain your focus on agreed-upon goals for work. If you were to become ill or injured, or die unexpectedly, your records could aid in maintaining service continuity (Kagle & Kopels, 2008).

Record keeping suggests at least a modicum of professionalism. They may also support the quality of your professional service. Accurate, complete, descriptive records are your single most important defense in the event of a malpractice lawsuit. Professional records that are absent, notations that are sparse, and those that appear altered after the fact can serve as evidence of inadequate care or perhaps even fraudulent behavior.

Duty to Respect Privacy

As a professional social worker, you have a duty to respect the privacy of people you serve. Under most circumstances, you are not entitled to intrude on the privacy of prospective or current clients. Privacy includes an individual's physical space (home or residence, locker, automobile, wallet or purse, or clothing), as well as those aspects of personal life that constitute a symbolic region (Everstine et al., 1980), which is that person's alone to share or reveal as he or she sees fit. Consider, for example, the case of a penniless traveler who seeks your professional help in locating transportation to her home in a neighboring state. If you were to ask her for information about her sexual history—a topic clearly unrelated to the issue of concern—you would probably violate her right to privacy.

Similarly, suppose you hold strong religious beliefs. Your personal faith provides much needed spiritual support and comfort in your daily life. However, you serve as a social worker in a public child and family welfare agency. If you were to proselytize your religious beliefs with clients, you would violate their privacy. In a sense, this would be similar to a telemarketer who calls your home or a door-to-door salesperson who, uninvited, tries to sell you a product. You have not requested the information but you get it anyway. Social workers must have sound professional reason for entry into these private physical or symbolic regions.

Although a right to privacy is more implicit than explicit in the U.S. Constitution, it has grown in significance both inside and outside the helping professions (Etzioni, 1999; McWhirter & Bible, 1992). Article 12 of the Universal Declaration of Human Rights indicates that "no one shall be subjected to arbitrary interference with his privacy, family, home or correspondence, nor to attacks upon his honor and reputation. Everyone has the right to the protection of the law against such interference or attacks" (General Assembly of the United Nations, 1948). As rights to privacy have evolved, so have the threats to them. Technological advances in the form of video and audio recording and other sensing devices; the explosion in computer software and hardware technology; cell phones, tablets, netbooks, laptops, desktops, and the GPS devices housed within them; the Internet; and, of course, developments in DNA, urine, and blood testing increasingly endanger privacy.

However, respect for privacy rights is not universal—even among helping professionals and consumers. For example, agencies and organizations now commonly place cameras in waiting areas, hallways, or parking areas. Governments, police, and security agencies record telephone conversations, and observe and record human activity with drone and satellite-based video cameras. Client records are stored on computers linked to the Internet, in electronic "clouds," or on computers that have WiFi connections. Some school systems monitor and sometimes videotape classroom activity, and many search students' school lockers—often without their direct consent. Especially in some substance abuse programs, individuals may be body searched and drug testing via blood or urine samples may be required as a condition for the receipt of service. Police may stop people on the street and search them for weapons or demand that they display identification papers. Dogs may be used to "sniff" out drugs or explosive materials. Media reporters and television or movie producers may be interested in the stories of clients and perhaps in your services to them. Educators may seek to audiotape or videotape worker–client interviews or to use clients' stories in books or other publications. Even when clients sign releases, they may not fully understand or appreciate the implications of the widespread publicity that may follow such publication. These actions and circumstances risk the privacy rights of clients and possibly their friends, neighbors, and family members as well.

Duty to Maintain Confidentiality

Professional social workers have a duty to maintain the confidentiality of information clients convey to them. Derived from the right to privacy, this obligation applies, in general, to all helping professionals. The laws that certify or license social workers require that information shared by clients remain confidential. Indeed, some laws use the term *privileged communication* in describing this legal obligation. "Confidentiality refers to the professional norm that information shared by or pertaining to clients will not be shared with third parties. Privilege refers to the disclosure of confidential information in court proceedings" (Reamer, 1994, p. 47). When laws specify that your communications with clients are privileged, you must meet an even higher standard of confidentiality. When clients' information is privileged, it becomes much more formidable, even for a judge, to force you to reveal confidential information without your clients' consent.

In 1996, the U.S. Supreme Court in *Jaffee v. Redmond* specifically upheld a U.S. Court of Appeals decision extending privilege for confidential client communications to licensed social workers during the course of psychotherapy. Redmond, a police officer, received psychotherapeutic counseling from a licensed social worker. Following an on-duty shooting death, the plaintiffs' lawyers attempted to subpoena the social worker's case records. The social worker and Redmond, the client, refused to provide the requested information. Based partly on that refusal, the court awarded damages to the plaintiffs. The Court of Appeals overturned that decision and the U.S. Supreme Court upheld the reversal. This decision is notable. It reinforces the doctrine of privilege for psychotherapy clients and specifically includes licensed social workers with psychiatrists and psychologists as professionals who might provide such services in a privileged context.

The advent of computerized record keeping, organizational networks, management information systems, agency, governmental, and insurance company databases, the Internet, and managed care systems has seriously complicated the confidentiality issue. Advances in computer and communications technology may have contributed to increased productivity and efficiency, and perhaps even to improvements in the quality of social services. However, as information about clients becomes increasingly easy to access, use, and share, it becomes more difficult to safeguard client records. Despite these complicated challenges, the basic duty remains intact. Indeed, in some areas the responsibilities of professionals to protect client privacy and confidentiality have increased.

The U.S. Health Insurance Privacy Protection Act (HIPPA) and the associated Standards for Privacy of Individually Identifiable Health Information (the Privacy Rule) reflect the importance society increasingly places on the confidentiality of health information.

> A major goal of the Privacy Rule is to assure that individuals' health information is properly protected while allowing the flow of health information needed to provide and promote high quality health care and to protect the public's health and well-being. The Rule strikes a balance that permits important uses of information, while protecting the privacy of people who seek care and healing. (Office for Civil Rights, 2003, p. 1)

All individually identifiable health information is protected under the Privacy Rule. Data such as names, addresses, telephone numbers, Social Security numbers, dates of birth or death, diagnoses, treatments, bank information, and any other information that could identify individual persons are considered confidential and must be protected.

"Individually identifiable health information" is information, including demographic data, that relates to "the individual's past, present or future physical or mental health or condition . . . the provision of health care to the individual . . . (and) . . . the past, present, or future payment for the provision of health care to the individual, and that identifies the individual or for which there is a reasonable basis to believe can be used to identify the individual" (Office for Civil Rights, 2003, p. 4).

In general, material shared by clients is their property not the social worker's. It is not yours or your sponsoring organization or agency, even though you record it in a case record. You are merely using the knowledge to serve clients. It does not become your property simply because you have heard and recorded it. Under most circumstances, clients must give informed consent before you may share information with another person or organization. Even when clients provide informed consent, you should carefully consider the nature, form, and extent of information to provide. Suppose, for example, a client is relocating across the country and requests that you forward a copy of her or his records to another social worker who will provide continuing services. If the case record contains information that is no longer accurate, comments about third parties, or other irrelevant information, you might inform the client that you would like to exclude such references from the records before sending them. Although it might represent more work for you, a summary of services rather than a duplicate set of the case records may provide more protection for the client and could actually be more useful to the new social worker.

Duty to Inform

As a professional social worker, you are obligated to educate clients and prospective clients concerning the nature and extent of the services you and your agency offer. Under HIPPA, you must also inform clients about privacy practices. In addition, helping professionals should address matters such as cost, length of treatment, risks, probability of success, and alternate services that may be appropriate. This is where knowledge of evidence-based practice, best practices, practice guidelines, and community resources are needed. You should also provide information concerning relevant policies and laws that could affect clients during the provision of social services. For example, early in the process, you should notify clients about your legal obligation to report indications of possible child abuse and neglect and certain other crimes (for instance, elder abuse or, in some locations, spousal abuse). You should also inform clients that, should a person's life be at risk, you intend to take action to protect that person, even if it means violating confidentiality.

Full disclosure to clients about these limitations and conditions represent a fundamental part of fair and due process. At times, it may also relate to individuals' rights regarding self-incrimination. If you recall from the Fifth Amendment of the U.S. Constitution, people cannot be compelled to testify against themselves. This provision is derived from the common law principle, *Nemo tenetur seipsum accusare* (that is, No one is obligated to accuse him or herself). This principle is reflected in the requirement that police officers must provide *Miranda* warnings to suspects (*Miranda v. Arizona*, 1966). Certainly, meetings with social workers are usually not equivalent to police arrests, interrogations, or courtroom proceedings. Nonetheless, clients have a right to know that, under some circumstances, you might share information that could, in effect, become incriminating evidence in some subsequent civil or criminal litigation.

Typically, you should also give clients information about your qualifications, fields of expertise, and, when relevant, areas about which you have limited knowledge or experience. Similarly, clients should be informed about any actions you might take that pertain to their care—such as consultation with a nationally renowned expert or the provision of information to an insurance company. Of course, you should inform clients well in advance before you discontinue services or transfer them to another helping professional.

Several fundamental human rights including due process, equal protection, privacy, and dignity support the duty to inform. This informed understanding between a social worker and a client constitutes an aspect of the agreement through which the client, in effect, employs the social worker to provide professional services within the context of a fiduciary relationship (Kutchins, 1991, 1998). "Fiduciary relationships emanate from the trust that clients must place in professionals. . . . The professional's obligations are far greater than those of a commercial vendor" (Kutchins, 1991, p. 106). Indeed, within the context of these special relationships, clients have a right to provide informed consent (O'Neill, 1998).

Informed consent involves the following dimensions: (1) *Disclosure:* Relevant information must be fully and clearly provided to the client by the helping professional; (2) *Capacity:* The client must be competent or capable of understanding, rationally evaluating, and anticipating implications and potential consequences of decisions and actions; and (3) *Voluntariness:* The client must have genuinely free choice to accept or reject proposed activities—direct or indirect coercion or intimidation confounds such freedom. If one or more of these aspects are absent or diminished, then clients cannot be considered to have provided fully informed consent (Koocher & Keith-Spiegel, 1990; Meyer & Weaver, 2006).

When you purchase services from an automobile mechanic or a house painter, you have certain rights. For example, you have a right to honest answers to questions you ask. In general, however, it is your responsibility to learn as much as you can before you buy. *Caveat emptor*—let the buyer beware—is a major principle. The mechanic or painter is not required to provide additional information or consider what might be in your best interest. Helping professionals, however, assume added responsibilities because of the vulnerability of clients and the potential for their exploitation. Therefore, social workers have an "affirmative obligation to disclose more information than is requested" (Kutchins, 1991, p. 106) to ensure that clients are fully aware of aspects of the services that they might not have asked about or even considered.

Duty to Report

Professional social workers have a legal obligation to report to designated governmental authorities indications of certain "outrages against humanity" (Everstine & Everstine, 1983, p. 240; Meyer & Weaver, 2006). Although the specific procedures for reporting may vary somewhat from place to place, as a social worker you must report suspicion of certain criminal behavior, including "child abuse, child neglect, child molestation, and incest" (Everstine & Everstine, 1983, p. 240). Increasingly, governmental bodies enact laws to expand the kinds of behavior that must be reported. These include abuse, neglect, and exploitation of persons who are elderly, physically or mentally challenged, or developmentally disabled.

The duty to report relates to several fundamental human rights. Article 1 of the Universal Declaration of Human Rights holds that "all human beings are born free and equal in dignity and rights." Article 3 declares that "everyone has the right to life, liberty and security of person." Article 4 states that "no one shall be held in slavery or servitude." Article 5 holds that "no one shall be subjected to torture or to cruel, inhuman or degrading treatment or punishment" (General Assembly of the United Nations, 1948).

The duty to report is perhaps most obvious in the case of child abuse and neglect. Within the United States, all states require that helping professionals report instances of suspected child abuse or neglect to governmental authorities. Along with medical doctors, psychologists, nurses, and teachers, social workers are typically included among the group of "mandated reporters" specifically mentioned in legislation. Mandated reporters who fail to notify authorities of suspected abuse may be subject to severe legal penalties.

Duty to Warn and Protect

Social workers also bear some responsibility to warn potential victims and take action to protect people a client might harm. This duty, derived from the same human rights that warrant reporting crimes against humanity, means that helping professionals should sometimes safeguard the lives of others who might be in danger. Of course, accurate prediction of future dangerousness is hardly a science. Despite the risk of false positives (concluding that someone is dangerous when he or she actually is not), public safety sometimes outweighs the rights of clients (VandeCreek & Knapp, 2001; Woody, 1997). The famous *Tarasoff v. Regents of the University of California* decision established that helping professionals are obligated to take some action to protect the lives of third parties (Kagle & Kopels, 1994). Suppose, for example, that during an interview, a client with a history of violence toward others reveals a specific intention to kill his former spouse. You ask additional questions and you conclude that the client indeed poses a clear and present danger to his ex-wife. Under such circumstances, you would (1) try to arrange for protective supervision of the client—perhaps, for example, through temporary hospitalization, (2) warn the intended victim of the threat, and (3) notify legal authorities of the danger. Of course, because such actions violate some aspects of the client's right to confidentiality and perhaps to privacy, you should clearly document why you have taken this course of action. In such instances, you would be wise to quote the client's words, cite his gestures, and provide related evidence to support your conclusion that the client is potentially dangerous to another person. Also, document when and how you notified the relevant parties and whom you contacted.

The duty to warn or the duty to protect others is similar but not equivalent to the duty to report. For example, legal statutes require social workers to report suspicions of child abuse. Indications of present or past child abuse are sufficient to warrant a report—which usually involves the identification of the alleged victim and/or alleged perpetrator if known. The social worker does not need to know that child abuse actually occurred to submit a report. Suspicion alone is sufficient, and social workers who report in good faith are typically immune from liability. In the case of potential violence toward others, however, suspicion alone is insufficient (*United States v. Hayes*, 2000). The social worker must have reasonable evidence to conclude that the client poses a real and significant threat of violence toward another (Recent cases, 2001). In such cases, social workers are not immune from liability, as is typical in cases involving reports of suspected child abuse. Therefore social workers must exercise due professional care in reaching decisions about clients' dangerousness and in carrying out their obligation to warn and protect.

Understanding the Fundamental Values and Ethics of Social Work

In addition to the legal obligations that apply to all helping professionals, social workers must also conform to the fundamental values and ethics of the social work profession. Social workers and social work educators have energetically discussed the topic of social work values since the emergence of the profession during the late 19th century. The discussion will undoubtedly continue throughout the 21st century, especially as the world becomes increasingly interconnected and interdependent through globalization and internationalization.

In discussing values, the International Federation of Social Workers (2000) states,

> Social work grew out of humanitarian and democratic ideals, and its values are based on respect for the equality, worth, and dignity of all people. Since its beginnings over a century ago, social work practice has focused on meeting human needs and developing human potential. Human rights and social justice serve as the motivation and justification for social work action. In solidarity with those who are disadvantaged, the profession strives to alleviate poverty and to liberate vulnerable and oppressed people in order to promote social inclusion. Social work values are embodied in the profession's national and international codes of ethics. (Values section, para. 1)

Although there is some divergence of opinion regarding the application of fundamental social work values, there is considerable consensus about the values themselves. For example, the National Association of Social Workers (2008) identifies the core values for social work in the Preamble to its Code of Ethics:

> The mission of the social work profession is rooted in a set of core values. These core values, embraced by social workers throughout the profession's history, are the foundation of social work's unique purpose and perspective:

◆ Service
◆ Social Justice

- Dignity and Worth of the Person
- Importance of Human Relationships
- Integrity
- Competence

This constellation of core values reflects what is unique to the social work profession. Core values, and the principles that flow from them, must be balanced within the context and complexity of the human experience. (Preamble section, paras. 3–4)

The Council on Social Work Education (CSWE, 2008) endorses the six core values identified in the NASW Code of Ethics and adds two more (p. 2):

- Human Rights
- Scientific Inquiry

These eight fundamental social work values (see Figure 5.1) serve as an extremely useful foundation for thinking critically about practice issues and ethical dilemmas. They are invaluable in helping social workers define a professional identity and establish a social work frame of reference. Abstract concepts, however, are not usually specific enough to guide ethical decision making. Codes of ethics serve that function. Ethical principles and standards derive from the fundamental

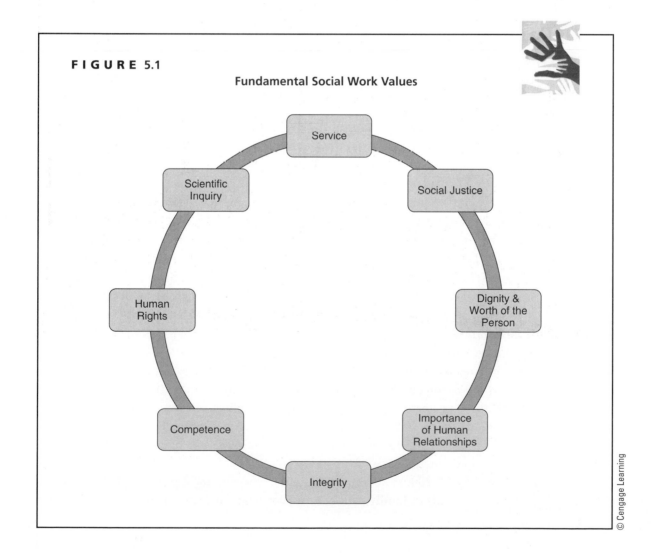

FIGURE 5.1

Fundamental Social Work Values

Service

Scientific Inquiry

Social Justice

Human Rights

Dignity & Worth of the Person

Competence

Importance of Human Relationships

Integrity

© Cengage Learning

social work values, but appear in more concrete and prescriptive form. Reference to a social work code of ethics should help you make practice decisions that are congruent with fundamental social work values.

To practice ethically, you need a thorough understanding of both the fundamental social work values and the principles and standards that guide ethical decision making. As suggested earlier, the Code of Ethics of the National Association of Social Workers (2008) serves as the primary reference throughout the United States. The preamble of the NASW code suggests that:

> The primary mission of the social work profession is to enhance human well-being and help meet the basic human needs of all people, with particular attention to the needs and empowerment of people who are vulnerable, oppressed, and living in poverty. A historic and defining feature of social work is the profession's focus on individual well-being in a social context and the well-being of society. Fundamental to social work is attention to the environmental forces that create, contribute to, and address problems in living.
>
> Social workers promote social justice and social change with and on behalf of clients. "Clients" is used inclusively to refer to individuals, families, groups, organizations, and communities. Social workers are sensitive to cultural and ethnic diversity and strive to end discrimination, oppression, poverty, and other forms of social injustice. These activities may be in the form of direct practice, community organizing, supervision, consultation, administration, advocacy, social and political action, policy development and implementation, education, and research and evaluation. Social workers seek to enhance the capacity of people to address their own needs. Social workers also seek to promote the responsiveness of organizations, communities, and other social institutions to individuals' needs and social problems. (2008, Preamble section, paras. 1–2)

To practice ethically, you should be thoroughly familiar with the Social Work Code of Ethics. Carry a copy with you during your professional activities. You will frequently need to refer to it throughout the course of your service with and for clients.

Violations of the code may serve as grounds for malpractice lawsuits or grievances filed with social work licensing boards or professional associations. The *NASW Procedures for Professional Review* (National Association of Social Workers, 2005) contains detailed descriptions concerning the processes by which complaints are submitted and adjudicated.

In studies of 894 of 901 claims of ethical misconduct by NASW members from 1986 to 1997, Strom-Gottfried (1999, 2000a, 2000b, 2003) identified some 66 categories of professional misbehavior and then organized them into 10 clusters. Among the cases with adjudicated findings, boundary violations were the most common form of misconduct (about 55 percent). Most of those involved sexual misconduct and many reflected dual relationships. Poor practice, such as failure to employ standard interventions or misapplication of professional standards and principles, was the second most common area of misconduct (about 38 percent). Incompetence caused by ignorance or inadequate supervision or impairment, inadequate record keeping, dishonesty or fraud, failure to maintain confidentiality or protect privacy, failure to describe policies necessary for clients to provide informed consent, improper behavior with colleagues, problems related to billing and reimbursement, and conflicts of interest between the worker and one or more clients constituted other forms of professional misconduct.

Strom-Gottfried (1999, 2000a, 2000b, 2003) found that about 52 percent of the misconduct claims were filed by clients or family members of clients, about 19.5 percent by employees or supervisees, about 10.4 percent by coworkers or colleagues, and about 4.5 percent by supervisors or employers. Slightly less than half of the complaints reached the hearing stage, although more than 60 percent of those that did resulted in findings of ethical violations against the respondents.

Strom-Gottfried (1999, 2003) found that the most common ethical violations included the following:

1. Sexual activity
2. Dual relationship
3. Other boundary violations
4. Failure to seek supervision or consultation
5. Failure to use accepted practice skills
6. Fraudulent behavior
7. Premature termination
8. Inadequate provisions for case transfer or referral
9. Failure to maintain adequate records or reports
10. Failure to discuss policies as part of informed consent

Identifying Ethical and Legal Implications

In addition to understanding the legal duties of professional helpers and the social work code of ethics, a social worker must identify those obligations, principles, and standards that might apply in a given practice situation. This requires critical thinking skills as you consider the facts in a specific situation and determine which ethical principles and legal obligations may be relevant. For example, imagine that you are a social worker in an agency that provides crisis intervention services. One day, while catching up on paperwork, a former client whom you had served some 8 months earlier telephones to say, "I have locked myself in my basement. I have a gun, and I am going to shoot myself today. I wanted to let you know that you did not help me at all! Goodbye."

In addition to managing the various emotions you would undoubtedly experience, you would also have to consider several values, ethical principles, and standards, as well as various legal obligations. The values, ethical principles, and standards described in the NASW Code of Ethics (2008) shown in Boxes 5.3–5.5 probably apply.

BOX 5.3
NASW Code of Ethics: Applicable Values

◆ Value: *Service*; Ethical Principle: Social workers' primary goal is to help people in need and to address social problems.
◆ Value: *Dignity and Worth of the Person*; Ethical Principle: Social workers respect the inherent dignity and worth of the person.
◆ Value: *Integrity*; Ethical Principle: Social workers behave in a trustworthy manner.
◆ Value: *Competence*; Ethical Principle: Social workers practice within their areas of competence and develop and enhance their professional expertise. (National Association of Social Workers, 2008)

BOX 5.4

NASW Code of Ethics: Applicable Ethical Principles

◆ Social workers' primary responsibility is to promote the well-being of clients. In general, clients' interests are primary. However, social workers' responsibility to the larger society or specific legal obligations may on limited occasions supersede the loyalty owed clients, and clients should be so advised. (Examples include when a social worker is required by law to report that a client has abused a child or has threatened to harm self or others.) (Section 1.01)

◆ Social workers respect and promote the right of clients to self-determination and assist clients in their efforts to identify and clarify their goals. Social workers may limit clients' right to self-determination when, in the social workers' professional judgment, clients' actions or potential actions pose a serious, foreseeable, and imminent risk to themselves or others. (Section 1.02)

◆ In instances when clients lack the capacity to provide informed consent, social workers should protect clients' interests by seeking permission from an appropriate third party, informing clients consistent with the clients' level of understanding. In such instances, social workers should seek to ensure that the third party acts in a manner consistent with clients' wishes and interests. Social workers should take reasonable steps to enhance such clients' ability to give informed consent. (Section 1.03.c)

◆ In instances when clients are receiving services involuntarily, social workers should provide information about the nature and extent of services and about the extent of clients' right to refuse service. (Section 1.03.d)

◆ Social workers may disclose confidential information when appropriate with valid consent from a client or a person legally authorized to consent on behalf of a client. (Section 10.7.b)

◆ Social workers should protect the confidentiality of all information obtained in the course of professional service, except for compelling professional reasons. The general expectation that social workers will keep information confidential does not apply when disclosure is necessary to prevent serious, foreseeable, and imminent harm to a client or other identifiable person. In all instances, social workers should disclose the least amount of confidential information necessary to achieve the desired purpose; only information that is directly relevant to the purpose for which the disclosure is made should be revealed. (Section 10.7.c)

◆ Social workers should inform clients, to the extent possible, about the disclosure of confidential information and the potential consequences, when feasible before the disclosure is made. This applies whether social workers disclose confidential information on the basis of a legal requirement or client consent. (Section 10.7.d)

◆ Social workers should discuss with clients and other interested parties the nature of confidentiality and limitations of clients' right to confidentiality. Social workers should review with clients circumstances where confidential information may be requested and where disclosure of confidential information may be legally required. This discussion should occur as soon as possible in the social worker–client relationship and as needed throughout the course of the relationship. (Section 10.7.e)

◆ Social workers should not disclose confidential information to third-party payers unless clients have authorized such disclosure. (Section 10.7.h)

(continued)

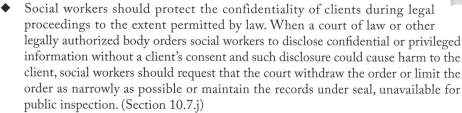

BOX 5.4 *(continued)*

♦ Social workers should protect the confidentiality of clients during legal proceedings to the extent permitted by law. When a court of law or other legally authorized body orders social workers to disclose confidential or privileged information without a client's consent and such disclosure could cause harm to the client, social workers should request that the court withdraw the order or limit the order as narrowly as possible or maintain the records under seal, unavailable for public inspection. (Section 10.7.j)

♦ When social workers act on behalf of clients who lack the capacity to make informed decisions, social workers should take reasonable steps to safeguard the interests and rights of those clients. (Section 11.4)

♦ Social workers should terminate services to clients and professional relationships with them when such services and relationships are no longer required or no longer serve the clients' needs or interests. (Section 11.6.a)

♦ Social workers should take reasonable steps to avoid abandoning clients who are still in need of services. Social workers should withdraw services precipitously only under unusual circumstances, giving careful consideration to all factors in the situation and taking care to minimize possible adverse effects. Social workers should assist in making appropriate arrangements for continuation of services when necessary. (Section 11.6.b)

♦ Social workers should seek the advice and counsel of colleagues whenever such consultation is in the best interests of clients. (Section 2.05.a)

♦ Social workers should keep themselves informed about colleagues' areas of expertise and competencies. Social workers should seek consultation only from colleagues who have demonstrated knowledge, expertise, and competence related to the subject of the consultation. (Section 2.05.b)

♦ When consulting with colleagues about clients, social workers should disclose the least amount of information necessary to achieve the purposes of the consultation. (Section 2.05.c)

♦ Social workers should refer clients to other professionals when the other professionals' specialized knowledge or expertise is needed to serve clients fully or when social workers believe that they are not being effective or making reasonable progress with clients and that additional service is required. (Section 2.06.a)

♦ Social workers who refer clients to other professionals should take appropriate steps to facilitate an orderly transfer of responsibility. Social workers who refer clients to other professionals should disclose, with clients' consent, all pertinent information to the new service providers. (Section 2.06.b)

♦ Social workers should take reasonable steps to ensure that documentation in records is accurate and reflects the services provided. (Section 3.04.a)

♦ Social workers should include sufficient and timely documentation in records to facilitate the delivery of services and to ensure continuity of services provided to clients in the future. (Section 3.04.b)

♦ Social workers' documentation should protect clients' privacy to the extent that is possible and appropriate and should include only information that is directly relevant to the delivery of services. (Section 3.04.c)

♦ Social workers should store records following the termination of services to ensure reasonable future access. Records should be maintained for the number of years required by state statutes or relevant contracts. (Section 3.04.d)

(continued)

BOX 5.4 *(continued)*

◆ When an individual who is receiving services from another agency or colleague contacts a social worker for services, the social worker should carefully consider the client's needs before agreeing to provide services. To minimize possible confusion and conflict, social workers should discuss with potential clients the nature of the clients' current relationship with other service providers and the implications, including possible benefits or risks, of entering into a relationship with a new service provider. (Section 3.06.a)

◆ If a new client has been served by another agency or colleague, social workers should discuss with the client whether consultation with the previous service provider is in the client's best interest. (Section 3.06.b)

◆ Social workers should accept responsibility or employment only on the basis of existing competence or the intention to acquire the necessary competence. (Section 4.01.a)

◆ Social workers should strive to become and remain proficient in professional practice and the performance of professional functions. Social workers should critically examine and keep current with emerging knowledge relevant to social work. Social workers should routinely review the professional literature and participate in continuing education relevant to social work practice and social work ethics. (Section 4.01.b)

◆ Social workers should base practice on recognized knowledge, including empirically based knowledge, relevant to social work and social work ethics. (Section 4.01.c)

◆ Social workers should not participate in, condone, or be associated with dishonesty, fraud, or deception. (Section 4.04)

◆ Social workers should critically examine and keep current with emerging knowledge relevant to social work and fully use evaluation and research evidence in their professional practice. (Section 5.02.c)

BOX 5.5
Applicable Legal Obligations

The legal obligations that deserve consideration in this situation are the:

◆ *Duty of Care* (including the responsibility to try to prevent suicidal action)
◆ *Duty to Inform*
◆ *Duty of Confidentiality*
◆ *Duty to Respect Privacy*

Even though this is, nominally, a former client who expresses anger toward you, social work ethics suggest that you should maintain your professional role and continue to provide high-quality service. His best interest continues to be your primary obligation. Because the client expresses disappointment in you and may not respond to your attempts to contact him, you should probably seek advice and consultation from your supervisor, colleagues, or other professionals competent in crisis intervention and suicide prevention. You should also try to respect the client's civil and legal rights. You should maintain the confidentiality of information that he reveals, or share such information with others only for compelling reasons, such as when he threatens to harm himself or someone else. These last three principles apply if or when you consider contacting the caller's family members, a medical doctor, an ambulance service, paramedics, or the police in your determined efforts to protect his life.

As a professional social worker, you should attempt to prevent the client from taking his life. This is consistent with the legal duty of care under which you are obligated to be available, to try to prevent suicidal action, to avoid causing suicidal action, and to ensure the physical protection of clients who are dangerous to themselves. You also have a duty to inform the client concerning actions you intend to take. Finally, you have a legal as well as an ethical duty to maintain confidentiality and respect the client's right to privacy.

When you consider the relevance of these various ethical principles, standards, and legal obligations, it becomes clear that you cannot possibly meet all of them. If you attempt to serve the client with devotion and meet your legal duty to try to prevent his suicide by telephoning family members, a physician, or the police, you violate his right to confidentiality and, potentially, his privacy. His right to privacy would obviously be lost at the point that police or emergency medical personnel enter his home. If you maintain his right to confidentiality and privacy, you neglect your legal duty to attempt to prevent his suicide. This is indeed an ethical dilemma. How do you decide what to do?

Addressing Ethical Dilemmas

Several authors have suggested sequential steps for the process of ethical decision making (Dolgoff, Loewenberg, & Harrington, 2009; Mattison, 2000; Reamer, 1995a; Rhodes, 1986, 1998) or ethical problem solving (Reamer & Conrad, 1995). Congress (1999, 2000), for example, encourages social workers to adopt the ETHIC Model of Decision Making and proceed through the following steps or processes:

E—Examine relevant personal, societal, agency, client, and professional values.

T—Think about what ethical standard of the NASW code of ethics applies, as well as relevant laws and case decisions.

H—Hypothesize about possible consequences of different decisions.

I—Identify who will benefit and who will be harmed in view of social work's commitment to the most vulnerable.

C—Consult with supervisor and colleagues about the most ethical choice. (Congress, 2000, p. 10)

Reamer (2000) suggests a seven-step process for ethical problem solving:

1. Identify the ethical issues, including the social work values and duties that conflict.
2. Identify the individuals, groups, and organizations that are likely to be affected by the ethical decision.
3. Tentatively identify all possible courses of action and the participants involved in each, along with possible benefits and risks for each.

4. Thoroughly examine the reasons in favor of and opposed to each possible course of action, considering the relevant ethical theories, principles, and guidelines; codes of ethics and legal principles; social work practice theory and principles; personal values (including religious, cultural, and ethnic values and political ideology), particularly those that conflict with one's own.

5. Consult with colleagues and appropriate experts (such as agency staff, supervisors, agency administrators, attorneys, ethics scholars).

6. Make the decision and document the decision-making process.

7. Monitor, evaluate, and document the decision. (p. 361)

The sequential steps identified by social work scholars such as Congress (1999, 2000), Dolgoff et al. (2009), and Reamer (1995a, 2000; Reamer & Conrad, 1995) reflect well-reasoned, logical processes—especially when you can adhere to all of the applicable ethical principles. Unfortunately, this is sometimes impossible. When numerous principles and legal duties apply and some conflict with each other, you are faced with an ethical dilemma. In other words, conforming to one standard (for example, duty to report) necessarily requires that you violate another (for example, duty to maintain client confidentiality). When ethical and legal obligations conflict, which do you ignore? Which do you respect? How do you decide?

How to address and resolve moral and ethical dilemmas has been the subject of philosophical discussion for centuries (Holmes, 2003). In contemporary times, many social workers have questions about whether to base ethical decisions on certain fixed values and principles through a deductive, deontological, absolutist process, or on analysis of individual cases via inductive, teleological, consequentialist, utilitarian, or relativistic reasoning. A social worker adopting a utilitarian perspective would consider the relative good versus harm of the probable consequences of the ethical decision and accompanying action in the particular case. A social worker adopting a deontological view would apply the chosen principle, rule, or law regardless of the potential consequences (Mattison, 2000).

Professional codes of ethics tend to reflect a strong deontological emphasis. Such rules are written and codified so that they may be precisely followed. Indeed, sanctions may be imposed when the "rules are violated." On the other hand, social work also emphasizes a person-in-environment perspective—suggesting that circumstances play a part in all processes, including those involving ethical dilemmas. In effect, the NASW Code of Ethics implicitly suggests that social workers adopt advanced and sophisticated critical thinking processes to address ethical issues in a professional manner. Note these passages:

> Specific applications of the Code must take into account the context in which it is being considered and the possibility of conflicts among the Code's values, principles, and standards.
>
> Further, the NASW Code of Ethics does not specify which values, principles, and standards are most important and ought to outweigh others in instances when they conflict. Reasonable differences of opinion can and do exist among social workers with respect to the ways in which values, ethical principles, and ethical standards should be rank ordered when they conflict. (National Association of Social Workers, 2008, Purpose of the NASW Code of Ethics section, paras. 3–4)

The NASW Code of Ethics does not assign a particular value, weight, or rank to each ethic. Therefore, you may and indeed should consider the array of applicable ethical principles, as well as the particulars of the situation, circumstances, and potential consequences of ethical decisions and actions. Of course, this complicates the decision-making process. The sheer number of factors inherent in each unique case situation is daunting. A clear ranking of the principles or an ethics hierarchy would certainly make it easier to apply the principles—from a deontological perspective. However, fixed application of ranked principles reduces our capacity to consider unique situational aspects.

Of course, there are risks associated with both the deontological and the teleological approaches—especially when taken to the extreme. Case-by-case, inductive reasoning may lead social workers to, in effect, justify or rationalize any decision on the basis of the exigencies of the situation (Jonsen & Toulmin, 1988). Conversely, strict deductive application of prioritized ethical principles can contribute to petty, bureaucratic-like thinking—a kind of *tyranny of principles*—that fails to appreciate the need to sometimes make exceptions to the "rules" (Toulmin, 1981). Complex, committed relativistic thinking may be required (Perry, 1970, 1981, 1982).

In considering the contextual or situational aspects of moral and ethical issues, you might wisely consider dimensions such as motives, means, ends, and likely effects (Fletcher, 1966). Explore your own motives, examine the means by which you plan to address the issues and implement the decision, assess the impacts of the ends you envision, and identify the probable effects of your proposed actions. These considerations reflect age-old intellectually challenging questions such as: "Do the ends justify the means?" "Are my motives pure?" "Have I considered the potential impact of my actions upon others?" "Who should participate in the decision-making process?" "Who should make the final choice?"

These lead to issues specific to social work: "Is a social worker ever justified in using 'bad means' to pursue a 'good end'?" "Should a social worker steadfastly adhere to 'good means' even when the outcome is likely to be 'bad'?" "Should a social worker ever make a decision that affects another without that person's knowledge and participation?" "Should a social worker ever place an ethical obligation above a legal duty or, conversely, a legal duty above an ethical standard?"

One of the hallmarks of professional social work status is continuous and ongoing consideration of value and ethical issues in service to others. Because you have the potential to harm as well as help, to exploit as well as empower, and to restrict as well as liberate, you must consciously, deliberately, and reflectively examine your thoughts, feelings, and actions in both moral and ethical terms (Goldstein, 1987; Schon, 1990).

Motives

In exploring motives, consider your primary and secondary purposes as both a person and a social worker. In accord with your status as a privileged professional, you assume weighty moral, ethical, and legal responsibilities for others and for society. Ideally, your primary motives and those that influence your decisions and action are consistent with professional values and ethics (for example, service, social justice, respect for people, integrity, scientific inquiry, and competence). However, you also reflect personal motives (for example, fear of legal action, desire to assert your own agenda or will, sympathy, pity, or spite). In carrying out your social work functions, you may and indeed should acknowledge your personal motives as you shift focus and emphasize your professional motives.

In addition, ask yourself questions such as: "If I was a client and my social worker acted on these motives, what would I think of that social worker and how would I feel?" "If social workers everywhere reflected these motives, how would society respond?"

Means

In exploring "means," consider the "ways" you might act. Determine who should participate in the decision and how you and other participants might implement the action plans. Means include both the processes of decision making as well as the nature of the plan of action. Ask yourself, "Are the means consistent with my professional values and ethics?" "Are the means likely to produce the desired end or outcome?" "How will people and situations likely be affected by my use of these means?" If the means are not consonant with social work principles or the associated effects appear potentially harmful, ask yourself, "Have I genuinely considered all other means to these ends that would enable me to adhere to my professional values and ethics and ensure that the effects are beneficial?" If acceptable means are indeed unavailable, ask yourself, "Do the ends justify these undesirable means and the potential associated effects?"

Finally, you might ask yourself, "If I were a client and my social worker adopted these means, what would be my reaction?" "If these means were applied routinely and universally by all social workers, how would society react?"

Ends

Consider the nature of the envisioned "ends" (goals) and determine if they are personal or professional. Ask yourself, "How were these goals determined?" "Who participated in their identification and definition?" "Toward whom or what are these goals targeted?" "Are the people affected by the pursuit and accomplishment of these goals aware of their existence and involved in their identification and pursuit?" "Would I be professionally proud to accomplish these goals?" "Are these goals consistent with our mutual understanding of the issues for work, the mission of the agency or program, and the purpose of the social work profession?"

You could also ask yourself, "If I were a client in similar circumstances, how would I respond to these goals?" "If these goals were pursued and achieved by all social workers and their clients, how would society respond?"

Effects

In exploring "effects," consider the additional consequences that could result from adoption of the identified means and accomplishment of the envisioned ends. Beyond the direct impact on the targeted people-in-environment, your decisions and actions may affect you, other clients, other persons, and related social systems. These "side effects" may be positive or negative and energy enhancing or energy depleting depending on their nature, intensity, duration, and a host of other factors. Sometimes, the side effects are potentially so damaging that they outweigh even the most desirable ends. For example, suppose that a social worker learned about a survey instrument that successfully identifies adult males who abuse children. However, the rate of "false positives" of this instrument is extremely high. In fact, there is at least one inaccurate identification for every accurate one. The goals (ends) are certainly desirable: to protect children from abuse and identify adult male offenders who need service. However, the side effects are so onerous (false identification of innocent people) that the means could not reasonably be used without several additional safeguards.

Consider another example: Suppose an intervention (means) designed to reduce or prevent drug abuse among urban adolescents successfully enables 42 percent of participants who previously abused drugs to discontinue drug usage altogether. What great news! However, 33 percent of participants who had not previously used drugs begin to do so—perhaps because of the information and connections established through involvement with other participants. If these figures are accurate, the severity of the side effects or the "collateral damage" would warrant suspension or alteration of the service (for example, limit the program to substance-abusing youth only).

Finally, you might ask yourself, "If I were subject to these side effects, how would I react?" "Would I personally be willing to accept the side effects to achieve the intended goal?" "If these side effects were experienced widely throughout the world, how would society react?"

Of course, we consider motives, means, ends, and effects in an integrative fashion. We explore them in relation to each other and within the context of personal views, laws and policies, and professional values and ethics.

Consider a social worker who hopes to protect a small child from physical harm (desirable motive). She or he decides to lie to the allegedly abusive parent (undesirable means) in an effort to prevent injury to the child (desirable end). In reaching the decision and taking the action, the social worker, in effect, decides that the undesirable means are justified by the desirable ends and willingly accepts responsibility for whatever happens.

This is contextual, teleological, or utilitarian thinking based on an estimation of the likely consequences of the action; in this case, the lie. A major danger in such analysis is that the means may or may not yield the intended ends. That is, the lie may not protect the child from harm. You cannot guarantee the future. The lie may achieve the anticipated ends, may have no effect whatsoever, or may exacerbate the problem through an unanticipated or adverse effect. Whatever happens, the social worker may conclude, "My intentions were good. I wanted to protect the child from injury, so I lied."

Another social worker in a similar situation may adopt a deontological approach and conclude that lying is always wrong. The social worker may think, "I cannot lie" (desirable means) to the allegedly abusive parent, even if I anticipate an adverse response that increases the likelihood of physical injury to the child (undesirable end). I cannot predict future events or guarantee outcomes. Therefore I should at least be honest." Whatever happens, the social worker may conclude, "At least I did not lie." However, the act of not lying may have been followed by physical harm to the child. The means may have been good but the ends unfortunate.

Relying solely on relevant ethical or legal standards, or exclusively on the characteristics of the situation, does not necessarily lead to a clear decision or plan of action. Both teleological and deontological approaches reflect strengths as well as weaknesses.

Despite the risks associated with efforts to rank moral or ethical values, some scholars have developed hierarchies to help social workers address ethical dilemmas in which one ethic conflicts with another. For example, Dolgoff et al. (2009) propose a seven-level hierarchy of ethical principles or "Ethical Principles Screen." In describing the screen, they suggest that the protection of human life is the paramount moral and ethical obligation. Ranked first or highest, this principle takes precedence over all other moral values or ethical principles. Therefore, social workers who learn that a client intends to kill a former lover would take action to protect the potential victim, even if they abridged other ethical principles in the process.

Dolgoff et al. (2009) place equality and inequality in the second position. This complex principle refers to fairness and justice by suggesting "that all persons in the same circumstances should be treated in the same way—that is, persons in equivalent situations have the right to be treated equally. At the same time, persons in different situations have the right to be treated differently if the inequality is relevant to the issue in question. Unequal treatment can be justified when other considerations such as beneficence (the duty to do good, not harm others) outweigh the equality principle or on the grounds that such unequal treatment will promote greater equality" (p. 67). Conceptually, this idea is similar to the *difference principle* that emerged in our exploration of social justice in Chapter 4.

Let's elaborate with an example. Competent adults of equivalent status usually have the right to engage in consensual sex. However, an adult does not have the right to engage in sexual activities with a child, even with the child's apparent consent, because their comparative status and power are obviously unequal. Similarly, because of the power associated with professional status and function, a social worker may not have sex with a client, even when the client is an adult and takes the initiative or provides full consent. This leads to a double standard where there is one rule for adults and another more favorable standard for less powerful and more vulnerable children; and one rule for professionals and another more favorable expectation for their clients. The unequal double standards are justified on the basis of the unequal power among the participants. In such circumstances, double standards that favor more vulnerable persons are quite warranted.

Consistent with social work's traditional emphasis on respect for individual rights and self-determination, respect for and acceptance of diversity and difference, and autonomy and freedom occupies the third position. This principle encourages social workers to "make practice decisions that *foster a person's autonomy, independence, and freedom*" (Dolgoff et al., 2009, p. 67). Of course, a client's right to independent action is not limitless. A person does not have an autonomous right to kill others, abuse or exploit a child, batter a spouse, or falsely scream "fire" in a crowded theater.

Consonant with the duty of care, the principle of least harm is ranked fourth, indicating that "when faced with dilemmas that have the potential for causing harm, a social worker should attempt to avoid or prevent such harm. When harm is unavoidable, a social worker should always choose the option that will cause the least harm, the least permanent harm, and/or the most easily reversible harm. If harm has been done, the social worker should attempt where possible to repair the harm done" (Dolgoff et al., 2009, pp. 67–68).

Consistent with our professional obligation to advance human rights and social justice, and promote social well-being, the fifth principle holds that a "social worker should choose the option that promotes a better *quality of life* for all people, for the individual as well as for the community" (Dolgoff et al., 2009, p. 68).

In line with our legal duties as professional helpers, the sixth principle involves privacy and confidentiality. Dolgoff and colleagues suggest that a "social worker should make practice decisions that strengthen every person's *right to privacy and confidentiality*. Keeping confidential information inviolate is a direct derivative of this obligation" (2009, p. 68).

Truthfulness and full disclosure occupies the seventh position. Consistent with our sense of professional integrity, this principle holds that social workers should be honest and "speak the truth and to *fully disclose all relevant information*" (Dolgoff et al., 2009, p. 68) to clients and others with whom we interact. "Social and professional relationships require trust in order to function well, and trust, in turn, is based on honest dealing that minimizes surprises so that mutual expectations are generally fulfilled" (Dolgoff et al., 2009, p. 68).

Dolgoff et al. (2009) offer their Ethical Principles Screen to social workers as an aid in organizing and ranking aspects of ethical dilemmas when two or more ethical obligations conflict. Facing such an ethical dilemma, a social worker would first classify the aspects of the situation according to the seven fundamental ethical principles. Once categorized, the social worker then applies the Ethical Principles Screen to determine which aspect should take precedence over others. In most cases, elements of the ethical dilemma classified according to the first ethical principle are superior to those associated with the second through seventh principles. Those aspects of the situation that fit into the second ethical principles are superior to those associated with the third through seventh principles, and so on. Of course, if you can conform to all dimension of the code of ethics, you do not need the Ethical Principles Screen. You would simply respond in the ethical manner. Ethical dilemmas arise when conflicts exist among various legal obligations and ethical standards. In such circumstances, you must make a decision about which duty should take precedence.

Dolgoff et al.'s (2009) hierarchical screen helps us think about specific dilemmas within the context of abstract principles. Indeed, philosophers have long argued that certain fundamental moral principles exist and that they can and should guide decision making in all aspects of life.

Some helping professions, notably medicine, have adopted these basic moral values in the following manner (Beauchamp & Childress, 1983; Koocher & Keith-Spiegel, 1990):

Beneficence. The principle of beneficence suggests that helping, protecting, and promoting the well-being and welfare of clients and others is a primary moral value. In other words, professionals engage in "good deeds" through "good works" and must sometimes accept personal risk or sacrifice to carry out their responsibilities. Beneficence incorporates Dolgoff et al.'s (2009) first principle by including the protection of human lives. Beneficence is reflected in the legal duty of care and the duties to inform, report, warn, and protect.

Nonmaleficence. The principle of nonmaleficence suggests that the professional should do everything possible to avoid harming clients or others in their efforts to serve. The value is often captured through the admonition, "First, do no harm!" It is reflected in ethical and legal codes concerning the quality of care so that clients and others do not suffer unnecessary harm as a result of services they receive. This moral value incorporates Dolgoff et al.'s (2009) fourth principle, that of least harm. The concept of utility is part of this value because the professional considers the nature and extent of potential harm in attempts to implement "good acts." In essence, utility involves a combination of beneficence and nonmaleficence by suggesting that we take actions to promote the greatest good with the least harm. Indeed, we may incorporate nonmaleficence within the legal duty of care. For example, if efforts to help one person resulted in injury to a dozen others, the question of utility must be considered. Similarly, a client and worker might decide that standing up for oneself by becoming more assertive is a desirable goal. However, if standing up to an employer leads the client to lose a desperately needed job, then the harm done might well outweigh the good.

Justice. The principle of justice suggests that people have a right to equal treatment unless a disparity of power or capacity warrants differential treatment. Equal access and equal opportunity are components of justice, as is consideration of extenuating or mitigating factors and environmental circumstances. Helping professionals are thus obligated to provide fair and equitable treatment to all. In social work, the value of justice applies to individuals, groups, communities, and societies. This moral value includes Dolgoff et al.'s (2009) second principle, that of equality and inequality—similar to Rawl's difference principle—and their fifth principle, that of quality of life. We may also implicitly consider justice as another part of the legal duty of care. Indeed, unjust practices may well fail to meet the reasonable standard of professional care criterion.

Autonomy. The principle of autonomy suggests that people generally have a fundamental right to liberty and self-determination. They have a right to govern their own affairs and make decisions about actions that may affect them or their well-being. This value reflects Dolgoff et al.'s (2009) third principle, that of autonomy and freedom, and is implicit in the legal duty to respect privacy.

Privacy. The principle of privacy derives partly from the right to self-determination. In the context of privacy, people have a right to control the nature and extent of intrusion into or publicity about their personal lives and homes. Even the publication of clients' names threatens privacy. We might ask, for example, if a social workers calls out the full name of a client in a waiting area so that other clients and visitors may overhear, have they abridged that client's right to privacy and violated their own legal duty to respect privacy?

Confidentiality. The principle of confidentiality is associated with those of autonomy and privacy. In essence, clients retain ownership of information shared with helping professionals. Therefore social workers may not share clients' information without their expressed permission. To do so would also violate the legal duty to maintain confidentiality. As illustrated in Dolgoff et al.'s (2009) sixth principle, clients maintain fundamental rights to privacy and confidentiality. Neither the assumption of the role of client nor the receipt of service diminishes these rights.

Fidelity. The principle of fidelity or "good faith" suggests that clients and others may expect helping professionals to be honest and to keep their commitments. This moral value incorporates

Dolgoff et al.'s (2009) seventh principle, that of honesty and full disclosure, and is inherent in the legal duty of care. Fidelity involves honesty, veracity, and integrity. We expect helping professionals to tell the truth, to refrain from any forms of dishonesty, fraud, and deception, and to honor commitments made to clients and others.

You can probably recognize the risks and limitations associated with attempts to rank-order the core moral values in advance of specific information about a particular ethical dilemma. However, once you understand the facts of a situation and identify the applicable duties and obligations, you may choose to create a case-specific values hierarchy that reflects your judgments about the relative importance of the relevant responsibilities and facilitates your decision-making process. For example, in one instance, a social worker, perhaps in conjunction with a client, may determine that autonomy is more important than beneficence. In another situation, the risk of harm (nonmaleficence) may outweigh the potential good (beneficence). Developing a case-specific values hierarchy requires more judgment and analysis than would applying a universal scheme such as that proposed by Dolgoff et al. (2009). However, ethical dilemmas tend to reflect complexities and idiosyncrasies that warrant modification of even the most well-conceptualized value hierarchies. Intellectual flexibility and integrity are consistent with a person-in-environment perspective and with the characteristics of professionalism. Of course, critical thought and careful judgment are hallmarks of professional social work practice and, perhaps especially, within the context of ethical decision making.

Return now to the case of the man who has locked himself in his basement and is threatening suicide. You have already identified several ethical principles, standards, and legal duties that may apply in this situation. You have undoubtedly found that several of these conflict with each other. To determine which of these conflicting responsibilities should take precedence in this particular instance, let's proceed to develop a case-specific values hierarchy.

If you examine the specifics of this situation in relation to the moral values, you would readily recognize the importance of beneficence. This is consonant with the principle of service, the ethical responsibility to "help people in need," and your obligation to safeguard human life. This moral value is consistent with the legal duty of care that includes the obligation to prevent suicidal action. Let's place that at the highest level of our case-specific values hierarchy. Based on evidence that your former client intends to attempt suicide[2] and the priority we have assigned to human life, you would take action to protect his life—even if it means violating some or all other ethical principles and legal duties. Of course, if possible, you would first try to intervene in a manner that did not infringe on other values and human rights. For example, in this situation, you or perhaps your supervisor—because the client has targeted you as a source of dissatisfaction—might attempt to engage him in conversation and defuse the situation before taking more invasive action.

An effort to intervene directly with the client by telephone is congruent with the moral value of autonomy. The man, however, may not answer the telephone—or it may become apparent that further contact by you or your supervisor would exacerbate the situation. If such is the case, you may have to infringe on the client's autonomy and his rights to privacy and confidentiality.

In your attempt to save the man's life, you may have to call his relatives to inform them about the situation and request their cooperation. You may have to telephone the local police or paramedics and ask them to go to the house. At some point in the process, you may need to provide evidence to a judge or magistrate, or perhaps to a court-appointed physician, to facilitate hospitalization. Such actions obviously infringe on several of the client's fundamental human and civil rights. They represent violations of some of your own ethical principles and legal duties.

---

[2] In certain locales (for example, Oregon), physician-assisted suicide does not necessarily constitute illegal or criminal behavior. However, a physician must first establish that the patient seeking such help is mentally and emotionally stable, and capable of autonomous decision making. The client described in this situation would not meet these standards.

Based on your case-specific values hierarchy, however, you would intervene in this situation even if such intervention involved risk of some harm to the client, loss of his privacy and autonomy, violation of his right to confidentiality, and denial of his rights to equal or preferred treatment. As an adult he has a right to equal treatment and as a client he has a right to preferred treatment because of the power differential. Nonetheless, you would abridge those rights because in this particular situation we placed the protection of human life above all the other ethical principles and legal duties.

Summary

The values, ethics, and legal obligations that guide social workers pertain to every aspect of professional practice. Indeed, you should consider ethical principles more important than theoretical knowledge, research findings, agency policies, and, of course, your own personal views.

To make sound ethical decisions in social work practice, you should be familiar with the fundamental human rights of all people and the basic moral values involved in ethical decision making. You also need to know and understand the values of the profession, the principles reflected in the social work code of ethics, and the legal obligations affecting your practice. In addition, you need to identify the ethical principles, standards, and legal duties that may apply to particular situations. Finally, when different values, ethical principles, or legal obligations conflict, you must be able to determine which ones take precedence over others.

The skill of ethical decision making is fundamental to social work practice. Without such skill, you cannot legitimately claim professional status. Indeed, attempting to provide social work services without regard for ethical principles would be unconscionable.

CHAPTER 5: SUMMARY EXERCISES

1. As a social work student, you sometimes experience feelings of substantial distress and pressure when faced with numerous demands and challenges of life and school. You and your fellow students may occasionally be tempted to cheat in some fashion, perhaps by plagiarizing a paper, taking a "cheat sheet" to an exam, collaborating with a colleague when you should be working alone, or lying to a professor to obtain a due-date extension. You are not alone in dealing with such temptations. In recent years as many as 70–86 percent of college students have cheated in college. The extent of college cheating has increased dramatically over the past several decades. In 1940, the percentage was in the range of 20–23 percent (Callahan, 2004; Simkin & McLeod, 2010).

   Assume that you are a student in a social work course. One of your classmates—a popular person in the program and one of your friends—purchased an essay from one of the Internet firms that sells college papers on various topics. With a sense of pride, she casually tells you that the paper cost only $50 and that when she submitted it for her social work course, the professor gave it an "A+" grade. Use a word-processing program to (a) list the specific ethical principles from the NASW Code of Ethics, your college or university's Code of Academic Conduct, and those legal duties that you believe apply to the case; (b) if a conflict between two or more legal or ethical obligations exist, develop a case-specific values hierarchy to help you analyze and resolve the ethical dilemma; (c) describe the actions you would probably take as a social work student in this situation; and (d) provide a brief rationale to support those actions. Save the document as "Summary Ex 5-1" and deposit it in your Social Work Skills Learning Portfolio.

2. Assume that you are providing social work services to Jeanne, a 35-year-old woman who has just been diagnosed with HIV. You also know that her longtime male partner sometimes physically and emotionally abuses her. Jeanne informs you that her partner does not have HIV and does not know that she now has the virus. Using a word-processing program, prepare brief responses to the following: (a) List the specific ethical principles from the NASW Code of Ethics and identify those legal duties that you believe apply to the case; (b) if a conflict between two or more legal or ethical obligations exists, develop a case-specific values hierarchy to help you analyze and resolve the dilemma; (c) describe the actions you would probably take as a social worker in this situation; and (d) provide a brief rationale to support those actions. Save the document as "Summary Ex 5-2" and deposit it in your Social Work Skills Learning Portfolio.

3. Assume that you lead a social work group for people affected by substance misuse. Prior to and again at the first meeting, you indicated that as group members worked together to pursue their individual goals, personal information would probably be shared. You asked that each group member keep confidential whatever is said in the group. Each participant committed to do so and signed a confidentiality agreement. A few weeks later, you learn that one of the group members repeated something that was said in the group and, as a result, another group member was fired from his job. Use a word-processing program to (a) list the specific ethical principles from the NASW Code of Ethics and identify those legal duties that you believe apply to the case; (b) if a conflict between two or more legal or ethical obligations exists, develop a case-specific values hierarchy to help you analyze and resolve the ethical dilemma; (c) describe the actions you would probably take as a social worker in this situation; and (d) provide a brief rationale to support those actions. Save the document as "Summary Ex 5-3" and deposit it in your Social Work Skills Learning Portfolio.

4. Assume that you serve as a social worker in an agency that provides counseling and other services to low-income families and children. Over the course of the last several weeks, you have been visiting a family of six: a heterosexual couple and their four children. The B. family has numerous needs but, together, you decided to work toward the goal of finding better paying and more stable employment.

In the first meeting, you learned that Mr. and Mrs. B. are members of a religious organization that prohibits the use of medicines, surgical procedures, and forms of modern medical care. As you chatted with 8-year-old Ruth during a recent visit, you noticed a tumor on her abdomen. You mentioned it to Mrs. B. who said that the entire family and other members of their religious group were praying daily for Ruth's health. She expected their prayers would shortly be answered. When you next visited the family about a week later, you observed that the tumor was much larger and appeared darker in color. Use word-processing software to (a) list the specific ethical principles from the NASW Code of Ethics and identify those legal duties that you believe apply to the case; (b) if a conflict between two or more legal or ethical obligations exists, develop a case-specific values hierarchy to help you analyze and resolve the ethical dilemma; (c) describe the actions you would probably take as a social worker in this situation; and (d) provide a brief rationale to support those actions. Save the document as "Summary Ex 5-4" and deposit it in your Social Work Skills Learning Portfolio.

5. As a social worker in the oncology unit of the general hospital, you frequently work with clients who are dying. An intelligent, articulate 88-year-old woman, Ms. T., who has suffered from intense pain for several months, informs you that she has hoarded powerful analgesic medicines and intends to take her life during the night. She says that she wants to say goodbye to you and to thank you for all your help during this time. However, she asks that you please refrain from interfering with her plans. Use word-processing software to (a) list the specific ethical principles from the NASW Code of Ethics and identify those legal duties that you believe apply to the case; (b) if a conflict between two or more legal or ethical obligations exists, develop a case-specific values hierarchy to help you analyze and resolve the ethical dilemma; (c) describe the actions you would probably take as a social worker in this situation; and (d) provide a brief rationale to support those actions. Save the document as "Summary Ex 5-5" and deposit it in your Social Work Skills Learning Portfolio.

6. Assume that you have been providing social work services to a married couple that has indicated a desire to improve the quality of their relationship. You and the clients have agreed that direct, open, and honest communication is a relationship goal. Each has also expressed that sexual fidelity is an important dimension of their marriage. Between the fifth and sixth meetings, you receive a telephone call from one of the partners who says, "I think it would help you to know that I am involved romantically with another person. My spouse does not know and I know that you will not reveal this information because of your legal obligation to maintain confidentiality. I want you to know about this other relationship because I think it will help you to help us. I have come to respect your expertise. You are doing a wonderful job. Thank you." Use a word-processing program to (a) list the specific ethical principles from the NASW Code of Ethics and identify those legal duties that you believe apply to the case; (b) if a conflict between two or more legal or ethical obligations exists, develop a case-specific values hierarchy to help you analyze and resolve the ethical dilemma; (c) describe the actions you would probably take as a social worker in this situation; and (d) provide a brief rationale to support those actions. Save the document as "Summary Ex 5-6" and deposit it in your Social Work Skills Learning Portfolio.

7. Please reflect on the content contained in this chapter and the exercises you completed. Based on your reflections, word-process a succinct one-to-two page essay titled "Challenges in Ethical Decision Making." Within the essay, discuss the personal and emotional, the intellectual and professional, and the social and cultural challenges associated with ethical decision making. When you have finished, include the report in your Social Work Skills Learning Portfolio.

PART 1 SUMMARY EXERCISE: PROFESSIONALISM

Of all the issues that pertain to professionalism, none is more important than the issue of the "goodness of fit" between one's personal beliefs, characteristics, motivations, and ambitions and the nature of social work practice. At some point, you must honestly address the following questions: "Am I personally suited for this profession? Are my beliefs, motives, attributes, and characteristics compatible with those needed by social workers? Am I capable of putting aside my own personal beliefs when they conflict with the values and ethics of the profession, and my service obligations as a social worker? Am I ready for the challenges and sacrifices that social work entails?" These questions are fundamental to the consideration of personal and professional integrity. As a way to address them, please complete the following summary exercise. It will help you explore your motives for selecting this profession and evaluate your overall readiness to pursue social work as a profession.

1. Reflect upon and integrate the results of the exercises you undertook as you completed Part 1 (Chapters 1–5) of the skills book by preparing a summary analysis and assessment of your overall readiness for professional social work. Prepare your assessment in the form of a four- to five-page, double-spaced, word-processed report (1,000–1,250 words) titled "Summary Assessment of My Motivation, Readiness, and Suitability for the Profession of Social Work." When you have finished, include the report in your Social Work Skills Learning Portfolio. In your report, be sure to address the following dimensions.

   a. Career Plans: Look ahead to the professional social work career to which you aspire after graduation. Describe the setting, the nature of the issues, and the kinds of people with whom you would prefer to work. Identify and describe the personal qualities and attributes that you think will be required of you to practice social work ethically and effectively in such a context.

   b. Client and Setting Preference: Identify those settings, issues, and people with whom you would prefer not to work. Discuss the reasons for these preferences. What are the implications of those reasons for your personal and professional development? Would you be able to manage and put aside your personal preferences, if and when needed, in order to provide professional services in such a situation?

   c. Critical Events: Identify one or two major factors or incidents in your personal, familial, or situational experience that contributed to your choice of social work as a career. Discuss how they affect your current readiness and motivation for professional social work practice.

   d. Satisfying and Challenging Aspects: What do you anticipate will be the single most rewarding or satisfying part of being a professional social worker? What will be the single most difficult, challenging, or unsatisfying part?

   e. Outstanding Questions: Based upon your reflection and responses, identify two or three questions that you would want to ask an outstanding, highly experienced social worker.

f. Readiness for Social Work: Consider your family genogram, eco-map, timeline, and the results of the self-efficacy, personality assessment, self-control, and social support instruments. Reflect upon your responses to the critical thinking, scientific inquiry, and career-long learning exercises as well as those related to valuing diversity and difference, advancing human rights and social justice, and promoting social well-being. Finally, review your responses to the exercises that involve understanding legal obligations and social work values and ethics, identifying legal and ethical obligations that might apply to professional situations, and addressing ethical dilemmas. Then, ask yourself,

◆ "Do I possess or can I develop the personal capacities necessary to function effectively as a professional social worker?"
◆ "Am I ready to accept the challenges and sacrifices that social work entails?"
◆ "All things considered, am I really suited for this profession?"

If your answers include a negative response, check out your conclusions by meeting with an adviser, a social work professor, or a vocational counselor. If your conclusions are confirmed through discussions with others, proceed to identify other careers for which you may be better suited. If your answers are all affirmative, make note of personal areas that require further exploration and identify those capacities you need to strengthen. Outline a plan to do so.

As you finish this chapter, please reflect on your learning by completing the following self-appraisal exercise.

SELF-APPRAISAL: THE ETHICAL DECISION-MAKING SKILLS

Please respond to the following items to help you undertake a self-assessment of your competency in the ethical decision-making skills addressed in this chapter. Read each statement carefully. Then, use the following 4-point rating scale to indicate the degree to which you agree or disagree with each statement. Record your numerical response in the space provided:

4 = Strongly agree;   2 = Disagree;

3 = Agree;   1 = Strongly disagree

4	3	2	1	Rating Statement
				At this point in time, I can
☐	☐	☐	☐	1. Discuss the purposes and functions of ethical decision making.
☐	☐	☐	☐	2. Identify and discuss the legal duties that apply to helping professionals.
☐	☐	☐	☐	3. Access the laws that regulate the practice of social work in my locale.
☐	☐	☐	☐	4. Identify and discuss the fundamental values of the social work profession.
☐	☐	☐	☐	5. Discuss the ethical principles and standards that guide social work practice.
☐	☐	☐	☐	6. Identify the relevant legal duties and ethical principles that might apply in various professional contexts and situations.
☐	☐	☐	☐	7. Analyze and determine the relative priority of competing legal and ethical obligations through the development and use of a case-specific values hierarchy.
☐	☐	☐	☐	8. Use critical thinking skills to reach ethical decisions and plan appropriate action.
☐	☐	☐	☐	9. Assess proficiency in the ethical decision-making skills.
☐	☐	☐	☐	10. Assess my readiness for the profession of social work.
				Subtotal

Note: These items are identical to those contained in the Ethical Decision-Making Skills section of the Social Work Skills Self-Appraisal Questionnaire presented in Appendix 3. If you completed that self-appraisal before beginning Chapter 1, you have already responded to these items once before. You may now compare the responses you made on that occasion with those you made this time. Also, compare the two subtotals. If you believe that you have progressed in terms of your proficiency, the more recent subtotal should be higher than the earlier one.

PART II
SOCIAL WORK SKILLS

TALKING AND LISTENING— THE BASIC INTERPERSONAL SKILLS

In this chapter (see Box 6.1), we explore the basic interpersonal skills of talking and listening. These include the processes social workers adopt in fully and accurately sending and receiving messages. They apply in our professional activities and, of course, in our personal lives as well. For convenience, we use the term *talking* to refer to the processes involved in sending and *listening* to refer to those used in receiving messages—regardless of the means of transmission.[1] These skills are especially significant for engaging diversity and difference. Unless social workers can both understand and be understood by the people we hope to serve, our knowledge and expertise are of limited value.

Social workers need well-developed communication skills in all phases and aspects of practice. Inadequate skills in sending and receiving messages can impede development of a productive professional relationship and prevent a successful outcome. Such deficiencies are especially problematic in intercultural and multicultural contexts with people who differ from ourselves. Proficient talking and listening skills contribute to clear expression and accurate understanding during exchanges with individuals, families, groups, organizations, and communities of diverse backgrounds and views. Indeed, highly developed competence in talking and listening are essential for engaging diversity and difference.

---

[1]People vary widely in their physical ability to speak, hear, see, read, or write. In this book, we use the terms *talking* and *listening* to refer to the transmission and reception of communication messages—regardless of the medium. Many superbly effective social workers communicate through alternate means (for example, sign language, mime, and through interpreters, speech synthesizers, TDD, voice recognition systems, and other forms of communication).

The purpose of this chapter is to help learners develop proficiency in the basic interpersonal skills of talking and listening (that is, sending and receiving messages).

Goals

Following completion of this chapter, learners should be able to demonstrate proficiency in:

- Describing and discussing the talking, listening, and active-listening skills
- Engaging diversity and difference through culturally sensitive communications
- Nonverbal communications and body language
- The talking skills—including written as well as verbal communication
- The listening skills
- Active listening
- Assessing proficiency in the talking, listening, and active-listening skills

Core EPAS Competencies

The skills addressed in this chapter support the following core EPAS:

- Identify as a professional social worker and conduct oneself accordingly (EP2.1.1).
- Apply social work ethical principles to guide professional practice (EP2.1.2).
- Apply critical thinking to inform and communicate professional judgments (EP2.1.3).
- Engage diversity and difference in practice (EP2.1.4).
- Engage . . . with individuals, families, groups, organizations, and communities (EP2.1.10[a]).

Cultural Sensitivity and Competence: Engaging Diversity and Difference

"Culture is a learned worldview or paradigm shared by a population or group and transmitted socially that influences values, beliefs, customs, and behaviors, and is reflected in the language, dress, food, materials, and social institutions of a group" (Burchum, 2002, p. 7). In a sense, the culture of a group, organization, or community is similar to an individual's personality. *Cultural sensitivity* refers to "the ability to recognize, understand, and react appropriately to behaviors of persons who belong to a cultural or ethnic group that differs substantially from one's own" (*Dictionary of Public Health* [Online], 2007). *Competence* refers to the ability to complete a task or activity, or to fulfill a responsibility correctly, effectively, or proficiently. In the context of professional social work practice, then, *cultural competence* is the awareness, knowledge, understanding, sensitivity, and skill needed to effectively conduct and complete professional activities with people of diverse cultural backgrounds and ethnic affiliations. However, the notion of cultural competence should not be misinterpreted to mean that anyone ever becomes fully or completely culturally competent—even in regard to people within his or her own cultures (Dean, 2001). Rather, cultural competence is an ongoing developmental process that is "never ending and ever expanding" (Burchum, 2002, p. 14).

In its Standards of Cultural Competence, the National Association of Social Workers (2001) indicates that:

> Cultural competence refers to the process by which individuals and systems respond respectfully and effectively to people of all cultures, languages, classes, races, ethnic backgrounds, religions, and other diversity factors in a manner that recognizes, affirms, and values the worth of individuals, families, and communities and protects and preserves the dignity of each. (p. 11)

In addition, the National Association of Social Workers (2008) emphasizes the importance of cultural competence by including in its Code of Ethics a discrete section titled Ethical Responsibilities to Clients: Cultural Competence and Social Diversity. That section includes the following passages:

1. Social workers should understand culture and its function in human behavior and society, recognizing the strengths that exist in all cultures. (Section 1.05.a)
2. Social workers should have a knowledge base of their clients' cultures and be able to demonstrate competence in the provision of services that are sensitive to clients' cultures and to differences among people and cultural groups. (Section 1.05.b)
3. Social workers should obtain education about and seek to understand the nature of social diversity and oppression with respect to race, ethnicity, national origin, color, sex, sexual orientation, age, marital status, political belief, religion, and mental or physical disability. (Section 1.05.c)

Ngo-Metzger and colleagues (2006) recognize the consumer's perspective in proposing a culturally competent framework for quality services in health care. They identify three general categories of factors. These include: (1) Consumer Factors, (2) Provider Factors, and (3) System Factors. Included among the *consumer factors* are race or ethnicity, age, gender, socioeconomic status including income and education, health literacy, insurance status, utilization aspects including availability of time and transportation, English proficiency, expectations, religion or spirituality, beliefs and values, and explanatory models. Among the *provider factors* are race or ethnicity, age, gender, training or specialty, experience with diverse populations, language competency, communication style, religion or spirituality, beliefs and values, and explanatory models. The *system factors* include access including ease of appointment scheduling, short wait list, and adequate time during visits; convenient location of the care facilities; diverse workforce that represents the consumer population; coordination of care between different providers and health care settings; and quality improvement environment with continued patient feedback. These factors interact throughout the service experience. Ngo-Metzger et al. (2006) identify five interactional aspects that affect the quality of culturally competent care (see Figure 6.1).

In 2001, the board of directors of the National Association of Social Workers approved standards for cultural competence in social work practice (see Box 6.2). A few years later, the NASW (2007) endorsed a set of indicators for assessing the level of achievement of the NASW standards for cultural competence in social work practice. These indicators, associated with the 10 standards, provide specific guidance concerning the knowledge, attitudes, and abilities that culturally competent social workers can demonstrate.

FIGURE 6.1
Ngo-Metzger's Five Aspects of Culturally Competent Practice

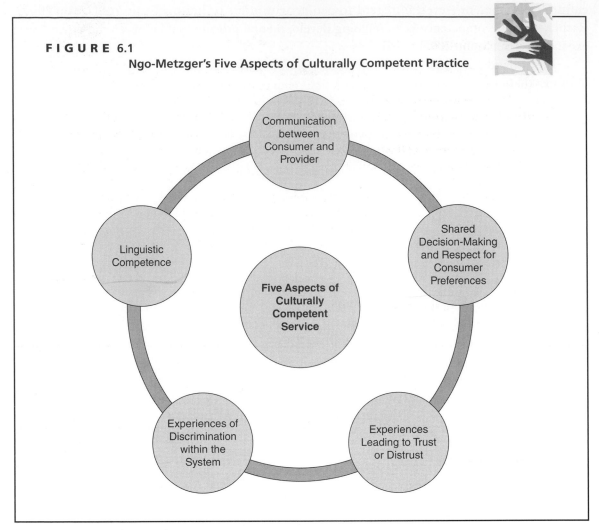

Adapted from Ngo-Metzger's conceptualization.

BOX 6.2
NASW Standards for Cultural Competence in Social Work Practice

Standard 1. Ethics and Values Social workers shall function in accordance with the values, ethics, and standards of the profession, recognizing how personal and professional values may conflict with or accommodate the needs of diverse clients.

Standard 2. Self-Awareness Social workers shall seek to develop an understanding of their own personal, cultural values and beliefs as one way of appreciating the importance of multicultural identities in the lives of people.

Standard 3. Cross-Cultural Knowledge Social workers shall have and continue to develop specialized knowledge and understanding about the history, traditions, values, family systems, and artistic expressions of major client groups that they serve.

Standard 4. Cross-Cultural Skills Social workers shall use appropriate methodological approaches, skills, and techniques that reflect the workers' understanding of the role of culture in the helping process.

Standard 5. Service Delivery Social workers shall be knowledgeable about and skillful in the use of services available in the community and broader society and be able to make appropriate referrals for their diverse clients.

Standard 6. Empowerment and Advocacy Social workers shall be aware of the effect of social policies and programs on diverse client populations, advocating for and with clients whenever appropriate.

Standard 7. Diverse Workforce Social workers shall support and advocate for recruitment, admissions and hiring, and retention efforts in social work programs and agencies that ensure diversity within the profession.

Standard 8. Professional Education Social workers shall advocate for and participate in educational and training programs that help advance cultural competence within the profession.

Standard 9. Language Diversity Social workers shall seek to provide or advocate for the provision of information, referrals, and services in the language appropriate to the client, which may include use of interpreters.

Standard 10. Cross-Cultural Leadership Social workers shall be able to communicate information about diverse client groups to other professionals. (National Association of Social Workers, 2001, pp. 4–5)

Development of these capacities and abilities tends to occur along a cultural competency continuum. Cross, Bazron, and Dennis (1989) propose a continuum that proceeds in the fashion suggested in Figure 6.2.

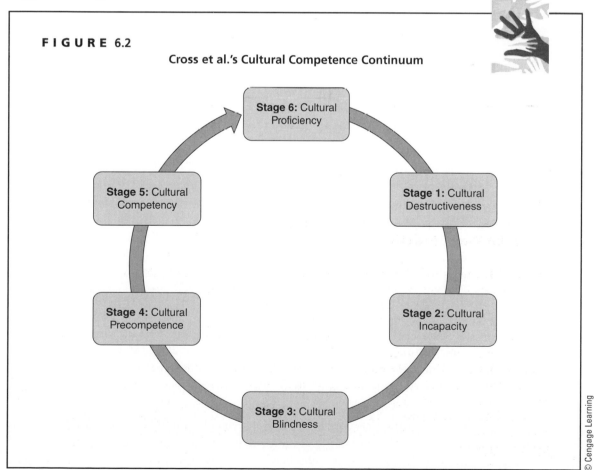

FIGURE 6.2

Cross et al.'s Cultural Competence Continuum

Stage 6: Cultural Proficiency

Stage 5: Cultural Competency

Stage 1: Cultural Destructiveness

Stage 4: Cultural Precompetence

Stage 2: Cultural Incapacity

Stage 3: Cultural Blindness

© Cengage Learning

Adapted from Cross, Bazron, and Dennis' conceptualization.

In Stage 1 of the cultural competency continuum, individuals, families, groups, organizations, and communities actively disrespect, deny, or diminish the culture of diverse others through their beliefs, attitudes, policies, practices, words, and behaviors. In Stage 2, diverse cultures are indirectly disrespected or diminished through forms of bias and discrimination that are routine, established, and institutionalized. In Stage 3, policies and practices are applied "blindly" without regard to the unique characteristics, needs, beliefs, and preferences of diverse others with the result that diverse minority or less-powerful cultures are disadvantaged. In a diverse and multicultural world where power and influence are disproportionately distributed, more dominant or powerful individuals and groups tend to apply their own cultural standards as if those standards were necessarily free from bias and fundamentally true, right, and universal. Stage 4 involves recognition of and familiarity with diverse cultures and their beliefs, practices, needs, and preferences. Stage 5 applies knowledge reflected in Stage 4 to action. That is, individuals, families, groups, organizations, and communities actively respect, affirm, and value the culture of diverse others through their beliefs, attitudes, policies, practices, words, and behaviors. In Stage 6, the knowledge and action reflected in Stages 4 and 5 are refined and enhanced so that cultural diversity becomes highly valued and celebrated as a focus for further growth, learning, and human and social development (Cross et al., 1989; National Center for Cultural Competence, 2004).

Culturally Sensitive Communications

Despite the fact that "everyone communicates," effective interpersonal communications are among the most difficult activities human beings undertake. The challenges facing workers and clients in their professional encounters are often even more extreme. People tend to ascribe various and sometimes unexpected meanings to the verbal and nonverbal, conscious and unconscious messages they express and receive. Culture plays such a large part in the process of effective communication that highly developed sensitivity is essential.

Furthermore, the importance of culturally sensitive communications with diverse groups and communities increases with each passing decade. According to population projections of the Census Bureau (2009), the estimated United States population of approximately 307 million as of July 19, 2009 will grow to about 440 million by the year 2050. The implications of a population that approaches half a billion are staggering—even in a country as resource-rich as the United States. Growth in overall size, however, reflects only part of the picture. The nation's racial and ethnic composition will change dramatically as well.

By 2050, members of minority ethnic groups will grow from one-third to 54 percent of the U.S. population. Indeed, for the first time, during 2010–2011 the number of white births was outnumbered by newborns from other racial groups: 49.6 to 50.4 percent of all births, respectively (Morello & Mellnik, 2012, May 17). When combined, minorities currently constitute the majority in several states (for example, Hawaii, Texas, California, New Mexico) and in 13 major cities. By 2042, minority ethnic groups are expected to reflect a majority in the nation as a whole. "The non-Hispanic, single-race white population is projected to be only slightly larger in 2050 (203.3 million) than in 2008 (199.8 million). In fact, this group is projected to lose population in the 2030s and 2040s and comprise 46 percent of the total population in 2050, down from 66 percent in 2008" (U.S. Census Bureau, 2008, para. 6). From 2008 to 2050, the Hispanic population is expected to grow from 15 percent to about 30 percent of the U.S. population whereas the black population should grow from 14 percent to about 15 percent. The Asian population will grow from 5.1 percent to 9.2 percent of the U.S. population by 2050. In addition, the "number of people who identify themselves as being of two or more races is projected to more than triple, from 5.2 million to 16.2 million" (para. 10).

By midcentury, about 88.5 million people in the U.S. population will be 65 and older. Indeed, some 19 million will be 85 and older. Meanwhile, the proportion of the "working age" population (18– 64 years) should decrease from "63 percent in 2008 to 57 percent in 2050" (U.S. Census Bureau, 2008, para. 12).

In earlier chapters, we considered various aspects of professionalism—including our obligations to value diversity and difference, advance human rights and social justice, and promote social well-being. Obviously, culturally sensitive communication skills are vital in these professional activities. When we interact with diverse others, that is when we engage diversity and difference, we must recognize that each person has culturally based views about all sorts of things, including roles related to the seeking, giving, and receiving of help; and expectations about beginning and ending social and professional encounters.

Language and communication may be among the most important dimensions of culture. Language, for example, affects our thoughts, feelings, and behavior and influences those of others. Language permits communication between and among people and profoundly affects both the processes and outcomes of interpersonal encounters. Within a few years, most social workers in the United States will require proficiency in at least one other language besides English. Schools and departments of social work might encourage or require their students to learn a second language. The growth of the Hispanic population suggests that many social workers should know Spanish as well as English, but competency in other languages is also needed to serve diverse populations, including the large numbers of first- and second-generation immigrants and refugees who come to North America.

Understanding the meaning of words is, of course, only one aspect of the numerous challenges and opportunities associated with intercultural communication. Recognizing our common humanity is another. Indeed, the objective of effective intercultural communication is much more than basic understanding. Rather, it is more akin to the notion of "inclusive cultural empathy" (Pedersen, Crethar, & Carlson, 2008)—a state that involves the processes depicted in Figure 6.3.

In seeking inclusive cultural empathy, we (1) accept and value those who belong to different cultural groups, (2) learn something about others' cultures, and (3) engage others in ways that convey respect for their cultural affiliations. Pedersen et al. (2008) also adopt a broad and expansive view of culture. Much like the concept of "intersectionality" that we introduced in Chapter 4, they recognize that each of us is a member of many communities and several cultures. In this sense, each

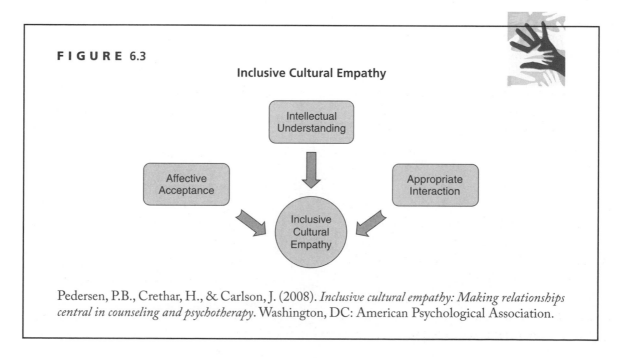

FIGURE 6.3

Inclusive Cultural Empathy

Pedersen, P.B., Crethar, H., & Carlson, J. (2008). *Inclusive cultural empathy: Making relationships central in counseling and psychotherapy*. Washington, DC: American Psychological Association.

of us is "multicultural." Social workers, therefore, require an inclusive conception of culture and an open, curious, and humble approach to diverse others. Though we may not share all the communities and cultures of other people, we certainly share some. Furthermore, as members of the same human species, we share many more similarities than we do differences. Indeed, DNA studies suggest that distinct, identifiable subspecies or "races" do not appear among modern human beings.

> While different genes for physical traits such as skin and hair color can be identified between individuals, no consistent patterns of genes across the human genome exist to distinguish one race from another. There also is no genetic basis for divisions of human ethnicity. People who have lived in the same geographic region for many generations may have some alleles in common, but no allele will be found in all members of one population and in no members of any other. Indeed, it has been proven that there is more genetic variation within races than exists between them. (Human Genome Project Information, 2008, Will genetic anthropology establish scientific criteria for race or ethnicity?, para. 1)

As we engage diversity and difference, let's appreciate our commonalities as well as value our distinctions. "DNA studies indicate that all modern humans share a common female ancestor who lived in Africa about 140,000 years ago" (Human Genome Project Information, 2008, Will genetic anthropology establish scientific criteria for race or ethnicity?, para. 1). In effect, we are all "brothers and sisters" in an extremely intelligent family. Of all the species, we humans should be able to develop the three major characteristics of inclusive cultural empathy.

Affective acceptance involves recognition, awareness, and acknowledgment "of culturally learned assumptions and a network of comemberships across cultural boundaries that include both cultural patterns of similarity and difference" (Pedersen, Crethar, et al., 2008, p. 54). Such emotional acceptance involves awareness of our own culturally based patterns, expectations, and perceptions as well of those of other cultures, and an appreciation of how cultures influence communication. We also accept the limitations of our self-awareness and knowledge about other cultural traditions. Indeed, humility helps us maintain a sense of genuine curiosity about cultures and a sincere interest in others.

Intellectual understanding involves factual knowledge of cultural similarities and differences among those involved in an exchange. Often this involves social workers and clients, but it may also include community members, representatives from other groups, organizations, or nations. Such cognitive understanding usually evolves from knowledge gained from the professional and scientific literature; conversations and experiences with people and groups from other cultures; findings from research about various communities and studies of intercultural communication; and outcomes of policies, programs, and practices that incorporate cultural components. We should also recognize the current state of our knowledge and its limitations (Goode, Dunne, & Bronheim, 2006). Each cultural group contains great diversity. Sometimes, the "within group" differences are even greater than the "between groups" differences. Let's remember that some individuals within any cultural group differ markedly from the average characteristics of the group as a whole. We can never assume that a member of any cultural group is necessarily like others in that group. This is especially true when we incorporate the notions of inclusiveness and intersectionality.

Appropriate interaction includes those interpersonal "skills and abilities to incorporate both similarities and differences in a plan for working together by reframing the culturally learned assumptions and information to bring about constructive change" (Pedersen, Crethar, et al., 2008, p. 54). Inclusive cultural empathic skills enable us to communicate effectively and serve people with whom we share cultural similarities as well as cultural differences.

In our desire to help, social workers need interpersonal competencies as well as attitudes of cultural acceptance, awareness of self and others, and relevant knowledge. We could be highly accepting and very knowledgeable; however, without communications skills we would be unable to engage others in meaningful and productive ways. Social workers must be able to communicate verbally and nonverbally with people from diverse communities and cultures and, when necessary, use interpreters in appropriate and effective ways (U.S. Department of Health and Human Services Office of Minority Health, 2009a).

The teaching and learning of intercultural communication skills for helping professionals has gained credibility and momentum in recent years. For example, the Office of Minority Health offers free online cultural competency education programs (2009b). Numerous scholarly publications also serve as resources. Indeed, the sheer quantity of scholarly work related to intercultural communication in counseling and social work is impressive indeed (Balgopal et al., 2008; Brammer, 2004; Deardorff, 2009; Fong, 2003; Fontes, 2008; Gudykunst & Kim, 2003; Hofstede & Hofstede, 2005; Hogan, 2012; Ivey, Ivey, & Zalaquett, 2010; Ivey, Ivey, Zalaquett, & Quirk, 2012; Lie & Lowery, 2003; Lum, 2008, 2003; Neuliep, 2012; Pedersen, Crethar, et al., 2008; Pedersen, Draguns, Lonner, & Trimble, 2008; Pope-Davis, Coleman, Liu, & Toporek, 2003; Roysircar, 2003; Roysircar, Sandhu, & Bibbins, 2003; Sorrells, 2013; Sue, 2006; Sue & Sue, 2008).

Whenever possible, search out scholarly materials about those diverse groups and communities you serve in your field practicum or expect to serve in your professional roles following graduation. Learn about the core assumptions, beliefs, and common practices of various religious and philosophical perspectives (Hinnells, 2010; Monahan, Mirola, & Emerson, 2011; Renard, 2002). Recognize the ways religious and cultural attitudes may divide or unite us (Haidt, 2012; Putnam & Campbell, 2010) and explore the relationships between religion and human rights (Witte & Green, 2012), social and economic justice, and social well-being. Try to gain some personal experience with various communities as well. Visit neighborhoods, attend religious services, view movies, and talk with community leaders and community members to gain a depth of understanding that you cannot get through scholarly materials alone. Approach others with humility and sincere curiosity. Most will be more than happy to help you learn about their communities and cultures.

Awareness and knowledge go hand in hand. Your initial thoughts, feelings, and attitudes about; and your social behavior with other cultures are very likely to change as you gain knowledge about their norms, values, history, religious beliefs, ceremonies, apparel, and social customs; and especially as you spend time with diverse others. Suppose, for example, that you experience negative judgmental thoughts about a culture that reflects a formally structured, patriarchal family structure where women and children assume lesser overt status and power. Your view might change if you learned that historically such a family structure served survival needs in a society where death was a common punishment for social deviance. You might also discover that within that culture's religious traditions, the father is viewed as the primary connecting link between women or children and God or heaven. Without such knowledge, you might be judgmental or dismissive; with it, you might be more understanding and better able to communicate with respect and inclusive cultural empathy. Absent an appreciation of their culture, you might begin an initial meeting with a family or community group by talking first with children or adolescents, rather than the fathers and elders. As a result, you might unwittingly express disrespect for their culture and alienate the family or the community. Your ignorance could lead them to withdraw from helpful services and perhaps reject needed resources.

Cultural insensitivity and communication deficits may lead members of some groups and communities to avoid human and social service organizations altogether. Does it surprise you that certain population groups seek psychological and social services at lower rates than do others? Are you aware that early dropout rates are much higher for some racial and ethnic groups than for others? Culturally insensitive communications may be part of the explanation.

As you proceed on the never-ending path toward enhanced cultural sensitivity, first learn about various facets of culture that directly relate to the services you provide. Regardless of your practice setting, you can probably readily identify a number of current or prospective clients from a cultural tradition that differs from your own and about which you know little. Once identified, you might seek to learn about the following:

> (1) [the group's] religious/spiritual orientations and views of metaphysical harmony, (2) cultural views of children, (3) cultural style of communication—whether information is transmitted primarily through spoken words or through the context of the situation, the relationship, and physical cues, (4) culturally prescribed and proscribed behaviors in formal and informal relationships, (5) family structures and roles; child-rearing practices including nurturing, meeting physical and psychosocial needs, methods of discipline (including use of corporal punishment), (6) norms of interdependency, mutuality, and obligation within families and kinship networks, (7) health and healing practices, and (8) views of change and intervention. (Samantrai, 2004, p. 34)

Of course, many other factors affect communication with diverse others. For example, in one culture, the concept of time as measured by "the clock" may be highly valued. Being "on time" may be associated with responsibility, reliability, courtesy, commitment, and perhaps wealth. In such a culture, the phrase "time is money" may be used. However, in another culture, clock time may hold much less value. The natural rhythms of the movement of the sun and moon, the changing of the seasons, and the ebbs and flows in human relationships may assume greater importance. There, the concept "when the time is right" may be evident in social relations and interpersonal communications.

Other culturally relevant dimensions of communication include preferences about proximity or the degree of space between people, the expression of emotion, the nature and extent of eye contact, the degree of hand or other physical movements, and the ease with which intimate or personal topics are discussed. History is often a remarkably significant aspect of culture that may be overlooked in our efforts to deal with current issues. For instance, suppose one cultural group experienced severe oppression by another for several generations. Their ancestors may have been enslaved or perhaps subject to "ethnic cleansing" or genocide. What might happen if your name or appearance reminds clients of people who oppressed, tortured, and decimated their ancestors? In such circumstances, the cultural history may emerge as a powerful part of the immediate present.

Indeed, powerfulness and powerlessness tend to remain significant phenomena for individuals and groups who have experienced either or both. Being a "somebody" or a "nobody" profoundly affects people and the way we communicate with others. The poet Emily Dickinson (1924/2000) understood this when she wrote: "I'm nobody! Who are you? Are you a nobody too?"

In discussing the attitudes and actions of "somebodies" toward "nobodies," Fuller (2002) uses the term *rankism* to refer to the uses and abuses of power by those of higher rank in relation to those of lower rank. The feelings of shame, humiliation, indignity, or inferiority felt by a "nobody" when abused, oppressed, enslaved, imprisoned, or exploited, or even when addressed with superiority, arrogance, or condescension by a "somebody" are pretty much the same whether it appears as racism, sexism, ageism, ableism, lookism, heterosexism, or other insidious "isms." When a professor demeans a student, a colonel ridicules a private, an employer humiliates an employee, a parent shames a child, a senator ignores a citizen, a social worker belittles a client, or the people of one culture denigrate those of another, the resulting dehumanization frequently has long-lasting effects.

Social workers' expression of cultural sensitivity involves awareness and management of rankism in all its myriad manifestations. The role of social worker involves a position of status and rank relative to clients. Of course, the difference in status is not, in itself, necessarily a negative. Indeed, as you learned in earlier chapters, the prestige and competence implicit in professional status are significant factors contributing to effective service outcomes. However, when we professionals begin to view ourselves as "somebodies" and clients as "nobodies," the beneficial aspects of the differential status can easily turn into the deleterious effects of rankism.

In communications with and about others, prominent signs of rankism involve the judgmental use of the terms *I* and *you*; and *us* and *them*—typically in a metaphorical sense—and the application of labels or classifications. Terms such as "ally" and "enemy"; "doctor" and "patient"; or even "social worker" and "client" can reflect obvious or subtle forms of rankism. In our efforts to understand and support clients, social workers may unwittingly adopt moralistic metaphors and labels or classifications that actually hinder our professional efforts.

Perhaps the best-known depiction of a common moralistic metaphor is the "dramatic triangle." Apparent in the Greek tragedies and many novels, plays, movies, TV soap operas, and common gossip, the triangle reflects tension or conflict among three parties, forces, themes, or perspectives. A typical form includes a hero or heroine who confronts a villain or overcomes an obstacle to rescue a worthy or desirable victim.

Karpman (1968, 1971) refers to a common triangle (see Figure 6.4) in families, groups, and organizations that includes the roles or positions of Persecutor, Victim, and Rescuer. Of course, these terms have judgmental connotations and also reflect rankism. The persecutor demeans and subordinates the victim, and the rescuer—sometimes from a position of moral superiority—attempts to liberate and safeguard the vulnerable person or group. Occasionally, a rescue may occur without the implicit or explicit consent of the rescued and, of course, the rescuer may need to combat, defeat, control, or subordinate the persecutor in the process.

The dramatic triangle is readily apparent in cultural mythologies (Campbell, 1972; Campbell & Moyers, 1988) and political philosophies (Morone, 2003). During wartime or times of struggle, leaders tend to emphasize moralistic metaphors and dramatic triangles where one country, ethnic community, people, or coalition is viewed as "good," another as "bad," and a third as "victimized." The European theater of World War II provides a clear example of a dramatic triangle—at least from a North American perspective: Great Britain, the United States, and their allies represent the "good" coalition, whereas Hitler and the Nazis represent the "bad." At first, the innocent victims included the nations Poland, Belgium, France, and other countries invaded by Hitler's forces. Much later, Jews, Gypsies, gay and lesbian people, and other cultural groups imprisoned and murdered during the Holocaust were identified and recognized as victims.

In his January 2002 State of the Union address, President George W. Bush used the term *axis of evil* to refer to North Korea, Iran, and Iraq. He said: "States like these and their terrorist

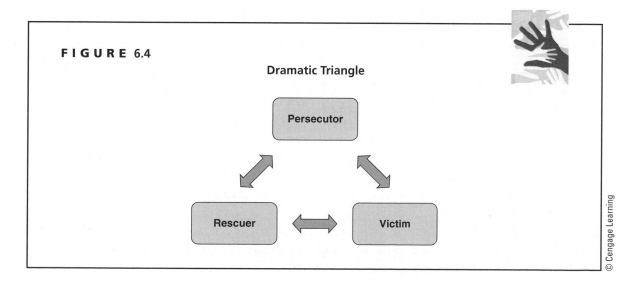

FIGURE 6.4

Dramatic Triangle

© Cengage Learning

allies constitute an axis of evil, arming to threaten the peace of the world" (Bush, 2002, para. 20). In so doing, he used a moral metaphor and established a triangle. In effect, he identified those three national governments as evil sponsors of terror, the residents of the United States and their allies (and perhaps the general populations of the three countries in question) as potential victims, and the United States and its allies as heroic protectors and perhaps rescuers. "Us-and-them" thinking is evident. As is common in such triangles, however, the roles often shift—sometimes quite rapidly. From a victim's perspective, a hero can quickly change to that of persecutor or oppressor. Indeed, a victim can sometimes feel quite victimized by a hero soon after a purported rescue. We might wonder how many Iraqis and Afghanis who initially viewed American soldiers as liberators (that is, heroes) later viewed them as occupiers (that is, persecutors). Similarly, we might ask how many U.S. soldiers have changed their view of themselves from that of heroic rescuers to that of unappreciated victims.

As opposed to moralistic triangles, however, some triangular relationships can contribute to motivation, cooperation, energy, productivity, love, and perhaps even peace in various contexts—including those that involve cross-cultural exchange. Whereas the dramatic triangle depicted in Figure 6.4 tends to reflect "I-and-you" or "us-and-them" orientations where "either/or" patterns emerge, other triangles may reflect a "we" perspective where "both/and" messages are common.

In "either/or" interactions, each person or group assumes a single role or position at a time (for example, rescuer, victim, or persecutor) and "I" and "you" or "us" and "them" are highly distinct; and labels are commonly assigned. Such interactions tend to involve some distrust and suggest a potential for conflict or competition (Whitfield, Whitfield, Park, & Prevatt, 2006). Sentences often contain "Yes, but . . ." phrases that challenge the value of another's message. Common themes might include: "It's either you or me." "It's us or them." "You're wrong; I'm right." "I win; you lose."

In "we" triangles, all parties tend to be inviting, trusting, and cooperative. Labels and classifications are used minimally and nonjudgmentally, or avoided altogether. All parties assume roles of nurturer and motivator, and nurtured and motivated, and do so at or near the same time. Sentences often contain "Yes, and . . ." phrases that support and elaborate upon another's words. For example: "Yes, that's a really good point and to that I'd like to add. . . ." Messages that involve "we" and "us" are also common: "All of us have something to contribute and we can all benefit." "You have an excellent idea *and* here's another one."

Especially when social workers know something about others' core beliefs and values, their wants and needs, and their cultural traditions, we can promote "we" relationships that de-emphasize both "I" and "you", and "us" and "them" perspectives. Indeed, learning about other peoples and their cultures, becoming aware of the many forms of rankism, and considering the nature and implications of various metaphors and conceptualizations are usually extraordinarily enriching endeavors—both personally and professionally. However, let's remain aware of the dangers of stereotypes and overgeneralizations. The power of mass media, public education, and mainstream society is such that minority cultures are sometimes assimilated by majority cultures. The often dramatic differences between first and third generations of immigrant families typify the speed with which humans adapt to new social environments. Similarly, the amount of wealth, extent of formal education, age, and degree of isolation from other groups all influence the rate and extent to which adaptation occurs. Members of cultural groups vary greatly from one another. Some welcome acculturation and assimilation whereas others resist them.

Let's balance our growing knowledge of diverse cultures with the reminder that extraordinary diversity exists within each cultural group. You might, for example, serve in an agency where interviewers routinely assign clients to a racial or ethnic category based on their physical characteristics. When completing an intake form, some workers might "check a box" to signify a racial or ethnic category because "he looks Hispanic" or, on the telephone, "she sounds African American." Such practices involve considerable risk. The person labeled Hispanic may think of himself as Puerto Rican or perhaps Latino. A woman classified as Asian might view herself as Thai, or that "white boy" might proudly consider himself Cherokee.

Acknowledge our strong human tendencies toward ethnocentrism, overgeneralization, rankism, and that extremely tempting process of "assumption making." The most respectful approach is to ask prospective clients for their input. If racial or ethnic classifications are truly useful for agency purposes, we might simply ask, "In terms of race or ethnicity, what do you consider yourself?" If the answer does not fit the list of categories, you might add a new one. Also, recognize that many people self-identify as multiracial, mixed, or interracial whereas others may include one or more racial identities and an ethnic identity as well (for example, white, Hispanic). You might also provide clients an opportunity to "decline to identify" themselves according to a racial or ethnic group. Furthermore, you might ask yourself and other agency personnel questions such as: "Why is this information needed and how might it be used?" "What are the risks and benefits associated with the collection and use of such information?" "How will clients who provide information benefit from its collection and use?" "Do the benefits outweigh the risks?"

EXERCISE 6-1: CULTURALLY SENSITIVE COMMUNICATIONS

Complete the following exercises to become more aware of the nature of your speech and language patterns.[2]

1. Imagine that you are working in an agency that provides a wide range of psychosocial services including individual, family, and group counseling. You are about to meet for the first time with a prospective client who remains unemployed after losing a long-term job; is now deeply in debt; and is about to lose his apartment. The client differs dramatically from you. If you are female, pretend that the client is male or transgendered. If you are white, imagine that the client is a person of color. If you are heterosexual, assume that the client is homosexual or bisexual. If you are tall, assume that the client is of shorter stature. If you are highly educated, imagine a client with limited formal education. If you are middle class, pretend that the client is virtually penniless. If you have a residence, presume that the client is homeless. If you believe in a god or higher power, you might imagine that the client is agnostic or atheist; or if you are Christian, assume that your client is Muslim, Hindu, or Buddhist. If you have normal hearing, imagine that your client is hearing-impaired. If you are sighted, assume that your client is blind. If you are able-bodied, imagine that your client uses a wheelchair to get around.

   Now, use a recording device (for example, audio or video) to capture yourself as you express the words you would say or sign as you begin work with this prospective client. Introduce yourself, describe something about the kinds of services your agency might be able to provide, and ask this imaginary person some of the questions you would like to ask. Continue this imaginary introduction for approximately 2 minutes.

   Replay the recording and review your language usage. Examine the words you said and consider them from the point of view of the imaginary person you have created for this exercise.

   Use the space below to discuss how your prospective client would likely experience the words and language you have chosen to use? Consider how people who differ from

---

[2] If you communicate primarily through sign language, computer-mediated speech, or another means, please approximate this exercise in the message-sending mode you use with clients. Be sure to consider the implications of your challenges in your analysis.

you in terms of age, gender, skin color, sexual orientation, educational background, socio-economic status, ethnicity, religious beliefs, physical appearance, and physical or mental ability might experience you, your speech, and your language. Finally, identify one or two aspects of culturally sensitive communication that you would like to strengthen in preparation for your roles and functions as a professional social worker.

2. Access the Internet and use a search engine to first locate a list of ethnic groups in the world and then a list of racial and ethnic groups in the United States. Alternately, you could go to your university or library to locate books or other print material containing such lists (Levinson, 1998). Recognize that various sources may use different definitions of *ethnic group* or *ethnolinguistic group*. For example, if you search the online version of *The World Factbook of the U.S. Central Intelligence Agency* using the keywords "field listing ethnic groups" you should find a tabular list of ethnic groups by percentage of population in the world's nations (Central Intelligence Agency, 2012). If you use the keywords "lists of ethnic groups" in a search engine such as Google, Yahoo, or Bing, you would probably locate the Wikipedia entry by the same title (Wikipedia, 2012). If you conducted a similar search using the keywords "Fact Sheet for a Race, Ethnic, or Ancestry Group," you would probably access the American Fact Finder website of the U.S. Census Bureau. That site permits you to search for demographic data related to a particular population group in the country as a whole, by state, or by city/town. You might notice that the list of racial, ethnic, and ancestry groups used by the U.S. Census Bureau differs somewhat from those used by other organizations.

   Once you have gained a sense of the hundreds of ethnic groups throughout the world and the country, select one that interests you and about which you know little. For example, you might decide to learn about the Hmong or perhaps the Navajo, the Amish, or the Druze, Persian, Armenian, Kurdish, Sikh, Haitian, or Bantu ethnic groups. Once you have made your choice, conduct a library, bibliographic, or Internet search to identify three or four cultural "do's and taboos" in verbal or written communication style or approach with members of that ethnic group. Be sure to include at least one "do" that conveys respect and at least one "taboo" that suggests disrespect (Axtell, 1998, 2007).

Use the space below to list the "do's" and "taboos" and to cite the source of the information. Finally, remember that members of a particular racial, ethnic, linguistic, cultural, or national group or tribe are not "all alike." Indeed, variations within groups might sometimes be greater than those between groups.

3. Access the Internet and use a search engine to locate the "Say Hello to the World" project of the Internet Public Library (2009).

Use the following space to write how you would say "Hello, my name is (your name)" in each of the following languages: (a) Arabic, (b) Cherokee, (c) Chinese, (d) Hindi, (e) Spanish, and (f) Swahili. Also, look to see how the phrase "Hello, my name is" appears in Braille and in American Sign Language.

4. Suppose you were about to meet with a family that recently entered the United States from another country. Because of a preliminary telephone call, you know that they are interested in learning about immigration laws and procedures for obtaining a "Green Card" (Form I-551). Access the Internet and search for the "Lawful Permanent Residence" ("Green Card") section of the U.S. Citizen and Immigration Services (USCIS) website (2009) to become familiar with key requirements.

Use the following space to outline what is involved in qualifying for green card status.

Talking and Listening

Effective communication requires skills in both talking and listening. That is, we must be able to transmit understandable messages to as well receive and comprehend messages transmitted by others. We also need skills in active listening. Active listening is a form of communication through which we expressively demonstrate that we have understood what others have said.

Most people find it extremely challenging to communicate fully and accurately with others. Social workers are no exception. Here is a list of some of the common errors we sometimes make in talking and listening:

- Interacting in a patronizing or condescending manner.
- Interrogating (rather than interviewing) by asking questions in rapid, staccato-like fashion.
- Focusing on ourselves (for example, formulating questions before understanding the other's message, self-consciously monitoring our internal experiences, evaluating our own performance).
- Attending predominantly to a single dimension of a person's experience (for example, just thoughts or just feelings; only the personal or only the situational; just the negative or just the positive).

- Interrupting frequently with a comment or question.
- Failing to listen or remember.
- Selectively listening with an "agenda" or "theory" so that we interpret others' messages to match our own beliefs and opinions, and confirm our own biases.
- Neglecting to use a person's name, mispronouncing or changing it (for example, referring to "Catherine" as "Cathy" or "Josef" as "Joe"), or assuming a degree of formality or informality that does not match that of the client's (for example, "Mr. Jones" when he would prefer "Bill," or "Jane" when she prefers "Mrs. Smith").
- Neglecting to consider the cultural meaning of the interview for a particular person or family.
- Failing to demonstrate understanding through active listening.
- Using terms that stereotype people or groups.
- Offering suggestions or proposing solutions too early in the process (on the basis of incomplete or inaccurate understanding of the person-issue-situation).
- Making statements in absolutist terms (through, for example, words such as always, never, all, or none).
- Prematurely disclosing personal feelings, opinions, or life experiences.
- Confronting or challenging a person before establishing a solid relationship and a genuine base of accurate understanding.
- Speculating about causes of issues before adequately exploring the person-issue-situation.
- Prematurely pushing for action or progress from a person who has not indicated a readiness for action.
- Using clichés and jargon, or using a single phrase over and over so that it seems insincere.
- Making critical or judgmental comments, including pejorative remarks about other people or groups (for example, other professionals, agencies, and organizations).
- Displaying inappropriate or disproportionate emotions (for example, acting extraordinarily happy to meet a new client or weeping excessively when a person expresses painful feelings).

Nonverbal Communications and Body Language

A great deal of human communication is nonverbal. As a social worker, you should be keenly aware of the significance of body language. Factors such as posture, facial expression, eye contact, gait, and body positioning represent important forms of communication (Ivey et al., 2010; Kadushin & Kadushin, 1997).[3] In professional encounters with others, your body language should be congruent with your verbal language. Clients often notice discrepancies and inconsistencies between what you say verbally and what you express nonverbally. When you present yourself in an incongruent fashion, others may be confused about you and your message. When you express yourself congruently, people are more likely to understand your communications and to experience you as genuine and sincere.

In addition to verbal and nonverbal congruence, social workers typically hope that their body language communicates attention and interest in the other person, as well as caring, concern, respect, and authenticity. On some occasions, social workers need to express messages in an assertive manner that conveys authority. To emphasize one element or another, changes in body language may be necessary.

---

[3] If you are visually or hearing challenged, or move about with assistance (for example, walking aids, guide dog), please reflect on the potential nonverbal communication effects on clients and colleagues. Also, consider how you might best address the nonverbal dimension of communication in your service to others.

In beginning interviews with prospective clients, you should typically adopt an open or accessible body position (Egan, 2010a; Evans, Hearn, Uhlemann, & Ivey, 2008; Ivey et al., 2010). If standing, you may hold your arms and hands loosely along your sides. If seated, you can place your hands on your lap. Arms held across the chest, behind the head, or draped over an adjoining chair may reflect inattention or nonreceptiveness. Tightly clasped hands, swinging legs or feet, pacing, looking at a watch or clock, or drumming one's fingers tend to communicate nervousness or impatience. Slouching in a chair may suggest fatigue or disinterest. Sometimes, however, you may need to assume an informal body position to increase the comfort and decrease the threat experienced by another person. For example, in working with children, you might sit on the floor and talk while playing a game. With teenage clients, significant encounters may occur while sharing a soft drink, shooting pool, or leaning against a fence or wall. Important exchanges may take place while you transport a client to a doctor's office or a food pantry, while you help carry groceries, or when you enjoy a snack together.

The frequency and intensity of eye contact varies according to the people involved, the purpose of the meeting, the topic under discussion, and a host of other factors. In general, you should adopt seating or standing arrangements that allow for but do not force eye contact between the participants. Although it is common for social workers to attempt rather frequent eye contact, especially when clients are talking, the degree and intensity should vary according to the individual and cultural characteristics of the person, the issues of concern, and the context of the meeting. People from many cultures experience regular eye contact as positive and rewarding, but those from several other cultures do not. "Some cultural groups (for instance, certain Native American, Eskimo, or aboriginal Australian groups) generally avoid eye contact, especially when talking about serious subjects" (Ivey, 1988, p. 27).

In certain cultures, dropping one's eyes to avoid direct eye contact conveys respect, whereas steady, direct eye contact signifies disapproval. For some groups, eye contact is more likely when talking than when listening, but the exact opposite is true in other cultures. In all cases, however, you should not stare. Staring can constitute a violation of the other's space and may be experienced as a challenge. Associated with dominance and patriarchy among several species (Smuts, 1995), staring often reflects a power differential. Many people of majority status and those affiliated with favored groups feel entitled to peruse, appraise, and glare at people of minority or less favored status. For example, many men believe it quite acceptable to stare or leer at women. In North America, many whites commonly watch and observe people of color in a different way than they do other whites. There are numerous other examples. However, as a social worker interested in relationships characterized by equality, mutual respect, and joint participation, your eye contact should never be so intense or continuous that it becomes an intrusion, a privacy violation, or a form of intimidation or superior rank.

Attending (Carkhuff & Anthony, 1979; Evans et al., 2008; Ivey et al., 2010) or "physically tuning-in" (Egan, 2010a) to others are terms frequently used to describe the process of nonverbally communicating to others that you are open, nonjudgmental, accepting of them as people, and interested in what they say. A general purpose of attending is, in fact, to encourage others to express themselves as fully and as freely as possible. During the beginning phase especially, your nonverbal presentation is at least as important as any other factor in influencing clients' responses to you.

There is substantial literature regarding the skill of attending. For example, Carkhuff and Anthony (1979) suggest that counselors face their clients squarely, at a distance of 3 to 4 feet, without tables or other potential obstacles between the participants. They further recommend regular eye contact, facial expressions showing interest and concern, and a slight lean or incline toward the other person. Using the acronym SOLER, Egan (2010a) also suggests that we *squarely* face the person, assume an *open* body position, sometimes *lean* slightly toward him or her, maintain *eye* contact, and do so in a *relaxed* manner.

Many of these guidelines are useful, but they tend to reflect nonverbal characteristics common among adult, majority-member, middle- and upper-class North Americans. Many children, members of ethnic-minority groups, and people of lower socioeconomic status commonly demonstrate quite different nonverbal characteristics in their social interactions. Facing some people too directly, too squarely, and too closely may infringe on personal territory and privacy. For others, a distance of 4 feet would be much too far for an intimate conversation. Therefore please be flexible in your attending and physical positioning. Closely observe the nonverbal expressions of the other person and respect them. Also, within these general guidelines, assume a comfortable body position. Trying to understand another person requires energy and concentration. Physical discomfort could distract you and you might become less attentive. However, do not assume such a comfortable position that you lose interest. Dozing off during an interview does not convey attention and concern!

When seated positions are desirable and available (for example, when interviewing an adult in an office setting), place the chairs so that they create an angle of between 90 and 135 degrees. This allows other people to direct their eyes and bodies toward or away from you as desired, and it affords you the same opportunity. Matching, movable chairs are preferred. They provide flexibility and suggest that you and your clients are "on the same level." Physically leaning toward clients at points when they are sharing emotionally charged material usually demonstrates concern and compassion. However, carefully observe their reactions. Some clients may find the added closeness too intimate or even intrusive, especially during the early stages of the working relationship.

Of course, many times you have limited control over the placement of chairs or even the location of the interview setting. Often an exchange occurs during a walk or an automobile drive, in a kitchen during mealtime, while the client is caring for children, and sometimes even while others are watching television. As a relationship develops and you begin to understand the meaning of various gestures to the client, it may become possible to ask to move a chair closer or lower the volume on the television. Such requests may be quite meaningful to clients, as they realize that you actually do want to hear what they say!

EXERCISE 6-2: NONVERBAL COMMUNICATIONS AND BODY LANGUAGE

1. Recruit a friend or colleague to join you in a few nonverbal experiments.[4] After you have completed them, use the space provided to summarize your observations, discoveries, preferences, and questions. Make note of your partner's as well.

   a. Maintaining eye contact, slowly move toward your partner, who remains in position, until it becomes uncomfortable for you. Then stop. Observe the approximate distance between you. What were your thoughts, feelings, and sensations as you moved closer and closer to your partner? What did your partner experience as you approached?

   b. Position yourself face-to-face with your partner at a distance of approximately 4 feet. Look directly into his or her eyes until you become uncomfortable. When that occurs, simply avert your eyes. Now, move to 3 feet, then to 2 feet, each time looking directly into your partner's eyes until you experience discomfort. Then turn away. Share your reactions with each other. Now, experiment with different kinds

---

[4] If you are visually or physically challenged in some way, please adapt these exercises accordingly. Be sure to incorporate the implications of your challenges in your discussions.

and degrees of eye contact within a 2- to 4-foot range. For example, try looking at your partner's cheekbone or mouth instead of directly into her or his eyes. Share your reactions. Experiment further by looking into your partner's eyes for several seconds and then slightly change your focus so that you look at a cheekbone for a few seconds; then return your gaze to the eyes. Follow that by looking at your partner's mouth for a few seconds, and then return to the eyes. Share your responses to this manner of eye contact.

c. Place two chairs squarely facing one another (front to front) approximately 2 feet apart. Be seated. Share your thoughts and feelings as you sit face-to-face and knee-to-knee. Is it comfortable for both of you, for only one, for neither? If it is uncomfortable, alter the distance until it becomes comfortable. Ask your partner to do the same. Finally, compromising if necessary, move the chairs until you arrive at a mutually comfortable distance. Change the placement of the chairs so that instead of directly facing one another, they now are side by side in parallel position, approximately 6 inches apart. As you and your partner take your seats, share your respective thoughts and feelings. Now increase the angle so that the chairs form a 90-degree angle. Share with one another your reactions to this arrangement. Now increase the angle an additional 45 degrees. Share your reactions to this position. Which arrangement does your partner prefer? Which do you?

d. Based on the results of your experimentation, place the chairs in the position and at the angle that is reasonably comfortable for both you and your partner. Some compromise may be necessary. Now, maintaining a more or less neutral facial expression and without saying a word, try to show through your body language, but without changing your facial expression, that you care about your partner and are interested in his or her thoughts and feelings. Continue to experiment with three or four different body positions, attempting to demonstrate concern and interest, for approximately a minute each. Following each position, seek verbal feedback from your partner concerning her or his reactions. What did you learn from the exercise?

e. Assume a position that your partner indicates reflects caring and interest. Now begin to experiment with different facial expressions. First, let your face become relaxed in its more or less usual state. Retain this facial expression for about a minute while your partner experiences the effect. After a minute, seek feedback from your partner about his or her observations and reactions. Then experiment with other facial expressions through which you hope to express silently, in turn, affection, compassion, joy, sadness, disappointment, disapproval, fear, and anger. Hold each facial expression for a minute or so while your partner tries to determine the feeling you are trying to express. Share your experience, observations, and discoveries.

Talking: Verbal and Written Communications

The words you choose, the sound and pitch of your voice, the rate and delivery of your speech, and your use of language may suggest a great deal to clients and others with whom you interact.[5] During a typical first contact—whether face-to-face, via telephone, or by letter, fax, or e-mail—use easily understandable words and phrases. Keep it simple. Save arcane and esoteric language for professors! Avoid evaluative terms. Even words such as *good, okay,* or *right*—through which you intend to convey support and encouragement—may suggest to a client that you are making evaluative judgments about people. A client may have thoughts such as: "If you judge me or my actions positively without knowing much about me, can you really be objective?" "At this point, you approve of me. I'd better not say anything that might lead you to disapprove. I guess I'll keep the real issues to myself." The same result can occur if we express premature judgments about other people, groups, organizations, or institutions. Clients might wonder, "If you so quickly judge others, will you also do the same to me?"

Especially during the early stages of work, be careful about sharing opinions or hypotheses. Use of diagnostic, medical, legal, or psychological terminology, or social work jargon may suggest to clients that you might label or classify them before fully understanding all the intricacies of their cir-

---

[5] If you use assisted communication systems or other forms of "talking" (for example, sign language) that do not involve voice and speech, please consider their potential effects on communication with others. Just as "tone of voice" may have meaning in a conversation between hearing people, a signed message may convey "tone" as well.

cumstances. Labels of all kinds, even positive ones, can significantly affect the tenor of your relationships with clients and the course of your work together. Variations of the verb *to be* often result in a labeling effect. Suppose, for example, that you were to say, "He is a child abuser." Because the word *is* suggests an equivalence between *he* and *child abuser* (that is, *he* equals *child abuser*), we would tend to view that human being through the conceptual screen of "child abuser." Rather than a human being who has abused a child, he becomes a child abuser who might possibly have some human qualities.

Of course, we should not tolerate the abuse or exploitation of children or other vulnerable people. Perhaps especially among social workers, such offenses tend to elicit strong emotional reactions. However, even terms that are not so emotionally laden can have deleterious labeling effects. When you think or say, "She is young," "They were foolish," "He was manipulative," "She is seductive," "He is aggressive," "They are poor," "He is white," "He is disabled," or "She is unmarried," you reflect conclusions that are primarily derived from your own rather than from others' experience of themselves.

The human being convicted of the crime of child abuse may experience himself as a weak, impulsive person guilty of a terrible sin. The person who appears to you to be young may experience herself as old beyond her years. Indeed, she may even question her own sexual identity and wonder whether she is truly female. The behavior that you consider foolish may have resulted from an excruciating examination of various possibilities. The manipulation that you infer may represent an attempt to maintain a sense of personal control or perhaps salvage some dignity by a person who feels humiliated. What you perceive as seductive may be naturally warm and friendly interpersonal expressions that are entirely consistent with that person's familial and cultural traditions. What you consider aggressive may constitute an effort to counter powerful feelings of fear and anxiety. What you view as poverty, someone else may consider as freedom from petty pursuit of money and material goods. The person you regard as a white male might view himself as Hispanic and may have adopted an androgynous philosophy in which the concepts of masculine and feminine have little relevance. The man you think is disabled may regularly play wheelchair basketball and tennis and possess computer skills beyond any you can imagine. The person you consider unmarried may have long ago determined for herself that the institution of marriage was anathema to a liberated perspective.

Inferences, speculation, and labels about people are risky at all times and especially so during the early phases of a relationship. As you interact with others, try to adopt the frame of reference of the person who is communicating, and be careful when you use forms of the verb *to be*. In general, use words that are descriptive rather than inferential and simple rather than complex.

We social workers seek to learn about sociological theories and research findings that pertain to different groups, especially cultural groups common in our communities, and populations at risk of oppression, exploitation, and discrimination. For example, in talking and listening with clients, you might benefit from research findings suggesting that men and women tend to adopt different conversational styles (Basow & Rubenfeld, 2003; Mulac et al., 1998; Tannen, 1990, 1994, 2001), that some Native American clients may find personal questions about their "individual identity" intrusive or foreign (Blount, Thyer, & Frye, 1992; Gilbert & Franklin, 2001; Good Tracks, 1973; Lewis & Ho, 1975; Weaver, 2004; Weaver & Bearse, 2008), and that some Hispanic or Latino clients may prefer an extended, informal beginning (Castex, 1996; Delgado, 2007; Longres, 1995; Wodarski, 1992; Zuniga, 2001, 2003). As a result of sociocultural knowledge, you may be tempted to generalize about people, perhaps because of their perceived membership in a certain class or group (for example, poor, rich, black, transgendered, disabled, diabetic, or Democrat). When tempted, however, be alert to the danger of stereotypes and our human tendency to engage in confirmation bias.

For example, many men use conversational styles quite different from those of many women, but some men adopt conversational styles that are quite similar to those of many women. Some Native Americans experience personal questions from a social worker as an expression of interest and concern, and some Latino clients prefer a direct, businesslike approach as they begin with a social worker. All women are not the same; nor are all men, all people of color, all children, all gay or lesbian people, all social workers, or even all professors. Be sensitive to and carefully consider factors of gender, class, ethnicity, ableness, sexual orientation, religion, and cultural affiliation but also recognize that, despite our nearly identical DNA, each individual person is unique. Each person differs, at least to some extent, from common characteristics of the "average" member of his or her class or group.

As an interview proceeds, you may attempt to match the client's language mode. Some people favor words associated with hearing; others prefer those identified with seeing; still others like words that indicate sensing or touching. For example, if you use words such as *hear, sound, noise, loud,* or *soft* with people who favor an auditory language mode, you enhance the likelihood of mutual understanding. Your potential value may also increase. A similarly favorable reaction is likely if you were to use *see, view,* and *perceive* with people who prefer a visual language mode, or *feel, sense,* and *touch* with those who favor tactile language (Bandler & Grinder, 1979).

In general, try to adopt a speaking style that is moderate in tone and speed of delivery. Through your speech, convey that you are truly interested in what the client has to say (Ivey, 1988, p. 22). Sometimes, however, you may deliberately increase or decrease your rate of speech to match the pace of the client. On other occasions, you may purposely slow your pace to lead a fast-talking client into a slower speaking mode. In some circumstances (for example, when working with a client with some loss of hearing), you may lower the pitch of your voice to be more audible. Generally, when you speak or write, active voice is preferable to passive voice, and each unit of speech should not be so long or complex as to impede understanding. Short messages and single questions are easier to comprehend, as are single questions. Multipart questions can confuse others.

In written communications, adopt a professional attitude consistent with the qualities and characteristics of professionalism discussed in earlier chapters. Badly written, poorly formatted documents that contain spelling and grammatical errors, logical fallacies, and fail to reflect critical thought, a scholarly perspective, or the universal intellectual standards are likely to be dismissed by recipients.

In general, write in relatively short sentences. Use active voice, get to the point, provide a rationale for or evidence to support your position and, when needed to strengthen a position, include one or more illustrative examples. Gear your language to your audience. If you are communicating with other helping professionals you may use relevant jargon to capture complex phenomena that are best described through sophisticated terminology. In other contexts and for other audiences, avoid jargon altogether. Use succinct, descriptive, and businesslike language. Unless your purpose requires an evaluation or professional judgment, avoid speculative language. Distinguish opinions and conclusions from observations and facts.

Organize your document in an orderly fashion. You may use actual section headings or simply conceptualize each paragraph or two as a section so that the heading is implied. Obviously, there are many various documents that social workers prepare. These include notations made as part of case records (written or, increasingly, electronic), agendas and minutes of meetings, formal position or "white papers," grant applications, business plans and, of course, a seemingly endless number of e-mail messages.

In addition to case records, the most commonly prepared documents are probably letters, memorandums, and e-mails. Professional letters are organized in "business letter" fashion. If you prepare letters as part of your role with an organization, use the agency's letterhead paper. However, if you are not writing as a representative of your agency but rather from your perspective as a professional social worker, use your personal letterhead paper—or include your name followed by earned credentials (for example, Sue Wong, MSW, LSW indicates that Ms. Wong has earned a Master of Social Work degree and is currently a Licensed Social Worker). Along with your name, place your address, center-justified, at the top of the first page.

As you prepare a professional letter, keep its purpose in mind. Ask yourself, "What do I hope to accomplish through this letter?" Once answered, outline the steps needed to accomplish it. Typically, the first paragraph contains a succinct summary of your purpose and, when needed, a brief introduction of yourself. The remaining paragraphs may be used to elaborate upon that purpose by, for example, summarizing factual information about the nature and extent of a problem or issue along with an illustrative example or two to provide a "human face" (without risking privacy or violating confidentiality); providing a rationale as to why action is needed; identifying a few reasonable approaches and then discussing the advantages and disadvantages as well as potential risks and potential benefits of each; and then recommending the approach you prefer. A concluding summary often helps to reinforce the message.

As in all professional documents, carefully edit and reedit the letter; be sure to credit sources, avoid plagiarization, and double check for spelling, grammatical, and logical errors. Avoid unusual fonts. Instead use a traditional font—such as Times New Roman—in 12-point size. Left justify all text (with the exception of your name and address which is centered at the top). Most professional letters reflect a structure similar to that illustrated in Box 6.3.

BOX 6.3
Professional Letter Format: Example

Sue Wong, MSW, LSW
1 Long Drive
Indianapolis, Indiana 46260

[Date (e.g., July 27, 2012)]

[Recipient's Personal Title, Name, and Credentials if applicable and known (e.g., Mr. Curt Blank, BSW)]
[Recipient's Position if known (e.g., Director of Homeless Services)]
[Name of Organization if applicable (e.g., City of Indianapolis)]
[Street Address (e.g., 3611 County Square Building, Suite #152)]
[City or Town, State or Province, and Postal Code (e.g., Indianapolis, Indiana 46202)]
[Country, if needed (e.g., USA)]

[Salutation and Name followed by a colon (e.g., Dear Mr. Blank:)]

[Introductory Paragraph(s)]
[Main Paragraph(s)]
[Summary or Concluding Paragraph(s)]

[Closing followed by a comma (e.g., Sincerely yours,)]

[Signature (e.g., Sue Wong]
[Your Printed Name (e.g., Sue Wong, MSW, LSW)]
[Your Professional Title (e.g., Licensed Social Worker)]

BOX 6.4
Memorandum Format

MEMO

To:

CC:

From:

Date:

Subject:

[text here]

Memorandums are intra-agency or interdepartmental communications. For example, a social worker might send a memorandum to the executive director of her agency. She might forward copies to her supervisor and colleagues within the agency who might find the information relevant to their roles and responsibilities. Similarly, a social work student might send a memo to a professor, an advisor, the dean or director of the program, or perhaps to colleagues in a class or to fellow members of a student association or organization.

Approach the preparation of memos with the same level of professional care that you do with letters. Keep the purpose and audience in mind, and remember that your professional reputation is often reflected in the nature and quality of the documents you prepare. Most memos reflect a structure similar to that illustrated in Box 6.4.

E-mail communication represents an increasingly widespread means for professional correspondence. There are, however, major risks associated with e-mail and, of course, other electronic forms of communication such as texting, tweeting, and posting through various social media forums. A primary danger involves the often short timespan between a thought, feeling, or sensation and its electronic expression and transmission. A major advantage of letters, memos, position papers, and other reports is that we can prepare drafts, put them away for an hour or a day while we reflect upon them, and then return to revise and edit—perhaps two or three times—before distributing them. Such a time-lapse allows for both System 1 ("fast") and System 2 ("slow") thinking (Stanovich, 1999). As Kahneman (2011) suggests, System 1 thinking "operates automatically and quickly, with little or no effort and no sense of voluntary control" whereas System 2 thinking "allocates attention to the effortful mental activities that demand it, including complex computations. The operations of System 2 are often associated with the subjective experience of agency, choice, and concentration" (pp. 20–21). Both thinking systems are incredibly important and needed by social workers. System 1 includes our automatic, intuitive thoughts and the immediate, often unconscious, application of various heuristics or algorithms or, sometimes, stereotypes. System 1 thinking also tends to engage our reactive emotions so that we become less likely to think deeply or from new or different perspectives. System 2 thinking is slower and deeper in nature; tends to involve conscious, logical processing, reflection and analysis, and can include hypothetical reasoning. System 2 thinking is hard work—requiring the use of, as Agatha Christie's Hercule Poirot might say, "a lot of little grey cells." Such deep thought, though, may lead to alternate, creative, and innovative perspectives or approaches—although the process may be quite slow. Many other animals reflect System 1 thinking; however, System 2 thinking may be unique to human beings. The exclusive application of one system without the other, however, would not benefit members of the species *Homo sapiens*; and certainly not social workers and our clients.

E-mail and other forms of electronic communication are especially amenable to fast thinking—which, in professional contexts, can have deleterious effects upon social workers, their agencies and colleagues, the profession and, unfortunately, sometimes clients and other people. To counter the temptation to "think fast, type fast, and press the send button," consider the following practices:

◆ Do not use your organization's e-mail or cell phone service to send private messages or to send professional messages that are not associated with your agency roles and functions (that is, when you are not serving as a representative of the agency). Create a personal e-mail account through a free service provider (for example, www.hotmail.com, www.gmail.com, and numerous others) and use your own phone for personal and for nonagency related professional correspondence.

◆ Do not send messages to clients via e-mail—unless a client clear and fully understands the numerous risks associated with electronic transmission of sensitive material; and provides informed consent for such communication. Simply put, e-mails are not and cannot be considered secure. Their confidentiality and privacy cannot be safeguarded.

◆ When sending e-mails to colleagues within and outside your agency, ensure that clients' identities and confidential materials are excluded. Also, remember that e-mails are retained somewhere in electronic storage and can be hacked or retrieved by others. Indeed, some organizations monitor the e-mail and computer activity of their employees. A few do so in a covert manner. Of course, e-mail correspondence may be used in legal proceedings, both criminal and civil, as well as in professional disciplinary reviews. As a result of "unprofessional" e-mail messages, social workers may be demoted or discharged, and their professional reputations tarnished.

◆ Create professional e-mail messages in a separate word-processing program. Review it carefully at least one time and use the spell-check and grammar-check features before you copy and paste the message into your e-mail system. You might also decide upon the routine use of a time-delay—say 10 or 15 minutes—before you transfer your message from the word-processing to the e-mail system. That way, you have at least some time to reflect upon the message and, perhaps, engage your capacity for slow, analytic, System 2 thinking.

EXERCISE 6-3: TALKING

1. Imagine that you are serving as a social worker in a community outreach program. The program seeks to locate homeless people in the area and inform them of community resources that might enhance their lives and well-being. Several services for

homeless individuals and families are available. These include: temporary housing and food preparation; medical and dental care; job training and placement; and ongoing counseling. Use a word-processing program to prepare a preliminary "script" to help you prepare what you might say to homeless people in introducing yourself and the services you can provide. Reflect upon the script and then revise as needed. Familiarize yourself with the script—but do not memorize it. Then, without reading the script, make a 2- to 3-minute audio recording of what you might say when you first meet a homeless person that you find living in a small wooded section near a downtown river and seek to introduce yourself and describe the services provided by the program.[6]

Replay the recording and review your language usage. Examine the words you said and consider them from the point of view of a person who has not sought your company. Reflect upon your speech and tone of voice. Use the space provided below to respond to the following questions: What might they suggest about your approach and attitude toward the person? Do your voice and speech convey the qualities of interest, respect, confidence, and hopefulness? Identify one or two aspects of verbal and nonverbal communication that you would like to strengthen in preparation for your roles and functions as a professional social worker.

Following that, imagine that you are that homeless person. A stranger approaches and begins to speak to you. You do not know the identity of the stranger nor the purpose for the visit. How might you experience the stranger's body language and movement, nonverbal expressions, speech, voice, and language? As a homeless person, how would you like to be approached, addressed, and engaged?

---

[6] If you are visually or physically challenged in some way, please adapt these exercises accordingly. Be sure to incorporate the implications of your challenges in your discussions.

2. As you know, the "talking" skills also include written as well as verbal forms of communication. Use a word-processing program to prepare two professional-quality documents: (a) a letter and (b) a memorandum. As a topic for both documents, select a social problem that has recently been the subject of local, national, or international news and also interests you. For example, you might be concerned about human trafficking, or the illegal procurement and sales of human organs, or perhaps injustices associated with application of the death penalty. You might question the practice of stoning or caning women accused of adultery, the forced marriage of girls to adult men, or the practice of female circumcision. You might be concerned about drought, famine, hunger, and starvation in parts of the world or perhaps about the social impact of climate change.

As social workers, we are well aware of a seemingly infinite number of major social problems. Choose one that engenders passion and energy. Then, draft either a "letter to the editor" or a letter to your legislative representative. You do not have to mail the letter. View the exercise as an opportunity to practice your written communication skills. In the letter, use a paragraph or two to introduce the nature and scope of the problem, and provide an illustrative example. Use the remaining paragraphs to suggest some action—perhaps in the form of a policy or program, legislation, or steps that other concerned people might take. Prepare the document in the form of a business letter.

After you edit and finalize the letter, prepare an alternate version in the form of a memorandum to colleagues. To do so, make an electronic copy of the letter that you prepared and then edit it so that it appears in the form of a memorandum. Label the word-processed documents "Draft Letter 1" and "Draft Memo 1" and include them in your Social Work Skills Portfolio.

Listening

Listening involves the use of your sensory capacities to receive and register the messages expressed verbally and nonverbally by others.[7] The listening skills include *hearing* or *receiving* others' words, speech, and language; *observing* (Carkhuff & Anthony, 1979; Ivey et al., 2010) their nonverbal gestures and positions; *encouraging* (Ivey, 1988; Ivey et al., 2010) them to express themselves fully; and *remembering* what they communicate.

Most of us are rather poor listeners, tending to pay more attention to our own thoughts and feelings than to the messages others are trying to convey. Competent listening rarely comes naturally. Yet listening, more than any other skill, is essential for effective social work practice. It requires two actions. First, you minimize attention to your own experiences (for example, thoughts, feelings, and sensations). Then, you energetically concentrate on the client with a determination to understand—rather than evaluate—what the client is experiencing and expressing.

For most of us, one of the genuinely humanizing events in life occurs when we feel truly understood by another person. When you listen attentively with intention to understand and empathize, you convey a special degree of respect. It demonstrates that you value others and are interested in what they have to say. In a sense, careful listening is a gesture of love. Because of this,

---

[7] If you are visually or physically challenged in some way, please adapt these exercises accordingly. Be sure to incorporate the implications of your challenges in your discussions.

empathic listening is a dynamic factor in social work practice. It has several purposes. First, effective listening enables you to gather information that is essential for assessment and planning. Second, it helps clients feel better—often reducing tension or anxiety, heightening feelings of personal safety and well-being, and encouraging greater hope and optimism. Third, attentive listening encourages clients to express themselves freely and fully. Fourth, effective listening usually enhances your value to clients. Finally, attentive listening often contributes significantly to positive change in clients' self-understanding and self-efficacy as well as their problem-solving and goal-seeking capacities.

To listen effectively, you need to manage your own impulses, tendencies, and predispositions. This is essentially a matter of self-awareness and self-discipline—those professional characteristics we discussed earlier. You hold back from fully experiencing and freely expressing your own reactions, ideas, or opinions. Such self-discipline involves temporarily suspending judgment and action so you can better hear and understand other people. As a social worker, you are probably highly motivated to help troubled people. In your desire to serve, you may sometimes be tempted to rush to conclusions and solutions. Although life-threatening situations often require immediate intervention, engaging in premature assessment, offering advice early, or proposing action before understanding the issues and the person-in-environment, typically interferes with effective, empathic listening. Frequently, it also has unintended adverse consequences. In most circumstances, you would be wise to listen carefully and fully before assessing or intervening. As Shulman (2009) suggests, "Workers who attempt to find simple solutions often discover that if the solutions were indeed that simple, then the client could have found them without the help of the worker" (p. 126).

Self-disciplined listening may involve some use of silence. Social workers "frequently perceive silence as a hindrance and a hazard to the progress of the interview. . . . The professional assumption is that talking is better" (Kadushin, 1983, p. 286). This is certainly not always the case. Periods of silence, pauses in the exchange, are vital elements in effective communication. Sometimes people need time to transition to System 2 thinking and reflect upon phenomena in more complex or deeper ways. Of course, you should not let silence continue so long that it becomes an anxious contest to see who will speak first. Do recognize, however, that with some clients, at certain moments, silence can be a powerfully helpful experience. "Instead of a threat, silence should be seen and utilized as an opportunity" (Kadushin, 1983, p. 294).

Hearing refers to the process of listening (that is, receiving messages), which involves attending to the speech and language of other people. Numerous factors can impede or obstruct hearing. A room might be noisy, or a person might talk softly or mumble. Someone may speak in a foreign language or adopt an unfamiliar dialect. Another person might use words you do not understand or use them in different ways than you do. Effective hearing involves diminishing the obstacles and focusing entirely on the words and sounds of the other person. It also involves reducing the tendency to hear selectively because of our inclination to judge the words and sounds of others, and confirm our own assumptions and preconceptions. In attempting to hear clearly, we hope to take in and remember the messages sent by the speaker. In listening, process is as important as content. Therefore try to hear more than the words themselves. Listen as well to the person's manner of speaking including pace, pauses, and intonations. Connect empathically as you try to hear the meaning and feeling just beyond or just beneath the words actually said.

Another vital element in the listening process is the skill of observation. *Observing* (Carkhuff & Anthony, 1979; Ivey et al., 2010) occurs when you pay attention to the client's physical characteristics, gestures, and other nonverbal behavior. Nonverbal communication is at least as informative as verbal expression and sometimes more so, especially in multicultural contexts. As a social worker, try to observe nonverbal manifestations of energy level, mood, and emotions as well as indirect signs and signals. Quite often, clients do not directly express their feelings through verbal speech. Without staring, try to observe carefully so you notice nonverbal expressions of feeling.

The purpose of observing is to gain a better and more complete understanding of the ways in which the client experiences the world. During interviews, attend to subtle or indirect communications. These may relate to themes of power or authority, ambivalence about seeking or receiving help, difficulties in discussing topics that involve a stigma or taboo, and inhibitions concerning the direct and full expression of powerful feelings (Shulman, 2009). You may pick up more indirect communications from nonverbal rather than verbal expressions, so observe closely. Be careful, however, to avoid the tempting conceptual trap of reaching premature conclusions. The most you can do is formulate tentative hypotheses about a theme based on the words and the nonverbal gestures a client has used. Such tentative hypotheses are not, in any sense, true or valid. They represent, rather, preliminary hunches!

Among the specific aspects to observe are (1) facial expression, (2) eye contact, and (3) body language, position, and movement. In observing, look for predominant facial expressions, head and body positions, physical gestures, and patterns of eye contact during communication exchanges. Consider them in light of cultural affiliations as well as the context. Also, look for the nature and timing of changes in these nonverbal indicators. These may suggest feeling states such as contentment, calmness, acceptance, joy, sadness, fear or anxiety, and anger. Based on these observations, consider what these expressions, gestures, and behaviors might suggest about how this person experiences herself or himself and feels about the problem or issue of concern. Also, imagine what they indicate about how the person thinks and feels about you and about this meeting.

Encouraging (Ivey et al., 2010) is a form of listening that involves some talking. You can encourage other people to continue expressing themselves by making very brief responses in the form of single words, short phrases, or sounds and gestures that invite them to continue their expression. Some examples of brief verbal encouragers include: Please go on. . . . and?. . . . Uh huh. . . . Mmmm . . . . Yes. . . . Please continue.

Nonverbally, you may further communicate encouragement by nodding, making attentive eye contact, gesturing slightly with your hands, and leaning or inclining slightly toward the client. Repeating a portion of a phrase or a key word that a client uses may also constitute encouragement. Such brief responses enable you to demonstrate that you want to hear more, but you do so without interrupting with a lengthy statement of your own. However, avoid using the same encouragers over and over. After a while, their repeated use may suggest a lack of sincerity. Also, recognize that the use of minimal encouragers alone is insufficient. Active-listening communications are necessary to demonstrate accurate empathic understanding.

The final dimension of listening involves *remembering* what the client communicates. Hearing and observing are skills without much inherent value unless you can retain the information received. Remembering is the process of temporarily storing information so that you may use it later—for example, to communicate understanding, make thematic connections between messages expressed at different times, prepare a written record, or develop an assessment.

EXERCISE 6-4: LISTENING

Recruit a friend or colleague to join you in a listening exercise. Indicate that the purpose of this exercise is to help you become a better listener. Ask your partner to identify a topic of interest that the two of you might discuss for approximately 10 minutes. As the listener, your tasks are to encourage your partner to discuss the subject; to hear and comprehend what she or he communicates; and to remember what was said and done. Keep in mind that your partner's perspective is paramount. Withhold your own opinions; refrain from judgments or evaluations in both speech and thought. This is your partner's time. Let the discussion proceed in whatever way and direction your partner wishes. Encourage him or her to communicate freely and fully, and try not to interfere with the flow of expression. As your partner talks, listen attentively and observe carefully. At the end of the 10-minute period, thank your partner and proceed with the following:

1. First, ask your partner to reflect upon her or his experience of the exchange. Then, ask your partner to give you truly honest feedback about how well you listened. Say that you sincerely want to become a better listener so that genuine feedback is needed. You might also say that whatever your partner says, your feelings will not be hurt because this is a practice exercise and you plan to improve.

   As you seek feedback from your partner, explore nonverbal as well as verbal factors. For instance, ask about eye contact, facial expressions, body positions and movements, physical gestures, tone of voice, rate of speech and its audibility in terms of their relationship to listening. Did your partner feel you were interested in what she or he had to say; that you understood and remembered what was said; and you were non-judgmental about her or him and what she or he said?

   Ask about points at which your partner felt that you listened especially well as well as those when you did not. Finally, ask your partner for suggestions about what you might do to improve upon your listening abilities and become a better listener.

   Thank your partner again and say goodbye.

   Reflect upon the exercise and your partner's observations, then use the space provided to: (a) summarize your partner's comments and suggestions; (b) identify aspects of your listening skills that you would like to strengthen; and (c) outline brief plans by which to become a better listener.

Active Listening

Active listening combines talking and listening skills in such a way that others feel both understood and encouraged to share more. It is a form of feedback. You listen carefully and communicate your understanding of a speaker's messages by reflecting or mirroring them back. In essence, you paraphrase the client's message. Ideally, your words should be essentially equivalent to or synonymous with, but not identical to, those of the client. If the client communicates factual content, your active-listening response should convey that factual information. If the client expresses feelings, reflect those feelings in your active-listening response and do so at an equivalent level of intensity. If the client shares conceptual ideas, paraphrase them through active listening so that you accurately capture his or her meaning.

Active listening represents a clear and tangible demonstration that you have understood or at least are trying to understand what a client has expressed. It indicates that you want to comprehend fully and accurately the messages communicated. Active listening shows that you are interested in the client's views, feelings, and experiences. Because it conveys empathy and furthers understanding, there is simply no substitute for active listening. It constitutes a major element of the vital feedback loop between you and your client. If you do not listen actively, you are more likely to miss part of a client's message and thereby misunderstand, distort, or misrepresent it. Furthermore, if you fail to listen actively or if you paraphrase in a consistently inaccurate fashion, you discourage the client from free and full expression. You also significantly diminish your own value in the relationship. Clients look forward to being understood. If you do not accurately communicate understanding, clients may feel unheard, disappointed, and alienated. Experiences of oppression, discrimination, abuse, or exploitation have left many clients feeling profoundly misunderstood throughout their lives. When you, as a professional social worker, communicate sincere and accurate understanding, the effect can be positive indeed. However, if the clients feel that you too, like so many before, also misunderstand, a powerfully adverse effect may result. Experiencing yet another repetition of alienation, such clients may wish they had never sought your services in the first place.

Active listening combines the talking and listening skills into three steps:

- ◆ Step 1: *Inviting*. Through your body position, facial expression, speech, and language, indicate that you are prepared to listen. Often, you can invite the other person to express himself or herself by asking a question such as "What happened?" or "How did this all come about?" It is not always necessary, however, to ask a specific question. Many clients begin to talk about themselves and their concerns as soon as you begin to attend to them with your eyes, face, and body.
- ◆ Step 2: *Listening*. When a client responds to your invitation to speak and begins to talk, you listen carefully by attempting to hear, observe, encourage, and remember. In this step, you essentially use your ears and brain to receive and retain the messages sent by the other person.
- ◆ Step 3: *Reflecting*. Periodically, as the client pauses at the conclusion of a message segment, paraphrase his or her statement. For example, a client might say, "I'm really frustrated with my boss. He says he wants production, production, production! But then he comes down to my shop and spends hours shooting the breeze." In active listening, you could say in response, "You're annoyed with him because he tells you he wants you to work harder and harder but then he interferes when you're trying to do so." Here is another example. Suppose a client says, "Ever since I was 7 years old, I felt fat and ugly." You might say, in active listening, "From the time of your childhood up through the present time, you've thought of yourself as overweight and unattractive." By communicating an equivalent message, you demonstrate empathic understanding.

Active listening is, of course, most useful when you have accurately understood and paraphrased the client's message, but it can be helpful even when you have not. Sometimes you may misunderstand a message or miss part of it as your attention wanders; or the client may misspeak and send an incomplete or confusing message. In such cases, your sincere attempt to understand by active listening almost always elicits further expression from the client.

A client may spontaneously express confirmation when your active listening response accurately reflects his or her message. The client may say something such as "Yeah, that's right." Then the client often simply continues to talk. On those occasions when your response is not entirely accurate but is close enough to demonstrate that you have heard some of the message and are genuinely trying to understand, the client may say, "Well, no. What I meant was . . ." He or she may then try to restate the message so that you can understand. However, when you are extremely inaccurate, perhaps due to your own lack of interest or attention, the client may very well respond with an emphatic "No!" and then become much less expressive. A similar phenomenon can occur when you do not listen actively often enough. If you only talk or only listen but do not actively listen, you may discourage clients from expressing themselves freely and fully.

When we are first developing skill in active listening, social workers tend to make several common errors:

- Using so many of the client's own words that your paraphrased reflections sound like mimicry.
- Repeatedly using the same lead-in phrases (for example, "I hear you saying . . ." "It sounds like . . .").
- Trying to be clever, profound, or interpretive—playing the role of "brilliant analyst" or "clever detective" tends to indicate that you are listening more to your own thoughts and speculations than to the client's message.
- Responding only to facts, thoughts, and ideas or just to feelings and emotions rather than listening actively to all dimensions of the client's expression.
- Interrupting frequently to reflect the client's message.
- Using active listening following every short phrase or statement.

EXERCISE 6-5: ACTIVE LISTENING

In the spaces provided, write the words you might say in active listening to the following statements:

1. CLIENT: My husband thinks I'm an alcoholic. I'm here because he made me come. Sure, I drink. I drink a lot. But he's the reason I drink.

2. CLASSMATE: I've missed the last three classes and don't know what's going on in here. Today is the day of the midterm exam and I know I'm going to flunk. I'm so uptight, I can't think straight.

3. WOMAN WHO LOST HER 12-YEAR-OLD CHILD TO GANG VIOLENCE: I never wanted to live in this cesspool. We just couldn't afford to move to another neighborhood. There are gunshots almost every night and the police rarely come by—that is, until after someone's been killed. Drug dealers and street walkers are everywhere. I feel so guilty that my lovely daughter had to live and to die here. It's just so unfair. If you don't have much, you have to live where you can and that means somebody, sometime is gonna die.

4. SUPERVISOR: I am disappointed that you did not follow up on the Sanchez case. You know those children are at risk and I expected you to visit them again last week.

5. PROFESSOR: I wonder if the match between your personal values and those of the social work profession is a good one. From your comments in class and the papers you've written, it seems to me that your views differ quite a bit from those of most social workers.

6. SOCIAL WORK COLLEAGUE: I am working with a family that is driving me up the wall. I know I have a problem here. I get so angry at the parents for being so passive. I work so damn hard and they don't do a thing!

7. CHILD: Sometimes my mommy's boyfriend is mean to her. He hits her and she ends up crying a lot. I don't like him at all.

8. COMMUNITY LEADER: I appreciate your offer to help with our community organization and development efforts. However, the social workers we've had before have never worked out.

9. CLIENT WHO SEEMS ANGRY OR FRUSTRATED: I have to tell you that I've been to a counselor before. All she did was repeat my words back to me and then ask me what I'd like to do. Well, I want advice from somebody who really knows something about this problem—not someone who just wants to be my friend. I need an expert who has helped other people resolve the same problem I'm dealing with.

Summary

The basic interpersonal skills of talking and listening (that is, sending and receiving messages) are fundamental to all aspects of human interaction, including the phases and processes of social work practice. To communicate effectively as a social worker, you use all the sensory faculties at your command in sending and receiving messages. In addition, you regularly combine the talking and listening skills in the form of active listening. Active listening conveys empathy by overtly demonstrating that you are making a genuine effort to understand.

Highly developed communications skills contribute to clear expression and accurate understanding during exchanges with individuals, families, groups, organizations, and communities. Integral to cultural sensitivity, they are essential for engaging diversity and difference with people of diverse views and traditions.

CHAPTER 6: SUMMARY EXERCISE

The following exercise should help you to refine your abilities in culturally sensitive talking, listening, and active-listening skills.

1. With the informed consent of a friend or colleague from a cultural tradition that differs in some substantial way from your own, make a video recording[8] of a 15-minute conversation. Indicate that you are trying to practice your interviewing skills and would like to conduct an interview about his or her choice of career. Tell your partner that she or he will not have to answer any questions that evoke discomfort. Also, be sure to indicate that your professor and perhaps some of your classmates may review the recording to provide feedback about the quality of your interviewing skills. Ask your colleague for permission to both record the interview and to use it exclusively for the purpose of your learning. In other words, obtain informed consent. You might mention that if your colleague is interested in viewing the recording and perhaps providing additional feedback once you have completed the assignment, you would truly welcome and appreciate that as well.

    During the interview, explore with your colleague how she or he came to make the career choice. Explore influential and motivational factors. Ask about your partner's hopes and aspirations as well as issues and concerns regarding the chosen career. Use the skills of talking, listening, and active listening to encourage your colleague to share as much as possible about the career decision. At the conclusion of the interview, ask your colleague to reflect upon the experience and then complete a copy of the Talking and Listening Skills Rating Form contained in Appendix 11.

    When your partner has completed the instrument, ask her or him for immediate reactions to and feedback about the experience—perhaps by elaborating upon responses to items included in the rating form. Ask about cultural sensitivity. At what points were aspects of his or her culture especially well recognized, appreciated, or respected; when were they not? Explore nonverbal factors such as your eye contact, facial expressions, body positions and movements, physical gestures, tone of voice, rate and volume

---

[8] Since the interview is recorded, maintain the anonymity of your partner as much as humanly possible. Erase or destroy the recording as soon as you complete the requirements for the learning exercises.

of speech as well as its modulation. Ask if you appeared genuinely interested in what she or he had to say. Ask how well your partner thinks that that you understood and remembered what was said, and that you fully accepted him or her? Ask about exchanges when she or he felt especially heard and understood; and those when she or he did not. Ask about your attempts to reflect back and paraphrase her words. Which times were you truly on target; when were you off? Finally, ask your partner to give you suggestions about what you might do to become more culturally sensitive and improve upon your talking and listening skills. When your partner finishes, express your gratitude, offer your thanks, and say goodbye.

2. Next, play the video recording. Prepare a word-processed transcript that accurately reflects what was said and by whom but **do not use your colleague's name**. Use *interviewee* to refer to his or her words. Title the document "Transcript of an Early Interview." Identify the talking and the listening skills you used during the conversation. For example, identify as talking a statement you made or a question you asked that came from your frame of reference. Identify as active listening your attempts to communicate your understanding of your partner's expressions. Use your word-processing software to organize the transcript according to the format outlined in Table 6.1, but **be sure to disguise the identity of the person you interviewed**.

TABLE 6.1
Transcription and Skill Identification Format

	Transcript	Skill Used
Interviewer	Record the words you said here.	Identify the talking and listening skill used—if any—here.
Interviewee	Record what your partner said here.	Use this space to make observations or comments to advance your learning.
Interviewer	Record the words you said here.	Identify the talking and listening skill used—if any—here.
Interviewee	Record what your partner said here.	Use this space to make observations or comments to advance your learning.

© Cengage Learning

After you have prepared the transcript, use it along with the video itself; your colleague's responses to the Talking and Listening Skills Rating Form and her or his comments and suggestions; and your own observations to evaluate your proficiency in the talking, listening, and active-listening skills. Word-process a two- to three-page (500–750 words) report titled, "Evaluation of an Early Interview." In your paper, respond to the dimensions suggested by statements in the Talking and Listening Skills Rating Form by addressing questions such as the following: How did your verbal and nonverbal communications reflect sensitivity and respect for various aspects of your colleague's culture? How did your facial expressions, head movements, tone of voice, body positions, and physical gestures communicate that you were genuinely interested in your partner and everything he or she said? How clearly and audibly did you speak, and what might your tone of voice and speech modulation suggest about your attitude toward your colleague? Were your words and language familiar to your colleague so that she or he could easily understand everything you said? How did your verbal communications and nonverbal expressions convey nonjudgmental interest in, attention to, and respect for your partner and everything he or she expressed? How well did you remember what was expressed during the interview? How did you summarize and reflect back your partner's messages so that she or he felt truly heard and understood?

Conclude the report by identifying those aspects of the talking and listening skills that you need to practice more and improve. Outline the dimensions of your plans to do so.

If you have your interview partner's permission and informed consent, ask one or two classmates or an instructor from the school or department of social work to review the videotape and offer evaluative feedback about your expression of cultural sensitivity and the nature and quality of your talking, listening, and active-listening skills. Consider the feedback. If constructive, revise your word-processed report to accommodate the new information. Once you have edited and finalized your report, include it and the transcript in your Social Work Skills Learning Portfolio.

3. Finally, reflect on the content and the exercises contained in this chapter; and your recently completed interview evaluation report. Based on your reflections, word-process a succinct one-to-two page letter to yourself. Prepare it as a formal business letter. Address it to yourself along with a note to read it again one year from now. In the letter, describe a plan by which you might become a more culturally sensitive and more empathic listener who can communicate with people in a warm, genuine, and respectful manner. Identify how you would know that you had progressed in these areas. When you have finished, title the file "One-Year Letter to Myself" and include the letter in your Social Work Skills Learning Portfolio. Make a note in your calendar to read the letter in one year's time.

CHAPTER 6: SELF-APPRAISAL

As you finish this chapter, please reflect on your learning by completing the following self-appraisal exercise.

SELF-APPRAISAL: THE TALKING AND LISTENING SKILLS

Please respond to the following items to help you undertake a self-assessment of your proficiency in the basic interpersonal skills addressed in this chapter. Read each statement carefully. Then, use the following 4-point rating scale to indicate the degree to which you agree or disagree with each statement. Record your numerical response in the space provided:

4 = Strongly agree	2 = Disagree
3 = Agree	1 = Strongly disagree

4	3	2	1	Rating Statement
				At this point in time, I can
☐	☐	☐	☐	1. Describe and discuss the talking, listening, and active-listening skills.
☐	☐	☐	☐	2. Engage diversity and difference through culturally sensitive communications.
☐	☐	☐	☐	3. Use nonverbal communications and body language in a professional manner.
☐	☐	☐	☐	4. Apply the talking skills—including written as well as verbal communication—in a professional manner.
☐	☐	☐	☐	5. Use the listening skills effectively.
☐	☐	☐	☐	6. Use the active-listening skills.
☐	☐	☐	☐	7. Assess my proficiency in the talking, listening, and active-listening skills.
				Subtotal

Note: These items are identical to those contained in the Talking and Listening Skills section of the Social Work Skills Self-Appraisal Questionnaire presented in Appendix 3. If you completed that self-appraisal before beginning Chapter 1, you have already responded to these items once before. You may now compare the responses you made on that occasion with those you made this time. Also, compare the two subtotals. If you believe that you have progressed in terms of your proficiency, the more recent subtotal should be higher than the earlier one.

PREPARING

This chapter (see Box 7.1) should help you learn the skills used in the preparing phase of social work practice. Initial meetings set the tone and influence the general direction of subsequent interactions. In fact, the nature of your first contacts with people often determines whether they actually become clients. Preparation is essential in this regard. Without it, we can easily lose our cognitive and emotional equilibrium as we encounter individuals, families, groups, organizations, and communities of diverse cultural traditions struggling with highly complex and challenging issues in often extraordinarily difficult circumstances (Branch Jr. & Gordon, 2004; Burke & Parker, 2007; Gleeson & Philbin, 1996; Hayes, Humphries, & Cohen, 2004; Kovacs & Bronstein, 1999; Sar, 2000).

In a meta-analysis of some 125 research studies, Wierzbicki and Pekarik (1993) found that the average early-dropout rate in outpatient mental health services was approximately 47 percent. Client factors associated with early dropout included limited formal education, lower socioeconomic status, and racial-minority status. A more recent meta-analysis of 669 studies of adult psychotherapy indicated an average early discontinuation rate of about 20 percent. Factors associated with early dropout include researchers' definition of "dropout," diagnosis and age of client, extent of provider experience, and type of study (Swift & Greenberg, 2012). In a study of nearly 14,000 people served in 17 mental health centers, Sue (1977) discovered that when compared with white clients, a significantly greater percentage of minority applicants did not return following an initial visit. Differences between the personal and cultural expectations of clients and professional helpers represent the clearest explanation for early dropout or discontinuation of needed services. Indeed, when professional helpers fail to express accurate understanding of clients' view of the problems (that is, how clients conceptualize the issues), the rate of dropout triples. Similarly, the actual length of service appears to be determined primarily by clients' expectations of anticipated duration (Epperson, Bushway, & Warman, 1983; Pekarik, 1988, 1991; Pelkonen, Marttunen, Laippala, & Lonnqvist, 2000; Wierzbicki & Pekarik, 1993).

Although several factors are undoubtedly involved with premature discontinuation, insufficient and ineffective preparation for first meetings is certainly part of the problem. Effective preparation and careful planning can make the difference.

Let's try to be personally and professionally ready to perform competently from the first moment of contact. Use the preparing skills before the first meetings with individuals, families, groups, organizations, and communities with whom you interact as part of your professional responsibilities. Then continue to use them in advance of each subsequent encounter. The preparing skills include (1) preparatory reviewing, (2) preparatory exploring, (3) preparatory consultation, (4) preparatory arranging, (5) preparatory empathy, (6) preparatory self-exploration, (7) centering, and (8) preliminary planning and recording.

Preparatory Reviewing

Preparatory reviewing involves examining and considering information available to you and your agency before an initial contact with another person or people (Kadushin, 1983). When an individual, family, group, organization, or community has previously received service from your agency, review the relevant case records. When a telephone contact or an intake interview has preceded the first meeting, examine notes concerning the nature and substance of that interaction. For first meetings with other people, such as an agency director, a client's medical doctor, or a new supervisee, thoughtfully review relevant materials concerning the general purpose of the meeting and any topics likely to emerge. When meeting with a family system or subsystem, a group, an organization, or a community, preparatory reviewing becomes, if anything, even more important as you consider intrasystem and intersystem factors and dynamics.

Preparatory reviewing helps you grasp significant facts and circumstances before meetings. This reduces the need for applicants, clients, or other people to repeat information they have previously provided. It allows for more efficient use of time and helps people feel that what they say is valued and remembered.

In some instances, failure to review available materials can constitute professional negligence or malpractice. For example, suppose a teenage boy contacts your agency. He has a history of making serious suicide attempts following conflicts in romantic relationships. Your agency has served him off and on during the past several years, and this pattern of suicidal action is documented in his case file. He requests an appointment for some time later that day, indicating that he needs help because his girlfriend recently "dumped" him, deciding that she wanted to date another boy. If you fail to review the case record, you may decide to give the teenager an appointment several days later, not realizing the serious, immediate risk of suicidal behavior.

As another example, suppose you are about to interview a family with a history of both spousal and child abuse. Both patterns are well-documented in agency files. Imagine the risks associated with failure to review those materials before the meeting.

Groups, organizations, and communities may also have factions or "histories" that pertain to the purpose for the meeting and our preparation. For instance, suppose you are about to meet with a small group of leaders to establish a direction and goals for your work with their community organization. Your agency has previously worked with the organization and the community it represents. Imagine what could happen if you did not know that since your agency's last contact, the organization had split into two because of a conflict over its mission and the misuse of funds by its director. There are now two subgroups—one led by the former director and another by former board members—purporting to serve the same community. Imagine a first meeting in which you were unaware of these current circumstances?

There are also numerous practical reasons for reviewing relevant information before a visit. You may learn, for example, that a prospective client is hard of hearing or does not speak any of the languages spoken in your agency, so that an interpreter will be required. You might find out that a person uses a wheelchair and has a canine companion. Such knowledge could enable you to rearrange your office to allow enough open space for the wheelchair and dog.

Although many benefits are associated with the preparatory review of materials, there are potential dangers as well. Some records and related documents contain hearsay information or opinions written as if they were undisputed facts. You may inadvertently accept at face value information that is essentially false, distorted, biased, or incomplete. Some records contain profiles, assessments, or diagnoses that can lead you to form a stereotypical impression of a person or group before you actually meet. Such profiles may have been inaccurate when initially recorded, or they may have since become so. The person or people, the issue, or the situation may have changed, sometimes dramatically, since the last entry. In preparatory reviewing, recognize that information contained in case records or other forms of written material may be incomplete or erroneous. It is vital that you maintain an open mind during the preparatory reviewing phase.

1. At 10:13 A.M. on January 12, Ruth Gordon, an agency social worker received a telephone call from a woman identifying herself as Mrs. Nancy Cannon. The social worker jotted a few notes concerning the call on a form entitled Telephone Contact (see Box 7.2). Ms. Gordon later gave the report to you, the social worker assigned to conduct the initial face-to-face interview and, if appropriate, provide needed professional services.

   Demonstrate your use of the preparatory reviewing skill by examining the contents of Box 7.2. Use a pen or pencil to highlight information that you, as the social worker, would want to remember for a first meeting with Mrs. Cannon. Use the space below the box to make note of potential themes or issues.

BOX 7.2

Telephone Contact

January 12, 10:13 A.M. Mrs. Nancy Cannon telephoned from her place of work (the Capital Insurance Company—phone 234-6213). She sounded concerned. She said that on the previous Saturday night, her 14-year-old daughter Amy had come home after her 9:00 P.M. curfew, smelling of alcohol. She says that she "grounded" her daughter but now wants to talk with a social worker about the situation. Mrs. Cannon requested an appointment for herself alone, indicating that she wanted to sort things out with someone before she dealt further with her daughter.

Mrs. C. reported that this was the first such incident. She said, "I've never had any trouble whatsoever from Amy. She's been a wonderful child." She stated that she had not sought professional help before and that this was her first contact with any social service or mental health agency. She indicated that her husband, Amy's father, had recently filed for divorce and had left the home approximately 6 weeks ago. Mrs. C. wondered whether that might be connected with Amy's misbehavior over the weekend.

Disposition: An appointment was scheduled with an agency social worker for tomorrow at 12:00 noon. Mrs. C. requested a lunch-hour appointment, if at all possible, to reduce the amount of time away from her job.

Ruth Gordon, BSW, LSW
Licensed Social Worker

Preparatory Exploring

The skill of preparatory exploring involves asking questions and seeking information about a prospective client or others, a problem or issue, and a situation—prior to the meeting. This is an important but often neglected skill. Receptionists, intake workers, or executives from your agency may talk with people before you first meet with them. They often have useful information that can improve the quality of the first contact. Similarly, referral sources from outside your agency may have knowledge that can help. As part of making a referral on behalf of another person or group, family members, physicians, judges, teachers, religious leaders, other helping professionals, and governmental officials often contact social service agencies. They may possess important information concerning the person or group, the presenting issue and situation, and sometimes even the nature of the service needs. As a natural part of the process of talking about the referral to your agency, you may appropriately inquire about the person or group, issue, and situation with the referral source. Usually, you would not have permission to seek information from other sources. For that, you would need the informed consent of the client. However, when someone makes a referral for another person, family, group, organization, or community, you may appropriately seek information from the referring source. Regardless of the source of information, however, realize that what you hear from others reflects their own perspectives. Other people may view things in quite a different way, and you may too.

Preparatory exploring is also applicable for people previously served by colleagues in your own agency. For example, by reviewing agency files, you may learn that another social worker in the agency, Ms. Castillo, had previously served a client you are about to see. Once you learn that, you could ask Ms. Castillo for pertinent information about the case.

The use of the preparatory exploring skill can result in a more positive and productive first meeting. However, information gained through the preparatory exploring process should not lead you to stereotype people or form fixed impressions about the nature of an issue and situation. You can resist such temptations by consciously distinguishing fact from opinion and recognizing that the views of one person usually differ from those of others.

In preparatory exploring, remain open to information that may help you be a more effective service provider. You may note names and relevant demographic data such as phone numbers, addresses, or special needs and circumstances. You may learn the preferred pronunciation of names. Details concerning the nature, severity, and urgency of the issue are, of course, extremely important, as are indications of the strengths and resources available to the people involved.

EXERCISE 7-2: PREPARATORY EXPLORING

1. At 3:15 P.M. on Wednesday, Father Julio Sanchez, a Catholic priest in a largely Mexican parish, telephones you at your agency. He indicates that a family of seven needs help. He says that the parents and older children are migrant workers. He reports that the family had been traveling to a new work site when their automobile broke down. In the space provided, write the questions you would ask and identify the information you would seek as you use the skill of preparatory exploring with Father Sanchez.

Preparatory Consultation

The skill of preparatory consultation may be used in two primary ways. The first involves seeking advice from a social work supervisor or professional colleagues within your agency concerning an upcoming visit with a prospective client or other people. The second involves consultation with experts or examination of published material related to a topic that appears relevant to a forthcoming meeting.

When engaging in preparatory consultation with agency-based colleagues, you may usually be fairly open about details that pertain to an upcoming meeting. Your supervisors and other members of your service program or unit are just as responsible for protecting the privacy and confidentiality rights of your clients as you are of theirs. When consulting with outside experts, however, social workers must be more circumspect and seek information in ways that do not compromise clients' rights. For example, suppose you are about to meet with a new client who mentioned during the initial telephone contact that she is an undocumented immigrant and expected to be deported within the next few weeks. However, her children are U.S. citizens and she wants them to remain in this country. She seeks your help exploring options and locating the best available care of her children during her absence. She anticipates being away for at least 1 year and perhaps many more.

Given this limited information, many social workers would wisely consult government websites to review up-to-date information about deportation policies and processes; as well as potential resources for children of deported parents. You might contact a governmental representative by phone or through an internet "live chat" service. In seeking information, however, you would avoid the use of her name, address, or other identifying characteristics—unless you had her expressed informed consent to do so. Otherwise, you could easily violate her rights to confidentiality and privacy.

Clients' rights are usually safer when social workers consult published works such as professional books, research articles, or legal statutes. However, be a bit careful in your choice of keywords so that your client's privacy and confidentiality rights are assured.

Commonly, social workers would seek consultation from professional colleagues to consider tentative objectives for an interview, seek advice, or to discuss other service-related issues. The specific nature of the consultation, however, varies from situation to situation. On one occasion, you might discuss possible locations for the interview. In another, you might inquire about cultural customs of a particular religious or ethnic group about which you have limited knowledge. On occasion, you might seek advice concerning how best to ensure your own safety when you are about to interview someone who has previously been physically violent toward people in positions of authority. In still another, you might focus on the agency policies or legal obligations that could apply in a particular case. By engaging in preparatory consultation, you can enhance the quality of initial meetings. The usually modest investment of time it takes to consult with a colleague or supervisor can pay significant dividends in effectiveness.

Similarly, a search for accurate information about legal regulations, governmental policies, and potential resources that might be pertinent to a potential client's needs and issues can dramatically accelerate progress toward a successful outcome. So might a search for intervention approaches or practices that reflect strong scientific evidence of effectiveness. For example, imagine that you are about to meet a new client for the first time. During the initial telephone contact, he mentioned that he has a few medical issues and sometimes experiences episodes of syncope when he meets people for the first time. Social workers who do not know the definition of syncope might be wise to conduct a search for the word's meaning, a description of how it occurs, and perhaps what might be done to help someone when they have an episode. In the absence of such knowledge, the client would have to spend quite some time providing an explanation to the social worker. And, the social worker who is ignorant about syncope might be ill-prepared to respond helpfully should the client experience an episode during the interview.

Obviously, social workers benefit when we can efficiently access valid, reliable, and relevant information about topics, issues, programs, practices, and resources that pertain to the people we serve. In general, clients benefit when their social workers are more rather than less knowledgeable. However, the ever-expanding Internet raises challenging questions about the extent of the privacy rights of prospective clients, clients, and other people with whom we interact in our roles and functions as social workers. The line between a legitimate and an illegitimate Internet search is not entirely clear. For example, people with access to a computer could use a person's name or address to conduct an Internet search for information about that person or family. Such a search might yield newspaper stories, links to social media entries, images, references to court appearances or legal documents, and perhaps to facts about economic status, religious or political affiliation, memberships in groups and organizations, and a great deal more. Social workers everywhere are grappling with the moral and ethical implications of such person-focused Internet searches. The issue may be captured in questions such as these: "Should I, as a social worker, conduct an Internet search about a particular client or prospective client without that person's consent?" "Does an Internet search that includes a client's name or other identifying characteristics constitute a violation of that client's right to privacy and confidentiality?" "If I do conduct such a search, should it be considered a professional social work activity and should the results of the search be incorporated in the client's case record? If it is not a legitimate social work activity, do I have the right to use my agency's computer resources and time in my workday to conduct such a search?" "If I conduct an Internet search using a client's name as a keyword and do so as a personal rather than a professional activity, will the information I garner affect the quality of my work and the nature of the working relationship with that client? What if I am under oath during a legal proceeding and I am asked if I had ever conducted an Internet search for information about a client, how should I answer?"

As you gain actual social work practice experience, you may begin to feel less need for preparatory consultation. Please be cautious about such an attitude. Preparatory and ongoing consultation with colleagues and supervisors is often incredibly useful and sometimes necessary to help us maintain emotional balance and equilibrium. Consultation with experts and review of relevant published professional literature can be invaluable and, in some instances, truly life-saving. Even after years of experience, there are unexpected, unusually complicated circumstances where preparatory and ongoing consultation can make the difference between effective and ineffective meetings; and between positive and tragic outcomes.

1. You work in an agency that serves an elderly population in the community. On Tuesday morning, a woman telephoned the agency and talked with you about her neighbor Mrs. Anderson. According to the caller, Mrs. Anderson is 82 years old and lives by herself in an apartment. The caller reported that Mrs. Anderson has not left her apartment in 3 days and would not answer her door or telephone. The neighbor did say, however, that she could hear someone moving about in the apartment. Immediately following the phone call, you examined agency files and discovered that Mrs. Anderson had not previously received agency services. Use the following space to identify the information you would seek and the issues you would address as you consult with your supervisor before taking action concerning Mrs. Anderson.

2. You work in an agency that serves people who are unemployed. Your major function is to help people obtain jobs or to secure regular incomes through grants or programs of various kinds. As you review a pile of intake forms, you learn that in about 2 hours you will meet with an unemployed man for the first time. According to the form, Mr. Gaines is about 47 years of age and served in the Gulf War. He was honorably discharged from the U.S. Army several years ago. Use the following space to describe how you would search for and consult credible published material as you prepare to meet with Mr. Gaines about unemployment-related issues.

Preparatory Arranging

The skill of preparatory arranging involves logistical preparation for a meeting. It includes scheduling an appointment, ensuring that there is adequate time and privacy, and organizing the physical environment. You may have to secure an interview room, locate an interpreter, rearrange furniture, or find a white-board or drawing tablet. It includes considering the appropriateness of your apparel, appearance, and perhaps even hygiene. Some people are put off by a social worker's noticeable body odors; other people are allergic to perfumes or colognes and react adversely to such scents. Some cultures reflect preferences that we can easily respect—if we know about them and make the necessary accommodations ahead of time. Avoiding cultural *faux pas* is much easier than rectifying them.

Preparatory arranging could involve any number of considerations. For example, you might locate transportation for a family or secure temporary child care so that you can meet separately with a parent. You might reserve a large room in a school or community building to meet with a group or a neighborhood organization. Be sure to consider the significance of the environment for people when making visits outside your agency (Kadushin, 1983). Many people assign special meaning to their homes and might feel ill at ease should you arrive before adequate preparations have been made. Food may also have special significance to a family, and family members may reserve certain chairs in a home for specific people. Groups and organizations often reflect similar characteristics. Imagine the potential reaction if you sat in the chair reserved for the leader of a group or the CEO of an organization. Pay close attention to the subtle signals and context so that you may convey respect and sensitivity for the familial, cultural, and systemic meanings associated with each unique encounter.

In agency settings, preparatory arranging includes considering the potential effects of the physical environment. Ensure that clients have a comfortable place to sit and children have a play area when they arrive at the agency. Check to see that interviewing rooms are sufficiently sound-proofed so that privacy can be assured. When you have office space assigned to you, arranging involves selecting and displaying pictures, posters, and other items such as college degrees, professional certificates, and your social work license. It may also include selecting paints or wallpapers and placing furniture.

The office environment can have a powerful impact on people. Suppose, for example, that you provide social services in an area where firearms are widely prized. You would be unwise to decorate your office wall with a poster that reads, "Ban handguns." The titles of books on your shelves can have a similar effect. You could needlessly alienate many people. Personal, political, or religious books and symbols may interfere with others' ability to experience you as an objective professional who genuinely respects them.

In sum, preparatory arranging should facilitate communication and diminish interference and distraction. Although it requires some time and reflection, ultimately such preparation improves efficiency and increases the probability of a successful engagement.

EXERCISE 7-4: PREPARATORY ARRANGING

1. Assume that you are a social worker in a high-security men's prison. You share an office with another worker. The office contains two desks, chairs behind and next to each desk, two bookcases, two telephones, and two file cabinets. In addition, there is a small area

containing a sofa, two comfortable chairs, and a coffee table. You have a 10:00 A.M. appointment scheduled with Mr. Somes, a prisoner. The topic for conversation is the serious illness of his wife of 23 years. According to a report you have just received from her physician, it appears that Mrs. Somes will die sometime within the next few days.

As the appointment time approaches, you notice that your social work colleague remains at his desk, actively engaged in paperwork. You had expected him to be out of the office, as he usually is at this time of day. Use the following space to discuss how you would use the skill of arranging before the meeting.

Preparatory Empathy

Preparatory or anticipatory empathy involves envisioning the world and the current circumstances from another person or group's perspective and experience. Try to anticipate what others are likely to sense, feel, think, imagine, and do as they meet with you; especially for the first time but for later meetings as well. Even before an initial face-to-face meeting, anticipatory empathy heightens your sensitivity to possible agendas, thoughts, feelings about themselves, feelings about you, the presenting problems and issues, and the circumstances. Through preparatory empathy, you try to anticipate others' subjective experience related to seeking or receiving social service and to this particular meeting with you. Put yourself in others' shoes to gain increased appreciation for their motivation for and feelings about the contact, their thoughts and feelings about engaging with an authority figure, and potential issues related to factors such as gender, sexual orientation, stage of life, culture, ethnic background, and socioeconomic status.

Preparatory empathy regarding cultural and ethnic aspects is especially important. Members of some cultural groups may be ambivalent or conflicted about social workers and about social services. Many have adopted negative stereotypes of social workers—which you may need to transcend. Certain people may prefer a slow and informal beginning. Others might find it difficult to share personal information about themselves and their families. Some may be concerned that you might challenge or criticize their culture-based, traditional gender and family roles. In most instances, visiting an agency or meeting with a social worker is hardly a simple request for service. The meaning of such contact can be extraordinarily complicated for most people and especially for members of diverse groups. Be sensitive to the potential cultural implications of upcoming meetings.

Preparatory empathy involves trying to experience what the other or others may be thinking and feeling before the meetings occur. Because you engage in preparatory empathy in advance of face-to-face contact and do so on the basis of often incomplete information, realize that you may be considerably off target. Preparatory empathy is therefore always tentative, always preliminary, and always subject to immediate change based on others' actual communications. Even when your preparatory empathy proves to be inaccurate, however, it remains a productive activity because it enhances your readiness to listen carefully to people when you finally do meet in person.

Let's return to the upcoming visit with our new client, Mrs. Nancy Cannon. A social worker engaging in preparatory empathy might review the telephone contact notes (see Box 7.2) and then go through a process such as described in Box 7.3.

BOX 7.3
Preparatory Empathy: Example

If I were in Mrs. Cannon's shoes, I might feel anxious for, concerned about, and disappointed in my daughter. I would also love her a great deal. I might feel responsible for her behavior and perhaps even guilty about my own parenting. I might feel uncertain about how to proceed. I could very well feel inadequate and maybe frightened. I would be concerned about what the future might hold for Amy and for me. I am aware that my husband's divorce petition and his recent departure from the home may have adversely affected my daughter, and I might feel angry at him—on both my daughter's behalf as well as my own. If I believed I could have been a better spouse or taken actions to prevent his departure, I might also feel guilty about the separation and upcoming divorce proceedings. I might perceive the divorce as the result of some misbehavior of my own. Alternately, I may have initiated the divorce process and experience conflicted feelings about the decision to do so.

Regardless of how the separation and divorce process began, I would feel a great deal of stress during this period. I would probably feel confused about the present and fearful about the future. I might be concerned about finances, after-school supervision of Amy, and my ability to guide and discipline Amy under these new circumstances. I might wonder if there is another person in my husband's life and if there is now or ever will be someone else in my life. I might question my capacity to assume the roles of single person and single parent, my ability to deal with my husband around parental issues concerning Amy, and dozens of other issues provoked by my husband's departure and Amy's recent behavior. I would probably feel highly distressed and perhaps overwhelmed by the events of recent weeks. If sadness and grieving have not yet occurred, I might begin to experience them soon. I may even have begun to anticipate that not only has my husband left the household, but eventually Amy will also leave. After all, she is already 14.

Mrs. Cannon seems to be of a different ethnic background than my own and I am at least 10 years younger. I have never been married and do not have children of my own. Mrs. Cannon may ask about my marital and parental status. Because of these cultural and status differences, she may experience me as unable to understand and appreciate her situation. She may even see me as less able to help her, because I have not personally experienced these same difficulties.

Engaging in the skill of preparatory empathy helps to sensitize you to what others might experience as meetings begin. By empathizing in advance, you increase the likelihood that you will approach people as unique human beings with all of the complexity that entails. A major challenge in this form of anticipatory empathy, however, is resisting the temptation to narrow your view of people so that it leads to a kind of stereotyping rather than to enhanced openness and sensitivity.

EXERCISE 7-5: PREPARATORY EMPATHY

1. Assume that you are a social worker in a general hospital. This morning, a physician contacts you and asks that you accompany her while she informs the mother and father of a 23-year-old man that their son has human immune deficiency syndrome (AIDS). The physician wants you to provide support and social services to the family after she informs them of the diagnosis and prognosis. Use the following space to discuss how you would engage in the skill of preparatory empathy in advanced of a meeting with the parents of the AIDS patient in this situation.

Preparatory Self-Exploration

In addition to preparatory empathy, social workers also engage briefly in preparatory self-exploration before meeting with others. Preparatory self-exploration is a form of self-analysis or introspection through which you, a human being who happens to be a social worker, identify how you might personally be affected by your interaction with this particular person, family, group, organization, or community; the specific issues of concern; and the unique circumstances. In self-exploring, you ask yourself questions such as: "How am I likely to feel about this person or these people in this context? How are the cultural and demographic similarities or differences between us likely to affect me? Given what I know about the issues and circumstances what personal reactions might I experience?"

The purpose of this skill is to identify the potential effects of your own personal history, characteristics, needs, biases, emotional tender spots, philosophical or religious views, and behavioral patterns on clients you are about to encounter. Self-exploration helps to bring into conscious focus those aspects of your personal self that might affect the nature and quality of your engagement with and service to people.

Preparatory self-exploration also involves identifying other factors that may affect your readiness to provide service. For example, there may be extraneous circumstances unrelated to the people or problems that might influence you. If you have a splitting headache, are dealing with the breakup of a significant relationship, are in the process of repairing your furnace, have just lost out on an opportunity for promotion, did not sleep last night, or are worried about a family member of your own, your readiness to engage could be affected. Identifying these factors and their effects on you constitutes the first step toward managing them so that they do not interfere with the high-quality professional service that all people deserve.

EXERCISE 7-6: PREPARATORY SELF-EXPLORATION

1. Assume that you are a social worker in an agency that provides psychosocial counseling services to sexually abused children. You have recently begun to work with Cathy, a 7-year-old whose biological father molested her for a period of 4 years. About a month ago, Cathy's father forced her to perform fellatio. The incident led to his arrest and departure from the family home until his trial begins. You are about to interview Cathy's father for the first time. The general purpose of the interview is to gather information on which to base a tentative assessment of his potential to benefit from a pretrial counseling program. Use the following space to summarize the results of your self-exploration before the meeting.

Centering

Preparatory self-exploration enables you to identify personal factors that might affect your ability to engage people and provide high-quality service. Once identified, you attempt to manage or contain them through centering. As part of this centering process, you ask yourself "What can I do to ready myself personally before the meeting begins?" Centering involves organizing your personal thoughts, feelings, and physical sensations so that they do not interfere with your professionalism, performance, and delivery of social services. Depending on the personal factors involved, centering might include various kinds of activities. Among the more common are brief stress-management exercises to reduce emotional reactivity and promote self-control. Positive self-talk, visualization, muscular relaxation, journal writing, and brief mindful meditation may be useful.

Suppose, for example, you had once been the victim of date rape. At the time of the violation, you somehow minimized its significance. Now, however, you are aware that you still have strong feelings and some unresolved issues about the event. You have decided to seek out a social worker for help in this matter. As you review the intake form of a new client you will meet later today, you read that 2 weeks earlier a man raped her on their first date.

Through preparatory self-exploration, you might recognize that you remain unsettled about your own experience, even though it happened years earlier. You could also realize that you will probably not serve this client well if your own emotions about rape interact with hers. Therefore, you might center yourself by taking a few deep breaths, engaging in a brief relaxation exercise, and compartmentalizing (temporarily putting into an enclosed area of yourself) your personal experience so that you will be able to give your full attention to the client. As part of the process, you say to yourself, "I'm still tender about being raped but I'm able to manage my feelings of rage, shame, and fear so that they don't get in the way of my service to this client. Because it is obvious, however, that I still have some unresolved issues, I hereby commit to schedule an appointment for myself with a social worker with expertise in the area. I promise to telephone her agency office at 11 o'clock, when I have a free hour."

In centering, do not deny or minimize your personal issues and strong feelings. Rather, manage them temporarily and develop specific plans to address them at another time and in a different place.

EXERCISE 7-7: CENTERING

1. Assume that you have an appointment to meet with a client in approximately 10 minutes. While finishing a brief coffee break with a colleague, you learn that everyone else in the agency received a pay raise of 7 percent. Despite the fact that you have earned outstanding evaluations and recently received a promotion, you know that you received a 3 percent raise. In the following space, describe how you would center yourself before the meeting.

Preliminary Planning and Recording

Social workers engage in preliminary planning before meetings, contacts, and interviews with individuals, families, groups, organizations, and communities with whom we interact as part of our professional responsibilities. We plan before initial meetings and subsequent meetings as well. Begin the process of formulating preliminary plans by asking and answering questions such as: "Why is this meeting occurring? What is its overall purpose? What do I hope to accomplish through this meeting? What is my tentative agenda? What might be the agenda of the people who will be involved or affected by the meeting? What might they hope to accomplish? What would I consider a successful meeting? What might other participants? What are my functions or roles in this meeting? How do I wish to begin? What things should I say? What questions should I ask? What might they want to ask of me? What kind of interactional process would I like to see? What kind might they? How would I like the meeting to conclude? How might they like to see it end?"

The specifics of preliminary planning for meetings vary somewhat according to the purpose for the meeting, the circumstances, how many people are involved, and who they are. In general, the number of considerations increases as size and complexity grow. Let's classify social work interviews into three common categories: (1) Information-gathering; (2) Information-giving; and (3) Change-making. In information-gathering interviews, social workers encourage people to discuss the problems or issues of concern and their circumstances; their aspirations and goals; their views and feelings about themselves; and their preferences and strengths. As they express themselves, they may share facts as well as opinions, thoughts as well as emotions; and they may reveal information verbally, nonverbally, and sometimes through other means as well. By listening well as people share information, social workers gather a great deal of information and gain some understanding of them and their situations. Interestingly, as others talk and we listen, they also "hear themselves." Consequently, many grow in self-understanding and do so primarily because they are encouraged to share by an attentive, interested listener.

In information-sharing interviews, social workers provide needed or useful knowledge or professional opinions. You might offer information about a program, policy, or resource in your attempt to respond to a request or address a perceived need. You might educate people about a topic of concern or about possible strategies and methods to address particular problems or pursue selected goals. You might share an appraisal, assessment, or evaluation based upon one or more testing instruments or obtained through one or more information-gathering interviews. And, sometimes, you might offer a professional opinion or suggestion, make a formal recommendation, or submit a proposal.

In change-making interviews, you engage others in attempts to modify aspects of the person-in-environment system. The targets of change may range from the personal to the political or from the individual to the society. For example, one client might seek change in an unwanted situation (for example, securing food or obtaining housing, relocating to a safer neighborhood, finding a lover, or separating from a spouse). Another client might want to accept an undesirable but inevitable reality (for example, by adjusting expectations, forgiving another, or becoming more mindful). Some clients hope to change their feelings or emotions (for example, become less anxious, less depressed, more passionate, or more content). Others want to alter their thinking or their thoughts (for example, think more deeply or more optimistically, or experience more gratitude); and some want to change their behavior (for example, speak more clearly, become more assertive or more self-controlled, discontinue consumption of alcohol, or make more frequent gestures of love and affection).

Change may also be directed toward various aspects of small and large social systems (for example, a couple, a mother and child, a family, a formal or informal group, an organization or institution, a community, or a society). Targets for change might include social systems' purpose or mission or their structure, cultural rules or operating principles and policies, communication or decision-making processes, or perhaps feedback mechanisms. Change targets may also include the human-made and natural physical/ecological environments as well (for example, increased lighting in heavy crime areas, clean air or water, reforestation, sustainable energy, public transit). Interviews may involve clients and significant others in their world, people who might become clients but have not yet done so, and nonclients (for example, legislators or government leaders, community representatives, business executives, potential funders). Change-making interviews may include direct or indirect action and frequently incorporate advocacy and aspects of policy practice. Social workers realize that changes to policies, programs, and practices can have profound effects upon social systems of all sizes—from the child of a young, unemployed, single mother to a starving population in a drought-stricken region of the world.

Most of the time, social workers can readily identify a tentative, general purpose for an upcoming interview. Sometimes, of course, a meeting serves more than one purpose. Many interviews involve aspects of information-gathering and information-sharing as well as change-making. Once the purpose or purposes are identified, however, you may sketch out preliminary plans for the meeting.

The primary purpose of many first meetings is information-gathering. In such instances, you might formulate general but flexible plans concerning what data to seek and from whom. For example, in planning for a first meeting with a family, you may have to decide whether to see all family members together or to see some of them separately. If you plan to see members individually or in the form of smaller subsystems (for example, mother–daughter dyad or parental dyad), you determine whom to interview first, second, and so forth. The same questions apply in work with groups, organizations, and communities.

Consider the case of a prospective client who telephoned to request a meeting. She expressed an interest in resolving a family problem. Your tentative plans might look something like those depicted in Box 7.4.

BOX 7.4

Preliminary Plans: Example of a Help-Seeking Family

- Engage in introductions.
- Share your ideas about the general purpose and direction for the meeting (that is, information gathering).
- Establish the ground rules for the process.
- Address any questions or uncertainties concerning the agency, you as the social worker, the purpose, the process, or the ground rules.
- Determine the identities and characteristics of the family or household members.
- Explore the presenting problem/issue that stimulated the phone contact.
- Explore the history and development as well as the consequences of the problem/issue.
- Explore risk and protective factors (that is, those factors likely to increase and decrease the probability of an occurrence of the problem/issue).
- Examine how the family has attempted to address this and other issues and determine the outcomes of those efforts.
- Explore strengths within the family or household system and identify available resources that might contribute to a resolution of the problem/issue.
- Explore the client's quality of life.
- Establish a preliminary goal for service.
- Conclude the interview with some sense of what will happen next in the process.

Preliminary planning enables you to begin meetings in a coherent and purposeful fashion. The process yields a flexible structure, which can help you come across as organized, professional, and competent. The written record that results from preparation may take several forms and include various components. Many agencies use a telephone contact form (see Box 7.2) to make relevant notations about the caller, the reason for the call, the substance of the conversation, and any agreed-upon goals and plans. A more extensive intake form provides space to record identifying characteristics of the people involved (for example, name, gender, age, occupation, family role, address, and phone numbers), the presenting problem or issue (for example, reason for contact, preliminary description of the issue of concern, indication of desired goals or outcomes), and the circumstances. Although you should always view notes based on telephone conversations as preliminary and tentative, they often provide valuable information when you subsequently engage a person, family, group, or organization in a face-to-face meeting. Many workers also develop, often in brief outline form, a summary of their preliminary plans for the meeting. For example, Rose Hernandez, the social worker scheduled to conduct the initial face-to-face interview with Mrs. Cannon, might make a few notes in advance of her first meeting (see Box 7.5). Notice how useful these brief notes could be in helping her to be prepared from the very first moment of contact.

BOX 7.5
Preliminary Notes: Mrs. Nancy Cannon

January 13

Mrs. Nancy Cannon—seems to prefer "Mrs."
Presenting concern: 14-year-old daughter Amy alleged to have drunk alcohol and come home after her 9:00 PM curfew. First such incident; Mrs. Cannon wonders if her daughter's behavior may be related to Mr. Cannon's (Amy's father) recent departure from the home and subsequent divorce petition. He left the home about 6 weeks ago. I am uncertain who initiated the separation and divorce process. Mrs. Cannon wants a noontime appointment to avoid time away from work. Could there be financial constraints or concerns about keeping her job?

Rose Hernandez, BSW, LSW
Licensed Social Worker

Ms. Hernandez might also prepare preliminary plans such as that depicted in Box 7.6. She will be ready to engage Mrs. Cannon. Imagine the likely differences in interview quality, efficiency, and effectiveness between their meeting and one with a social worker who does not engage in preliminary planning.

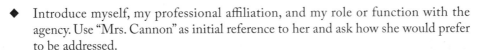

BOX 7.6
Preliminary Plans: Mrs. Nancy Cannon

◆ Introduce myself, my professional affiliation, and my role or function with the agency. Use "Mrs. Cannon" as initial reference to her and ask how she would prefer to be addressed.

◆ General purpose for the meeting appears to be information gathering. Collect relevant information related to Mrs. Cannon, her daughter Amy, the issue of concern, and the situation. Explore the separation and divorce issue as well as the nature of Mr. and Mrs. Cannon's relationship as Amy's parents. For example, are they both concerned about the drinking? Are they both interested in addressing Amy's drinking; and are they together in their views about how it should be addressed? In exploring, realize that Amy's drinking behavior may or may not be related to her parent's marital situation. Also, recognize that Mrs. Cannon may also want help in regard to the marital relationship or its dissolution.

◆ Make sure that Mrs. Cannon understands the limits of confidentiality, including duty to report indications of child abuse or neglect. Indicate the mutual nature of this working relationship and invite her active participation.

◆ Explore the apparent presenting issue (that is, Amy's drinking episode) as well as other aspects of Amy's social world (for example, her school performance, friendships, and social and recreational activities). Track the history and development of Amy's drinking behavior and the Cannons' marital conflict. Attempt to identify risk and protective factors vis-à-vis the drinking problem/ issue.

(continued)

BOX 7.6 *(continued)*

♦ Clarify Mrs. Cannon and Amy's current household situation and their quality of life; inquire about Mr. Cannon's circumstances as well. Identify significant others who are involved with the three family members.

♦ Explore strengths of Mrs. Cannon, Amy, and perhaps Mr. Cannon. Identify available resources that might relate to a resolution.

♦ Explore in detail how Mrs. Cannon, Amy, and Mr. Cannon have attempted to deal with Amy's drinking or other "misbehavior" and how they are coping with the separation and divorce. Identify approaches that have been helpful and those that have been ineffective.

♦ Explore what Mrs. Cannon would consider an optimal resolution to the problems of concern.

♦ Conclude the interview with a specific next step. Consider the possibility of a second appointment, perhaps with Amy and Mrs. Cannon together, Amy alone, Mr. Cannon alone, or possibly Mr. and Mrs. Cannon together.

Rose Hernandez, BSW, LSW
Licensed Social Worker

EXERCISE 7-8: PRELIMINARY PLANNING AND RECORDING

Use a word-processing program to prepare notes and preliminary plans for the meeting or meetings you would have with the various parties involved in the following situations. When finished, label the document "Preliminary Plans for 3 Clients" and deposit it in your Social Work Skills Learning Portfolio.

1. Assume that you are a social worker who works with a court that handles child custody disputes. You are responsible for collecting information and formulating a recommendation about the placement of a 12-year-old boy whose parents are divorcing. Each parent wants custody of the child.

2. Assume that you are a social worker with a military veterans' center. You receive a telephone message from Ms. Francine Rivera concerning her brother Hector. Ms. Rivera reports that Hector is 37 years of age. He completed two tours of combat duty in Iraq and one in Afghanistan. She reports that, since his discharge from the Army, he drinks a great deal of alcohol (beer) every day, has nightmares, and occasionally has violent outbursts. He has been unable to keep a job for more than a few weeks and has lost most of his friends. Ms. Rivera has become especially concerned lately because her brother has begun to talk about ending "his own miserable life." She says that he refuses to go to an agency but he might be willing to talk with someone if a counselor came to the house. You agree to go for a first visit at 5:30 P.M. on the next afternoon.

3. Assume that you are a social worker with a community outreach agency. Five mothers in a low-income neighborhood want your help in organizing their community in an effort to reduce violence, crime, and drug dealing and use. Two of the mothers have lost children through drug-related violence and the other three are concerned that their children

might be at risk. You agreed to meet with them in a private room at a nearby church. They are concerned about what might happen if the drug gangs learn about their efforts before they're ready for the gangs' likely threatening or violent response. They want to keep everything as quiet and low-key as possible. The meeting is scheduled for 7:00 P.M. on the following evening.

Summary

The preparing skills enable you to provide professional social work services efficiently and effectively from the first moment of contact. The preparing skills are used extensively before initial meetings and in advance of subsequent ones as well. The preparing skills include (1) preparatory reviewing, (2) preparatory exploring, (3) preparatory consultation, (4) preparatory arranging, (5) preparatory empathy, (6) preparatory self-exploration, (7) centering, and (8) preliminary planning and recording.

CHAPTER 7: SUMMARY EXERCISES

Use word-processing software to describe the actions you would take and to record how you would use the preparing skills in advance of meetings with the clients reflected in the following three case vignettes. In other words, use those preparing skills (preparatory reviewing, preparatory exploring, preparatory consultation, preparatory arranging, preparatory empathy, preparatory self-exploration, centering, and preliminary planning and recording) that apply in these particular situations. Be sure to consult credible published materials when that would aid in your preparation. When finished, label the document "Preparing for 3 Clients" and deposit it in your Social Work Skills Learning Portfolio.

1. Earlier in the day, a woman telephoned your agency and said she wanted to talk with someone about a recent incident. About a week earlier, she met a man in a bar. He drove her home and then raped her. She thought that she would be able to manage her feelings about the crime by herself. However, she now realizes that she needs professional help to cope. During the telephone conversations, she said, "I'm falling apart." You have an appointment with her in a few hours but have some time now to prepare. As part of your preparation, consult credible published materials regarding victims of rape as well as laws and legal procedures that pertain to "date rape."

2. Recently, a 14-year-old African American girl told her schoolteacher that she was pregnant by her 15-year-old white boyfriend. She also told the teacher that she needs to get an abortion quickly, or "my parents will kill me if they find out I'm pregnant." The teacher urged her to talk with you, the school social worker, and secured the girl's permission to tell you about the situation. The teacher did so and arranged for a meeting with you later today. As part of your preparation, consult credible published materials to clarify the legal rights of 14-year-olds and those of their parents in your locale. Locate credible answers to the following questions: (a) Would a school social worker in your city or town be legally justified in talking with the 14-year-old about the pregnancy and the possibility of an abortion before securing her parents' permission to do so? (b) Would the 14-year-old's communications with a social worker be considered privileged in this

situation? (c) Would the teenager's parents have a legal right to information that their daughter shared with a school social worker? (d) Would the apparent sexual relationship between the 14-year-old and the 15-year-old constitute sexual abuse, statutory rape, or any other crime that should be reported to authorities? (e) What do the laws in your locale suggest about the pregnancy termination rights of women in general and rights of 14-year-old girls in particular?

3. An 8-year-old girl has recently been the victim of sexual molestation. Medical personnel in the emergency room of the local hospital examined the girl, and confirmed that vaginal penetration of some kind had occurred. The alleged perpetrator, a 15-year-old neighbor, is under arrest in a juvenile detention center while awaiting a judicial hearing. The young girl seems to be in a state of emotional shock. She has not spoken a single word or expressed feelings since the incident several days earlier. The child-protection caseworker tried to encourage the child to talk about what happened, but her efforts were unsuccessful. As a social worker who specializes in work with victimized children, you received a request to help the child and family.

You have scheduled a home visit to talk with the girl's mother and then meet with the child. As you engage in preparatory consultation in advance of the meeting, be sure to explore credible literature about the particular form of emotional shock apparent in the young girl.

CHAPTER 7: EXPERIENTIAL INTERVIEWING EXERCISE

At this point you have gained some familiarity with the characteristics of professionalism; learned about culturally sensitive communications, and practiced the basic skills of talking and listening; and experimented with the preparing skills. It is now time to prepare for an experiential interviewing exercise. The multiweek learning activity is intended to help you gain proficiency in the social work skills within a safe and fairly realistic context. For this experience, you assume the role of social worker while a classmate or colleague assumes the role of "practice client." The exercise occurs over the course of several weeks. If your professor or field instructor does not assign a classmate or provide a "standard client"[1] to serve that function, you need to recruit someone to serve as your "practice client." You also must gain the consent of a social work instructor or other professional social worker to serve in the dual role of your supervisor and the client's advocate. If you are completing *The Social Work Skills Workbook* as part of a course, your professor is an obvious choice for the role. In accepting the role of supervisor, she or he agrees to be available to consult with you, respond to questions, and provide suggestions and advice as you function as a student social worker during the process. In serving as client advocate, he or she agrees to be available to the practice client who may have questions, concerns, problems, or complaints during the multiweek exercise. If the book accompanies a practicum experience, your field instructor would probably fulfill these functions. If you are working in an agency, your actual supervisor or another professional social work colleague might do so. Regardless of the setting, however, do not undertake this learning exercise until you secure someone to serve these essential roles.

---

[1] Some programs employ people to serve as "standard clients" for students. Students in the dramatic arts or graduates with some acting talent can often provide realistic learning opportunities. Standard clients can be extremely helpful in that they can all operate from a prescribed role description and identify the same problems, personal characteristics, and environmental circumstances for each social work student. Also, they are usually unknown to social work students, which add a sense of realism to the interview series.

In regard to the role of practice client, a classmate or another student[2] who is completing or has already completed the *Social Work Skills Workbook* might be receptive to your request. However, do not ask peers who are in a fragile or highly distressed state—perhaps due to a major loss or conflict, a serious medical condition, a significant life change, or a personal or family crisis. After all, you are practicing skills here, not actually providing social work services. Your colleague should realize that he or she is helping you to learn. Practice clients may or may not derive some personal benefit from the exercise. The purpose is educational in nature. It is not intended to help people dealing with serious concerns and we certainly do not want to add additional stress or pressure to people who are currently quite vulnerable.

Before you make contact with and attempt to recruit a classmate or colleague, use applicable preparing skills such as preparatory reviewing, preparatory exploring, preparatory consultation, preparatory arranging, preparatory empathy, preparatory self-exploration, centering, and preliminary planning and recording. In the case of a recruitment contact with a potential practice client, you need to clarify the purpose for the contact and understand in detail the guidelines for the experiential interviewing exercise; including the nature and scope of your responsibilities, and the expectations of the practice client (see Appendix 12). You also need information materials to provide the prospective practice client. These include a summary description of the exercise, a succinct description of the practice client role, contact information for the supervising social worker/client advocate, and a "consent to participate" (see Appendix 12).

As you begin the process of preparing and planning for a practice client recruitment contact, first review the requirements of the exercise. Highlight those aspects that are especially significant and make notations about aspects that are unclear as well as any questions that you might raise with your instructor or classmates. In other words, think critically about the exercise and, for example, identify any ethical issues that might warrant additional consideration. Second, use the skills of preparatory exploring and preparatory consultation, as needed, with your instructor and classmates. Obviously, you would use the basic skills of talking and listening in this and other aspects of preparation; and do so with cultural sensitivity. Third, make necessary arrangements for the exercise. Although you do not need to make an audio or video recording of recruitment contacts, you do require an informed consent form for your colleague to sign and other documents to help orient him or her to the exercise. Later, when you first meet with your colleague in the role of practice client, you will need audio or video recording[3] equipment, a quiet and private meeting location with chairs, time for the meetings, and perhaps pencils, notepads, drawing paper, or other materials. Fourth, engage in self-exploration and then in preparatory empathy to heighten your sensitivity to both your own as well as your colleague's possible thoughts, feelings, sensations, and behaviors about the recruitment contact and the possibility of subsequently undertaking the experiential learning exercise. Fifth, identify or develop and then practice some means to center yourself in advance of the first and the subsequent meetings with your colleague. As a way to practice, you might adopt the habit of centering yourself before encounters with friends, family members, classmates, instructors, and others with whom you interact. It is conceivable that by doing so, your interactions

---

[2] It is usually wise to recruit a classmate or colleague whom you know only slightly if at all. Avoid close friends and acquaintances as the temptation to lose "role integrity" is greater when they serve as practice clients. With unfamiliar practice clients, such temptations are usually fairly weak and the experience quite realistic as you learn about people and explore topics for the very first time.

3 Note: Video recordings are especially valuable for learning purposes because they contain so much information. Nonverbal communications such as facial expressions as well as physical movements and gestures of both social worker and client are sometimes more informative than the stated words. However, video recordings also involve considerable risk to the privacy and confidentiality rights of the parties involved—and especially to those of the practice client. Obviously, if a practice client appears on video, she or he can be recognized—even though a fictitious name is used. Therefore, if you video record the meetings, you must be extraordinarily protective of the recording; ensure that no copies are made; and, if the practice client prefers, destroy the recording when you have completed the exercise.

with others might become more constructive and satisfying, and perhaps even more enjoyable. Finally, prepare written preliminary plans for the recruitment contact. Be sure to identify a preliminary purpose for the exercise, identify and clarify your role or roles, your colleague's role, and those of your professor or other professional social worker serving as supervisor and client advocate. Use a word-processing program so that you can readily access and revise the plans as needed. Label the document "Preliminary Plans for a Practice Client Recruitment Contact" and deposit it in a private and secure electronic folder. Label the folder "Experiential Interviewing Exercise." That folder will serve as a place to keep notes and documents related to the learning exercise.

As you finish this chapter, please reflect on your learning by completing the following self-appraisal exercise.

SELF-APPRAISAL: THE PREPARING SKILLS

Please use the following items to help you undertake a self-assessment of your proficiency in the preparing skills addressed in this chapter. Read each statement carefully. Then, use the following 4-point rating scale to indicate the degree to which you agree or disagree with each statement. Record your numerical response in the space provided:

4 = Strongly agree   2 = Disagree

3 = Agree   1 = Strongly disagree

4	3	2	1	Rating Statement
				At this point in time, I can
☐	☐	☐	☐	1. Discuss the purposes and functions of preparing.
☐	☐	☐	☐	2. Engage in preparatory reviewing.
☐	☐	☐	☐	3. Engage in preparatory exploring.
☐	☐	☐	☐	4. Engage in preparatory consultation.
☐	☐	☐	☐	5. Engage in preparatory arranging.
☐	☐	☐	☐	6. Engage in preparatory empathy.
☐	☐	☐	☐	7. Engage in preparatory self-exploration.
☐	☐	☐	☐	8. Center myself.
☐	☐	☐	☐	9. Engage in preliminary planning and recording.
☐	☐	☐	☐	10. Assess my proficiency in the preparing skills.
				Subtotal

Note: These items are identical to those contained in the Preparing Skills section of the Social Work Skills Self-Appraisal Questionnaire presented in Appendix 3. If you completed that self-appraisal before beginning Chapter 1, you have already responded to these items once before. You may now compare the responses you made on that occasion with those you made this time. Also, compare the two subtotals. If you believe that you have progressed in terms of your proficiency, the more recent subtotal should be higher than the earlier one.

CHAPTER 8

BEGINNING

This chapter (see Box 8.1) should help you learn skills needed during the beginning phase of social work practice. This phase formally begins when you, in your role as a social worker, and another person or other people first encounter each other. Because first impressions are so important, the initial contact often affects all future encounters. Similarly, the beginning portion of each subsequent interview tends to influence the course of those meetings as well.

The beginning skills are commonly used quite extensively during the first few meetings. Whether the meetings involve clients or other people, be clear about purposes and expectations. Such clarity and transparency facilitate engagement and communication with referral sources, colleagues from your own or other agencies, government officials, parents, community representatives,

BOX 8.1

Chapter Purpose

The purpose of this chapter is to help learners develop proficiency in the beginning skills.

Goals

Following completion of this chapter, learners should be able to demonstrate proficiency in:

♦ Discussing the purposes and functions of beginning
♦ Introducing yourself

(continued)

- Seeking introductions
- Describing an initial purpose
- Orienting clients to the process
- Discussing policy and ethical factors
- Seeking feedback
- Assessing proficiency in the beginning skills

Core EPAS Competencies

The skills addressed in this chapter support the following core EPAS:

- Identify as a professional social worker and conduct oneself accordingly (EP2.1.1).
- Apply social work ethical principles to guide professional practice (EP2.1.2).
- Apply critical thinking to inform and communicate professional judgments (EP2.1.3).
- Engage diversity and difference in practice (EP2.1.4).
- Engage . . . with individuals, families, groups, organizations, and communities (EP2.1.10[a]).

and others with whom you interact as part of your professional responsibilities. Typically, you also use several beginning skills during the early portions of subsequent encounters. The beginning skills include (1) introducing yourself, (2) seeking introductions, (3) describing initial purpose, (4) orienting clients, (5) discussing policy and ethical factors, and (6) seeking feedback.

Competent use of the beginning skills helps ensure that meetings are purposeful and productive, and that relationships are positive. An effective beginning results when you and a prospective client or others accomplish the purpose for which you first meet (for example, information gathering, information sharing, or change making) and reach a mutual agreement concerning a next step in the process (for example, conclude your relationship, continue to work together, or arrange for service from another professional or agency).

Typically, social workers make contact with people in one of these ways:

- Individuals, families, groups, organizations, and communities may reach out to a social worker or agency for help with a problem they have identified as being beyond their means of solution.
- A social worker may reach out to offer services to people who are not initially seeking help.
- Someone else may conclude that an individual, family, group, organization, or community is affected by a serious problem that threatens their own or others' welfare and request that a social worker or agency intervene to provide services. (Compton, Galaway, & Cournoyer, 2005, pp. 165–166)

Contact may occur, for example, when a supervisor or agency executive assigns you responsibility for organizing and leading a task force or committee. A judge may order that a defendant or someone convicted of a crime or misdemeanor receive services from you and your agency. A community group might seek your help in developing a program, preparing a funding proposal, or advocating for a change in a governmental policy. Someone panhandling on the street may ask you for money—providing you with an opportunity to educate him about various social service programs and perhaps help to arrange a first meeting.

In addition, the nature of the contact may vary somewhat according to the number of people involved and their relationships with one another. First contacts with individuals differ somewhat from those with families and groups, which in turn vary from those with organizations and communities. Similarly, initial encounters via telephone, e-mail, instant message, text, webcams, or assorted Web-based social networks differ from those that involve face-to-face interaction in the same physical space. Nonetheless, regardless of the particular mode of communication, during the early part of most first meetings with systems of all sizes, we hope to facilitate an exchange of introductions, establish a tentative direction or purpose for the gathering, outline the usual expectations of clients or involved others, describe the policies and ethical principles that might apply during this and any subsequent encounters, and ensure that prospective clients and others understand the parameters within which the meeting takes place. This is a crucial part of the beginning process because it addresses your legal and ethical obligations with respect to informed consent; and it facilitates development of a transparent relationship context. When beginning, social workers commonly provide prospective clients and others an overview of relevant agency policies, as well as information about pertinent laws and ethical principles. That way, the people involved can truly understand the context within which the helping endeavor takes place. Throughout the beginning phase, regularly seek feedback concerning information discussed. Prospective clients and others sometimes need additional clarification about complex or confusing policies and principles.

Introducing Yourself

At the beginning of any first meeting, be sure to identify yourself by full name and profession, and by agency or departmental affiliation. For example, at the beginning of a meeting in the agency where he works, a social worker might say as he holds out his hand in greeting, "Hello Mr. and Mrs. Adabu. My name is Dan Majors. I'm a social worker here at the family service agency. I specialize in helping people who are dealing with family issues of one kind or another."

At the start of a visit to the home of a prospective client, another social worker might say, "Hello Mrs. Perez [offers hand to shake]. I'm Joanna Kapoor. I'm a social worker with the local school system. I specialize in service to families of the students in our school district. Please call me Joanna." In meeting a bilingual Mexican-American family for the first time, an English-speaking social worker might nonetheless say a few words of greeting in Spanish along with a brief statement of regret that she is not fluent in that beautiful language. At first contact with some Asian clients, a respectful lowering of the head to approximate a modest bow may augment the introductory ritual.

At the start of a community group meeting, a social worker might say, "Welcome everyone! My name is Leslie Nguyen. I'm a social worker with the city. I work with people in neighborhoods interested in developing a sense of community and increasing both safety and well-being throughout the area. Please call me Leslie."

In most circumstances, a friendly facial expression and a warm handshake serve as helpful welcoming gestures. A few informal comments about everyday topics (for example, the weather, transportation) may also help people feel more at ease; but do not overdo it. Spending too much time with chitchat may frustrate clients who are grappling with serious concerns and urgently wish to discuss them. Always consider your introduction and informal remarks in light of the context and purpose. Be especially sensitive to cultural factors. People that you meet for the first time fully realize that you do not yet truly know them as individuals. Too much informality or excessive enthusiasm may be premature and, in some cultures, quite rude. In many contexts, you would use your surname rather than your given name. For example, "Ms. Grandbois" may seem less culturally intrusive than "Judy."

In addition to identifying yourself by name, profession, and agency affiliation, you might also provide formal identification. For example, as part of her introduction to families, Joanna Kapoor routinely gives out her business card.

Joanna Kapoor, BSW, MSW, LSW
Licensed Social Worker
Center Township School District
902 W. New York Street
Indianapolis, IN 46202-5156
Telephone 317-274-6705

© Cengage Learning

In office settings, a display of your university degrees, social work license, and professional certificates can contribute to the introductory process. Clients may notice where you earned your college degree and that you have a license to practice social work in your locale. Indeed, some licensing laws specifically require the public display of your social work license. Along with pertinent agency materials, you might offer clients a brief printed biographical summary of your professional background, training, and your areas of expertise.

EXERCISE 8-1: INTRODUCING YOURSELF

The following exercises afford you with opportunities to practice the skill of introducing yourself. In the spaces provided, write the words you would say and describe the actions you would take in introducing yourself in the following circumstances.

1. Assume that you are a social worker in a residential nursing facility for elderly people. You have an appointment with family members concerning the possibility of placing an 85-year-old parent there. What would you say and do in introducing yourself?

2. Assume that you serve as a social worker in a training center for intellectually challenged children and young adults. Today you are about to lead a group of six or eight teenage residents. You've reviewed their case records and know that each has numerous talents and reflects intelligence in various ways. In terms of traditional IQ, they score between about 60 to about 70. The students have already taken their seats by the time you arrive. Although a few of them may have seen you walking around campus, none of them actually knows you and you do not know any of them. What would you say and do in introducing yourself?

Seeking Introductions

People's names tend to hold special significance. Early in first meetings, encourage people to say their names, and then try to pronounce them correctly. Thereafter, periodically throughout the interview, refer to them by name. For example, after introducing yourself, you might say, "And your name is . . . ?" If you already know the person's name, you might ask, "And you're Mr. Benoit?[1] Is that right? Am I pronouncing your name correctly?" Then ask how the person prefers to be addressed (Miss, Ms., Mrs., Mr., Reverend, first name, or nickname). People from cultural groups that have experienced oppression may be especially sensitive to premature informality. In the United States, for example, white slave owners commonly addressed adult slaves by first name or by calling them "boy" or "girl." Over time, the slave owners' surnames replaced the slaves' original African names. In a similar vein, some European Americans called male Native Americans "chief" in a form of rankism and sometimes ridicule. Although most social workers would never intentionally insult another person, sometimes ignorance and insensitivity lead to just such a result.

Frequently, clients may share additional forms of identification during the exchange of introductions. Suppose, for example, a new client introduces herself by saying, "I'm Mrs. Jones. I'm the mother of this mob." From her words, you might infer that she prefers to be called "Mrs. Jones" and that the role of parent represents a significant part of her personal and social identity. In some organizational contexts, a person's title or role may be preferred. For instance, if you testify in a court or in a legislative committee meeting, you would be wise to refer to the judge as "your honor" or "Judge Sanchez" and to the legislative representatives as "Madam Chairperson," "Senator Yung," or "Representative Jabbar."

---

[1] You might experiment with different ways that the Benoit surname could be pronounced.

In family and group contexts, you may ask members to introduce themselves through a "go around." In a group context, the introductions can actually proceed in clockwise or counter-clockwise fashion. In family contexts, however, especially in many cultures, it is often more respectful to seek introductions in order of age or status. For example, you might begin with the parents and then move to the children in order of age from old to young. In some formal group contexts, for example when meeting with a board of directors, a legislative committee, or a community association, you might begin with the leadership and then proceed in "go around" fashion. Frequently, in such settings, you may simply request that the formal leader or your contact person introduce the other members to you. Because initial group meetings often provoke anxiety, you could incorporate a stress-reducing, ice-breaking dimension to the introduction process. For example, you might ask family members to introduce themselves and share a few of the thoughts they had as they anticipated coming to this first meeting. In formal contexts, however, it is often wise to move right on to the purpose for the meeting.

EXERCISE 8-2: SEEKING INTRODUCTIONS

For these exercises, assume that you are a social worker at a multipurpose social services agency. Respond in the spaces provided by writing the words you would say in each situation.

1. You are about to begin a first meeting with a 23-year-old man. As you walk together to your office, you smell a strong odor of alcohol. How would you introduce yourself and seek an introduction from him? Why would you do so in that way?

2. You are about to begin a first interview with a family of six members. You know that it is a blended family and that not all of the children have the same last name. However, you do not actually know which children are from which relationships. How would you introduce yourself and seek introductions from the family members? Why do so in that way?

3. You are about to begin a first meeting with a group of community leaders from different neighborhoods throughout the city. You realize that they do not all know each other and, indeed, you do not know all of them. How would you introduce yourself and seek introductions from the other participants? What else would you say or do? Discuss your rationale for the words you choose and the action you propose.

Describing Initial Purpose

As part of the preparation process (see Chapter 7), social workers anticipate a tentative general purpose for a meeting (Schwartz, 1976; Shulman, 1992). Then, when you actually begin, you can suggest that purpose as a possible focus for the meeting. Especially in initial meetings, prospective and actual clients typically tend to look to you for leadership. After all, you are the professional person in a position of authority. The same holds true if you are convening a group of community members, chairing a committee meeting, or leading a task force or advocacy group. Therefore, clearly but succinctly discuss your view of the purpose for the meeting. Without some beginning guidance from you, people are likely to feel quite uncertain about a process that is usually quite stress provoking. By tentatively sharing a general purpose, other participants usually feel a sense of relief as they conclude that you possess some competence and might, indeed, know what you are doing.

Building on the work of Vinter (1963) and Hansenfeld (1985), Garvin (1997) identified the following overarching purposes for most social work agencies, programs, and services:

♦ *Socialization* "involves helping persons viewed as 'normal' and who are progressing from one status to another. Examples of this are assisting adolescents to assume adult responsibilities, middle-aged persons to plan for retirement, and school children to make better use of their learning environments" (p. 40).

   ● *Identity development* is an aspect of a socialization service in which social workers help people clarify their own goals and roles. Supporting adolescents as they explore social identity issues or consider career goals, facilitating a women's consciousness-raising group, or helping gay, lesbian, or bisexual people decide whether or not to come out are examples of identity development purposes.

   ● *Skill development* involves helping people develop the abilities needed to achieve the goals they establish. Educational counseling, training or "coaching" activities (for example, assertiveness training, social and communication skills, parenting skills, budgeting skills, time-management skills, study skills), and transition facilitation activities (for example, retirement preparation, divorce adjustment for both adults and children, helping adults entering or returning to college) contribute to skill development. Such socialization activities help people to acquire the knowledge and skills associated with the roles and goals to which they aspire.

◆ *Resocialization* involves "helping people viewed as not experiencing 'normal' phases of development or role transitions. Such people are often labeled 'deviant,' and therefore experience conflict with others" (p. 40).

● *Social control* activities may occur in agencies that have a relationship with one or more aspects of the criminal and juvenile justice, child and adult protection, educational, and some medical systems. Typically, the "targets" of social control activities have not yet decided to accept a nondeviant, socially acceptable role. Although many social workers are reluctant to consider themselves agents of social control, the purpose of such activities and the objectives of the agencies that sponsor them (or those of the funding sources) sometimes involve the control and management of unwanted behaviors; and, obviously, the people who exhibit them. Activities offered in prisons, training schools, alcohol and drug treatment centers, many residential organizations, certain mental health agencies, and some hospitals are often solely or primarily social control in nature. People associated with crime and delinquency, sexual offenses, violence, substance abuse, and deviance often receive services intended to serve the purpose of social control. Indeed, in many educational, mental health, and social service agencies, social control is frequently an unspoken but strong element of a, supposedly hidden but often quite public, agenda. As you might imagine, in many contexts the purpose of social control overlaps with the purpose of punishment—perhaps accompanied by the idea that infliction of pain or discomfort is "for their own good."

● *Rehabilitation* services and activities may occur in agencies and institutions such as psychiatric facilities, mental health centers, social service agencies, and the treatment programs of correctional settings. Typically, people who voluntarily seek rehabilitation services identify certain behavior patterns as problematic (for example, as deviant, maladaptive, dysfunctional, or sick) and choose to pursue a more functional, healthful, or socially acceptable path. Rehabilitation services help the members develop the knowledge, skills, and attitudes necessary to fulfill functional, accepted, and socially desirable roles. Many social, psychiatric, educational, and substance abuse services fall into this category, as do many self-help programs where members openly acknowledge their faults, failures, or addictions (for example, sex, relationship, drugs, alcohol, and so on) and undertake personal efforts to overcome them. In traditional Alcoholics Anonymous (AA) meetings, people usually begin to speak with a phrase such as, "Hello, I'm Paul. I am an alcoholic." Such introductions reflect personal ownership of a problem, illness, personal flaw, or moral failing from which the person hopes to recover.

In addition to information gathering, information sharing, and change making, these four overarching social work purposes may provide further context for the general reasons for initial meetings with clients. For example, when it is clear from a preliminary contact that a main issue requires rehabilitation or recovery services, you might identify that your purpose involves helping people develop new ways of thinking, feeling, and behaving so that they can recover from current problems and prevent them from recurring in the future.

In some instances, the general purpose for the meeting is clear, and so are the professional social work roles that support that purpose. When such a strong degree of clarity exists, you may also appropriately describe one or more of the professional social work roles that you expect to assume during the course of your work together (Schwartz, 1976; Shulman, 1992).

Among the more common direct social work roles are *advocate, broker, case manager, counselor, educator, evaluator, facilitator, investigator, mediator,* or *therapist.* In serving as an advocate, you represent, defend, or champion the rights of clients and others who might be in need or at risk. As a broker, you help to locate community resources and link people with them. As a case manager, you coordinate delivery of several different services provided by personnel from one or more agencies or programs. As a counselor, you provide support and guidance to people in their efforts to address and resolve problems and accomplish goals. As an educator, you provide information, teach, train, coach, or socialize people in the development of knowledge, attitudes, or abilities to enhance their psychosocial functioning. As an evaluator, you make judgments and recommendations based on careful, fair, and systematic collection and analysis of pertinent information (for example, recommending child custody arrangements, determining the effectiveness of a social service program, or assessing an applicant's eligibility for services). As a facilitator, you help bring people together, enhance their interaction and communication, and encourage them to cooperate in their efforts and actions. As an investigator (for example, child- or adult-protective services worker), you carefully and systematically search to uncover hidden or secret information pertaining to the safety and well-being of potentially vulnerable people. As a mediator, you serve as a communication link or go-between to help various parties address differences or conflicts and to interact more productively. As a psychotherapist or social therapist, you use advanced knowledge, extensive training, and specialized strategies and techniques to help people cope with or resolve specific social, physical, or psychological problems, conditions, disorders, symptoms, illnesses, or disabilities.

In beginning with involuntary, nonvoluntary, and other ambivalent or reluctant participants, both the purpose for the meeting and your roles warrant more complete and lengthy description. This is also the case in situations where clients seek a specific service offered through your agency. For example, your agency may sponsor an educationally oriented 6-week group experience for teenagers considering marriage. Because such structured, socialization groups tend to follow a predictable agenda, your social work roles are clear. You will serve as an educator and facilitator within the context of an information-gathering, information-sharing, and change-making group designed to help young people become more aware, more knowledgeable, and perhaps more able to function within the "normal" opportunities and constraints of marriage. Therefore you may appropriately describe to prospective members both an initial purpose and the professional roles that you expect to fulfill during the group experience.

Frequently, however, the exact nature of your professional role is unclear at the time of the first meeting. This often occurs with voluntary clients who seek service from organizations that have several programs and serve a variety of functions; or when social workers are asked to serve as consultants to agencies or community groups. When the professional roles you might assume remain uncertain, the tentative description of general purposes should suffice.

In the following examples, a social worker tentatively describes an initial purpose for a first meeting.

CASE SITUATION: The client is a 30-year-old woman who called the agency a few days earlier to ask for help with a troubled marriage. The worker and client have already exchanged introductions. The worker begins to describe a tentative general purpose for this initial meeting.

WORKER: When you phoned the agency the other day, you said that your marriage is on the brink of collapse. You also mentioned that you and your husband argue all the time. Is that correct? Yes? During our meeting today, I'd like to explore in detail with you what's going on in your marriage and how it developed to this point. As we both gain a better understanding of the circumstances, together we can consider what to do next.

CASE SITUATION: The divorcing parents of a 9-year-old boy are involved in child custody proceedings. The juvenile court hires a social worker to make recommendations to the judge about the placement of the child. At an initial meeting with the boy's father, the worker exchanges introductions and describes a purpose and role.

WORKER: Judge Bloom asked me to meet with you, your wife, and your son Kevin about the issue of custody arrangements. My job will be to gather information from all parties and make recommendations to the judge about the best possible arrangements for Kevin. I'll be meeting with Mrs. Brown [spouse] this afternoon and with Kevin [son] tomorrow morning. After these three meetings, I should have considerable understanding of the situation. At that time, I'll let you know if any additional meetings will be needed.

I certainly recognize that this is a difficult time for you and for everybody involved. You may feel a bit like you're on trial here. It may seem that way. I'll try my best to make it as reasonable a process as possible. You should know, however, that your son Kevin will be fully considered in these processes. His well-being is our primary focus. I will gear my efforts toward determining what is best for him and his development. I'm sure that you are also concerned about the consequences of the divorce and the upcoming court proceedings for Kevin too. I'd like to approach this interview with Kevin in mind as we try to determine the best custody arrangements.

CASE SITUATION: This is the first meeting of an educational group for people arrested for driving under the influence (DUI) of alcohol. The participants range in age from 16 to 62 and cross gender, ethnic, and socioeconomic-class lines. The group experience involves 12 weekly meetings of approximately 2 hours each. Members participate to decrease the chance of a jail sentence. If they complete the program successfully, their jail sentence is deferred. The worker and group members have exchanged introductions and engaged in some small talk. The worker now proceeds to describe an initial purpose and role.

WORKER: The county prosecutor asked me to lead this educational group for the next 12 weeks. I understand that each of you was arrested for driving under the influence of alcohol and that you have chosen to participate in the group in order to reduce the chances of a term in the county jail. I imagine that you all have other places that you would rather be at this time. Some of you may be grateful for this opportunity to avoid a jail sentence. Others may be annoyed that you have to attend these meetings. If I were in your shoes, I'd probably have mixed feelings too. Whatever you feel, I hope the series of group meetings will help you learn a great deal about alcohol use and its consequences. Most importantly, however, I hope the experience will lead you to never ever decide to drive a car under the influence of intoxicating substances. I also hope that you will become passionate advocates who do what's possible to stop your family members and friends from the deadly practice of impaired driving.

CASE SITUATION: The interview setting is the front doorstep of the Frankel residence. It is a large home in an upper-middle-class neighborhood. The social worker knocks on the door. A woman who appears to live there opens the door. Employed by the Child-Protection Service (CPS) Division of the Department of Human Services, the worker is visiting the home unannounced because the agency received a complaint that Mrs. Frankel had severely beaten her 4-year-old son. At the door, the worker exchanged introductions, learned that the woman is indeed Mrs. Frankel, and gave her a business card along with a brochure about CPS.

WORKER: Child-Protection Services is responsible for investigating all allegations of abuse or neglect of minor children in this county. We have received a complaint concerning the treatment of your 4-year-old son. I'd like to discuss this situation with you and meet your son. May I come in?

EXERCISE 8-3: DESCRIBING INITIAL PURPOSE

Use the following case situations to practice the skill of describing a tentative initial purpose for the meeting and, where you think appropriate, identifying your social work roles as well. Please respond to each situation in the spaces provided.

1. Assume that you are a social worker with a public housing agency. You are trying to interview all residents of a building in an effort to determine their social service needs. You have just knocked on the door of Mrs. Strong, a single mother with five children who range in age from 6 months to 9 years. Write the words you would say to her as you describe an initial purpose for the meeting. If you think your social work roles would be clear in this situation, identify them as well.

2. You are a social worker in the emergency room of a general hospital. Paramedics have just brought in the victim of an automobile accident. Doctors and nurses are providing life support as the patient's family members arrive. Your function is to find them a private place to wait and to inform them in general terms about what is happening to the patient. You go up to the family, introduce yourself, and guide them to a more private waiting area. Write the words you would say in describing an initial purpose for the meeting. In this case, your roles are likely to be quite clear. Identify them as well.

3. Along with other professional duties, you lead counseling groups for sexually abused children. You are about to begin working with a new group of five girls ranging in age from 7 to 10 years. Earlier, you conducted an individual interview with each of them and talked with them at length. However, the girls have not met each other before and none has had any group experience. You ask each girl to share only her first name with the others. They all do so, although several introduce themselves in a subdued and tentative manner. You want to begin the group in a warm, safe, and secure manner. Write the words you would say in describing an initial purpose of the meeting. Then identify the professional role or roles that you might assume.

4. In your role as a social worker with a city police department, you assume multiple roles and functions. A primary function, however, is to arrange and facilitate communication between various community groups and the police. This is part of a department-wide effort to reduce crime, promote safety, and improve relations. You are beginning a first meeting with a group of community leaders from different neighborhoods throughout the city. You know that they are extremely concerned about an increase in gang and drug-related crime in their communities. Emotions are high as several people in the

group have recently lost family members due to such violence. You want to begin the group in an empathic, compassionate, and respectful manner. Write the words you would say in describing an initial purpose for the meeting. Before identifying the professional role or roles that you might assume, imagine how the community leaders might respond to your statement about initial purpose. Think about their response as you then proceed to identify a professional role or roles.

Orienting Clients

During the beginning phase of the working relationship, many clients are quite unclear about what to expect. Certain aspects of the anxiety and ambiguity may be the result of cultural factors, but others may be associated with potential vulnerability or simple ignorance. Prospective clients are certainly concerned about the issues that led to the contact, but many are also worried that they may not be able to do what is needed to address those issues (Garvin & Seabury, 1997). In particular, prospective clients may be confused about how they can best help you help them. Ambiguity about what they are "supposed to do" is probably associated with the relatively high premature dropout rates for clients generally, and especially for members of minority status, racial, ethnic, cultural, religious, or linguistic groups; and for those of lower socioeconomic status (Claus & Kindleberger, 2002; Kubetin, 2003; Pelkonen, Marttunen, Laippala, & Lonnqvist, 2000; Sue, 1977; Swift & Greenberg, 2012; Swift, Greenberg, Whipple, & Kominiak, 2012; Wierzbicki & Pekarik, 1993).

Although mass media have contributed to popular familiarity with some facets of social services through television series and motion pictures, and, of course, various talk radio and television "therapists" such as *Dr. Phil*, the actual history of formal "for hire" helping relationships with professionals is relatively short indeed. Throughout the centuries, family members, friends, community leaders, elders, and shamans or other religious leaders have helped people deal with various psychosocial issues. Indeed, the family and local community addressed problems of all kinds. Except for visiting religious leaders and indigenous healers, outsiders provided service only on rare occasions.

Although social norms and mores have changed dramatically during the last several decades, most people still find it anxiety-provoking to seek and receive help for psychological and social issues from paid strangers. Such interactions are sometimes associated with a sense of shame and perhaps stigma. You may help clarify the situation by describing how clients can join you as active, collaborative participants in the helping process (Garvin, 1987, 1997). Indeed, orienting clients to the process and preparing them for likely activities may lower the early dropout rate and improve service outcomes (Atkins & Patenaude, 1987; Kovacs & Bronstein, 1999; Lambert & Lambert, 1984; Sar, 2000; Shuman & Shapiro, 2002; Swift et al., 2012; Yalom, Houts, Newell, & Rand, 1967).

For example, in the first meeting of a group for adolescents having school problems, you might orient group members in a manner such as illustrated in Box 8.2. You might attempt to orient an individual client in the manner depicted in Box 8.3.

In orienting clients, recognize that expectations necessarily vary according to the reasons clients seek or receive social work services. They also differ in relation to agency setting, its mission and programs, and the composition of the client system—its size and the ages, capabilities, and motivations of its members. As you can imagine, the expectations for an adult client about to begin an intensive 3-month educational and therapeutic group experience for men who batter women would be quite different from those for an 8-year-old child who witnessed her father shoot and kill her mother.

When serving as convener or chairperson of committees, task forces, boards, or community groups or as leader of organizations, we engage in a similar process of orienting fellow members to the roles and expectations associated with participation. After introductions and a description of initial purpose, we help others explore how they may work together toward their desired outcomes.

BOX 8.2
Orienting Clients (Group Members)

We all have problems at some point in our lives. It's part of being human. We've found that talking with other people who are in similar situations often helps resolve those problems. We've planned this group so you can share with each other your issues and concerns as well as your hopes and dreams. Although you are not required to say anything that you wish to keep to yourself, we hope that you will talk openly with one another, listen carefully to what others say, and share your thoughts and feelings about the issues we discuss. We expect all group members to follow the rule of confidentiality. That means that whatever any of you say in the group setting stays here. Things we talk about in the group should not be discussed outside this room.

BOX 8.3
Orienting Clients (Individual)

You can best help in this process by sharing your thoughts and feelings as freely and as fully as you possibly can. Please ask questions when you do not understand, offer suggestions about what might work better, and give feedback about what helps and what does not. Finally, you can be helpful in this process by trying as hard as you can to take the steps that we plan together. If we work together, there is a good chance we will be able to resolve the issues that led to this visit.

EXERCISE 8-4: ORIENTING CLIENTS

Use the following case situations to practice the skill of orienting clients. Please respond to each situation in the spaces provided.

1. Assume that you are a social worker meeting for the first time with a couple that wants help in dealing with relationship difficulties. Mr. and Mrs. Koslow have been married for 10 years. They have two children (8 and 10 years of age) and an adequate income. You have introduced yourself, secured introductions from Mr. and Mrs. Koslow, and suggested that one purpose for this first meeting might be to explore the problems and concerns that led the couple to come to the agency. They readily concurred with this idea. You now want to orient them to the process. What would you say?

2. Assume that you are a social worker meeting for the first time with a family of four (a single parent and three children, ages 11, 13, and 16 years). The eldest child, a daughter, has reportedly begun to use marijuana and has also adopted a gothic style of dress and appearance where black is the dominant theme. She has written poetry about death and created pencil drawings that depict violent scenes in a school yard. Multiple corpses are drawn in detail and pools of blood are prominent. The mother is very concerned. Therefore she brings the entire family to the agency to meet with you. You introduce yourself, secure introductions from each of the family members, and indicate that the purpose of this first meeting is to explore the problems and concerns that led the family to come to the agency. They agree with the suggested purpose. You now want to orient them to the process. What would you say?

3. Assume that you are a social worker meeting for the first time with a group of community members who have expressed concern about the increasingly high cost of energy for heating or cooling their apartments and homes. As the cold season approaches, they worry about their ability to heat their homes and keep their families comfortable when the temperature falls. These are low-income families earning minimum wage or less, and several are currently unemployed. You introduce yourself, secure introductions from each of the community members, and tentatively propose as a purpose of this first meeting to gather information and begin to consider action steps that might be taken to address the problem. They agree with the suggested purpose. You now want to orient them to the process. What would you say to do so?

Discussing Policy and Ethical Factors

An extremely important beginning skill involves discussing potentially relevant legal, policy, and ethical factors. Mutual understanding of the ground rules is critical for the development of an authentic, honest, and trusting relationship. Describing and discussing these factors constitutes part of the informed consent process and represents an essential element of professional service to clients. Failure to explore these factors with clients may seriously damage the working relationship and may sometimes constitute grounds for malpractice or disciplinary action.

Meetings with people who are not, formally, "clients" may not require detailed description of the legal and ethical factors associated with client status. However, agency policies and usual operating practices warrant discussion. In general, when meeting with people, describe the parameters and ground rules that do or might apply. It helps make things more transparent and less mysterious, and conveys respect to participants in the process. In a sense, such disclosure relates to the honesty, integrity, and fairness aspects of professionalism.

As a social worker, you are guided by certain policies and procedures in the performance of your duties. Some of these originate with the organization with which you are affiliated (for example, agency policies and procedures), others are promulgated by the social work profession (for example, ethical codes and standards), and still others are formulated by governmental bodies and courts (for example, laws, regulations, and legal precedents). People have a right to information about the policies and ethical principles that may apply to them during the course of your work together. Many agencies wisely provide prospective clients with brochures and other publications describing relevant policies. Box 8.4 shows a sample document that a social worker in an agency might provide to prospective clients and use to complement discussion of policy and ethical issues.

BOX 8.4
Agency Policies

As a general guideline, whatever clients say during sessions remains confidential among agency personnel. There are, however, a few exceptions. If a client wants the agency to provide information to another person or agency (for example, to a medical doctor), he or she may sign a *Release of Information* form that specifies which information to transfer and to whom. Also, as required by law, indications of possible child abuse or neglect will be reported to child-protection authorities. Similarly, we will not keep confidential information that a person represents a danger to himself or herself or to others. In such cases, we will take action to protect the lives of the people involved. In potentially life-threatening circumstances, the value of human life takes precedence over that of confidentiality.

The agency operates on a *sliding fee* basis. This means that the cost of each individual or family session varies according to clients' ability to pay: the higher the family income, the higher the cost—to a maximum of $55 per session. Group sessions are lower. Reimbursement from insurance companies, where applicable, is the responsibility of the client. However, agency staff members can help clients complete the necessary claim forms.

If you must cancel a scheduled meeting, the agency should be notified at least 1 day before the appointment.

In this agency, we regularly seek evaluative feedback about the nature and benefit of meetings with agency professionals. At the beginning of each meeting, we ask clients to complete short evaluation forms in our attempt to maintain and improve the quality of our services. In addition, we have a procedure for expressing concerns about the services clients receive or any of the agency policies or practices. If, for any reason whatsoever, you are uncertain about or dissatisfied with the service you receive, please discuss it with your service provider. If you do not receive an adequate explanation, if the service remains unsatisfactory, or if you feel uncomfortable talking directly about the issue with your helping professional, please contact our agency's client representative, Ms. Sheila Cordula, in Room 21 (telephone 789-5432). She will talk with you about your concerns and attempt to address them.

However, some clients do not or cannot truly understand the full meaning of such written material. You should therefore discuss key policies with most or all prospective clients.

Suppose, for example, an adult male client assumes that everything he says to you will remain confidential. During a counseling session, he tells you that he sometimes uses a wire coat hanger to "spank" his 2-year-old child. Operating on an assumption of "absolute confidentiality," he would probably feel profoundly betrayed when you informed him that you were legally required to report to local child-protection authorities what he told you about the "spankings."

Social workers are very concerned about protecting children from abuse and may sometimes wonder if discussion of policy and ethical factors may inhibit people from revealing pertinent information. Although such discussions probably have little adverse effect on communications, some social workers believe that they do and consequently skim over policies that might provoke discomfort. A few may even avoid them altogether. These are risky practices that not only endanger the basic rights of clients, but also place social workers at risk of malpractice or other disciplinary action. In general, failure to discuss policy and ethical factors may actually reduce the likelihood of learning about reportable activities such as child abuse. If consumers conclude that social workers cannot be trusted to tell the whole truth or to keep our promises, they may well avoid seeking professional help altogether.

In discussing relevant policy and ethical factors, however, social workers consider several aspects of the person-in-environment, including the relative urgency of the issue or problem and the context of the meeting. Suppose, for example, you serve as a social worker in the emergency room of a hospital. An ambulance delivers a severely injured young child who has been in an automobile accident. When the visibly distraught parents arrive, you decide to defer discussion of policy and ethical factors while you provide information about their child and try to offer comfort, compassion, and social support. In such instances, a social worker might reasonably decide that the parents' immediate needs take precedence over our obligation to discuss policies. Actually, we should consider all social work skills within the context of the person-in-environment. Such considerations are not limited to discussing policy and ethical factors. Frequently, a skill that is perfectly applicable in one circumstance is completely inappropriate in another. Because social work practice is a professional rather than a technical or bureaucratic endeavor, we must continually make judgments about when and how to best use our social work knowledge and skills.

EXERCISE 8-5: DISCUSSING POLICY AND ETHICAL FACTORS

Use the following case situations to practice the skill of discussing policy and ethical factors. Please respond to each situation in the spaces provided.

1. Assume that you are a social worker meeting for the first time with a 42-year-old woman, beaten nearly to death by her husband several times over the past 10 years. After the most recent episode, she sought refuge in a shelter for battered women, where you serve as a social worker. She wants help in dealing with her situation. You have introduced yourself and learned that she prefers to be called Luci. You have also described a tentative initial purpose; that is, to explore the nature of her concerns, consider various courses of action, and come up with plans to address the situation. She concurred with the purpose so you then oriented her to the process. At this point, you are ready to discuss policy and ethical factors. What would you say to do so?

2. As a social worker with the local police department, you have begun a first meeting with a group of community leaders from different neighborhoods throughout the city. They are extremely concerned about gang- and drug-related crime in their communities. Emotions are high as several people in the group have recently lost family members due to such violence. You have already introduced yourself, sought introductions

from participants, described a tentative initial purpose, and oriented them to the process. At this point you are ready to introduce the topic of policy and ethical factors in terms of the general parameters for this and any subsequent meetings. Consider the context and write the words you would say in doing so.

3. You are a social worker for an agency that serves sexually abused children. You are about to begin working with a new group of girls ranging in age from 7 to 10 years. You have introduced yourself, sought introductions from them (using first names only), described an initial purpose for the group, and outlined your professional roles in the process. As you oriented them to the process, you took extra time to lessen their anxiety and encourage them to view the group experience as a "place of safety." Continue this beginning process by writing the words you would say in discussing policy and ethical factors as they might relate to this group of girls.

Seeking Feedback

In using the skill of *seeking feedback* (Schwartz, 1976; Shulman, 1992), social workers encourage clients to comment about the proposed purpose for the meeting and our roles, their roles, policy or ethical factors, or any other aspects of our introductory remarks. An important part of effective communications involves checking to see if others have understood your messages and you have understood theirs. Seeking feedback serves this function. As social workers, we routinely seek feedback throughout the entire course of our work with people and do so formally[2] as well as informally. By asking for feedback about your initial description of purpose and roles, and your discussion of policy and ethical factors during the beginning phase, you continue the process of informed consent. You also further promote the idea that this is a collaborative, reciprocal kind of relationship that genuinely involves the active participation of both client and social worker. You invite clients to identify areas that are unclear, share thoughts that have occurred to them, introduce new topics, express disagreement with your comments, and evaluate the process. By seeking feedback, you effectively send a message that workers and clients are cooperative partners who are working toward a common purpose. You convey that you are genuinely interested in what they have to say about what you have said or done, and that you hope they will actively contribute their thoughts, reactions, and suggestions throughout the process.

Typically, social workers seek feedback about purpose, roles, and policy factors through questions such as: "How does that sound to you? What do you think about what we've talked about so far? What questions or comments do you have?" Often, people respond to requests for feedback by asking for clarification. This gives you an opportunity to elaborate about purpose, roles, or policy and ethical factors. In general, people who clearly understand these ground rules and believe that you sincerely want their feedback are likely to feel both informed and respected.

EXERCISE 8-6: SEEKING FEEDBACK

Use the following case situations to practice the skill of seeking feedback. Please respond to each situation in the spaces provided.

1. You, a social worker in an agency that serves children and their families, are meeting for the first time with a 32-year-old mother and her 8-year-old daughter. They have voluntarily sought help regarding problems with the child's schoolwork. At this time you do not know anything more about the school or family situation. You have introduced yourself and elicited introductions from them. You have learned that Ms. Pomerantz prefers to be called "Joan" and that her daughter prefers "Emily." You have asked them to call you by your first name as well. You have also outlined an initial purpose for this first meeting by saying, "In today's meeting I hope that we'll gain a beginning understanding of the concerns that led to this visit. Then, together, we'll try to find out how best to address those concerns."

    Write the words you would use in seeking feedback from Joan and Emily regarding your proposed purpose for the meeting.

---

[2] In Chapter 12, when we explore the processes and skills associated with evaluating, we consider formal, systematic means of eliciting, gathering, and analyzing evaluative feedback about the quality of the relationship and process, and progress toward goals and outcomes.

2. As you continue to interact with Joan and Emily Pomerantz, you state, "Almost everything that you and Emily say during our meetings will be treated as confidential. No one outside the agency will have access to information you share. The major exception to this policy of confidentiality is when you specifically and in writing request that we provide information to someone else. Of course, when someone's life is in danger or there are indications of possible child abuse or neglect, we'll take action to protect the safety of those involved—even if that means violating our basic rule of confidentiality."

   Write the words you would use in seeking feedback from Joan regarding these policy and ethical factors.

3. You are a social worker in an agency that serves adults and children who have been involved in child abuse. You are meeting for the first time with a 22-year-old man who has been charged with severely beating his 4-year-old son. He is required to receive counseling as part of an adjudicated court agreement that, depending on the results of your work together, may enable him to lessen the length of a prison sentence or perhaps avoid incarceration altogether. Thus far, you have introduced yourself and elicited an introduction from him. You sense from the nature of his body position that you should address him in a formal manner. You refer to him as "Mr. Battle" and identify yourself in a similar fashion. You have also outlined an initial purpose for this first meeting by

saying, "In today's meeting I hope that we will be able to gain a beginning understanding of your current situation and identify some preliminary goals for our work together. It is my understanding that you are required by Judge Koopman to participate in counseling sessions at least once per week for a minimum of 6 months."

Write the words you would use in seeking feedback from Mr. Battle concerning your statements thus far.

Summary

During the beginning phase of social work service, you introduce and identify yourself and seek introductions from prospective clients and involved others. Following the exchange of introductions, you describe a tentative initial purpose for the meeting, possibly identify one or more professional roles that you might undertake, orient participants to the process, and identify relevant policy and ethical factors that might apply. Throughout this beginning process, you regularly seek feedback concerning others' understanding of and reactions to your introductory comments. By using the beginning skills, you help to clarify the nature and boundaries or ground rules of the helping process, lessen the initial ambivalence people often experience, and establish a tentative direction for work.

CHAPTER 8: SUMMARY EXERCISES

Assume that you are a social worker with a multipurpose social services agency. Prepare for a first meeting in each of the situations described below. Use a word-processing program to write the words you would say and describe the actions you would take as you meet for the first time. Among the skills that may apply in this series of exercises are introducing yourself, seeking introductions, describing an initial purpose and (sometimes) your professional social work roles, orienting clients, discussing policy and ethical factors, and seeking feedback. Please *label* each of the beginning skills you use in each case situation. Also, discuss your rationale for the words you choose and actions you propose. When finished, combine your word-processed responses into a document titled "Beginning Skills Responses and Rationales" and include it in your Social Work Skills Portfolio.

1. Earlier in the day, a woman telephoned your agency and said she wanted to talk with someone about a recent incident. About a week earlier, she met a man in a bar. He drove her home and then raped her. She thought that she would be able to manage her feelings about the crime by herself. However, she now realizes that she needs professional help to cope. She said, "I'm falling apart." Build upon the preparations you have previously undertaken to describe the words you would say and the actions you would take in beginning with the woman.

2. Recently, a 14-year-old African American girl told her schoolteacher that she was pregnant by her 15-year-old white boyfriend. She also told the teacher that she needs to get an abortion quickly, or "my parents will kill me if they find out I'm pregnant." The teacher urged her to talk with you, the school social worker, and obtained the girl's permission to tell you about the situation. The teacher did so and arranged for you to meet with the teenager at this time. Build upon the preparations you have previously undertaken to describe the words you would say and the actions you would take in beginning with the young woman.

3. An 8-year-old victim of sexual molestation seems to be in a state of emotional shock. She has not spoken a word or expressed any feelings since the incident several days earlier. The child-protection caseworker tried to encourage the child to talk about what happened, but her efforts were unsuccessful. As a social worker who specializes in work with victimized children, you received a request to help the child and family.

   You are now making a scheduled home visit. You drive to the girl's home, where she resides with her mother. Build upon the preparations you have previously undertaken to describe the words you would say and the actions you would take in beginning with the child's mother; and then in beginning with the child.

CHAPTER 8: EXPERIENTIAL INTERVIEWING EXERCISE

Now that you have prepared for the recruitment contact, it is time to meet with a prospective practice client. Before doing so, ensure that you have gained a firm commitment from your professor, field instructor, or other professional social worker to serve in the dual roles of your supervisor and the practice client's advocate.

When you meet with a prospective practice client, use the beginning skills of introducing yourself and seeking introductions. Identify yourself as a social work student. Share your tentative purpose by informing your colleague that you are learning a large number of social work skills and wonder if she or he might be willing to be interviewed one time per week over the course of the next several weeks so that you can practice the skills and perhaps become more proficient. Tell your colleague that you would assume the role of a social worker and that he or she would serve in the role of client. Orient your peer to the process by indicating that she or he would behave as if voluntarily seeking help about one or two personal problems or issues. Provide the prospective practice client with a copy of the Guidelines and Consent Form for the Practice Client: Experiential Interviewing Exercise that is available in Appendix 12. Other relevant materials contained in that appendix may also be useful. Indicate that you will meet together five times. Your colleague should understand that you may not be of any actual help with the identified concerns except to the extent that talking about them might be beneficial. The primary purpose is to help you practice skills needed in social work practice.

You might mention that it is often professionally useful for social workers and social work students to take on a client role. By assuming the role of client, social workers may become more sensitive to the experience of seeking help. It is not always easy to ask for and receive assistance. Being a client can also significantly heighten social workers' awareness of things to do and things to avoid in their own social work practice. The experience often leads to greater understanding of how to be an effective social worker. Of course, assuming the role of social worker in a relatively safe, learning environment is usually extremely beneficial as well. You could mention that you hope to learn a great deal over the course of the next several weeks.

Discuss policy and ethical factors by informing your colleague that you plan to audio- or video-record the meetings and that you will prepare a written recording based on the interviews. Indicate that you might discuss the interviews with your supervising social worker but that you will not reveal your colleague's name or other identifying characteristics. Mention that, as the practice client, he or she may read your written records when they are completed. Assure your colleague that to ensure privacy you will together come up with a fictitious name to use in the recording and in your notes about the interviews. Reconfirm that you will not reveal his or her full name to anyone without his or her consent. Indicate that your colleague will not have to discuss any aspect of her or his personal life that she or he would prefer to keep private. Mention that if you happen to address a topic that he or she does not want to talk about, he or she may simply say, "I prefer not to talk about that." Notify your colleague that this exercise is entirely voluntary. It is perfectly all right to decline this invitation. Finally, advise your colleague that you are still learning about social work and have not perfected the social work skills. You will almost definitely make mistakes. The primary purpose of the exercise is for you to practice the social work skills. It is certainly not to provide actual social work services.

Be certain to inform your prospective practice client that a professor or other professional social worker has formally agreed to serve as your supervisor and will provide guidance as needed. Identify that person by name. Also mention that your supervisor will also serve as a client advocate so that your colleague may contact him or her if there are questions, issues, complications, conflicts, or complaints at any point during the learning exercise.

Inform your colleague that if she or he agrees to participate as a practice client, he or she should be prepared to identify and discuss an actual issue for which he or she might conceivably talk with a close, trusted friend or perhaps even consult a social worker. However, the issue should be modest and manageable. Ask your colleague to avoid issues that have the potential to overwhelm her or his natural coping mechanisms. If the issue involves other people (for example, parents, siblings, spouses, children, classmates, professors) either create pseudonyms or refer to them in general terms such as "my boyfriend."

If your colleague understands what is expected and provides formal consent to participate (see Appendix 12), arrange for a time and place during the next week to meet privately for approximately 45 minutes. Exchange contact information in case a meeting must be rescheduled or information shared during intervals between meetings. Also provide the practice client with contact information for the supervisor/client advocate.

The first 30 minutes of each meeting are reserved for the social work interview. After concluding, you and your colleague will step out of your respective roles of social worker and practice client to become collaborators in learning. During the remaining 10–15 minutes, you and your colleague will discuss the interview. She or he can share thoughts and feelings about the experience and provide evaluative feedback to you. The post-interview processing can substantially enhance learning. Plan to take notes during those exchanges.

Inform your colleague that, with the exception of the post-interview processing discussions, you intend to assume the role of social worker throughout each and every meeting. Remind your partner to assume the role of client from the moment you come together at the time of the scheduled meeting and to be prepared to discuss one or two true but relatively modest and definitively manageable issues or concerns for which she or he might conceivably seek help.

Record the time, date, and place of the scheduled meeting. If, by chance, you and the practice client have identified a fictitious name or pseudonym that she or he plans to use, mention that as well. Keep contact information about your colleague (telephone numbers or e-mail addresses) in a separate place—perhaps in your personal calendar or address book. In order to maintain confidentiality, do not indicate that this information relates to your practice client and do not include it in your Social Work Skills Learning Portfolio.

As you finish this chapter, please reflect on your learning by completing the following self-appraisal exercise.

SELF-APPRAISAL: THE BEGINNING SKILLS

Please use the following items to help you undertake a self-assessment of your proficiency in the beginning skills. Read each statement carefully. Then, use the following 4-point rating scale to indicate the degree to which you agree or disagree with each statement. Record your numerical response in the space provided:

4 = Strongly agree   2 = Disagree

3 = Agree   1 = Strongly disagree

4	3	2	1	Rating Statement
				At this point in time, I can
☐	☐	☐	☐	1. Discuss the purposes and functions of beginning.
☐	☐	☐	☐	2. Introduce myself.
☐	☐	☐	☐	3. Seek introductions.
☐	☐	☐	☐	4. Describe an initial purpose.
☐	☐	☐	☐	5. Orient clients to the process.
☐	☐	☐	☐	6. Discuss policy and ethical factors.
☐	☐	☐	☐	7. Seek feedback.
☐	☐	☐	☐	8. Assess my proficiency in the beginning skills.
				Subtotal

Note: These items are identical to those contained in the Beginning Skills section of the Social Work Skills Self-Appraisal Questionnaire presented in Appendix 3. If you completed that self-appraisal before beginning Chapter 1, you have already responded to these items once before. You may now compare the responses you made on that occasion with those you made this time. Also, compare the two subtotals. If you believe that you have progressed in terms of your proficiency, the more recent subtotal should be higher than the earlier one.

CHAPTER 9

EXPLORING

As the beginning phase ends, social workers engage clients in a mutual exploration of the problem or issue from a person-in-environment perspective. This chapter (see Box 9.1) should help you develop proficiency in the exploring skills, which encourage people to share information, thoughts, and feelings about themselves; the problems or concerns that led to the contact; and the social and environmental context in which they function. Through this collaborative process of exploration, you and clients usually learn a great deal. You and they often gain a more complete and realistic understanding of the problem or issue of concern as well as its impact upon them and their circumstances. In addition, clients often enhance their own self-understanding. Indeed, greater self-awareness is a common result because talking openly with other people also involves listening to oneself. As people share their thoughts, ideas, and feelings, they not only perceive your reactions to them and what they say, but also more fully experience their own. In group contexts, the effects are enhanced as people experience the reactions of others as well their own. Through this process, you collaboratively consider information regarding clients, involved others, problems or issues, and circumstances. You review risk and protective factors. This helps you both identify factors associated with the origin, development, and maintenance of the problems as well as those strengths, attributes, and resources that may be useful in working toward resolution. Such information, in conjunction with your own professional knowledge and, of course, the full participation of your clients, contributes to the development of an assessment, service contract, and plans for your work together.

The skills most applicable to the exploration phase are (1) asking questions, (2) seeking clarification, (3) reflecting content, (4) reflecting feelings, (5) reflecting feelings and meanings, (6) partializing, (7) going beyond what is said, (8) reflecting issues, and (9) reflecting hypotheses. Consistent with a person-in-environment perspective, we use these skills in exploring the person or people involved; the identified issues, problems, or aspirations; the social and physical/ecological circumstances; and any potential personal or environmental strengths, assets, and resources.

BOX 9.1

Chapter Purpose

The purpose of this chapter is to help learners understand and apply the exploring skills within the context of contemporary social work practice.

Goals

Following completion of this chapter, learners should be able to demonstrate proficiency in:

◆ Discussing the purposes and functions of exploring
◆ Exploring relevant aspects of the person-issue-situation and looking for strengths
◆ Asking questions
◆ Seeking clarification
◆ Reflecting content
◆ Reflecting feelings
◆ Reflecting feelings and meanings
◆ Partializing
◆ Going beyond what is said
◆ Reflecting issues
◆ Reflecting hypotheses
◆ Assessing proficiency in the exploring skills

Core EPAS Competencies

The skills addressed in this chapter support the following core EPAS competencies:

◆ Identify as a professional social worker and conduct oneself accordingly (EP2.1.1).
◆ Apply social work ethical principles to guide professional practice (EP2.1.2).
◆ Apply critical thinking to inform and communicate professional judgments (EP2.1.3).
◆ Engage diversity and difference in practice (EP2.1.4).
◆ Apply knowledge of human behavior and the social environment (EP2.1.7).
◆ Respond to contexts that shape practice (EP2.1.9).
◆ Engage . . . (and) . . . assess . . . with individuals, families, groups, organizations, and communities (EP2.1.10[a–b]).

In undertaking the exploration process, we enlist clients or others in a collaborative examination of the current state of the presenting problems or issues of concern as well as an overview of their origin and history. We also review previous attempts to address or overcome them along with the outcomes of those efforts. In addition to needs, problems, or issues, we also engage clients in collaborative consideration of wants, aspirations, and goals. In terms of goals, we seek clients' conception of two kinds: (1) goals that, if achieved, would naturally result in the elimination, reduction, or management of the presenting problems, and (2) goals that, if achieved, would contribute to a better quality of life and an enhanced sense of well-being.

As social workers, we view each client as a unique and significant individual, family, group, organization, or community that functions within the context of a social and physical/ecological environment. The characteristics and attributes of the client and those of the environment

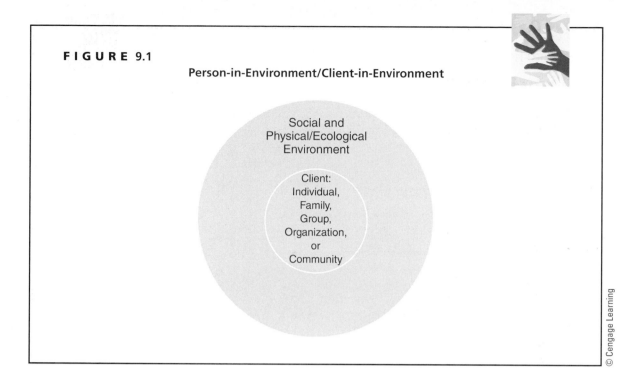

FIGURE 9.1

Person-in-Environment/Client-in-Environment

Social and Physical/Ecological Environment

Client: Individual, Family, Group, Organization, or Community

© Cengage Learning

bear upon the presenting problems and goals. Therefore, we adopt a person-in-environment[1] (or client-in-environment) perspective (see Figure 9.1) and attempt to learn about the client and the situation as well as the issues of concern. In exploring the client-in-environment, we consider strengths or assets as well as challenges or obstacles. We also gather information about two kinds of goals (that is, problem resolving and life quality enhancing) that often emerge within the client's biopsychosocial life spheres (see Figure 9.2) and the physical/ecological environment.

Problems and goals may be viewed as partly or wholly personal or as partly or wholly environmental, or partly or wholly interactional (that is, interactions within or between the person and environmental systems). Similarly, clients and social workers may conceptualize personal problems and goals as partially or completely sociological, psychological, or biological in nature. Environmental problems and goals may be viewed as physical or ecological. Of course, the particular biopsychosocial aspects or dimensions of the problems and goals, and the life spheres or domains within the environmental context, vary from client to client. Social workers, however, maintain a person-in-environment perspective and recognize that personal and environmental factors interact in an interdependent manner. We do so even when exploring *biological dimensions* such as heredity (for example, genetic factors), health and wellness, illness, injury, physiological sensations, and ingested or absorbed chemical substances (for example, medicines, substances such as alcohol and street drugs, environmental chemicals such as lead, pesticides, air and water pollutants that reside within a person's body); *psychological dimensions* such as perceptions, cognitive beliefs, attitudes, expectations (for example, thoughts about self and others, cultural views, religious and spiritual beliefs; beliefs about problems and problem solving), images, and individual behavior; and *social dimensions* such as interpersonal encounters, relationships, and patterns of communicating and relating that occur

---

[1] In the context of a "person-in-environment" perspective, a person is a client. In social work, a client can be an individual, family, group, organization, community, or perhaps an entire society. However, the PIE perspective suggests that all people—clients and nonclients alike—can truly be understood only within the context of their social and physical/ecological environment.

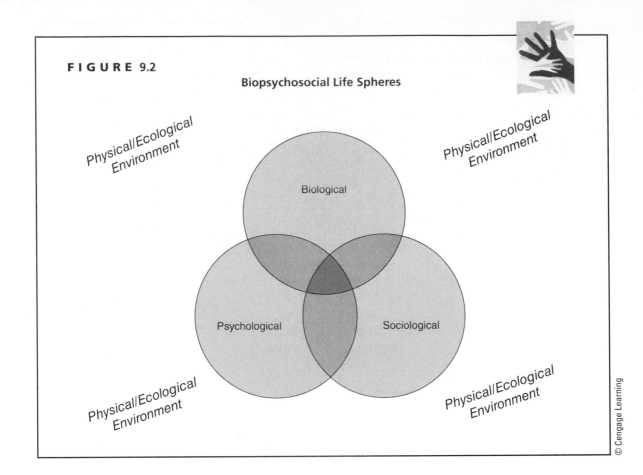

FIGURE 9.2

Biopsychosocial Life Spheres

Physical/Ecological Environment

Physical/Ecological Environment

Biological

Psychological

Sociological

Physical/Ecological Environment

Physical/Ecological Environment

© Cengage Learning

within the context of primary and secondary social systems (for example, families, households, various groups, organizations, neighborhoods, communities, cultures, and societies) as well as practices and traditions common within the client's social environment. Of course, problems and goals within the *physical/ecological environment* (for example, housing, air and water quality, noise levels, access to food and clothing, energy resources, personal privacy, and physical safety) as well as the *social environment* are common. Indeed, as social workers, we consider the physical/ecological as well as the social context and recognize that social policies and practices may affect, for better or worse, the biological, psychological, social, and environmental aspects of people's lives.

As you and your clients explore problems and goals from a person-in-environment perspective, you might consider biopsychosocial and environmental dimensions such as those outlined in Table 9.1. As an alternative or supplement to a tabular outline, you could also create a concept map (Mueller, Polansky, Foltin, Polivaev, & Other Contributers, 2010) to illustrate potentially relevant biopsychosocial and environmental dimensions.[2] Figure 9.3 contains selected dimensions of a concept map that social workers and clients might use to guide the process of exploring key biopsychosocial and environmental dimensions of problems and goals from a client-in-environment perspective.

When social workers prepare individualized concept maps, we replace the categorical dimensions with client-specific information. Figure 9.4 depicts a partially completed concept map of a homeless man who lives just outside the city center under a bridge by a small river. He has declined

---

[2] Many word-processors allow you to create conceptual maps and graphic illustrations of various kinds. You could also use a dedicated mind-mapping software program such as FreeMind (available at http://freemind.sourceforge.net).

TABLE 9.1
Outline of Selected Biopsychosocial Dimensions

Biological	Psychological	Sociological	Environmental (Physical/Ecological)
◆ Hereditary Predispositions ◆ Health and Physical Ability ◆ Illness, Disease, Injury ◆ Ingested or Absorbed Chemical Substances	◆ Individual Behavior ◆ Feelings and Emotions ◆ Cognitive Beliefs and Expectations ◆ Images and Visualizations ◆ Perceptions ◆ Sensations	◆ Friendship Systems ◆ Family Systems ◆ Employment Systems ◆ Neighborhood System ◆ Cultural Systems ◆ Educational Systems ◆ Religious or Spiritual Systems ◆ Health Care Systems ◆ Organizational Systems ◆ Community Systems ◆ Legal Systems ◆ Societal Systems	◆ Safety/Danger ◆ Air ◆ Water ◆ Food ◆ Shelter/Housing ◆ Clothing ◆ Privacy ◆ Noise/Quiet ◆ Transportation ◆ Energy ◆ Biodiversity ◆ Stimulation: Intellectual, Emotional, Social, Physical

© Cengage Learning

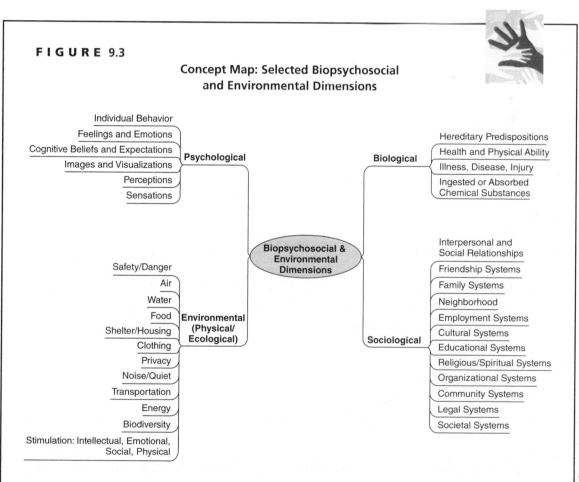

FIGURE 9.3

Concept Map: Selected Biopsychosocial and Environmental Dimensions

© Cengage Learning

FIGURE 9.4

Concept Map: The "Homeless Pacer"

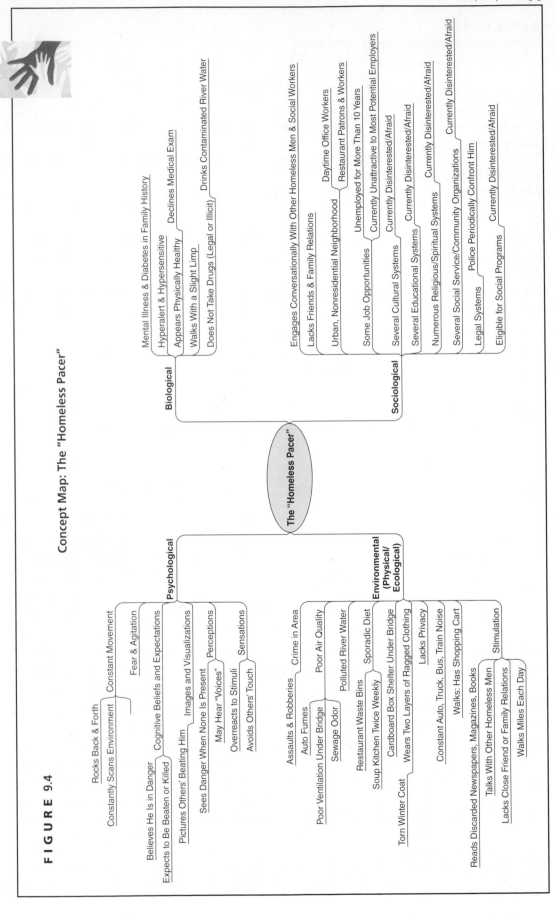

T A B L E 9.2
Exploration Matrix

	Present	Past	Future
Problem/Issue & Goal	1	2	7
Person/Client (Biopsychosocial)	3	4	8
Situation (Social & Physical/Ecological Environment)	5	6	9

to identify himself by name, so we refer to him as the "homeless pacer" because he constantly moves—walking, pacing, or, if seated, rocking back and forth—and he lives in Indianapolis, home of the Pacers basketball team.

Following the introductions and other parts of the beginning phase, people often feel a strong motivation to discuss the most pressing problems or issues[3] of concern. As the matrix shown in Table 9.2 suggests, you often begin by exploring a problem as currently experienced (cell 1). You might then trace its emergence, history, and development (cell 2). As you do so, many people naturally begin to describe aspects of themselves personally as well as dimensions of the situation. As needed, you may next explore their present view of themselves (cell 3), followed by a review of past experiences (cell 4). Then, to the degree that further information is needed, you can return to the present situation, including the social context and physical/ecological environment (cell 5), before exploring the situation as it has been in the past (cell 6). Finally, encourage clients to envision what the future might be like if they, the problem, and the situation remained as it is; and how the future might be if things were to change for the better; or for the worse (cells 7, 8, and 9).

Of course, these nine dimensions overlap; and they naturally involve consideration of relevant biopsychosocial and environmental factors. As you explore problems, clients often share information about themselves and their situations; and as clients discuss their circumstances, they frequently talk about the problems. While exploring the present, clients may reveal material from the past or hopes and fears about the future. You do not need to interrupt to maintain a particular order or sequence. Generally, you may simply encourage people to share relevant information in their own way. Resist any temptation to view the exploration matrix as a fixed interview schedule. Instead, see it as a flexible guide to help you organize the exploration of relevant aspects of the person-issue-situation over time.

Exploring the problem/issue involves examining the present status of the problem or issue of concern—its intensity, frequency, and duration—and the context in which it tends to happen (see Table 9.3). As social workers, we hope to discover what happens before, during, and after an occurrence or episode of the problem. In addition, you would commonly explore the issue as it has been in the past. Trace or track its development from the time of its initial occurrence to the present. In your exploration, include a careful examination of clients' attempts to resolve, cope with, or avoid the issue (see the later discussion on looking for strengths). Discuss efforts that have been successful, those that were partially successful, and those that were unsuccessful. Identify strengths and resources that clients used in earlier attempts at resolution. As part of this exploration, encourage people to share thoughts, feelings, and actions associated with the issue or problem of concern.

---

[3] We use the term *issue (or problem)* to refer to a topic of concern or interest to the client, the social worker, or other interested parties. In this context, an issue may be a problem, need, dilemma, symptom, aspiration, goal, or objective of relevance to participants in the professional relationship.

TABLE 9.3
Exploration of the Problem/Issue

Onset	Explore the origin of the problem; the circumstances under which it first occurred.
Evolution	Explore the development and course of the problem/issue; when and how it was better or worse; and when and how the client addressed or coped with the problem/issue.
Frequency	Explore how often episodes of the problem/issue occur.
Situational Context	Explore when, where, and how episodes of the problem/issue emerge.
Intensity/Severity	Explore the severity or intensity of the problem/issue.
Duration	Explore how long each episode of the problem/issue lasts.

© Cengage Learning

The exploration process also typically involves identification and review of those risk and protective factors that function to increase or decrease the probability that a problem will emerge. In developing a conceptual scheme for viewing risky behavior among adolescents, Jessor (1991; Jessor, Bos, Vanderyn, & Turbin, 1995) proposed "a relationship between risk and protective factors in five domains (biology/genetics, social environment, perceived environment, personality, and behavior)" (Astatke, Black, & Serpell, 2000, p. 66).

We can define risk factors "as individual or environmental markers that are related to the increased likelihood that a negative outcome will occur" (Small, 2000, para. 2). The concept of risk factors has been common in epidemiological and public health research related to disease, injuries, and risky behaviors (for example, unprotected sex, inadequate diets, limited physical or mental exercise, poverty, violence). Indeed, the Centers for Disease Control and Prevention (CDC) sponsor a Behavioral Risk Factor Surveillance System (BRFSS) to identify and monitor risk factors (Centers for Disease Control and Prevention, 2012).

In addition to risk factors, we may also identify protective—sometimes called "resilience"—factors. Protective or resilience factors are:

individual or environmental safeguards that enhance a person's ability to resist stressful life events, risks or hazards and promote adaptation and competence. An important but often overlooked aspect of protective processes is that they only operate when a risk factor is present.

Risk and protective factors can exist both within individuals and across various levels of the environment in which they live. Diverse problems can share common risk factors.

Risk factors often co-occur, and when they do, they appear to carry additive and sometimes exponential risks. It is often the accumulation of multiple risks rather than the presence of any single risk factor that leads to negative outcomes. (Small, 2000, paras. 3–5)

Research involving risk and protective factors associated with various social problems has been quite extensive over the course of the past several decades. Factors associated with the development of psychopathology received early interest (Garmezy, 1985, 1986; Masten, 1994; Rutter, 1979, 1985, 1987; Werner, 1986, 1989). Those associated with contraction of HIV/AIDS have received

TABLE 9.4
Selected Risk and Protective/Resilience Factors Table for HIV/AIDS

Risk Factors	Protective/Resilience Factors
Unprotected sex (for example, oral, anal, vaginal)	Sexual abstinence
	Sex with a single partner who is HIV-negative and monogamous
	Protected sex (for example, sex with condom)
Sharing needles, syringes, drug equipment or "works," or other objects that could retain blood or bodily fluids	Single use of needles and syringes (including those used to inject medicine, steroids, or vitamins; body piercing; and tattooing)
	Exclusive use of drug equipment or "works," or other objects that could retain blood or bodily fluids
Blood transfusions from HIV-positive blood supply	Tested, safe blood supply

Note: Adapted from the Behavioral Risk Factor Surveillance System (Centers for Disease Control and Prevention, 2012).

more recent research attention (Amaro, Raj, Vega, Mangione, & Perez, 2001; Langer, Warheit, & McDonald, 2001; Mullen, Ramirez, Strouse, Hedges, & Sogolow, 2002; Ramirez-Valles, 2002) and substance abuse has a similarly rich research base (Catalano, Hawkins, Berglund, Pollard, & Arthur, 2002; Center for Substance Abuse Prevention, 2001; Epstein & Botvin, 2002; Hawkins, Catalano, & Miller, 1992; Petraitis, Flay, Miller, Torpy, & Greiner, 1998; Wright, 2004). As you can readily imagine, the concepts of strengths, competencies, resilience, and quality of life relate to the notion of protective factors. As you explore problems and issues with clients, you may organize risk and protective factors in tabular format such as depicted in Table 9.4 (Centers for Disease Control and Prevention, 2012). Clients, of course, are often able to identify risk and protective factors based upon their own experience. In addition, scholarly social workers may also consider specific risk and protective factors observed in epidemiological research studies.

In exploring issues and problems, people often share their hypotheses or "theories" about causes and sometimes about "solutions." Indeed, once we have a solid grasp of the person or people involved, the issues, and the circumstances, we encourage clients to share their ideas, hypotheses, or theories about the problems and issues. Many clients readily offer ideas and explanations about "why" something happens or "how" a problem might be resolved. Let's refer to these as *explanatory hypotheses* and *change-oriented hypotheses*, respectively. Of course, social workers also generate hypotheses based upon our knowledge of theoretical models of human behavior, practice experience, and familiarity with relevant research studies. Our familiarity with risk and protective factors often leads us to generate implicit or explicit hypotheses based on the following assumption: If more risk factors and fewer protective factors are associated with problem emergence, then a decrease in risk factors and an increase in protective factors may contribute to its resolution. However, as Table 9.5 illustrates, we highly value clients' as well as our own hypotheses.

Clients' explanatory and change-oriented hypotheses frequently contribute to our understanding of risk and protective factors, as well as clients' ways of viewing themselves, the problems and goals, and their circumstances. Sometimes, however, the hypotheses appear unrelated to actual

TABLE 9.5
Clients' and Social Workers' Explanatory and Change-Oriented Hypotheses

	Explanatory Hypotheses	Change-Oriented Hypotheses
Client's		
Social Worker's		

© Cengage Learning

events or potential solutions. Regardless of their relevance, we note clients' explanatory and change-oriented hypotheses because they may contribute to or hinder progress toward resolution. Indeed, some clients have fixed views about causes or solutions that represent genuine obstacles to change. For example, a teenage boy might view his mother's nagging as the cause of the problems for which he wants your help—that is his explanatory hypothesis. He may also identify his mother as the solution to the problem: "If she would change, things would be better." That is his change-oriented hypothesis. If the teenager retains that fixed view—or if you unquestioningly accept the validity of his hypotheses—the locus of responsibility and control shifts from the adolescent to the mother.

From the boy's perspective, he is a "victim," his mother is a "persecutor," and you as the social worker are the potential "hero" who might convince mom to change her ways. While you should express your understanding of the teenager's hypotheses, you might be wise to test out their credibility. For example, suppose you had a separate conversation with his mother and learned that he had been arrested and convicted for possession, use, and sales of illicit substances; and, that his meetings with you are a required condition of his probation. Might that enlarge your perspective? Might the "mother's nagging" also be viewed as her concerned attempt to help him acknowledge and recover from substance misuse; and keep him from additional legal trouble? If you prematurely endorsed the boy's hypotheses, you might inadvertently reinforce the problematic behaviors that led to the agency visit in the first place.

Ideally, the client's and the worker's explanatory and change-oriented hypotheses are identical, similar, or at least compatible. The greater the congruence or overlap between the two sets of hypotheses (see Figure 9.5), the greater is the likelihood that the client and the social worker

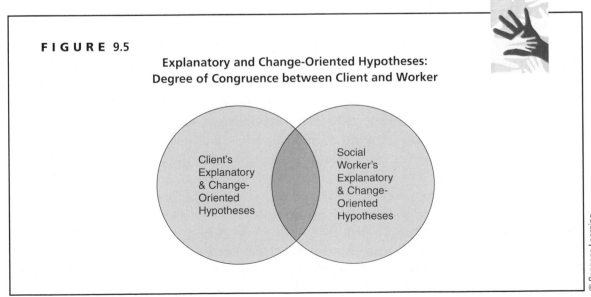

FIGURE 9.5

Explanatory and Change-Oriented Hypotheses: Degree of Congruence between Client and Worker

Client's Explanatory & Change-Oriented Hypotheses

Social Worker's Explanatory & Change-Oriented Hypotheses

© Cengage Learning

will have a positive and productive working relationship. Conversely, when the client and worker's hypotheses diverge, a successful outcome becomes markedly less likely.

In exploring hypotheses, excessive speculation about possible reasons for problems and issues may limit the exploratory process. Some clients and social workers prefer intellectual analysis over factual description and emotional expression about events and circumstances. Unfortunately, this preference for ideas may contribute to inadequate exploration of details or expression of feelings about the issues of concern. Through a process called intellectualization, people sometimes attempt to protect themselves from or defend against perceived powerful feelings by engaging in abstract, cognitive thought. In most cases, clients and social workers wisely explore descriptive information before examining possible reasons for phenomena. The quality of reflective thought tends to improve when a solid understanding of the facts and circumstances serves as a foundation. The worker postpones questions such as "Why do you think that happens?" or "What do you think causes that?" until the client has shared feelings and explored details about the person-issue-situation in sufficient depth and breadth. In general, descriptive exploration precedes and forms the basis and context for the development of hypotheses.

Exploring the person involves encouraging clients to explore aspects of themselves as individual human beings and, when relevant, as members of a family, group, organization, or community. Of course, we do so within the context of the problems and issues of concern. In this dimension, we are especially interested in the *thinking, feeling,* and *doing* aspects of clients' experiences. Seek information about strengths and assets, as well as weaknesses and deficiencies. Explore both the substance of clients' thoughts—whether they occur as beliefs (the words people say to themselves) or as images (the mental pictures people have); and the thought processes (the cognitive steps people take as they move from one idea to another). Within the dimension of feeling, consider clients' emotions (for example, anger, fear, or sadness) as well as physical sensations (for example, energy, fatigue, muscular tension, nausea, or light-headedness). Within the dimension of doing, explore overt behavior (for example, walking, speaking, hitting, or looking) as well as deficits in behavior (for example, behaviors such as assertive statements that clients might adopt but fail to do so).

Sometimes the nature of a problem warrants exploration of personal style or personality characteristics. Clients may discuss traits or attributes that contribute to understanding. For instance, a middle-aged woman may describe herself as being "extraordinarily sensitive to criticism" or remark that "my feelings are easily hurt." An older man might report that he is "emotionally shut down" or perhaps that he has "lost the ability to feel." An appreciation of these characteristics may help in understanding the person-issue-situation and in developing plans to pursue goals.

In addition, the biological or medical history and condition of clients may be pertinent to the exploration process. For instance, diabetes, epilepsy, cardiac problems, and chemical addictions are among the health-related factors that often contribute to an understanding of the person-issue-situation. Similarly, a deeper understanding of the issue may require exploration of clients' spiritual or religious beliefs. Indeed, some religions prohibit the application of certain medical procedures. Others may sometimes consider misfortunes to be the result of sinful behavior. Core beliefs about life's meaning and how to live a good and proper life often influence clients' understanding of themselves and others, their circumstances, and the issues they face.

Because most if not all issues have social aspects, social workers usually encourage clients to share information about their significant relationships and their typical ways of relating to others. For example, clients may describe their preferred relational styles (for example, direct or assertive, passive or indirect, slow or quick to speak or act) and how they react socially during encounters involving conflict or intense emotion (for example, confrontation, immobilization, withdrawal).

Clients' preferred coping processes and their problem-solving strategies are often relevant. Questions such as "How do you cope with stress, disappointment, or frustration?" may lead to deeper understanding and reveal potential directions for work or perhaps avenues for resolution. Similarly, queries such as "When you confront problems such as this one, how do you usually go about trying to solve them?" may contribute to an understanding of problem-solving patterns and strategies.

Exploring the situation involves examining current and, when applicable, past circumstances. Collect pertinent information about social and cultural factors, as well as economic, environmental, and legal aspects of situations that may relate to the issue of concern, or to those assets or resources that might be useful for resolution. Gather information about significant other people, family systems, communities, ethnic affiliations, religious involvement, housing, education, employment, and finances.

Just as individuals think, feel, and act, families and other social systems reflect cultural beliefs, norms and mores (for example, family or group "rules"); dominant emotional climates; preferred ways of communicating and relating, and decision making and problem solving; and habitual behavioral patterns. Systems typically reflect an organizational structure as well. Some are hierarchical, others are more or less egalitarian, and many are chaotic—varying according to the immediate circumstances.

Exploring the future involves examining the issue, the person, and the situation as they may emerge in the future. Explore a continuum of possible future scenarios. For example, you might first explore with the client how the problem and situation would probably be at some point in the future if everything continued along as it is now. What would the client be thinking, feeling, and doing in such a future. Then, you might examine how they might be in a "worst possible case" scenario, where things seriously deteriorate. Finally, you could explore a "best possible case," where the issues are completely resolved. The latter process is often quite enlightening, as it helps you and your clients clarify possible directions for work as well as revealing implicit strengths, assets, resources, and protective factors. Exploring the future also frequently yields an array of potential indicators or benchmarks of a successful outcome.

As you and clients explore the person-issue-situation together, you may recognize an imbalance in the degree of attention to problems, troubles, or risk factors versus strengths, resources, and protective factors. Occasionally, clients deny or minimize problems and stridently assert that everything is "just fine." Involuntary and nonvoluntary clients sometimes exhibit just such a "rosy" view—at least at first. Other clients, however, seem to focus primarily on problems, dilemmas, and distressing events. This is quite understandable. Many clients are so distraught that they focus almost exclusively on things that cause them the greatest distress. Helping professionals are frequently educated to do much the same, that is, to attend primarily to symptoms, problems, illnesses, pain, or disorders. Several factors contribute to this "tilt toward troubles." As a social worker, however, ensure that you and clients adequately explore strengths and resources—as well as problems and needs. Otherwise, you and your clients could conclude the exploration process with an incomplete understanding of both the factors associated with the development and continuation of the problems, as well as the potential resources that might be used to address them.

By *looking for strengths,* you gently—without denying or minimizing the client's reality—explore the strengths, capacities, assets, and competencies within the person-in-environment. Looking for strengths overlaps with the process of identifying protective or resilience factors (Fraser, Richman, & Galinsky, 1999; Gilgun, 1998, 2004a, 2004b; Smokowski, Mann, Reynolds, & Fraser, 2004). You may look for strengths by asking questions, seeking responses to "incomplete" or "fill-in-the-blank" sentences, or through active listening. As they cope with challenging problems and circumstances, clients often reflect extraordinary strength and resilience. Indeed, the term *heroic* applies to many clients.

Of course, there are downsides associated with a strengths perspective—just as there are with other conceptual models. A major danger arises when social workers prematurely force clients to look for positive attributes before they have explored the problems and circumstances of greatest concern. You may recall a brief reference in Chapter 5 to dramatically increased dropout rates when helping professionals do not communicate an accurate understanding of clients' views about and experiences of the presenting problem or issue (Epperson et al., 1983; Pekarik, 1988, 1991; Wierzbicki & Pekarik, 1993). Determined searches for strengths that prevent or impede clients' ability to describe and discuss issues of concern in their own way can leave them feeling unheard, misunderstood, and extremely frustrated. Many may not return following an initial visit. Paradoxically, a premature search for strengths may leave clients feeling diminished rather than supported. The effects can be similar to those experienced by a child who has just scraped her knee. It hurts and she is just about to cry. Suppose an adult (for example, a parent or teacher) were to say, "You're so grown-up! You just skinned your knee and I'm sure it hurts a lot. But you're such a big girl you're able to keep yourself from crying!"

That statement might motivate the girl to control her tears and, as a result, she might feel more grown-up. However, she would probably not feel understood. Indeed, the position "I know what you think and feel better than you do" is anathema to empathic understanding. The girl would almost certainly inhibit full and accurate expression of what she really experiences in order to avoid the censure of the adult or perhaps to maintain the image of herself as a "big girl."

Imagine how this pattern might play out between a social worker and a client of any age. Minimizing or denying the other's feelings and experiences—even in an effort to identify strengths—can negatively affect clients' willingness to share. Incomplete exploration of experiences, events, and circumstances—including the feelings associated with them—may interfere with the development of a constructive working relationship and a positive outcome.

Therefore, as you look for strengths, keep the client's perspective and the timing of the exploration in mind. Typically, looking for strengths should occur after the worker has accurately communicated understanding of the client's views and experiences of the problems and issues, and relevant aspects of the person and environment.

Strengths may appear in people, situations, or in responses to problems, issues, and other challenges. We may look for strengths in the areas of competencies, social support, successes, and life lessons (see Table 9.6).

All clients have many abilities, capacities, and talents. They also hold various beliefs about them. Social workers seek to help clients identify and explore strengths in both dimensions: *beliefs* as well as *realities*. For example, an optimistic attitude, a basic belief in one's own value and goodness, or a religious or philosophical perspective can contribute to a sense of inner peace or contentment under the most trying of circumstances. By *looking for competencies*, you and your clients may

TABLE 9.6
Looking for Strengths

	Person	Situation	Issue
Competencies			
Social Support			
Successes			
Life Lessons			

© Cengage Learning

discover an incredible array of useful traits and attributes. Unless you consciously seek them out, however, they may never become apparent.

You can look for competencies by asking questions such as: "When people praise or compliment you about your talents and abilities, what things do they mention?" "If people were to brag about your special qualities and characteristics, what would they say?" "Some people have special talents or abilities that they keep pretty much to themselves; what are some of yours?" You can also help clients explore competencies by using "incomplete" sentences. You could ask clients to complete sentences that begin with phrases such as "I am very good at . . ." or "I am especially talented when it comes to . . . ." Try to extend the exploration by considering how clients' talents, abilities, and competencies become manifest in social roles and situations (for example, family, work, and other social systems or during times of stress, conflict, or crisis). "Of all the things you do with your family, what gets you the most praise or credit?" "What qualities or abilities do you possess that you wish your boss knew about?" "When it comes to relationships, which of your personal qualities help you the most?" Competencies also relate to the issue of concern. "Over the course of time that you've been dealing with this issue, what talents or abilities of yours have been most helpful?" "What things do you say to yourself that help you address or cope with problems such as these?"

Social workers tend to recognize the importance of social support in all aspects of human life.[4] By *looking for social supports,* we encourage clients to identify and reflect on those individuals and groups within the social environment that have been or could be resources. Ask questions such as, "Over the course of your life, who have been the people that provided the greatest support?" or "Where do you feel the most support?" Of course you would also consider how those social supports have been helpful in the past or might yet favorably affect the person and contribute to resolution of the issue of concern.

Experiences of accomplishment and achievement tend to contribute to feelings of competency and optimism. By *looking for successes* we try to identify and recognize those positive outcomes. Questions such as the following may help: "When you reflect back upon your life, what do you consider your greatest successes or achievements?" "When you were a child, what were your biggest accomplishments? When you were a teenager? When you were a young adult?" Discovery of successes may lead to the creation of a "success timeline."

Over time, people tend to gain perspective and make their significant life experiences meaningful in some way. Successes and failures, good times and bad, pain and pleasure, all become part of a personal philosophy. By *looking for life lessons,* you encourage clients to consider what they have learned and realized. In effect, you help clients to acknowledge their own wisdom. Frequently, lessons learned earlier, perhaps in different circumstances, can be applied to current issues and concerns. You can look for life lessons by asking questions such as: "You've been through a great deal and somehow survived. What have you learned about life from these experiences? What have you learned about yourself? What have you learned about people?" As you proceed, you may find opportunities to look for life lessons that might apply to the current issue of concern. "Of all the things you've learned from these experiences, which lessons might help you address this issue?"

Usually, within one or two meetings, you and the client have discussed the more pressing issues, explored a good deal about the client system and the circumstances, identified relevant risk and protective factors, and discovered various strengths, assets, and resources. At this point in the process, you can decide whether you and your agency have the authority, resources, and expertise necessary to provide the needed social work services to this particular client system. Because of a lack of familiarity with social service, health, and mental health networks, prospective clients sometimes contact providers and organizations that are not well prepared to help them address their

---

[4] Please see the discussion of social support in Chapter 2 and the Social Support Appraisal Scale in Appendix 6.

particular issues. Through exploration of the person-issue-situation, you may be able to determine that another organization in the community would be better prepared to provide helpful service. Then, if the client concurs, you could contact the other agency to initiate a professional referral. Of course, you should conduct the referral process with great care, so that the client does not feel rejected by you or your agency. Furthermore, treat the other agency's personnel with professionalism and courtesy. The nature of your relationships with other community professionals often determines whether prospective clients receive a warm or cool reception. Therefore, approach your colleagues in other agencies with the same high degree of professionalism you show to clients.

When the issue of concern is congruent with your agency's mission and range of services and falls within your areas of expertise, you and your clients may appropriately continue the working relationship. Before long, the collaborative process of exploration should lead to a clear sense of direction for the work that you will do together.

Asking Questions

Questions serve to elicit facts, ideas, and feelings concerning the person, the issue, the situation, and potential means or processes for resolution. Questions help identify risk and protective factors as well as strengths, competencies, assets, and resources. They often yield information necessary for mutual understanding, assessment, decision making, planning, working and evaluating, and ending. Indeed, we use questions throughout the entire process of work with and on behalf of clients. However, they are especially useful during the exploring phase.

The first primary use of the questioning skill typically occurs as you and the client conclude the beginning phase. By this time, you have introduced yourselves, reached a tentative understanding of the purpose for meeting and possibly your respective roles, discussed relevant policies and ethical principles, and sought feedback.[5] The initial exploratory question represents the first substantive consideration of the issue or problem that led to the contact (Perlman, 1957, p. 88). Commonly, we phrase the question in such a way as to allow clients maximum opportunity to express themselves freely, fully, and in their own way. For example, you might ask, "When you telephoned the other day, you mentioned something about family problems. What's happening with the family that concerns you?" It may also be useful to ask about precipitating events related to the presenting concern. For instance, you might ask, "What led you to contact us about the family problems at this time?"

Helping professionals occasionally phrase questions as requests or directives. For example, you could say, "Please share your concerns about the difficulties that trouble you at this time." In the case of an involuntary client, you might say, "I understand that the judge required you to come here for counseling. I know quite a bit about the situation, but I'd like to hear the full story from you. Please describe what happened." In general, however, questions are preferred because directives may implicitly suggest a power or status differential. "Tell me . . ." or "Describe . . ." is, in effect, a command that may subtly indicate that the social worker is the most important person in this encounter.

"Tell me . . ." requests also tend to imply that the primary reason for clients' sharing is for you, the social worker, to acquire information that you will then use to formulate an assessment and prescribe a solution—that is, come up with "the answer." However, in most circumstances, social workers hope to foster a collaborative working relationship where clients function as full

---

[5] The skill of seeking feedback represents a specialized form of questioning that social workers routinely use to ensure that participants clearly understand all facets of the process.

participants in the process. Indications that the social worker is the expert authority who provides answers and solutions often lead clients to assume a passive, subordinate role akin to a "doctor–patient" or "parent–child" relationship, rather than to a genuine partnership of equals.

As you might expect, the questioning skill is applicable at many points throughout the exploration phase and, of course, all other phases as well. We use questions to explore relevant aspects of the person-issue-situation, including the circumstances surrounding the origin, development, and status of the presenting concerns. Examples of some common questions include: "How did these difficulties begin?" "Who were the members of your family as you were growing up?" "What were your parents like?" "Who lives with you now?" "What did you feel when she left?" "What were you thinking about when that happened?" "What would you like to be different?" "What did you do then?"

The questions you ask derive from your active pursuit of information regarding the person-issue-situation over time. There are two general types of questions: _closed-ended_ and _open-ended_. Closed-ended questions (Goodman & Esterly, 1988, pp. 123–127) are phrased to elicit short responses, sometimes simply yes or no. Closed-ended questions can yield a great deal of information in a brief amount of time. They are especially useful in crises, when we need to gather vital information quickly.

Here are a few examples of closed-ended questions: "What is your phone number?" "What's your address?" "Do you have a car?" "Do you live at home?" "When were you born?" "How old are you?" "Where do you work?" "Who is your family doctor?" "When was your last physical exam?" "Does anyone live with you?" "Is somebody there in the house with you right now?" "Which do you prefer?" "Have you taken some medicine?" "How many pills did you take?"

"Either–or" and "multiple-choice" questions are also usually closed-ended: "Is your mother or father more supportive?" "Do you prefer Mr. Johnson or Mrs. Xavier?" "How difficult is it to complete that step: (1) Extremely difficult, (2) Difficult, (3) Somewhat difficult, (4) Not at all difficult?" Answers to such questions are usually quite brief. This can be advantageous or not, depending on the purpose of the meeting and the needs of the situation. Sometimes the rapid collection of specific information is so important that you postpone free and full exploration of other aspects of the person-issue-situation. However, too many closed-ended questions, asked one after another, may lead clients to feel like suspects in a criminal investigation. They may feel interrogated rather than interviewed, and the quality of the professional relationship may suffer. Therefore, unless the situation is immediately life threatening or otherwise urgent, you would usually be wise to intersperse closed-ended questions with many more open-ended questions and active-listening responses.

Some closed-ended questions are, in legal terminology, leading. A leading question is phrased in a way that elicits (that is, "leads to") a specific answer—one that the questioner wants to hear. For example, suppose a social worker asked a client, "Haven't you experienced lots of pain in your pelvic area? Yes? Haven't you felt that pain since you were a young child? Yes? Aren't these painful symptoms common among people who were sexually abused as children? Yes? So, isn't it likely that you were sexually abused as a child?" Such a series of questions would clearly lead or suggest to a client that a certain conclusion held by the social worker was the right and valid one. During the exploration phase, such leading questions are generally counterproductive because they tend to narrow a process that should usually be quite open and expansive. In particular, whenever you serve an investigative function in your service as a social worker, choose your words and the phrasing of questions carefully. If you frequently ask leading questions in such interviews, your courtroom testimony could easily be challenged and perhaps disallowed. During the exploring phase especially, try to avoid leading or suggestive questions.

Open-ended questions (Goodman & Esterly, 1988, pp. 127–137) are phrased in a manner that encourages people to express themselves expansively and extensively. Open-ended questions tend to further exploration on a deeper level or in a broader way. They are usually not leading questions because they enable the client to respond in any number of ways. We may phrase them as "how" questions, which nearly always yield open responses from clients. For example, "How did that come to happen?" "How did he react?" "How do you feel right now?" "How did he act in that situation?"

We may also use "what" questions to elicit expansive responses from clients. For example, "What is the nature of your concern?" "What is she like?" "What happened then?" "In what way did you . . . ?" "What did you say then?" Recognize, however, that certain "what" questions are closed-ended. "What is your phone number?" "What is your date of birth?"

"What" questions tend to produce descriptive information. To elicit feelings, you often have to ask directly for them. For example, "What feelings did you experience when you realized that?" or "What are you feeling right now?" encourage clients to identify and perhaps share emotions. Indeed, some evidence indicates that open questions about feelings may encourage clients to share more emotion than do active-listening responses (Hill & Gormally, 1977, 2001). In exploring emotions, it may help to combine active-listening responses with specific open questions about feelings.

Directives can serve the functions of open- or closed-ended questions. For example, "Please say more about that," "Please elaborate," "Please continue," "Please share more about that part of your life," all encourage open responses. "Please spell your name," "Please tell me your street address," serve as closed-ended requests for brief responses. Remember, however, our earlier caution about the potential negative effects of directives on the working relationship. In most circumstances, social workers seek to develop a collaborative partnership rather than a hierarchical relationship in which we are the "experts in charge." Use directives sparingly and try to avoid indications that you are the superior party in the relationship.

"Why" questions may also encourage clients to express themselves in a full and open fashion. However, they can also generate defensiveness. Clients may conclude that you are judging them negatively and feel compelled to justify some aspect of their behavior or circumstances. Therefore, be cautious about the use of "why" questions. Use them in a tentative fashion and adopt a gentle tone of voice combined with warm, open, and accepting facial expressions. The way you phrase "why" questions can also help. For example, you may moderate the defensiveness-eliciting quality of a "why" question by qualifying phrases such as "I wonder why (that is)?" or "Why do you think that happens?" In asking "why" questions, be certain to communicate attitudes of interest and acceptance.

During the exploration process, intersperse your questions with active-listening responses. Otherwise, an interview can quickly turn quite unpleasant. When clients must answer one question after another—even when they are open questions—they often begin to feel interrogated rather than interviewed. Realize that questions can suggest blame, judgment, evaluation, or advice. They are not always simply neutral requests for information. For example, "Have you talked with your mother yet?" might imply that you expected a client to talk with his or her mother. "Have you completed that form?" may convey a similar message. Although it is sometimes useful to express a statement of opinion or preference in the form of a question, be aware that you are doing so. Sharing your personal or professional views within the context of a question does not relieve you of responsibility for the substance of the message. Also, try to avoid asking a string of questions at the same time. For example, "Are you still going with Jackie or have you given up on her and are now dating only Jill? And what about Cathy?" would confuse most clients. They would not know whether to respond to your first, second, third, or fourth question. Try to avoid multiple-choice questions. Instead, ask one question at a time.

Questions can be extremely useful for providing a sense of coherence and continuity to the exploration process. As clients talk about themselves, the issues of concern, and their situational contexts, they quite understandably sometimes focus a great deal on one topic while avoiding or only briefly touching on important related information. When that occurs, you can ask questions that guide clients toward an exploration of other pertinent aspects of the person-issue-situation. For example, to gather information about an aspect of a client's family and social situation that had been neglected, you might ask, "How would you describe your relationship with your older sister?" Be careful, however, to respect clients' psychological and interpersonal sensitivities. This is particularly important during the exploring phase. When a client is especially sensitive about a particular topic or theme, we usually postpone inquiry into that specific dimension until our working relationship becomes more established. Then, when the client feels more secure, we can return to those areas that require further exploration.

You may use the exploring skill of asking questions to gather and consider information about the person-issue-situation and to look for strengths and resources. As you might imagine, however, we commonly ask questions throughout the entire helping process.

EXERCISE 9-1: ASKING QUESTIONS

For these exercises, assume that you are a social worker with a multipurpose social service agency. In the spaces provided, write the words you would say in each situation.

1. You are in the midst of the first interview with Mr. K., a recently divorced 55-year-old man. You have introduced yourself and have addressed the other aspects of the beginning phase of practice. You are now ready for an initial exploratory question. At this point, you know only that Mr. K.'s concern relates in some way to the divorce. Therefore, you want to encourage him to explore that topic in depth. Write the words you would say in asking this first question. Once written, specify whether the question is open- or closed-ended. Outline your rationale for choosing this particular question and anticipate how Mr. K. might respond.

2. As a city-employed social worker for homeless and "street" people, you notice a woman standing alongside the intersection of a highway. As cars stop, she displays a cardboard sign that reads, "Homeless and Hungry—Will Work for Food." One of your functions is to reach out to people in such situations, educate them about available resources, and, if they agree, arrange for them to obtain food, shelter, and a fairly wide range of social and medical services. You have a cell phone which allows for immediate contact with various organizations and service providers as well as a large, city-owned car that allows you to offer free transportation.

You walk up to the woman and smile. She backs up a step and warily watches as you approach. You smile again, introduce yourself by name, and indicate that you serve as a city social worker who helps people find food and shelter. You show her your city identification and hand her one of your business cards. At that point, you ask about her name. She says that her name is Loretta and appears slightly more comfortable than she did earlier. You ask Loretta to call you by your first name too and extend your arm in an offer to shake hands. You mention again that your job is to help people obtain food and shelter, and that you can give her a ride to a place where both are available. At this point, you are ready to ask Loretta your first exploratory question. Write the words you would say in doing so. Once written, specify whether the question is open- or closed-ended. Outline your rationale for choosing this particular question and anticipate how Loretta might respond.

3. You have begun the first interview with the S. family, a seven-member blended family that sought your help with problems of family tension and conflict. You have gone through the introductions and addressed other aspects of the beginning phase. Your initial question was "What do you see as the major issues within the family?" The father responded to this question first. Then the mother answered, followed by other family members. Although the specific nature of the responses varied somewhat, there appeared to be considerable agreement that the strained relationship between the two teenage boys (biological children of the father) and their father's wife (the boys' stepmother) is a major issue. Their relationship appears to involve a great deal of tension, conflict, and anger. As the social worker, you now want to explore the origin and development of the difficulties in this relationship. Use the space below to write the words you would say in doing so. After you have written your question, determine whether it is open- or closed-ended. Are you directing the question to the boys, the other children, Mrs. S., Mr. S., or

the entire group? Outline your rationale for choosing this particular question and selecting the person or people you decided to address? How do you think the boys would react to the question? How might Mr. or Mrs. S. respond?

Assume that you continue to explore the issue, the family, and the situation. What would you say in formulating three additional questions? For each one, determine whether it is open- or closed-ended. Which aspect of the exploration process (person, family, issue, situation; present, past, future) does each question address? Finally, anticipate how various family members might react to each question.

4. You have begun to interview a prospective client of Latino background. She fluently speaks both Spanish and English. You have completed the introductions, addressed the policy and ethical factors, and established a tentative purpose for the meeting: to explore the concerns Mrs. F. has about her two children, 7 and 9 years old. According to Mrs. F., they are the only Latino children in their school, and several teenage boys have periodically harassed them. Mrs. F. is worried that her children might be in physical danger. She is also concerned that these experiences may undermine their positive attitude toward school.

As the social worker, you are now ready to explore the issue further. Write the words you would say in asking an initial exploratory question. What might you say in asking three additional questions concerning the issue, the children, Mrs. F., the family system, or the school situation? Identify whether each question is closed- or open-ended. Outline the rationale for the questions you created. Finally, predict the reaction that Mrs. F. might have to each question.

5. You have begun a first meeting with a group from a local social service agency. The participants include several members from the agency's board of directors, the director of the agency, three program directors, four social workers, two administrative staff members, and two consumers (that is, two current clients). The agency has hired you to serve as an organizational consultant to help them address several problems within the agency. Apparently, there are several areas of conflict and tension, poor communication, and low morale. Sometimes, clients of the agency are negatively affected by these problems. Indeed, some were scheduled for appointments with social workers who were not informed of the meetings. Other clients' records have been lost. Clinical supervision of social workers is sporadic if it occurs at all, and a systematic audit of case records has not taken place in more than a year.

   You have completed the introductions, addressed the policy and ethical factors, and established a tentative purpose for the initial meeting; that is, to explore the concerns about the agency that participants in the group identify. As a consulting social worker, you are now ready to explore the issues and organizational context. Write the words you would say in asking an initial exploratory question. What might you say in asking three additional questions concerning the agency, the problems, or the circumstances? Identify whether each question is closed- or open-ended. Clarify your rationale for the questions you created.

Seeking Clarification

During an interview, clients sometimes make statements that seem unclear or that you do not fully understand. They may communicate in an apparently contradictory fashion, skim over a relevant issue, or neglect some significant aspect of themselves, the issue, or the circumstances. Such indirect, unclear, or incomplete messages often involve important aspects of the client's experience. Therefore, the manner in which you respond may substantially affect the nature of the relationship, the direction of your work together, and the outcome of the helping endeavor. In such instances, you may use the skill of *seeking clarification*. That is, you attempt to elicit a more complete expression of the meaning of particular words or gestures. In effect, you ask clients to elaborate about something they have just said or done. During the early portion of an interview, you seek clarification to generate more complete and comprehensible information about particular aspects of the person-issue-situation. Seeking clarification also subtly suggests that a particular term or topic may be of some special relevance.

Obviously, social workers do not always completely understand everything that clients say. Sometimes this is because we are not listening well. At other times, clients do not clearly express themselves because they are uncertain about what they actually think and feel. After all, one purpose of exploring is to help clients understand themselves better. Also, clients sometimes send indirect messages that they hope you will notice. Many people are reluctant to ask directly for help. Such hesitancy is quite common among members of some groups and may be greater if the social worker and clients are from different cultures. In addition, many issues are so embarrassing or emotional in nature that clients find them difficult to talk openly about. Therefore subtle or ambiguous communications are common. Be sensitive to indirect expressions in the form of hints, nonverbal gestures, or incomplete or mixed messages, and recognize that considerable anxiety may be associated with such communications. Some clients may send extremely significant messages in an indirect manner because they are not yet fully aware of or comfortable with some aspects of their thinking or feeling, or because they fear that you might disapprove.

In responding to indirect expressions, move carefully toward a greater degree of specificity and clarity by asking for further information about the term, phrase, or topic. For example, during a first meeting, a 50-year-old client says to a 25-year-old social worker, "I've never had much luck with young social workers. You're all so innocent." The worker might respond to such a statement by asking, "When you talk about not having 'much luck' with other young social workers, it sounds like there have been some problems. What sorts of difficulties have you had with young social workers before?"

You may use the skill of seeking clarification to encourage clients to explain a term or elaborate about the specific aspects of a thought, feeling, action, or situation (Shulman, 1992). People often communicate in vague or general terms. Seeking clarification about detailed aspects of an experience or the specific meaning of a term may enable you and the client to gain a more complete and realistic understanding.

Seeking clarification may be especially helpful in circumstances where the social worker and the client reflect cultural differences. Words, phrases, and gestures commonly used in one culture may be nonexistent in another, or their meaning may differ dramatically. Although the client may know exactly what she or he means by a particular term, you may not—at least when it is first used. Even when a client uses a standard form of English, a term may have a unique meaning to him or her. Clients may use words that you have never heard before, or they may use a familiar term in an unusual manner. The skill of seeking clarification can help in these circumstances. In seeking clarification, you are looking for additional specific information about a particular word or phrase or some other aspect of a client's verbal or nonverbal communication.

Seeking clarification usually occurs as a discrete form of open-questioning, although it may occasionally appear in the form of a closed question or a directive. Rather than encouraging clients to provide more general information about a current or new topic, its purpose is to gain further understanding of specific aspects of a previous message. To practice this skill, use the following formats.

PRACTICE FORMATS: SEEKING CLARIFICATION

What, specifically, do you mean when you say _____?

or

Would you please elaborate on _____?

or

Please explain what you mean by _____?

EXAMPLE: SEEKING CLARIFICATION

CLIENT: My spouse and I just don't get along. We haven't for years. The relationship stinks.

WORKER: What do you mean when you say "The relationship stinks"?

As is the case with most exploring skills and the skill of seeking feedback, seeking clarification is useful throughout the entire helping process. It is especially relevant when exploring aspects of problems from a person-in-environment perspective, establishing goals, during the working and evaluating phases, and when concluding your relationship with clients. Often, you can effectively precede your request for clarification with an active-listening response.

EXERCISE 9-2: SEEKING CLARIFICATION

For these exercises, assume that you are a social worker with a multipurpose social services agency. Respond in the spaces provided by writing the words you would say to seek clarification in each situation.

1. You are in the midst of the first interview with Mr. K., a recently divorced 55-year-old man. You have introduced yourself and addressed other aspects of beginning. You are currently exploring the person-issue-situation. Mr. K. says, "I feel so bad. It really hurts. I miss her terribly. I'm not sure I can go on." Write the words you would say in seeking clarification of what he has just said. Outline your rationale for the words you chose. How do you think he might react to this question? Now try preceding your attempt to seek clarification with an active-listening response. What effect does that have?

2. You are an outreach worker for homeless and "street" people in your city. You have approached a woman who had been displaying a cardboard sign that reads, "Homeless and Hungry—Will Work for Food." You learned her name. Loretta responded to your initial question about her current situation by saying, in part, "I've been like this since I lost my kids." Write the words you would use to seek clarification in this situation. Outline the rationale for the words you chose. How do you think Loretta might react to this attempt to gain greater clarity?

3. You have begun the first interview with the S. family, a seven-member blended family. You are in the midst of exploring the nature and development of the issue when one of the teenage boys (biological children of the father) angrily refers to their father's wife (their stepmother) as a "home wrecker." In reaction, Mrs. S. lowers her eyes and becomes very quiet. Write the words you would say in seeking clarification from the teenager. What is your rationale for the words you chose? How do you think the teenager who made the remark might react? How might Mrs. S.? Mr. S.? The other members of the family? What would you say in seeking clarification from Mrs. S. concerning her nonverbal reaction to the term *home wrecker*? How do you think she and the other family members might react to your request for clarification from her?

4. Assume that you are exploring issues with Mrs. F., who is of Latino background and fluently speaks both Spanish and English. Mrs. F. is concerned about her children's safety at school. During the course of the exploration, Mrs. F. says angrily, "White men control this whole country and don't care about anybody but themselves!" Write the words you might say in seeking clarification. Briefly describe your rationale for the words you selected. How do you think Mrs. F. might react to your question? What is another way you might seek clarification in this situation?

5. You are serving as a consulting social worker for a local social service agency that has a number of organizational problems (for example, conflicts, tensions, poor communication, low morale). Your first meeting involves a fairly large group of people: four members from the agency's board of directors, the director of the agency, three program directors, four social workers, two administrative staff members, and two consumers. Early in the meeting, the agency director says, "As you probably know, these problems are not new. They did not suddenly emerge when I became director about 3 months ago. Most of these issues began long ago under the previous administration." Write the words you might say in seeking clarification. Outline your rationale for the words you selected. What is another way you might seek clarification in this situation?

Reflecting Content

Reflecting content (Carkhuff, 1987) is the empathic skill of communicating your understanding of the factual, descriptive, or informational part of a message. In exercising this skill, a form of active listening, you paraphrase or restate the client's words. By accurately reflecting content, you demonstrate that you have heard and understood what the client is trying to convey.

This skill is most applicable when a client communicates factual or descriptive material, or shares ideas that lack an emotional dimension. If the client does not express feelings, you do not add them to the content reflection. Accurately communicating your understanding of what clients say is crucial for several reasons. If clients do not believe that the social worker understands their view of the issues of concern, they may become less open and expressive, or they may even prematurely discontinue services. Accurate restatement of clients' expressions about the problems or issues that led to the contact demonstrates that you understand their concerns. Accurate reflections of content can also contribute to the development of a positive working relationship and promote a sense of collaborative partnership. Without accurate reflections, clients are likely to assume a passive, subordinate role in the process and view the social worker as an expert who asks questions, collects information, diagnoses problems, gives answers, and prescribes solutions.

To practice this skill, use the following format:

PRACTICE FORMAT: REFLECTING CONTENT

You're saying _____.

EXAMPLE: REFLECTING CONTENT

CLIENT: I'm a househusband. Every day, I cook the meals, clean the house, and do the laundry. That's my job now.

WORKER: You're saying that your current responsibilities include taking care of the family needs and doing the household chores.

In using the practice format, recognize that repeated use of the same lead-in phrases might begin to sound artificial and mechanical. Imagine how it would seem to you if someone started six or seven sentences in a row with the words, "You're saying." Indeed, the phrase "I hear you saying" has become a cliché. Therefore vary the lead-in phrases or avoid them altogether. If you accurately reflect the content of the person's message, such lead-in phrases are usually unnecessary.

Try to use your own words to reflect, restate, or mirror the information the client has conveyed. If you repeat too many of the client's words, he or she may begin to feel that you are "parroting" or "mimicking" rather than truly listening. You can sound more like a tape recorder than a concerned human being.

EXAMPLE: REFLECTING CONTENT

CLIENT: Several years ago, I lost my job. They closed the plant where I had worked for years and years. There was a huge layoff. Most of my buddies and I were let go. Since then, my wife has worked part-time, and that keeps some food on the table. My unemployment compensation ran out long ago. We've not been able to pay the mortgage on the house for about the last 6 months. I think the bank is going to foreclose on us soon.

WORKER: Mr. C. You haven't had an adequate income for a long time and it's beginning to look like you may lose your home.

Mr. C. is probably experiencing some emotion as he expresses himself. Although he has not actually mentioned his feelings, he may do so nonverbally by shedding tears or dropping his head and shoulders. In using the skill of reflecting content, you stay with the factual content of the message. Even when a client explicitly expresses emotions along with facts or opinions, you might choose to use the skill of reflecting content rather than a more complete form of active listening. By reflecting only the content of the message rather than both content and feeling, you highlight your understanding of the informational portion of the message. You might do so when the urgency of a situation requires you to elicit facts, ideas, or preferences quickly; when you determine that the content of a client's message is more relevant at that particular point than the feelings; or when you are trying to help a client maintain emotional self-control. In general, during the early stages of the exploration process, you should carefully respect clients' coping strategies. Follow their lead. If a client primarily expresses facts and opinions in an unemotional or intellectualized fashion, use the skill of reflecting content. At this stage, there is usually no pressing need to reflect feelings that clients have not directly expressed. Mr. C., for example, may be trying to maintain control of his emotions by expressing himself in a matter-of-fact, businesslike fashion. He may not yet trust the worker enough to risk full and free expression of his true feelings. The worker could further develop the relationship by accurately reflecting the content of Mr. C.'s stated message and then, perhaps later during the interview, return to an exploration and reflection of his feelings.

EXERCISE 9-3: REFLECTING CONTENT

For these exercises, assume that you are a social worker with a multipurpose social services agency. Respond in the spaces provided by writing the words you would say in reflecting content in each situation.

1. You are in the midst of the exploration process with Mr. K., a recently divorced 55-year-old man. He says, "The divorce was final about 3 weeks ago. She said she'd had enough of my constant criticism and sarcastic comments and that she was leaving me." Write the words you would say in reflecting the content of what he has said. Outline your rationale for the words you chose. How do you think he might react to your reflection?

2. You are in the midst of an exchange with Loretta, an apparently homeless woman on the street. In response to your question about her situation, she says, "I've been sleeping in a wooded area near the west side park. I made up this sign because I needed food. I'm hungry but I'm willing to work." Write the words you would use in reflecting the content of Loretta's message. Briefly describe your rationale for the words you chose. How do you think Loretta might react to your content reflection?

3. You are in the midst of an interview with the seven-member blended S. family. During the course of the exploration, Mrs. S. says, "I fell in love with Hank [Mr. S.], and when we married I hoped that his children and mine would come to love one another as brothers and sisters. I also wanted his kids to know that I would love and treat them as if I had given birth to them myself." Write the words you would say to reflect the content of Mrs. S.'s message. Outline your rationale for the words you chose. How do you think Mrs. S. might react? What is another way you might reflect the content of her message in this situation?

4. You are interviewing Mrs. F., a Latino mother of two children who have been harassed at school by several boys. During the course of exploration, Mrs. F. says, "I have talked to the teachers and the guidance counselor. They listen politely but they don't care about what this does to my children. They won't do a thing about it." Write the words you might say in reflecting content. Outline your rationale for the words you selected. How do you think Mrs. F. might react to your response? What is another way you might reflect the content of Mrs. F.'s message in this situation?

5. You are serving as a consulting social worker for a local social service agency that has a number of organizational problems (for example, conflicts, tensions, poor communication, low morale). Your first meeting involves a fairly large group of people. During the first few minutes of the meeting, one social worker says, "I haven't had a clinical supervision meeting in more than a year. In fact, unless it is my program director, I don't even know who my supervisor is." Write the words you might say in reflecting content. Outline your rationale for the words you selected. How do you think the social worker would react to your response? What is another way you might reflect the content of the social worker's message in this situation?

Reflecting Feelings

Reflecting feelings (Carkhuff, 1987) is another of the empathic, active-listening skills. It usually consists of a brief response that communicates your understanding of the feelings expressed by a client. Some of the more effective responses consist of a simple sentence containing a single feeling word. For example, phrases such as "You feel ashamed," "You're really hurting," or "You're terrified!" can be powerful empathic reflections of feeling. Despite the brevity and utility of such phrases, some workers are hesitant to reflect clients' emotions. The skill of reflecting feelings requires that you, at least to some extent, feel those same emotions yourself. Empathy can be uncomfortable, even painful. Partly because of such discomfort, you may be tempted to convert feeling reflections into content reflections by neglecting to use words that convey emotions. For instance, suppose a client says, "I am devastated." You might reflect the feeling by saying, "You feel crushed." If, however, you were to respond by saying, "It feels like you've been hit by a freight train," you imply the feeling; you do not actually say it. The message conveys an idea rather than a feeling. Although *hit by a freight train* is an apt phrase to amplify the feeling of devastation, it is much more effective when used in conjunction with one or more feeling words. For example, "You feel crushed. It's like you've been hit by a freight train" includes both a feeling word and a powerful idea that amplifies the emotion. Certain lead-in phrases, such as "You feel like . . . ," tend to be followed by ideas, analogies, similes, or metaphors rather than words that connote actual feelings. Therefore, until you develop proficiency, practice by using a format such as the following:

PRACTICE FORMAT: REFLECTING FEELINGS

You feel _____ (*appropriate feeling word*).

The single most important aspect in reflecting feelings is to capture accurately the primary emotion experienced by a person and mirror it back so that she or he *feels* your empathic understanding. When two feelings are in evidence, you may respond to both. For example: "You feel _____ and _____." Sometimes, you may be able to identify a single word that communicates both feelings. For example, *burdened* and *discouraged* might be reflected as *overwhelmed*.

EXAMPLE: REFLECTING FEELINGS

CASE SITUATION: His former wife remarried about a year ago. Last month she and her current husband left the area with the client's 5-year-old son. They moved 2,000 miles away. The client tried to stop their relocation by filing a motion with the court, but his former spouse won the right to move with her son.

CLIENT: I just can't stand it. I miss my son terribly, I know that he'll gradually lose interest in me and I can't do a thing about it.

WORKER: You feel sad and powerless.

EXAMPLE: REFLECTING FEELINGS

CASE SITUATION: A 16-year-old girl wanted desperately to be selected to the school's cheerleading team. She was not chosen.

CLIENT: It's awful. I can't go back to school. I can't face them. I wanted to be on the team so bad. It hurts. It really hurts.

WORKER: You feel terribly rejected and you're awfully disappointed.

During the early portions of our work together, we typically reflect only those feelings that clients verbally express. After establishing a foundation of accurate reflections, or when the nonverbal, emotional message is very clear, try to reflect what you perceive as the unspoken feeling message. Nonverbal messages in the form of facial expressions, body positions and movements, gestures, and tone of voice are important means for communicating emotions. Notice them.

As forms of expression, you may appropriately use the reflecting feelings skill. However, when you do so, recognize that you are taking a modest risk. Use the skill in an especially tentative fashion because the client has not actually expressed the feelings in words. Also, a client may not be ready to acknowledge certain feelings even though she or he expresses them nonverbally. Of course, members of certain cultural groups may feel especially vulnerable when feelings are directly recognized. Therefore please be cautious when reflecting unspoken emotions, particularly early in the working relationship. When you do so, use a gentle, tentative tone of voice. Be prepared to return to the skills of reflecting content, questioning, or seeking clarification if the client overtly or covertly indicates that your feeling reflections are premature or off target.

Effective use of the reflecting feelings skill requires a large and sophisticated vocabulary of terms that connote emotions. Without such a vocabulary, we would find it extremely difficult to mirror back or paraphrase the feelings, emotions, and sensations experienced and expressed by others. Of course, there are hundreds of words used to communicate feelings. Several scholars have proposed organizational schemes and some have attempted to identify fundamental emotions that are universal to humans from all cultures and societies. For example, Ekman[6] suggests that there are six universal emotions reflected in humans' facial expression: (1) happiness, (2) anger, (3) surprise, (4) sadness, (5) disgust, and (6) fear (Ekman, 1982; Ekman & Friesen, 1975).

As a social worker attempting to reflect clients' feelings accurately and at various levels of intensity, you should be familiar with a wide range of feeling words commonly used by the cultural groups in your community. Otherwise you could find it difficult to mirror the feelings expressed. For example, everyone experiences anger to one degree or another. A person who is mildly annoyed or irritated would probably not feel understood if you were to say, "You feel enraged." The words you use should match both the kind as well as the intensity of the feelings expressed by clients. As in other forms of active listening, your reflection should be essentially equivalent to the client's message.

EXERCISE 9-4: REFLECTING FEELINGS

1. Use word-processing software to create a table similar to Table 9.7. To begin to develop a feeling vocabulary of your own, consider the six categories of emotional experiences listed in Table 9.7. Identify at least 10 feeling words that connote some degree of the emotion listed for each of the six categories of feelings. For example, under the happiness category, you might include the word *satisfied;* under the fear category, you might list *stress* as an associated term. If you become stuck, review the alphabetized list of feeling words in Appendix 13. That should help you generate 10 English feeling words for each category. However, be sure to include feelings words of cultural groups common to your area. Once you have listed them, rate each one in terms of relative intensity (*1 = mild; 2 = moderate; 3 = strong*). For example, under the anger category, you might assign a 3 (strong) rating to the words *enraged* and *furious.* Similarly, you might assign a 2 (moderate) to the term *irritated;* and a 1 (low) to *annoyed.* Save and label the document "Feelings Vocabulary" and deposit it in your Social Work Skills Learning Portfolio.

---

[6] Subsequently, Ekman (1999, p. 52) expanded his array of basic emotions to include the following: amusement, anger, contempt, contentment, disgust, embarrassment, excitement, fear, guilt, happiness, pride in achievement, relief, sadness, satisfaction, sensory pleasure, shame, surprise.

Happiness	Anger	Surprise	Sadness	Disgust	Fear

TABLE 9.7
English Feeling Words

© Cengage Learning

Now that you have gained some familiarity with a range of feeling words, begin to practice the skill of reflecting feelings. Assume that you are a social worker with a multipurpose social services agency. Use the spaces provided to respond as requested to each exchange.

2. During your first interview with Mr. K., a recently divorced 55-year-old man, he says, "I am absolutely lost. There is no reason to go on. I feel like someone reached into my gut and wrenched out my insides." Write the words you would say in reflecting the feelings Mr. K. has expressed. Outline your rationale for the words you chose. How do you think he might react to your reflection? What are two alternative feeling reflections that might also apply in this situation?

3. You are in the midst of an exchange with Loretta, an apparently homeless woman on the street. In response to a question about her situation, she says, "I am afraid sometimes. A few days ago, a man drove by and said he had work for me. He took me to some woods and made me do a sex act on him. I didn't want to but I couldn't fight him off. I hope that doesn't happen again. He did give me 5 bucks though." Write the words you would use in reflecting feelings contained in Loretta's message. Briefly describe your rationale for the words you chose. How do you think Loretta might react to your feelings reflection? What implicit feelings might Loretta experience that she does not express in actual words?

4. You are interviewing the seven-member, blended S. family. Mrs. S. has just said, "I fell in love with Hank [Mr. S.], and when we married I hoped that his children and mine would come to love one another as brothers and sisters. I also wanted his kids to know that I would love and treat them as if they were my own children." Following her statement, she hangs her head as tears fall down her cheeks. Mr. S.'s eyes are also watery. Although specific feeling words were not used, write the words you would say in reflecting the feelings suggested by Mrs. S.'s nonverbal messages. Then do the same for Mr. S. What was your rationale for the words you chose for each feeling reflection? How do you think Mrs. S. might react to your response? Mr. S.? What is another way you might reflect the feelings suggested by their communications in this situation?

5. You are interviewing Mrs. F., a Latino mother who is concerned about the safety at school of her two children. At one point, Mrs. F. says, "I'm so angry. Talking with the teachers and the guidance counselor does not help at all. It's so frustrating having to fight so hard for fair treatment. My kids deserve to be protected." Write the words you might say in reflecting her feelings. Outline your rationale for the words you selected. How do you think Mrs. F. might react to your response? What is another way you might reflect the feelings indicated by Mrs. F.'s message in this situation?

6. You are serving as a consulting social worker for a local social service agency that has a number of organizational problems (for example, conflicts, tensions, poor communication, low morale). Your first meeting involves a fairly large group. During the first few minutes of the meeting, one administrative assistant says, "The other secretaries and I are blamed for everything that goes wrong around here. The so-called professionals treat us like dirt. I cannot tell you how many times I've been yelled at for something that isn't my responsibility. I love the clients but every morning I dread coming to work!" Use the space below, to write the words you might say in reflecting feelings. Outline your rationale for the words you selected. How do you think the administrative assistant would react to your response? What is another way you might reflect the feelings of the staff person's message in this situation?

Reflecting Feelings and Meanings

Reflecting feelings and meanings (Carkhuff & Anthony, 1979) is probably the most complete form of active listening. It is certainly the most complex. By reflecting both emotional and informational or ideational elements of a message, you convey a great deal of empathy.

For practice purposes, use the following formats:

PRACTICE FORMAT: REFLECTING FEELINGS AND MEANINGS

You feel _____ because _____.

or

You feel _____ and _____.

or

You feel _____ but/yet/however _____.

Reflecting feelings and meanings mirrors clients' emotions along with the facts or beliefs associated with them. As with other reflections, your response should represent an accurate and equivalent form of the client's message. Do not speculate or interpret. Rather, paraphrase or mirror the feelings and meanings as expressed. Even when you personally believe that clients' views about the causes of feelings they experience are incomplete or inaccurate, reflect their perspectives anyway. Often the meanings that clients convey suggest external or situational causes for their feelings (for example, "My mother makes me feel guilty"). At other times, clients refer to aspects of themselves (for example, attitudes, habits, traits, psychological patterns, fears, or physiological conditions) as the reason for their feelings (for example, "I'm basically a lazy person"). Whether the meaning associated with the feelings is externalized or internalized, try to remain congruent with the client's expressed experience when you reflect feelings and meanings. Resist the temptation to modify the meaning. As with other empathic reflections, accuracy is fundamental. Your response should be essentially equivalent to the message communicated by the client. Here are two examples:

EXAMPLE: REFLECTING FEELINGS AND MEANINGS

CASE SITUATION: A 60-year-old man who has just lost his job after 35 years of employment.

CLIENT: I have nowhere to turn—no job—no income—no nothing. They just let me go after 35 years of pain and sweat for them. I'm scared and angry.

WORKER: You feel desperate because the company has turned you out after so many years of hard work, and it does not look like you'll be able to find something else.

EXAMPLE: REFLECTING FEELINGS AND MEANINGS

CLIENT: I'm a wreck. I can't sleep or eat; I can't concentrate. I know my head is really messed up.

WORKER: You feel awful. You're anxious and confused, and you know you're not thinking straight right now.

For these exercises, assume that you are a social worker with a multipurpose social services agency. In the spaces provided, write the words you would say in reflecting feelings and meanings in each situation.

1. In the midst of your first interview with Mr. K., a recently divorced 55-year-old man, you are exploring his feelings about the situation. He says, "I was so used to her being there. I needed her but I never told her so. Now that she's gone, I realize just how much she meant to me." Write the words you would say in reflecting the feelings and meanings contained in what Mr. K. has said. Outline your rationale for the words you chose. How do you think Mr. K. might respond? What are two additional feelings and meanings reflections that could also apply to Mr. K's statement?

2. You are in the midst of an exchange with Loretta, an apparently homeless woman on the street. In response to a question about a recent sexual assault, she says, "When that man forced me to give him sex I first felt terrified for my life. I thought he'd kill me if I didn't do what he wanted. Then, I felt disgusted about what I was doing. I've never been a whore and I tried oral sex only once before—and that was with my husband on our wedding night. After it was all done though, it didn't seem so bad and I did get some money for food. That was the first time in several days that I had something to eat." Write the words you would use in reflecting the feelings and meanings contained in Loretta's message. Create three or four different versions to capture the different feelings and meanings. Briefly describe your rationale for the words you chose. How do you think Loretta might react to your reflection of her feelings and meanings?

3. You are interviewing the seven-member, blended S. family. Following a moment when both Mr. and Mrs. S. began to cry, one of Mr. S's teenage sons says, "Well, it just seems that she came into the house expecting to be Mom. She'll never be my mother, and I resent it when she tries to be." Write the words you would say in reflecting the feelings and meanings contained in his statement. Outline your rationale for the words you chose. How do you think the teenager might react to your response? Mr. S.? Mrs. S.? What is another way you might reflect the feelings and meanings suggested by the boy's words?

4. You are interviewing Mrs. F. While exploring the issue, Mrs. F. says, "I'm frustrated with the whole system! This society is racist to the core! Money and power are the only things they respect." Write the words you might say in reflecting feelings and meanings. Outline your rationale for the words you selected. How do you think Mrs. F. might react to your response? What is another way you might reflect the feelings and meanings indicated by Mrs. F.'s words?

5. You are serving as a consulting social worker for a local social service agency that has a number of organizational problems. During a meeting, a social worker says, "I've worked here about 5 years now. When I first arrived I noticed that many of the social workers were way behind in their record keeping. In fact, some didn't even keep records. I asked the program directors and the agency director about the policies about record keeping and was told that 'all professionals are responsible for maintaining their own case records and that if they are not doing so, they should be.' During that first year, I tried several times to organize staff meetings to discuss the issue of record keeping. I even developed a format and a sample to show everyone. Well, nothing happened. I continue to keep good-quality case records, but it's frustrating and frightening to know that not everybody does." Use the space below to write the words you might say in reflecting feelings and meanings. Outline your rationale for the words you selected. How do you think the social worker would react to your response? What is another way you might reflect the feelings and meanings of the social worker's message in this situation?

Partializing

The skill of *partializing* (Perlman, 1957; Shulman, 1992) is used to help clients break down multiple or complex aspects and dimensions of the person-issue-situation into more manageable units so you can address them more easily. Partializing is especially helpful during the exploration phase. If you and a client tried to deal with a multitude of facts, ideas, or feelings simultaneously, one or both of you would probably end up quite confused. Sometimes, there are simply too many phenomena to explore effectively all at once. The partializing skill helps you and clients to maintain a sense of coherence by considering smaller, more manageable units of information one at a time. For practice purposes, please use a format such as the following:

PRACTICE FORMAT: PARTIALIZING

You've addressed a number of topics here. You've talked about _____, _____, _____, and _____. There are so many aspects of what you've said that we could lose track if we try to consider them all at once. Could we explore them one at a time? (Yes) Which would you like to consider first?

or

Would it make sense to start with _____? That seems to be very important to you right now.

EXAMPLE: PARTIALIZING

CLIENT: My whole life is a mess. My husband drinks two six-packs every night and even more on weekends. I think he's an alcoholic. He's out of work—again! My teenage son smokes dope. I've found marijuana in his room. And he's just been expelled from school for stealing money from another kid's locker. So, both of them are at home now. I'm the only one working and I'm falling apart. I'm a nervous wreck. And, I'm angry as hell!

WORKER: You sure have a lot happening all at once. It sounds like everybody in the family has their own share of problems—and you're affected by all of them. I wonder, because there are so many issues to address—your husband's behavior, your son's, and your own feelings about it all—could we start by looking at them one at a time? Does that make sense to you? Okay? Which of these concerns you most right now? Let's start with that one.

EXERCISE 9-6: PARTIALIZING

Assume that you are a social worker at a multipurpose social services agency. In the spaces provided, write the words you would say in using the skill of partializing in each situation.

1. You are interviewing Mr. K., a recently divorced 55-year-old man. He says, "I think I'm on the brink of a nervous breakdown. I can't do my work. I can't sleep at night. I don't eat. All I do is think about her. I wonder what she's doing and whether she ever thinks of me. It's affecting my job. I think my boss is getting tired of my mistakes. I've also forgotten to pay some bills. Creditors are calling all the time. My life is a train wreck." First, separate and identify each of the elements in the client's message. List them in outline fashion. Which do you think is most important? Now write the words you would say in attempting to partialize what Mr. K. has said. Outline your rationale for the words you chose. How do you think Mr. K. might react to your words?

2. You are in the midst of an exchange with Loretta. In response to a question about her current needs, she says, "Well, first I need food. I'm really hungry. Then, I need to clean up, put on a decent dress, and find a job. It would be nice to have a roof over my head—but I can stay at my little campsite for a while longer. Once I save enough money to travel, I'll continue on my way to visit my youngest daughter. She lives about 1,300 miles from here." First, separate and identify each of the elements in Loretta's message. List them in outline fashion. Which do you think is most important? Now write the words you would say in attempting to partialize what she said. Outline your rationale for the words you chose. How do you think Loretta might react to your words?

3. You are interviewing the seven-member blended S. family. During the course of the exploration, Mr. S. says, "Since we married, we've had troubles with both my kids and hers.

Basically, they dislike each other, they seem to hate us, and lately my wife and I have begun to fight. Finances have become a problem, and there's no time for anything. I don't think I've had a single minute to myself in 6 months. My wife and I haven't been out of the house on a weekend evening since our wedding." First, separate and identify each of the elements in the client's message. List them in outline fashion. Which do you think is most important? Now write the words you would say to partialize the complex message communicated by Mr. S. Outline your rationale for the words you chose. How do you think Mr. S. might react to your words?

4. You are interviewing Mrs. F. During the conversation, she says, "I've had troubles ever since I moved into this community. The school system is totally insensitive to the Latino population. My kids have begun to disrespect me and berate their own heritage. All the neighbors are white and haven't even introduced themselves to us. My mother is seriously ill in Peru, but I don't dare leave the children here while they're in danger." First, separate and identify each of the elements in the client's message. List them in outline fashion. Which do you think is most important? Now write the words you might say in partializing this message. Outline your rationale for the words you selected. How do you think Mrs. F. might respond?

5. You are serving as a consulting social worker for a local social service agency that has a number of organizational problems. At one point an agency board member says, "As I see it, our agency has a long history of laissez-faire leadership, unprofessionalism at all levels of the organization, some incompetence, and a nearly complete absence of mission-driven, purposeful, and focused effort." Use the space below to separate and identify each of the elements in the client's message. List them in outline fashion. Which do you think is most important? Now write the words you might say in partializing this message. Outline your rationale for the words you selected. How do you think the board member might respond? How might other participants?

Going Beyond

Going beyond what is said (Hammond Hepworth, & Smith, 1977) occurs when you use your empathic understanding of clients' messages to extend slightly what they express. Instead of mirroring exactly what clients say, you use your knowledge, experience, logic, and intuition to add modestly to the feelings or meanings actually communicated. Through a process called additive empathy, you take a small leap beyond the expressed message to bring into greater awareness or clarity information that a client already knows. Your responses "go beyond what the client has explicitly expressed to feelings and meanings only implied in the client's statements and, thus, somewhat below the surface of the client's awareness" (Hammond et al., 1977, p. 137).

Going beyond sometimes involves combining what clients say verbally with what they express nonverbally. In this process, however, continue to remain congruent with clients' overall direction and perspective. Although departing somewhat from their actual words, stay within their frame of reference. Rather than changing directions, build on the agenda your client has previously established.

For example, during the early part of a first meeting, a client who recently immigrated to the United States from Haiti might say to a white worker, "Do they have any black social workers at your agency?" This may be an indirect communication (Shulman, 1992, pp. 42–44) by a client who wonders whether a white worker has the capacity to understand him and to value his culture. He might prefer a black social worker. Perhaps he has had a negative experience with a white social worker at some point in the past. A white worker might respond to this question by saying something such as "Yes, we have several black social workers [sharing information], although not as many as we should [sharing opinion]. Because you ask that question though, I wonder if you might be saying that you'd prefer to work with an African American social worker [going beyond]?"

EXAMPLE: GOING BEYOND

CLIENT: About 6 months ago, my son was killed in a motorcycle crash. We had a fight just before he left home that morning. I yelled at him and called him a "spoiled brat." He swore at me and tore out of the yard on that bike.

WORKER: You feel guilty because the last conversation with your son was so bitter. Do you sometimes think that the fight had something to do with the accident?

Going beyond is not an interpretation, nor is it a wild speculation or guess. Rather, it involves putting into words those thoughts and feelings that a person probably thinks or feels but that have not yet been verbally expressed.

EXAMPLE: GOING BEYOND

CASE SITUATION: A 12-year-old girl who was sexually molested by her mother's male friend.

CLIENT: My mother loved him very much and now he's gone.

WORKER: You sometimes wonder whether you should have said anything. You think that maybe your mom might be happier and still have her boyfriend if you had just kept quiet about what he did to you?

EXERCISE 9-7: GOING BEYOND

For these exercises, assume that you are a social worker with a multipurpose social services agency. Respond in the spaces provided by writing the words you would say in using the skill of going beyond what is said.

1. You are interviewing Mr. K., a recently divorced 55-year-old man. You are in the process of exploration when he says, "I guess I'm a real wimp! I'm desperate for her to come back home. All I do is think of ways to get her back. I make these plans about how to contact her; how to persuade her to change her mind. I constantly wonder what she's doing and whether she ever thinks of me." Write the words you would say in going beyond what Mr. K. has said. Outline your rationale for the words you chose. How do you think he might react to your response? What is another way you might go beyond what he said?

2. You are in the midst of an exchange with Loretta. In response to a question about her youngest daughter, she says, "Well, I haven't seen or talked with her in more than 15 years. When my husband divorced me, he got custody of the children. That destroyed me and I began to slide downhill from there. He remarried and his wife became their mother." Write the words you would use in attempting to go beyond Loretta's verbal statement. What is your rationale for the words you chose? How do you think she might respond? What is an alternative means for going beyond what she said?

3. You are interviewing the seven-member, blended S. family. During the course of the exploration, Mrs. S. says, "Things are so bad between my kids and his kids that I've begun to wonder whether it's worth trying anymore. Maybe my children and I should just leave. We made it on our own before, and we can do it again." Write the words you would say in going beyond what Mrs. S. has said. Outline your rationale for the words you chose. How do you think Mrs. S. might react to your response? What is another way you might go beyond what she said?

4. You are interviewing Mrs. F. At one point, she says, "Maybe it's not worth fighting this racist system. Maybe I should just accept things as they are. I'm just one person—just one woman—what can I do?" Write the words you might say in going beyond her verbal message. Outline your rationale for the words you selected. How do you think Mrs. F. might respond? What is another way in which you might go beyond Mrs. F.'s statement?

5. You are serving as a consulting social worker for a local social service agency that has a number of organizational problems. At one point during a meeting, the agency director says, "Look, I'm the director and, ultimately, I'm responsible for what happens here. I know things have been bad for a long time and I also know that in the 3 months I've been here I have not been active enough in addressing the problems. I have clearly been part of the problem and would like to be part of the solution. However, if it would help the agency, I would be willing to submit my resignation." Use the space below to write the words you might say in going beyond the director's verbal message. Outline your

rationale for the words you selected. How do you think the director might respond? What is another way in which you might go beyond the director's statement?

Reflecting Issues

By reflecting issues, you demonstrate to clients that you understand their view of identified problems or other topics of concern. An important form of active, empathic listening, reflecting issues represents a more specific application of the reflecting content skill. In this case, you paraphrase and highlight those problems or issues that clients indicate they wish to address in your work together. In effect, when you reflect issues, you take an early step toward the processes of assessment and contracting. When you empathically communicate your understanding of clients' experience of the issues that concern them, both the working relationship and clients' motivation to work with you tend to improve. By expressing empathic appreciation of the nature of the problems as clients see them, you simultaneously convey respect for clients as people of worth and value, and endorse their right to autonomy and self-determination.

Of course, reflection of an issue does not necessarily suggest moral approval or professional agreement to work toward its resolution. Occasionally, clients identify problems or goals that social workers could not morally, ethically, or legally help to address. For instance, suppose you serve as a school social worker in a high school. One of the students—a 16-year-old girl—says she wants your advice. She states:

> *Everybody drinks at the school dances. It helps people feel better and have more fun. But the new regulations prevent us from going out to our cars during dances. It's a good policy. Everybody had to go out to the parking lot to drink and then come back into the gym to dance. It was, like, back and forth all night long. It would be so much better if we could just spike one bowl of punch with whiskey. It would be safer and we wouldn't have to leave the building.*

As a school social worker, you obviously could not condone this action. Indeed, as you consider the student's comments, you might wonder if they might represent a "test" to see if you are susceptible enough to consent to the idea or perhaps to see if you would react with anger or judgment. Indeed, her words might constitute an attempt to provoke an emotional or irrational response. Regardless of the student's motivation, however, you could easily communicate your understanding of the student's expressed view of the issue so that she feels heard and understood. You need not approve of her words to demonstrate empathy. Such understanding can form the basis for further exploration and perhaps reconsideration of the issue. Furthermore, if you respond in a nonreactive, nonjudgmental way, you might pass the student's "test."

Clients, especially those who voluntarily seek social services, are usually quite ready to share their issues and concerns. However, some clients may need support, guidance, and encouragement to do so. In certain involuntary circumstances or when clients lack competence to participate in the process, you may have to assume major responsibility for both issue identification and goal establishment. We will address those skills later on.

Regardless of the context, do not assume that the issues clients initially identify will necessarily remain the focus for work. During exploration with an attentive social worker, clients often identify different concerns that are more "real," more urgent, or more essential than those they initially mention. Some clients test workers by trying out a relatively modest issue first. Based on the nature of your response, they may then move on to identify a problem of greater significance. In addition, the collaborative process of assessment may lead clients to reconsider and reformulate the issues for work.

As you begin to practice the skill of reflecting issues, please use the format outlined here. Later, when you gain greater proficiency, experiment with alternate formats.

PRACTICE FORMAT: REFLECTING ISSUES

As you see it, one of the issues you'd like to address in our work together is _____

_____ .

EXAMPLE: REFLECTING ISSUES

CLIENT: My wife left me—sure, for very good reasons—but I'm really down about it. She has left me before but always came back. This time I know she won't. She's gone for good, and I don't know what to do. I can't go on the way things are. I'm so sad and lost without her.

WORKER: As you see it, there are two major issues you'd like to address in our work together. First, you feel terrible. You're lonely and depressed, and you find it hard to function well when you feel that way. Second, you're unsure of how to get on with your life without your wife.

As a form of active listening, if you accurately paraphrase the issue as experienced by clients, they are likely to respond with something like "Yeah, that's right" to verify your reflection. Nonetheless, it is often useful to precede issue reflections with reflections of feeling, content, or feelings and meanings to show you understand multiple aspects of clients' experiences. It may help to seek feedback following your reflection of the issue. For instance, following the response in the example just shown, the social worker might ask the client, "Are these the major issues you'd like to work on?"

EXERCISE 9-8: REFLECTING ISSUES

For these exercises, assume that you are a social worker with a multipurpose social services agency. In the spaces provided, write the words you would say in reflecting issues.

1. During an interview with Mr. K., a recently divorced 55-year-old man, he begins to discuss the problems he would like to address in your work together. He says, "I guess my major problem is that I can't seem to get over her. I keep hoping when there is no hope." Write the words you would use in reflecting issues as Mr. K. sees them.

2. During an interview with Loretta, a homeless woman you first noticed on the street, she says, "I'm most concerned that when I finally arrive at my daughter's doorstep, she won't recognize me as her mother and will simply turn me away." Write the words you would use in reflecting issues as Loretta views them.

3. You are in the midst of an interview with the blended S. family. Mr. S. says, "I guess I can say this in front of the children—they know so much already. Anyway, today at work, I learned that there will soon be massive layoffs. It's likely that I will lose my job within the next 3 or 4 weeks. It's just what we need, to top off the rest of our problems!" Write the words you would say in reflecting issues as Mr. S. sees them.

4. You are conducting an interview with Mrs. F., the Latino woman who is concerned that her children are being mistreated. She says, "I guess I've never felt we really belong in this town. Nobody really seems to like us or want us here. I guess we just don't fit in." Write the words you might say in reflecting issues as Mrs. F. sees them.

5. You are working as an organizational consultant with a group from a local social service agency. Board and staff members and the agency director are participants with you in an effort to address several problem areas. During the meeting, one professional staff member says, "I'm almost 60 years old and have worked in eight different agencies since I received my social work degree 32 years ago. I can honestly say that my morale is the lowest it has ever been and that this place is toxic. Some people refuse to talk to others—even when it's needed for the job. Nasty rumors about people spread like wildfire, and I believe it's fair to say that some administrators have 'favorites' who receive special perquisites. Last year, a few of them received extremely large salary increases while the rest of us had our salaries frozen." Use the space below to write the words you would say in reflecting issues as the professional staff member sees them.

Reflecting Hypotheses

Just as social workers have ideas and "theories" about "why" problems occur and "what to do" to resolve them, so do clients. Indeed, clients' hypotheses often contribute to our collaborative understanding of the factors associated with the origin, development, and continuation of particular problems. We refer to these as *explanatory hypotheses*—ideas used to explain or understand the reasons that a problem exists and the factors that contribute to its persistence. When you empathically and accurately communicate your understanding of clients' explanatory hypotheses, they not only feel heard and understood they also feel like genuine collaborators in the helping process.

When you reflect clients' explanatory hypotheses, you demonstrate respect for the way they think about issues. Of course, like other forms of active listening, reflecting an explanatory hypothesis does not necessarily indicate endorsement of the "theory." Sometimes clients' explanatory hypotheses are based upon invalid assumptions and popular but unsubstantiated views about the causes of biopsychosocial and environmental phenomena. People sometimes adopt implausible or superstitious beliefs in their attempts to make sense of problems and concerns. For instance, clients sometimes hold themselves fully and unreasonably responsible for things clearly beyond their personal control. Though we may reflect our understanding of such views, we need not validate the invalid. However, to the degree that clients' hypotheses reflect consistency with research findings and empirically supported theories, we can endorse their views and build upon them with compatible hypotheses of our own.

In addition to explanatory hypotheses, many clients have ideas about what should be done to resolve the problem. In effect, they adopt *change-oriented hypotheses.* These are predictions about how resolution of problems or achievement of goals could or should occur. For example, some clients believe that they can resolve complex, long-standing multisystem problems through acts of personal willpower alone. Although we might sometimes wonder about their credibility, we empathically reflect clients' change-oriented hypotheses in our attempt to demonstrate understanding and respect.

Although many clients have well-conceptualized explanatory and change-oriented hypotheses, some do not. In such cases, you may encourage clients to think aloud about "why" the problems occur and "what might work" to resolve them.

Regardless of the context, do not assume that clients' "hypotheses" necessarily remain fixed and unalterable. As do social workers, clients often develop more sophisticated, more accurate, and more relevant explanatory and change-oriented hypotheses as they collect more information, reconsider facts, engage in change-focused activities, and monitor outcomes.

As you begin to practice the skill of reflecting hypotheses, please use the formats outlined here. Later, when you gain greater proficiency, experiment with alternate versions.

PRACTICE FORMAT: REFLECTING EXPLANATORY HYPOTHESES

As you see it, the reasons for this problem include _____.

_____

or

As you see it, one explanation for this issue is _____

_____

EXAMPLE: REFLECTING EXPLANATORY HYPOTHESES

CLIENT: My wife left me for another man. Of course, I drank too much, was away from home a lot, and neglected her needs. Basically, I was a lousy husband. I certainly cannot blame her for leaving me. It was my fault and I feel guilty as sin about it. I'm pretty sure that's why I'm so depressed. How could I have been so selfish?

WORKER: As you see it, she left because of your selfishness. She was entirely justified because you drank heavily and frequently neglected her. You feel guilty about your self-centered behavior and the depression is a natural result of that realization.

(continued)

PRACTICE FORMAT: REFLECTING CHANGE-ORIENTED HYPOTHESES

As you see it, you could address this particular problem by _____.

_____

EXAMPLE: REFLECTING CHANGE-ORIENTED HYPOTHESES

CLIENT: She had every right to leave. I was the one at fault and I feel so guilty and ashamed. This didn't have to happen. So far, I haven't given up hope for reconciliation; and I haven't forgiven myself for my selfish behavior. I guess if I'm going to get over this depression, I'll have to do both of those things.

WORKER: So, you think that if you accept the fact that the marriage is truly over and you also begin to forgive yourself, the depression will start to lift and you could have a life again.

Reflecting clients' explanatory and change-oriented hypotheses represents, of course, forms of active listening. If you accurately paraphrase clients' hypotheses, they are likely to respond, "Yes. That's how I see it," or "Yeah, that's right," to confirm the accuracy of your reflection.

EXERCISE 9-9: REFLECTING HYPOTHESES

For these exercises, assume that you are a social worker with a multipurpose social services agency. In the spaces provided, write the words you would say in reflecting hypotheses in response to the clients' statements.

1. You are interviewing Mr. K., a recently divorced 55-year-old man. He says, "I think the major reason that I can't get over her is that I don't truly believe it's over. I can't seem to accept the facts of the situation. The truth is that the marriage has ended and she will not take me back. Once I accept that reality, I'll begin to recover." Write the words you would say in reflecting hypotheses (explanatory, change oriented, or both) as Mr. K. sees them. Outline your rationale for the words you chose. How do you think Mr. K. might react to your reflections?

2. During an interview, Loretta says, "If my daughter does reject me when I show up on her doorstep after all these years, I guess I'll be able to understand why. I've been a mess for so long that I thought it would be better for both my kids if I were simply out of their lives. Their father is a good man and I'm pretty sure he married a kind and decent woman. They've been better off without me. But now, I think, I'm almost well enough to reconnect with them and perhaps even add something to their lives." Write the words you would say in reflecting hypotheses (explanatory, change oriented, or both) as Loretta expressed them. Outline your rationale for the words you chose. How do you think she might react to your reflections?

3. You are working with the blended S. family. Mr. S. says, "I'm incredibly worried and stressed. I'll probably be laid off from my job in the next few weeks. I can't eat or sleep. I'm constantly irritated and often fly off the handle with my wife and children. As best I can tell, the only way out of this mess is to find another job—one that pays at least as much as this one does." Write the words you would use to reflect Mr. S.'s explanatory and his change-oriented hypotheses. Outline your rationale for the words you chose. How do you think he might react to your reflections?

4. You are working with Mrs. F., the Latino woman who is concerned that her children are being mistreated during and after school. She says, "I guess I've had to acknowledge that there is a lot of prejudice and discrimination in this town and especially in this school. I think that's the reason for the abuse my kids have taken. I'm not optimistic that the school officials could or would do anything to correct the situation so I think my only option is to move away from this place." Write the words you would use to reflect Mrs. F.'s explanatory and her change-oriented hypotheses. Outline your rationale for the words you chose. How do you think she might react to your reflections?

5. You are working as an organizational consultant with a group from a local social service agency. During a meeting, one of the staff members says, "I'm an employee here so I realize I'm taking a risk in saying what I'm about to say—but here it is anyway. All of these problems are a direct result of passive, indecisive, and sometimes incompetent leadership from both our past and present directors and from board members. In my opinion, active, hands-on, competent leadership is needed to resolve these long-standing problems." Write the words you would use to reflect the staff member's explanatory and change-oriented hypotheses. Outline your rationale for the words you chose. How do you think she or he might react to your reflections?

Summary

During the exploration phase of social work practice, you encourage clients to share thoughts and feelings, and to describe experiences about the issue or concerns that led to the contact. Through the process of exploration, you and the client gather and review information regarding the person-issue-situation from a biopsychosocial perspective and from the perspective of time: present-past-future. Both the social worker and the client participate in an attempt to understand the development, maintenance, and status of the issues of concern. You seek to determine their frequency, intensity, and duration, as well as the risk and protective factors that might increase or decrease the probability of occurrence. By looking for strengths, you and your client identify assets, talents, abilities, and resources that could help in resolution efforts. In particular, you look for strengths in the areas of competencies, social support, successes, and life lessons. When combined with your professional knowledge and the client's input, the information collected contributes to the development of an assessment and plans for work.

Although the exploring skills of (1) asking questions, (2) seeking clarification, (3) reflecting content, (4) reflecting feelings, (5) reflecting feelings and meanings, (6) partializing, (7) going beyond, (8) reflecting issues, and (9) reflecting hypotheses are especially useful for encouraging mutual consideration of information regarding the person, issue, situation, and strengths, they also apply throughout the entire helping process. Along with the beginning skill of seeking feedback, you may use the exploring skills repeatedly as you and your clients work together toward resolution of the issues of concern.

CHAPTER 9: SUMMARY EXERCISES

Assume that you are a social worker with a multipurpose social services agency. You are actively exploring various aspects of the problems and issues of concern, the client system, and the social and physical circumstances. For each of the following cases, use the space provided to write the words you would use and describe the actions you might take in using the requested skills.

1. You serve as a community organizer in a low-income, high-crime area of town. A large percentage of the community is unemployed; neighborhood gangs patrol the area; drug sales and use are widespread; and pimps and prostitutes operate openly on the streets. You hope to help the members of the community organize themselves in order to address these concerns and develop their community. You have made individual contact with many concerned parents; several ministers, priests, rabbis, and imams; school principals and teachers; social workers and social service agency directors; police officials; local legislators; and several members of the mayor's council. Almost all of them have agreed to meet together with you to help address the problems.

    The time for the first meeting has arrived. You're meeting in a large room in a local school. You've introduced one another, described a tentative preliminary purpose of (a) assessing the state of the community, (b) identifying its problems and needs, and (c) developing plans to address the problems, meet the needs, and improve the social and economic conditions throughout the community.

    a. Write the words you would say in asking an initial exploratory question of the group.

b. Write five open-ended questions you would want to ask at some point during this first meeting.

2. You are in the midst of the first interview with a teenage couple (an Arab American male and European American female) who have sought counseling in advance of their forthcoming marriage. They differ in religious affiliation: he is Muslim and she is Southern Baptist. She says, "I know there are going to be lots of difficulties, and that's why we're here. We don't want the problems to get in the way of our feelings for each other."

   a. Write the words you would say in reflecting the content of her statement.

   b. Formulate an open-ended question to follow her statement.

   c. Write the words you would say in seeking clarification of her statement.

3. Following your response, she says, "One of the biggest problems has to do with my parents. My mom is fit to be tied and my dad is even worse. He's ready to kill Amir and he doesn't even know him. I'm afraid my parents won't even come to the wedding. That would really hurt."

   a. Write the words you would say in reflecting the feelings and meanings contained in her message.

b. Write the words you would say in going beyond the words she said.

c. Write the words you would say in reflecting issues.

4. You are interviewing a family of six (two parents and four children, ranging from 1 to 7 years of age) who had been sleeping in their dilapidated Chevy in a rest area on the highway. En route to another part of the country, where they hoped to find work, they ran out of money and food and nearly out of gas. A police officer referred them to the agency. During the interview, Mrs. Z. says, "We don't want charity. We just need enough money and food to make it there."

a. Write the words you would say in seeking clarification following her statement.

b. Write two open-ended questions and one closed-ended question that might yield useful information in your effort to understand and help the family.

c. Write the words you would say in reflecting issues.

5. Following one of your questions, Mrs. Z. says, "The baby hasn't been eating well. She's sleeping all the time and has a fever. She has diarrhea and yesterday she vomited three times. I think she must be sick. She needs a doctor and maybe a hospital ... but ... we don't have documents and I'm afraid we'll be arrested if we seek medical help."

a. Write how you would seek clarification following her statement.

b. Write the words you would say in asking two closed-ended questions and one open-ended question concerning the baby's health.

c. Write the words you would say in reflecting the feelings and meanings contained in her message.

d. Write the words you would say in going beyond the words she said.

e. Write the words you would say in reflecting issues.

f. Write the words you would say in reflecting hypotheses.

6. You are interviewing Mr. T. for the first time. He stands accused of molesting the 13-year-old daughter of his woman friend. Mr. T. is required to receive counseling to stay out of jail while the judge considers whether to proceed with felony charges. Mr. T. had been living with the girl's mother but now must stay away from the house during this period. During the interview, Mr. T. says, "I don't know why she said that I did those things. It really hurts me. I've been good to her and her mother. She's just lying and I don't know why. Maybe she's jealous."

   a. First, write the words you would say in seeking clarification concerning his message.

   b. Write three open-ended questions that might follow his statement.

   c. Reflect the content of his statement.

   d. Reflect the feelings and meanings contained in his message.

   e. Write the words you might use in reflecting feelings in response to his statement.

f. Write how you might go beyond the words he has said.

g. Write the words you would say in reflecting issues.

h. Write the words you would say in reflecting hypotheses.

CHAPTER 9: EXPERIENTIAL INTERVIEWING EXERCISE

At this point you have secured the commitment of a professor, field instructor, or other professional social worker to serve as your supervisor and as advocate for the practice client. You have successfully recruited a colleague to assume the role of practice client and have his or her consent to participate in the several-session experiential interviewing exercise. You have also become familiar with and gained some experience with the exploring skills. These are, in many respects, elaborations of the basic talking and listening skills and should complement the characteristics of professionalism as well as the preparing and beginning skills that you learned about earlier. You are now almost ready to engage your practice client in the first meeting. First, however, use applicable preparing skills to increase the probability that the crucial initial interview is positive and constructive.

You might start by assuming the role of social worker and recognizing that your function is to help the clients address and resolve problems or issues and make progress toward or achieve identified goals. Although this is an educational experience and the practice client is a colleague, she or he is a real human being with actual feelings that can be affected for better or for worse through this series of interviews. Furthermore, the identified issues are true and genuine. Therefore, you should adopt the characteristics of professionalism through all aspects and phases of the exercise. You might begin your preparation by engaging the following skills: preparatory reviewing, preparatory exploring, preparatory consultation, preparatory arranging, preparatory empathy, preparatory self-exploration, centering, and preliminary planning and recording. You might also anticipate using the talking and listening skills, the beginning skills, and several of the exploring skills during the first meeting with the practice client. As you recall, the beginning skills include: introducing yourself, seeking introductions, describing initial purpose, orienting clients or others, discussing policy and ethical factors, and seeking feedback. The exploring skills include: asking questions, seeking clarification, reflecting content, reflecting feelings, reflecting feelings and meanings, partializing, going beyond, reflecting issues, and reflecting hypotheses.

By the time of the first interview with the practice client, be familiar with the parameters of the several-week exercise. If needed, consult with your supervising social worker about the upcoming interviews. Make arrangements for a private place to meet and secure the necessary recording equipment. Obtain pencils, notebooks, and perhaps drawing paper that may be of use. You might prepare to share written material about the ethics and policies that guide the interview series. Definitely take the time to engage in preparatory empathy and imagine what it could be like for a colleague to take the risks associated with assuming the role of practice client and sharing personal thoughts, observations, and feelings about actual issues with a colleague who is assuming the role of social worker. Consider the possible implications and complications inherent in the client role. The fact that, in this instance, the practice client is a colleague makes relatively little difference. Sharing personal information and personal experiences with a relative stranger is a challenging and often frightening experience—perhaps especially when it is recorded. Through preparatory empathy, you should be better prepared to be culturally sensitive, to respect the personhood of the practice client, and to recognize the potential vulnerabilities involved in this process. Also engage in self-exploration and discover means to center yourself in advance of encounters with your practice client. Finally, prepare preliminary plans for the first meeting. Label the word-processed document "Preliminary Plans for the First Interview with a Practice Client." Deposit it in the "Experiential Interviewing Exercise" folder of your Social Work Skills Portfolio.

Before the first meeting, prepare yourself to use some or all of the beginning skills. Consider how you might introduce yourself and seek introductions from the practice client. For example, you might state your name and indicate that you are a social work student. You might then ask the practice client for her or his (fictitious) name or, if you know the pseudonym, you could use it first and then ask if you are pronouncing it correctly. Identify a tentative initial purpose and perhaps the social work role or roles that you might assume. For example, you might be prepared to suggest that your purpose is to help clients address and attempt to resolve problems and issues of various kinds and you are ready to serve as a consulting partner with the client in that process. You might also be prepared to orient the practice client to the role of client—perhaps by suggesting that he or she could best help in this process by being as open and forthright as possible; by letting you know if and when you misunderstand something that's said; and by giving feedback about what is helpful and what is not. Definitely be prepared to discuss relevant policy and ethical factors—such as the involvement of your professor or another professional social worker in providing supervision and in serving as client advocate, as well as confidentiality assurances and limitations. Indeed, you may word-process much of this and include it within your preliminary plans for the meeting.

At the time of the meeting, you should be ready to begin service as a well-prepared social worker. Since you already have your practice client's consent to record the interviews, turn on the equipment and then proceed to use the appropriate beginning and exploring skills that could help the practice client provide relevant information, describe situations, or share thoughts, feelings, and perhaps even identify sensations or other subjective experiences. Limit the interview to the beginning and exploration phases only. Do not attempt to assess, contract, or in any way try to work toward resolution. Resist temptations to speculate about underlying reasons or causes. Do not offer theoretical interpretations and, at this point, refrain from giving advice.

As this is a first meeting, your initial responsibilities are to commence the beginning process by ensuring that the client knows your name and credentials and that you know his or hers. You should also exchange contact information. Occasionally, meetings must be rescheduled or some other information should be exchanged in between your meetings. Share a tentative purpose for your work together. In this context, the purpose probably involves the exploration of the practice client's self-identified issues or concerns and your collaborative attempt to resolve them. You will certainly also explore aspects of the client and her or his situation that may have relevance to the issues. You might suggest a social work role or roles that you could fulfill in your collaborative efforts. For instance, you might function as a collaborative partner in addressing problems and pursuing goals. Educate the client about how he or she might actively participate in the process and discuss relevant policy and ethical factors. Be sure to seek feedback from the client at various points during the beginning process to ensure clear and accurate understanding.

Once you have completed the beginning tasks, proceed to ask an initial exploratory question about the problem or issue for which the practice client is seeking your help. As the client responds to that question, follow up with appropriate exploring skills as you seek to enhance mutual understanding of the focal issues from a person-in-environment perspective. During the interview, you might use some or all of the skills of asking questions, seeking clarification, reflecting content, reflecting feelings, reflecting feelings and meanings, partializing, going beyond what is said, reflecting issues, and possibly reflecting hypotheses. As you end the meeting, be sure to arrange for another in the near future. As you say goodbye, you might suggest a tentative starting point for the next meeting. For example, if you are still exploring the identified issues or the person-in-environment context, you might say something such as, "Next time, let's continue to explore your situation and try to reach some understanding about why and how these things seem to occur. How does that sound?"

Although the interview is only 30 minutes in length, when it is complete, you and the client will probably have gained a fairly clear conception of the focal problems or issues as well as considerable information about their origin and development, and their impact upon the client and others in his or her world.

When you've finished the interview, undertake the following:

1. Leave your respective social worker and client roles. Request that your colleague complete a copy of the Talking and Listening Skills Rating Form, the Preparing and Beginning Rating Form, and the Exploring Skills Rating Form (see Appendix 11). When your colleague has completed the rating forms, inquire about today's interview experience. Ask general open-ended questions so that you might get as much evaluative feedback as possible and, through that, enhance your learning. For example, you might ask your colleague questions such as:

   ◆ What thoughts, feelings, or other reactions do you have about today's meeting?
   ◆ What do you think about the process of working together that we discussed today?
   ◆ What parts of the interview affected you the most—either positively or negatively?

- What do you wish had happened during the interview that did not occur?
- What suggestions do you have about how the interview could have been better, more helpful, or more constructive for you?
- What suggestions do you have about how I could have been a better or more helpful social worker today?

Summarize your partner's feedback in a word-processed document titled "First Meeting with a Practice Client." Label this particular section "Practice Client Feedback."

2. Next, play the audio or video recording. Take notes as you go along. When you have completed your review of the recording, undertake the following:

   a. Use your word-processing program to create a table like the exploration matrix shown in Table 9.8. Once created, use the table to indicate the approximate degree to which you have explored various dimensions of the person-issue-situation. Recognize that we are especially interested in information that helps both the social worker and client understand the person, the issue, and the situation. Use approximate percentages to reflect the extent of exploration within each category. For example, if you believe you have explored about one-half of the issue as it currently is, write "50%" in that cell. If you have not talked at all about the issue in the past, place "0%" in that category. When you have completed the table, insert it as a section of a document titled "First Meeting with a Practice Client." Label the section "First Meeting Exploration Matrix." Next, reflect upon the matrix to identify those aspects of the person-issue-situation that you would like to explore further in the next interview. Word-process at least three open-ended questions for each matrix category that requires additional exploration. Include them below the exploration matrix in a section entitled "Additional Exploration Questions to Consider." Include both the matrix and the questions in the "First Meeting with a Practice Client" document for later inclusion in the "Experiential Interviewing Exercise" folder of your Social Work Skills Learning Portfolio.

TABLE 9.8
Exploration Matrix

	Present	Past	Future
Issue			
Person			
Situation			

© Cengage Learning

   b. Use your word-processing program to create a table like the one shown in Table 9.9. Once created, use the table to indicate the degree to which you and your colleague discussed the onset, evolution, frequency, situational context, intensity/severity, and duration of the identified issue of concern. As you did with the exploration matrix, use approximate percentages to reflect the extent of exploration within each category. When you have completed the table, insert it as a section of the "First Meeting with a Practice Client" document. Label the table "Exploration of the Problem/Issue."

TABLE 9.9
Exploration of the Problem/Issue

		Percentage Explored
Onset	Explore the origin of the problem; the circumstances under which it first occurred.	
Evolution	Explore the development and course of the problem/issue; when and how it was better or worse; and when and how the client addressed or coped with the problem/issue.	
Frequency	Explore how often episodes of the problem/issue occur.	
Situational Context	Explore when, where, and how episodes of the problem/issue emerge.	
Intensity/Severity	Explore the severity or intensity of the problem/issue.	
Duration	Explore how long each episode of the problem/issue lasts.	

© Cengage Learning

c. Use your word-processing program to create a Risk and Protective Factors Worksheet such as shown in Table 9.10. Once created, use it to outline the key risk and protective factors associated with the client-identified issues or problems. If you lack sufficient information to complete the worksheet, word-process several questions you might ask to gather needed additional information. Include the worksheet and your list of questions in the "First Meeting with a Practice Client" document. Label the section "Risk and Protective Factors." It should prove useful as your prepare for the next interview.

TABLE 9.10
Risk and Protective/Resilience Factors Worksheet

Risk Factors	Protective/Resilience Factors

© Cengage Learning

d. Use your word-processing program to create a Looking for Strengths matrix like the one shown in Table 9.11. Once created, use it to indicate the degree to which you looked for strength in the areas of competencies, social support, successes, and life lessons. Also, word-process at least one open-ended question for each strengths dimension needing further exploration. When you have finished, label the table "Looking for Strengths." Include the table and your additional strength-seeking questions as a section of the "First Meeting with a Practice Client" document. Label the section "Strengths."

TABLE 9.11
Looking for Strengths

	Person	Situation	Issue
Competencies			
Social Support			
Successes			
Life Lessons			

© Cengage Learning

3. Now, refer to the active-listening, beginning, and exploring sections of The Social Work Skills Interview Rating Form (see Appendix 15) to evaluate your performance of those skills. Use your word-processing program to identify the skills you performed well, those that need improvement, those that you should have used during the interview but did not, as well as those that you used but probably should not have. Also, describe and discuss your own reactions to the interview. How prepared were you? How did you feel about it? What did you like and what did you dislike about it? Discuss what you would do differently if you had a chance to conduct the interview again and outline what you might do in the next interview to improve the quality of the interview. Summarize your ratings, reactions, and reflections in a section of the "First Meeting with a Practice Client" document. Title the section "My Ratings, Reactions, and Reflections" and save the entire document for deposit in the "Experiential Interviewing Exercise" folder of your Social Work Skills Portfolio.

4. Finally, reflect upon the entirety of the first interview experience and use relevant preparing skills to prepare for the next meeting with the practice client. Draw upon what you learned and the documents you created to word-process tentative plans for the meeting. Label the document "Preliminary Plans for the Second Interview with a Practice Client" and deposit it in the "Experiential Interviewing Exercise" folder of your Social Work Skills Portfolio.

CHAPTER 9: SELF-APPRAISAL

As you finish this chapter, please reflect on your learning by completing the following self-appraisal exercise.

SELF-APPRAISAL: THE EXPLORING SKILLS

Please respond to the following items. Read each statement carefully. Then, use the following 4-point rating scale to indicate the degree to which you agree or disagree with each statement. Record your numerical response in the space provided:

4 = Strongly agree   2 = Disagree

3 = Agree   1 = Strongly disagree

4	3	2	1	Rating Statement
				At this point in time, I can
☐	☐	☐	☐	1. Discuss the purposes and functions of exploring.
☐	☐	☐	☐	2. Explore relevant aspects of the person-issue-situation and look for strengths.
☐	☐	☐	☐	3. Ask questions.
☐	☐	☐	☐	4. Seek clarification.
☐	☐	☐	☐	5. Reflect content.
☐	☐	☐	☐	6. Reflect feelings.
☐	☐	☐	☐	7. Reflect feelings and meanings.
☐	☐	☐	☐	8. Partialize.
☐	☐	☐	☐	9. Go beyond what is said.
☐	☐	☐	☐	10. Reflect issues.
☐	☐	☐	☐	11. Reflect hypotheses.
☐	☐	☐	☐	12. Assess proficiency in the exploring skills.
				Subtotal

Note: These items are identical to those contained in the Exploring Skills section of the Social Work Skills Self-Appraisal Questionnaire presented in Appendix 3. If you completed that self-appraisal before beginning Chapter 1, you have already responded to these items once before. You may now compare the responses you made on that occasion with those you made this time. Also, compare the two subtotals. If you believe that you have progressed in terms of your proficiency, the more recent subtotal should be higher than the earlier one.

ASSESSING

Assessment is a fundamental process in professional social work practice (Jordan, 2008; Meyer, 1993; Perlman, 1957; Richmond, 1944; Sowers & Dulmus, 2008). When the exploration process has progressed well, you and the client have gathered and begun to reflect on a substantial amount of relevant information about the person, the issues, and the circumstances. You have traced the origin and development of the issues and identified factors that might be associated with their occurrence. You have learned about aspects of the client system and the situation in both the present and the past, and even considered various scenarios in the future. You have explored risk factors as well as protective factors, strengths, assets and resources of various kinds (for example, competencies, social support, successes, and life lessons)—some of which might be useful later in planning problem-solving and goal-pursuing action. Importantly, you have communicated your understanding of the clients' identified problems and perhaps their explanatory and change-oriented hypotheses as well. During the assessment phase, you collaborate with members of the client system in trying to make sense of this information so that you and your client can effectively address the problems, issues, or needs that emerged through the exploration process.

Aspects of the assessment process typically begin during the exploring phase and continue on into the contracting phrase as well. Through collaborative assessment, social workers and clients move toward clarification of the problems for work. Having reflected and considered the client's hypotheses, you may now share your professionally based hypotheses about how personal and situational factors influence the problems and vice versa—how the problems affect the involved people and circumstances. You consider the relative urgency with which certain issues should receive attention; and, sometimes, you share your hypotheses about how the issues of concern might be addressed, often drawing on strengths and resources both within the client system and within the social and physical or ecological environment as well.

Understanding gained from these reflective and analytic processes usually leads to a relatively clear focus or direction for the work that you and your client will undertake together. Ideally, the assessment process leads to client-and-worker consensus about explanatory and change-oriented hypotheses. These hypotheses usually serve as the basis upon which you and the client establish a clear and detailed service agreement or "contract" for your work together (Dziegielewski, 2008; Maluccio & Marlow, 1974; Seabury, 1975, 1976). When all goes well, the data collected during the exploration phase logically lead to an assessment and case formulation, which, in turn, logically leads to a service contract. The contract guides both worker and client during the working and evaluating phase. Ideally, these processes reflect internal consistency (see Figure 10.1). Indeed, you should be able to discuss how the information collected through exploration supports the tentative assessment and case formulation, and how the assessment and case formulation in turn support the agreed-upon service contract, which contains goals, action plans, action steps, and plans for evaluation. As workers and clients collaboratively pursue the service goals and evaluate progress toward their achievement, they may sometimes need to recycle the process. For example, if progress toward achievement of a goal is not apparent, a presenting problem worsens, or an issue of greater urgency arises, workers and clients typically reengage in the exploring, assessing, and contracting processes to improve the probability that their revised action plans will yield favorable results.

This chapter (see Box 10.1) is designed to help learners develop proficiency in the social work skills commonly involved in the assessment process: (1) identifying issues, (2) sharing hypotheses, (3) clarifying issues for work, (4) organizing descriptive information, and (5) preparing an assessment and case formulation.

Assessment involves both career-long learning and critical thinking as you bring your professional knowledge together with the client's firsthand experience in a collaborative process of reflection, analysis, and synthesis. Using theoretical and empirical knowledge within the context of biopsychosocial and person-in-environment perspectives, you conjointly assess individuals, dyads, families, groups, organizations, communities, or societies. You or your clients may adopt conceptual or assessment tools of various kinds. For example, concept maps and diagrammatic representations such as family genograms, eco-maps, or timelines (refer to Chapter 2) could be helpful. You might use scales or questionnaires such as the Social Support Appraisals Scale, the General Self-Efficacy Scale, the "Big Five" Personality Test (see Chapter 2), or any of the hundreds of valid and reliable instruments that might pertain to an issue of concern (Fischer & Corcoran, 2007a, 2007b; Hudson, 1982).

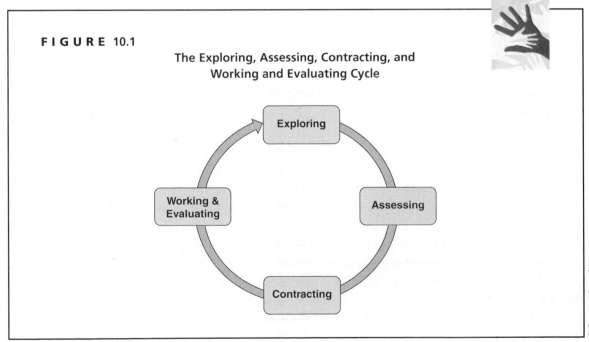

FIGURE 10.1

The Exploring, Assessing, Contracting, and Working and Evaluating Cycle

© Cengage Learning

You might examine a phenomenon in relation to a set of criteria or guidelines derived from research studies or validated protocols. For example, in assessing the relative risk of recidivism among people who have committed sexual offenses, you might consider findings from a meta-analysis such as Hanson and Morton-Bourgon's (2009). In assessing child sexual abuse, you might refer to *The Evaluation of Sexual Abuse in Children* (Kellogg & The American Academy of Pediatrics Committee on Child Abuse and Neglect, 2005). Although prepared for pediatricians, social workers would benefit from an understanding of the biophysical as well as psychosocial risk factors. In terms of psychosocial risk factors for child sexual abuse, you might review Levenson and Morin's article (2006). For the assessment of child abuse in general, you might consider empirical factors such as those summarized by Herring (1996). Certain conditions tend to be associated with a greater risk of child abuse. Among these are a history of child abuse or neglect reports, a parent who was abused as a child, a youthful parent, a single-parent or an extended-family household, domestic violence in the household, the lengthy separation of parent and child, substance abuse by parent or caretaker, impairment (for example, physical, intellectual, psychological) of the child, and impairment of the parent or caretaker (Brissett-Chapman, 1995, pp. 361–362). Using factors such as these as a guide, the worker thoughtfully considers the information learned during the exploring phase to determine the risk of child endangerment. The outcome of the assessment may powerfully affect, for better or worse, the well-being of a child and family. The consequences of both false positives (for example, where the worker concludes there is high risk but the true danger is low) and false negatives (for example, where the worker concludes there is low risk but the true danger is high) can be serious. In some cases, an inaccurate assessment may endanger lives.

Of course, social workers also serve couples, families, groups, organizations, and communities as well as individuals. Assessment guidelines and instruments are just as useful in work with these larger-size client systems. For example, the Inventory of Family Protective Factors (Gardner, Huber, Steiner, Vazquez, & Savage, 2008) may help families identify factors that foster family resilience. Moos and Moos' (2009) Family Environment Scale has long been used in family-environment-related research. In work with groups, scales such as the Group Attitude Scale (Evans & Jarvis, 1986) or the Perceived Group Cohesion Scale (Chin, Salisbury, Pearson, & Stollak, 1999) may be quite useful. In terms of organizational culture, Cooke and Lafferty's Organizational Culture Inventory (Szumal, 2003), the Organizational Culture Survey (Glaser, Zamanou, & Hacker, 1987), or Cameron and Quinn's (1999) Organizational Culture Assessment Instrument can complement individual and small group interviews.

The Community-Oriented Programs Environment Scale (Moos & Otto, 1972) may be used to evaluate change in communities. The World Values Survey (2009) and several of the indices used by the United Nations are helpful in assessing large communities and societies. Perspectives related to the concepts of social capital, social cohesion, and "well-being" may be useful in both large- and small-community contexts. Based in large part on the work of Robert Putnam (Putnam, 1995, 2001, 2002; Putnam & Campbell, 2010; Putnam, Feldstein, & Cohen, 2003), the Saguaro Seminar on Civic Engagement in America at Harvard University's Kennedy School of Government created a Social Capital Community Benchmark Survey (2000, 2002, September). The Saguaro Seminar completes large-scale national studies (2000, 2006). Other tools include the Social Capital Inventory (Narayan & Cassidy, 2001), the Social Capital Integrated Questionnaire, and the Social Capital Assessment Tool—the latter two developed by the World Bank Social Capital Thematic Group (2009).

Although social work assessments tend to have much in common, the specific forms vary considerably according to client system size and characteristics as well as practice setting, agency or program purpose, and presenting problem or issue. For example, a social worker serving an elderly client might refer to government guidelines in helping to determine whether a nursing home has adequate physical facilities and sufficient social stimulation to meet the basic needs of an elderly client. A psychiatric or clinical social worker might refer to criteria published in a recent edition of *Diagnostic and Statistical Manual* [*DSM*] (American Psychiatric Association, 2000a, in press) to help consider whether a client might be depressed, and if so, how seriously (Williams, 2008). A social worker serving in a crisis and suicide-prevention program might use guidelines to estimate a distraught client's risk of suicidal action as low, moderate, or high (American Psychiatric Association, 2003; Berman, Jobes, & Silverman, 2006; Rogers, Lewis, & Subich, 2002; Rutter & Behrendt, 2004; Verwey et al., 2010).

A social worker working with community members seeking to enhance conditions in their neighborhood might conduct a needs assessment. A social worker working with a representatives from two competing youth gangs—each with a history of violence toward the other—might spend weeks or longer meeting separately with gang leaders to determine conditions that could (1) permit safe, nonviolent correspondence between representatives of each group and (2) reflect a reasonably high probability of productive dialogue. In such circumstances, well-intentioned outsiders—even professional social workers—can sometimes make things worse. An unsafe, nonproductive encounter between competing gang members could trigger a violent reaction that results in injuries and death to many people, including uninvolved bystanders and family members.

Certain kinds of issues commonly surface in almost all social work practice settings. Violence toward self or others, child physical and sexual abuse, exploitation of vulnerable people, and mental health or substance abuse issues are likely to emerge as concerns wherever you serve. All social workers, therefore, need to be alert to their possible presence. Indeed, some agencies make it standard operating procedure to assess for substance abuse, child abuse and domestic violence, and risk of suicide or violence against others. As a social worker making such assessments, you might consider various sources. The *DSM-IV-TR* (American Psychiatric Association, 2000a) and the *DSM-5* (American Psychiatric Association, in press), for example, contain criteria for distinguishing between substance dependence and substance abuse. Although both dependence and abuse involve dysfunctional patterns of use contributing to problems in psychological and social functioning, the former includes the development of physical tolerance to the substance whereas the latter does not.

The *DSM* is a multiaxial classification manual of psychiatric disorders. The emphasis is on classification rather than on understanding risk and protective or other factors associated with the onset or the treatment of disorders. Clinical disorders and "other conditions that may be the focus of attention" are recorded on Axis I whereas personality disorders and forms of "mental retardation" appear on Axis II (American Psychiatric Association, 2000a, p. 27). General medical conditions are recorded on Axis III. Indeed, many health conditions are associated with various psychological and social problems as well. Consider, for example, the medical problems associated with lead poisoning—especially among children. Many older homes and apartments contain lead-based paints (DeRienzo-DeVivio, 1992) and some candies and their wrappers contain lead as well (Medlin, 2004). Children who ingest products containing lead can suffer serious health and psychosocial problems, including "decreased intelligence, impaired neurobehavioral development, stunted physical growth, hearing impairment, and kidney problems" (Medlin, 2004, p. A803).

"Psychosocial and Environmental Problems" (for example, lead-based paints, polluted air or water) such as those mentioned earlier may be recorded on Axis IV and organized according to the following subcategories:

- Problems with primary support group
- Problems related to the social environment
- Educational problems
- Occupational problems
- Housing problems
- Economic problems
- Problems with access to health care services
- Problems related to interaction with the legal system/crime
- Other psychosocial and environmental problems (American Psychiatric Association, 2000a, p. 32)

Axis V of the *DSM-IV-TR* (American Psychiatric Association, 2000a) includes a Global Assessment of Functioning (GAF) scale through which a client's "psychological, social, and occupational functioning" may be rated "on a hypothetical continuum of mental health–illness" (p. 34). Axis V may also be used to record other aspects of functioning. For example, in the appendices, the *DSM-IV-TR* contains several provisional tools such as the Defensive Functioning Scale (pp. 307–813), the Global Assessment of Relational Functioning (GARF) Scale (pp. 814–816), the Social and Occupational Functioning Assessment Scale (SOFAS) (pp. 817–818), and an Outline for Cultural Formulation and Glossary of Culture-Bound Syndromes (pp. 897–903).

Although the *DSM* is extremely well-known and widely used by practitioners from several professions, it remains a controversial classification system. Allegations of cultural bias have been made and findings of numerous studies add to questions about its validity and reliability

(Dalal, 2009; Kirk & Kutchins, 1994; McLaren, 2008; Spitzer, Williams, & Endicott, 2012). Some have examined the potential conflicts of interest associated with the identification of "new" disorders (a process sometimes called "disease mongering") for which pharmaceutical drugs may be created, and medical and psychiatric treatments prescribed (Cosgrove, 2011; Cosgrove & Krimsky, 2012; Cosgrove, Krimsky, Vijayaraghavan, & Schneider, 2006; Wakefield, 2012). Psychiatric and psychotherapeutic interventions for many of the disorders contained within the *DSM* manuals are often covered by private and public medical insurance. If they were not so classified, most health plans would not pay for their treatment. The massive amount of money directly or indirectly associated with the health care, pharmaceutical, and health insurance industries may contribute to the medicalization of social problems and common life challenges, and to their description in psychiatric or psychological terms. Rather than social problems, they may become psychiatric disorders or illnesses. As the number of such disorders increase, the health care–related professions and industries tend to expand and costs tend to rise (Caplan, 2012, April 27; Kirk & Kutchins, 1992; Kutchins & Kirk, 1997).

As an alternative or supplement to the *DSM*, social workers may consider the person-in-environment (PIE) classification system (Karls & O'Keefe, 2008a, 2008b). The PIE approach gives practitioners, presumably with the input and participation of clients, an opportunity to classify or code problems within the following dimensions or factors (Karls & O'Keefe, 2008a, p. 1):

- Factor I: Social Functioning Problems: type, severity, duration, coping ability, and strengths
- Factor II: Environmental Problems: severity, duration, and resources or strengths
- Factor III: Mental Health Problems and Strengths
- Factor IV: Physical Health Problems and Strengths

Problems in *Factor I—Social Role and Relationship Functioning* (for example, family roles, other interpersonal roles, occupational roles, special life situation roles) may be identified and then classified and coded by type (for example, power conflict, ambivalence, obligation/responsibility, dependency, loss, isolation, oppression, mixed, other) as well as severity (for example, *1* or *L = Low, 2* or *M = Moderate, 3* or *H = High, 4* or *H+ = Very High, 5* or *C = Catastrophic*), duration (for example, *1* or *Y: 5+ = 5* or *more years, 2* or *Y: 1–5 = 1–5 years, 3* or *M: 6–12 = 6–12 months, 4* or *M: 1–6 = 1–6 months, 5* or *W: 1–4 = 1–4 weeks*), coping ability (for example, *1* or *A = Outstanding, 2* or *B = Above average, 3* or *C = Adequate, 4* or *D = Somewhat inadequate, 5* or *F = Inadequate, 6* or *I = Unable to judge at this time*), and strengths (for example, *1* or *N = Notable Strengths, 2* or *P = Possible Strengths*) (Karls & O'Keefe, 2008a).

Social workers may then use the classifications within the *Factor II—Problems in the Environment* dimension to identify those situational conditions that affect or are affected by the identified problems in social role functioning (Factor I). Environmental problems are categorized according to the following major systems (Karls & O'Keefe, 2008a, p. 17):

1. Basic Needs System
2. Education and Training System
3. Judicial and Legal System
4. Health, Safety, and Social Services System
5. Voluntary Association System
6. Affectional Support System

Each of these major systems contains problem areas (for example, food/nutrition, shelter, employment, economic resources, transportation, and discrimination) and each problem area contains a list of specific problems. For example, the discrimination problem area includes: discrimination on the basis of age, ethnicity, color, language, religion, gender, sexual orientation, lifestyle, noncitizen status, veteran status, dependency, disability, marital status, body size, political affiliation, and other. Once an environmental condition or problem has been identified, its severity, duration, and strengths index are determined and coded (Karls & O'Keefe, 2008a).

For example, a social worker and client using the PIE Classification Manual might assign a classification such as:

- Factor I: Parent Role Problem, ambivalence type, very high severity (5), duration of 6 months to 1 year (3), somewhat inadequate coping ability (4), and notable strengths (1) [1120.5341]
- Factor II: Absence of Affectional Support, high severity (4), duration of 6 months to 1 year (3), and possible strengths (2) [10101.432] (Karls & O'Keefe, 2008a).

The PIE classification system has generated considerable interest among social work academicians and researchers (Williams, 1994; Williams, Karls, & Wandrei, 1989). Social work practitioners, however, appear to be less intrigued. Many may not be aware of the system, and others, especially those in health and mental health settings, may not see the value of additional classification beyond the *DSM* or the International Classification of Diseases (*ICD*) systems (World Health Organization, 2007). The potential utility of the PIE classification scheme may become apparent only in years to come, when epidemiological and demographic studies establish the incidence and prevalence rates of various problems involving social role functioning and environmental conditions. Like the *DSM*, the PIE classification system is primarily problem focused in nature. To be truly useful to helping professionals and consumers, each problem classification or diagnosis must reflect both validity and reliability; and effective interventions for each must be established.

This seems to be the case for certain disorders included within the *DSM*. The condition identified as Panic Disorder, for example, seems to reflect coherent cluster of systems and can be identified with a reasonable degree of reliability. Perhaps most importantly, however, numerous research studies have yielded psychosocial treatment protocols that are remarkably effective in ameliorating or eliminating symptoms of panic (Sánchez-Meca, Rosa-Alcázar, Marín-Martínez, & Gómez-Conesa, 2010a, 2010b). You may expect much time to pass before effective prevention or intervention services can be established for many of the problems involving social role functioning and environmental conditions included in the PIE Classification Manual (Karls & O'Keefe, 2008a, 2008b).

In addition to classification manuals such as the *DSM* and the PIE system, rapid assessment instruments (RAIs) of various kinds may complement the assessment process and sometimes serve as potential indicators or measures of goal attainment (Fischer & Corcoran, 2007a, 2007b; Hudson, 1982; Rush, First, & Blacker, 2008; Schutte & Malouff, 1995). In the case of substance abuse issues, instruments such as the CAGE Screening Test for Alcohol Dependence (Ewing, 1984), the Michigan Alcoholism Screening Test (MAST) (Selzer, 1971; Selzer, Vinokur, & van Rooijen, 1975), or the Drug Abuse Screening Test (Skinner, 1982), in conjunction with other information, can be used as aids in determining, for instance, whether a client might be physically addicted, perhaps indicating a need for detoxification in a hospital setting. Judgments of this nature and magnitude require perspective, objectivity, and well-developed critical thinking skills. A great deal of career-long learning is also required because of continuing advances in the scientific knowledge on which assessment criteria are based.

Indeed, during the last decade or two, many helping professionals have become concerned that exclusive or excessive focus on problems may interfere with clients' motivation and impede progress toward resolution. Several scholars (De Jong & Berg, 2002; de Shazer, 1988; de Shazer et al., 1986; Miller, Hubble, & Duncan, 1996) have questioned the assumption that detailed exploration of clients' personal and social histories and in-depth understanding of the contributing causes of psychosocial problems are necessary for effective resolution of those problems. Partly because of these concerns, professional helpers have become extremely interested in concepts and perspectives related to strengths, capacities, protective factors, assets, resiliencies, and solutions.

Dozens of books, book chapters, and journal articles have been published on the topic of strengths in social work practice (Chapin, 2007; Cowger, 1994, 1996; Dybicz, 2011; Gilgun, 2004b; Greene & Lee, 2011; Rapp & Goscha, 2006; Saleebey, 2009). Indeed, Saleebey (2001) advocates for the development of a diagnostic strengths manual to counterbalance the symptom perspective reflected in the American Psychiatric Association's *DSM* classification system.

Locating, enhancing, and promoting resilience and hardiness have generated similar interest (Fraser et al., 1999; Gilgun, 2005; Kamya, 2000; Maddi, Wadhwa, & Haier, 1996; Peters, Leadbeater, & McMahon, 2005; Smokowski, 1998; Walsh, 2006; Whittaker, 2001), as has solution-focused or solution-oriented practice (Baker & Steiner, 1996; Berg & De Jong, 1996; Berg & Reuss, 1998; De Jong & Berg, 2002; Greene & Lee, 2011; Lee, 1997; Mattaini & Thyer, 1996; Miller et al., 1996; O'Connell, 2005; Sundman, 1997). The positive psychology initiative represents an analogous trend. Stimulated initially by Martin Seligman (2002, 2011), virtues and strengths are emerging in psychology as a focus for both research and practice. Numerous publications reflect this phenomenon (Carr, 2003; Compton, 2004; Csikszentmihalyi & Csikszentmihalyi, 2006; Frisch, 2005; Linley, Joseph, & Seligman, 2004; Ong & Dulmen, 2006; Peterson, 2006; Seligman & Csikszentmihalyi, 2000; Snyder & Lopez, 2005). In addition, Peterson and Seligman (2004) published a classification handbook of character virtues and strengths. They provide an overall list of 24 strengths that support the following six overarching virtues (pp. 29–30):

1. *Wisdom and knowledge*—cognitive strengths that entail the acquisition and use of knowledge
2. *Courage*—emotional strengths that involve the exercise of will to accomplish goals in the face of opposition, external or internal
3. *Humanity*—interpersonal strengths that involve tending and befriending others
4. *Justice*—civic strengths that underlie healthy community life
5. *Temperance*—strengths that protect against excess
6. *Transcendence*—strengths that forge connections to the larger universe and provide meaning

Hardly a threat to the dominance of the *DSM* among helping professionals, this effort to classify virtues and strengths nonetheless represents a significant opportunity to acknowledge positive aspects of human behavior and experience. The strengths reflected in these virtues may represent protective or resilience factors of relevance to many people, problems, and aspirations.

Another theme or trend in contemporary psychosocial services involves the assessment and enhancement of motivation, particularly as it relates to the transtheoretical or "stages of change" model (Miller & Rollnick, 2002; Prochaska, 1999; Prochaska, Norcross, & DiClemente, 1994; Prochaska & Velicera, 1998; Rollnick & Miller, 1995). According to the transtheoretical perspective, long-term change tends to proceed sequentially in five stages (Prochaska, 1999):

1. Precontemplation
2. Contemplation
3. Preparation
4. Action
5. Maintenance

Prochaska and colleagues (Prochaska & Norcross, 2007; Prochaska et al., 1994) suggest that people who make significant changes in their behavior proceed through all stages of the

Transtheoretical Model (TTM). Although, the process may sometimes be spiral rather than linear in nature, they conclude that people who make durable change eventually address each stage.

Precontemplation is the first TTM stage of change. People in this stage tend to reflect ambivalence, uncertainty, disinterest, or denial. For example, suppose you had agreed to help an unemployed, paraplegic client find a job. Your client is highly motivated and has already taken numerous steps. He's in the action stage. When you first contact a prospective employer who has never employed someone who uses a wheelchair, you might anticipate a precontemplative response. Despite the Americans with Disabilities Act, the employer could be quite reluctant to consider the request seriously. As a social worker, your first step toward change might be to help the employer consider the idea of moving toward the next stage—contemplation.

Contemplation is the second stage of the change process. People in this stage tend to engage in data collection, reflection, and analysis. The possibility of change is considered. There may even be a general sense of direction or a vague plan. Let's return to the situation of your paraplegic client (action stage) and the "reluctant employer." Suppose you supply the employer with scholarly papers that outline the benefits of a diverse workforce and describe businesses that became successful after employing disabled workers. When the "precontemplative employer" reads those materials and entertains the idea of hiring a person affected by a spinal cord injury, you might begin to see signs of contemplation and reflection. Unfortunately, thinking about change in general terms does not usually produce it. In trying to serve your client, you encourage the employer toward the preparation stage.

Preparation is the third stage of change. The transition from contemplation to preparation is associated with at least two notable shifts in thinking. First, there is a significant increase in thinking about solutions and resolutions, accompanied by a decrease in contemplation about the problem, issue, or need. Second, thoughts about the future increasingly replace those about the past and present. "The end of the contemplation stage is a time of anticipation, activity, anxiety, and excitement" (Prochaska et al., 1994, p. 43). Plan making characterizes the onset of the preparation stage. People might outline specific steps and set short-term dates. Importantly, they share with others and publicly "announce" their intent to change. You would notice signs of preparation when the "contemplative" employer tells colleagues, "We will hire at least one disabled worker this month and at least one more each month for the next 6 months." However, even extremely well-conceived plans do not automatically lead to change. Change requires action of some kind.

Action, the fourth stage, is characterized by motivation, purposefulness, activity, and optimism. You notice actual differences in the person, the situation, or aspects of both. Indeed, the most long-lasting change tends to occur when action involves several dimensions of the person and the environment. However, the activities of this stage may not lead to durable change. The intensity may fade, sometimes remarkably quickly, and change-related activities may not continue. The action stage can be short-lived and disappointing. Despite the public announcements, the plans, and the flurry of initial activity, your client may not be hired or, if he is, additional disabled workers may not become employed. "Many people . . . erroneously equate action with change, overlooking not only the critical work that prepares people for successful action but the equally important (and often more challenging) efforts to maintain the changes following action" (Prochaska et al., 1994, p. 44).

Maintenance is the fifth stage in the change process. In some ways, it represents the greatest challenge of all. Requiring ongoing motivation, commitment, stamina, persistence, and follow-through, maintenance lacks the excitement of the preparation stage and the intensity of the action stage. Maintaining lasting change usually requires ongoing, detailed attention to small steps on a day-to-day and week-to-week basis. Human systems tend to reflect powerful forces of inertia that return them to traditional behaviors and processes. Without continuous attention and consistent routines designed to maintain change, you may anticipate a return to previously established patterns. The recently "enlightened employer," who appears so motivated and "ready" to diversify the workforce, can easily become distracted by unrelated problems and challenges, and fail to monitor progress on a day-to-day basis. The person leading the effort to employ disabled workers may leave the company or be transferred to another area. There may be a downturn in the economy. When there is a surplus of applicants, workforce diversification may not seem as important or attractive as it does when a scarcity of dependable workers exists. Unless you persistently attend to maintenance, change is unlikely to last. However, if maintenance activities continue, the potency of the older forces of inertia gradually decreases as the once-new changes become part of the established and traditional routine, reflecting their own forces of inertia. Indeed, they would be quite difficult to change (Prochaska et al., 1994).

West (2005) and others have challenged the transtheoretical stages of change on theoretical and empirical grounds. Indeed, it is not certain that all people proceed through all five "stages," and the descriptions of the stages are far from precise. These issues call for further development and additional research. Nonetheless, the TTM represents a potentially useful addition to the array of conceptual models available to social workers and clients in their efforts to understand how change occurs, and to incorporate such understanding in their plans.

In addition to the transtheoretical model, you may be interested in aspects of the Health Belief Model (Applewhite, 1996; Becker, 1974; Harrison, Mullen, & Green, 1992; Rosenstock, 1990; Rosenstock, Strecher, & Becker, 1994, 1988), the theory of reasoned action (TRA) and its successor the theory of planned behavior (TPB) (Ajzen, 1991; Ajzen & Fishbein, 1980; Albarracin, Johnson, Fishbein, & Muellerleile, 2001; Fishbein & Middlestadt, 1989; Fishbein, Middlestadt, & Hitchcock, 1994), and, as we explored earlier, "self-efficacy" (Bandura, 1977, 1992, 1997, 1995b; Holden, 1991; Schwarzer, 1992; Schwarzer & Fuchs, 1995) to help you and clients consider aspects of the change process that relate to psychosocial factors. As social workers know, motivation is not the exclusive result of personal factors. Situational factors also affect clients' expectations about eventual outcomes as well as their readiness to take action.

Failure to consider motivational dimensions may lead social workers to presume that once clients identify an issue, they are necessarily ready to take action to ameliorate its adverse effects. Given our long-standing belief in "starting where the client is," social workers in particular recognize that clients often hold complex thoughts and conflicting feelings about problems, and especially about actions that might be required to address them. Furthermore, when clients experience multiple problems, their degree of motivation to address one problem may differ substantially from that of another. When we fail to incorporate clients' readiness, motivation, and beliefs and expectations regarding change, we may inadvertently obstruct rather than enhance problem resolution. Clearly, many clients are not "ready" or "motivated" to take action as soon as they share an issue with a social worker. In such cases, we should respect our clients and "start where they are" rather than where we might want them to be.

Different levels of readiness and motivation call for different helping activities—ones that "match" the stage of change. For example, people who are "preparing to change" typically experience marginal benefit from additional exploration into historical events or examination of the problems of concern. They are ready to consider potential solutions and begin the process of formulating plans. Helping them to develop plans and identify steps is likely to match their stage of change and contribute to goal-oriented action.

Conversely, people who are only beginning to contemplate the possibility and value of change would probably find examination of relevant intervention strategies premature and perhaps even insulting. Helping them to explore problems or issues and facilitating discussion about the pros and cons associated with change would better match their level of readiness for change.

Motivational enhancement or motivational interviewing approaches can encourage and facilitate clients' progression through the stages of change (Miller, 1995; Miller & Rollnick, 1991, 2002). However, they focus primarily on the person's readiness, motivation, beliefs, and expectations. There is little attention to situational factors. Nonetheless, focusing on these personal factors may help clients assume greater responsibility for addressing the issues they identify. Such processes reflect a traditional social work theme of "helping clients to help themselves." However, there are times when social workers should or must take action on behalf of clients—often in an effort to influence change in the client's environment. In such circumstances, the social worker's own motivation becomes highly relevant to the change process. In adopting a person-in-environment perspective, social workers attend to situational and contextual factors, as well as personal or psychological factors, that relate to client-identified problems. Of course, other people in the "situation" also reflect their own levels of readiness and motivation regarding changes asked or expected of them.

Interestingly, almost 60 years ago, leading social work scholars at the University of Chicago School of Social Service proposed a triadic model of assessment that included motivation, capacity, and opportunity (Ripple, 1955; Ripple & Alexander, 1956; Ripple, Alexander, & Polemis, 1964). Using this framework, social workers and clients considered ways and means to solve problems and accomplish goals by intervening within these dimensions of the person-in-environment.

In contemporary social work, we may integrate several of these perspectives for the purposes of assessment. Recognize, however, that knowledge is increasing at an exponential rate and the conceptual tools, classification schema, and theoretical perspectives used today will probably change within a few years as researchers produce more valid, reliable, and relevant knowledge.

Although social work assessment is an ongoing process rather than a finished product, a formal record is usually required. This record may be handwritten, digitally recorded, or word-processed. Keep in mind, however, that assessments change, sometimes frequently and occasionally dramatically, during work with or on behalf of a client system. Also remember to exercise caution with terminology that may label or unnecessarily stigmatize people (see "Culturally Sensitive Communications" in Chapter 6).

Social work assessments are multidimensional in nature and serve many purposes. They may be structured in different way and recorded according to various organizational schemes. The Description, Assessment, and Contract (DAC) outline that you will soon consider, represents a comprehensive integrated format that might be useful in certain contexts. You will probably discover that some sections are irrelevant for use with some clients or in certain agency settings. In addition, recognize that numerous other models are readily accessible in the professional literature. Some may be especially applicable to your particular social work role and function in your service to specific population groups or in assessing specific problems of concern.

As you engage in assessment activities, please approach them as professional rather than technical endeavors, as collaborative rather than singular undertakings, and as dynamic rather than static processes. Avoid the temptation to pursue a bureaucratic or technical approach to assessment. Whenever possible, adopt a conversational style that reflects the core facilitative conditions of empathy, respect, and genuineness. Use available professional knowledge and judgment to determine the particular nature and style of assessment. It is highly unlikely that all clients would have the same assessment experience. The unique nature of each person-issue-situation virtually requires certain adaptations or innovations. When possible, incorporate valid and reliable assessment instruments, but be sure to consider their cultural implications and other potential limitations. Regularly seek feedback and encourage clients to participate with you in formulating assessments. When clients collaborate in the assessment process, their sense of empowerment and self-efficacy tend to grow and their motivation for change usually increases.

Assessments, like other professional activities, must be recorded in some coherent fashion. The DAC represents one, but only one, approach to organizing the results of the exploring, assessing, and later, the contracting processes. As its title suggests, the DAC includes three major sections. First, you organize the information gained through the exploration process into a description. Second, you translate the ideas and hypotheses concerning plausible causes and potential solutions that you and the client generated into a tentative assessment. Third, you summarize the agreement about goals and plans that you and the client negotiated into a service contract.[1]

Completion of the description portion of the DAC helps to organize a great deal of information about a client system, the situational context, and the issues of concern. The assessment section contains information that you and the client generate through analysis, synthesis, and the formulation of questions or hypotheses concerning the descriptive data. At first glance, the DAC may appear exhaustingly inclusive. It certainly does include a large array of sections. However, several of these are obviously inappropriate for work with many clients. When that is so, certain sections may be ignored and the format of the DAC adapted to fit the unique needs and functions of your specific social work setting. Realize that numerous alternate schemes are available. Ultimately, in consultation with your supervisors and agency colleagues, you determine the utility of any format for the particular circumstances of your social work practice.

Identifying Issues

On some occasions, you may identify issues that clients did not mention during the exploration process. Based on the emerging assessment of the person-issue-situation, you may recognize an area of concern that relates to the presenting problem but was not noticed or not acknowledged by the client. At other times, you may have a different view of the problem or issue that a client has introduced. For example, a client may say that her spouse's "laziness" is a major problem. After seeking clarification about what she means by the term, you might ask, "I wonder, might what you call laziness be a sign of something else? Could it be that your spouse is quite unhappy with life just now; perhaps as unhappy as you are?"

Sometimes, you must assume primary responsibility for both issue and goal identification. For instance, when the situation is immediately life threatening (for example, an individual client is suicidal, homicidal, psychotic, or heavily intoxicated), the client is seeing you on an involuntary basis (for example, required to seek counseling or face felony charges), and she or he remains unwilling to share her or his views, you may identify at least some of the issues for work. Once you do so, seek feedback so that the client might propose modifications or suggest other issues.

Even when the situation is neither life threatening nor involuntary, you may sometimes legitimately share your view of possible issues. Based on the tentative assessment, you may suggest that the client consider additional issues or different views of a problem. You may have professional knowledge or prior experience that leads you to point out an issue not previously discussed. For example, suppose a client describes feelings of constant fatigue, difficulty sleeping, loss of appetite, decreased interest in pleasurable activities, and diminished social involvement. You would probably wonder whether the client might be mourning the loss of someone or something, be physically ill (for example, suffer from a diabetic or infectious condition), or perhaps be experiencing a significant depressive episode.

Social workers naturally form opinions about factors that contribute to clients' presenting issues. Clients often appreciate it when you share these ideas. However, if and when you do so, express them in the same way you share all your professional opinions. That is, communicate them as ideas to consider rather than as indisputable facts. In addition, acknowledge clients' right to agree, disagree, or suggest alternatives. As a part of this process, routinely seek feedback from clients concerning these newly identified or redefined issues.

In practicing the skill of identifying issues, follow the format outlined here. Notice how we incorporate the skill of seeking feedback at the end.

---

[1] We explore the description and assessment parts of the DAC in this chapter and the contract portion in Chapter 11.

PRACTICE FORMAT: IDENTIFYING ISSUES

As we have talked about you and your situation, I have been wondering about _____

_____

(*identifying issues*). What do you think—is that an issue we should consider too (*seeking feedback*)?

EXAMPLE: IDENTIFYING ISSUES

CASE SITUATION: Lisa and Ruth have sought help to address problems in their relationship.

CLIENT: We fight all the time. We have a knock-down drag-out fight virtually every single day. We moved in together 2 months ago. Ever since we've fought like cats and dogs. We were so great together before we decided to share the apartment. We don't hit each other, but there sure is a lot of yelling and screaming.

WORKER: As we've talked about your relationship and how moving in together has affected it, I've been wondering about the question of expectations. It seems to me that moving from a dating relationship to a live-in relationship represents a very significant change—one that might leave each of you uncertain about what the other wants and needs in this new form of relationship. What do you think—could this issue of unclear expectations now that you live together be something we should address too?

EXERCISE 10-1: IDENTIFYING ISSUES

For these exercises, assume that you are a social worker with a multipurpose social services agency. Use the space provided to write the words you would say in identifying issues.

1. You have spent nearly a full hour talking with Mr. K., a recently divorced 55-year-old man. He has explored a number of issues, expressed feelings, and shared ideas about how and why the divorce occurred and what he might do to recover from the loss. Based on this summary of concerns and a review of exchanges that occurred earlier (see Exercises 9-1 through 9-9), write the words you would use in identifying one or more issues that Mr. K did not explicitly mention but, based upon your social work perspective, you conclude might apply to him or his situation.

2. You have spent several hours with Loretta, a homeless woman. You first arranged for her to eat a large meal. Then, you drove her to your agency office where you continued to explore issues from a person-in-environment perspective. She has mentioned

a number of concerns, some aspirations, and shared thoughts and feelings about various aspects of her life and circumstances. Based on this summary of concerns and a review of exchanges that occurred earlier (see Exercises 9-1 through 9-9), write the words you would use in identifying one or more issues that Loretta did not explicitly mention but, based upon your social work perspective, you think might apply to her and her situation.

3. You have spent approximately 75 minutes talking with the seven-member blended S. family. You and the family members have identified several issues: strain and conflict between Mr. S.'s children and Mrs. S., financial difficulties, marital distress, and most recently the threat to Mr. S.'s job. Based on this summary of concerns and a review of exchanges that occurred earlier (see Exercises 9-1 through 9-9), write the words you would use in identifying one or more issues that members of the S. family did not explicitly mention but, based upon your social work perspective, you believe might apply to them or their situation.

4. You have now talked with Mrs. F. for quite some time. You've explored several issues, including her doubts that she and her family could fit in this community, her children's apparently increasing disrespect for her and for their Latin heritage, and, most importantly, the concern for her children's safety at school. Based on this summary of concerns and a review of exchanges that occurred earlier (see Exercises 9-1 through 9-9), write the words you would use in identifying one or more issues that Mrs. F. did not explicitly mention but, based upon your social work perspective, you believe might apply to her or her family and their situation.

5. In your role as organizational consultant to a troubled social service agency, you have now met with a large group of staff and board members and other stakeholders in an attempt to clarify and then develop plans to resolve several problem areas. Numerous issues have already been identified and you have observed people as they interacted with each other during earlier meetings. Based on these issues, your observations, and a review of exchanges that occurred earlier (see Exercises 9-1 through 9-9) write the words you would use in identifying one or more issues that participants did not explicitly mention but, based upon your social work perspective, you believe might apply to the agency; its personnel, structure, or administrative processes; or to current circumstances.

Sharing Hypotheses

Like many clients, social workers also have ideas and "theories"[2] about "why" problems occur and "what to do" to resolve them. Unlike many clients, however, social workers usually possess sophisticated knowledge of scientific theories and empirical research about the causes for and the risk and protective factors associated with various social problems. We also often understand the research-based evidence about the policies, programs, practices, and interventions that serve to prevent, ameliorate, or resolve many social problems. Many social workers keep up-to-date with systematic reviews and meta-analyses of service effectiveness. Indeed, our professional education and our emphasis on scientific inquiry, critical thinking, and continuous learning help to prepare us to view phenomena from various theoretical lenses and perspectives that are supported by research-based evidence. Because social workers embrace a person-in-environment perspective, the explanatory and change-oriented hypotheses[3] that we employ tend to reflect multidimensional facets. Most of our assessment hypotheses involve elements of the client system, elements of the environmental system, and aspects of the problems or issues themselves.

As social workers engage in assessment processes, we apply the primary critical thinking skills of *analysis* and *synthesis*. Analysis involves examining in fine detail various pieces of information about the client system, issues, and circumstances. For example, consider a 30-year-old woman who reports that she "feels anxious in the presence of men." Together, you consider how different dimensions of

---

[2] When used scientifically, the term "theory" has a much different meaning than it has in everyday, popular usage. When your neighbor says, "I have a theory about why kids today are so messed up. It's because they have never had to work for anything—everything has been handed to them on a plate," he is not sharing a theory in the scientific sense. When conversing with clients, social workers sometimes use the term in a colloquial rather than a scholarly manner. However, we recognize that we are doing so.

[3] Later, in the working and evaluating chapter, we introduce the skill of "educating." Sharing explanatory and change-oriented hypotheses that have solid foundation in scientific theory and research evidence as well as critical thought and analysis represent a specific form of the skill of educating.

anxiety interact. After collecting information about what the client thinks, feels, senses, imagines, and does when she experiences anxiety, you might piece together or track the sequence of events leading up to and following the upsetting feelings. Such a functional analysis might reveal that the anxious feelings usually occur in the presence of men who are her own age or older, are confident and appear successful, and whom she thinks are eligible for romantic consideration. Further analysis might enable you to uncover that the client does not feel anxious when she interacts with men in business or professional contexts, men who are married or gay, or those who are much younger or less successful than she is. You and your client might also discover that when she first notices the early signs of anxiety, she immediately begins to say certain things to herself. For example, in such contexts, she might think, "I must not become anxious right now; if I become anxious, I will not say what I want to say and I will embarrass myself." She also seems to focus intently on physiological symptoms of anxiety such as flushing, perspiration, hyperventilation, and rapid heart rate.

Analysis often leads you and the client to pinpoint critical elements from among the various pieces of information. These become cornerstones in the formulation of *explanatory hypotheses* and, subsequently, *change-oriented hypotheses* as well. Synthesis builds on what you gain from analysis. It involves assembling significant pieces of information into a coherent whole by relating them to one another and to elements of your theory, knowledge, and experience base. For example, you might hypothesize that the client's anxiety in the presence of certain men may reflect a learned pattern resulting from her experience of growing up as an only child, attending girls-only grammar and high schools, and later enrolling in a college for women only. Such an explanatory hypothesis might help address the "why" question that many clients (and many social workers) ask themselves. However, we are usually even more interested in formulating hypotheses that involve contemporary factors. Often enlightening, factors from the past are not as amenable to change as are those in the present.

For example, in the case of a community that reflects growing crime rate, an increase in high school dropout rates, and an upward spike in food stamp (SNAP) applications, you and community members might hypothesize that the recent closing of a local manufacturing plant and the resulting loss of employment may contribute to these phenomena. Such a hypothesis would help to explain, in part, "why" the incidence rates of these social problems have increased. Later, based in part on our explanatory hypotheses, we also seek to generate *change-oriented hypotheses* to guide our efforts to resolve problems and achieve goals. In this instance, you might hypothesize that returning jobs to the community could help to alleviate the identified social problems and contribute to community development.

We use analysis and synthesis skills to generate explanatory and change-oriented hypotheses. In synthesis, we take certain bits of data or certain aspects of the analysis and combine them into a coherent whole. Usually, social workers apply research-supported theoretical concepts and perspectives to link certain pieces of information with others and to incorporate them within the context of a unifying theme. Our professional knowledge and expertise contribute to the generation of relevant, plausible hypotheses. However, in this process, we cannot neglect clients' knowledge, experience, and wisdom. Clients and other stakeholders often have ideas, opinions, and theories of their own. Based as they are on firsthand experience, their contributions add realism, practicality, and depth to assessment hypotheses.

Assessment leads to greater understanding by both worker and client. Coherent, plausible explanations about how and why identified problems occur also tend to enhance motivation and encourage optimism. However, our primary purpose for assessment goes well beyond enhanced understanding, hope, and readiness. As social workers, our fundamental purpose is to help clients resolve problems and achieve goals.

In the case of the woman who becomes anxious in the presence of certain men, you might consider a two-part explanatory hypothesis that (1) "distorted thoughts and beliefs" trigger anxious feelings, and (2) her intense focus upon physiological sensations serves to exacerbate them.

In other words, when she is in the company of an "eligible" man, she experiences thoughts and beliefs that have the following effects:

1. They inflate the importance of "having a romantic relationship with a man" or "being married to a man."
2. They exaggerate the significance of each moment of each encounter with any and all potential romantic partners.
3. They intensify her focus on herself (how she appears, what she says, what she does) so that she becomes highly self-conscious.
4. They increase her attention to physiological signs and symptoms of anxiety.

Such an explanatory hypothesis involves contemporary rather than historical factors and naturally leads to ideas about how to resolve the problem. That is, it guides us toward change-oriented hypotheses for possible inclusion in a case formulation. We might hypothesize that if she learned to think and focus somewhat differently in the presence of men she views as eligible, she would probably experience fewer signs and symptoms of anxiety. Therefore you and the client might well consider hypotheses and intervention strategies derived from them to change: (1) the patterns of intensely focusing on interoceptive signs and symptoms of anxiety; and (2) the distorted thoughts and beliefs she has about herself, about men and relationships, and about the future. The approach would probably also include increasing the frequency and duration of interaction with men whom she considers eligible. Increased exposure to available men might help her learn to think, feel, and focus differently in their presence.

In this particular instance, we use cognitive and behavioral concepts to develop change-oriented hypotheses to decrease or eliminate the woman's anxiety in the presence of eligible men. These hypotheses are central to our formulation and reflect our "theory of the case." They logically lead to change-oriented predictions such as the following:

1. If she places less intense emphasis upon "having a romantic relationship with a man" or "being married to a man," she will experience less anxiety in the presence of men she finds attractive.
2. If she places less significance on each moment of each encounter with a potential romantic partner, she will experience less anxiety in the presence of men she considers "eligible."
3. If she focuses less on herself (how she appears, what she says, what she does) and more on people she's with, she will be less self-conscious and less anxious in their presence.
4. If she pays less attention to the physiological sensations and symptoms of anxiety when they occur, she will experience fewer of them and at lower levels of intensity.
5. If she spends more time in the presence of attractive, "eligible" men (that is, more "exposure"), she will, over time, experience fewer and less intense signs and symptoms of anxiety.

In addition to cognitive and behavioral perspectives, however, there are dozens of theoretical perspectives and thousands of research studies that might apply to particular people, issues, and situations. Indeed, scholarly social workers typically first consider change-oriented hypotheses and intervention approaches that reflect research-based evidence of relevance and effectiveness. That is, we start with those intervention models shown through research studies to be safe and effective in helping people like our clients address problems similar to those they hope to resolve. If sufficient high-quality research-based evidence exists—as it does in the case of psychosocial services for people affected by anxiety and panic—we call the approach evidence based. Currently, however, we do not have evidence-based practices (EBP) for all social problems, all population groups, and all circumstances. There does not seem to be a single "silver-bullet" practice theory or policy approach that works well for everybody everywhere. Indeed, helping professionals will probably never be able to rely on a single theoretical perspective in our attempts to help diverse populations, living in diverse circumstances, and affected by diverse problems. Consequently, we must continue to review research studies that pertain to the clients we serve and the problems they address; and we must think critically about which theoretical perspectives and conceptual models best apply to particular clients.

On those occasions when we lack strong research-based evidence of the effectiveness of services for particular people, issues, and situations, we may generate hypotheses from strong scientific theories. For example, when certain interpersonal relationship issues are the target of concern, you might apply concepts from social learning theory. When strain and conflict within or between groups or organizations are the focus of attention, we might apply aspects of social systems theory. Fundamental concepts within social role theory—role ambiguity, role change, and role conflict—may be considered in relation to signs of frustration and distress. Crisis theory may help during emergencies, such as natural disasters, violent experiences, and other circumstances that involve sudden change. Family systems concepts may lead you to consider the effects of enmeshed boundaries or the absence of feedback processes within a family unit. Family structural models help us appreciate the significance of power and function. Understanding development theories may allow you to identify tasks necessary for further growth in individual, family, group, organizational, and community systems. Ecological and evolutionary perspectives may help explain how a particular phenomenon could represent an understandable adaptation to social and environmental circumstances. Behavior theories may enrich our understanding of the power of negative reinforcement (that is, the removal of aversive stimuli) in addictive processes and how the absence of reinforcement opportunities may contribute to emotional issues (such as depression), existential issues (such as alienation and despair), and social issues (such as criminal or antisocial activities). Economic models, particular contemporary versions that incorporate social and behavioral elements (Belsky & Gilovich, 2000), are often extremely relevant. Indeed, a plethora of theories may prove useful as you and your clients seek to understand and synthesize significant information about the concerns and circumstances. When supported by and combined with research-based knowledge, such theoretical understanding can contribute to the preparation of well-reasoned and well-supported hypotheses and the case formulations that emerge from them.

In the early stages of work with clients, the analysis and synthesis processes of assessment are tentative and speculative. You and your client do not usually have conclusive support or confirmation for a particular "theory of the case." Therefore, continue to view the results of your critical analysis as hypotheses or questions rather than as conclusions. When viewed in this tentative way, your hypotheses serve to guide the collection of additional information and sometimes help to identify possible interventions. For example, suppose you and members of your client system generate the following change-oriented hypotheses as part of your case formulation: (1) if community leaders and city officials offer a recently closed factory building to another company at a discounted rent and a lower tax rate, that company will relocate to our community; (2) if recently unemployed adults receive education and training in skills needed by that company, they will secure employment there; and (3) if the rate of community employment increases, there will be a decrease in crime, a decrease in high school dropout rates, and a decrease in SNAP (food stamp) applications. Such change-oriented hypotheses lead you and your clients to actions that might address and resolve the issues of concern.

During the assessment process, resist the temptation to conclude that you have "the key" or "the solution." Very few problems have one right answer. Most of the time, there are many plausible hypotheses and numerous potential solutions. Your professional challenge is to collaborate with clients to identify those change-oriented hypotheses most likely to be relevant and useful for each problem, each unique client system, and each set of circumstances.

Frequently, clients express hypotheses that both make logical sense and reflect reasonable consistency with your professional knowledge. When that occurs, you may wisely adopt or perhaps slightly adapt those hypotheses for use during your work together. Sometimes, however, clients' explanatory hypotheses and perhaps especially their change-oriented hypotheses constitute an obstacle to progress. For example, many clients (as well as many social workers) tend to view other people's (mis)behavior as the cause of identified problems. It logically follows that, if others' behavior causes the problem, then all we need to do is change their behavior and the problem will be resolved. That seems reasonable. Indeed, seeking to change others' behavior does, at times, seem to make good sense (for example, educating an elected official to vote for fair and just policies; helping a child learn a language; encouraging young people to adopt safe-sex practices). At other times, however, an attempt to change others constitutes a profoundly counterproductive and disempowering endeavor. For instance, suppose a woman holds herself in positive regard only when other people view her as physically attractive. Consequently, she regularly engages in compulsive and sometimes frantic behavior to elicit favorable reactions from others. That is, she tries to change others as a way to help herself feel better. However, her approach places the locus of power in other people's hands rather than in her own. Through their behavior, other people control her views and feelings about herself. Obviously, this is an extremely vulnerable position. Clothing, makeup, extreme diet and exercise, and cosmetic surgeries may become routine; as may various forms of seductive behavior. Nonetheless, when others do not notice or fail to acknowledge her attractiveness, or when another woman garners greater attention, her self-regard plummets and despair sets in. In such instances, the woman might benefit from consideration of alternate hypotheses—ones that place greater power and control in her own hands. For example, she might consider the hypothesis that she could decide to believe that she is inherently valuable simply because she exists rather than because others think she is attractive. She might hypothesize that she could judge her self-worth independently without regard to the views of others. Or, she might hypothesize that she could accept the assumption that questions of attractiveness are simply irrelevant to decisions about one's self-worth.

Fixed explanatory perspectives and limited ideas about potential solutions can be as problematic as the problems themselves. Indeed, we humans frequently seek to resolve problems by using the same problem-solving approaches that we have consistently used in the past. In fact, we sometimes repeat those very strategies that abjectly failed us in the past. In other words, we often do the same thing over and over again while expecting a different outcome.[4] When clients' explanatory and change-oriented hypotheses constitute part of the problem rather than part of the solution,[5] you may share one or more alternate hypotheses for their consideration. However, adopt a tentative and cautious approach. If your hypotheses obviously conflict with those of the client, they can negatively affect the working relationship and introduce another issue to address. The client may believe strongly that her or his views are correct or true and that yours are incorrect or false. Clients may vigorously defend their positions and view social workers who hold different perspectives as adversaries or opponents rather than collaborators. Sometimes, social workers also strongly believe that we are right; that our hypotheses are true; and that clients ought to defer to us, give up their beliefs, and accept ours. Unfortunately, when social workers adopt such positions, we risk damage to the cooperative, collaborative nature of our work with the people we call "clients."

Therefore, before you share yours, first reflect clients' hypotheses so that they know that you truly understand what they mean. Then, use the exploring skills to help clients examine their hypotheses in greater depth. Encourage them to ask questions about the validity, relevance, and utility of their views about why and how the issues occur; and about how to resolve them. In other words, ask them, in effect, to think critically about their own thinking. As a result of such exploration, clients may begin to see flaws in their hypotheses and become more receptive to alternate views. Then, you may ask them if they would be interested in hearing about another "theory."

---

[4] "Insanity is repeating the same mistakes and expecting different results" (Narcotics Anonymous, 2008, p. 23).
[5] In 1967, Charles Rosner wrote the following slogan for the Volunteers in Service to America (now AmeriCorps VISTA) program as part of a campaign to recruit volunteers: "If you're not part of the solution, you're part of the problem."

The simple act of asking, especially when preceded by hypothesis reflections and exploratory questions, can often increase clients' openness and cognitive flexibility.

Finally, before you share explanatory hypotheses ensure that they actually do a better job of explaining phenomena than do your client's. Insufficient, easily refuted explanations do not usually contribute to progress. Similarly, when you offer change-oriented hypotheses make sure that they are considerably more likely to contribute to goal attainment than are those of your client. Ideally, any change-oriented hypotheses that social workers share should reflect a strong rationale and a solid foundation in scientific theory, critical thought, or empirical evidence. And, as you share hypotheses, do so in a tentative manner; as something for clients to consider for themselves. Convey them in such a way that clients may freely evaluate their relevance and usefulness for themselves and their particular circumstances. Recognize clients' right to accept, reject, or propose alternative hypotheses. One way to emphasis clients' autonomy is to immediately follow the skill of sharing hypotheses with the skill of seeking feedback.

As you begin to practice the skill of sharing hypotheses, please use the formats outlined here. Later, when you gain greater proficiency, experiment with alternate versions.

PRACTICE FORMAT: SHARING EXPLANATORY HYPOTHESES

Would you be interested in considering another "theory" about how and why problems such as this one might occur? Yes? Okay. Well, in addition to your theory, we might also explain the problem in this way: _____. How does that sound to you?

EXAMPLE: SHARING EXPLANATORY HYPOTHESES

CLIENT: I'm sorry to say so but our 4-year-old son is basically a lazy and selfish child who does whatever he wants whenever he feels like it. He has just started preschool and the teachers report that he doesn't pay attention and often misbehaves. He's disobedient at home now too.

WORKER: (reflecting explanatory hypotheses) As you see it, your son has at least two fundamental flaws in his character. First, he's selfish and, second, he's lazy; and those two characteristics lead to problematic behavior both at home and in preschool. (seeking feedback) Is that accurate? Yes? Your theory about your son makes some sense—many children do seem to exhibit traits during childhood that continue on throughout their lives. (closed-ended question) However, I wonder if you might be interested in considering another possible explanation for such misbehavior? Yes? Okay. (sharing explanatory hypotheses) Well, if it's alright with you, I'd like to offer an alternate explanation for your son's behavior at home and school; an explanation that might also include what you consider to be his selfish and lazy traits. Briefly, I wonder if it might be possible that your 4-year-old son could be reacting to the fact that he has recently begun to attend preschool; that this represents a major change from the first 3 years of his life; and that the adjustment to that change might be reflected in what appears to be selfishness, laziness, and misbehavior? (seeking feedback) How does that sound to you?

PRACTICE FORMAT: SHARING CHANGE-ORIENTED HYPOTHESES

(*closed-ended question*) Would you be interested in considering another theory about how we might attempt to resolve this issue? Yes? Okay. Well there are, of course, many ways to make changes and sometimes, we must engage in a process of trial and error. However, in the case of addressing problems such as those you identified, there's a theory that seems to apply quite well. In brief, the theory goes something like this: (*sharing explanatory hypotheses*) ————————————————————. (*seeking feedback*) How does that sound to you?

EXAMPLE: SHARING CHANGE-ORIENTED HYPOTHESES

CLIENT: I think it's time to use the belt—just as my grandfather did with my father, and my father did with me. What's that biblical saying, "Spare the rod and spoil the child?"[6] I think we need to get serious here and punish him until he gets the message.

WORKER: (*reflecting change-oriented hypotheses*) So, you think that if you punish your 4-year-old son with a belt, he will become more obedient and improve his behavior. (*seeking feedback*) Is that accurate? Yes? (*reflecting change-oriented hypotheses*) Well, it's certainly possible that more severe punishment might help. (*closed-ended question*) I wonder, though, would you be interested in hearing about another theory about how parents might help their children learn to control their behavior? Yes? Okay. (*sharing change-oriented hypotheses*) Well, this theory is based on numerous research studies of childhood discipline. Some of that research does suggest that punishment can reduce misbehavior— especially in young children and particularly when the people who delivered the punishment are present. Following severe punishment, children usually become fearful of the people delivering the punishment, the location where the punishment takes place, and the instrument of punishment (for example, a paddle or belt). If the people who punished them are close by, the punished children may be able to refrain from misbehavior; although they often display signs of fear and agitation when doing so. Sometimes the children become so anxious about not misbehaving that they slip up and do so anyway. It's similar to people who are so concerned about making mistakes when speaking in public that they keep saying to themselves, "Don't make a mistake! Don't make a mistake!" The added stress and the emphasis on "mistakes" often increase the likelihood of making those very mistakes.

   On the other hand, when parents routinely look for, notice, and praise their children's positive behaviors and their growing abilities and do so in an enthusiastic manner, the kids tend to manage their behavior whether or not

---

[6] The phrase "spare the rod and spoil the child" is not an exact quote from the King James Bible. However, Proverbs 13:24 reads: "He that spareth his rod hateth his son: but he that loveth him chasteneth him betimes." Proverbs 23:13-14 reads: "Withhold not correction from a child: for if thou beatest him with the rod, he shall not die. Thou shalt beat him with a rod, and shalt deliver his soul from hell" and Proverbs 29:15 reads: "The rod and reproof give wisdom: but a child left *to himself* bringeth his mother to shame."

(continued)

their parents are present. Of course, consequences for misbehavior are needed. The consequences that seem to work best for young children are relatively modest ones—such as brief 2- to 3-minute periods in a chair that faces a blank wall. Instead of focusing only on rewards or only on punishments, a combination of both may be more effective. If that makes sense to you, we would figure out ways to deliver brief, modest consequences for misbehavior and provide lots and lots of enthusiastic praise for positive behavior. In fact, the emphasis would be on "catching him being good." (*seeking feedback*) How does that sound to you?

When sharing explanatory and change-oriented hypotheses, do so in a tentative fashion so that clients recognize that you do not expect nor need them to accept blindly whatever you say. In response to your use of the seeking feedback skill, many clients might respond, "Oh, that's interesting" or "I've never thought about it like that before" or "Let me think about that for a while" or, even, "My, that makes a lot of sense. The way I've been approaching this problem obviously hasn't worked; maybe your ideas might help."

EXERCISE 10-2: SHARING HYPOTHESES

For these exercises, assume that you are a social worker with a multipurpose social services agency. In the spaces provided, share hypotheses that you think might apply in these situations.

1. You have spent quite some time talking with Mr. K., a recently divorced 55-year-old man. He has explored a number of issues, expressed feelings, and shared ideas about how and why the divorce occurred and what he might do to recover from the loss. Reflect on the exchanges that occurred earlier (see Exercises 9-1 through 9-9; and 10-1), and then write the words you would use in sharing at least one explanatory and at least one change-oriented hypothesis that differs distinctly from any that Mr. K expressed. The hypotheses you share should relate to a problem, issue, or phenomenon reflected in the earlier exchanges and can reasonably be supported on the basis of strong logical, theoretical, or empirical grounds.

2. By now, you have spent quite a long time with Loretta, a homeless woman. She has mentioned a number of concerns, some aspirations, and shared thoughts and feelings about various aspects of her life and circumstances. Reflect on the exchanges that occurred earlier (see Exercises 9-1 through 9-9; and 10-1), and then write the words you would use in sharing at least one explanatory and at least one change-oriented hypothesis that differs distinctly from any that Loretta expressed. The hypotheses you share should relate to a problem, issue, or phenomenon reflected in the earlier exchanges and can reasonably be supported on the basis of strong logical, theoretical, or empirical grounds.

3. You have spent quite some time with the seven-member blended S. family. You and the family members have identified several issues: strain and conflict between Mr. S.'s children and Mrs. S., financial difficulties, marital distress, and most recently the threat to Mr. S.'s job. Reflect on the exchanges that occurred earlier (see Exercises 9-1 through 9-9; and 10-1), and then write the words you would use in sharing at least one explanatory and at least one change-oriented hypothesis that differs distinctly from any that members of the S. family expressed. The hypotheses you share should relate to a problem, issue, or phenomenon reflected in the earlier exchanges and can reasonably be supported on the basis of strong logical, theoretical, or empirical grounds.

4. You have now talked with Mrs. F. for quite some time. You've explored several issues, including her feeling that she and her family do not fit in this community, her children's apparently increasing disrespect for her and their Latin heritage, and, most importantly, the concern for her children's safety at school. Reflect on the exchanges that occurred earlier (see Exercises 9-1 through 9-9; and 10-1), and then write the words you would use in sharing at least one explanatory and at least one change-oriented hypothesis that differs distinctly from any that Mrs. F. expressed. The hypotheses you share should relate to a problem, issue, or phenomenon reflected in the earlier exchanges and can reasonably be supported on the basis of strong logical, theoretical, or empirical grounds.

5. In your role as organizational consultant, you have now met quite a few times with a large group of staff and board members and other stakeholders in an attempt to clarify and then resolve several problems within the agency. Numerous issues have already been identified and you have observed people as they interacted with each other during earlier meetings. Reflect on the exchanges that occurred earlier (see Exercises 9-1 through 9-9; and 10-1), and then write the words you would use in sharing at least one explanatory and at least one change-oriented hypothesis that differs distinctly from any that participants expressed. The hypotheses you share should relate to a problem, issue, or phenomenon reflected in the earlier exchanges and can reasonably be supported on the basis of strong logical, theoretical, or empirical grounds.

Clarifying Issues for Work

Clarifying issues for work constitutes the first definitive indication that you and the client agree to work together toward resolving certain problems. Simply stated, clarified or focal issues are those that the participants agree to address. The focal issues assume a prominent place in the contract portion of the Description, Assessment, and Contract (DAC).[7] Usually, you derive the problems or issues for work from those the client has identified, those you have contributed, or some negotiated combination or compromise of the two. Whatever their source, these agreed-upon issues provide a focus and context for all your subsequent professional activities. Whenever possible, state the focal issues for work in clear and descriptive terms. Record them in the contract portion of the DAC.

Clarifying issues for work follows naturally from the processes of exploration and assessment. Typically, you use the skills of reflecting and identifying issues before you and clients jointly agree on the specific problems or issues to address. When you clarify issues, you make a commitment that your work together will focus primarily on these particular areas. In practicing this skill, consider the format outlined below.

PRACTICE FORMAT: CLARIFYING ISSUES FOR WORK

I think we agree about the primary issues that we will address in our work together. Let's review them, and write them down so that we can refer to them as we go along. First, there is the issue of _____. Second, the issue of _____. Third, _____. What do you think? Is this an accurate list of the issues that we'll focus upon?

EXAMPLE: CLARIFYING ISSUES FOR WORK

CASE SITUATION: A woman has identified two major issues for which she sought help from your agency. You have contributed a third issue. You have explored them all in considerable detail and done so from a person-in-environment perspective.

CLIENT: Well, that's my story. I hope you can help with the mess I'm in.

WORKER: I hope so too. It seems to me that we have identified three major issues to address during our work together. Let's review them once more, and jot them down so that we can refer to them as we go along. First, there is the issue of housing. You have been living on the street now for 3 weeks and the weather is beginning to turn cold. Second, there is the diabetes. You have been without medicine for a week now and you have no insurance or money to pay for it. Third, you lost your job 2 months ago and need to find work so you can make some money. What do you think? Is this an accurate list of the issues that we'll address together?

As you and your clients clarify issues for work, record them in a coherent fashion for ready reference. You could prepare a simple outline (like the one presented in Box 10.2) or a concept map (see Figure 10.2). Both forms serve that purpose well. Be sure to provide a copy to all clients—even to those who have written them in their own notebooks.

---

[7] Appendix 14 contains an example of a completed DAC.

F I G U R E 10.2

Sample Concept Map of Focal Problems/Issues for Work

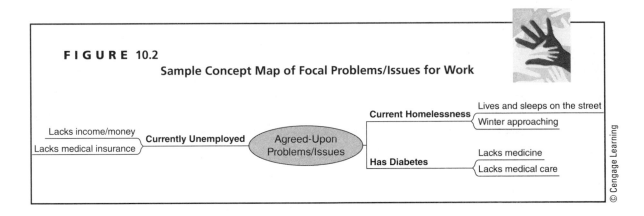

© Cengage Learning

EXERCISE 10-3: CLARIFYING ISSUES FOR WORK

For these exercises, assume that you are a social worker with a multipurpose social services agency. Review relevant earlier exercises and your responses to them and then, in the spaces provided, write the words you would say in clarifying issues with each client. Use the format suggested earlier. However, feel free to be somewhat creative in your response. You cannot actually exchange ideas with these clients so you must adopt a certain amount of flexibility in clarifying issues for work.

1. Refer to Exercises 9-1 through 9-9, and 10-1 and 10-2, and then write the words you would use to clarify issues for work as they might apply to Mr. K.

2. Refer to Exercises 9-1 through 9-9, and 10-1 and 10-2, and then write the words you would use to clarify issues for work as they might apply to Loretta.

3. Refer to Exercises 9-1 through 9-9, and 10-1 and 10-2, and then write the words you would use to clarify issues for work as they might apply to the seven-member S. family.

4. Refer to Exercises 9-1 through 9-9, and 10-1 and 10-2, and then write the words you would use to clarify issues for work as they might apply to Mrs. F. or her family.

5. Refer to Exercises 9-1 through 9-9, and 10-1 and 10-2, and then write the words you would use to clarify issues for work as they might apply to the troubled social service agency that has retained you as a social work consultant.

Organizing Descriptive Information

Most social work interviews do not occur in such a logical fashion that a transcript of the interaction between worker and client would represent a coherent description of the available information. Therefore your first step in the assessment process is to organize the information gained through exploration into a form that allows for efficient retrieval and examination. Typically, this involves arranging data according to certain categories that you and agency professionals consider significant.

Regardless of the organizational format used, be sure to distinguish clearly between reported and observed information. Indicate that ideas or conclusions resulting from speculation or inference, and deduction or induction, are opinions or hypotheses. Differentiate them from factual data. Assertions or opinions are not facts and we should never present them as such.

Descriptive organization allows you to present information that you read, observe, or hear in a coherent fashion. Note the date and source of data. In settings where a particular individual is identified as the formal client,[8] you may include information in the description part of the DAC in accordance with the guidelines contained in Box 10.3 (see Appendix 14 for a completed example). Remember, however, that many portions of the format will not apply to some of the individuals, dyads, families, groups, organizations, and communities that you serve. Ultimately, our purpose for the descriptive section is to organize relevant data gathered during the exploration phase into a coherent, understandable representation of the client system; the issues or problems of concern; and various situational factors that pertain to the client system and those concerns. The structure of any particular format used to organize the descriptive data is not especially important. What is important is that the data be presented in a coherent and easily accessible fashion.

BOX 10.3

Guidelines for Completion of the DAC Description: Individual

I. **Description**
   A. **Identification and Contact Information**

   In this section, place information that identifies the individual client and other relevant members of the person-in-environment systems. Data such as names and ages of household members, birth dates, insurance identification numbers, home addresses, places of work, telephone numbers, e-mail addresses, names and contact information of family doctors, and people to notify in case of emergency may be included. Note the date and place of the interview. Record your own name as the interviewer.

   B. **Person, Family and Household, and Community Systems**
      1. **Person System**

      In this section, provide additional biopsychosocial information about the client. Whenever possible, use information that comes from clients, referral sources, and your direct observations, rather than from your inferences. Also, identify the source of the information (for example, "Mr. M. stated that he has been a member of the local

   (continued)

---

[8] In many contexts, an entire family may be served even though one member of that family is formally designated as "the client" (for example, a child or teenager). Similarly, each participant in a social work group is commonly considered an "individual client," and relevant descriptive, assessment, and contracting information about him or her is included in a case record.

BOX 10.3 *(continued)*

congregational church since he was a child and serves as an elder on the church board of directors." Or, "I observed that the client walked with a limp. She seems to have some difficulty with her left leg." Or, "Mrs. Jimenez says that she has a heart condition."). Quote significant words or phrases that the client uses in self-description. Be careful to use language that enhances the description rather than stereotypes the person. For example, the statement "Mary is a 45-year-old, white, divorced female" tends to emphasize age, race, and marital status in a manner that could unnecessarily narrow the focus. Contrast that with this description, "Mary describes herself as a person with a 'great deal of energy and zest for life.' She describes herself as 'single and happy to be so.' She says she 'just turned 45 years old but feels 30.'"

Information based on your own observations of clients, such as their approximate height and weight, physical appearance, striking or characteristic features, speech patterns, and clothing may be included in this section. However, ensure that such information is actually relevant for the purpose of assessment and mention that it derives from your own observations.

2. **Family and Household System**

In this section, describe the client's family and household, or primary social system. If you have not included them elsewhere, include names, ages, and telephone numbers and addresses of significant people. Family genograms and household eco-maps are useful tools for organizing this information. Cite the source of information and quote significant words and phrases. It may be easier to attach a genogram to the document rather than trying to include it within the description. When you do so, simply insert a notation such as "See attached genogram dated January 13."

3. **Community System**

In this section, describe the community system within which the identified client functions. Indicate the source of the information and include systems such as school, work, medical, recreational, religious, neighborhood, ethnic, cultural, and friendship affiliations whenever appropriate. The eco-map is an especially valuable tool for presenting this kind of information and can be included in this section. It may be easier to attach an eco-map to the document rather than trying to include it within the description. When you do so, simply insert a notation such as "See attached eco-map dated January 13."

C. **Presenting Problems/Issues of Concern**

In this section, describe the presenting problems or issues of concern as identified by the client or responsible party (for example, parent, guardian, judge, teacher, or medical doctor). Clearly identify the source of the information and summarize the origin, development, and status of each primary problem/issue. Quote significant words and phrases that help to describe needs, problems/issues, concerns, or goals. In this section, outline how the prospective client came to seek social services at this time. Also, if identified, record the initial, desired outcome or goal as envisioned by the client or responsible party. Unless the situation is of such an urgent or life-threatening nature that you must take immediate action, postpone your own view of the problems/issues and goals until you and the client undertake a more thorough exploration and assessment.

D. **Assets, Resources, and Strengths**

In this section, record information concerning the assets, resources, and strengths available within the client-and-situation systems. You may make note of competencies, social

(continued)

BOX 10.3 *(continued)*

supports, successes, and life lessons, along with specific resources such as the involvement of concerned relatives, sufficient financial assets, optimistic attitudes, or high energy levels. Be sure to include those aspects that might influence or moderate the presenting problems and issues. Identify the source of this information about assets, strengths, and resources. The source might be the client, a family member, a previous social worker, or your own observations. Where possible, quote significant descriptive words and phrases. As a social worker, you encourage identification of strengths and resources to provide a balanced picture—one not solely characterized by needs, problems, concerns, and deficiencies. In addition, certain assets, strengths, competencies, and resources often become extremely relevant later when we seek to identify and use protective factors during the assessing, contracting, and the working and evaluating phases of work.

E. **Referral Source and Process; Collateral Information**
Summarize information concerning the source of the referral (who suggested or required that the identified client make contact with you) and the process by which the referral occurred. You may present information provided by sources other than the identified client or the client system (for example, family member or a close friend) here. Cite the source by name, role, or position, and phone number. Try to quote specific words and phrases used in describing the person-issue-situation and the events that prompted the referral (for example, "When Dr. Muhammad called to refer Mrs. Malbi, he said she is severely depressed.").

F. **Social History**
In this section, include summary information about the identified client's social history and current social circumstances. You may include or attach one or more timelines in this section. Include data that is relevant to the purpose for your involvement. Do not include extraneous information just because "it is interesting." It should relate to the person-issue-situation. Cite the source of the information (for example, the client, a family member, or your own observations) and quote significant words and phrases wherever possible. In describing historical information, recognize that experiences may have consequences that are energy enhancing, growth promoting, liberating, and empowering, as well as energy depleting, growth limiting, oppressive, disenfranchising, or traumatic. As you describe historical information, be sure to reflect, where indicated, those aspects that represent strengths or successes. You may use a "successes timeline" in this context. Other kinds of timelines may be used to summarize relevant historical information (for example, developmental, relationship, familial, critical events, sexual, alcohol or drug use, educational, or employment).

Depending on the agency program, your social work function, and the specific circumstances of the person-issue-situation, this section could contain some or all of the following subsections.

II. **Developmental**
A. You might include a description of a client's developmental history. You might provide information such as the nature of the client's birth, infancy, childhood, adolescent, and adult developmental processes. Specific information regarding events or experiences might be included here.

1. **Personal, Familial, and Cultural**
You may summarize here information concerning the significant past and present personal, familial, and cultural relationships. You may include significant processes and events that influenced the client's biopsychosocial development and behavior.

(continued)

BOX 10.3 *(continued)*

2.   **Critical Events**

Summarize events or situations that might have been significant in some way. Identify liberating, empowering, or growth-enhancing processes and events such as successes, accomplishments, achievements, and experiences that may have enhanced psychosocial functioning. Also identify critical events such as violence, abuse, rape or molestation, suicides or suicide attempts, victimization, oppression, and discrimination that may have had traumatic effects. Describe how these experiences affected the client.

3.   **Sexual**

You may include here, if relevant to the social work purpose, information related to the person's sexual development and history.

4.   **Alcohol and Drug Use**

Because alcohol and drug abuse is so prevalent in our society, unless this topic is clearly irrelevant to the social work purpose, it is frequently useful to explore and summarize clients' history in these areas.

5.   **Medical/Physical/Biological**

Summarize here the person's medical and physical history. This might include identification of illnesses, injuries, disabilities, and current physical health and well-being. If relevant, you may refer to the medical history of family members or conditions that appear to have some genetic or hereditary influence. When applicable, you could include or attach a family medical genogram or pedigree. Be sure to include the date and results of the client's most recent physical examination. If not recorded earlier, the client's family doctor or source of medical care should be identified.

6.   **Legal**

Include here, as relevant, history of involvement in the criminal justice and legal system as well as pertinent information such as citizen or residency status, custody, or guardianship.

7.   **Educational**

Summarize the client's educational history. Both formal and informal educational experiences may be noted.

8.   **Employment**

Include here the client's employment history, including military and volunteer experiences.

9.   **Recreational**

Where applicable, summarize recreational and avocational activities that the client has undertaken over the years. Often, these endeavors constitute strengths or resources.

10.   **Religious/Spiritual**

Summarize current and past religious and spiritual affiliations and activities, and their meaning and significance for the client. Aspects of this dimension often represent strengths or resources. Sometimes, however, certain religious beliefs or practices relate to the problem/issue.

11.   **Prior Psychological, Social, or Medical Services**

Summarize here previous involvement with psychological, social, and medical services that may relate to the person-issue-situation. Where relevant, identify the names, addresses, and telephone numbers of agencies and service providers.

12.   **Other**

Include here any additional, relevant historical and developmental information.

Appendix 14 contains an example of a completed DAC. Review it now to see how information about the case of Mrs. Lynn Chase might be organized into the description section of the DAC. Please recognize, however, that most individual or family descriptions are not nearly as comprehensive in nature as the one created for Mrs. Chase. You should not view the format as a guide for data collection. Rather, the format represents one possible way to organize relevant data that has been gathered. There are many other formats. Indeed, several of the subsections contained in this particular format could easily be merged into one or two. Also, remember that a key focus for the organization of data remains the problems, issues, or goals as presented by clients. Our clients' aspirations remain central. As a result, many dimensions suggested as possible subsections in Box 10.3 (and illustrated in the example contained in Appendix 14) would be irrelevant to clients concerned with different issues.

In working with larger systems (for example, naturally formed groups, organizations, and communities), different formats may help us organize relevant information. Box 10.4 contains one—but only one—possible structure.

BOX 10.4

**Guidelines for Completion of the DAC Description:
Natural Group, Organization, or Community**

I. **Description**
   A. **Identification and Contact Information**
      In this section, place information that identifies the people with whom you first interact and those expected to join you in your collaborative work together. In the case of a community group or organization, it might be the formal leaders or a subgroup that initiated contact or responded to your invitation. Data such as names, home addresses, places of work, telephone numbers, e-mail addresses, may be included. Sometimes, for example, in work with a group of street-based sex workers or members of a youth gang, participants may prefer to remain partially or completely anonymous. Note the date and, if useful, the place of the interview. Record your own name as the interviewer.

   B. **Client System**
      In this section, provide additional psychosocial information about the natural group, organization, or community with which you expect to work. Include information that comes from others as well as your direct observations. In the descriptive section, avoid opinions, conclusions, or hypotheses based on your own inferences. Also, identify the source of the information (for example, "Ms. P stated that she and several other sex workers in the 11th Street area have been hit with stones thrown by passersby. She said it has happened about three or four times weekly for the last month or so." Or, "Mrs. Johnson, the president of the organization's board of directors, stated that their agency will close within 6 months if they fail to secure additional funding." Or, "I observed that as we talked about the stone throwing, the women routinely scanned the street and sidewalks. Sometimes, one or two would briefly step away to talk with potential customers."). Quote significant words or phrases that the client uses in self-description. Use language that enhances the description rather than stereotypes people or groups.

      You may include social network maps, or organizational charts. Cite the source or sources of information. It may be easier to attach graphical data to the document rather than trying to include it within the description. When you do so, simply insert a notation such as: "See attached organizational chart dated October 24."

      Information based on your own observations of the people involved may be included in this section. However, ensure that such information is actually relevant for the purpose of assessment and mention that it derives from your own observations.

      (continued)

BOX 10.4 *(continued)*

C. **Social and Physical/Ecological Environment**

In this section, describe the social and physical/ecological environment within which the natural group, organization, or community exists and functions. Indicate the source of the information and include systems such as competing and cooperating groups, organizations, and communities with which the client system does or could interact. Eco-maps are often valuable tools for presenting this kind of information and can be included in this section. Geographical maps may be included (for example, to identify the territory of a particular gang or the boundaries of a community). It may be easier to attach an eco-map to the document rather than trying to include it within the description. When you do so, simply insert a notation such as "See attached map dated January 13."

D. **Presenting Problems/Issues of Concern**

In this section, describe the presenting problems or issues of concern as identified by members of the client system. Clearly identify the source of the information and summarize the origin, development, and status of each primary problem/issue. Quote significant words and phrases that help to describe needs, problems/issues, concerns, or goals. In this section, outline how contact was initiated and by whom; also, if identified, record the initial, desired outcome or goal as envisioned by members of the client system. Unless the situation is of such an urgent or life-threatening nature that you must take immediate action, postpone your own view of the problems or issues and goals until you and members of the natural group, organization, or community undertake a more thorough exploration and assessment.

E. **Assets, Resources, and Strengths**

In this section, record information concerning the assets, resources, and strengths available within the client system and the social and physical/ecological environment. You may make note of competencies, social supports, successes, and life lessons, along with specific resources such as the involvement of concerned others, sufficient financial assets, optimistic attitudes, or high energy levels. Be sure to include those aspects that might influence or moderate the presenting problems and issues. Identify the source of this information about assets, strengths, and resources. The source might be one or more members of the client system or others who value them. It might be a previous social worker or consultant, or your own observations. Where possible, quote significant descriptive words and phrases. As social workers, we encourage identification of strengths and resources to provide a balanced picture—one not solely characterized by needs, problems, concerns, and deficiencies. In addition, certain assets, strengths, competencies, and resources often become extremely relevant later when we seek to identify and use protective factors during the assessing, contracting, and the working and evaluating phases of work.

F. **Referral Source and Process; Collateral Information**

Sometimes others make the first contact with you or your agency on behalf of a natural group, organization, or community. When that occurs, summarize information concerning the source of the referral and the process by which it occurred. You may present information provided by referral sources. Cite the source by name, role, or position, and phone number. Try to quote specific words and phrases used in describing the problems, situation, and the events that prompted the referral (for example, "When Rabbi Cohen called to express his concern about a group of youths congregating near the Hebrew Academy, he mentioned that several of the boys wore Nazi swastikas.").

(continued)

BOX 10.4 *(continued)*

G. History

In this section, include summary information about the history and current circumstances of the natural group, organization, or community. You may include or attach one or more timelines in this section. Include data that are relevant to the purpose for your involvement. Do not include extraneous information just because "it is interesting." It should relate to the client system, the identified issues, or goals. Cite the source of the information and quote significant words and phrases wherever possible. In describing historical information, recognize that historical experiences may have present-day or potential consequences that are energy enhancing, growth promoting, liberating, and empowering, as well as energy depleting, growth limiting, oppressive, disenfranchising, or traumatic. As you describe historical information, be sure to incorporate, where indicated, those aspects that represent strengths or successes. You may use a "successes timeline" in this context. Other kinds of timelines may be used to summarize relevant historical information (for example, developmental, critical events, or "eras").

Depending on the agency program in which you serve, your social work function, and the specific circumstances of the client system, this section could contain some or all of the following subsections.

1. **Developmental**

   You might include a description of the origin and development of the group, organization, or community. You might provide information about the original formation of the group, establishment of the organization, or foundation of the community. Specific information regarding notable development-related events or experiences might be included here.

2. **Social and Cultural**

   You may summarize here information concerning the cultural aspects of the client system. For example, a natural group of young people hanging out outside a neighborhood thrift store may be of working-class background. Many of their fathers or mothers lost their jobs in a recent plant closure. The group of sex workers on 11th Street may be first- or second-generation immigrants—perhaps from a particular region of the world. An organization's board of directors may reflect a single ethnic group, the executive director another, whereas the staff members may reflect considerable ethnic diversity. A community may include three more or less distinct neighborhoods. One is predominantly European American, Catholic, and working class in composition. A second is racially, ethnically, and religiously mixed and includes people from both the working and professional classes. The third is almost exclusively European American, Protestant, and well-to-do.

3. **Critical Events**

   If not described earlier, you may summarize events or situations of significance to the client system in some way. Identify liberating, empowering, or growth-enhancing processes and events such as successes, accomplishments, achievements, and experiences that may have enhanced social functioning. Also identify events that negatively affected the system. In work with youth gangs, for example, the murder of a beloved leader may have triggered a war with a rival gang believed responsible for his death. An organization may have once laid off 25 percent of its staff to forestall bankruptcy. A neighborhood may have been flooded by a hurricane, flattened by a tornado, or destroyed by a fire. A community may have been hit by a dangerous epidemic of influenza. These and other such events may have seriously affected the group, organization, or community. Include descriptive information about these critical events.

(continued)

BOX 10.4 *(continued)*

4. **Legal**

    If not included in other sections, describe relevant contact with the criminal justice and legal system as well as pertinent information such as citizen or residency status of members of the client system. For example, a previous director of an organization may have embezzled funds and a trial is about to start. Key members of a gang may be in jail or prison, or a police task force may be targeting violent youth gangs for special attention, arrest, and prosecution. Two homes in a neighborhood may have been foreclosed by banks and another may recently have been burglarized. A community association may have filed a lawsuit to restrain the city from building a highway that would split a neighborhood in half—fragmenting a community that originated nearly two centuries earlier.

5. **Financial**

    If relevant to the purpose for your involvement, you may include here the client system's sources of and amounts of income as well as expenditures. Sometimes financial factors are associated with the onset or continuation of problems or could be involved in the achievement of goals. For example, a youth gang may acquire money through drug sales, theft, or the "protection" of businesses and neighborhoods. An organization may secure funding through grants and fees, or sales of goods and services. A community may depend upon a local factory for employment.

6. **Prior Social Services**

    Summarize here previous involvement with social or consultative services that may relate to the client system and its presenting issues and goals. Where relevant, identify the names, addresses, and telephone numbers of service providers.

7. **Other**

    Include here any additional, relevant information.

EXERCISE 10-4: ORGANIZING DESCRIPTIVE INFORMATION

1. For this exercise, assume that you are your own client. Use a word-processing program to draft the description section of a written record as if you are a social worker who learned what you know about yourself as a person and about your situation. Identify one or two problems/issues or goals for which you might conceivably consult a social worker. As do all human beings, social workers also confront problems and issues of various kinds throughout the course of life. Such challenges are inevitable. Therefore, build on the self-understanding exercises that you undertook in Chapter 2 by organizing information about yourself and your situation into a descriptive record. Use the DAC format to prepare the description portion of a personal case record for inclusion in a separate part of your Social Work Skills Learning Portfolio. Be sure to attach your genogram, eco-map, and critical events timeline. In creating your case record, it might be prudent to disguise your own identity. After all, these materials reflect a great deal about yourself and your own personal life. Instead of your full name, you might create pseudonyms to identify yourself and the significant people in your life. Create a separate folder entitled "A Personal Case Record" to hold these materials in your portfolio.

Preparing an Assessment and Case Formulation

After recording the available descriptive information, begin to prepare an assessment and preliminary case formulation (that is, a "theory of the case"). As you do with descriptive data, organize the results of your analysis and synthesis into a coherent structure. The particular format varies from agency to agency, program to program, and indeed from client to client. Nonetheless, virtually all social work assessment schemes refer in one way or another to various theoretical dimensions and include consideration of the client system, problems and issues, and circumstances. The organizing structure may be derived from a single theoretical perspective or, eclectically, from several. On occasion, the assessment may even be atheoretical. Sometimes you and clients apply common sense and logic to develop: (1) explanatory hypotheses to understand particular problems, people, and circumstances, and (2) change-oriented hypotheses that lead to goals and plans for action and evaluation.

Whether theoretical or atheoretical in nature, the assessment process enables you and your clients to reach agreement about a "theory of the case." You develop explanatory hypotheses about risk factors and those conditions that affect and maintain problems. You hypothesize about strengths, assets, competencies, resources, and protective factors that could help in resolution. In addition, you seek to determine the client's current readiness and motivation to address particular problems or issues.

Building upon your explanatory hypotheses, you and your client develop change-oriented hypotheses to identify other people or systems that could or should be involved in the helping process. You collaboratively determine potential targets for change—those aspects that, if altered, might resolve the issue. You identify potential obstacles or barriers to progress as well. You predict probable consequences if things remain the same and assess risk to determine how urgently intervention must be undertaken. In addition, you jointly consider potentially applicable intervention approaches, modalities, strategies, tasks, activities, and techniques and assess their probability of success. Finally, you determine a time frame for work and develop ways and means to evaluate progress.

We mentioned concept maps when we discussed the exploring phase. Similar to genograms and eco-maps in form, concept maps are graphic illustrations that capture significant and relevant ideas or information. You might use them to organize thoughts and observations about various phenomena related to the biopsychosocial aspects of the person-issue-situation (for example, problems, goals, hypotheses, action steps, evaluation processes). Concept maps are especially useful in the assessment and contracting phases as you and the client develop a theory of the case—often with the aid of a functional analysis.

Functional analyses, also known as functional assessments or functional behavioral assessments, help the worker and client recognize and highlight those factors that bear a functional relationship to a particular problem or issue of concern and, potentially, to its resolution. Notice that we generally avoid the term *cause* or *causal* to refer to these relationships. Based on the data collected during the exploring phase, we cannot reasonably support a claim that particular factors "cause" a problem or issue. However, we can usually identify factors—including risk and protective factors—that are associated with the problematic phenomena. Based on these functional relationships, clients and workers can begin to generate change-oriented hypotheses. That is, we hypothesize that a change in one or more of these associated factors will lead to a change in the problem or issue. Of course, unless tested, change-oriented hypotheses remain hypothetical. We cannot be certain of the outcome until action takes place. Nomothetic research evidence may provide information about the relative probability that a certain intervention or action will lead to a particular outcome. However, we also need idiographic evidence to "test" our change-oriented hypotheses. In other words, we must evaluate progress to determine if our hypotheses are credible.

Functional analyses contribute to an understanding or tentative explanation of the relationship of various biopsychosocial and environmental factors to the focal issues. They also lead to change-oriented hypotheses about how best to pursue the established goals (Cone, 1997; Haynes, 1998; Haynes, Leisen, & Blaine, 1997; O'Neill et al., 1997; Virués-Ortega & Haynes, 2005). Functional analysis builds upon the data collected during the exploring phase of work as the worker and client address questions such as:

◆ "How did the problem/issue begin?" "When?" "Under what circumstances?"
◆ "How has the problem/issue changed since it first began?" "When has it been better?" "When has it been worse?"
◆ "How often does the problem/issue occur now?"
◆ "Where and when does the problem/issue occur?"
◆ "How intense, serious, or severe is the problem/issue?"
◆ "How long does an episode of the problem/issue last?"

As suggested by Table 10.1, completion of the exploration phase of work should result in considerable information about the onset, development, and evolution of the problem/issue; its frequency, intensity, and duration; and the situational context in which it occurs. Adopting biopsychosocial and environmental perspectives, we also organize information about those phenomena that precede, accompany, and follow occurrences of the problem. In work with individuals, we are interested in beliefs, behaviors, feelings, and sensations (that is, biological phenomena) associated with problematic episodes. In addition to person-related factors, we also seek to identify situation-related factors that occur before, during, and following an occurrence. You may gather this information during the exploring phase when you and your clients address questions such as:

◆ "What thoughts or images go through your mind just before an episode of the problem/issue?"
◆ "What thoughts or images go through your mind during an episode of the problem/issue?"
◆ "What thoughts or images go through your mind just following an episode of the problem/ issue?"
◆ "What are you doing just before an occurrence of the problem/issue?"
◆ "What are you doing during an occurrence of the problem/issue?"
◆ "What are you doing just following an occurrence of the problem/issue?"

T A B L E 10.1
Focal Issue: Excessive Alcohol Consumption—John C.

Onset	Onset 16 months ago when wife initiated divorce proceedings
Evolution	Gradual worsening; better for about 1 week when he and spouse attempted reconciliation
Frequency	Daily episodes
Situational Context	Drinks exclusively in his living room in the evening; falls asleep afterward
Intensity/Severity	7–10 ounces of vodka each episode
Duration	Each episode lasts about 3–4 hours

© Cengage Learning

- "What feelings or emotions do you experience just before an occurrence of the problem/issue?"
- "What feelings or emotions do you experience during an occurrence of the problem/issue?"
- "What feelings or emotions do you experience just after an occurrence of the problem/issue?"
- "What sensations[9] do you experience just before an episode of the problem/issue?"
- "What sensations do you experience during an episode of the problem/issue?"
- "What sensations do you experience just following an episode of the problem/issue?"

In work with individuals alone or as members of a family or group, it may help to organize your functional analysis in tabular form (see Table 10.2).

TABLE 10.2
Functional Analysis Focal Issue: Excessive Alcohol Consumption—John C.

	Distant or Historical Antecedent Factors	Proximate Antecedent Factors	Co-occurring Factors	Subsequential Factors
Self-Statements, Beliefs or Images	Remembers what happened during his childhood when his father and mother divorced.	"I'm alone again." "I'll always be alone." "Life is unbearable without my wife." "When can I get a drink—it will help me feel better?" Pictures his father's bitterness and unhappiness.	"Ahh, that feels better." "It's her (my wife's) fault." "Someday she'll realize what she's done."	"I'm not an alcoholic." "I'm not going to end up like my father. This is just temporary with me."
Behaviors	Remembers unsuccessful attempts to comfort his father—who sat every night in front the TV drinking beer.	Enters living room.	During weekdays, he drinks vodka with tonic water continuously from about 6:00 P.M. until he falls asleep at about 11:00 P.M. On weekends, he begins drinking at about 1:00 P.M.	Loses consciousness and falls asleep.
Feelings	Remembers feeling pity for his father and anger at his mother for initiating the divorce.	Anger, loneliness, stress, sadness	Becomes less angry and stressed. Sadness remains but less intense.	Guilt and remorse upon awakening.

(continued)

---

[9] Clients' experience of their own bodily sensations is most relevant when working with individuals and in some multimember systems. In work with dyads, families, small groups, communities, organizations, and societies, we are often interested in factors such as commonly held beliefs and attitudes, norms, mores, and emotional climate.

T A B L E 10.2 *(continued)* **Functional Analysis Focal Issue: Excessive Alcohol Consumption—John C.**				
Sensations	Remembers headaches, stomachaches, and tension during childhood.	Agitation, tension, tearfulness	Senses become dulled; bodily tension seems to lessen; tears stop.	Awakens next morning feeling somewhat hung over with increasingly strong urge for an alcoholic drink.
Situational Context	John C.'s wife filed for divorce from him 18 months earlier.	Arrives home from work in the early evening. Stays home on weekends.	Watches TV in larger reclining chair.	Falls asleep.

© Cengage Learning

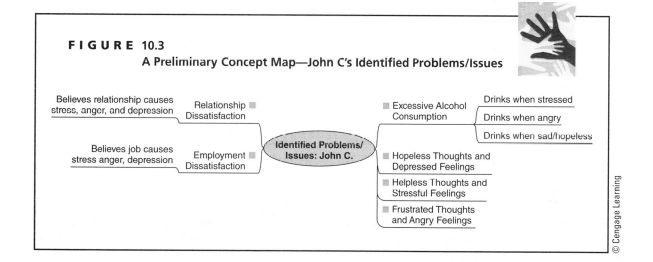

FIGURE 10.3

A Preliminary Concept Map—John C's Identified Problems/Issues

© Cengage Learning

You may prepare a similar table for those times or circumstances when a problem or issue is "not a problem," "less of a problem," or when clients are "coping well with the problem." Concepts maps may help as well. Figure 10.3 contains a preliminary concept map of how a worker and client might track aspects of the problems and issues John C. identifies. In this example, he reports feeling dissatisfied in his relationship and in his work. He frequently experiences thoughts and feelings associated with stress, anger, and sadness or depression; and drinks excessively when he feels stressed, angry, or sad. Together the worker and client establish that excessive drinking represents the highest priority focal issue, and negative thoughts and feelings represent the next most important. They also decide to defer work related to the job and relationship dissatisfaction until they make progress on the others.

Box 10.5 contains guidelines for completing the assessment and case formulation parts of the DAC (see Appendix 14 for a completed example). The assessment derives from information presented in the description portion of the DAC. However, do not use the assessment section to repeat material. Instead, refer to descriptive information to support explanatory and change-oriented hypotheses that you and the client generate. In a sense, the assessment and case formulation portion of the DAC represent an argument that involves "claims" supported by descriptive evidence.

BOX 10.5

Guidelines for Completion of the DAC Assessment and Case Formulation

II. Tentative Assessment[10]
  A. **Problems or Issues**
    1. **Nature, Duration, Frequency, Severity, and Urgency**

Analyze information gained during the exploration phase and reported in the description section to capture the nature and essence of the problems or issues of concern. Go beyond the earlier description to offer explanatory hypotheses about "why" they are of concern and "how" they came to be so at this particular time. Include the client's as well as your own explanatory hypotheses about the problems or issues of concern. Incorporate professional and scientific knowledge to enhance understanding of the identified problems or issues.

Where available, include the results of questionnaires, surveys, and other assessment instruments as well as "pretest" or baseline rating data (for example, frequency or intensity of problem occurrence during the interval between initial contact and first face-to-face meeting). In your assessment of issues and problems, incorporate or make reference to tables or concept maps and to narrative discussion about their duration, frequency, severity, and urgency.

    2. **Risk and Protective Factors; Exceptions**

In this section, propose explanatory hypotheses about risk factors and conditions that contribute to the onset, development, or continuation of the problems/issues. Specify factors that seem to trigger, accompany, and follow occurrences of the problems or issues of concern. You may incorporate or attach a functional analysis table as a summary (see Table 10.2 for an example).

If relevant, assess the risk of suicide, homicide, violence, abuse, neglect, and substance misuse. Generate hypotheses about risks to the client system, and to other people and social systems if things continue as they are. That is, what is likely to happen if the problems or issues remain unresolved? Also, anticipate potential consequences of successful resolution. How will the client system change when the problems are resolved? How will other people and social systems react to those changes? Recognize that certain negative effects may accompany positive change.

Hypothesize about circumstances and conditions that inhibit, impede, or prevent emergence or reemergence of the problems/issues. Refer to protective factors, strengths, and to exceptions—those times when and where the problems/issues do not occur—and offer explanatory hypotheses about these exceptions. Support your explanatory hypotheses by incorporating or referencing tables, concept maps, or narrative information contained in the descriptive section. However, avoid unnecessary repetition of descriptive content.

Hypothesize about aspects of the client system and circumstances that represent challenges, obstacles, or barriers to resolution of the problems/issues. If applicable, make reference to deficiencies in basic needs for money, shelter, food, clothing, and social and intellectual stimulation, as well as to social, political, and cultural obstacles such as oppression and discrimination. As needed, hypothesize about the impact of environmental conditions such as overcrowding, inadequate or excessive stimulation, and the presence of toxic materials.

---

[10] Appendix 14 contains an example of a completed DAC.

(continued)

BOX 10.5 *(continued)*

B. **Contributing Factors**
  1. **Client System Factors**

     If the problems or issues of concern involve specific individuals (for example, someone is unemployed, a family member misuses alcohol or drugs, a person has been victimized and traumatized), there may be personal factors[11] associated with the problems or issues of concern. In such cases, you and your client may appropriately generate explanatory hypotheses about the relationship between relevant individual factors and the problematic issues.

     When the client system includes more than one person (for example, family, formed group, natural group, organization, or community), you and your clients may generate explanatory hypotheses about the relationship between client system factors and the problems or issues of concern. Hypothesize about aspects of the client system that relate to the problems/issues of concern. Incorporate concepts from theoretical and research-based knowledge. Include your own hypotheses as well as those of the client. The nature of the professional knowledge that might apply varies according to the unique characteristics of the problems, client system, and circumstances. At times, hypotheses about an individual's personality style and characteristics, or a client system's approach to problem solving, may be useful. At other times, hypotheses about self-, family, group, organizational, or community efficacy can further understanding. Sometimes, interpersonal or relational styles or social skill deficits may apply. Frequently, hypotheses about familial, cultural, social, and occupational role identities, along with the extent of congruence or conflict among them, may be noted. Hypotheses about a person's (or group's) beliefs about oneself (or itself), others, the world, and the future may serve both to explain the how and why of a particular problem and to provide some indication about how to proceed and what to do.

     Hypothesize about how client system factors may affect the problems/issues and, in turn, how the problems/issues affect the client systems' thinking, feeling, and doing. If relevant, hypothesize about possible biochemical or physical factors and effects. Consider personal or group assets, strengths, and competencies vis-à-vis the problems/issues and the preliminary goals. Hypothesize about the effects and effectiveness of strategies the client system tends to adopt to cope with or respond to the problems/issues. Anticipate potential effects if the problems/issues are resolved or remain unresolved. Where applicable, consider the problems/issues in relation to the client system's spiritual, religious, and cultural beliefs.

     At times, the relative flexibility or rigidity of a client system's boundaries and decision-making strategies, as well as the nature, strength, and functionality of defensive and coping processes may be considered. Sometimes the client system's relative ability to control desires and impulses and to manage temptations may apply. Often, explanatory hypotheses about the client system's emotional states and traits are useful, as are those about the phase of life cycle development and maturity level. At times, it helps to consider hypotheses about the client system's competence to make significant life decisions, fulfill time- and situation-appropriate roles and tasks, function autonomously, and participate in the helping process.

     Sometimes, the results of specific assessment processes such as mental status or substance abuse examinations, questionnaires, surveys, and baseline ratings may warrant

---

[11] In work with natural groups, organizations, and communities, "personal" or "individual" factors may not be relevant for the purposes of assessment and case formulation. If so, you may simply exclude that section.

(continued)

BOX 10.5 *(continued)*

analysis and elaboration. Hypotheses about results may further understanding about the client system (or the problems or issues and the social and physical circumstances).

2. **Situational and Systemic Factors**

Propose explanatory hypotheses about the relationship between the problems/issues and the situational and systemic factors. Hypothesize about potential effects of the problems/issues upon the client system, other people and social systems, and the environment. Analyze the systemic patterns, structures, and processes of social systems associated with the promotion and maintenance of the problems/issues. Appraise the strategies used to cope with or adapt to the problems. Assess the degree of energy, cohesion, and adaptability of primary social systems. Analyze relevant life cycle developmental issues and the maturity of pertinent social systems. Consider how the needs and aspirations of other people and social systems relate to the problems/issues and the people involved.

When pertinent, propose explanatory hypotheses about the social system's predominant emotional climate; operating procedures; communication styles and process; affection and support patterns; distribution of power and availability of resources; assignment of roles; boundaries between members, subsystems, and other systems; and processes of decision making. Similarly, hypotheses about systemic structures, patterns, and processes; developmental life cycle issues; external stressors; and other situational factors may be relevant.

You may refer to genograms, eco-maps, concept maps, and timelines presented in the description section, as they often provide evidentiary support for explanatory hypotheses. Tables that present risk and protective factors and strengths, and especially functional analysis tables, may be particularly relevant. If applicable, consider the legal and ethical implications that may pertain to service in this case.

Hypotheses about capacities, abilities, strengths, competencies, and resources within the social and environmental context may add depth to the assessment; and so might those about the spiritual, religious, and cultural beliefs and practices of significant others, groups, organizations, and communities. Include hypotheses about the potential effects on the client system and on significant others if the problems or issues of concern (1) remain as they are and (2) are resolved.

3. **Motivation and Readiness; Stage of Change**

Generate hypotheses about the client system's motivation to address and resolve the problems/issues, and to work collaboratively toward change. In your assessment, refer to assets, strengths, and competencies and determine the transtheoretical stage that best reflects the client system's current readiness for change vis-à-vis each identified problem/issue. Hypothesize about factors associated with the readiness level and, if applicable, those that might serve to enhance motivation. Hypothesize about significant other people and social systems' motivation to contribute to resolution of the problems/issues. You might try using a 10-point subjective rating scale *(1 = low; 10 = high)* to estimate various aspects of motivation (for example, motivation to address particular problems/issues; motivation to take action; motivation to work with you). Realize that an individual's or group's level of motivation to address one issue may differ dramatically from their motivation to address another. Such information can be invaluable in conjointly deciding which problems to address first.

(continued)

BOX 10.5 (*continued*)

C. **Case Formulation**

The earlier portions of the assessment section primarily involve analysis. The case formulation, however, tends to require synthesis. We piece together various elements derived from analysis to identify or create one or more strategies for change. We seek to identify those factors within the client system and the social and physical/ecological environment that, if changed in some way, might help to resolve the identified problems. In other words, we propose change-oriented hypotheses.

The case formulation typically follows logically from the analyses of the problems/issues, the client system, and the social and physical/ecological environment. As social workers, we commonly target factors both within the client system (for example, individual, family, group, organization, or community) and outside the client system (for example, social and physical/ecological environment) for change. Occasionally, however, the focus may be primarily on the people or primarily on the situation.

We can think of the case formulation as a set of change-oriented hypotheses or strategic predictions. Based upon our analytic assessment, we predict that, working together, the social worker and client will resolve the problems/issues by changing one or more aspects of the client system, one or more aspects of the environment, or some combination of the two. We often include an estimate of the probability that our predictions will turn out to be true or accurate. That is, we provide a prognosis that the problems/issues can be successfully resolved through our strategic actions.

Appendix 14 contains an example of a tentative assessment and case formulation, organized as part of the DAC. As you review the example in the appendix, realize that most written assessments and case formulations are not as lengthy as the example and do not contain as many subsections. Often, you will be able to integrate the results of analysis and synthesis into fewer subsections. Furthermore, if your client system is a natural group, an organization, or a community, the assessment and case formulation would usually look quite different from the one completed with Mrs. Lynn B. Chase.

EXERCISE 10-5: PREPARING AN ASSESSMENT AND CASE FORMULATION

1. For this exercise, please review the information that you organized into the description section of your case record as part of Exercise 10-4. Based on what you know about yourself and what you included in the description portion of your DAC, proceed to word-process a tentative assessment and case formulation through analysis and synthesis of the available data. Record it in your case record. In completing your assessment and case formulation, remember that much of what you record remains tentative and speculative—even in this case, where you are assessing yourself and your situation. These hypotheses await later support and confirmation. Formulate your ideas in accord with the format provided in the assessment and case formulation section of the DAC. Continue to disguise your identity and any people you might reference in the record. When complete, place the assessment and case formulation portions of the DAC into the "A Personal Case Record" section of your Social Work Skills Learning Portfolio.

Summary

During the assessment phase of social work practice, you and the client attempt to make sense of the data gathered during the exploration phase. The assessment provides the parties a perspective from which to initiate the process of contracting (that is, reaching consensus about a service agreement). The following skills are especially pertinent to the assessment phase: (1) identifying issues, (2) sharing hypotheses, (3) clarifying issues for work, (4) organizing descriptive information, and (5) preparing an assessment and case formulation.

CHAPTER 10: SUMMARY EXERCISES

Assume that you are a social worker with a multipurpose social services agency. You are working with several people and have been actively exploring various aspects of the problems and issues of concern, the client system, and the social and physical circumstances. For each of the following case situations, use the space provided to write the words you would use and describe the actions you might take in using the requested skills.

1. You work as a community organizer in a low-income, high-crime area of town. A large percentage of the community is unemployed; neighborhood gangs patrol the area; drug sales and use are widespread; and pimps and prostitutes operate openly on the streets. You are trying to help the members of the community organize themselves to address these concerns and develop cohesiveness and unity. At this point, you are working primarily with a group of concerned parents; several ministers, priests, rabbis, and imams; school principals and teachers; social workers and social service agency directors; police officials; local legislators; and several members of the mayor's council. This larger group has separated into subgroups according to targeted social problems. One subgroup is focusing on unemployment, a second on gangs, a third on drug sales, a fourth on drug use, and a fifth on prostitution. Because the problems overlap, the large group meets periodically so that everybody is aware of subgroup activities.

    a. Use the space below to generate at least one explanatory hypothesis for each of the following issues: (1) many children and adolescents from the community join neighborhood gangs; (2) many youth and young adults sell illegal drugs; and (3) some adolescent girls and boys perform sexual acts in exchange for money. Use scientific theories, empirical research findings, and logical analysis to formulate hypotheses. For example, you might consider attachment theory and economic theory to help explain youngsters' need for belonging and drug dealing and prostitution, respectively. In relation to gang membership, you might propose an explanatory hypothesis such as, "Some children and adolescents experience gangs as a kind of family substitute" or "Some kids learn that membership in a gang is a natural part of social development" or "For some kids, it seems more dangerous not to belong to a gang than to belong to one." In relation to the sales of drugs and sex, you might offer an explanatory hypothesis such as, "When unemployment is high and jobs are scarce, some youngsters may conclude that drug dealing and prostitution are among the few ways to earn money."

b. After creating explanatory hypotheses, build upon them to formulate change-oriented hypotheses about how each of these social problems might be resolved.

2. You are working with a young couple (an Arab American male and European American female) who have sought counseling in advance of their forthcoming marriage. In their mid-twenties, both are college educated and have excellent, well-paying jobs. Nevertheless, each partner is concerned about potential problems that might ensue following their interracial marriage.

    a. Identify one problem that young interracial couples sometimes face. You might locate common problems through a quick review of the relevant research literature. Alternately, you might use your own knowledge and experience to anticipate possible problems. Once you have identified an issue, generate an explanatory hypothesis about how or why it might occur. Use scientific theories, empirical research findings, and logical analysis to formulate hypotheses. For example, suppose you anticipate that rejection of apartment rental applications could become a problem for a young interracial couple. You might then propose an explanatory hypothesis that "some landlords believe that young interracial couples (1) are undependable tenants and (2) lead other tenants to leave the building. Therefore, they reject interracial couples to avoid these predicted negative consequences."

b. Now, with the identified problem and your explanatory hypothesis in mind, formulate a change-oriented hypothesis about how the problem might be addressed. You might conduct a brief search for research studies that pertain to the effectiveness of programs, practice, or interventions that target that particular problem. Alternately, you might apply concepts from a relevant practice theory. Or, you could base a change-oriented hypothesis upon logic and reason. If you do the latter, be sure to include a rationale. Finally, laws, ordinances, court decisions, regulations, and policies may sometimes relate to the problem and help in the generation of a policy-related change-oriented hypothesis.

As an illustration, let's build upon the explanatory hypothesis that "some landlords believe that young interracial couples (1) are undependable tenants and (2) lead other tenants to leave the building. Therefore, they reject their applications." A change-oriented hypothesis might be, "If the couple's offer to rent an apartment is rejected—and the rejection appears to result from their status as a young interracial couple—and if they still want the apartment under those circumstance—an appeal to the landlord on the basis of their good character, fine references, healthy deposit, and adequate income may secure the rental. If that appeal fails and they still want the apartment, providing the landlord a copy of the city ordinance prohibiting housing discrimination on the basis of race may lead the landlord to reconsider. If the landlord fails to accept their application following this aspect of their appeal, complaints with the Office of Fair Housing and Equal Opportunity (FHEO) of the United States Department of Housing and Urban Development (HUD), the Civil Rights Commission of the state, and the city's Fair Housing Commission may either secure them the apartment or serve to prevent others from discrimination in the future."

3. You are working with a family of six (two parents and four children, ranging from 1 to 7 years of age) who had been sleeping in their dilapidated Chevy in a rest area on the highway. En route to another part of the country, where they hoped to find work, they ran out of funds to continue the trip. As you explore the circumstances with the parents, you learn that the mother has disabling diabetes and the father is unemployed in part due to an economic slowdown in his industry and in part due to increased police and governmental efforts to identify and deport undocumented workers. He has been unsuccessful in his search for work for the last few months. You also learn that the family does not have friends or relatives in their intended location. Rather, they base their hopes for employment there on rumors that jobs are available.

   a. In the space below, identify any one of the several problems apparent in the case description. Once you specify a problem, generate at least one explanatory hypothesis about how or why it might occur.

   b. Now, with the problem and your explanatory hypothesis in mind, formulate a change-oriented hypothesis about how that particular problem might be resolved.

4. You are working with Mr. T. Accused of molesting a 13-year-old girl—the daughter of his woman friend—he must participate in counseling services for 12 months or return to jail on felony charges. Mr. T. must not have any contact with the woman and her daughter during this period. During the first several meetings, Mr. T. consistently states that the girl is lying about the molestation. He says that he never touched her.

   a. Assume that the allegation of child abuse is factually true. Mr. T. may be lying when he says he did not molest the girl. Or, he may truthfully be unable to recall the events. Use the space below to generate at least one explanatory hypothesis about how or why Mr. T. might (1) lie about or (2) repress (forget) the abuse.

b. Now, with the problem and your explanatory hypothesis in mind, formulate a change-oriented hypothesis about how the problem of deception or the problem of repression might be resolved.

5. Following allegations that Mr. and Mrs. D. have neglected and abused their children (ages 1 and 3 years), you have begun to work with the couple. Based upon strong evidence collected by the state's child-protection services, both children have sometimes been left alone and unsupervised in a filthy yard that contains animal waste and potentially dangerous materials—pieces of glass and sharp and rusty metal objects. The investigation also confirmed that Mr. D. had a drinking problem and had beaten Mrs. D. on more than one occasion.

a. Use the space below to generate at least one explanatory hypothesis about one of the following issues: (1) Mrs. D. sometimes lets the children play unsupervised in the dangerous yard; (2) Mrs. D. remains in a relationship with a man who drinks heavily and sometimes beats her; (3) Mr. D. drinks heavily; or (4) Mr. D. sometimes beats Mrs. D.

b. Now, with your explanatory hypothesis in mind, formulate a change-oriented hypothesis about how the problem you selected might be resolved.

CHAPTER 10: EXPERIENTIAL INTERVIEWING EXERCISE

At this point, you have completed your first meeting with a practice client and are planning to undertake a second interview. In the initial meeting, you probably used some or all of the beginning skills and perhaps several exploring skills as well. As a result, you and the client probably gathered some information about the presenting issues as well as their origin and development, and their impact upon the client and others in the client's world. You may have discussed other aspects of the client's life circumstances as well. After the initial meeting, you reflected upon the meeting, obtained evaluative feedback from the practice client, identified areas to explore further, and engaged in preliminary planning for the second meeting.

Well before the second meeting—preferably immediately or shortly after the first one—you should begin to organize the descriptive information you gathered into a word-processed record. You are now somewhat familiar with the first two sections of the Description, Assessment, and Contract (DAC). Before your second meeting, word-process the descriptive information gathered during the first meeting. Use the DAC structure or some other coherent format. Remember to disguise the identity of the practice client. Refer to the date and time of the first interview and make note of the date you completed the written record. Identify yourself as a student social worker. Label the document "Description." After you have completed a draft of the initial description, replay the recording. Make note of exchanges that may enhance its quality or accuracy and revise the document accordingly. When finished, place the revised Description document into a new subfolder within the "Experiential Interviewing Exercise" folder. Label that subfolder "Practice Client Case Record."

Building on the previous meeting with your practice client, conduct the second interview. Once again, ensure that the interview setting is private and record the meeting. You might begin by briefly referring to what you accomplished in the first meeting and identifying a tentative purpose or agenda for this one. For example, if you completed much of the exploration of the problem-issue-situation, a reasonable purpose for the second interview might be to continue that process with a view toward reaching some explanation for the problems or issues of concern and identifying a direction for work. Be sure to seek feedback from the client about your ideas for today's meeting. If the practice client agrees with your tentative purpose, proceed to use exploring, assessing, and other relevant skills in your interview. In addition to seeking feedback, the most applicable exploring skills might be asking questions, seeking clarification, reflecting content, reflecting feelings, reflecting feelings and meanings, partializing, going beyond what is said, reflecting issues, and reflecting hypotheses. The most applicable assessing skills might be identifying issues, sharing hypotheses, and clarifying issues for work. Toward the end of the session, arrange for another meeting in a week or so. You might also share your preliminary ideas about what may happen in the next meeting.

When you've finished the interview, complete the following:

1. Leave your respective social worker and client roles. Request that your colleague complete a copy of the Exploring Skills Rating Form and the Assessing Skills Rating Form (see Appendix 11). Aspects of the Talking and Listening Skills Rating Form may also apply. When your colleague has completed the rating forms, inquire about today's interview experience. Ask general open-ended questions so that you might get as much evaluative feedback as possible and, through that, enhance your learning. For example, you might ask your colleague questions such as:

   ◆ What thoughts, feelings, or other reactions do you have about today's meeting?
   ◆ What do you think about the problems or issues we identified as the primary focus for our work together?
   ◆ What parts of the interview affected you the most—either positively or negatively?
   ◆ What do you wish had happened during the interview that did not occur?
   ◆ What suggestions do you have about how the interview could have been better, more helpful, or more constructive for you?
   ◆ What suggestions do you have about how I could have been a better or more helpful social worker today?

   Summarize your partner's feedback in a word-processed document titled "Second Meeting with a Practice Client." Label this particular section "Practice Client Feedback."

2. Next, describe and discuss your own reactions to the interview in a word-processed document. How did you feel about it? What did you like and what did you dislike about it? Refer to the active-listening, beginning, exploring, and assessing sections of The Social Work Skills Interview Rating Form (see Appendix 15) to evaluate your performance of the social work skills. Identify those skills you performed well, those that need improvement, those that you might or should have used during the interview, and those that you used but probably should not have. Identify additional aspects of the person-issue-situation that might contribute to a more complete assessment. You might have a chance to explore those in a subsequent meeting. Finally, discuss what you would do differently if you had a chance to conduct the interview again and outline what you might do in the next interview to improve the quality of the interview. Summarize your ratings, reactions, and reflections in a section of the "Second Meeting with a Practice Client" document. Label the section "My Ratings, Reactions, and Reflections" and then save the entire document for deposit into the "Experiential Interviewing Exercise" folder of your Social Work Skills Portfolio.

3. Next, reflect upon the entirety of the interview experience and use relevant preparing skills to prepare for the next meeting with the practice client. Draw upon what you learned and the documents you created to word-process tentative plans for the meeting. Label the document "Preliminary Plans for the Third Interview with a Practice Client" and deposit it in the "Experiential Interviewing Exercise" folder of your Social Work Skills Portfolio.

4. Record information gained during this meeting into a coherently organized word-processed document. You might use the relevant sections of the DAC format. After word-processing the description section, label the document "Description-Supplement." Record the date of the interview as well as the date you prepare the record. Then, proceed to formulate a tentative assessment through thoughtful reflection about the

available data. After analyzing and synthesizing the information, word-process an assessment entry for the case record. Label the document "Assessment." Record the date of the interview as well as the date you prepare the record. Identify yourself as the social worker but continue to disguise the identity of the practice client. Also, recall that much of what you determine remains tentative and speculative. These are ideas or hypotheses, not facts. Generated by the client or the social worker, or collaboratively by both, they nonetheless require further support and confirmation. After you have completed drafts of these documents, replay the recording. Make note of exchanges that may enhance their quality or accuracy. Revise the documents accordingly. When finished, place them into the "Practice Client Case Record" subfolder of your Social Work Skills Learning Portfolio.

CHAPTER 10: SELF-APPRAISAL

As you finish this chapter, please reflect on your learning by completing the following self-appraisal exercise.

SELF-APPRAISAL: THE ASSESSING SKILLS

Please respond to the following items. Your answers should help you assess your proficiency in the assessing skills. Read each statement carefully. Then, use the following 4-point rating scale to indicate the degree to which you agree or disagree with each statement. Record your numerical response in the space provided.

4 = Strongly agree;   2 = Disagree;

3 = Agree;   1 = Strongly disagree

4	3	2	1	Rating Statement
				At this point in time, I can
☐	☐	☐	☐	1. Discuss the purposes and functions of assessment.
☐	☐	☐	☐	2. Identify issues.
☐	☐	☐	☐	3. Share hypotheses.
☐	☐	☐	☐	4. Clarify issues for work.
☐	☐	☐	☐	5. Organize descriptive information in the form of a written record.
☐	☐	☐	☐	6. Prepare an assessment and case formulation.
☐	☐	☐	☐	7. Assess proficiency in the assessing skills.
				Subtotal

Note: These items are identical to those contained in the Assessing Skills section of the Social Work Skills Self-Appraisal Questionnaire presented in Appendix 3. If you completed that self-appraisal before beginning Chapter 1, you have already responded to these items once before. You may now compare the responses you made on that occasion with those you made this time. Also, compare the two subtotals. If you believe that you have progressed in terms of your proficiency, the more recent subtotal should be higher than the earlier one.

CONTRACTING

Contracting[1] follows integrally from the exploring and assessment processes and leads to the development of a service agreement between the worker and the client. This chapter (see Box 11.1) will help you develop proficiency in the contracting skills. Competent use of these skills enables social workers and clients to: establish goals, develop plans to pursue and achieve those goals, and create plans to evaluate progress toward goal achievement.

Aspects of the contracting process typically begin during the exploring phase and continue throughout the assessment process. They culminate in a service agreement or contract for service. Skills especially applicable to contracting include the following: (1) establishing goals, (2) developing action plans, (3) identifying action steps, (4) planning for evaluation, and (5) summarizing the contract.

---

[1] We use the term *contracting* to convey that the process involves an interaction between worker and client that leads to a more or less formal agreement concerning the nature, scope, and focus of the services to be provided. Although it is not, strictly speaking, a legal document, we refer to the written or unwritten outcome of this process as a *service agreement* or *service contract*.

The purpose of this chapter is to help learners develop proficiency in the contracting skills.

Goals

Following completion of this chapter, learners should be able to demonstrate proficiency in:

- Discussing the purposes and functions of contracting
- Establishing goals
- Developing action plans
- Identifying action steps
- Planning for evaluation
- Summarizing the contract
- Assessing proficiency in the contracting skills

Core EPAS Competencies

The skills addressed in this chapter support the following core EPAS competencies:
- Identify as a professional social worker and conduct oneself accordingly (EP2.1.1).
- Apply social work ethical principles to guide professional practice (EP2.1.2).
- Apply critical thinking to inform and communicate professional judgments (EP2.1.3).
- Engage diversity and difference in practice (EP2.1.4).
- Apply knowledge of human behavior and the social environment (EP2.1.7).
- Respond to contexts that shape practice (EP2.1.9).
- Engage . . . (and) . . . assess, . . . with individuals, families, groups, organizations, and communities (EP2.1.10[a–b]).

Establishing Goals

Following clarification of issues; consideration of how and why they occur; and generation of ideas about how best to address and resolve them, social workers encourage clients to participate in establishing goals for their work together. Setting effective goals is a critical element in the contracting process. First, social workers and clients agree upon the issues to address and then we develop goals that, if accomplished, would resolve those issues. Goal setting is a vital step toward change. Goals are the aims toward which the social worker and client direct their cognitive, emotional, behavioral, and situational actions. Goals are essential. Consider the title of a book by David Campbell: *If You Don't Know Where You're Going, You'll Probably End Up Somewhere Else* (1974). Without clear goals, you and your clients are indeed likely to end up somewhere other than where you intend.

In co-constructing goals with clients, we often attempt to phrase goals in a SMART format. SMART stands for:

- Specific
- Measurable
- Action oriented
- Realistic
- Timely

Objectives defined in a SMART manner are usually easier to understand, undertake, accomplish, and assess. As Egan (1982) suggests, effective goals are:

- Stated as accomplishments
- Stated in clear and specific terms
- Stated in measurable or verifiable terms
- Realistic (that is, have a reasonable chance of success)
- Adequate, if achieved, to improve the situation
- Congruent with clients' value and cultural systems
- Time-specific (that is, include a time frame for achievement)

According to Egan, effective goals meet the criteria just outlined. First, well-formed goals appear as accomplishments rather than processes. "To lose weight" is a process. "To achieve a weight of 125 pounds and maintain that weight for 6 months" is an accomplishment. Second, effective goals are clear and specific. They are not vague resolutions or general mission statements. "Securing employment" is nonspecific. "To secure employment as a waiter in a restaurant within 6 weeks" is much more clear and specific. Third, well-stated goals appear in easily understood, measurable, or verifiable terms. Clients can easily recognize when they have reached their goals. "To feel better" is hard to recognize and not sufficiently measurable. "To feel better as indicated by sleeping the night through (at least 7 hours per night on at least five nights per week), completely eating three meals daily, and scoring at least 15 percent better on the Hamilton Depression Rating Scale (HAM-D)" is much more measurable. Fourth, effective goals are realistic and reasonable. Given the motivations, opportunities, strengths, resources, and capacities of the person-issue-situation systems, the established goals reflect a reasonably high probability of attainment. A goal "to get all straight A's" would not be realistic for a student who has never before received a single "A." Fifth, effective goals are adequate. A goal is adequate to the degree that its accomplishment would represent progress toward the resolution of an agreed-upon problem or issue. Goals that do not contribute to problem resolution are therefore inadequate. Sixth, effective goals are congruent with the client's value and cultural systems. Unless a life-threatening situation exists, you should generally neither ask nor expect clients to forsake their fundamental personal or cultural values. Seventh, effective goals include a time frame. Both you and your clients need to know when achievement of the goals is expected.

Although specification of goals in a SMART manner consistent with Egan's criteria represents a useful ideal, this is not always desirable or feasible. Do not become so focused on defining goals in a precise manner that you lose touch with the client's reality. Some clients are in such a state of uncertainty and confusion that pushing too hard toward goal specificity would exacerbate their state of distress. As we discussed earlier in relation to the transtheoretical model and the stages of change (Prochaska, 1999; Prochaska, Norcross, & DiClemente, 1994; Prochaska & Velicera, 1998), people are at different levels of readiness and motivation to take action. Pushing for SMART goals with clients who are just beginning to contemplate the idea that a problem might exist could interfere with the process of exploring and clarifying issues. On occasion, therefore, you may postpone precise goal specification and instead establish a general direction for work. Indeed, sometimes the general direction involves "working toward clarifying goals for our work together" or "figuring out where we want to go from here." Later, when the confusion and ambiguity subside, you may appropriately return to encourage identification of clear and precise goals that conform more closely to a SMART format.

Whether stated in specific or general terms, effective goal statements follow logically from and relate directly to the identified issues for work. Usually, you and your client identify at least one goal for each identified focal problem (see Figure 11.1). Social workers and

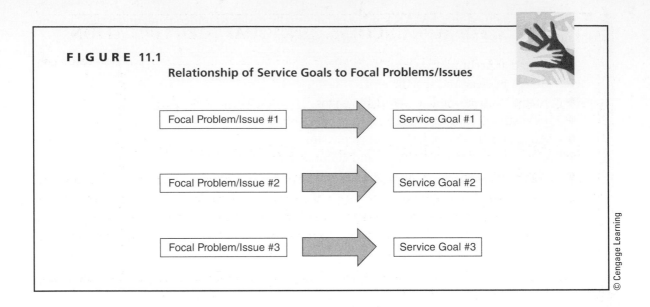

FIGURE 11.1

FIGURE 11.1

Relationship of Service Goals to Focal Problems/Issues

Focal Problem/Issue #1 → Service Goal #1

Focal Problem/Issue #2 → Service Goal #2

Focal Problem/Issue #3 → Service Goal #3

© Cengage Learning

clients sometimes begin the process of creating goals by converting a focal problem into its opposite. Many issues appear as a surplus or deficit of knowledge, skill, or resources. For example, a social worker and client could readily convert a problem of insufficient knowledge about family planning (that is, a knowledge deficit) into a goal "to increase client's knowledge of family planning." A client's excessive anxiety—a surplus of anxiety—could become "to decrease client's excessive anxiety." A client's insufficient income could become "to increase client's income."

Sometimes accomplishing one goal resolves more than one focal problem, so it may not always be necessary to create a separate goal for each issue. Nonetheless, be sure that accomplishing the service goals would resolve all the agreed-upon issues for work. Be cautious, however, about attempting to pursue too many goals all at once. A large number of goals may diminish motivation (Dalton & Spiller, 2012) and decrease the probability of success.

Consistent with the values of the profession, social workers define goals through a collaborative process with clients and gain full, informed consent to work toward their achievement. In effect, when you and a client establish goals, you implicitly agree to a contract in which both parties commit to work toward their accomplishment. Most of the time, clients are quite capable of active participation in goal identification. As part of that process, you encourage them to identify a goal for one or more issues for work. However, some clients focus so intently on problems that they simply cannot respond to a direct question such as "What are your goals?" or "What is your goal for resolving this issue?" Therefore, we generally engage clients in the goal-setting process by asking questions about how specifically they will know when a particular issue has been resolved (Berg, 1994; De Jong & Berg, 2002; Lipchik, 2002; O'Connell, 2005). In addition to furthering the purposes of goal establishment identified earlier, these questions serve another extremely important function. They tend to enhance clients' hope and optimism. Such questions encourage clients to envision, in considerable detail, a future in which the issue has indeed been resolved. In so doing, clients often begin to feel better, more energized, and more motivated to work toward goal attainment. To yield such results, however, we must phrase these questions in a certain way. We adapt the exploring skill of seeking clarification to encourage clients to both establish a goal and to imagine a future without the problem or issue. Clarification-seeking questions, phrased in the following format, tend to yield these dual results.

PRACTICE FORMAT: ENCOURAGING GOAL IDENTIFICATION

In specific terms, how will you know when the issue of _____ is truly resolved?

or

What would indicate to you that this problem is truly a thing of the past?

EXAMPLE: ENCOURAGING GOAL IDENTIFICATION

WORKER: Now that we have a pretty clear list of the problems, let's try to establish specific goals for each one. The first issue we've identified is that your 14-year-old son skips school 2 or 3 days each week. Let's imagine that it is now some point in the future and this issue has been completely resolved. What would indicate to you that your son's truancy is truly a thing of the past?

CLIENT: Well, I guess I'll know when Johnny goes to school every day and his grades are better.

WORKER: (*reflecting goal; seeking feedback*) When Johnny goes to school daily and improves his grades, you will feel that it's no longer an issue. Is that right?

CLIENT: Yes.

WORKER: (*seeking clarification*) Okay, now let's try to be even more specific. When you say, "Johnny will go to school every day," do you also mean that he will attend all his classes when he's there?

CLIENT: Yes.

WORKER: (*seeking clarification*) What do you think would be a reasonable period for accomplishing this goal?

CLIENT: Well, I don't know. I'd like him to start now.

WORKER: (*sharing opinion; seeking feedback*) That would be great progress! But I wonder if that might be expecting too much. Let's see, it's now 1 month into the school year. As I understand it, Johnny skipped school some last year too and this year he is skipping even more. What do you think about a 2-month period for accomplishing the goal?

CLIENT: That sounds really good.

WORKER: (*establishing goal*) Okay, how does this sound as our first goal: "Within 2 months from today's date, Johnny will go to school every day and attend all his classes except when he's sick enough to go to a doctor?"[2] Let's take a moment to write that down. ... Now about the grades, as I understand, he is currently failing most of his courses. How will you know when that is no longer an issue?

---

[2] Note that this example involves goals for Johnny—a person who is not present. And, the goals are derived from problems in Johnny's behavior as identified by his mother; not by Johnny himself. If Johnny does not view his school-related behavior as problematic, and if he does not concur with these goals, the chances for progress diminish. It is perfectly reasonable for parents to express concern about their children's behavior and to establish goals for its improvement. However, when the children are old enough to participate and it is safe for them to do so, social workers encourage parents to involve the children themselves. In this case, the social worker and client would probably seek Johnny's input and reaction to the identified issues and proposed goals, and attempt to secure his voluntary and active participation.

As should be apparent from this last example, social workers must often be quite active in encouraging goal identification. Notice that the questions reflect an implicit optimism. They require the client to envision a future in which the issue is indeed resolved. Therefore, in seeking goal identification, try to avoid phrases such as, "If the issues were resolved. ..." This could suggest to a client that you are pessimistic about the chances of success. In expressing optimism, however, be careful to avoid making promises that you cannot keep. Most of the time social workers cannot guarantee that their services will result in successful outcomes.

Sometimes, in response to your questions, clients formulate clear goals with which you can readily concur. When this happens, you may simply reflect the goal by paraphrasing the client's words. You may use a format such as the following.

PRACTICE FORMAT: REFLECTING GOALS

As you see it, one goal for our work together is _____.

EXAMPLE: REFLECTING GOALS

CLIENT: (*responding to worker's request to state a goal*) Well, I guess I'd like to improve the quality of the communication between us.

WORKER: (*reflecting goals*) As you see it then, one goal for our work together is for the two of you to become better at talking pleasantly and respectfully with one another. (*seeking feedback*) Is that right?

CLIENT: Yes.

Reflecting goals involves communicating your empathic understanding of clients' views about goals that they would like to pursue. As are all reflecting skills, it is a form of active listening. When you reflect their goals, you demonstrate that you have heard and understood the direction clients' want to go. In reflecting goals, you may paraphrase or mirror the client's words even when they are expressed in general terms. Alternately, you can modestly extend what the client said by phrasing your response so that the goal is clear and specific.

Sometimes, despite your active encouragement, a client cannot or will not identify a goal. In such instances, you may simply postpone the goal-setting process and engage in additional exploration of the person-issue-situation. Alternatively, you may propose a tentative goal, which the client may accept, reject, or modify. In proposing a goal, you may adopt a format such as the following:

PRACTICE FORMAT: PROPOSING A GOAL

I wonder, would it make sense to establish this as one goal for our work together: _____
_____?

(continued)

EXAMPLE: PROPOSING A GOAL

WORKER: Now that we have a pretty clear understanding of the issues and a sense of the direction we'd like to go, let's establish goals for our work together. We've agreed that your pattern of alcohol consumption is a significant problem that we'll address. I wonder, would it make sense to establish as a goal for our work together to limit the amount of daily alcohol intake to one 12-ounce can of beer each day?

EXAMPLE: ESTABLISHING GOALS

CLIENT: Yes. It does feel like I've lost everything I had hoped for. I guess it's normal to feel sad when a marriage fails.

WORKER: (*reflecting feelings and meanings*) Your dreams for the future of the marriage have been shattered, and you feel a powerful sense of loss and sadness.

CLIENT: Yes, my marriage meant a lot to me.

WORKER: (*encouraging goal identification*) I wonder if it might be possible for us to identify a goal in relation to these feelings of sadness and loss. Let's imagine that it's now sometime in the future when you have fully recovered. What will you be thinking, feeling, and doing when these depressed feelings are no longer a problem for you?

CLIENT: Gee, I don't know exactly. I guess when I'm finally over her I'll feel a lot better.

WORKER: (*reflecting content; encouraging goal specificity*) So it will be a positive sign when you begin to feel better. And what will indicate to you that you're feeling better?

CLIENT: I guess once I'm over this, I'll be able to sleep and eat again and not think about her so much, and I might even be dating someone else.

WORKER: (*reflecting content; proposing a goal; seeking feedback*) So when you begin to eat and sleep better, and you think about her less, we'll know that things have taken a positive turn. Let's make the goals even more specific so that we will know when you have completely achieved them. How does this sound to you? "Within 6 months, to (1) sleep 6 or more hours per night at least five nights per week, (2) regain the weight that you lost, (3) think about things other than your wife at least 75 percent of the time, and (4) go out on at least one date." What do you think?

CLIENT: Real good. Right now, I probably think about her 95 percent of the time, and the idea of going on a date sounds just awful. If I were thinking about other things, doing other things, and dating someone else, I'd know that I'd finally be over her.

WORKER: (*establishing goal*) Okay. Let's jot that down so we can remember it.

In the same way you previously recorded the agreed-upon problems or issues for work, we now do the same for the established goals. Typically, the goals bear a close relationship to the problems or issues of concern. Table 11.1 reflects the relationship between the focal problems and the service goals. If we converted the general goals reflected in Table 11.1 into SMART goals, they might appear as presented in Box 11.2.

TABLE 11.1
Sample: Relationship of Service Goals to Focal Problems/Issues

Focal Problems/Agreed-Upon Issues for Work	Service Goals
◆ Currently homeless	◆ Client has permanent housing.
• Lives on the street	• Client has shelter.
• Winter approaching	• Client has warm shelter.
◆ Diabetes	◆ Client manages diabetic symptoms.
• Without medicine for a week	• Client has medicine.
• Lacks medical care	• Client has medical care.
◆ Currently unemployed	◆ Client is employed.
• Lacks money	• Client has stable income.
• Lacks medical insurance	• Client has medical insurance.

© Cengage Learning

BOX 11.2
Service Goals in SMART Form

1. Client has warm temporary shelter by 7:00 P.M. this evening.
2. Client has warm, permanent housing within 3 months of today's date.
3. Client receives at least 1-week's supply of diabetes medication within 4 hours of this time.
4. Client meets with a medical doctor within 1 week of today's date.
5. Client has ongoing relationship with health care system within 3 months of today's date.
6. Client has regular employment within 3 months of today's date.
7. Client has medical insurance within 5 months of today's date.
8. Client receives income from employment within 3 1/2 months of today's date.

EXERCISE 11-1: ESTABLISHING GOALS

For these exercises, assume that you are continuing in your role as a social worker with a multipurpose social services agency. In the spaces provided for each case situation, complete three tasks. First, used the provided spaces to write the words you would say in encouraging the client to identify a goal. Second, prepare a general goal statement that reasonably follows from one or more of the issues that you specified in Exercise 10-3. Third, prepare a specific goal statement that reasonably follows from one or more of these same issues. Try to write it so that it meets Egan's ideal criteria for effective goal statements.

Of course, the nature of this exercise does not allow you to interact with clients in establishing goals. Therefore, simply formulate appropriate questions and then share your view of goals that might match the identified issues. The primary purpose here is to practice asking questions that encourage goal identification and to gain experience in preparing two forms of goal statements.

1. Write the words you would say in asking questions that encourage Mr. K., the 55-year-old man who experienced post-divorce issues, to identify goals for your work together. Then, on behalf of Mr. K., write (a) a general goal statement and (b) a SMART goal statement that relate to one or more of the issues clarified in Exercise 10-3.

2. Write the words you would say in asking questions to encourage Loretta, the homeless woman, to identify goals for your work together. Then, on behalf of Loretta, write (a) a general goal statement and (b) a SMART goal statement that relate to one or more of the issues clarified in Exercise 10-3.

3. Write the words you would say in asking questions to encourage members of the S. family to identify goals for your work together. Then, on behalf of the S. family, write (a) a general goal statement and (b) a SMART goal statement that relate to one or more of the issues clarified in Exercise 10-3.

4. Write the words you would say in asking questions that encourage Mrs. F., the Latino mother who is concerned about her children, to identify goals for your work together. Then, on behalf of Mrs. F., write (a) a general goal statement and (b) a SMART goal statement that relate to one or more of the issues clarified in Exercise 10-3.

5. Write the words you would say in asking questions that encourage members of the social service agency group with whom you provide consultation services to identify goals for your work together. Then, on behalf of the social service agency group, write (a) a general goal statement and (b) a SMART goal statement that relate to one or more of the issues clarified in Exercise 10-3.

6. When you have completed these exercises, review the SMART goal statements that you wrote and then ask yourself the following questions. Have I described the goals as accomplishments rather than processes? Are the goals clear and specific? Are they measurable or verifiable in some way? Are they realistic, given the circumstances? Are they adequate? Do they appear to be consistent with the fundamental values and cultural preferences that you might expect of these clients? Finally, are the goals congruent with the issues clarified in Exercise 10-3? If your answer to any of these questions is no, revise your SMART goal statements so that they do meet Egan's ideal form.

Developing Action Plans

Once you and your clients have established goals, engage them in the process of developing action plans. Sometimes called "service plans," "treatment plans," or "intervention plans," action plans address the questions of who, what, where, when, and especially how you and the client will pursue the agreed-upon goals. In planning action, you and the client identify pertinent others who will meet with you and who or what will be the target for change. Together, you also determine who will be involved in the change efforts and how those efforts might affect others. For example, consider a case in which the mother of an 8-year-old boy expresses concern about his disobedience and aggression. You and the client would determine who could and who should be involved and in what context. Will it be the mother and boy together; the mother independently; the boy separately; sometimes one, sometimes the other, sometimes both; the boy in a group with other boys; or the mother in a group with other mothers? There are numerous possibilities, and many decisions are required. Clients participate in the process and, of course, must provide informed consent before any intervention or action may be undertaken.

Lifelong learning and critical thinking abilities become particularly relevant in this process. Sometimes you may be highly knowledgeable about nomothetic research studies concerning the effectiveness of services intended to address problems and pursue goals such as those you and your clients identify. At other times, you may need to search, review, and analyze current research studies before you can competently explore potential action plans.

You and the client also determine what social work role or roles you will play (for example, advocate, broker, case manager, counselor, educator, evaluator, facilitator, investigator, mediator, therapist, consultant, researcher, or policy analyst or planner) and what theoretical approach or intervention protocol to adopt in pursuing established goals. If, for example, you and a client decide that you will serve in the role of counselor, you also need to determine a theoretical model or approach, change strategy, or intervention protocol that will guide your actions (for example, task centered, family systems, ecological, behavioral, problem solving, cognitive-behavioral, or some combination thereof). You also select one or more counseling formats (for example, individual, dyadic, family, small group, or some combination of them). You and the client also determine how to implement the change efforts. How active should you be? How direct should you be? Should you encourage the client to take the initiative, or should you assume primary leadership responsibility? You and the client decide how fast to proceed with change efforts and how to approach other people who could or should be involved.

You and the client decide where and when to hold your meetings and where and when the change efforts will occur. Sometimes it is easier for clients or potentially more effective, to meet in their homes rather than in your agency office. On other occasions, an entirely neutral location may be the best choice. You and the client also determine when you will meet (for example, morning, afternoon, evening; on which days), how often (for example, once per week, three times weekly, once per month), and how long (for example, 15 minutes, 30 minutes, 1 hour, 2 hours). Usually, you and the client establish a time frame for your work together. Will you plan to work together toward these goals for 6 weeks, 9 sessions, 3 months, 12 meetings, 6 months, or longer?

In addition, social workers and clients discuss the nature of a typical meeting so that those involved understand the general expectations. In an extension of the skill of orienting clients, you might initiate such a discussion by saying, "Here's what we usually do in our regular meetings. ..." It also helps to discuss expectations about activities between meetings. Some clients are unaware that much of the work toward goal attainment actually occurs during the time between one meeting and another. You could introduce this topic by saying, "Between meetings, we'll each engage in various tasks or activities and take steps to accomplish these goals. In fact, we'll do much of our work between meetings. Some people call these activities 'homework.'"

As you flesh out aspects of the plan, engage the client in identifying possible obstacles as well as potential resources that might influence the outcome of your plans. You might think of these as risk and protective factors for the service plan. Importantly, you also review and reflect on the likely benefits of a successful outcome.

Most social work action plans involve change of some kind—change that would help resolve an issue and achieve a goal. Sometimes a single decision or action is sufficient. More commonly, however, we focus on change that requires several decisions and numerous actions. We may direct these change efforts toward some biological or psychological aspect of a person, some part of the social or environmental situation, or, as is usually the case, toward elements of both the person and the situation. For example, change in a person's thinking might be a focus (for example, to think more favorably about oneself, to develop a more optimistic attitude, or even to accept that certain things will probably remain pretty much as they are). Alternately, change in a client's feelings (for example, to reduce the frequency and intensity of angry feelings or to become more relaxed) might be the focus. Often, we attempt to produce a change in a client's behavior (for example, speak more often in a group context or become more proficient in certain parenting skills). As social workers, we also focus a great deal on situational, policy, and environmental change of various kinds. For instance, you might attempt to secure housing for a homeless person or to improve the quality of care for someone living in a foster home. You might try to find employment for someone out of work or obtain an exception for someone deemed ineligible for the SNAP (food stamps) program, health insurance, or Social Security benefits. Regardless of the focus of change, recognize that individuals, dyads, families, groups, organizations, communities, or societies that are not ready for planned change or motivated to take action rarely do so. If you expect that change naturally and easily results from a cooperative process of goal setting and action planning, you will be quite disappointed. Social workers realize that human beings and social systems vary in their readiness and motivation for change (Prochaska, 1999; Prochaska et al., 1994; Prochaska & Velicera, 1998). Indeed, an individual client might be anxious to take action to resolve one problem but reluctant to consider the possibility of change with regard to another.

In developing action plans, you and the client address a number of factors, including the stages of change, and develop an approach to guide your work together. The following is an example of how action plans might appear as part of the contract portion of the DAC.

BOX 11.3

Example: Action Plans

Florence Dupre (client) and I (Susan Holder—social worker) plan to meet together for weekly 1-hour sessions over the course of the next 8 weeks. Our purpose is to accomplish the goals identified above. In particular, we will work to secure a full-time job for Florence that pays $15 or more per hour and includes medical and retirement benefits. We will approach this work as a cooperative effort with each of us contributing ideas and suggestions and each of us taking steps toward goal achievement. I (Susan Holder) will serve in the roles of counselor, educator, and advocate in attempting to help Florence Dupre reach the identified goals for work. Sometimes we will meet at the agency, sometimes at Ms. Dupre's apartment, and sometimes at other locations within the community. In approaching this work, we will adopt a collaborative problem-solving approach in which we will jointly analyze the potential pros and cons associated with various courses of action and undertake various actions or steps intended to pursue the agreed-upon goals. Throughout the 8-week period, we will keep track of the tasks we undertake and their impact, and generally monitor progress toward goal achievement. At the end of that time, we will determine whether to conclude our work, consult with or refer to someone else, or contract with each other for further work together.

Susan Holder
Licensed Social Worker

EXERCISE 11-2: DEVELOPING ACTION PLANS

For these exercises, assume that you are continuing your work with the five client systems described in the previous exercises (Mrs. K., Loretta, the S. family, Mrs. F., and the troubled social service agency). Review your responses to Exercises 10-3 (clarifying issues for work) and 11-1 (establishing goals). Then, in the spaces provided following each vignette, outline action plans for your work with each client. Of course, it should be congruent with the identified issues and goals, and consistent with the dimensions discussed earlier.

1. Outline action plans for your work with Mr. K.

2. Outline action plans for your work with Loretta.

3. Outline action plans for your work with the S. family.

4. Outline action plans for your work with Mrs. F.

5. Outline action plans for your consultative work with the troubled social service agency.

6. When you have completed these exercises, review the action plans you have formulated. Ask yourself whether the plans adequately describe who is to be involved; who or what are the targets of change; where, when, and how long the meetings are to occur; how active you are to be; what role or roles you are going to assume; what strategy or approach is to be used; and what the time frame is to be. In addition, ask whether the action plans in any way infringe on the personal values and cultural preferences you might expect of these particular clients. Finally, determine whether the action plans are logically congruent with the issues identified in Exercise 10-3 and the final goals established in Exercise 11-1. Estimate the probability that successful implementation of the plans will lead to achievement of the goals. In the following space, specify those aspects of the action-planning process that you need to strengthen.

Identifying Action Steps

Sometimes the goals that social workers and clients formulate are simply too large to accomplish through single actions. When it is unrealistic and impractical to undertake simultaneously all the actions needed to accomplish a particular goal, we engage clients in identifying small action steps or tasks (Reid, 1992) that are consistent with the action plans and likely to contribute to goal accomplishment. In a sense, these tasks or action steps are subordinate goals or objectives. Regardless of their form, we anticipate that their completion will constitute progress toward the achievement of one or more agreed-upon service goals. You may record them in the Plans portion of the Contract section of the DAC.

In identifying action steps, you and the client use information gained and hypotheses generated during the description and assessment phases. You attempt to foster a flexible, creative, brainstorming atmosphere where various ideas are identified and examined. We commonly use the skills of questioning, seeking clarification, reflecting, going beyond, and seeking feedback during this process. As a collaborative partner in the process, you may also share your own professional knowledge and expertise. Indeed, the theory- and research-based hypotheses generated during assessment often lead to the identification of specific action steps associated with one or more evidence-based practice approaches. Completion of action steps (sometimes referred to as *instrumental objectives*) increases the probability of goal accomplishment. In other words, action steps are *instrumental* in the achievement of the service goals. For example, people who believe they are powerless or helpless in certain life circumstances often become passive, inactive, reclusive, and withdrawn. They might even be called "depressed." Numerous research studies suggest that when people who feel depressed increase their level of activity, become more engaged in meaningful individual and social endeavors, and begin to change what and how they think about themselves and their circumstances, they usually become less depressed and more satisfied (Nieuwsma et al., 2012). Based upon such research-based evidence, a social worker might encourage clients whose goals are to become less depressed and more satisfied with life to consider instrumental objectives or actions steps designed to increase the frequency and duration of (1) physical activity, (2) meaningful activity, (3) social activity, and (4) thoughts of personal self-efficacy. Based upon our knowledge of the research findings, social workers might hypothesize that such action steps would be instrumental in achieving the goals of reducing clients' levels of depression and increasing their degree of life satisfaction.

Of course, there are many ways to resolve issues and achieve goals. Some approaches require changes in the person, others involve changes in the social situation or the ecological environment, and many entail changes in multiple dimensions. Changes such as increasing one's knowledge about parenting or increasing one's skill in communicating assertively are examples of person-focused change. Securing adequate food and shelter or organizing a tenants' union to lobby for improved building conditions exemplify situation-focused or environmental change. In social work practice, changes are rarely limited to the individual person. We usually seek changes in the situation as well. When you engage in policy practice and whenever you serve as an advocate, broker, or mediator, you are working toward situational change. For example, an unemployed client's situation could improve dramatically if you intercede with a prospective employer to help the client secure a new job; or, if you engage in collective efforts to improve the overall health of the economy and create many new jobs.

Consider the example of a female client living with a man who periodically beats her. With your help, several situational changes might be possible. Her male companion could be encouraged to join in a process of relationship counseling designed to enhance direct verbal communication and decrease the risk of future violence. Alternately, he might begin to participate in a program for abusive men. The client might file a criminal complaint with the police and courts, or she might leave the household for a safe shelter. All these steps involve changes in the situation, and all would affect the person as well. Although an action step in any given case may be primarily person focused or primarily situation focused, you should be aware of the following systemic principle: Changes in one aspect of the person-issue-situation nearly always result in changes in other aspects as well.

In other words, person-focused change will probably affect the situation in some way—just as situation-focused change will likely affect the person in some way.

Completion of tasks or action steps contributes to the achievement of larger goals. Because they usually involve relatively small steps, they tend to have a higher probability of success than would be the case if someone attempted to achieve a large goal in a single action. For example, suppose you are 50 pounds overweight and wanted to lose that much to improve your health. You commit to a goal of losing 50 pounds as soon as possible. Except by surgery, it is physically impossible to lose 50 pounds through a single action. Reducing by 1 pound, then another, and then another, however, is conceivable. It is similar to the "one day at a time" principle of Alcoholics Anonymous (AA). Abstaining from alcohol for the rest of one's life is indeed a large order for anyone who has drunk large quantities of alcohol every day for many years. Abstaining for 1 day, 1 hour, or even for 1 minute is more manageable and certainly more probable. By putting together and accomplishing several smaller tasks or action steps (instrumental objectives), a large goal that otherwise would seem insurmountable may be achieved (see Figure 11.2).

Identifying action steps involves determining what will be done, when, and by whom. These actions constitute steps, tasks, or activities that you or the client will take in your efforts toward goal accomplishment. Various action steps may be referred to as *client tasks*, *worker tasks*, *in-session tasks*, *between-session tasks* (Tolson, Reid, & Garvin, 1994), or *maintenance tasks*. Client tasks or between-session tasks are action steps that clients take during the intervals between your meetings. Sometime social workers refer to client tasks as "homework" activities or assignments. However, the term *task* may better convey that the worker and client jointly determine the activity. Usually, the worker does not "assign" the task as a teacher might assign homework to a student. Rather, social workers and clients together decide what tasks to undertake.

Worker tasks are those that the social worker completes before meeting again with a client. In-session tasks are procedures, activities, or intervention techniques that you or clients undertake during your meetings together. Maintenance tasks are those regularly occurring personal or situational activities that become routine or institutionalized by clients to promote long-term change. Although maintenance tasks may occur within sessions, clients more often complete them between sessions or after the conclusion of their work with a social worker.

In attempting to specify tasks or action steps, you and the client first engage one another in generating a first small step toward the goal. You may initiate this process by asking questions such as "What would represent a first step toward achieving this goal?" or "What needs to change for you to be able to make a small step toward achieving this goal?"

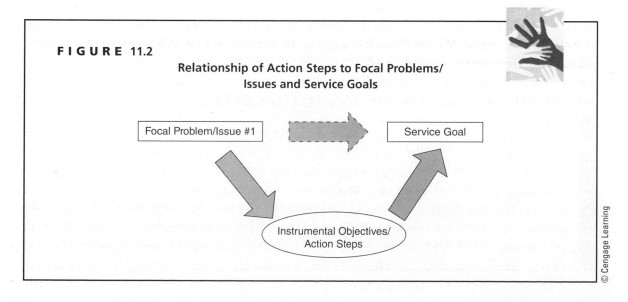

FIGURE 11.2

Relationship of Action Steps to Focal Problems/ Issues and Service Goals

Focal Problem/Issue #1 → Service Goal

Instrumental Objectives/ Action Steps

© Cengage Learning

Questions such as the following may also help to generate action steps and, simultaneously, to identify ways to evaluate progress: "What will be the first sign that you are beginning to make progress toward this goal?" "What will be the very first indication that there is progress in this matter?" "What will be the very first sign that you are taking steps to reach your goal?" Such questions tend to increase clients' optimism and motivation. They do so by bringing the near future into clients' present thinking. You ask clients to imagine or visualize the situation as somewhat improved and to identify signs of that improvement. These signs often reveal the kinds of specific action steps that might produce progress toward goal attainment.

Notice the emphasis on identifying actions to take. Your focus is on doing something that represents movement toward goal achievement. Depending on the nature of the agreed-upon goals, you may encourage clients to identify steps leading to changes in their thoughts, feelings, or behaviors, or in their situations.

When the agreed-upon goals require long-term change (for example, maintain a 50-pound weight loss for 1 year, or abstain from all alcohol use for 6 months), you engage the client in identifying action steps that directly relate to the maintenance of durable change. We do not require such maintenance tasks in circumstances where a single decision or short-term action is the goal. Lasting change, however, requires ongoing attention. Therefore, social workers and clients identify ways and means to maintain change over the long term. Durable change is most likely when personal or situational policies, practices, or activities become routine or institutionalized. The most effective maintenance tasks occur regularly (for example, hourly, daily, weekly, or biweekly) and function as reminders, incentives, or rewards for the affected individuals, families, groups, organizations, or communities.

In identifying maintenance tasks, you and the client anticipate that positive changes have occurred and the service goals have been achieved. Together you address the question, "How do we maintain these changes over the long term?" You ask yourselves, "How can these changes become a natural and routine part of everyday life?" Building on the mutual understanding gained earlier, you jointly generate possible maintenance tasks within each relevant sphere of the person-in-environment.

During the contracting phase, you ask questions and share information that leads to the identification of small and manageable tasks that, when completed, contribute to the accomplishment of one or more service goals. As you and the client reach consensus concerning action steps, reflect them in clear terms and then seek feedback from the client. Record them in your case notes.

In practicing the skill of identifying action steps, use a format such as the following:

PRACTICE FORMAT: IDENTIFYING AN ACTION STEP

So, the (first or next) step that (you, I, or we) will take is _____. (You, I, or We) will complete this task by (date) and talk about it at our next meeting.

EXAMPLE: IDENTIFYING AN ACTION STEP

CLIENT: (*identifying an action step*) I'll go ahead and talk with her to see if she'd be interested in the idea of joint counseling.

WORKER: (*identifying an action step*) Okay, the next step that you will take is to talk with your partner and ask her if she might be interested in joining us for a few meetings. You'll talk with her within the next few days in order to give her a chance to think about it and give you her response before our next meeting. How does that sound? Fine, let's jot that down so we can keep it in mind.

By identifying an action step, you firmly cement the contract for your work with clients. The following are some examples of typical processes by which a worker might engage clients in establishing action steps.

EXAMPLE: ESTABLISHING ACTION STEPS

WORKER: (*reflecting a goal; seeking an action step*) You want to improve your sleeping patterns. Right now, you sleep through the night only about 1 out of every 7 days. You want to be able to do so at least 5 days per week. Going from 1 to 5 nights is a pretty large jump. It might be helpful to start with something a bit smaller. What would represent a good first step toward achieving the goal?

EXAMPLE: ESTABLISHING ACTION STEPS

WORKER: (*reflecting a goal; seeking an action step*) You want to improve your sleeping patterns. Right now, you sleep through the night through about 1 day per week and you want to be able to do so at least five times per week. What will be the first signs that you are beginning to sleep better?

If the client cannot or does not respond to your encouragement by identifying a small action step, you may tentatively propose one for consideration. Of course, as always, be sure to seek the client's reactions to the idea. In proposing a task, you might use a format such as the following:

PRACTICE FORMAT: PROPOSING ACTION STEPS

As a first step toward the goal of _____, what do you think about _____ (client task, worker task, or in-session task as needed)?

EXAMPLE: PROPOSING ACTION STEPS

WORKER: (*proposing a client task*) We have identified the goal of graduating from high school by completing your General Education Diploma (GED) within the next 12 months. As a first step toward that goal, what do you think about contacting the school that you attended through the ninth grade to ask for your academic records?

EXAMPLE: PROPOSING ACTION STEPS

WORKER: (*proposing a worker task*) We have identified the goal of graduating from high school by completing your GED within the next 12 months. As a first step toward that goal, I'd like to contact the department of education on your behalf and ask for information about local GED programs. How does that sound to you?

(continued)

EXAMPLE: PROPOSING ACTION STEPS

WORKER: (*proposing an in-session task*) Here's a copy of the application form for the GED program. I thought we might try to complete it together during our meeting today. What do you think?

The social worker typically assumes responsibility for making a formal record of the jointly agreed-upon tasks or action steps (see Table 11.2). In the recording, the worker identifies the person or people responsible for undertaking each task and the time frame for completion. Record keeping is a professional responsibility. Social workers must maintain accurate notes. Many clients, however, also make notes for themselves. In doing so, they often feel a greater sense of active participation in the process. To encourage this, some social workers provide notebooks to clients during their first meeting together.

TABLE 11.2
Action Steps Associated with Agreed-Upon Service Goals

Service Goals	Action Steps
Client has warm temporary shelter by this evening.	*Client Task:* Gather together belongings. *Worker Task:* Contact temporary housing shelters; make arrangements for short-term shelter.
Client has warm, permanent housing within 3 months of today's date.	*Client Task:* Complete necessary application forms. *Worker Task:* Locate low-cost or subsidized housing.
Client receives at least 1 week's supply of diabetes medication within 4 hours of this time.	*Client Task:* Describe medical condition. *Worker Task:* Contact medical clinic to secure interim supply of medication.
Client meets with a medical doctor within 1 week of today's date.	*Client and Worker Tasks:* Schedule appointment with medical clinic; arrange for transportation if needed.
Client has ongoing relationship with health care system within 3 months of today's date.	*Client Task:* Arrange for follow-up visit with medical clinic. *Worker Task:* Facilitate arrangement of follow-up visit if needed.
Client has regular employment within 3 months of today's date.	*Client Task:* Search for job openings; make application; secure employment, preferably with company that provides health insurance. *Worker Task:* Search for job openings; help client with application and preparation for job interview; help arrange for transportation if needed.
Client has stable income from employment within 3 1/2 months of today's date.	*Client Task:* Share information with worker. *Worker Task:* Seek information from client.
Client has medical insurance within 5 months of today's date.	*Client Task:* If employment does not include health insurance, make application with low-cost carrier. *Worker Task:* Locate low-cost health insurer— if employment does not include health insurance.

EXERCISE 11-3: IDENTIFYING ACTION STEPS

Review your responses to Exercises 11-1 (establishing goals) and 11-2 (developing action plans). Then, in the spaces provided, write the words you might use to encourage Mr. K., Loretta, the S. family, Mrs. F., and the troubled social service agency to identify an initial small task or action step. Then, write three different action steps that you might propose to each client. Of course, they should be congruent with the identified issues and goals and, if completed, clearly represent progress toward goal achievement.

1. Write the words you might say in encouraging Mr. K. to identify one or more action steps. Then, record what you might say in proposing a client task, a worker task, and an in-session task.

2. Write the words you might say in encouraging Loretta to identify one or more action steps. Then, record what you might say in proposing a client task, a worker task, and an in-session task.

3. Write the words you might say to help members of the S. family to identify one or more action steps. Then, write how you might propose a client task, a worker task, and an in-session task to the S. family.

4. Write the words you might say in encouraging Mrs. F. to identify one or more action steps. Then, record how you might propose a client task, a worker task, and an in-session task to her.

5. Write the words you might say in encouraging the group at the troubled social service agency to identify one or more action steps. Then, write what you might say in proposing a client task, a worker task, and an in-session task to the group.

6. When you have completed these exercises, review the tasks or action steps identified and ask yourself the following questions: Do you describe the steps so that they involve actually doing something? Are the steps clear and specific? Would they in any way infringe on the personal values and the cultural preferences that you might expect of these clients? Finally, are the action steps congruent with the specified issues, the goals, and the action plans identified in Exercises 10-3, 11-1,

and 11-2? Are the action steps consistent with the strategies and interventions used in evidence-based practices and services? In particular, what is the probability that, if completed, the action steps would indeed contribute to and maintain the achievement of the identified goals? Use the space below to specify those aspects of action step identification you need to strengthen.

Planning for Evaluation

As professionals, we are responsible for evaluating progress toward problem resolution and goal achievement. Regardless of the nature of the agency setting, the presenting issues, or the client's circumstances, you should be able to identify some means to measure progress toward goal attainment. In doing so, be sure to consider the "goodness of fit" between the evaluation tools or procedures and clients' capacities and resources. For example, some clients are unable to create frequency charts or to complete lengthy paper-and-pencil instruments. Nonetheless, start with the presumption that you can locate or create some reasonable and relevant form of evaluation. In many practice contexts, failure to evaluate progress would constitute negligence and perhaps malpractice.

You can measure progress toward goal attainment in several ways. One of the more applicable methods is called goal attainment scaling (Kiresuk & Sherman, 1968; Kiresuk, Smith, & Cardillo, 1994). Goal attainment scaling (GAS) is particularly well suited to social work practice because the dimensions for measurement are not predetermined, as is the case with standardized tests and questionnaires. In GAS, the dimensions for assessment evolve from the goals negotiated by you and the client. Therefore they are specific to each person-issue-situation. Kagle and Kopels (2008) provide a useful summary of GAS procedures as do several others (see, for example, Compton et al., 2005; Cox & Amsters, 2002; Fleuridas, Leigh, Rosenthal, & Leigh, 1990). In addition, Marson and Dran (2006) sponsor an extraordinary website on the topic of Goal Attainment Scaling.

In developing a Goal Attainment Scale (see Table 11.3), social workers and clients identify and "weight" the importance of each of the agreed-upon goals. Use a 1- to 10-point scale, where 10 reflects the "most important." Record each goal in the appropriate cell. Then collaborate with the client to generate a series of five descriptive predictions concerning the possible outcomes of work toward achievement of each goal. Record those in the appropriate cells as well. These predictions provide you and your client with markers on which to base your evaluation of progress. The possible outcomes range from "most unfavorable" to "most favorable."

TABLE 11.3
Blank Goal Attainment Scale Form

Client: _____ Session Number or Date _____

Outcomes	Goal 1 Weight (1–10) ____	Goal 2 Weight (1–10) ____	Goal 3 Weight (1–10) ____	Goal 4 Weight (1–10) ____	Goal 5 Weight (1–10) ____
−2 Most unfavorable results thought likely					
−1 Less than expected success					
0 Expected level of success					
+1 More than expected success					
+2 Most favorable results thought likely					

© Cengage Learning

Other means for evaluating progress toward goal achievement include frequency counting and subjective rating. In counting, you, the client, or another person in the client's environment keeps track of the frequency of a goal-related phenomenon (see Table 11.4). For example, consider self-esteem: people who have low self-regard often think disparaging and critical thoughts about themselves.

TABLE 11.4
Frequency Count Form: Self-Approving Thoughts per Day

Client: _____

Date	Frequency
Day 1	2
Day 2	5
Day 3	4
Day 4	8
Day 5	11
Day 6	9
Day 7	12
Day 8	14
Day 9	14
Day 10	15

© Cengage Learning 2014

You and such a client might identify as a final goal to increase the frequency of self-approving thoughts. You might provide the client with a small notepad in which to keep track of the number of self-approving thoughts during a given period (for example, each day for 1 week). You could then transfer the frequency counts onto graph paper, with the expectation that the change program will lead to a higher frequency of self-approving thoughts per day. We often use frequency counting to establish a baseline for the targeted phenomenon, before implementing intervention plans. Then, we use the baseline as a benchmark for evaluating the effectiveness of the service approach. You can apply frequency-counting procedures to many different phenomena in various person-in-environment dimensions.

Subjective rating requires that you, the client, or another person make a relative judgment concerning the extent, duration, frequency, or intensity of a targeted phenomenon. For example, you might ask a client to create an imaginary 10-point scale that runs from "worst" or "least" (number 1) to "best" or "most" (number 10). The client may then use this subjective scale to rate the target phenomenon. For example, suppose a client is concerned about the quality of the relationship with her partner. You could make a request in this fashion: "Would you please imagine a scale that runs from 1 to 10, with 1 being the lowest possible and 10 being the highest possible? Now let's rate the quality of each encounter you had with your partner yesterday. We'll use this form [see Table 11.5] to record your ratings." By using the form with the client during your meeting, you increase the likelihood that she will understand how to use it and improve the chances that she will use it to record the quality of daily encounters between sessions. Suppose the client reports she had four interactions with her partner yesterday. The first interaction was positive (Level 8), the second was unpleasant (Level 3), the third was okay (Level 5), and the last was extremely positive (Level 9). You could then ask the client and perhaps her partner as well to use subjective rating forms (see Table 11.5) to track the quality of their interactions throughout the day. You could phrase the request in this manner: "I'll give you several blank copies of the Subjective Rating Form. Following each encounter with your partner, use a row in the form to indicate the date and time, provide a brief description of the interaction, and record your rating of its quality. Please do not share your ratings with your partner until we meet together again. When we have several weeks' worth of ratings, we will create a graph so we can determine how your views change as we work toward improving the quality of the relationship. How does that sound?"

Subjective ratings also work well for problems that involve the intensity of unpleasant personal feelings or sensations. We often call this a Subjective Units of Distress Scale (SUDS). For example, suppose you have a teenage high school student as a client. The teenager reports intense anxiety when she talks in front of her peers in classroom contexts. In this case, we plan to track progress by recording subjective ratings of the relative intensity of her anxious feelings in various classroom situations. Table 11.6 illustrates how you might use subjective ratings of distress for evaluation purposes.

TABLE 11.5
Sample Subjective Rating Form: Quality of Relationship Encounters

Client: _____

Date/Time	Encounter	Subjective Rating (1–10)
Day 1: 7:30 A.M.	Early morning conversation	8
Day 1: 11:30 A.M.	Phone conversation	3
Day 1: 6:17 P.M.	Early evening conversation	5
Day 1: 10:30 P.M.	Nighttime interaction	9

© Cengage Learning

TABLE 11.6
Sample Subjective Units of Distress Scale (SUDS)

Client: _____ Issue: Classroom Anxiety

Date/Time	Situation	SUDS Rating (1–10)
Day 1: 9:15 A.M.	English class: Teacher calls on me to answer a question. I know the answer.	7
Day 1: 11:20 A.M.	Math class: Teacher asks me to complete a problem on the board in front of the entire class.	9
Day 1: 1:12 P.M.	Speech class: I give a 1-minute preview of a 10-minute speech I'm supposed to give next week.	9
Day 1: 2:30 P.M.	Science Class: Teacher calls on me to answer a question from today's required reading. I don't know the answer.	10
Day 2:		

© Cengage Learning

Subjective ratings can be used in relation to almost all forms of human phenomena (for example, physiological, psychological, or social). Of course, because they are subjective by definition, they are susceptible to individual bias and other forms of human error. Nonetheless, subjective ratings can be extremely useful when used to complement objective measures or when objective tools are inappropriate or impractical.

Frequency counts and subjective rating tables can easily be converted into graphic form through spreadsheet software programs. Figure 11.3 reflects a graphic illustration of the data contained in Table 11.4.

In addition to frequency counts and subjective ratings, social workers may also select from a vast array of widely available, valid, and reliable paper-and-pencil measurement tools—often called rapid assessment instruments (RAIs). For example, *The Clinical Measurement Package: A Field Manual* (Hudson, 1982) contains nine scales that are useful to social workers. These scales relate to phenomena that often affect our clients. The Clinical Measurement Package (CMP) scales address

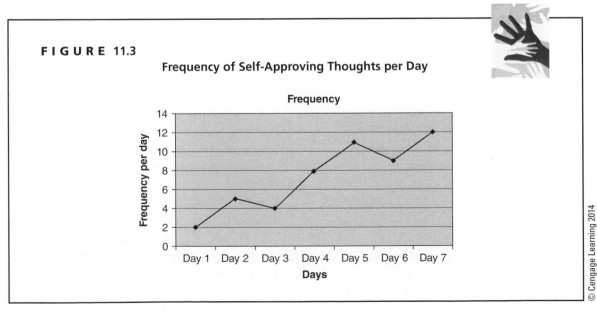

FIGURE 11.3

Frequency of Self-Approving Thoughts per Day

© Cengage Learning 2014

dimensions such as self-esteem, generalized contentment, marital satisfaction, sexual satisfaction, parental attitudes, child attitudes toward mother, child attitudes toward father, family relations, and peer relations. Each of the scales may be completed and scored quickly.

Measures for Clinical Practice: A Sourcebook (Fischer & Corcoran, 2007a, 2007b) is another extraordinary resource. The sourcebook contain two volumes of rapid assessment instruments relevant for many aspects of social work practice. Volume 1 contains more than 100 measures relevant for assessing various dimensions of couples, families, and children (Fischer & Corcoran, 2007a). Volume 2 includes more than 200 instruments relevant for adults (Fischer & Corcoran, 2007b). Among the measures are instruments to aid assessment of various kinds of abuse, acculturation, addiction, anxiety and fear, assertiveness, beliefs, children's behavior, client motivation, coping, couple and marital relationships, death concerns, depression and grief, ethnic identity, family functioning, geriatric issues, guilt, health issues, identity, impulsivity, interpersonal behavior, locus of control, loneliness, love, mood, narcissism, pain, parent–child relationship, perfectionism, phobias, posttraumatic stress, problem solving, procrastination, psychopathology and psychiatric symptoms, rape, satisfaction with life, schizotypal symptoms, self-concept and -esteem, self-control, self-efficacy, sexuality, smoking, social functioning, social support, stress, suicide, treatment satisfaction, and substance abuse. The two volumes of *Measures for Clinical Practice* represent a rich resource of easily administered and rapidly scored instruments.

EXERCISE 11-4: PLANNING FOR EVALUATION

Review the earlier exercises that involve Mr. K., Loretta, the S. family, Mrs. F., and the troubled social service agency. Then, in the spaces provided, describe two means for evaluating progress toward goal achievement in each of those case situations. First, plan an evaluation process that is more objective in nature. Then, plan a subjective method to measure progress. The primary purpose is to encourage you to consider various means for measuring progress in your work with clients. Of course, whatever evaluation plans you generate should relate directly to the identified issues and goals so that progress can be determined.

1. Prepare brief plans by which you might subjectively evaluate progress toward goal attainment in your work with Mr. K. Then, outline plans by which you might objectively evaluate progress toward goal achievement in your work with him.

2. Prepare brief plans by which you might subjectively evaluate progress toward goal attainment in your work with Loretta. Then, outline plans by which you might objectively evaluate progress toward goal achievement in your work with her.

3. Prepare brief plans by which you might subjectively evaluate progress toward goal attainment in your work with the S. family. Then, outline plans by which you might objectively evaluate progress toward goal achievement in your work with the S. family.

4. Prepare brief plans by which you might subjectively evaluate progress toward goal attainment in your work with Mrs. F. Then, outline plans by which you might objectively evaluate progress toward goal achievement in your work with Mrs. F.

5. Prepare brief plans by which you might subjectively evaluate progress toward goal attainment in your work with the troubled social service agency. Then, outline plans by which you might objectively evaluate progress toward goal achievement in your work with the organization.

6. When you have completed these exercises, please consider the means of evaluation you have identified and ask yourself the following questions: How subject to evaluator bias and other forms of error are these evaluation procedures? What are the ethical implications of these forms of evaluation? Do the procedures appear to be respectful of the personal values and the cultural preferences you might expect of these clients? Finally, are the procedures likely to yield an accurate indication of progress toward the goals established in Exercise 11-1? In the following space, specify those aspects of evaluation planning you need to strengthen.

Summarizing the Contract

Summarizing the contract involves a concise review of the essential elements of the service agreement that you and the client approved. The service contract covers issues for work, goals, action plans, tasks or action steps, and the means by which you and the client intend to evaluate progress. Written agreements are generally preferred so that all involved parties may have copies and can refer to them as needed (Hanvey & Philpot, 1994). The service agreement may be organized in accordance with the framework shown here (see Box 11.4) and incorporated into a DAC. Alternately, they may be prepared separately as formal contracts, using letterhead paper, with spaces for you and the client to sign. Whether formal or informal, written or unwritten, the service agreement provides for the description of issues, goals, and plans. The service contract reflects your commitment to work together with the client toward achievement of the agreed-upon goals. Of course, the specific dimensions of the format shown here may not be relevant for practice in all social work settings or with all clients, issues, or situations. As a professional social worker, you are responsible for adopting contract guidelines that best match the needs and functions of your agency program and your clients. Regardless of the setting, however, you will probably find that service agreements or contracts represent a key component of effective social work practice.

BOX 11.4
Guidelines for Completion of the Service Contract

III. Service Contract

    A. Problems/Issues

        1. **Client-Identified Issues**
        In this section, clearly outline the problems/issues that the client identifies.

        2. **Worker-Identified Issues**
        In this section, outline the issues that you identify.

        3. **Focal Problems/Agreed-Upon Issues for Work**
        In this section, outline the issues that both parties agree to address. These are the issues that remain the focus for work unless subsequently renegotiated by you and the client. Of course, either party may request revisions to the service agreement.

    B. Service Goals

        In this section, outline the final outcome goals that you and the client select. Of course, they should relate directly to the problems or issues for work. If possible, define the final goals in a SMART format. Sometimes, of course, only general goal statements are possible or advisable. Whether specific or general, you may record the service goals in this part of the contract.

    C. Plans

        1. **Action Plans/Service Approach**
        In this section, build upon the case formulation to summarize the general parameters of the action plans or service plans that you and your client have devised. Make note of factors such as who will be involved; where, when, and how often the work will occur, and for how long; and how the process will unfold. Identify, where applicable, the social work role or roles you will assume, and the theoretical approach, perspective, or model selected for use in work with this particular client as you collaboratively pursue the service goals.

            a. **Client Tasks/Action Steps**
            In this section, outline the initial tasks or action steps that the client agrees to undertake in his or her attempt to achieve the agreed-upon goals.

            b. **Worker Tasks**
            In this section, outline the initial tasks or activities that you plan to undertake in your effort to help achieve the agreed-upon goals.

(continued)

   c. **In-Session Activities**

     In this section, outline the initial tasks or activities that you and the client agree to undertake during your meetings together.

   d. **Maintenance Tasks**

     If the goals involve long-term change, use this section to outline the tasks or activities that you agree will occur on a regular, ongoing basis to promote lasting change.

2. **Plans to Evaluate Progress**

   In this section, outline the means and processes by which you and the client will evaluate progress toward goal accomplishment. Whenever possible, incorporate valid and reliable objective evaluation instruments to accompany subjective means and processes.

Social workers typically prepare service contracts or service agreements in narrative form for inclusion in the case record. However, the addition of graphic representations (for example, logic models, concept maps, or tables) to the agreement can serve multiple purposes (Alter & Egan, 1997; Alter & Murty, 1997; Julian, 1997; Julian, Jones, & Deyo, 1995; Mattaini, 1993a, 1995). Indeed, preparation of an Action-Planning Table (APT) enables you and your clients to refer regularly to the focal problems and service goals, and to the action plans and the evaluation plans for each goal. You can also incorporate specific action steps, the results of those steps, and the results of various outcome indicators (for example, subjective rating scores, or scale scores). In a sense, such a planning table is another kind of "concept map" or "logic map." However, we typically arrange the components in a linear fashion to highlight the relationship of problems to goals, goals to plans, plans to action steps, and action steps to outcomes.

An abbreviated Action-Planning Table to guide service activities in work with Mrs. Chase might look something like the one presented in Table 11.7.

TABLE 11.7
Action-Planning Table: Mrs. Chase

Problem/Issue	Service Goal	Action Plans	Evaluation Plans

Issue 1:
  Arguments with son and husband
	Goal 1a:
	  Decrease frequency of arguments by 50% within 4 weeks.
		Service Plans 1a:
		  8 weekly cognitive-behavioral and task-centered service sessions
			Evaluation Plans 1a:
			  Argument log (completed daily)

	Goal 1b:
	  Increase frequency of satisfying exchanges with son and husband by 50% within 4 weeks.
		Service Plans 1b: 8 weekly cognitive-behavioral and task-centered service sessions	Evaluation Plans 1b:
			  Satisfying exchanges log (completed daily)

© Cengage Learning

(continued)

Issue 2: Irritable, critical, angry feelings toward son and husband	Goal 2a: Decrease frequency and intensity of negative feelings of irritation and anger toward son and husband by 50% within 4 weeks.	Service Plans 1a: 8 weekly cognitive-behavioral and task-centered service sessions	Evaluation Plans 1a: Argument log (completed daily)
	Goal 2b: Increase frequency and intensity of positive feelings of comfort and acceptance of son and husband by 50% within 6 weeks.	Service Plans 1b: 8 weekly cognitive-behavioral and task-centered service sessions	Evaluation Plans 1b: Satisfying exchanges log (completed daily)

EXERCISE 11-5: SUMMARIZING THE CONTRACT

1. For this exercise, please review the information you organized into the description and assessment sections of your own DAC (see Exercises 10-4 and 10-5). Based on what you know about yourself and what you included in the description and assessment sections, word-process a written contract as if you are your own social worker. In creating your contract, be aware that you, despite your considerable self-understanding, may miss one or more key issues that a professional social worker might help you to identify. Therefore—even though it concerns you rather than someone else—view the contract as a dynamic document, subject to later revision. Prepare the contract in accordance with the format provided in the contract section of the DAC. When complete, place the assessment and case formulation portions of the DAC into the "A Personal Case Record" section of your Social Work Skills Learning Portfolio. At this point, you have completed all three sections of a DAC—the Description, the Assessment, and the Contract.

Summary

Based on the exploration and assessment processes, social workers collaborate with clients to reach consensus about a service contract that specifies the goals for work and describes the plans to achieve them. Skills that are especially applicable to this phase of practice include (1) establishing goals, (2) developing action plans, (3) identifying action steps, (4) planning for evaluation, and (5) summarizing the contract.

CHAPTER 11: EXPERIENTIAL INTERVIEWING EXERCISE

At this point, you have completed two interviews with a practice client and are planning to undertake a third. Thus far, you probably used some or all of the beginning skills and many or most of the exploring skills as well. As a result, you have probably demonstrated a high level of empathy with, respect for, and understanding of the practice client as a person as well as his or her circumstances. You might have acknowledged some of the client's strengths and abilities. You have probably also collaboratively examined the client-identified problems or issues of concern and know a good deal about how they originated, when and how they occur, and their impact on the client's life. You may have summarized the practice client's ideas or hypotheses about why or how those issues occur.

Following the second interview, you and the practice client stepped out of your respective roles and reflected upon and reviewed the experience. You sought feedback from the practice client, prepared word-processed entries for the practice client case record, and probably engaged in preliminary planning for this upcoming third meeting.

Building on the previous meetings with your practice client, conduct the third interview. Ensure that the setting is private, and again record the meeting. You might begin by proposing a tentative agenda and then, of course, seek feedback from the client about it. When you and the practice client agree upon a direction for today's meeting, proceed to use exploring, assessing, and contracting skills with an aim of reaching consensus about a few primary goals for your work together. Goals phrased in SMART format are usually preferable. However, some clients are not yet ready for that degree of specificity. If so, general goals or directions should suffice. In addition to exploring and assessing skills, the most applicable contracting skills include establishing goals, developing action plans, identify action steps, planning for evaluation, and summarizing the contract. Be sure to seek feedback from the practice client about all aspects of the service agreement (contract). If the practice client's views about the goals and plans differ from yours, continue discussion until you reach genuine consensus. Major difficulties occur when social workers adopt one set of goals and plans, and clients adopt another. As you conclude, arrange for another meeting and share with the practice client your preliminary ideas about what may happen in the next meeting.

When you've finished the interview, complete the following:

1. Leave your respective social worker and client roles. Request that your colleague complete a copy of the Contracting Skills Rating Form (see Appendix 11). Aspects of the Talking and Listening, Exploring, and Assessing Skills Rating Forms may also be applicable. When your colleague has completed the rating forms, inquire about today's interview experience. Ask general open-ended questions so that you might get as much evaluative feedback as possible and, through that, enhance your learning. For example, you might ask your colleague questions such as:

   ◆ What thoughts, feelings, or other reactions do you have about today's meeting?
   ◆ What do you think about the goals that we established?
   ◆ What do you think about the plans we discussed?
   ◆ What parts of the interview affected you the most—either positively or negatively?
   ◆ What do you wish had happened during the interview that did not occur?
   ◆ What suggestions do you have about how the interview could have been better, more helpful, or more constructive for you?
   ◆ What suggestions do you have about how I could have been a better or more helpful social worker today?

Summarize your partner's feedback in a word-processed document titled "Third Meeting with a Practice Client." Label this particular section "Practice Client Feedback."

2. Next, describe and discuss your own reactions to the interview. How did you feel about it? What did you like and what did you dislike about it? Refer to the active-listening, beginning, exploring, assessing, and contracting sections of The Social Work Skills Interview Rating Form (see Appendix 15) to evaluate your performance. Identify those skills you performed well, those that need improvement, those that you should have used during the interview, and those that you used but probably should not have. Evaluate the quality of the service agreement or contract. Identify aspects that might be missing or ways it might be improved. You might have a chance to address those in a subsequent meeting. Finally, discuss what you would do differently if you had a chance to conduct the interview again and outline what you might do in the next interview to improve the quality of the interview. Summarize your ratings, reactions, and reflections in a section of the "Third Meeting with a Practice Client" document. Label the section "My Ratings, Reactions, and Reflections" and then save the entire document for deposit into the "Experiential Interviewing Exercise" folder of your Social Work Skills Portfolio.

3. Next, reflect upon the entirety of the interview experience and use relevant preparing skills to prepare for the next meeting with the practice client. Draw upon what you learned and the documents you created to word-process tentative plans for the meeting. Label the document "Preliminary Plans for the Fourth Interview with a Practice Client" and deposit it in the "Experiential Interviewing Exercise" folder of your Social Work Skills Portfolio.

4. Record information gained during this meeting into a coherently organized word-processed document. You might use the relevant sections of the DAC format. If you have gathered additional descriptive information, organize into a word-processed document labeled "Description-Supplement." If additional analysis and synthesis requires alteration or supplementation to the assessment, word-process a new entry for the case record. Label the document "Assessment-Supplement." Record the date of the interview as well as the date you prepare the record. Identify yourself as the social worker but continue to disguise the identity of the practice client. Label the document "Contract." After you have completed drafts of these documents, replay the recording. Make note of exchanges that may enhance their quality or accuracy. Revise the documents accordingly. When finished, place them into the "Practice Client Case Record" subfolder of your Social Work Skills Learning Portfolio.

CHAPTER 11: SELF-APPRAISAL

As you finish this chapter, please reflect on your learning by completing the following self-appraisal exercise.

SELF-APPRAISAL: THE CONTRACTING SKILLS

Please respond to the following items. Your answers should help you to assess your proficiency in the contracting skills. Read each statement carefully. Then, use the following 4-point rating scale to indicate the degree to which you agree or disagree with each statement. Record your numerical response in the space provided.

4 = Strongly agree;   2 = Disagree;

3 = Agree;   1 = Strongly disagree

4	3	2	1	Rating Statement
				At this point in time, I can
☐	☐	☐	☐	1. Discuss the purposes and functions of contracting.
☐	☐	☐	☐	2. Establish goals.
☐	☐	☐	☐	3. Develop action plans.
☐	☐	☐	☐	4. Identify action steps.
☐	☐	☐	☐	5. Plan for evaluation.
☐	☐	☐	☐	6. Summarize the contract.
☐	☐	☐	☐	7. Assess proficiency in the contracting skills.
				Subtotal

Note: These items are identical to those contained in the Contracting Skills section of the Social Work Skills Self-Appraisal Questionnaire presented in Appendix 3. If you completed that self-appraisal before beginning Chapter 1, you have already responded to these items once before. You may now compare the responses you made on that occasion with those you made this time. Also, compare the two subtotals. If you believe that you have progressed in terms of your proficiency, the more recent subtotal should be higher than the earlier one.

WORKING AND EVALUATING

As you engage clients in the process of working toward the goals you jointly agree to pursue, you make a transition. Until this point in the helping process, you use social work skills primarily for collecting information, developing a relationship, formulating an assessment, and negotiating a service contract. Once you agree on a contract, however, you may legitimately use skills to promote change within various aspects of the person-issue-situation. This chapter (see Box 12.1) should help you develop proficiency in the working and evaluating skills. These skills build on clients' experience and frames of reference by introducing, in a much more active and expressive fashion, your professional knowledge and expertise.

The skills covered in earlier chapters are primarily empathic, exploratory, and contractual in nature. You use them to clarify policies under which you operate; explore factors associated with the origin, development, and maintenance of the issues of concern; learn about and understand clients' experience from their own perspective; collaboratively develop an assessment; and agree on plans to pursue and evaluate progress toward the jointly determined goals for work. Throughout these processes, you listen actively to convey empathic understanding, reflect hypotheses, ask questions, and seek feedback. This encourages further self-expression and self-exploration by clients while also strengthening your working relationship. You may sometimes go slightly beyond clients' literal statements, but your primary focus is on their experience and frame of reference.

The working and evaluating skills are significantly different. Here, you may appropriately proceed from your social work frame of reference; your professional knowledge, experience, and expertise; and your capacity to think critically, rationally, and free from superstition and prejudice. These skills tend to be more active and expressive than empathic in nature. Through the working and evaluating skills, you express your professional agenda; your thoughts, feelings, beliefs, opinions, hypotheses, deductions, and conclusions. You first use such an active and expressive skill during the beginning phase of practice, when you suggest a tentative purpose for meeting and outline relevant

BOX 12.1
Chapter Purpose

The purpose of this chapter is to help learners develop proficiency in the working and evaluating skills.

Goals

Following completion of this chapter, learners should be able to demonstrate proficiency in:

◆ Discussing the purposes and functions of the working and evaluating skills
◆ Rehearsing action steps
◆ Reviewing action steps
◆ Evaluating
◆ Focusing
◆ Educating
◆ Advising
◆ Representing
◆ Responding with immediacy
◆ Reframing
◆ Confronting inconsistencies
◆ Pointing out endings
◆ Progress recording
◆ Assessing proficiency in the working and evaluating skills

Core EPAS Competencies

The skills addressed in this chapter support the following core EPAS competencies:

◆ Identify as a professional social worker and conduct oneself accordingly (EP2.1.1).
◆ Apply social work ethical principles to guide professional practice (EP2.1.2).
◆ Apply critical thinking to inform and communicate professional judgments (EP2.1.3).
◆ Engage diversity and difference in practice (EP2.1.4).
◆ Apply knowledge of human behavior and the social environment (EP2.1.7).
◆ Respond to contexts that shape practice (EP2.1.9).
◆ Intervene, and evaluate with individuals, families, groups, organizations, and communities (EP2.1.10[c–d]).

policy and ethical factors. You also express your knowledge and experience when you identify an issue, suggest a goal, or propose an action step during the assessing and contracting processes.

Occasionally, the expressive skills bear little obvious relationship to clients' words or actions. However, most of the time, use of the expressive skills reflects an attempt to expand or extend clients' experience. You take what you have learned from the client and process it through your knowledge of research findings and science-based theoretical perspectives. Then, you apply the results in words and actions that you reasonably anticipate will help clients progress toward their goals.

Because the working and evaluating skills tend to be expressive rather than empathic, you must have a clear and justifiable rationale for their use. Your motivations should be professional, not personal. Resist temptations to share your knowledge, feelings, or opinions simply because they occur to you in the moment. Rather, the working skills you apply should consistently relate to the contract for work. That is, use your knowledge, intelligence, and expertise to help clients in their pursuit of agreed-upon goals. Indeed, unless you can demonstrate a clear relationship to the goals, it would be quite difficult to establish a logically defensible rationale for the use of an expressive skill. To determine whether an expressive work-phase skill is appropriate and applicable, you might critically consider the following questions:

◆ Have we adequately explored the person or people, the issue or issues, and the circumstances?

◆ Have I sufficiently communicated empathic understanding of the client's experience so that I may now reasonably consider using an expressive work-phase skill?

◆ Do we have a clear service agreement or contract?

◆ What is my objective in choosing one or more expressive work-phase skills at this particular time?

◆ Will my use of one or more expressive work-phase skills at this point help the client progress toward resolution of at least one of our agreed-upon problems or issues and goals?

◆ Will the use of a particular work-phase skill convey respect for the client's personal values and cultural preferences?

◆ How will the client likely react to my use of a particular expressive work-phase skill?

◆ What is the risk that using an expressive work-phase skill at this point in this context might endanger the client's personal or social well-being?

◆ What might be the risks that using an expressive work-phase skill now might endanger other people?

◆ How might my personal thoughts and feelings about this client at this time influence my selection or application of one or more expressive work-phase skills?

◆ Am I tempted to use an expressive work-phase skill now to express a personal view of my own, satisfy an individual need, or fulfill my own impulses?

If you think critically about these questions and consider their implications, you should be able to determine the appropriateness and applicability of a particular expressive work-phase skill. If you remain uncertain, however, you may choose a skill that is clearly more appropriate or return to an empathic exploring skill until you and the client are ready to take interventive action.

During the work and evaluation phase, social workers continue to use many of the empathic skills previously discussed. Indeed, we use skills of reflecting feelings, reflecting meanings, reflecting feelings and meanings, reflecting hypotheses, and going beyond what is said throughout the entire helping process. We also regularly use the skills of seeking feedback, asking questions, and seeking clarification. During the working and evaluating phase, however, skills such as rehearsing, reviewing, focusing, reframing, educating, and advising are increasingly used. In using expressive work-phase skills, maintain your focus on the assessment and service contract. In particular, shape your efforts according to the agreed-upon goals and the service approach you and the client have established. Each application of a working skill should relate in some way to one or more of the identified goals or their associated instrumental objectives and action steps.

The skills especially applicable to this phase include (1) rehearsing action steps, (2) reviewing action steps, (3) evaluating, (4) focusing, (5) educating, (6) advising, (7) representing, (8) responding with immediacy, (9) reframing, (10) confronting inconsistencies, (11) pointing out endings, and (12) recording progress.

Rehearsing Action Steps

As part of the contracting process, clients often agree to attempt an action step. In the work phase, social workers prepare and encourage clients to carry out agreed-upon tasks. Unfortunately, clients' good intentions during a meeting are not always realized. Life's demands and challenges sometimes get in the way so that certain action steps remain unattempted or incomplete. When this happens, you and your clients identify and confront those biopsychosocial or environmental obstacles that interfere with task accomplishment. You may do several things within the context of your meetings with clients to increase the chances that steps will be taken. Various in-session activities such as role play, guided practice, and visualization bridge the gap between the special circumstances of the social work interview and the more common environment of everyday life. Involving more than talk alone, rehearsal activities constitute action step practice. By engaging several dimensions of experience (for example, thinking, feeling, and doing) in the rehearsal activity, clients move closer to what is necessary in the real-world context.

Rehearsing an action step decreases anxiety associated with the idea of taking action, enhances motivation, and increases the probability that the task will be undertaken. It also improves the chances that the action step will be successful. Through rehearsal, social workers help clients identify what needs to take place, anticipate what could happen, consider probable scenarios, and prepare various ways and means to complete the task. Although many clients are quite capable of creatively generating alternate scenarios and potential courses of action, some are not. When clients need such help, you may appropriately assume a more active role to anticipate possible circumstances and identify various options. You might propose a few different ways to undertake the step or present examples of how other people might do so. As part of the rehearsal process, you could model an action step for clients by saying or doing what they could say or do in various circumstances. In similar fashion, you might engage clients in role play. For example, you could assume the role of a person who will be involved in a client's action step. During or following the role play, you provide the client with guidance, feedback, support, and encouragement.

Another form of rehearsal involves clients visualizing themselves undertaking an agreed-upon action step (Lazarus, 1984). Before encouraging clients to engage in visualization, however, first determine whether they have the capacity to create mental images or "pictures." You might explore this by asking, "If I were to ask you to imagine in your mind's eye the kitchen in the place where you live, could you do so?" If the client says, "Yes," you could then say, "Good, some people aren't able to imagine as well as you do. Your mental capacity in this area will help in our work together." You might then say, "Please assume a relaxed position and take a few slow, deep breaths. You may close your eyes if you wish but closing your eyes is not essential—many people can visualize just as well with their eyes open." Then you might go on to ask, "Please imagine a movie screen on which you can see the context where the step you'll take will occur. Now see yourself actually taking the action we have discussed." You might pause for a moment to ask the client to study the visualized scene in detail, noticing all aspects of the action step.

You may use visualization to identify clients' fears and to anticipate potential obstacles to successful action, as well as for the purpose of rehearsal. Once your clients generate clear ideas (that is, mental pictures) about what needs to be done, you may ask them to imagine overcoming obstacles and successfully completing the action step. Following that, you may also ask clients to identify the positive thoughts and feelings that accompany imaginary completion of the action step.

The following is an excerpt from an interview in which Susan Holder helped Lynn Chase to rehearse an action step through role play.

EXAMPLE: REHEARSING AN ACTION STEP

WORKER: (*identifying an action step; seeking feedback*) One of the steps we identified is to express your affection for both Robert and Richard at least once each day. If I understand the usual patterns correctly, this would represent a change from the way you have recently related. Is that right?

CLIENT: (*MRS. CHASE*) Yes, it would be a big change.

WORKER: Making changes such as this usually requires some preparation and planning. By practicing ahead of time, we increase the likelihood that we will actually do it. With that in mind, what do you think about taking a little time to plan and practice with me what you are going to say and do each day with Robert and Richard?

CLIENT: Okay.

WORKER: Thanks. Now, when you think of where and when you might make your first caring statement to Robert, what comes to mind?

CLIENT: Well, I think that I'd like to start off the day with something positive.

WORKER: Good idea! Where do you think you will be when you make your first affectionate statement?

CLIENT: Well, I think it will probably be in the kitchen.

WORKER: In the kitchen. . . . Okay, let me assume the role of Robert. And, if you would, let's imagine that it is now tomorrow morning and we are in your kitchen. What will you say to him?

CLIENT: Well, I think I'll say something like, "Robert, I know that we have been on each other's nerves lately. I now recognize that a lot of it has been my fault. I guess I've been more stressed out than I realized. Anyway, I want to say I'm sorry and I want you to know that I have never loved you more than I do now."

WORKER: (*AS ROBERT*) Geez. Thanks, Mom. I love you too.

WORKER: (*AS HERSELF*) Thanks, Lynn. When you say those words to Robert, I can really see your love for him. It shows especially when you look right into his eyes with gentleness and affection. How does it feel to you?

CLIENT: It feels really good. I feel warm inside. I feel loving toward him and also better about myself.

WORKER: How do you think Robert will respond to your words?

CLIENT: I'm not sure. But I do think he'll like it, and it should bring us closer.

WORKER: That's exactly what you want to happen, isn't it?

CLIENT: Yes, it sure is.

WORKER: How do you feel when you realize that Robert will probably appreciate your comments and feel very loved?

CLIENT: Really good. I can't wait until tomorrow morning!

The following excerpt illustrates how Ms. Holder, the social worker, helps Mrs. Chase rehearse an action step using visualization.

EXAMPLE: REHEARSING AN ACTION STEP

WORKER: (*identifying the step; exploring probability of action; seeking feedback*) One of the steps we identified as a means to decrease stress and increase feelings of personal comfort is to spend 15 minutes each day planning for or working in your garden. I must admit to wondering about your ability to actually do that. You are very busy. You do so many things that I wonder whether you will really take the time to do the 15 minutes of gardening each day. What do you think?

CLIENT: (*MRS. CHASE*) Well, to be honest, I have known for some time that I need to get back to gardening and I just haven't done it. I keep on making promises to myself and I keep on breaking them.

WORKER: Thanks for being frank with me. If we're going to get anywhere with these issues, honesty and openness is the best policy. If you don't think you will actually take a step that we identify, please share that so we can make better plans.

CLIENT: Okay, I will.

WORKER: Thanks, Lynn. Making changes such as this usually requires some preparation and planning. Unless we practice ahead of time, things tend to stay the same. With that in mind, shall we try a little experiment that may make it a little easier to actually do the gardening that you'd like to do?

CLIENT: Well, I guess so. What kind of experiment?

WORKER: I'm sure that you've heard the old saying "Practice makes perfect." Well, for many people, practicing in one's imagination is nearly as effective as actually practicing in real life. If you happen to be one of the people who can form mental pictures, then we can use that capacity to visualize the steps you plan to take. By visual practicing, you increase the likelihood that you will actually begin to garden for real. Does that make sense to you?

CLIENT: Yes, I think so. How do I do it?

WORKER: First, let's find out about your picture-making ability. Please try now to imagine your garden as it used to be when it was in full bloom. Can you picture it?

CLIENT: Yes. I can see it now.

WORKER: Can you see it in color or is it black and white?

CLIENT: It's in color.

WORKER: Wonderful. Now, please imagine yourself in the garden tilling the soil around the growing plants. Is that the sort of thing you might be doing?

CLIENT: Yes. I'd be down on my knees, working the soil.

WORKER: Can you visualize that in your mind's eye?

CLIENT: Yes.

WORKER: Now, please describe what you are feeling, what you are experiencing, as you work the garden.

(*continued*)

CLIENT: Well, I feel warm and relaxed. I feel content. I feel happy. Working the soil is, well, it's pleasurable.

WORKER: Now, please picture yourself in the garden this very evening. Can you do that?

CLIENT: Yes.

WORKER: And does that feel as good as the other picture did?

CLIENT: Yes.

WORKER: Now, let's shift to a different picture. Suppose it rains. Can you imagine planning or preparing for the garden in a way that would also be relaxing or pleasurable?

CLIENT: Yes. I can work on my drawings of the garden. I draw a kind of map to show which plants, fruits, and vegetables go where in the garden. I also work out what to plant, when to plant, and the approximate dates they should be harvested.

WORKER: And what do you feel in this picture?

CLIENT: I feel just as relaxed and content as when I'm in the garden itself.

WORKER: Let's create a picture of you actually doing that on rainy days when you cannot go out into the garden.

CLIENT: Okay.

As a result of rehearsing—whether through role play, guided practice, visualization, or some combination of them—clients are more likely to carry out the activity in their own natural environment.

EXERCISE 12-1: REHEARSING ACTION STEPS

Review the earlier exercises that involve Mr. K., Loretta, the S. family, Mrs. F., and the troubled social service agency. Respond in the spaces provided by describing what you would do and say in using the skill of rehearsing the action steps you identified as part of Exercise 11-3.

1. You are in the midst of an interview with Mr. K. You have agreed on the issues and goals for work and have identified action steps (see Exercise 11-3). In the following space, describe what you would do and say in rehearsing the action step with this client. In formulating your description, anticipate what the client might say or do in response to your statements and actions.

2. You are in the midst of an interview with Loretta. You have agreed on the issues and goals for work and have identified an action step (see Exercise 11-3). In the following space, describe what you would do and say in rehearsing the action step with this client. In formulating your description, anticipate what the client might say or do in response to your statements and actions.

3. You are in the midst of an interview with the seven-member blended S. family. You have agreed on the issues and goals for work and have identified an action step (see Exercise 11-3). In the following space, describe what you would do and say in rehearsing the action step with this client system. In formulating your description, anticipate what the clients might say or do in response to your statements and actions.

4. You are interviewing Mrs. F. You have agreed on the issues and goals for work and have identified an action step (see Exercise 11-3). In the following space, describe what you would do and say in rehearsing the action step with this client. In formulating your description, anticipate what the client might say or do in response to your statements and actions.

5. You are meeting with the executive director of the agency for which you are providing social work consultative services. You and the director have agreed on the issues and goals for work and have identified an action step (see Exercise 11-3). In an initial effort to turn the troubled agency in a positive direction, the director intends to make a presentation to the board of directors outlining the major components of a strategic plan. In the following space, describe what you would do and say in rehearsing the action step with the agency director. In formulating your description, anticipate what the director might say or do in response to your words and actions.

Reviewing Action Steps

There are three possible outcomes when a client agrees to undertake an action step: (1) the client may complete it, (2) the client may partially complete it, or (3) the client may not attempt any portion of the action step. The first two outcomes typically represent progress; the third does not. Even the third outcome, however, may be useful if you and the client carefully review the process to improve the chance of success in the future. In working with clients, try to increase the probability that they will attempt and complete agreed-upon action steps. If clients rehearse an action step before attempting it for real, they are more likely to try it. Clients may also become more motivated to take action when they understand that they will subsequently review the action step with you. Demonstrate your interest in the process and outcome of their action steps by asking about them. By reviewing what happened following the attempt, you also gather information that contributes to the evaluation of progress toward goal achievement and the identification of subsequent action steps.

In reviewing action steps, adopt an attitude of supportive curiosity. Share your pleasure when clients partially or fully complete the task or activity. On the other hand, avoid disapproval or criticism when clients fail to attempt an action step. Rather, convey your interest through questions such as "What do you think got in the way of the attempt?" In such circumstances, explore with clients the thinking and feeling experiences that led them to defer action. Also inquire about situational factors that may have contributed to a change in plans. Often, it will become clear that unanticipated obstacles interfered with completion of the action step. You and your clients can use that information to devise alternate plans that address the obstacles. Then, you can rehearse the revised action steps. When clients complete an action step, you may appropriately express both pleasure and curiosity as you inquire about the factors contributing to the accomplishment. "What was different this time that enabled you to take this step?" For clients who have partly completed the activity, inquire with pleasure and interest about those differences that made it possible to take this "step in the right direction." Later, you may explore what factors blocked a more complete attempt and then collaborate to adjust the plans. When clients partially or fully complete the action step, encourage them to identify and express the satisfying thoughts and feelings that accompany action toward goal achievement. In most circumstances, you may also appropriately share your positive impressions about the client's efforts. Following such encouragement, you and your clients may then proceed to identify and rehearse additional action steps.

EXAMPLE: REVIEWING A COMPLETED ACTION STEP

WORKER: (*MS. HOLDER*) Last time we talked, you agreed to spend 15 minutes each day in gardening activities. If you recall, we went through the process of visualizing those activities in your mind's eye. How did that work out?

CLIENT: (*MRS. CHASE*) It was great! I gardened every day, sometimes more than 15 minutes, and I enjoyed it enormously. It spread out into other parts of my life too. I felt more calm and content throughout the day.

WORKER: Wonderful! So, it was truly effective in increasing your feelings of contentment?

CLIENT: Yes. It really worked. I had only one headache all week, and I felt much better.

WORKER: Terrific! Now is there anything about the gardening activity that we should change to make it better?

CLIENT: No. It's working just fine. Let's not change anything about it.

WORKER: Agreed. Let's keep the gardening activity just the same. That is, each day you will spend 15 minutes in a gardening activity. Is that right?

CLIENT: Yes.

EXAMPLE: REVIEWING A PARTIALLY COMPLETED ACTION STEP

WORKER: (*MS. HOLDER*) Last time we talked, you agreed to spend 15 minutes each day in gardening activities. If you recall, we went through the process of visualizing those activities in your mind's eye. How did that work out?

CLIENT: (*MRS. CHASE*) Well, I gardened on 2 days this week but I couldn't find the time to do any more than that. I was just too busy.

WORKER: You were able to find time to do the gardening on 2 of the 7 days. That's a very good beginning. On the 2 days that you gardened, what was it like?

CLIENT: Well, I guess at the beginning of the week I was just determined to do the gardening. I did it and I liked it. It's a lot to do, to start up a garden when you haven't worked on it for a long time. But I enjoyed it a lot and I felt good on those 2 days. On the third day, I just couldn't find the time.

WORKER: It sounds like the 2 days that you did the gardening were very good days for you. You enjoyed those days at lot. On the third day when you did not garden you didn't feel as well. Would I be correct in saying that the gardening is definitely a helpful activity?

(continued)

CLIENT: Oh, yes! If only I would do it!

WORKER: Let's see if we can figure out some way to make it easier for you to do the gardening and gain the benefits from it. What was different about the days that you did garden from the days that you didn't?

CLIENT: Well, I was really motivated on the first 2 days. On the third day, I had a tough time at work, and I was exhausted when I got home. I just slumped onto the sofa and went to sleep. I guess I was tired every night after that.

WORKER: Let's assume then that when you come home from work really tired, it's much harder for you to do the gardening, even though it leads to relaxing and contented feelings. I wonder, when you fall asleep on the sofa after work, do you awaken feeling as rested and relaxed as you do when you garden?

CLIENT: Actually, I feel much worse after dozing on the sofa. I'm kind of grouchy for the rest of the evening. And I don't sleep very well at night. It's better when I garden.

WORKER: Now that we know that, let's see what we can do to help you garden even when you're tired and exhausted from work. Imagine that you have just come home from a stressful day at work. You're exhausted. Your usual pattern has been to crash on the sofa. This time, however, imagine instead that you take a drink of ice water and walk out to the garden. You sit in a chair and look at your garden while drinking the ice water. You don't do anything. You just sit there. After 10 minutes or so, you can feel the stress and exhaustion begin to lessen. You decide to do just a little bit of gardening. After 15 minutes, you pause, and notice that you feel calm and relaxed. You're no longer tired. Instead, you're ready to go on with the rest of your evening.

How about it, Mrs. Chase, could you imagine that pretty clearly?

CLIENT: Yes. And I can see myself really relaxing during the gardening. I don't relax as well when I sleep on the sofa.

WORKER: In that case, what do you think about trying the 15 minutes of gardening again during this next week—only, let's go for 4 days instead of all 7?

CLIENT: That sounds good. I think I'll do it this week.

EXAMPLE: REVIEWING AN UNATTEMPTED ACTION STEP

WORKER: (MS. HOLDER) Last time we talked, you agreed to spend 15 minutes each day in gardening activities. If you recall, we went through the process of visualizing those activities in your mind's eye. How did that work out?

CLIENT: (MRS. CHASE) Well, I thought about it but I couldn't find the time to do any gardening at all. I was just too busy.

WORKER: You were unable to find time to do the gardening at all during this past week. Tell me, during this past week, have there been any signs that things are getting better?

CLIENT: Well, no. Things are about the same. I did feel a lot better after talking with you last time, but that lasted only a day or so.

(continued)

WORKER: It sounds like there was some temporary relief from talking about the problems with me, but there hasn't been any real progress, is that right?

CLIENT: Yes, I'm afraid so.

WORKER: Let's talk some about the gardening activity itself. In our discussion last time, you were quite sure that when you begin to garden again, even for a little bit, you will soon feel better. Do you think that still holds true, or have you reconsidered whether gardening would actually be helpful to you?

CLIENT: Well, I know it would help me, but I just can't find the time.

WORKER: If you still think the gardening would be helpful, let's see if we can identify what gets in the way of taking time to do it. During this past week, what did you end up doing instead of the gardening?

CLIENT: Well, on the first evening I planned to garden, Robert injured his knee playing basketball and I had to take him to the emergency room. He has been in bed all this week. I've been nursing him each evening after I get home from work.

WORKER: Your son's injury got in the way. How is his knee now?

CLIENT: Well, it's much better. He should be able to get out of bed about the middle of next week. Then he'll start walking around the house. By the first part of the following week, he should be able to return to school.

WORKER: It sounds as if your son is well on the way to recovery, and you will soon have more time once he can get around on his own. Do you think that when he does start to walk again, you will be more likely to do the gardening?

CLIENT: I think so. It depends upon how much help he needs.

WORKER: It sounds like you'll be nursing him at least for another several days. What is involved when you care for him in the evening?

CLIENT: Well, first I make him supper and then I take it to his room. Then we talk for a while. Then I clean up the kitchen and do the dishes. Then I check on Robert again. We usually talk some more. By that time, it's time for bed.

WORKER: Lynn, it seems to me that we have a choice to make here. First, if you really believe that once Robert is better you will begin the gardening, we can simply delay our start date for the gardening activities. If you believe, however, that if it were not Robert's injury it would be something else that would prevent you from gardening, then perhaps we should take this opportunity to challenge the pattern of excessive caretaking. When we explored this before, we used the phrase "over-mothering" to refer to the way you sometimes care so much for others, especially Richard and Robert, that it interferes with their ability to care for themselves. If your decision not to garden is a matter of neglecting yourself and over-mothering rather than simply a matter of unusual circumstances, then perhaps we might begin to address that right now while Robert is still injured. What do you think?

CLIENT: Well, honestly, I think it's some of both. Robert's injury gives me an opportunity to care for him. I'm not sure it's over-mothering but I certainly do more than is really necessary. And, focusing so much on him this past week kept me away from the gardening activities that I was truly looking forward to.

(continued)

> WORKER: Then, what do you think? Should we delay the start date for the gardening activities, or should we start now in order to challenge the tendency to avoid caring for yourself?
>
> CLIENT: Well, I guess I'd like to start right now. Even with Robert's injury, I should be able to find 15 minutes at some point during the evening.
>
> WORKER: All right. I wonder, though, because of the extra responsibilities caused by Robert's injury, should we change the plans from 15 minutes every single day to 15 minutes three times during the next week? That might be more reasonable, given the current circumstances.
>
> CLIENT: Yes, yes. I think that would be just about right. I know I can garden three times during the next 7 days.
>
> WORKER: Okay. We've changed the plans for gardening from once every day to three times during the next week. Now, what do you think about rehearsing this a little bit?

As a result of reviewing action steps, clients are more likely to believe that you genuinely care about between-session tasks and are serious about helping them progress toward agreed-upon goals. Reviewing action steps increases the probability that clients will attempt and complete more tasks in the future.

EXERCISE 12-2: REVIEWING ACTION STEPS

Review the earlier exercises that involve Mr. K., Loretta, the S. family, Mrs. F., and the troubled social service agency. In the spaces provided, create simulated dialogues between yourself and the client to demonstrate the skill of reviewing action steps. Follow up on the action steps identified in Exercise 11-3 and rehearsed in Exercise 12-1.

1. You are in the midst of reviewing action steps with Mr. K. He reports that he has fully completed the action step (client task) that you had previously agreed upon and rehearsed. What might you say in reviewing the action step with this client?

2. You are in the midst of reviewing action steps with Loretta. She reports that she attempted but did not fully complete the action step (client task) that you had previously agreed upon and rehearsed. What might you say in reviewing the action step with this client?

3. You are in the midst of reviewing action steps with the seven-member S. family. The family indicates that they partly carried out the action step (client task) that you had previously agreed upon and rehearsed. What might you say in reviewing the action step with them?

4. You are in the midst of reviewing action steps with Mrs. F. She reports that she did not attempt the action step (client task) that you had previously agreed upon and rehearsed. What might you say in reviewing the action step with this client?

5. You are working with the executive director of the social service agency for which you are providing social work consultative services. The director reports completion of the action step (client task) that you had previously agreed upon and rehearsed. What might you say in reviewing the action step with the director? Anticipate what the director might say or do in response to your statements and actions.

Evaluating

Evaluation of progress is crucial during the work and evaluation phase. It often occurs while you are reviewing action steps. Through the skill of evaluating, you engage the client in reviewing progress toward goal attainment. You and the client may identify progress through changes in such indicators as goal attainment scales, frequency counts, individualized or subjective rating scales, rapid assessment instruments, or other paper-and-pencil and online instruments. Include the results of evaluations in case records. Also, track results so that you may note the presence or absence of progress as well as the rate of change. If you use a spreadsheet software program, you can readily convert numerical scores into tables, line graphs, pie charts, bar graphs, forest plots, and other graphic forms that clients can easily understand. Such graphic evidence of progress may enhance clients' self-efficacy and increase their motivation to take further action. Over time, if evaluation reveals little or no progress, or suggests a deteriorating trend, you and your clients would reconsider the assessment, the contract, and the action steps that you planned. Obviously, when progress toward goal achievement is not forthcoming, you need to reexamine the approach to change.

Through the skill of evaluating, you engage clients in examining data in accordance with the plans for evaluating progress. You determine whether the evaluation data reflect progress toward goal attainment, no change, or a change in the wrong direction. As you do when reviewing action steps, you may appropriately express your pleasure when there is clear evidence of progress. Encourage clients to identify those factors that contribute to positive change. When there is no evidence of progress, enlist clients in a collaborative exploration of the reasons why. Then, jointly consider whether you need to make a major revision to the plans or whether relatively minor adjustments might suffice. Frequently, the evaluation instruments provide useful information to supplement clients' experiences and your own observations. When problems worsen, an intensive reanalysis is needed. You and your clients attempt to determine if the planned action steps, rather than helping, actually contribute to the deteriorating situation. Occasionally, initial negative effects are an expected but temporary phenomenon, subsequently followed by positive results. Because of the systemic nature of many issues, at first "things may sometimes become worse before they get better." However, this phenomenon—if it occurs at all—should be short-lived. If it continues for any length of time, it represents a problem that must immediately be addressed. Also, negative effects are not always the result of either your professional efforts or the action steps undertaken by clients. Rather, they may be the effects of changes in circumstances. Of course, sometimes the change program itself produces negative consequences. When this occurs, a major revision to the contract is imperative.

As an example, consider Mrs. Chase's sleep log, in which she records the number of hours she sleeps each night. Susan Holder, the social worker, has reviewed these daily logs and converted the sleep data into the graph displayed in Figure 12.1.

As the line graph reveals, Mrs. Chase slept approximately 4 hours nightly during the period between January 13 and January 19. According to her, 4 hours has been the approximate amount she slept each night over the last several months. On the evening of January 20, following the second interview with Susan Holder, Mrs. Chase implemented the change program they had jointly devised. From that night on, Mrs. Chase's daily log reflects general progress toward the goal of sleeping 8 hours nightly. She slept less than 7 hours on only one night.

In evaluating progress, Mrs. Chase and Susan can reasonably infer that, in regard to the goal of sleeping more, the plans are working successfully. Of course, they would also review Mrs. Chase's subjective ratings concerning how refreshed she feels when she awakens each morning. Susan could also convert these subjective ratings into graphic form for ready review.

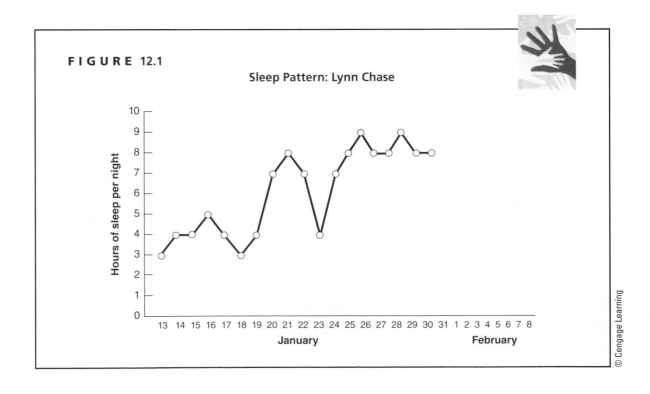

FIGURE 12.1

Sleep Pattern: Lynn Chase

EXERCISE 12-3: EVALUATING

For these exercises, assume that you are a social worker with a multipurpose social services agency. In the spaces provided, create simulated dialogues between yourself and the client, showing how you might use the skill of evaluating progress toward goal attainment. Use your responses to Exercise 11-4 to recall how you planned to evaluate progress for each of our five clients.

1. You are in the midst of evaluating progress toward goal attainment with Mr. K. The measurement data clearly reflect overall progress toward goal achievement. However, during the past week, the scores reflected a sharp decline. In fact, the data suggest that things are worse. Write the words you would use to initiate a review of the data and discuss the implications with Mr. K.

2. You are in the midst of evaluating progress toward goal attainment with Loretta. The measurement data clearly indicate that some progress toward goal achievement has occurred. However, the extent of progress is modest. Write the words you would use to initiate a review of the data and discuss the implications with Loretta.

3. You are in the midst of evaluating progress toward goal attainment with the S. family. The measurement data for the previous week indicate that progress toward goal achievement has not occurred. In earlier weeks, there had been consistent positive improvement. However, last week the data suggest that there was no change in either a positive or a negative direction. Write the words you would use to initiate a review of the data and discuss the implications with the S. family.

4. You are in the midst of evaluating progress toward goal attainment with Mrs. F. The measurement data clearly indicate that progress toward goal achievement has occurred. There is a definitive change in a positive direction. Write the words you would use to initiate a review of the data and discuss the implications with Mrs. F.

5. You are in the midst of evaluating progress toward goal attainment with the board of directors of the agency for which you are providing social work consultation services. The measurement data clearly reflect progress toward goal achievement. There is a definitive change in a positive direction. Communications among staff members have improved, staff members now receive weekly supervision, the agency director is pursuing an active and engaged approach to leadership, and morale is improving. Write the words you would use to initiate a review of the data and discuss their implications with the board.

Focusing

Focusing (Perlman, 1957) is a skill used to direct or maintain attention to the work at hand. Occasionally, both workers and clients wander away from the agreed-upon agendas. These diversions are sometimes productive, leading to greater understanding and improving the chances for effective change. At other times, however, such departures are clearly unproductive. Through the skill of focusing, you redirect energy to relevant topics. Also, clients sometimes miss the significance of phenomena that relate to targeted problems and goals. By directing attention to them, you may heighten their awareness. For example, in working with a family, you may observe that just as plans for an action step are about to be finalized, one sibling interrupts with a complaint about another family member's past misbehavior. As a social worker, you might hypothesize that the interruption may represent a defensive or self-protective act, ambivalence about change, or perhaps an attempt to maintain family-system equilibrium. However, you regard it theoretically; you may use the skill of focusing to respond to the interruption. You could say to the family member who interrupts, "Would you please hold on to that thought so that we can come back to it later? Let's complete our plans first. Thanks." Through such a form of focusing, you guide the family back to the work at hand. To accomplish a different purpose, that of enhancing process awareness, you might focus in a different way: "I noticed that just about the time we were reaching consensus on a step to address one of the issues, Johnny brought up his concern about Sheila's past behavior. I wonder, Johnny, what do you think led you to raise the topic at this particular time?"

EXERCISE 12-4: FOCUSING

For these exercises, assume that you are a social worker with a multipurpose social services agency. In the spaces provided, write the words you would say in using the skill of focusing.

1. You are reviewing action steps with Mr. K. In the midst of this process, he begins to reminisce about a childhood friend. Based upon the service goals, you believe that he would benefit if you were to complete the process of reviewing action steps. You intend to return later to his childhood memories. Write the words you would say in using the skill of focusing with Mr. K.

2. You are meeting with Loretta to discuss her current circumstances. In the midst of this, she mentions her eldest daughter. However, she stops abruptly and returns to the topic of her new housing arrangement. Based upon the service goals, you believe that she would benefit if you were to encourage her to continue to talk about her daughter. Write the words you would say in using the skill of focusing with Loretta.

3. You are in the midst of exploring a new topic of importance to the S. family. Only the parents and the teenage children are present for this meeting. The subject involves the emerging sexuality of one of the adolescents. As the discussion begins, you observe that Mrs. S. changes the subject to a less anxiety-provoking issue. This pattern seems to occur whenever the adolescent family members begin to express sexual concerns. Based on your professional judgment, you conclude that continuing with the topic of adolescent sexuality would be congruent with the values and cultural background of the family, would be helpful to the family, and would represent a step toward goal achievement. You therefore decide to use the skill of focusing. Write the words you would say to redirect the discussion back to the topic of adolescent sexuality. Then indicate how you might refocus to enhance the family's awareness of the pattern of shifting away from difficult topics.

4. You are in the midst of role-playing an action step with Mrs. F. She has assumed the role of her own daughter. A few moments after taking the part of her daughter, Mrs. F.'s eyes begin to water, and then tears start to fall onto her cheeks. Mrs. F. shrugs and continues in the role of her daughter. You make a professional judgment that Mrs. F. would benefit from a more complete expression of her feelings and an exploration of the meaning of the tears. You also realize that such steps would be entirely consistent with the contract for work. In the space provided, write the words you would say in using the skill of focusing to call attention to the tears as well as to the thoughts and feelings behind them.

5. You are in the midst of evaluating progress toward goal attainment with the board of directors of the agency for which you are providing social work consultation services. Following your summary presentation of data regarding progress, the board members begin an active discussion of the implications of these positive findings. Suddenly, one of the participants introduces the topic of the former director's misbehavior. In your professional judgment, a shift away from the current discussion at this time would detract from the board's work. Write the words you would say to help the board members continue to discuss the implications of the positive evaluation data.

Educating

During the work phase, it may become apparent that clients lack valid information or relevant skills that could contribute to the achievement of the agreed-upon goals for work. In such circumstances, you may appropriately assume the role of teacher or educator. The skill of educating involves several dimensions. Often, you share knowledge and professional opinions. For example, you might inform parents about major developmental milestones to anticipate in an infant's first year of life. You could share your ideas about how parents might facilitate childhood development through, for instance, mutual play activities. In educating, convey the information in such a way that clients may freely consider its relevance for their particular situation and decide whether to accept it. This is particularly true when sharing professional opinions rather than facts. Even when you present factual information, however, continue to respect the right of clients to disagree and choose their own course of action.

In educating clients, realize that all people do not learn in the same way. There are several different learning styles; some of your clients are likely to have learning styles that differ from your own preferred manner of teaching or learning. Therefore, individualize your educational approach so you can reach each client. For example, some clients have an affinity for deductive thinking. They enjoy theoretical concepts and principles. Once they comprehend an abstract principle, they can apply it through deductive reasoning to everyday life. Other clients possess strength in inductive thinking. They can take a specific incident or situation and reach a clear understanding of it. Sometimes, they can apply this understanding to similar circumstances in the future, but at other times, these clients may have to go through the learning process all over again. Such clients often benefit more from examples, illustrations, and specific guidelines than from abstract principles. Many clients also learn better when you tell a story, use a metaphor, or share an analogy. For example, in working with an adult male client who feels trapped by circumstances, you might realize—having thoroughly explored the situation with the client—that he is, in many ways, trapping himself. There are options, but the client has not really seen or seriously considered them. At such a time, you might tell a story in the following fashion.

EXAMPLE: EDUCATING

I remember a comic strip I once saw. In the first frame, there is a desperate-looking man, staring out between the iron bars of a jail. His eyes and head are absolutely still. He looks only through the bars and nowhere else. He seems to be highly anxious, afraid, and depressed all at the same time. In the second frame, we see the scene from a more distant perspective. Again we notice the desperate man looking out from between the bars. But then we notice that there are iron bars on one side of the room only. The other three sides don't have bars at all; there aren't even any walls. It's completely open. The prisoner, if he would only move his head out from between the bars and look in another direction, could easily see that he could walk away any time he wanted.

Some clients learn best by hearing, others by seeing, and others through a multisensory learning approach (a combination of hearing, seeing, and physically experiencing). Some people learn best by working independently and some by working cooperatively with others, receiving guidance and feedback throughout the process. Certain individuals are more receptive to learning during the morning, others during the afternoon, and still others during the evening hours. Some people enjoy moving around while learning, whereas others prefer stillness. Some prefer to have stimulation in the form of music or background noise, whereas others learn best when it is absolutely quiet. As you try to educate clients, discover their preferred learning styles and adapt your teaching approach accordingly.

Sometimes, you can serve important educational functions by sharing personal feelings and experiences. It is very much like telling a story, but it is a story about yourself. This process is known as self-disclosure. In self-disclosing, you typically become a more genuine human being to the client. In addition, the personal experience may carry special meaning to the client, who might attribute considerable significance to the message or moral of your personal story. In sharing your personal feelings and experiences, however, be careful not to become the client's client. There should be a clear relationship between your self-disclosures and the identified problems and established goals for work. Also, do not take so much time in sharing your experiences and feelings that it detracts significantly from clients' opportunities for self-expression. If you share too much of yourself, especially personal difficulties or tragedies, clients may begin to view you as troubled or needy rather than as competent. If your clients begin to see you in this light, it could seriously diminish your effectiveness. Clients might abruptly end the relationship with you and look for a "healthier" professional. Alternately, clients may start to take care of you, assuming the role of caretaker or surrogate parent. In addition, your clients might begin to protect you from the full impact of the truth about their situations. Therefore be cautious about speaking of yourself too often or at too great a length. Remember, social work services are primarily for clients, not for you.

EXERCISE 12-5: EDUCATING

For these exercises, assume that you are a social worker with a multipurpose social services agency. In the spaces provided, write the words you would say in using the skill of educating.

1. You are in the midst of exploring the current status of some of Mr. K.'s symptoms. You notice that he has lost quite a bit of weight in the last few weeks. He reports that he has lost his appetite. Foods that he had previously enjoyed are no longer pleasurable. He says he drinks a lot of coffee and makes sandwiches. He hasn't eaten in a restaurant since the divorce. He says that he hates to eat alone but hasn't felt motivated to either invite friends or to accept invitations from others to join him for meals. You and Mr. K. agree that his poor appetite and restricted eating patterns, and perhaps especially his social isolation, may be symptomatic of grief or perhaps depression. You then begin to educate him about the role of social engagement and social activity in reducing depressive symptoms. Write the words you would say as you begin to educate Mr. K. about these protective factors. (You may find it helpful or necessary to conduct a search of the relevant professional literature to ensure that your words are based on credible theory and research.)

2. You are talking with Loretta about her plans to secure employment. You notice that she has begun to prepare her hair differently, apply some makeup, and wear appealing clothing that she obtained from Goodwill and Salvation Army sources. You celebrate her progress and mention that employers sometimes (rightly or wrongly) consider applicants' appearance during job interviews. She says that she'd like to know more about what employers want and how she should prepare for job interviews. You say that you'd be happy to talk with her about these things and then begin to use the skill of educating to do so. Write the words you would say as you begin to educate Loretta about the qualities that contemporary employers look for in their employees and about how to prepare for job interviews. (You may find it helpful or necessary to conduct a search of the relevant professional literature to ensure that your words are based on credible theory and research.)

3. You are in the midst of an individual meeting with a teenage member of the S. family. She reports to you in confidence that she is sexually active and "will continue to have sex with my boyfriend no matter what my mother says!" She reports that she and her boyfriend do not practice birth control but that she would like to have some protection. She also mentions that she has recently begun to feel some unusual itching and discomfort "down there" (in her vaginal area). What would you like to communicate to her? How would you begin to educate the teenager about birth control possibilities and about medical care?

(You may find it helpful or necessary to conduct a search of the relevant professional literature to ensure that your words are based on credible theory and research.)

4. You have just rehearsed an action step with Mrs. F. She assumed the role of her daughter while you played the part of Mrs. F. Through this experience, Mrs. F. became aware of her feelings of extreme guilt about the way she has reared her children. She sobs and says, "I tried not to repeat the bad things my parents did to me, but it looks like I did so anyway." How might you educate her about the human tendency to repeat intergenerational family patterns even when trying to avoid them? (You may find it helpful or necessary to conduct a search of the relevant professional literature to ensure that your words are based on credible theory and research.)

5. You are in the midst of evaluating progress toward goal attainment with the board of directors of the agency for which you are providing social work consultation services. The

measurement data clearly indicate that progress toward goal achievement has occurred. The board members report their satisfaction with this news. However, you are well aware that maintenance of positive organizational change usually requires continued attention over a considerable period of time. Without clear, continuing plans to maintain change, reversion to previous, long-established patterns is quite likely. How might you educate the board members about the potential to return to previous, dysfunctional organizational patterns and the need for continued engagement? (You may find it helpful or necessary to conduct a search of the relevant professional literature to ensure that your words are based on credible theory and research.)

Advising

In working with clients, it is sometimes proper for you to provide advice. Making a suggestion or recommendation can be a perfectly appropriate action by a social worker. In using the skill of advising, you should almost always convey that the client may freely accept or reject your advice. As Maluccio (1979) observes, many clients very much value and appreciate professional advice. Nonetheless, particularly during the early stages of your professional development, you may experience conflict about advising. You may be tempted to give too much advice or perhaps too little. As a social worker, you are probably keenly aware of the values of self-determination, autonomy, and respect for the uniqueness of each person. In interpreting these values, you might conclude that you should never offer any advice at all. Conversely, you might decide that clients are entitled to all the knowledge you possess; you might therefore provide a great deal of advice, whether or not clients request or need it. These two positions represent the extremes of a continuum. Most likely, you will take a more moderate stance, giving advice in certain circumstances but not in all. Some advice is usually appropriate and helpful. The challenge for social workers is to know when to, when not to, and especially how to give advice.

Resist the temptation to offer advice based on your own personal feelings, attitudes, ideology, and preferences. This can be difficult in situations when a client asks, "What should I do?" or

"What would you do if you were in my place?" For example, suppose you have worked for several weeks with a 19-year-old man who is gay. Through your exploration together, the young man has become much more self-accepting and comfortable with his sexual orientation. Recently, he raised the issue of whether to tell his parents the truth about his sexual orientation. He asks you, "Should I tell them?"

Of course, you could deftly avoid answering his question by responding with a question of your own: "What do you think?" Alternately, you could respond directly and share your personal opinion: "Of course. Tell them. You have nothing to be ashamed about." Or, not knowing what to do or say, you might become confused and uncertain. On the one hand, you might expect that the client would probably feel less distressed and more personally integrated if he were to tell his parents about his sexual orientation. On the other hand, you might also anticipate that such an encounter between the young man and his parents could be extremely stressful. It could conceivably lead to the loss of his parents' approval and support; he might even lose all contact with them. You might conclude that this decision is ultimately his and his alone to make. Following that line of thinking, you might respond directly to his question, but without advising him what to do: "I'd be more than glad to explore this issue with you and help you make a decision. However, I cannot simply give you an easy, direct answer to that question. I cannot advise you what to do. The final decision is yours and yours alone to make."

Of course, there are also many occasions when you clearly should offer direct and specific advice. For example, suppose that you have been helping an adult female client become more assertive with her lover. You and the client have rehearsed assertive communication during your meetings together. The client is about to take a step toward greater assertion in her intimate relationship. Based upon your understanding of relationship theory and research, you believe that soft or caring expressions tend to strengthen relationships and provide a basis for moving toward hard or confrontational assertions. You therefore advise the client to begin with affectionate, caring assertions and later, after some experience, to initiate assertive expressions that involve requests that her partner make changes.

Advising is involved in many aspects of practice. For example, you might advise an adult male client who grew up in a household where his father was regularly intoxicated and abusive to read selected books on the topic of children of alcoholic families. You might suggest that the client consider attending Adult Children of Alcoholics (ACOA) or Al-Anon meetings as an adjunct to your work together. You might advise a client to seek medical care. You might appropriately give advice concerning a variety of life circumstances. In so doing, you would phrase the advice in slightly different ways to accomplish different objectives. Unless life-threatening circumstances exist, however, you should nearly always express advice in the form of a suggestion or perhaps a strong recommendation. Avoid communicating advice as commands or directives, such as an authoritarian boss might deliver to a subordinate employee or an angry parent might say to a disobedient child.

As you begin to practice the skill of advising, please use the format outlined here. As you become more proficient in using the skill, experiment with alternate formats.

PRACTICE FORMAT: ADVISING

I have an idea that I'd like you to consider. I'd like to suggest that you _____
_____.

EXERCISE 12-6: ADVISING

For these exercises, assume that you are a social worker with a multipurpose social services agency. In the spaces provided, write the words you would say in using the skill of advising.

1. You have educated Mr. K. about the role of social engagement and social activity in reducing depressive symptoms. However, Mr. K. seems uncertain and ambivalent about becoming more socially active. In the space provided, write the words you would say in advising Mr. K. to do so.

2. As you role play practice job interviews with Loretta, you observe that when she talks about her positive characteristics and abilities she tends to tilt her face downward, lower her eyes, and clasp her hands together. She also begins to speak in a softer voice and in a less expressive manner. In the space provided, write the words you would say in advising Loretta about body posture, facial expression, eye contact, and speaking voice when trying to "sell oneself" to potential employers.

3. During an individual meeting with a teenage member of the S. family, she describes symptoms that strongly suggest she has contracted a sexually transmitted disease (STD). In the space provided, write the words you would say in advising the teenager to seek medical care.

4. As you and Mrs. F. have explored more about the relationship between her parenting patterns and the childhood experiences in her own family of origin, you conclude that she might benefit from the construction of a family genogram. In the space provided, write the words you would say in advising Mrs. F. to help you complete her family genogram.

5. You are in the midst of evaluating progress toward goal attainment with the board of directors of the agency for which you are providing social work consultation services. The measurement data clearly indicate that progress toward goal achievement has occurred. However, there is one area where the positive trend is not apparent. On average, clients' satisfaction with the agency and the quality of services has not improved. Of course, if clients were highly satisfied before changes were implemented and their degree of satisfaction simply continued as before, you and the board members might not be concerned. Unfortunately, in general, clients have not been very satisfied and that has not changed—despite the positive trends in other areas. The board members ask for your advice. They want to know what you think should be done to improve client satisfaction with the agency and the services they receive. Use the space below to write what you would say in advising the board of directors in this matter.

Representing

The skill of representing includes those actions social workers take on behalf of clients in pursuit of agreed-upon goals. We usually engage in representational activities to facilitate clients' interaction with members of various social systems. Representing incorporates the interventive roles of the social broker, advocate, and mediator (Compton, Galaway, & Cournoyer, 2005). Therefore, representing is a complex process indeed. It builds on many of the skills of the preparing, beginning, and exploring phases, as well as those of assessing, contracting, and working. Instead of working directly with the client, however, you intervene with others on behalf of the client. For example, suppose an unemployed adult woman is currently homeless and desperately needs immediate shelter, food, clean clothes, and financial support. Based on your joint assessment, you and the client concur that a particular resource agency would probably deny her application if she applied directly and in person. Therefore, the client asks you to represent her in this matter. You agree to make an initial contact with the appropriate agency. Then, with the support of the client, you sketch out several action steps. As you would use the preparing skills in advance of a first meeting with a client, you also carefully prepare for the contact with the agency to improve your chances of effectively representing the client.

During the course of your social work career, collect the names, phone numbers, and e-mail addresses of other social workers and representatives of various community resources. Get to know people at churches, temples, mosques, community centers, hospitals, neighborhood associations, government and nongovernmental organizations, and other systems that might serve as resources for clients. Make notes about such people and keep them in a card file or computerized database for easy access. Periodically send them friendly thank-you notes and mail letters of praise to their supervisors and agency administrators. Such actions tend to enhance your value within the helping community and improve the chances that your clients will receive the high-quality service they deserve.

In the instance of the woman in need of food and shelter, you might decide that a good first step would be to contact a social work colleague at the agency in question. Once you make telephone contact, proceed in much the same manner as if you were beginning with a client. Introduce yourself and secure an introduction in return. Depending on the circumstances, you might make a few informal, friendly remarks to put your colleague at ease. Then outline the purpose for the contact: "I have a client here with me who needs assistance. She is unemployed, without money. She hasn't eaten for 2 days and has no place to stay tonight. I'm calling to determine whether she might be eligible to receive some help from your agency." Following this description of purpose, you may seek feedback to confirm that your message has been understood. At this point in the process, you could invite your colleague to provide information about eligibility requirements or to inquire further about your client's circumstances.

Representing clients in such cases is often extremely satisfying. Interactions with resource people may be both pleasant and productive. Your clients may be treated well and receive what they need. If you cultivate positive relationships with resource people and know something about the mission and programs of various service organizations, you are more likely to be effective in representing your clients.

However, representing clients is not always enjoyable or satisfying. Sometimes, you must become an assertive advocate on behalf of clients that receive unfair or poor-quality treatment. It can be frustrating. For example, consider the situation of a client who seeks your help in dealing with a property owner. In the middle of a cold winter, heat, which all tenants are supposed to receive as part of their rent, is not reaching into the client's apartment. Despite several complaints, the property owner has taken no action to correct the situation. The client then asks you to represent her by contacting the property owner on her behalf.

First, you would use the preparing skills to formulate preliminary plans. You explore the situation more fully with the client, securing detailed facts about the heating problem and learning about her experience as a tenant there. You might then consult city officials who are knowledgeable about housing regulations and landlord–tenant laws, expanding your own knowledge base. You also prepare for the initial contact with the property owner. In this instance, suppose you decide to telephone first. You might telephone, give your name, and say, "I am a social worker with the tenants' advocacy program of the city social services agency. One of your tenants, Mrs. Wicker, has contacted us about a problem with the heating system. It seems that the family has been without heat for 5 days. Could you tell me what's being done to repair the problem and how much longer it will be before their apartment is warm enough for them to live there?"

If the property owner does not acknowledge the problem and, for example, begins to denigrate the client, you might respond, "Regardless of the complaints you have about Mrs. Wicker and her family, they still need heat. As you know, it's dangerously cold, and the lives of the family members could be in serious jeopardy if heat is not restored soon." If the landlord remains unresponsive, you might outline the steps you could take should the heating system remain unrepaired and the family continues to be in danger. In several respects, your comments are similar to those you might share in beginning with a client. You state your purpose, describe your role as client advocate, and discuss the actions you could take should your client continue to be in need or at risk (that is, your policies and procedures). You also make a specific request for action from the property owner (that is, you outline the property owner's role).

If the property owner acknowledges the problem, outline plans and a timetable for repair, and makes a commitment to provide the family with sufficient heat, you may appropriately express your thanks and credit him for being responsive to your request. You would then apprise the client of the property owner's proposal and request that she notify you about the outcome. If the property owner follows through as promised, you might communicate appreciation for the positive action. If the property owner does not do so, however, you would probably contact him again, report that the apartment is still dangerously cold, and inform him specifically about the steps you will now take to ensure the safety and well-being of your client.

You will probably represent clients quite frequently as a regular part of social work practice, to link clients with needed community resources and to secure fair and equitable treatment, as part of the processes of mediation and conflict resolution. In representing, ensure that you have clients' informed consent to act on their behalf, always keep their best interests in mind, and regularly update them about your activities.

EXERCISE 12-7: REPRESENTING

For these exercises, assume that you are a social worker with a multipurpose social services agency. In the spaces provided, outline the action steps you might take in representing the clients in the following situations. Describe how you would prepare to represent the client, and then write the words you would say in beginning with the person or organization contacted on behalf of the client.

1. With his consent, you are representing Mr. K. in relation to his former wife. He believes that if he could apologize to her, express his sincere hope that her future will be bright, and say goodbye, it would help him complete the progress he's made toward emotionally, as well as cognitively, accepting the fact that the marriage is over. You are about to contact the former Mrs. K. to advocate for a meeting that would include her, Mr. K., and you in your role as his social worker. In the space provided, outline the steps you would take before making contact, and then write the words you would say as you begin to represent Mr. K. with the former Mrs. K.

2. With her consent, you are representing Loretta in regard to a possible job opportunity. The position involves answering phones and serving as a receptionist for a nonprofit, nongovernmental agency. You are about to contact an administrator of the agency on Loretta's behalf. In the space provided, outline the steps you would take before making contact, and then write the words you would say as you begin to represent Loretta and advocate for her employment with the agency.

3. With her consent and that of her parents, you are representing Gloria, a teenage member of the S. family, in relation to certain sexual issues. You have jointly decided that you will contact the office of her family physician to arrange for a prompt appointment to deal with a sexually transmitted disease. Outline the steps you would take before making contact with the doctor's office, and then write the words you would say in beginning to represent Gloria in this matter.

4. With the informed consent of Mrs. F., you are representing her during interactions with the principal of the school where her daughters report that several teenage boys have harassed them. According to the girls, the boys spit on them and used ethnic epithets in referring to their Latino heritage. Outline the steps you would take in preparing for contact with the principal and then write the words you would say in representing Mrs. F. and her daughters.

5. As part of your consultative work with a social service agency, you recruited a group of about 10 current and former clients to meet together with you and with the agency's newly appointed "consumer advocate" about once per month in an effort to improve service quality and advocate for agency consumers. During the most recent consumers' group meeting, one participant—a current client—expressed her disappointment and frustration with the fact that her social worker has not returned any of the several telephone calls she has made over the course of the past 2 weeks. She wanted to schedule an appointment to talk about an urgent matter involving her 8-year-old daughter. First, you ask the client if she would prefer to handle the matter herself or might she want the help of the agency's consumer advocate. The client says she would love the help and provides permission for the advocate to represent her in this matter. Then, you turn to the consumer advocate and ask, "What might be done to help here?" What do you think the agency's consumer advocate might say in outlining preliminary plans to represent the client in: (a) providing feedback regarding her dissatisfaction and (b) securing an early appointment with a social worker to help her with the urgent matter involving her 8-year-old daughter?

Responding with Immediacy

The skill of responding with immediacy (Carkhuff & Anthony, 1979) involves exploring clients' experiences and feelings about you, your relationship, or your work together as they occur. In responding with immediacy, you focus on clients' experience of what is occurring right here and right now between you. These thoughts and feelings become the subject for immediate exploration. Responding with immediacy makes things real. It intensifies the relationship and encourages clients to explore relational concerns as they emerge. When you respond in an immediate manner, you also demonstrate or model an open communication style. Such openness may promote greater honesty and authenticity on the part of clients, increase their understanding of interpersonal patterns, and reduce any hesitation to address issues and goals. One format for responding with immediacy is as follows.

PRACTICE FORMAT: RESPONDING WITH IMMEDIACY

Right here and now with me you seem to be (thinking/feeling/doing/experiencing) _____.

Usually, the skill is applied directly to clients' immediate experience about you, your relationship, or the nature and utility of your work together. Your response becomes less immediate and less powerful as you move away from the context of "right here and right now with me." Responding with immediacy occurs in the present tense. Whenever the discussion shifts into the past or future tense, the interaction becomes less immediate. For example, if you comment about something that happened a week or two earlier, clients may recall it differently or not at all, or they may process the information intellectually without feeling its full impact. Although it may still be a useful comment to make, exploring a previous exchange rarely has the powerful effect of responding immediately to something that is occurring right here and right now.

In many cases, the manner in which clients relate to you is representative of their general pattern of relating with people. Clients sometime re-create in the working relationship the same patterns that emerge in other relationships. By responding immediately to such relational patterns as they emerge, you can help clients learn to recognize them and perhaps develop new, more useful styles of interaction.

Responding with immediacy is not appropriate for use with all clients. It depends on the nature of your contract, including the goals for work and your plans for change. In general, you would not respond with immediacy unless clients' reactions are clearly relevant to the issues and goals for work. Also, social workers differ in the degree to which they emphasize and attend to immediate interactions in their relationships with clients. Some social work practice approaches regard worker–client relational factors as extremely important, whereas others consider them less so. Nonetheless, most social workers recognize that client reactions within the working relationship are often relevant to the helping process. Responding with immediacy is a skill for addressing and exploring client experiences as they occur.

For example, suppose that you have begun to work with an adult female client who is troubled because her spouse reports that he does not like to spend time with her. Indeed, her spouse confirms this: "It's true. I'm sorry to say that I don't like her company. Every time we start to talk, she drifts off into the ozone—into some daydream world." During your meetings with this client, you notice that her attention frequently does seem to wander in a fashion similar to her spouse's description. She seems to focus on her own thoughts and listens just enough to your comments to stay distantly aware of the conversation. You begin to observe and to feel that when you talk, she essentially tunes you out. Because this pattern relates to the agreed-upon contract, you might appropriately respond with immediacy: "Right here and now as I'm talking, I notice that your eyes are turned away from me. You seem to be looking off into the distance and thinking about something else. What are you experiencing right now?"

Responding with immediacy often results in a significant increase in energy between you and your clients. Both social workers and clients are likely to become much more oriented to the present moment and more engaged with one another. Because immediate responses often heighten intensity and interpersonal intimacy within the professional relationship, use the skill only after rapport is well established and, of course, a contract has been negotiated. Also, refer to observable phenomena in descriptive terms. Avoid judgmental language. "You're ignoring me" involves a judgment about another's behavior. "I notice that your eyes are directed away from my eyes" is descriptive. Your clients should know that you genuinely have their interest at heart before you move into the intimate realm of immediacy.

EXERCISE 12-8: RESPONDING WITH IMMEDIACY

For these exercises, assume that you are a social worker with a multipurpose social services agency. In the spaces provided, write the words you would say in using the skill of responding with immediacy.

1. Mr. K. begins to cry as he tries unsuccessfully to express his feelings about the way you advocated for him and arranged for the meeting with his former wife. Although he cannot put his emotions into words, it is apparent that he is touched by your loyalty to him and feels extremely grateful to you for your efforts on his behalf. Write the words you would say in responding with immediacy to Mr. K.'s nonverbal expressions.

2. During a discussion with Loretta, you ask a question about her eldest daughter. At that point, Loretta abruptly jumps up from her chair and begins to pace back and forth. She seems agitated and extremely uncomfortable with the topic, and appears annoyed with you for mentioning her daughter. Write the words you would say in responding with immediacy to Loretta's reaction.

3. In the midst of an individual meeting with Gloria, a teenage member of the S. family, she confides to you that although she is sexually active with her boyfriend, she often fantasizes about another person. As she says that, she looks deeply into your eyes, blushes, and then looks away in an apparently embarrassed reaction. You suspect that she has had sexual fantasies about you. You know that it would be quite consistent with your contract to discuss this directly. In the space provided, write the words you would say in responding with immediacy to the teenager's expression.

4. As Mrs. F. talks with you about her own parenting practices and those that she experienced as a child in her own family of origin, you observe that she sits back in her chair, crosses her arms in front of her, and appears to frown. You're not entirely certain what this reaction means, but you suspect that she may be feeling ashamed and vulnerable. You think she is afraid that you might be critical of her. In the space provided, write the words you would say in responding with immediacy to Mrs. F.

5. As part of your consultative work with a social service agency, you meet regularly with the executive director to review actions taken, consider the results of evaluation data, and plan next steps to take. During today's meeting you and the director discuss findings from client satisfaction evaluation data. Some of the data reflect unfavorably upon the agency's current administration. Learning of this, the director's facial expression and body language begin to change, and both the volume and pace of speech increase as the director says, "You're encouraging clients to criticize agency administration in general and me in particular. I don't think that's fair. As a consulting social worker, you're supposed to be helping—not making things harder for me." Use the space below to write the words you would say in responding with immediacy to the director's words.

Reframing

The term *reframing* (Bandler & Grinder, 1979, 1982; Hartman & Laird, 1983; Tingley, 2001) refers to the words you say and the actions you take in introducing clients to a new way of looking at some aspect of themselves, the issue, or the situation. Usually, reframing involves sharing a different perspective from that which clients had previously adopted. Clients sometimes embrace a point of view in such a determined fashion that the perspective itself constitutes an obstacle to goal achievement. Of course, fixed views are not always problematic. Do not indiscriminately attempt to challenge or reframe clients' perspectives. Reframing is applicable when clients' viewpoints constitute a fundamental part of the issue for work. Similar to the skill of educating, it differs in that the overall purpose of reframing is to liberate the client from a dogmatic perspective. As a result of reframing, clients may reconsider strongly held beliefs. This may, in turn, affect their feelings and behavior as well.

There are several forms of reframing. One of the more common is *reframing a negative into a positive*.

EXAMPLE: REFRAMING A NEGATIVE INTO A POSITIVE

When you say that you're "stupid" and "indecisive" because you find it difficult to choose from among various courses of action, I feel confused. I mean, what you refer to as indecisive appears to me to be the ability to see different points of view. It seems to me that you're willing to consider many perspectives and options. This sounds like flexibility—not indecisiveness. And what you call stupidity sounds a great deal to me like carefulness, thoroughness, and patience. These are attributes that I find extremely appealing and functional. Are you sure they are so bad?

Personalizing meaning (Carkhuff & Anthony, 1979) is another form of reframing through which you encourage clients to shift the attribution of responsibility away from other people, organizations, or external forces (that is, the situation) and toward themselves (that is, the person). Personalizing meaning can help people assume greater responsibility for effecting change. It can be liberating, even empowering. Personalizing meaning can help clients see a relationship between their own beliefs, values, attitudes, and expectations, on the one hand, and the feelings they experience or the behavior they enact on the other. This form of reframing involves going beyond the communication directly expressed by the client. You slightly alter the client's expression to shift an externalized meaning toward a more internalized or personalized meaning, for which the client is likely to feel greater responsibility, personal power, and control. In personalizing meaning, you may use a format such as the following.

PRACTICE FORMAT: PERSONALIZING MEANING

You feel (do/experience) _____ because you think (believe/value/perceive/expect) _____.

Because the skill of personalizing meaning derives from your frame of reference rather than the client's, it constitutes an expressive rather than an empathic skill. Therefore you should phrase your comments in a tentative manner. Personalizing meaning suggests that the client's thoughts, feelings, or actions are more associated with conscious individual processes than with external or situational factors. Occasionally, it may leave clients feeling greater guilt or more burdened with responsibility. Conversely, however, it also may convey a sense of considerable optimism, because such feelings result from one's own values, beliefs, or thoughts. These are aspects of a person that are not necessarily permanent—one's beliefs and attitudes can and do change—and, unlike many situational factors, they are largely within one's own control. Such a view reflects an enormous potential for change—much more so than do explanations that people feel a certain way because they are jinxed, have a deficient superego structure, had a lousy childhood, suffer from a personality disorder, or have a biochemical deficiency.

Here is an example of a social worker talking with a client who happens to be a social work student.

EXAMPLE: PERSONALIZING MEANING

CLIENT: I'm devastated! I got a C+ in my social work field placement. I'll never make it through the program. I'm a total failure.

WORKER: You're disappointed in yourself because you believe you should do better than C+ work, and you're afraid that getting a C+ means that you won't be able to graduate?

Situationalizing meaning is another form of reframing through which you change the meaning suggested by clients' expressions. Although there is certainly an empathic element, in this form of reframing you also begin slightly to alter the meaning as presented by the client. In the case of situationalizing meaning, you reflect understanding of the client's feelings or behaviors but then suggest that they may also be viewed as a result of external, societal, systemic, situational, or other factors beyond the client's individual control or responsibility. Frequently, situationalizing meaning results in an expansion of clients' perspectives and a lessening of their sense of guilt, self-blame, or personal responsibility.

EXAMPLE: SITUATIONALIZING MEANING

CLIENT: I'm a wreck. I can't sleep or eat; I can't concentrate. I know my head is really messed up. I've been kind of crazy.

WORKER: You feel awful; you're anxious and depressed and you have lots of issues. I wonder, though, might these feelings be an understandable reaction to the recent changes in your life? Wouldn't even the best-adjusted person feel out of sorts and have some difficulty sleeping after losing a good job without any immediate prospects for another?

For these exercises, assume that you are a social worker with a multipurpose social services agency. In the spaces provided, write the words you would say in using the skill of reframing.

1. During a meeting with you, Mr. K. says, "The fact that she's gone hurts a lot less than before and I actually went on a date! I know I'm making progress but, it's clear to me that I'll never ever find anyone that I'll love as much as I loved her." Write the words you would say in reframing Mr. K.'s statement so that it reflects a personalized meaning.

2. Loretta is sharing, tentatively, some new information about her personal and family history. She says, "The fact is that I was terribly mean to my husband and I abused my kids—especially my oldest. They are all better off without me but I'm sure the girls will be emotionally damaged for the rest of their lives." Write the words you would say in reframing Loretta's statement so that it reflects a personalized meaning.

3. You are in the midst of an individual meeting with Gloria, a teenage member of the S. family. She says, "My mother is always on my case. She's so controlling. I can't do anything I want to do. She thinks that I'm 5 years old." Reframe her statement from a negative to a positive. Then, reframe her statement so that it has a personalized meaning.

4. During a meeting with Mrs. F., she confirms that she is indeed feeling guilty and ashamed that she may have harmed her children. She says, "I feel so ashamed. I've done

just what I've always criticized my parents for." Reframe Mrs. F.'s statement so that it reflects a situationalized meaning. Then reframe her statement so that it has a personalized meaning. Finally, reframe it from a negative into a positive.

5. As part of your consultative work with a social service agency, you meet regularly with a group of about eight professional social workers. During today's meeting, one social worker expresses concern that the recent changes (for example, more active and engaged leadership by the agency director, clear and complete communications throughout the agency, regular supervisory meetings, and emphasis on quality control) may limit the professional autonomy of the social work staff. She says, "I'm becoming increasingly concerned and worried about these changes. If these trends continue, before long the other social workers and I will become little more than glorified technicians and bureaucrats. We'll have to check with a supervisor before we take any action with clients. We won't be able to exercise our independent professional judgment and do what we think is best for our clients." Reframe the social worker's statement so that it reflects a situationalized meaning. Then, reframe it so that it has a personalized meaning. Finally, use the skill of reframing a negative into a positive.

Confronting Inconsistencies

In *confronting inconsistencies* (Carkhuff & Anthony, 1979), you directly and without judgment point out discrepancies, incongruities, or contradictions in clients' words, feelings, and actions. In confronting, you gently encourage clients to consider apparently incongruent aspects of themselves or their behavior. For example, suppose an adult male client has requested help from you regarding a troubled marriage. The client says, "I am willing to do whatever is necessary to improve this relationship." Following a joint meeting with you and his spouse, during which he promised "to go out for a date with my spouse this week," he voluntarily worked overtime at his job and arrived home 3 hours late—too late for the date. After the client subsequently misses another planned date night, you might use the skill of confronting inconsistencies by saying, "You said you want to improve the relationship and you agreed to two dates with your spouse. However, you worked late on the nights you had planned to go out with your wife. What do you think this might mean?"

In confronting inconsistencies, you may use the following format (Carkhuff & Anthony, 1979, p. 117).

PRACTICE FORMAT: CONFRONTING INCONSISTENCIES

On the one hand you say (feel, think, or do) _____ but (and/yet) on the other hand you say (feel/think/do) _____.

Confrontation can have a powerful effect on clients. It has the potential to cause severe disequilibrium in people who are highly stressed or have fragile coping skills. Therefore, before confronting inconsistencies with a particular client, be certain that person has the psychological and social resources to endure the impact. Certainly you should establish a solid relationship with the client before any confrontation. When you do confront inconsistencies, try to be descriptive about the incongruities or discrepancies that you observe. Avoid judgmental or evaluative speculations and conclusions. Finally, it is usually wise to "precede and follow confrontations with empathic responsiveness" (Hammond, Hepworth, & Smith, 1977, p. 280).

EXERCISE 12-10: CONFRONTING INCONSISTENCIES

For these exercises, assume that you are a social worker with a multipurpose social services agency. In the spaces provided, write the words you would say in using the skill of confronting inconsistencies.

1. As you and Mr. K. prepare for the upcoming meeting with his former wife, he says, "This meeting should help a lot. I'll say I'm sorry, wish her well, and say goodbye. It should be very interesting. I wonder if she'll view me in a different way after that; she might even give me another chance." Write the words you would say in confronting Mr. K. about the apparent inconsistencies evident in his expressed intentions.

2. As you talk with Loretta about her new job, she says, "I really enjoy my work. The other employees are great and the boss—well, he's okay too." As she spoke about the boss she, apparently quite unconsciously, shook her head side-to-side and pursed her lips in what seemed to be an expression of disgust. Write the words you would say in confronting Loretta about the apparent inconsistencies in her communication.

3. You are in the midst of an individual meeting with Gloria, a teenage member of the S. family. She reports that her physician had prescribed medication for treating the sexually transmitted disease. The doctor told her to abstain from sexual intercourse during the 2-week period she is to take the medication. She was also told to inform her boyfriend that he should see his doctor and be treated before he resumes any sexual relations. Otherwise Gloria and her boyfriend would continue to infect each other. The girl says that her boyfriend will not go to the doctor and continues to want to have sex with her. She says, "I'll probably just let him have what he wants because if I don't, he'll go somewhere else." Write the words you would say in confronting Gloria about the apparent inconsistencies in what she knows and what she thinks she will do.

4. During the course of your interaction with the principal of the school where Mrs. F.'s daughters have been harassed by several teenage boys, the principal says, "There is no racism at this school. The F. girls are simply too sensitive. They are the only Latino students we have in the school, and they will just have to learn to deal with the boys. We never had any trouble before they enrolled here." Write the words you would say in confronting the principal about the inconsistencies between his words and the apparent reality of the situation.

5. As part of your consultative work with a social service agency, you meet regularly with the executive director. During today's meeting, the director says, "I'm blamed and criticized whatever I do. I'm viewed as weak and incompetent because of the situation I inherited from the former director. He defrauded the agency, treated people unfairly, and failed to fulfill his responsibilities. I've been doing the best I can and I'm still guilty by association." Write the words you would say in confronting the agency director about the apparent inconsistencies in his words and his aspirations as a leader.

Pointing Out Endings

In *pointing out endings,* you remind the client "some time before the last session that the working relationship is coming to a close" (Shulman, 1992, p. 206). In most cases when you and clients agree to work together and establish a service contract, you also determine a time frame. This occurs as a significant part of the goal setting and planning processes (see Chapter 9). Periodically during the work phase, you refer to this time frame. Of course, you and clients may renegotiate the timetable when the situation warrants. Ideally, however, you and the client carefully consider and openly discuss any such revision. Extending a time frame does not necessarily increase the probability of goal achievement. Additional time could imply that the goals are just too difficult to accomplish. Also, time extensions may leave an impression that your work together can go on indefinitely.

Social work in several practice settings (for example, hospitals, residential facilities, prisons) has natural ending points that are partially or completely beyond either clients' or social workers' control. There are numerous legal as well as practice implications related to ending processes (*Lawsuit seeks discharge treatment-planning at NYC jails,* 1999). Consider, for example, the process of discharge following a stay in a medical or psychiatric hospital. Discharge planning is a complex ending process that often involves additional assessment, contracting, and working activities (Christ, Clarkin, & Hull, 1994; Cox, 1996; Morrow-Howell, Chadiha, Proctor, Hourd-Bryant, & Dore, 1996; Proctor, Morrow-Howell, & Kaplan, 1996; Tuzman & Cohen, 1992).

By pointing out endings, you may help motivate clients to work hard on the action steps so as to complete them within the established period. As Perlman (1957) suggests, the social work relationship is time limited. After all, as a social worker you are not marrying or adopting your clients. You are a professional helper, not a member of the family. By establishing time limits and pointing out endings, you help clients to prepare psychologically for the process of concluding the working relationship. If you and your clients avoid the topic of the forthcoming conclusion to the relationship, both of you can deny the immediacy of the feelings. Such denial may allow temporary emotional respite from strong feelings, but it also prevents the parties from psychologically anticipating and preparing themselves for ending. Therefore, despite feelings of discomfort, you should occasionally refer to the upcoming conclusion to the working relationship.

You may undertake the skill of pointing out endings in several ways. Regardless of the specific form it takes, this skill helps clients begin to prepare consciously and emotionally for the conclusion of your work together. Whether it involves a transfer, a referral, or a termination, you gently remind the client that there will soon be an ending and that he or she may very well have some thoughts and feelings about the change.

For example, suppose you and several family members contract to meet for eight sessions. The agreed-upon goal is to improve communication within the family. The work has proceeded quite well. By the fourth meeting, the family members have progressed to such an extent that they are able to express differences of opinion without feeling devalued or rejected. There has also been a noticeable decrease in tension and an increase in humor. Toward the end of the session, you say, "We're now finishing up our fourth session. There are four meetings left. We're halfway there."

Following such a reminder, you might explore thoughts and feelings associated with the idea of ending. You might ask, "As we think about concluding our relationship, some thoughts or feelings may come up. I wonder, what comes to mind when you think about finishing our work together?" Or you might ask, "How will things be different once we have concluded our work together?" Although a specific format is not universally applicable, the primary element in pointing out endings is the reminder. Statements such as "We have _____ meetings left" or "We will be meeting for another _____ weeks" serve this function. In the case of transfers or referrals, clarify what will happen following your ending with the client. You might say, "We have _____ meetings left before you begin to work with _____," or "We will be meeting for another _____ weeks before you begin the program at _____."

EXERCISE 12-11: POINTING OUT ENDINGS

For these exercises, assume that you are a social worker with a multipurpose social services agency. In the spaces provided, write the words you would say in using the skill of pointing out endings.

1. You have been working with Mr. K. for approximately 2 months. He has met with his former wife and said goodbye, and has begun dating someone. His appetite has improved and he has become more active socially and recreationally. He exercises daily and, in a decisive gesture, donated his television to a charity. He says he now listens to music and reads books. He reports that when he thinks about his former wife, he does so fondly but no longer hopes they will get back together. A few weeks earlier, as you and Mr. K. discussed his progress, you collaboratively decided that you would conclude your relationship in 1 month. Today's meeting is the next to last one. Your next meeting will conclude your work together. Write the words you would say in pointing out endings with Mr. K.

2. Over the course of the last few months, Loretta has blossomed. She is doing extremely well in her job, has been saving money, and enjoying life. She has friends that she spends time with and activities outside of work. She has submitted an application to serve as a volunteer to help homeless women in the community. She thinks they'll approve her request and she looks forward to helping others reclaim their lives. A few weeks earlier, as you evaluated progress with her, you wondered aloud about when you should conclude your work together. She said, "Three more times and I should be good to go." Today's meeting represents the second of the three. Your next meeting will conclude your work together. Write the words you would say in pointing out endings with Loretta.

3. You are in the midst of the next-to-last meeting with the S. family. During the past several months, many productive changes have occurred. Two sessions before, the family members indicated that they were well on their way to accomplishing their goals. At that time, you had agreed to meet three more times. Next week you will have the concluding session. Write the words you would say in pointing out endings with the S. family.

4. Through a joint discussion 2 weeks earlier, you and Mrs. F. concluded that she could best complete work toward goal attainment by participating in a 10-week assertiveness training group sponsored by another community agency. The group begins in 3 weeks. Next week will be your last meeting together. Write the words you would say in pointing out endings with Mrs. F.

5. For the past 11 months, you have provided consultation services to an agency that is trying to recover from incompetent management and fraudulent behavior under a previous administration. About every 5 or 6 weeks, you meet with a large group of agency personnel, board members, and key stakeholders to apprise them of progress, seek their feedback, and gather their input. Your 12-month contract with the agency expires in 3 months' time. You will meet with this group one more time after today's meeting. What would you say in pointing out endings with the group in this next-to-last meeting?

Recording Progress

As a professional social worker bound by numerous legal and ethical obligations, you must keep records throughout all phases of practice. During the work phase, you should keep track of any revisions to the initial assessment and contract. Include notes about action steps and progress toward goal achievement. Incorporate the results of evaluation procedures such as goal attainment scaling, individual or subjective rating scores, rapid assessment instrument and other test scores, as well as graphics that reflect trends. Describe phenomena and events and identify issues or themes that might relate to the process of working toward goal accomplishment. In some instances, you should provide a rationale for an action you are taking or a recommendation you are making. Suppose you were to learn from an adult male client that he sometimes sexually molests his infant son. Of course, you must report this information to relevant authorities. Usually, this means a telephone call to the child-protection services division of the department of welfare or human services. Because you acquired this information during a meeting protected by laws and ethics concerning client confidentiality, you should meticulously record the data (that is, the words the client said) that led you to conclude that the child may be at risk of abuse. You should also record what you said to the client in response. You may have informed him that you, as a professional social worker, have a legal obligation to report this information to child-protection authorities.

You should note this. You may also have indicated that you would like to continue to serve as his social worker during this time; you should record this as well. When you make the phone call to the relevant authorities, be sure to record the date and time, the person contacted, and the contents of the conversation. Of course, unless the client provides informed consent to do so, you refrain from sharing information about the client beyond that which is relevant to the issue of possible child abuse.

In many settings, social workers use a problem-oriented recording (POR) approach during the work phase (Biagi, 1977; Burrill, 1976; Johnson, 1978; Martens & Holmstrup, 1974). The well-known SOAP format (subjective data, objective data, assessment, and plan) is commonly used in medical settings and has been widely used in social services as well. The DAR (data, action, and response) and APIE (assessment, plan, implementation, and evaluation) are fairly common, and there are several variations to the traditional SOAP structure. For example, SOAPIE stands for subjective, objective, assessment, plan, implementation or interventions, and evaluation. SOAP-IER adds "revisions" to the format. The SOAIGP format represents another derivation (Kagle & Kopels, 2008). SOAIGP stands for:

> **S**—supplemental information from clients or family members
> **O**—your observations and, if applicable, those of other agency staff
> **A**—activities that you, the client, or others undertake
> **I**—your impressions, hypotheses, assessments, or evaluations
> **G**—current goals
> **P**—plans for additional activities or action steps

In the supplemental category, you may include new or revised information provided by clients, family members, or other people in the client's primary social systems. In the observation section, you may describe your own observations of the person, issue, and situation. If applicable, you may also include observations of other agency staff members. In the activities category, you may summarize client tasks, worker tasks, and in-session tasks that have occurred. In impressions, you may summarize your current evaluation of progress toward goal achievement and make note of your tentative impressions and hypotheses. You may also summarize results of frequency counts, subjective ratings, and test results in this section. Under goals, you may record goals that are the current focus of work or revise original goals. In the plans section, you may make note of changes in your approach and identify additional action steps that you or your client intend to take. For example, following an interview with Mrs. Chase, Susan Holder might prepare a SOAIGP entry as shown in Box 12.2.

Problem-oriented recording formats serve many valuable functions. The SOAPIE, SOAPIER, and SOAIGP adaptations improve on the earlier SOAP system with their greater emphasis on implementation or intervention and evaluation and, in the case of SOAIGP, specific recognition of the importance of goals. To further that trend, please consider the preliminary, experimental version of a goal-focused format, tentatively called GAAP, as shown in Box 12.3.

Progress recordings are legal as well as professional documents. Prepare them as if they could become public knowledge—perhaps in the context of a review committee or even a courtroom hearing or trial. Organize them in a coherent manner. Prepare them in a well-written, legible, and timely fashion. Include descriptive and factual information that pertains to the purposes and goals for work. Avoid complex abstractions that cannot be substantiated. Ensure that your records reflect accurate, objective, unbiased reporting, along with respect for the individual and cultural characteristics of clients and their active participation in decisions and processes. While maintaining the confidentiality rights of third parties, identify the sources of information and support the reasons for decisions and actions. Finally, ensure that your records reflect compliance with legal and agency policies (Kagle, 2002).

BOX 12.2

Example: Progress Recording—SOAIGP

SOAIGP Entry for Meeting with Lynn Chase February 10

Supplemental. Mrs. Chase indicated that she had accomplished the action step we had identified for this week. She reported that it was a great help. She stated that she has felt in better spirits than she has for months. Before the meeting, Mr. Chase had telephoned to report that things are much better at home. He said, "Everybody has begun to help out at home, and we're all much happier. Thanks a lot."

Observations. Mrs. Chase does indeed appear to be in much better spirits. She speaks with energy and expressiveness. When talking about her family life and her gardening, her face becomes bright and animated. When she discusses work, there is a slight change to a more "businesslike" quality.

Activities. During today's meeting, Mrs. Chase and I talked at length about her childhood. On several occasions, she referred to her mother's drinking and the mixed feelings she experienced as a child when she dealt with her intoxicated mother. She sobbed when she talked of the embarrassment and rage she felt when a friend had visited while her mother was drunk and verbally abusive. She also revealed that she felt "somehow to blame" for her mother's drinking. She said, "I used to feel that if I were somehow better or less of a problem, then Mother wouldn't need to drink so much."

I reminded Mrs. Chase that we had three more meetings together. She said that she would miss me, but already "things were much better."

Impressions. Mrs. Chase's daily logs (attached) reflect progress toward two of the goals: sleeping better and arguing less with Robert and Richard. It is my impression that the change program continues to be viable. There is no need to revise it at this time.

Goals. The previously established goals remain in effect.

Plans. We identified a new action step. In addition to those already identified last week, Mrs. Chase agreed to read Janet Woititz's book *Adult Children of Alcoholics* (1983) within 2 weeks of today's date.

Susan Holder, BSW, MSW

BOX 12.3

Example: Progress Recording—GAAP

Goals. Summarize the goals and objectives reflected in the contract.

Activities. Describe the tasks, activities, and interventions undertaken by participants (for example, social worker, client, others) during or in between meetings in pursuit of the goals.

Assessment. Report the results of assessment and evaluation processes related to effects and outcomes of activities and progress toward goal achievement. Incorporate or attach the results of subjective and objective evaluation instruments (for example, RAIs, frequency counts, subjective ratings).

Plans. Based on the assessment and evaluation, outline plans for additional goal-related tasks and activities including, when necessary, changes to the agreed-upon goals and objectives.

EXERCISE 12-12: RECORDING PROGRESS

For these exercises, assume that you are a social worker with a multipurpose social services agency. Use a word-processing program to prepare simulated progress notes about the following interviews. Prepare them as if you intended to include them within a formal case record. When finished, label the document "Progress Notes for Five Clients" and deposit it in your Social Work Skills Learning Portfolio.

1. Today's meeting with Mr. K. is the next to last one. Next time, you will conclude your work together. During this meeting, he discussed the meeting with his former wife with considerable satisfaction and pride. He was especially pleased with himself for sincerely experiencing and truthfully sharing his pleasure that his wife seemed happier than she had for years and was enjoying life. Initially cautious, she also said that he looked and seemed better than he had for a long time as well. Although you had been somewhat concerned that the meeting might reactivate feelings of loss and remorse, it had the desired outcome. That is, Mr. K. used the meeting to say goodbye to both his former wife and to the marriage itself. He reported that when he now thinks about his former wife, he does so fondly but no longer hopes they will get back together. He seemed quite resolved about that. He reported that he is now dating someone, is eating better, and is active socially and recreationally. He said that he exercises daily and reads books—something that he loved to do as a child but had not done for the past 40 years. Prepare a progress note regarding the interview. Use the SOAIGP format.

2. Today's meeting with Loretta is the next to last one. Next time, you will conclude your work together. During this meeting, she described how well she is doing in her job and in her life outside of work as well. She said that she spends time with friends and regularly takes long walks with two other women. She reported that she submitted an application to serve as a volunteer to help homeless women in the community. She thinks they'll approve her request and she looks forward to helping others reclaim their lives as she has her own. Loretta also described an encounter that she had with her boss. She said that she had felt uncomfortable around him since she began work there but she desperately wanted the job and did not want to "rock the boat." She reported that it became clear during the previous week exactly why she felt uneasy with him. She said the boss "came on to her and asked her to have a drink with him after work." At that point, she thought to herself, "Oh, I remember this kind of thing from many, many years ago." She said that she told him this: "Thanks so much for the invitation. That's very nice of you but I know you need to get home to your wife and family, and I want to keep our relationship friendly and professional. So, thanks again but no thanks." She giggled as she described the shocked look on his face and reported that since that encounter he has treated her with courtesy and respect. Prepare a progress note regarding the interview. Use the SOAIGP format.

3. Earlier today, you completed an interview with Gloria, a teenage member of the S. family. She reported that following your last meeting together, she had told her boyfriend that he would have to see his doctor and receive treatment before she would again have sex with him. She appeared to be pleased that she could report this to you. You praised her for taking that action and asked about her boyfriend's response. She said that he had left in a huff, but she thought that he might be back. Prepare a progress note regarding the interview. Use the SOAIGP format.

4. Earlier today, you completed a meeting with Mrs. F., her daughters, and the principal of their school. During the course of the meeting, the girls described in detail what the teenage boys had said and done to them. They talked of the boys spitting at them and calling them names that referred to their Latino heritage. The girls were able to identify the boys by name. The principal appeared surprised and disturbed by what the girls had to say. He apparently believed the girls because he said that he was indeed sorry that this had happened. Furthermore, he said that he would talk with the boys later that day. He also asked the girls to tell him right away if anything like this ever happened again. Prepare a progress note regarding the interview. Use the GAAP format.

5. For approximately 11 months, you have been providing social work consultation services to an agency attempting to recover from the consequences of incompetent management and fraudulent behavior under a previous administration. Change in a positive direction is now apparent. Communications among staff members have improved and they now receive weekly supervision. The agency director is pursuing an active and engaged approach to leadership, and morale is improving. Today, you met with the board of directors to review these positive trends and to outline your intentions to support the executive director, the administrators and supervisors, and other staff members in their efforts to improve. Although the board members were extremely pleased with your report and encouraged you to continue your fine work, they requested that you complete an evaluation of the executive director's performance and submit a recommendation to the board concerning his fitness to continue in that role. Prepare a progress note regarding the meeting. Use the SOAIGP format.

Summary

During the work and evaluation phase of social work practice, you and the client take action toward resolving the identified issues and achieving the established goals. In this process, you use both empathic skills and work phase expressive skills. Skills pertinent to the work phase include (1) rehearsing action steps, (2) reviewing action steps, (3) evaluating, (4) focusing, (5) educating, (6) advising, (7) representing, (8) responding with immediacy, (9) reframing, (10) confronting inconsistencies, (11) pointing out endings, and (12) progress recording.

CHAPTER 12: EXPERIENTIAL INTERVIEWING EXERCISE

At this point, you have completed three interviews with a practice client and are planning to undertake the fourth. Thus far, you have used numerous social work skills and probably have a clear conception of the agreed-upon issues for work, the goals, and plans to pursue those goals as well as means to evaluate progress toward their accomplishment. By this time, you and the practice client may have considered various explanatory and change-oriented hypotheses and perhaps shared some ideas in common. As a result of your frequent communication of empathic understanding and open-ended questions, you may have established a warm and trusting relationship. The practice client may feel quite safe and secure with you and may have shared thoughts, feelings, and observations freely and fully. Indeed, she or he might have been so actively involved as to commit to undertake one or more action steps during the interval between meetings. The practice client may have also planned to monitor and measure progress toward the agreed-upon service goals.

Following the third interview, you and the practice client reviewed the experience. Your colleague shared evaluative feedback and you reflected on ways you might improve. You also prepared word-processed entries for the practice client case record, and presumably engaged in preliminary planning for this upcoming fourth meeting.

Building on the previous meetings with your practice client, conduct the fourth interview. Ensure that the setting is private, and again record the meeting. You might identify a tentative agenda for today's session and seek feedback about it from your practice client. Assuming consensus about an agenda, proceed to use the working and evaluating skills during the meeting. Of course, seeking feedback, many of the exploring skills and possibly some of the assessing, and the contracting skills may be applicable as well. As you know, the working and evaluating skills include: rehearsing action steps, reviewing action steps, evaluating, focusing, educating, advising, representing, responding with immediacy, reframing, confronting inconsistencies, and pointing out endings. Remember that you will complete a progress recording shortly after the meeting.

When you've finished the interview, complete the following:

1. Leave your respective social worker and client roles. Request that your colleague complete a copy of the Working and Evaluating Skills Rating Form (see Appendix 11). If items from other rating forms such as the Talking and Listening, the Exploring, the Assessing, or the Contracting Skills Rating Forms are applicable, you may use those as well. When your colleague has completed the ratings, inquire about today's interview experience. Ask general open-ended questions to obtain as much evaluative feedback as possible and, through that, enhance your learning. For example, you might ask your colleague questions such as:

   ◆ Did we work on what you wanted to work on today?
   ◆ Do you think that the approach we took today in working toward the goals was effective?
   ◆ What do you think about the way we evaluated progress today?
   ◆ What parts of the interview affected you the most—either positively or negatively?
   ◆ What do you wish had happened during the interview that did not occur?
   ◆ What suggestions do you have about how the interview could have been better, more helpful, or more constructive for you?
   ◆ What suggestions do you have about how I could have been a better or more helpful social worker today?

   Summarize your partner's feedback in a word-processed document titled "Fourth Meeting with a Practice Client." Label this particular section "Practice Client Feedback."

2. Next, describe and discuss your own reactions to the interview. How did you feel about it? What did you like and what did you dislike about it? Refer to the working and evaluating sections of The Social Work Skills Interview Rating Form (see Appendix 15) to evaluate your performance. Items in the active-listening, beginning, exploring, assessing, and contracting sections may be applicable as well. Identify those skills you performed well, those that need improvement, those that you might or should have used during the interview, and those that you used but probably should not have. Evaluate the quality of the work you did together. Consider how you evaluated progress. Identify aspects of the interview that might be missing or ways you might enhance its quality. You might have a chance to address those in a subsequent meeting. Finally, discuss what you would

do differently if you had a chance to conduct the interview again and outline what you might do in the next interview to improve the quality of the interview. Summarize your ratings, reactions, and reflections in a word-processed section of the "Fourth Meeting with a Practice Client" document. Label the section "My Ratings, Reactions, and Reflections" and then save the entire document for deposit into the "Experiential Interviewing Exercise" folder of your Social Work Skills Portfolio.

3. Next, reflect upon the entirety of the interview experience and use relevant preparing skills to prepare for the next meeting with the practice client. Draw upon what you learned and the documents you created to word-process tentative plans for the meeting. Label the document "Preliminary Plans for the Fifth Interview with a Practice Client" and deposit it in the "Experiential Interviewing Exercise" folder of your Social Work Skills Portfolio.

4. Record information gained during this meeting into a coherent progress record. You might use the SOAIGP format that we discussed in this chapter to organize your word-processed document. Record the date of the interview as well as the date you prepare the record. Identify yourself as the social worker but continue to disguise the identity of the practice client. Label the document "Progress Note." After you have completed a draft of the progress note, replay the recording. Make note of exchanges that may enhance the quality or accuracy of the note. Revise the document accordingly. When finished, place the revised progress note into the "Practice Client Case Record" subfolder of your Social Work Skills Learning Portfolio.

As you finish this chapter, please reflect on your learning by completing the following self-appraisal exercise.

SELF-APPRAISAL: THE WORKING AND EVALUATING SKILLS

Please respond to the following items. Your answers should help you to assess your proficiency in the working and evaluating skills. Read each statement carefully. Then, use the following 4-point rating scale to indicate the degree to which you agree or disagree with each statement. Record your numerical response in the space provided.

4 = Strongly agree   2 = Disagree

3 = Agree   1 = Strongly disagree

4	3	2	1	Rating Statement
				At this point in time, I can
☐	☐	☐	☐	1. Discuss the purposes and functions of working and evaluating.
☐	☐	☐	☐	2. Rehearse action steps.
☐	☐	☐	☐	3. Review action steps.
☐	☐	☐	☐	4. Evaluate progress.
☐	☐	☐	☐	5. Provide focus during meetings.
☐	☐	☐	☐	6. Educate others.
☐	☐	☐	☐	7. Advise others.
☐	☐	☐	☐	8. Represent clients.
☐	☐	☐	☐	9. Respond with immediacy.
☐	☐	☐	☐	10. Reframe messages.
☐	☐	☐	☐	11. Confront inconsistencies.
☐	☐	☐	☐	12. Point out endings.
☐	☐	☐	☐	13. Prepare written progress recordings.
☐	☐	☐	☐	14. Assess proficiency in the working and evaluating skills.
				Subtotal

Note: These items are identical to those contained in the Working and Evaluating Skills section of the Social Work Skills Self-Appraisal Questionnaire presented in Appendix 3. If you completed that self-appraisal before beginning Chapter 1, you have already responded to these items once before. You may now compare the responses you made on that occasion with those you made this time. Also, compare the two subtotals. If you believe that you have progressed in terms of your proficiency, the more recent subtotal should be higher than the earlier one.

CHAPTER 13

ENDING

This chapter (see Box 13.1) should help you develop proficiency in the *ending skills*. Social workers use these skills as we conclude our working relationships with clients. Although the particular form of ending may vary, several skills are important to the process. Drawing on the work of Schwartz (1971, 1976) and Kubler-Ross[1] (1969), Shulman (1992) discusses several skills associated with the dynamics of the ending process. The skills presented here derive in part from those. The social work ending skills include (1) reviewing the process, (2) final evaluating, (3) sharing ending feelings and saying goodbye, and (4) recording the closing summary.

The four most common forms of concluding relationships with clients are (1) transferral, (2) referral, (3) termination, and (4) client discontinuation. In the first three, you and your clients openly discuss the ending process and jointly determine the best course of action given the circumstances. These are the preferred modes of ending. The fourth form, quite common in many agency settings, is exclusively client initiated. Often with good reason, clients may decide to stop meeting with you. They may do so by informing you during a meeting, in a telephone conversation, or even by letter. They may also discontinue without notification, perhaps by failing to attend a scheduled meeting. Their absence conveys the message. In such cases (assuming that you can make contact by phone or in person), it is often very useful to seek clarification from clients who discontinue in this manner. However, you should be extremely sensitive to clients' indirect expressions during these contacts. Sometimes, in response to your inquiry, clients might say they will resume meeting with you "because you were so nice as to call," when in fact they have

---

[1] The validity of the Kubler-Ross "Stages of Grief" model has been challenged in several research studies. We cannot assume that clients necessarily respond to loss according to any or all of the five stages of denial, anger, bargaining, depression, and acceptance—or do so in any particular sequence (Konigsberg, 2011).

BOX 13.1
Chapter Purpose

The purpose of this chapter is to help learners develop proficiency in the ending skills.

Goals

Following completion of this chapter, learners should be able to demonstrate proficiency in:

- Discussing the purposes and functions of ending
- Reviewing the process
- Final evaluating
- Sharing ending feelings and saying goodbye
- Recording the closing summary
- Assessing proficiency in the ending skills

Core EPAS Competencies

The skills addressed in this chapter support the following core EPAS competencies:

- Identify as a professional social worker and conduct oneself accordingly (EP2.1.1).
- Apply social work ethical principles to guide professional practice (EP2.1.2).
- Apply critical thinking to inform and communicate professional judgments (EP2.1.3).
- Engage diversity and difference in practice (EP2.1.4).
- Apply knowledge of human behavior and the social environment (EP2.1.7).
- Respond to contexts that shape practice (EP2.1.9).
- Intervene, and evaluate with individuals, families, groups, organizations, and communities (EP2.1.10[c–d]).

decided to discontinue. If you listen carefully during such contacts, you may learn something about the ways you presented yourself or how you intervened that played a role in their decision to discontinue. This information may be helpful with other clients in the future. Providing clients with an opportunity to provide feedback about the nature and quality of service may also help them conclude the relationship in a more satisfying manner. It may sufficiently expand their view of you, the agency, and the experience to enable them to seek services again at some point in the future.

Clients are more likely to discontinue without notification at certain times. There is an increased probability of client discontinuation whenever changes occur. Changing from a customary meeting time or relocating from one meeting place to another may lead clients to discontinue. The transfer of a client to another social worker within the same agency can also involve a stressful transition, which the client may resolve through discontinuation. Perhaps the most difficult of all involves a referral to another professional in a different agency. This involves many changes—a new location; another agency with at least somewhat different policies, procedures, and mission; a new meeting schedule; and, of course, a different helping professional. Many clients, perhaps quite understandably, cope with these numerous changes through discontinuation. Although the dynamics of transfers and referrals are similar, transfers are generally easier to manage. Referrals involve more change, and the psychosocial demands on the client are greater. Nonetheless, transfers and referrals, like termination and discontinuation, bring about a conclusion to the relationship between you and the client.

Ending a significant relationship is often a difficult and painful experience. It is certainly challenging for social workers. Concluding a relationship with a client can stimulate strong feelings of sadness, loss, and other emotions as well. For clients, the process of ending may be even more intense. By this time, clients usually view you as a kind, caring, and understanding person who listens well and has their best interests at heart. Often, clients have shared personally intimate thoughts and feelings. This may lead them to feel both safe and vulnerable. They may have entrusted their secrets to you, a person with whom they may never again have contact. They may have successfully addressed a major issue, turned their lives around, or reached a significant goal. They may experience intense gratitude and want to express it to you—perhaps with a tangible or symbolic gift. The conclusion of the relationship may elicit a host of deep feelings. Some clients may feel intensely sad, as if they had lost a best friend, which may in fact be the case. They may feel frightened and dependent as they ask themselves, "How can I make it without you?" They may feel guilty that they did not work as hard as they might have or that they did not take as much advantage of the opportunities for change and growth as they could have. They may feel rejected by you or angry that the relationship is ending. They may think, "If you really cared about me, you wouldn't end the relationship—you must not care about me at all. You're glad to be rid of me!" Clients may also deny or minimize feelings that lie just beneath the surface of awareness. They may present themselves as being quite ready to terminate, when they are actually struggling with strong feelings that they do not acknowledge or express. There are many manifestations of the psychological and social processes associated with ending—a transition that often provokes significant reactions from both you and your clients. Ideally, we explore these responses as part of the ending process.

Reviewing the Process

Reviewing the process involves a summary retrospection of what has occurred between you and your clients during the time you have worked together. It is a cooperative process; all parties participate in the review. Typically, you invite clients to share their reflections about the work you have undertaken together and perhaps identify some exchanges or events that were especially significant or meaningful or had the greatest impact.

Following the responses to your request, you might ask about additional thoughts and feelings. This often stimulates discussion of other experiences. After the client shares, take a few moments to mention some of your own significant recollections. When you do so, highlight something the client realized, said, or did that, you think, contributed to progress or made a difference of some kind.

> **PRACTICE FORMAT: REVIEWING THE PROCESS**
> **(Encouraging Clients)**
>
> I've been thinking about the work we've done together during these last several months. We've covered a lot of ground, and you have made changes in your feelings and emotions, the way you think about things, and how you approach others and the world. You've also made changes in your situation. As you think back over all that we've done together, what strikes you as especially significant or meaningful?
>
> *or*
>
> *(continued)*

Reviewing the process may be useful and potentially beneficial even when progress has been modest or nonexistent. Encourage the client to share significant moments—positive or negative—and then explore those to highlight lessons that can be learned. When you share, try to find strengths or positive aspects in the client's actions and experiences that might, in the future, serve as stepping stones for further progress or growth.

EXERCISE 13-1: REVIEWING THE PROCESS

For these exercises, assume that you are a social worker with a multipurpose social services agency. In the spaces provided, write the words you would say in reviewing the process with each client.

1. You have been working with Mr. K. for approximately 2 months. When he first met with you, he said that his major problem was that he couldn't seem to "get over" his former wife; that he kept hoping for reconciliation when their chances were virtually non-existent. During the time of your work together, he has made considerable progress. He has resolved the major problem—he no longer obsesses about his ex-wife and has cognitively and emotionally accepted the fact that the marriage is truly over. He is moving forward in several areas, including his social and recreational life. He is extremely pleased with the resolution of the original problems and the achievement of the goals that you collaboratively identified. He is also proud of his own personal growth. He views himself as a more complete person who now feels quite content with himself and his life. You are also pleased with the work you have done together. As this is your last meeting, please write the words you would say in encouraging Mr. K. to review the process with you. After that, refresh your memory of those exercises that you completed in earlier chapters to write the words you might say in sharing something that you believe could have been especially significant, meaningful, or impactful for Mr. K.

2. You have now worked with Loretta for nearly 4 months. During that time, she has found a job—where she now regularly receives excellent evaluations; secured an apartment; made friends; and enjoys an active social and recreational life. When you first met, Loretta said that she was traveling to visit her youngest daughter whom she hadn't seen, spoken, or corresponded with in more than 15 years. She has decided to postpone her travel plans until she decides how best to contact both of her daughters to determine if either of them is interested in resuming some kind of a relationship. As this is your last meeting, please write the words you would say in encouraging Loretta to review the process with you. After that, refresh your memory of those exercises that you completed in earlier chapters to write the words you might say in sharing something that you believe could have been especially significant, meaningful, or impactful for Loretta.

3. You are in the midst of the final meeting with the S. family. During the past several months, many productive changes have occurred. Mr. and Mrs. S. are happier with each other and have adopted a consistent approach to parenting. They enjoy the children much more than they had before and the children, in turn, seem to have gained respect for them. The children are also doing well, perhaps especially Gloria who is growing into a self-confident, independent, and assertive young woman. As this is your last meeting, please write the words you would say in encouraging the S. family to review the process with you. After that, refresh your memory of those exercises that you completed in earlier chapters to write the words you might say in sharing something that you believe could have been especially significant, meaningful, or impactful for the family as a whole or for any individual members.

4. This is your concluding session with Mrs. F. The school situation has dramatically improved. In large part due to Mrs. F. and the girls, the school has initiated an anti-bullying program which has been embraced by the community at large. Within the family, Mrs. F. and her daughters are communicating in a much more satisfying way. In 2 weeks, the three of them will begin a 10-week assertiveness-training group sponsored by another community agency. As this is your last meeting, please write the words you

would say in encouraging Mrs. F. to review the process with you. After that, refresh your memory of those exercises that you completed in earlier chapters to write the words you might say in sharing something that you believe could have been especially significant, meaningful, or impactful for Mrs. F. or her daughters.

5. For nearly a year now, you have been providing social work consultation services to an agency that is trying to recover from the consequences of incompetent management and fraudulent behavior under a previous administration. During that time a number of positive changes have occurred and the agency is ready to attempt to continue on without your direct involvement. As this is your last meeting, please write the words you would say in encouraging the agency group to review the process with you. After that, refresh your memory of those exercises that you completed in earlier chapters to write the words you might say in sharing something that you believe could have been especially significant, meaningful, or impactful for the group as a whole or for any individual members.

Final Evaluating

In addition to reviewing the process, you also engage clients in a final evaluation of progress toward problem resolution and goal attainment. For this discussion, you may draw on the results of measurement instruments such as questionnaires, various individual or subjective rating scales, and the graphic reflections of trends and patterns (for example, line graphs). You may also share your own impressions of progress toward goals; or overall growth and development. Be sure to seek feedback from clients when you summarize evaluative data or make observations. Although they usually concur, clients sometimes hold different views that deserve consideration and acknowledgment.

As part of this process, express your pleasure concerning positive changes that have occurred. Credit clients for the work they have undertaken and help them identify issues that have not been completely resolved, goals that have been only partially achieved, and new aspirations that may have emerged during the course of your time together. Work toward such goals does not have to stop because you and your client are ending your working relationship. Clients, often with the support of friends, family members, and colleagues may continue to take action steps toward desirable outcomes—including those that involve overall quality of life. By the time clients conclude the working relationship with a social worker, many have become competent problem solvers in their own right. They are often quite capable of defining goals and identifying and taking action on their own. This phenomenon, when it occurs, is enormously satisfying for social workers. When clients become effective problem solvers who are skilled at self-help, you may reasonably conclude that you have indeed helped them to help themselves. If, because of their association with you, clients acquire skills with which to address future issues and pursue aspirations, they have gained a great deal indeed.

Like most of the ending skills, final evaluating is a cooperative process. You and the client share your respective evaluations of progress and jointly identify areas for additional work. As part of the process, provide clients with a summary of the results of subjective and objective evaluation instruments; in graphical form if possible. When clients see tangible evidence of progress in a graphic illustration, they often experience feelings of success and accomplishment in a different way than they do when we talk only verbally about their progress.

PRACTICE FORMAT: FINAL EVALUATING

Let's now take a final look at where we stand in regard to progress toward the goals that we identified. One of our major goals was _____. Let's look at our evaluation data. How far do you think we have come toward its achievement?

Join clients in celebrating largely or completely accomplished goals with appropriate pleasure and satisfaction. Encourage them to experience and enjoy the sense of personal competence, self-efficacy, and satisfaction that accompanies goal achievement. Help clients identify areas that need additional work and encourage them to plan additional action steps to take after you conclude your relationship together. Of course, this discussion is not nearly as extensive or as detailed as when you and clients established action steps as part of the contracting and work processes. Rather, you encourage clients to look forward to future activities that can support continued growth and development. You may initiate this process by asking a question such as "What kinds of activities do you think might help you to continue the progress you've made so far?"

PRACTICE FORMAT: FINAL EVALUATING (Considering the Future)

Now that we're concluding our time together, you may have some ideas about goals you'd like to pursue or steps you'd like to take in the future. What do you think you'll do next?

As part of the final evaluation, you may seek feedback from clients about things you said or did that were helpful and things that were not. This kind of evaluation may help clients to identify behaviors they can adopt for their own future use. It may also provide an opportunity for clients to share their gratitude to you for your help. However, an important purpose for seeking feedback about helpful and unhelpful factors is to aid you in your own professional growth and development.

In a sense, you request that clients evaluate your performance as a social worker. By seeking such evaluative feedback, you may gain valuable information about yourself that may prove useful in your work with other current and future clients. In asking for feedback, you might say, "I would appreciate it if you would tell me about those things I did that were particularly helpful to you during our work together. . . . And could you also identify things I did that were not so helpful?"

EXERCISE 13-2: FINAL EVALUATING

In the spaces provided, write the words you would say to engage each client in the process of final evaluating. Prepare statements to encourage each client to identify future action steps. Finally, write the words you might say in seeking evaluative feedback from each client concerning what has been helpful and what has not.

1. This is your last meeting with Mr. K. He has made considerable progress. He no longer obsesses about his ex-wife and has cognitively and emotionally accepted the fact that the marriage is truly over. He is more socially active and engages in several recreational pursuits as well. He feels quite content with himself and his life. You are also pleased with the work you have done together. You have evaluation data in graphic form that reflect significant decrease in the frequency and intensity of disturbing thoughts about the marriage, improvement in overall mood, and increase in personal satisfaction. You also have several evaluative observations about his progress as well as his personal growth and development. With this information in mind, please write the words you would say to engage Mr. K. in the process of final evaluating.

2. Loretta has made remarkable progress during the time you have worked together. This is your last meeting together. She now has secure and satisfying employment, a decent and safe apartment, and she enjoys an active social and recreational life. She has accomplished virtually all of the basic goals of securing income, food, and shelter and has grown personally as well. You provide Loretta with a Goal Attainment Scale that summarizes progress toward these goals. The single major goal that remains involves the relationship with her daughters. Originally, Loretta said that she was traveling to visit her youngest daughter whom she hadn't seen, spoken, or corresponded with in more than 15 years. Partly as a result of your work together, she has decided to postpone her plans to visit her youngest daughter and has slightly revised her goals. She realized she was afraid to meet her eldest daughter because she felt so guilty about her behavior as a

mother. Her current plan is to decide how best to contact both of her daughters to determine if either of them is interested in resuming some kind of a relationship. Once she makes that decision, she'll take action. With this information in mind, please write the words you would say to engage Loretta in the process of final evaluating.

3. You are meeting for the last time with the S. family. During the past several months, many productive changes have occurred. At times, modest strain is apparent between some of the children. In general, however, the family seems to be coping well with the complex demands of blending and growing together. You have observed numerous ways in which they are communicating more directly and honestly with one another, and experiencing more satisfying relationships. In addition, weekly scale scores reveal a modest but consistent trend toward greater family cohesion and satisfaction. In addition, the family has achieved more than half of their agreed-upon goals. You have graphics that reflect both data sets. With this information in mind, write the words you would say to engage the S. family in the process of final evaluating.

4. You are meeting for the last time with Mrs. F. She and her daughters have made noticeable gains. The school and community have embraced the anti-bullying initiative that the F. family instigated. The F. daughters are now actively involved in school and after-school activities, and have developed a strong, inclusive, and accepting social network. The subjective scales that Mrs. F. rated each week reveal a marked improvement in overall quality of life, family life, work life, and social life scores. You have a line graph that displays upward trends in all four areas. The F. family is extremely satisfied with the changes that have occurred and they are looking forward to the assertiveness-training

group they will join in another week or so. With this information in mind, write the words you would say to engage Mrs. F. in the process of final evaluating.

5. This is your last meeting as a social work consultant with a social service agency that is recovering from the consequences of incompetent management and fraudulent behavior under a previous administration. The agency has made substantial progress toward achievement of almost all goals. You have a Goal Attainment Scale that summarizes these results. You also have observed numerous ways in which the agency has progressed—notably in its relationships with the community and especially in the way agency personnel interact with and engage current and former clients as ongoing "consultants" in their efforts at continuous improvement of service quality. Data from client satisfaction surveys have begun to show substantial improvement. Write the words you would say in initiating the process of final evaluating with the agency group.

Sharing Ending Feelings and Saying Goodbye

The nature and intensity of the feelings clients experience as they conclude a relationship with you vary according to their personal characteristics, the duration of service, the issue and goals, the roles and functions you served, and the degree of progress (Hess & Hess, 1999). Because ending is a significant event in the lives of most clients, social workers usually provide opportunities to share feelings related to the ending process.

Clients may experience several emotional responses as they end their relationship with you: anger, sadness, loss, fear, guilt, dependency, ambivalence, gratitude, and affection. Clients may hesitate to express their emotions freely at this time. If they conclude the relationship without sharing some of these feelings, they may experience a sense of incompleteness. This "unfinished" quality may impede the appropriate process of psychological separation from you and inhibit the client's movement toward increased autonomy and independence. Therefore, we usually encourage clients to express their ending feelings.

PRACTICE FORMAT: SHARING ENDING FEELINGS (Encouraging Clients)

We've reviewed our work together and evaluated progress, but we haven't yet shared our feelings about ending our relationship with one another. As I realize that this is our final meeting together, I am touched by so many things and have several competing emotions. I wonder if you might have some feelings about this as well.

Social workers, of course, also experience various feelings as we end our working relationships with clients. You may have spent several weeks or months with a person, a couple, a family, or a group. During your work together, a client may have shared painful emotions, discussed poignant issues, or made significant progress. Despite your professional status and commitment to an ethical code, you are also human. It is entirely understandable and appropriate that you also experience strong feelings as you end your relationships with clients. During the ending process, you may find yourself feeling guilty, inadequate, proud, satisfied, sad, angry, ambivalent, relieved, or affectionate. The kind and degree of your feelings may vary because of many factors. Like clients, you will probably experience some kind of emotional reaction during the ending phase. It is often useful to share some of these feelings. Unlike clients, however, you retain your professional responsibilities, even in ending. You cannot freely express whatever feelings you experience. You must consider the potential effects on clients. For example, suppose you feel annoyed at an adult male client because he did not work as hard toward change as you had hoped he would. You should not share these or any other such feelings, unless to do so would help the client progress toward any remaining goals or conclude the relationship in a beneficial manner. Even during the final meeting, you choose which feelings to express and how to express them. However, do not simply suppress feelings that are inappropriate to share with clients. Rather, engage in the skills of self-exploration and centering (see Chapter 7) to address them in a personally and professionally effective fashion.

When they are relevant and appropriate, you may share your personal feelings about ending the relationship. Often, when you do share your feelings, clients respond by sharing additional emotions of their own. You may then reflect their feelings and perhaps share more of your own. Finally, however, you and the client complete the ending process by saying goodbye.

PRACTICE FORMAT: SHARING ENDING FEELINGS (Worker)

When I think about the fact that we will not meet anymore, I feel _____
_____.

EXAMPLE: SHARING ENDING FEELINGS (Worker)

WORKER: Now that we're concluding our work together, I feel a real sense of loss. I have truly valued our time together and have come to admire you and the way you're approaching life's challenges. I'm feeling sad about saying goodbye but also happy that you're moving forward. I'm really going to miss you.

EXERCISE 13-3: SHARING ENDING FEELINGS AND SAYING GOODBYE

In the spaces provided, write the words you would say to encourage each client to share feelings about ending. Also, prepare statements in which you share your own ending feelings with each client. As part of your own sharing, please specify those feelings that you think you might experience had you actually worked with each client. Identify those that would be appropriate to share and those that would not. Finally, note the exact words you would use in saying goodbye.

1. After working with Mr. K. for more than 2 months, you have completed your review of the process and conducted a final evaluation. You have approximately 15 minutes left in this very last meeting. Write the words you would say to encourage Mr. K. to share his feelings about ending; to express your own feelings; and finally to say goodbye to Mr. K.

2. After working with Loretta for several months, you have completed your review of the process and conducted a final evaluation. You have approximately 15 minutes left in this very last meeting. Write the words you would say to encourage her to share her feelings about ending; to express your own feelings; and finally to say goodbye to this fascinating woman.

3. You have reviewed the process and engaged in a final evaluation of progress with the S. family. In the last several minutes remaining in this final meeting, you would like to share ending feelings and say goodbye. Write the words you would say to encourage family members to share their feelings about ending; to express your own feelings; and finally to say goodbye to the S. family.

4. You are in the process of winding down your final session with Mrs. F. You have reviewed the process and engaged in a final evaluation of progress. Now it is time to move toward closure. Write the words you would say to encourage her to share her feelings about ending; to express your own feelings; and finally to say goodbye to Mrs. F.

5. For the past 11 months, you have been providing social work consultation services to an agency that is trying to recover from the consequences of incompetent management and fraudulent behavior under a previous administration. You are meeting with a large group of agency personnel, board members, and key stakeholders for the last time. You are in the process of winding down this final meeting. You have reviewed the process and engaged in a final evaluation of progress. Now it is time to finish up. Write the words you would say to encourage group members to share their feelings about ending; to express your own feelings; and finally to say goodbye to the people you've worked with for nearly a year.

Recording the Closing Summary

Following your final meeting with a client, you synthesize what occurred into a written closing summary. This final entry is usually somewhat more extensive than the typical progress recording. When the ending session has included a review of the process, a final evaluation, and a sharing of ending feelings, you will probably have most of what you need to complete a closing summary. Include the following information in the final record: (1) date of final contact; (2) your name and title as well as the name of the client; (3) beginning date of service; (4) the reason contact between you and the client was initiated; (5) the agreed-upon issues and goals for work; (6) the approach taken, the nature of the services that you provided, and the activities that you and the client undertook; (7) a summary evaluation of progress and an identification of issues and goals that remain unresolved or unaccomplished; (8) a brief assessment of the person-issue-situation as it now exists; and (9) the reason for closing the case (Wilson, 1980).

You may use the following section headings to organize your closing summary:

- Process and issues
- Evaluation
- Continuing goals
- Current assessment
- Ending process

As an illustrative example, consider how social worker Susan Holder might prepare a closing summary following the final interview with Mrs. Chase (see Box 13.2).

BOX 13.2

Example: Recording—Closing Summary—Lynn Chase

Process and Issues. Mrs. Lynn B. Chase and I, Susan Holder, MSW, met together today for the eighth and final time. Mrs. Chase and I first met almost 3 months ago. At that time, we agreed on the following issues for work: (1) frequent arguments with and feelings of irritability and anger toward son and husband; (2) stress, tension, and anxiety; (3) sleep disturbance; (4) ambivalence about job; (5) thoughts and feelings of excessive responsibility and possibly of control; and (6) role strain and possibly conflict among the roles of mother, wife, homemaker, and employee. Based on these issues, we established several related goals and developed an 8-week plan by which to approach our work together.

Evaluation. In reviewing the work process and evaluating progress, Mrs. Chase reported today that the feelings of stress and anger have decreased substantially since the time of the first contact. She also indicated that relations between her and her son, her and her husband, and even her husband and her son have greatly improved since the family more evenly redistributed housework responsibilities. Her reports are consistent with the other evaluation measures we used.

   She also said that she assumes less of a caretaker role with her husband and son. She said that she now believes that they have actually benefited from the assumption of greater family and household responsibility. She stated that she now sleeps fine and rarely has a headache. Mrs. Chase reported that her job at Fox Manufacturing is now quite satisfying; she said she is glad she kept it. And she has been engaging in more playful and pleasurable activities, particularly gardening.

(continued)

BOX 13.2 *(continued)*

Mrs. Chase indicated that the single most helpful aspect of our work together was when I said to her that "doing too much for your husband and son may prevent them from developing their full potential."

Continuing Goals. Mrs. Chase indicated that she is still working on issues related to excessive caretaking and intends to do further reading. She reported that she might attend an Adult Children of Alcoholics (ACOA) meeting to see what it's like. She said that she is also considering taking an assertiveness-training course.

Current Assessment. Based on the available evidence, Mrs. Chase, her son, and her husband are communicating more directly, sharing household responsibilities, and experiencing considerable satisfaction in their relationships with one another.

Robert seems to be negotiating the demands of adolescence in a constructive fashion, and Mrs. Chase has made considerable progress in reversing her long-held patterns of excessive responsibility and control.

Mrs. Chase and her family reflect numerous personal strengths that should serve them well in the future. I anticipate that Mrs. Chase will continue to grow and develop now that she has permitted herself to consider more expansive and flexible personal and familial roles.

Ending Process. Mrs. Chase and I concluded our work together in a positive manner. She expressed her gratitude, and I shared my affection for her as well as my pleasure at the progress she has made. We closed the case in the 8-week time frame as contracted.

Susan Holder, BSW, MSW   February 27

EXERCISE 13-4: RECORDING THE CLOSING SUMMARY

Use a word-processing program to prepare brief closing summaries for each of the following clients. The numerous earlier exercises about these five clients should provide most of the needed information related to issues, goals, action steps, and progress. Prepare the closing summaries as if you intended to include them within a formal case record. When finished, label the document "Closing Summaries for Five Clients" and deposit it in your Social Work Skills Learning Portfolio.

1. You have just completed your final meeting with Mr. K. Use information from previous exercises to prepare a closing summary of your work with him.

2. You have just completed your final meeting with Loretta. Use information from previous exercises to prepare a closing summary of your work with her.

3. You have completed the final meeting with the S. family. Use information from previous exercises to prepare a closing summary of your work with the family.

4. You have concluded the last session with Mrs. F. Use information from previous exercises to prepare a closing summary of your work with her.

5. You have concluded your last meeting with members of the troubled social service agency. Use information from previous exercises to prepare a closing summary of your work with the group.

Summary

The ending phase of social work practice provides an opportunity for you and your clients to look back on your relationship and the work you undertook together. You have a chance to evaluate overall progress and to identify directions for future work. However, concluding these working relationships can be both a joyful and a painful experience for you and your clients. Each of you may experience satisfaction concerning the progress achieved, regret about actions that were not taken, and sadness at the departure of a person who has been important. In optimal circumstances, you can explore these feelings as part of the ending process.

The particular form of ending may be transferral, referral, termination, or discontinuation. Several skills are important to the process, including (1) reviewing the process, (2) final evaluating, (3) sharing ending feelings and saying goodbye, and (4) recording the closing summary.

CHAPTER 13: EXPERIENTIAL INTERVIEWING EXERCISE

Conduct a final interview with your colleague who has served as your practice client during these past several weeks. As you did previously, ensure that the interview setting is private, and once again record the meeting. Using empathic, working, and especially ending skills, interview your colleague with a view toward concluding the relationship. This is your last meeting. Therefore use the relevant ending skills of reviewing the work process, final evaluating, and sharing ending feelings and saying goodbye. Remember that you will complete a closing summary shortly after the meeting.

When you have finished the interview, complete the following:

1. Leave your respective social worker and client roles. Request that your colleague complete a copy of the Ending Skills Rating Form (see Appendix 11). If items from other rating forms such as the Talking and Listening, the Exploring, the Assessing, the Contracting Skills, or the Working and Evaluating Rating Forms are applicable, you may use those as well. When your colleague has completed the ratings, inquire about today's interview experience. Ask general open-ended questions to obtain as much evaluative feedback as possible and, through that, enhance your learning. For example, you might ask your colleague questions such as:

   ◆ Did we work on what you wanted to work on today?
   ◆ Do you think that the approach we took today in working toward the goals was effective?
   ◆ What do you think about the way we evaluated progress today?
   ◆ What parts of the interview affected you the most—either positively or negatively?
   ◆ What do you wish had happened during the interview that did not occur?
   ◆ What suggestions do you have about how the interview could have been better, more helpful, or more constructive for you?
   ◆ What suggestions do you have about how I could have been a better or more helpful social worker today?

   Because this is your last meeting together as part of this exercise, also ask your partner to provide you with feedback concerning the entire five-session experience. You may adapt the session-focused open-ended questions (above) so that they refer to the complete series of meetings. For example, you might ask:

- Over the course of our five meetings together, did we work on what you wanted to work on? Were there issues that you would have preferred to address that we did not address? If so, what do you think caused that?
- How effective was the approach we took in addressing the problems and pursuing the goals that we identified for our work together?
- What do you think about the way we evaluated progress toward the goals we identified?
- What parts of the five-session experience affected you the most—either positively or negatively?
- What do you wish had happened during our five interviews that did not occur?
- What suggestions do you have about how our meetings could have been better, more helpful, or more constructive for you?
- What suggestions do you have about how I could have been a better or more helpful social worker in our work together?

Summarize your partner's feedback in a word-processed document titled "Fifth Meeting with a Practice Client." Label the section "Practice Client Feedback."

2. Following this last session, record your own reaction to the final meeting. How did you feel about the interview? What did you like and what did you dislike about it? Do you believe that you used all the relevant empathic, expressive, and ending skills during the interaction? How well did you use the ending skills? What would you do differently if you were to redo this final interview? Which of the ending skills should you practice further? Summarize your ratings, reactions, and reflections in a section of the "Fifth Meeting with a Practice Client" document. Label the section "My Ratings, Reactions, and Reflections."

3. Now consider the entire series of interviews. Summarize your overall impressions, reactions, and reflections about the experience in a section of the "Fifth Meeting with a Practice Client" document. Label the section "My Reactions to and Reflections on the Five-Session Experience" and then save the entire document for deposit into the "Experiential Interviewing Exercise" folder of your Social Work Skills Portfolio.

4. Word-process a written closing summary of your work with the colleague who served as your practice client. After you have completed a draft of the closing summary, replay the recording. Make note of exchanges that may enhance the quality or accuracy of the closing summary. Revise the document accordingly. When finished, place the closing summary in your Social Work Skills Learning Portfolio.

CHAPTER 13: SELF-APPRAISAL

As you finish this chapter, please reflect on your learning by completing the following self-appraisal exercise.

SELF-APPRAISAL: THE ENDING SKILLS

Please respond to the following items. Your answers should help you to assess your proficiency in the ending skills. Read each statement carefully. Then, use the following 4-point rating scale to indicate the degree to which you agree or disagree with each statement. Record your numerical response in the space provided.

4 = Strongly agree   2 = Disagree

3 = Agree   1 = Strongly disagree

4	3	2	1	Rating Statement
				At this point in time, I can
☐	☐	☐	☐	1. Discuss the purposes and functions of ending.
☐	☐	☐	☐	2. Review the process.
☐	☐	☐	☐	3. Engage clients in a process of final evaluation.
☐	☐	☐	☐	4. Share ending feelings and say goodbye.
☐	☐	☐	☐	5. Prepare a closing summary record.
☐	☐	☐	☐	6. Assess proficiency in the ending skills.
				Subtotal

Note: These items are identical to those contained in the Ending Skills section of the Social Work Skills Self-Appraisal Questionnaire presented in Appendix 3. If you completed that self-appraisal before beginning Chapter 1, you have already responded to these items once before. You may now compare the responses you made on that occasion with those you made this time. Also, compare the two subtotals. If you believe that you have progressed in terms of your proficiency, the more recent subtotal should be higher than the earlier one.

SUPPLEMENTAL EXERCISES: FINAL LESSONS

Congratulations! You have now complete all the chapters in the workbook, undertaken many, many exercises, and created a large Social Work Skills Learning Portfolio. You have done a lot! Please acknowledge the extraordinary amount of time and effort you expended in all the various activities. You deserve a great deal of credit!

Completion of this workbook represents a kind of ending too. In a way, it resembles the ending processes that social workers and clients experience. Some of the skills you recently practiced may be adapted for this last set of exercises—the Final Lessons. Use a word-processing program to respond to each of the tasks described below. Create section headings to organize the document in a coherent fashion. When finished, label the file "Final Lessons" and deposit it as the final document for inclusion in your Social Work Skills Learning Portfolio.

1. Compare the contents of your Social Work Skills Learning Portfolio with the checklist contained in Appendix 1. These documents represent tangible evidence of your learning. Identify any documents that are missing from the portfolio. Also, make note of those documents that could be improved through careful revision.

2. The portfolio materials, however, are only a part of the skills development story. From the time you first opened this workbook until now, you undertook a great many learning exercises. You practiced the social work skills a number of times and did so in various ways. Reflect about what you have learned. Then, briefly discuss the most important lessons gained from the various learning experiences.

3. Following your identification of important lessons learned, conduct a final evaluation of your proficiency in the social work skills. To do so, please turn to Appendix 2 and complete the Social Work Skills Test. The items are geared toward the comprehension level of understanding and are derived directly from the text. At this point in time, most learners who have carefully read the text and completed many of the exercises will correctly answer 70 percent or more of the items.[2] If you completed the test previously, the exam should be much easier to complete and your score should be considerably higher.

4. Now go to Appendix 3 and complete the Social Work Skills Self-Appraisal Questionnaire. You may have completed the questionnaire quite some time ago—before beginning Chapter 1. If you did so, you will be able to compare your item ratings and overall scores from the two events in pretest—posttest fashion. As such, it should provide you with a reasonable indication of the degree to which you gained increased proficiency in the social work skills. If this is the first time you completed the entire instrument, you may compare your items ratings and scores from the self-appraisal exercises that conclude each chapter with those in the relevant sections of the Social Work Skills Self-Appraisal Questionnaire in Appendix 3. The end-of-chapter appraisals represent sections of the Questionnaire as a whole.

5. After you have analyzed the results of the Social Work Skills Test and the Social Work Skills Self-Appraisal Questionnaire, identify those skills that require a lot of additional practice, those that need some, and those for which you have developed high levels of proficiency. Identify a list of relevant learning goals and develop plans to pursue them.

---

[2] The correct answers to the items in Part 1 of the Social Work Skills Test may be found through a careful review of the text. These items are written at the comprehension level and should not require much thought; knowledge of the text alone should suffice. The items in Part 2, however, do require application, analysis, synthesis, or evaluation. Answers to those items may involve discussion with professors or colleagues—after, of course, you have completed the test.

THE SOCIAL WORK SKILLS LEARNING PORTFOLIO

Portfolios are widely used in many contexts to demonstrate talents, competence, achievement, and potential. Artists and photographers, for example, commonly maintain selections of their artistic work in portfolios. Then, when applying for jobs, bidding on contracts, applying to graduate schools or institutes, or seeking to display their work in art galleries, they may present examples of their artistic products as part of the process. You may use portfolios within learning contexts as well. A collection of written products, especially those that have been assessed or evaluated, can contribute to and reflect the depth and breadth of your learning. The documents you prepare as you complete the exercises contained in this workbook are especially well suited for incorporation into your own Social Work Skills Learning Portfolio.

Prepare the Social Work Skills Learning Portfolio in word-processed, computerized format. It should contain several completed exercises, assignments, self-assessments, and products that reflect and represent your learning. At various points during the learning process, "interim portfolios" may be self-assessed or submitted to someone else (for example, a social work colleague, a professor, or a supervisor) for evaluation and feedback. You may later prepare a "final" portfolio that includes a selected collection of products that you have carefully revised and reworked to reflect your very best work. Such final portfolios may be used for various purposes, including job interviews. Most importantly, however, they can represent a foundation for ongoing lifelong learning and skill development throughout your entire social work career.

As a first step in creating a Social Work Skills Learning Portfolio, please consider the products you might include. The following represents a list of selected learning exercises contained in the workbook. You may use the "Yes" or "No" boxes to keep track of those products you decide (or are assigned) to include in your portfolio. Use the "Document Quality" boxes, where applicable, to rate the quality of each relevant document.

THE SOCIAL WORK SKILLS LEARNING PORTFOLIO: CONTENTS

Document Enclosed?		Documentation	Document Quality (5=Excellent; 4=Superior; 3=Good; 2=Fair; 1=Poor; N/A=Not Applicable)					
Yes	No		5	4	3	2	1	N/A
☐	☐	Preface: Responses and Scores on The Social Work Skills Test (Appendix 2)						
☐	☐	Preface: Ratings and Scores on the Social Work Skills Self-Appraisal Questionnaire (Appendix 3)						
☐	☐	Preface: Ratings and Scores on the Self-Appraisal of Proficiency in the EPAS Core Competencies, Practice Knowledge, and Practice Behaviors (Appendix 18)						
☐	☐	Preface: Ratings and Scores on the Self-Appraisal of Proficiency in the ASWB Knowledge, Skills, and Abilities (Appendix 19: Bachelor's or Appendix 20: Master's)						
☐	☐	Chapter 1 (Summary Exercise 1-1): "Introduction to Social Work: Preliminary Thoughts and Ideas"	☐	☐	☐	☐	☐	☐
☐	☐	Chapter 1: Ratings and Scores on the end-of-chapter Self-Appraisal: Introduction Subscale						
☐	☐	Chapter 2 (Summary Exercise 2-1): Snapshot Report and Score on the Integrity and Work Ethics Test						
☐	☐	Chapter 2 (Summary Exercise 2-2): Item Ratings and Score on the General Self-Efficacy Scale (see Appendix 4)						
☐	☐	Chapter 2 (Summary Exercise 2-3): Ratings and Scores on the Self-Control Schedule (see Appendix 5)						
☐	☐	Chapter 2 (Summary Exercise 2-4): Multigenerational Genogram	☐	☐	☐	☐	☐	☐
☐	☐	Chapter 2 (Summary Exercise 2-5): Eco-Map	☐	☐	☐	☐	☐	☐
☐	☐	Chapter 2 (Summary Exercise 2-6): Critical Events Timeline	☐	☐	☐	☐	☐	☐
☐	☐	Chapter 2 (Summary Exercise 2-7): Scores on the Big Five Personality Instrument						

Yes	No		5	4	3	2	1	N/A
☐	☐	Chapter 2 (Summary Exercise 2-8): Ratings and Scores on the Family Subscale, the Friends Subscale, and the Overall Social Support Appraisals Scale (see Appendix 6)						
☐	☐	Chapter 2 (Summary Exercise 2-9): "Implications of Integrity, Professional Knowledge and Self-Efficacy, Self-Understanding and Self-Control, and Social Support for Social Work Practice"	☐	☐	☐	☐	☐	☐
☐	☐	Chapter 2: Ratings and Scores on the end-of-chapter Self-Appraisal: Professionalism Subscale						
☐	☐	Chapter 3 (Summary Exercise 3-1): Ratings and Scores on the Critical Thinking Questionnaire (see Appendix 7)						
☐	☐	Chapter 3 (Summary Exercise 3-3): Ratings and Scores on the Lifelong Learning Questionnaire (see Appendix 8)						
☐	☐	Chapter 3 (Summary Exercise 3-5): Learning Goal and Plans for Learning and Evaluation Table	☐	☐	☐	☐	☐	☐
☐	☐	Chapter 3 (Summary Exercise 3-6): Table of Synonyms and Keywords for a Social Problem	☐	☐	☐	☐	☐	☐
☐	☐	Chapter 3 (Summary Exercise 3-7): "Implications of Critical Thinking and Scientific Inquiry, and Career-Long Learning for Social Work Practice"	☐	☐	☐	☐	☐	☐
☐	☐	Chapter 3: Ratings and Scores on the end-of-chapter Self-Appraisal: Critical Thinking, Scientific Inquiry, and Career-Long Learning Skills Subscale						
☐	☐	Chapter 4 (Summary Exercise 4-1): Ratings and Scores on the Acceptance of Others Scale (see Appendix 9)						
☐	☐	Chapter 4 (Summary Exercise 4-4): Ratings and Scores on the Satisfaction With Life Scale (see Appendix 10)						
☐	☐	Chapter 4 (Summary Exercise 4-8): "Implications of Valuing Diversity and Difference, Accepting Others and Respecting Autonomy, Advancing Human Rights and Social Justice, and Promoting Social Well-Being through Policy Practice."	☐	☐	☐	☐	☐	☐

Document Enclosed?		Documentation	Document Quality (5=Excellent; 4=Superior; 3=Good; 2=Fair; 1=Poor; N/A=Not Applicable)					
Yes	No		5	4	3	2	1	N/A
☐	☐	Chapter 4: Ratings and Scores on the end-of-chapter Self-Appraisal: Valuing Diversity, Advancing Human Rights and Social Justice, and Promoting Social Well-Being through Policy Practice Subscale						
☐	☐	Chapter 5 (Summary Exercise 5-1): "Summary Ex 5-1"	☐	☐	☐	☐	☐	☐
☐	☐	Chapter 5 (Summary Exercise 5-2): "Summary Ex 5-2"	☐	☐	☐	☐	☐	☐
☐	☐	Chapter 5 (Summary Exercise 5-3): "Summary Ex 5-3"	☐	☐	☐	☐	☐	☐
☐	☐	Chapter 5 (Summary Exercise 5-4): "Summary Ex 5-4"	☐	☐	☐	☐	☐	☐
☐	☐	Chapter 5 (Summary Exercise 5-5): "Summary Ex 5-5"	☐	☐	☐	☐	☐	☐
☐	☐	Chapter 5 (Summary Exercise 5-6): "Summary Ex 5-6"	☐	☐	☐	☐	☐	☐
☐	☐	Chapter 5 (Summary Exercise 5-7): "Challenges in Ethical Decision-Making."	☐	☐	☐	☐	☐	☐
☐	☐	Chapter 5 (Part 1 Summary Exercise): "Summary Assessment of My Motivation, Readiness, and Suitability for the Profession of Social Work"	☐	☐	☐	☐	☐	☐
☐	☐	Chapter 5: Ratings and Scores on the end-of-chapter Self-Appraisal: The Ethical Decision-Making Skills Subscale						
☐	☐	Chapter 6 (Exercise 6-3.1): "Introduction Script"	☐	☐	☐	☐	☐	☐
☐	☐	Chapter 6 (Exercise 6-3.2a): "Draft Letter 1"	☐	☐	☐	☐	☐	☐
☐	☐	Chapter 6 (Exercise 6-3.2b): "Draft Memo 1"	☐	☐	☐	☐	☐	☐
☐	☐	Chapter 6 (Summary Exercise 6-1): Client's Completed Copy of the Talking and Listening Skills Rating Form (see Appendix 11)						
☐	☐	Chapter 6 (Summary Exercise 6-2a): "Transcript of an Early Interview"	☐	☐	☐	☐	☐	☐
☐	☐	Chapter 6 (Summary Exercise 6-2b): "Evaluation of an Early Interview"	☐	☐	☐	☐	☐	☐

Yes	No		5	4	3	2	1	N/A
☐	☐	Chapter 6 (Summary Exercise 6-3): "One-Year Letter to Myself"						
☐	☐	Chapter 6: Ratings and Scores on the end-of-chapter Self-Appraisal: The Talking and Listening Skills Subscale						
☐	☐	Chapter 7 (Exercise 7-8.1 through 7-8.3): "Preliminary Plans for 3 Clients"	☐	☐	☐	☐	☐	☐
☐	☐	Chapter 7 (Summary Exercise 7-1 through 7-3): "Preparing for 3 Clients"	☐	☐	☐	☐	☐	☐
☐	☐	Chapter 7 (Experiential Interviewing Exercise): "Preliminary Plans for a Practice Client Recruitment Contact"	☐	☐	☐	☐	☐	☐
☐	☐	Chapter 7: Ratings and Scores on the end-of-chapter Self-Appraisal: The Preparing Skills Subscale						
☐	☐	Chapter 8 (Summary Exercise 8-1 through 8-3): "Beginning Skills Responses and Rationales"	☐	☐	☐	☐	☐	☐
☐	☐	Chapter 8 (Experiential Interviewing Exercise): Recruitment of a Practice Client: Consent Forms and Other Relevant Documentation	☐	☐	☐	☐	☐	☐
☐	☐	Chapter 8: Ratings and Scores on the end-of-chapter Self-Appraisal: The Beginning Skills Subscale						
☐	☐	Chapter 9 (Exercise 9-4.1): "Feelings Vocabulary"	☐	☐	☐	☐	☐	☐
☐	☐	Chapter 9 (Experiential Interviewing Exercise 9): "Preliminary Plans for the First Interview with a Practice Client"	☐	☐	☐	☐	☐	☐
☐	☐	Chapter 9 (Experiential Interviewing Exercise 9-1): "First Meeting with a Practice Client" (Practice Client Feedback Section)	☐	☐	☐	☐	☐	☐
☐	☐	Chapter 9 (Experiential Interviewing Exercise 9-2a): "First Meeting with a Practice Client" (First Meeting Exploration Matrix Section; and Additional Exploration Questions to Consider Section)	☐	☐	☐	☐	☐	☐
☐	☐	Chapter 9 (Experiential Interviewing Exercise 9-2b): "First Meeting with a Practice Client" (Exploration of the Problem/Issue Table Section)	☐	☐	☐	☐	☐	☐
☐	☐	Chapter 9 (Experiential Interviewing Exercise 9-2c): "First Meeting with a Practice Client" (Risk and Protective Factors Table Section)	☐	☐	☐	☐	☐	☐

Document Enclosed?		Documentation	Document Quality (5=Excellent; 4=Superior; 3=Good; 2=Fair; 1=Poor; N/A=Not Applicable)					
Yes	No		5	4	3	2	1	N/A
☐	☐	Chapter 9 (Experiential Interviewing Exercise 9-2d): "First Meeting with a Practice Client" (Strengths Table Section)	☐	☐	☐	☐	☐	☐
☐	☐	Chapter 9 (Experiential Interviewing Exercise 9-3): "First Meeting with a Practice Client" (My Ratings, Reactions, and Reflections Section)	☐	☐	☐	☐	☐	☐
☐	☐	Chapter 9 (Experiential Interviewing Exercise 9-4): "Preliminary Plans for the Second Interview with a Practice Client"	☐	☐	☐	☐	☐	☐
☐	☐	Chapter 9: Ratings and Scores on the end-of-chapter Self-Appraisal: The Exploring Skills Subscale						
☐	☐	Chapter 10 (Exercise 10-4): "A Personal Case Record" (Description Section of a DAC with Genogram, Eco-Map, and Critical Events Timeline Attached)	☐	☐	☐	☐	☐	☐
☐	☐	Chapter 10 (Exercise 10-5): "A Personal Case Record" (Assessment and Case Formulation Section of a DAC)	☐	☐	☐	☐	☐	☐
☐	☐	Chapter 10 (Experiential Interviewing Exercise 10): "Description Section of a DAC" for inclusion in the "Practice Client Case Record"	☐	☐	☐	☐	☐	☐
☐	☐	Chapter 10 (Experiential Interviewing Exercise 10-1): "Second Meeting with a Practice Client" (Practice Client Feedback Section)	☐	☐	☐	☐	☐	☐
☐	☐	Chapter 10 (Experiential Interviewing Exercise 10-2): "Second Meeting with a Practice Client" (My Ratings, Reactions, and Reflections Section)	☐	☐	☐	☐	☐	☐
☐	☐	Chapter10 (Experiential Interviewing Exercise 10-3): "Preliminary Plans for the Third Interview with a Practice Client"	☐	☐	☐	☐	☐	☐
☐	☐	Chapter 10 (Experiential Interviewing Exercise 10-4): "Description-Supplement Section of a DAC" and "Assessment Section" for inclusion in the "Practice Client Case Record"	☐	☐	☐	☐	☐	☐
☐	☐	Chapter 10: Ratings and Scores on the end-of-chapter Self-Appraisal: The Assessing Skills Subscale						

Yes	No		5	4	3	2	1	N/A
☐	☐	Chapter 11 (Exercise 11-5): "A Personal Case Record" (Add a Contract Section to the Description, and the Assessment and Case Formulation Sections of a DAC)	☐	☐	☐	☐	☐	☐
☐	☐	Chapter 11 (Experiential Interviewing Exercise 11-1): "Third Meeting with a Practice Client" (Practice Client Feedback Section)	☐	☐	☐	☐	☐	☐
☐	☐	Chapter 11 (Experiential Interviewing Exercise 11-2): "Third Meeting with a Practice Client" (My Ratings, Reactions, and Reflections Section)	☐	☐	☐	☐	☐	☐
☐	☐	Chapter11 (Experiential Interviewing Exercise 11-3): "Preliminary Plans for the Fourth Interview with a Practice Client"	☐	☐	☐	☐	☐	☐
☐	☐	Chapter 11 (Experiential Interviewing Exercise 11-4): "Description-Supplement Section of a DAC"; "Assessment Supplement Section"; and "Contract Section" for inclusion in the "Practice Client Case Record"	☐	☐	☐	☐	☐	☐
☐	☐	Chapter 11: Ratings and Scores on the end-of-chapter Self-Appraisal: The Contracting Skills Subscale						
☐	☐	Chapter 12 (Exercise 12-12): "Progress Notes for Five Clients"	☐	☐	☐	☐	☐	☐
☐	☐	Chapter 12 (Experiential Interviewing Exercise 12-1): "Fourth Meeting with a Practice Client" (Practice Client Feedback Section)	☐	☐	☐	☐	☐	☐
☐	☐	Chapter 12 (Experiential Interviewing Exercise 12-2): "Fourth Meeting with a Practice Client" (My Ratings, Reactions, and Reflections Section)	☐	☐	☐	☐	☐	☐
☐	☐	Chapter 12 (Experiential Interviewing Exercise 12-3): "Preliminary Plans for the Fifth Interview with a Practice Client"	☐	☐	☐	☐	☐	☐
☐	☐	Chapter 12 (Experiential Interviewing Exercise 12-4): "Progress Note" for inclusion in the "Practice Client Case Record"	☐	☐	☐	☐	☐	☐
☐	☐	Chapter 12: Ratings and Scores on the end-of-chapter Self-Appraisal: The Working and Evaluating Skills Subscale	☐	☐	☐	☐	☐	☐

Document Enclosed?		Documentation	Document Quality (5=Excellent; 4=Superior; 3=Good; 2=Fair; 1=Poor; N/A=Not Applicable)					
Yes	No		5	4	3	2	1	N/A
☐	☐	Chapter 13 (Exercise 13-4): "Closing Summaries for Five Clients"	☐	☐	☐	☐	☐	☐
☐	☐	Chapter 13 (Experiential Interviewing Exercise 13-1): "Fifth Meeting with a Practice Client" (Practice Client Feedback Section)	☐	☐	☐	☐	☐	☐
☐	☐	Chapter 13 (Experiential Interviewing Exercise 13-2): "Fifth Meeting with a Practice Client" (My Ratings, Reactions, and Reflections Section)	☐	☐	☐	☐	☐	☐
☐	☐	Chapter 13 (Experiential Interviewing Exercise 13-3): "Fifth Meeting with a Practice Client" (My Reactions to and Reflections on the Five-Session Experience Section)	☐	☐	☐	☐	☐	☐
☐	☐	Chapter 13 (Experiential Interviewing Exercise 13-4): "Closing Summary" for inclusion in the "Practice Client Case Record"	☐	☐	☐	☐	☐	☐
☐	☐	Chapter 13: Ratings and Scores on the end-of-chapter Self-Appraisal: The Ending Skills Subscale						
☐	☐	Chapter 13 (Supplemental Exercises 1-5: Final Lessons): "Final Lessons"	☐	☐	☐	☐	☐	☐

THE SOCIAL WORK SKILLS TEST

The Social Work Skills Test[1] contains two major parts. Part 1 includes true-false and multiple-choice items that refer directly to descriptive content contained within the book. These items are written primarily at the comprehension level of intellectual development. That means that correct responses require you to have read, understood, and remembered material presented in the book.

Part 2 includes short-answer items in which you must apply what you have learned to practice scenarios. More intellectually challenging than Part 1, these items are framed at the application, analysis, synthesis, and evaluation levels of intellectual development. Many of these items approximate contexts and exchanges that commonly occur in social work practice. You must invest considerable thought, judgment, and care in responding to items in Part 2 of The Social Work Skills Test.

The Social Work Skills Test—Part 1[2]

Carefully read each of the following true-false and multiple-choice items and choose the best response from among the available answers. You may use the answer sheet provided in Appendix 21 to record your responses to Part 1 of The Social Work Skills Test. Use a #2 pencil to record your answers by filling in the bubble below the letter that reflects the best answer to each item. Record the date you completed this part of the test.

    1. There is more genetic variation within races than exists between them. Indeed, DNA studies in the Human Genome Project suggest that distinct, identifiable subspecies or "races" do not appear among modern human beings.
       A. True
       B. False

---

[1] The Social Work Skills Test (Ver. 1.2). Copyright © 2009 and 2013 by Barry R. Cournoyer. For information about the test, email the author at bcourno@iupui.edu.

[2] In order to enhance learning, correct answers to Part 1 of The Social Work Skills Test are not provided. Since the true-false and multiple-choice items are primarily comprehension-level in nature, answers may be found within the text itself. The items in Part 2 do require application, analysis, synthesis, or evaluation. Answers to those items may require discussion with professors or colleagues—after, of course, you have completed the test.

2. Failure to discuss relevant legal, policy, and ethical factors with clients may be grounds for malpractice action.
   A. True
   B. False

3. In the U.S. all 50 states have adopted the federal minimum wage standard as their own.
   A. True
   B. False

4. Surveys indicate that service as a social worker remains one of the most satisfying careers.
   A. True
   B. False

5. Usually appearing in the form of negative or unfavorable opinions about a person, phenomenon, or group, prejudice may occur in a positive or favorable direction as well.
   A. True
   B. False

6. Several experimental research studies have demonstrated that false memories are quite difficult to produce.
   A. True
   B. False

7. If researchers do not obtain favorable findings through the statistical procedures incorporated as part of the original research design, they may legitimately run the figures through a series of various other statistical procedures to determine if the anticipated findings can be established through one or more of them.
   A. True
   B. False

8. Researchers who seek to determine the outcomes of policies, programs, and change-oriented interventions are increasingly expected to include _____ statistics in addition to more traditional statistics in their published studies.
   A. significance level   C. epidemiological
   B. demographic   D. effect size

9. The legal *duty of care* applies to social workers and other helping professionals. This legal principle requires the professional to
   A. meet a minimal standard of care.   C. adopt practice methods, models, and procedures that reflect the best research-based evidence of safety and effectiveness.
   B. possess advanced expertise in a practice method, model, technique, or procedure before using it with clients.   D. meet a reasonable standard of care.

10. People sometimes adjust their aspirations to current conditions. For example, within a few years following the windfall, those major lottery winners who do not quickly spend everything adapt to their newfound lifestyle and adjust their aspirations upward—so

that the "gap" between what is and what they aspire to remains about the same. This process is sometimes described as

A. the aspiration differential.   C. aspirational adaptation.

B. the hedonic treadmill.   D. the have-want gap.

11. Suppose a social worker asked a client, "Haven't you experienced lots of pain in your pelvic area? So, isn't it likely that you were sexually abused as a child?" Such questions would best be characterized as

A. assessment-focused.   C. leading.

B. theme building.   D. open-ended.

12. Multiple content areas are addressed in the standardized social work licensing examinations used throughout most of the 50 states, the District of Columbia, Puerto Rico, the U.S. Virgin Islands, and some Canadian provinces. The two content areas or domains that contain the largest percentage of items in the exams are

A. Supervision in Social Work; Practice Evaluation and the Utilization of Research.   C. Assessment in Social Work Practice; Direct and Indirect Practice.

B. Human Development and Behavior in the Environment; Service Delivery.   D. Issues of Diversity; Professional Values and Ethics.

13. During the beginning phase of the working relationship, many clients are quite unclear about what to expect and what they are "supposed to do." When social workers clarify the ambiguous situation by describing what's likely to happen and how clients can join you as active, collaborative participants in the helping process, they are using the social work skill of

A. *clarifying expectations.*   C. *socialization.*

B. *orienting clients.*   D. *clarifying processes.*

14. Suppose a client (a high school senior) says, "I've been accepted by two universities. One offers the academic program that perfectly matches my career goals and interests. The other is located close to where my boyfriend will go to school. I'm hopelessly torn between the two options." The social worker responds to the client's statement by saying, "You don't know whether to pursue your academic goals or your relationship goals." In responding in this way, the social worker is probably using the skill of

A. *focusing.*   C. *reflecting feelings and meanings.*

B. *reflecting feeling.*   D. *reflecting content.*

15. Belief in one's ability to organize or plan a course of action, implement that plan, and achieve a successful outcome is best described as

A. ego-strength.   C. problem solving.

B. self-esteem.   D. self-efficacy.

16. In advance of all meetings and especially before initial meetings, social workers try to envision clients' current circumstances, their perspectives, and their expectations. We attempt to experience what our clients are likely to sense, feel, think, imagine, and do in the encounter. Through _____ social workers seek to better appreciate others'

subjective experience related to seeking or receiving social service and to this particular meeting.

A. *anticipatory assessment*
B. *preparatory empathy*

C. *preparatory planning*
D. *preparatory anticipation*

17. A client says, "The company laid me off about 8 months ago and I haven't been able to make the mortgage payments on the house for the last six. I've looked and looked for work but I can't find anything. I'm so discouraged that I've just about given up." In response, the social worker says, "As you see it, there are at least three major issues you'd like to address in our work together. First, you're unemployed and can't find work. Second, you haven't paid your home mortgage in several months. Third, you're close to giving up hope that things will improve." In this situation, the social worker is probably using the skill of

A. *reflecting content.*
B. *reflecting feelings and meanings.*

C. *reflecting issues.*
D. *going beyond what is said.*

18. As human beings, we tend to see what we hope or expect to see and find what we hope or expect to find. In research, these human tendencies may lead to misapplication of research designs or misinterpretation of data such that our own anticipated findings are "discovered." When such tendencies are not controlled or managed in some way, research would likely be subject to the effects of

A. attrition.
B. confirmation bias.

C. maturation.
D. reactivity.

19. According to the Educational Policy and Accreditation Standards of the Council on Social Work Education (2008), there are four "phases" of social work practice that competent social workers undertake in their service with individuals, families, groups, organizations, and communities. The second of these four phases is

A. Evaluation.
B. Assessment.

C. Ending.
D. Intervention.

20. Occasionally, people who believe they were negatively affected by a social worker's professional behavior submit grievances to the National Association of Social Workers (NASW). Most claims of ethical misconduct are filed by

A. supervisees or employees of the social worker.
B. supervisors or employers of the social worker.

C. coworkers or colleagues.
D. clients or their family members.

21. Well-designed, practice-relevant outcome studies often produce information about the relative probability that a certain program, practice, policy, protocol, or interventive action will lead to a particular outcome. These studies typically involve good size samples and random assignment of participants into "treatment" and "control groups." Such studies often yield _____ of great value to social workers and clients as they consider how to address problems and pursue goals.

A. projective evidence
B. idiographic evidence

C. nomothetic evidence
D. predictive evidence

22. Toward the end of a series of 12 scheduled meetings, a social worker draws on the results of measurement instruments such as questionnaires, various individual or subjective rating scales, and the graphic reflections of trends and patterns (for example, line graphs) to share her or his estimate of progress toward achievement of the agreed-upon goals for work. In doing so, the social worker is probably using the skill of

A. *reviewing the process.* C. *final evaluating.*

B. *pointing out endings.* D. *seeking clarification.*

23. Among the classification schemas that some social workers use as part of an assessment process are the *DSM* and

A. *Bloom's Taxonomy.* C. the *PIE system.*

B. *Gorman's Grid.* D. the *CARP Scale.*

24. When social workers seek advice from a social work supervisor or colleague concerning an upcoming visit with a prospective client or other persons, they are engaged in

A. *anticipatory supervision.* C. *preparatory consulting.*

B. *preparatory exploring.* D. *preparatory advice-seeking.*

25. A(n) _____ is a simple table that reflects, in shorthand fashion, important events or experience in chronological order during a designated period.

A. Timeline C. Ecogram

B. Genomap D. Chronograph

26. Triangles of various kinds may emerge in families, groups, organizations, communities, and societies. Many of these reflect moral judgments and metaphors. The famous "dramatic triangle" involves three roles or positions. Which of the following is *not* one of them?

A. Persecutor C. Rescuer

B. Victim D. Mediator

27. *Hearing* or *receiving* others' words, speech, and language; *observing* their nonverbal gestures and positions; *encouraging* them to express themselves fully; and *remembering* what they communicate are elements of the social work skill of

A. *registering.* C. *understanding.*

B. *reflecting.* D. *listening.*

28. In legal terms, malpractice, or *mal praxis*, by professional social workers is

A. a tort. C. a misdemeanor.

B. a violation of contract law. D. a felony.

29. When social workers encourage clients to consider occurrences of problems in terms of their distant as well as proximate antecedent factors, co-occurring factors, and subsequential factors, they are probably engaged in a process of

A. functional analysis. C. factor analysis.

B. situational assessment. D. systems analysis.

30. In its *Code of Ethics*, the National Association of Social Workers (NASW) identifies a set of six core values. These core values serve as the foundation of social work's unique purpose and perspective. The first of these is

A. social justice.

B. dignity and worth of the person.

C. integrity.

D. service.

31. The term _____ may be used to refer to the uses and abuses of power by those of higher status in relation to those of lower status. The feelings of shame, humiliation, indignity, or inferiority felt by a "nobody" when abused, oppressed, enslaved, imprisoned, or exploited, or even when addressed with superiority, arrogance, or condescension by a "somebody" are pretty much the same whether it appears as racism, sexism, ageism, ableism, lookism, heterosexism, or other insidious "isms."

A. Elitism

B. Xenophobia

C. Rankism

D. Ethnocentrism

32. _____ includes formal and informal relations and activities that address and often meet significant human needs for inclusion, social identity, socialization, understanding, and encouragement.

A. Social welfare

B. Social support

C. Social consensus

D. Social intelligence

33. Beliefs that individual happiness is based, in part, upon genetic and biological factors, and tends to remain quite stable over time supports the hypothesis that each person has a

A. relatively fixed happiness quotient.

B. happiness floor.

C. happiness set-point.

D. happiness ceiling.

34. A social worker is meeting with Sharon Oh. The client says, "I'm glad I've come here. Last time I needed help, I went to the North Central Social Services Center. They were just awful. They didn't know what they were doing and didn't help me at all." Which of the following would be the best example of a social worker's optimum use of the talking and listening skills in responding to this client's statement?

A. "You didn't have a positive experience when you sought help before and you're looking forward to better service here."

B. "Ms. Oh, you're hoping that we're more competent than that other agency."

C. "Sharon, I'm glad you've come here too."

D. "Yes, I've heard other people say they have had bad experiences at that agency."

35. A social worker says to a client, "I think we agree about the primary issues that we'll address in our work together. Let's review them and write them down so that we can refer to them as we go along. First, there is the problem of unemployment and finding work. Second, there's the problem of the overdue mortgage payments. Third, there's the problem of your own discouragement. How about it—is this an accurate list of the problems that we should address in our work together?" In this situation, the social worker is probably using the skill of

A. *partializing.*

B. *clarifying issues for work.*

C. *identifying issues.*

D. *reflecting issues.*

36. As described in the Educational Policy and Accreditation Standards (EPAS) of the Council on Social Work Education (2008), the purpose of the social work profession is actualized through the profession's quest for social and economic justice, the prevention of conditions that limit human rights, the _____, and the enhancement of the quality of life for all persons.

    A. equitable distribution of food and material resources

    B. promotion of democratic political processes

    C. development of job and educational opportunities

    D. elimination of poverty

37. Suppose a new client says to a social worker, "I'm facing a whole lot of problems all at the same time. One of my kids needs surgery but I just lost my job and my health insurance. My husband just left us and moved across the country with a woman half my age. Good riddance to him but, of course, he's not providing us any financial support. I'm hoping to get another job—one with insurance—but my 18-year-old car just broke down and I can't go anywhere. I don't know what to do. I'm frightened and desperately need your help." After first responding empathically to ensure that the client feels respected and understood, the social worker would then be wise to use the skill of

    A. *focusing.*

    B. *advising.*

    C. *partializing.*

    D. *educating.*

38. A client says, "Well, I guess the first thing I'd like to accomplish is to get a job so I can pay some bills." The social worker responds by saying, "As you see it then, your most important goal is to find work." In this situation, the social worker is probably using the skill of

    A. *seeking clarification.*

    B. *proposing goals.*

    C. *reflecting goals.*

    D. *going beyond what is said.*

39. When considering moral and ethical issues or dilemmas, a social worker would wisely consider dimensions such as _____, *means*, *ends*, and *effects*.

    A. *motives*

    B. *integrity*

    C. *justice*

    D. *fairness*

40. During the early phases of practice, social workers often seek to explore clients' reasons for making contact with the agency at this particular time. For example, in some circumstances, a social worker might ask, "What led you to call us at this particular time—rather than, say, 6 months or a year ago?" Such a question would best be characterized as

    A. open-ended.

    B. explanatory.

    C. leading.

    D. closed-ended.

41. The concept of "inclusive cultural empathy" involves at least three central processes. Which of the following is *not* one of the three?

A. *Cultural Matching:* Adopt the gestures, speech patterns, and slang or jargon of the diverse cultural groups with whom we interact.

B. *Appropriate Interaction:* Engage others in ways that convey respect for their cultural affiliations.

C. *Intellectual Understanding:* Know something about others' cultures.

D. *Affective Acceptance:* Accept and value those who belong to different cultural groups.

42. During the assessment phase of work, social workers and clients commonly generate a "theory of the case" that includes two kinds of hypotheses:

A. Ad Hoc and Predictive.

B. Explanatory and Change-Oriented.

C. Causal and Correlational.

D. Descriptive and Diagnostic.

43. During the exploration phase of work, social workers and their clients commonly review three general aspects or dimensions: (1) the problem or issue, (2) the person, and (3) the

A. development of the problem.

B. person's history.

C. situation.

D. family.

44. Social workers often estimate both the likelihood that a policy, program, or practice will yield beneficial results as well as the likelihood it will cause harm. Familiarity with odds and probabilities helps social workers in such processes. For example, suppose that approximately 67 percent of clients who enroll in a particular program resolve their problems and achieve their goals. Another 33 percent fail to do so. However, about 3 percent of that 33 percent are harmed by the program. Given such information, a social worker might inform a prospective client that, generally speaking, the chances that anyone enrolling in that program might be harmed are approximately

A. 2 in 100.

B. 3 in 100.

C. 1 in 100.

D. 4 in 100.

45. Arguments typically contain a claim or a conclusion along with one or more premises. Consider the following argument:

- The bodies of all human males contain testosterone.
- Testosterone causes violence.
- Therefore all human males are violent.

This particular argument is

A. invalid but sound.

B. invalid and unsound.

C. valid but unsound.

D. valid and sound.

46. Typically, the last entry in a completed case record is a

A. *terminal assessment.*

B. *final evaluation.*

C. *closing summary.*

D. *final progress note.*

47. Human beings are generally remarkably resilient. In time, following stressful life events and difficult circumstances, most people return to their previous levels of happiness. This phenomenon is often referred to as the
    A. adaptation theory of well-being.
    B. adjustment process.
    C. restoration of equilibrium.
    D. process of accommodation.

48. When social workers introduce clients to a new way of looking at some aspect of themselves, the issue, or the situation by sharing a different perspective from that which their clients had previously adopted, she or he is probably using the skill of
    A. *reflecting meaning*.
    B. *reframing*.
    C. *going beyond what is said*.
    D. *paraphrasing*.

49. Suppose someone attempts to persuade you to adopt their position by suggesting that only two options apply to a complex issue. For instance, in regard to the topic of universal health care coverage, someone might frame the issue in "either/or" fashion such as, "Do you prefer a free-market or a socialistic approach to health care?" In doing so, she or he is probably reflecting the _____ logical fallacy.
    A. false dilemma
    B. straw man
    C. red herring
    D. same cause

50. Many clients readily offer ideas and explanations about "why" something happens. We can refer to these as their
    A. explanatory hypotheses.
    B. theoretical hypotheses.
    C. change-oriented hypotheses.
    D. exploratory hypotheses.

51. Which of the following nations reflected the highest prison population (per 100,000 residents) during the mid-to-late 2000s?
    A. Russia
    B. Rwanda
    C. United States
    D. Turkey

52. In *The Social Work Skills Workbook*, the author describes nine universal intellectual standards that apply to both formal and informal learning. When social workers resist tendencies to view complicated matters in an overly simplistic manner or straightforward topics in an excessively complex way, and instead approach professional topics and issues in a manner that adequately addresses their relative complexity, they demonstrate the standard of
    A. relevance.
    B. intellectual sophistication.
    C. fairness.
    D. logic.

53. In *The Social Work Skills Workbook*, the author outlines seven phases of practice that elaborate the four introduced in the Educational Policy and Accreditation Standards (EPAS) of the Council on Social Work Education. The second of the seven phases is
    A. Beginning.
    B. Assessing.
    C. Working and Evaluating.
    D. Exploring.

54. A single statistical measure or indicator can never adequately capture the complexities associated with income and wealth inequality. The Gini is a useful, but far from perfect

index. Other types of measures may complement the Gini. These include, for example, _____ indicators.

A. recovery

C. progressive

B. regressive

D. mobility

55. After a client and social worker agree upon goals and plans for work, the social worker may appropriately engage in the skill of _____ if it becomes apparent that clients lack useful or valid information or skills that could contribute to the achievement of the agreed-upon goals for work.

A. *informing*

C. *reframing*

B. *interpreting*

D. *educating*

56. The probability that a particular statistical procedure will correctly detect a difference in a sample when such a difference actually exists in the larger population is often referred to as

A. a significance level.

C. an effect size.

B. statistical power.

D. a population estimate.

57. Social workers sometimes have an opportunity to talk with referral sources or previous helpers before meeting clients for the first time. When social workers do ask questions about incoming clients' issues, circumstances, and needs or wants before actually meeting with them, they are probably engaged in

A. *preliminary questioning.*

C. *preparatory investigating.*

B. *preparatory exploring.*

D. *preparatory reviewing.*

58. When a social worker encourages a client to explore the experiences and feelings about what is occurring right here and right now between the client and the social worker, she or he is probably using the skill of

A. *responding with immediacy.*

C. *focusing.*

B. *exploring.*

D. *questioning.*

59. Occasionally, both workers and clients wander away from the agreed-upon issues and goals. These diversions are sometimes productive, leading to greater understanding and improving the chances for effective change. At other times, however, such departures are clearly unproductive. When social workers redirect attention and energy to relevant topics, they are probably using the skill of

A. *focusing.*

C. *restructuring.*

B. *reframing.*

D. *attending.*

60. Sponsored by the United Nations Development Programme, the Gender Inequality Index (GII) measures three general dimensions: (1) health—as measured by the mortality and adolescent fertility rates, (2) empowerment—as measured by level of education and percentage of parliamentary seats, and (3) labor—as measured by participation in the workforce. Which of the following nations reflected the highest level of gender equality (or lowest level of gender inequality) in 2011 as measured by the GII?

A. Germany

C. Yemen

B. Canada

D. United States

61. During a meeting with a client, a social worker says, "When we began this process, we decided to meet 12 times. At first, we met twice per week, then once per week, and recently once per month. According to my calendar, we have two more meetings to go: one in another month and the last one a month after that." In this situation, the social worker is probably using the skill of

A. *pointing out endings.*   C. *confronting.*

B. *clarifying.*   D. *focusing.*

62. Toward the conclusion of their work together, social workers typically provide clients an opportunity to express their feelings about the experience, their relationship, and about ending. Social workers also often share their own feelings as they conclude their work with clients. In doing so, the social worker is probably using the skill of

A. *reviewing the process.*   C. *self-disclosure, questioning, and educating.*

B. *pointing out endings.*   D. *sharing ending feelings and saying goodbye.*

63. The United Nations' Human Development Index (HDI) is a composite indicator of three measures of human development. Which of the following is *not* one of the three?

A. education   C. personal property

B. standard of living   D. health

64. A social worker says, "We've agreed that finding work is the first and most important goal for our work together. As a step toward that goal, I'd like to ask one of our employment consultants to review your resume and provide suggestions for improvement. How does that sound to you?" In this situation, the social worker is probably using the skill of

A. *proposing an action step.*   C. *advising.*

B. *planning.*   D. *proposing a goal.*

65. During the initial stages of exploring the problem or issue, social workers most often encourage clients to

A. consider epidemiological research findings concerning the problem or issue.   C. describe their previous attempts to resolve or cope with the problem or issue.

B. talk with friends and family members to gain alternate perspectives about the problem or issue.   D. imagine how others would resolve the problem or issue.

66. During the exploration phase of work, social workers and their clients commonly examine temporal aspects of the problem or issue. That is, they consider the problem as it was in both the past and the present. In this context, they may also consider the problem or issue

A. as if it had never appeared.   C. as it could appear in the future.

B. as if it were a strength.   D. as if another person or people experienced it.

67. Bloom's taxonomy is often used in the preparation of learning objectives. The taxonomy proceeds through six categories or levels of learning. The first or basic level involves *recollection*, while the sixth level involves *evaluation.* The third level involves

A. *synthesis.*   C. *analysis.*

B. *comprehension.*   D. *application.*

68. The standardized social work licensing examinations used throughout most of the 50 states, the District of Columbia, Puerto Rico, the U.S. Virgin Islands, and some Canadian provinces are developed under the aegis and sponsorship of the

A. International Federation of Social Workers.

B. Association of Social Work Boards.

C. Council on Social Work Education.

D. National Association of Social Workers.

69. When you as a social worker share your name and profession, and your agency or departmental affiliation, you are using the social work skill of

A. *orientation.*

B. *self-identification.*

C. *self-disclosure.*

D. *introducing yourself.*

70. During the early phases of practice, social workers sometimes seek to gather specific information. For example, in some circumstances, a social worker might ask questions such as, "What is your phone number?" "What's your address?" "What's your date of birth?" Such questions would best be characterized as

A. data gathering.

B. detail oriented.

C. open-ended.

D. closed-ended.

71. Suppose a social worker visits a household to determine if a child has been abused by her parents or older siblings. Based upon the available evidence, the social worker concludes that child abuse has not occurred. Subsequent information, however, reveals that the social worker's conclusion was incorrect. In fact, the child had been abused on several occasions. The social worker's inaccurate conclusion represents a

A. false positive.

B. true positive.

C. false negative

D. true negative.

72. Which social work skills build on clients' experience and frames of reference by introducing, in a much more active and expressive fashion, social workers' professional knowledge and expertise?

A. The *assessing* skills

B. The *exploring* skills

C. The *working and evaluating* skills

D. The *contracting* skills

73. In addition to the three essential facilitative qualities, four categories of common, non-specific factors account for much of the variation in counseling and psychotherapy outcomes. These categories include: (1) client and situational factors, (2) relationship factors, (3) _____, and (4) model and technique factors.

A. socioeconomic factors

B. professional identity factors

C. education and experience factors

D. expectancy factors

74. During the exploration phase of practice, social workers often engage clients in *looking for strengths.* In doing so, social workers and clients typically look for (1) *competencies,* (2) *social support,* (3) *successes,* and (4) _____

A. *dreams.*

B. *life lessons.*

C. *fortunate events.*

D. *happiness.*

75. When a social worker schedules an appointment, secures an interview room, locates an interpreter, or repositions furniture to better accommodate an incoming client who

speaks a foreign language or is accompanied by a guide dog, she or he is reflecting the skill of

A. *environmental preparation.*
B. *preparatory planning.*
C. *preparatory organizing.*
D. *preparatory arranging.*

76. Suppose a social worker responds to a client's statement in this way: "You mention that you and your partner are no longer intimate. What do you mean by the phrase, 'no longer intimate?'" In responding in this way, the social worker is probably using the skill of

A. *going beyond what is said.*
B. *focusing.*
C. *questioning.*
D. *seeking clarification.*

77. A group of agency social workers are consulting with each other to improve the quality of their service to their clients. One social worker discusses a family she's serving. She describes a situation in which three young children were physically and sexually abused by their mother's boyfriend. The boyfriend confessed to the crimes, was convicted, and is now in jail. Which of the following would be the most accurate way for the social worker to refer to the boyfriend?

A. "He's a predator."
B. "He's a sex offender."
C. "I think he's a pedophile."
D. "He abused those children."

78. During an initial meeting, a social worker learns that a client has recently begun to consider the possibility that she may have a problem with the excessive consumption of alcohol. Although she has not taken any steps yet to change the pattern and has not developed a plan for change, she has begun to keep a record of when, where, what, and how much alcohol she drinks each day. In relation to the issue of alcohol consumption at this point in time, you and the client would probably consider her to be in the _____ stage of change.

A. Maintenance
B. Contemplation
C. Preparation
D. Action

79. The following graphic representation indicates that

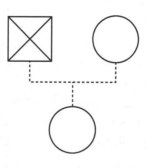

A. the biological father of a female child is deceased.
B. a marital relationship that ended in divorce produced a female child.
C. the biological mother of a male child is deceased.
D. a casual relationship resulted in the birth of a male child who died.

80. Toward the end of a series of 16 scheduled meetings, a social worker says to a client, "As we conclude our work together, I've been thinking about what we've done during these last several months. We've covered a lot of ground together, and you have made changes in both your own behavior as well as in your situation. As you think back over all that

we've done together, what memories come to mind?" In this context, the social worker is probably using the skill of

A. *final evaluating.*

B. *seeking clarification.*

C. *reviewing the process.*

D. *pointing out endings.*

81. According to the United States Census Bureau, the nation's racial and ethnic composition will change dramatically during the 21st century. When combined, members of minority ethnic groups will probably constitute a majority of the U.S. population by the year

A. 2042.

B. 2082.

C. 2022.

D. 2062.

82. Within the United States criminal justice system, there are many causes of wrongful convictions. However, more than 60 percent of defendants who were wrongfully convicted but subsequently exonerated involved _____ making it the single most common cause of wrongful convictions (Gross, Jacoby, Matheson, Montgomery, & Patil, 2004).

A. defense attorney incompetence

B. prosecutor misconduct

C. witness perjury

D. eyewitness misidentification

83. During the previous meeting, a client agreed to undertake an action step each day until the next meeting. In today's meeting, the social worker says, "Last time we met, you said that each day before you went to sleep, you would get out your notebook and write down five things about which you're grateful. How did that work out?" In this situation, the social worker is probably using the skill of

A. *focusing.*

B. *reviewing action steps.*

C. *responding with immediacy.*

D. *evaluating.*

84. To encourage others to express themselves as fully and as freely as possible, a social worker would typically seek to communicate nonverbally that she or he is open, nonjudgmental, and interested in and accepting of them as people. This process is commonly referred to as

A. empathy.

B. attending.

C. matching.

D. proxemics.

85. During a meeting with a long-time client, a social worker says, "On the one hand you say you want to improve the relationship with your children and on the other hand you report that you cannot spend time with them because of your work responsibilities." In this situation, the social worker is probably using the skill of

A. *confronting inconsistencies.*

B. *reflecting meaning.*

C. *going beyond what is said.*

D. *reframing.*

86. Evidence-based practice (EBP) involves five sequential steps. The second step in the EBP process involves the

A. application of the evidence in practice with clients.

B. evaluation of the effects of the application in collaboration with clients.

C. search for and discovery of relevant research-based evidence.

D. analysis of evidence in light of clients' needs, goals, culture, and preferences.

87. Humans' tendency to view their own racial, ethnic, cultural, or national group as superior to others' is called

A. bias.

B. ethnocentrism.

C. discrimination.

D. prejudice.

88. During a meeting, a social worker and client examine a graphic representation of the number of caring gestures the client made toward his teenage son each day. As they review the graph (below) together, the social worker is probably using the skill of _____.

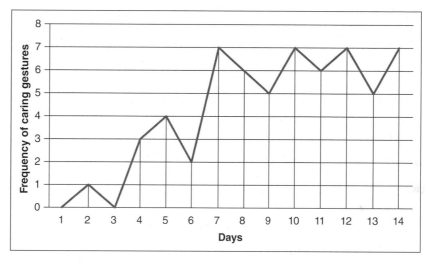

A. *evaluating.*

B. *educating.*

C. *reviewing action steps.*

D. *reframing.*

89. To identify the potential effects of their own personal histories, characteristics, needs, biases, emotional tender spots, philosophical or religious views, and behavioral patterns, social workers often engage in _____ in advance of meetings with others.

A. *preparatory self-management*

B. *preparatory sensitization*

C. *preparatory self-control*

D. *preparatory self-exploration*

90. In its *Educational Policy and Accreditation Standards* (EPAS), the Council on Social Work Education (CSWE) endorses the six core values identified in the *Code of Ethics* of the National Association of Social Workers (NASW) and adds two more. These two are

A. honesty and professionalism.

B. knowledge and expertise.

C. human rights and scientific inquiry.

D. equality and community.

91. The following graphic representation is an element of

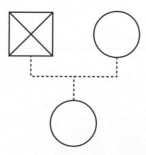

A. a genogram.

B. a famframe.

C. an eco-map.

D. a social systems map.

92. The social worker has been working with a client for a few weeks now. At this point, they are discussing factors associated with the client's current unemployment. In exploring possible reasons for her unemployment, the client shares a theory, "I believe I'm unemployed because I did not complete my degree in engineering. If I had, I'd still have a job or I'd have an easier time finding one." The social worker says, "As you see it, one of the reasons you're unemployed is because you didn't finish your college degree in engineering." In this situation, the social worker is probably using the skill of

A. *reflecting meaning.*
B. *going beyond what is said.*
C. *reflecting hypotheses.*
D. *reflecting issues.*

93. A social worker's responsibility to *warn and protect* a potential victim of violence may be distinguished from the *duty to report* child abuse in terms of the standard or level of evidence required. For example, the standard of evidence needed to take protective action in the case of an adult male client's threat to kill or harm his boss would _____ than that required to report possible child abuse.

A. be higher than
B. be the same as
C. be lower than
D. sometimes be higher and sometimes lower than

94. There are three common forms of malpractice. Which of the following is *not* one of the three?

A. Masfeasance
B. Misfeasance
C. Nonfeasance
D. Malfeasance

95. As it had for the preceding 2 years, the federal minimum wage for 2012 remained at _____ per hour.

A. $9.75
B. $8.50
C. $10.25
D. $7.25

96. A social worker tells other staff members they should not believe a client's story about being sexually harassed because that client "is a liar." However, the social worker fails to provide evidence that the client is currently lying or has done so in the past. Which of the following logical fallacies does the social worker's statement best represent?

A. Personal Experience
B. Begging the Question
C. *Ad Hominem* Attack
D. Popular Belief

97. In *The Social Work Skills Workbook*, the author describes several formats that social workers might use to organize written progress notes. Which of the following is *not* one of these formats?

A. GAAP
B. GRAF
C. APIE
D. SOAPIER

98. When social workers engage other people or social systems on behalf of clients in pursuit of agreed-upon goals, they are typically using the skill of

A. *advising.*
B. *interpreting.*
C. *educating.*
D. *representing.*

99. A social worker and client agree to work toward finding employment for the client. Together, they have developed a plan for pursuing that goal and are now engaged in

planning ways to evaluate progress toward its achievement. They identify a range of possible outcomes that range from "most unfavorable" to "most favorable." In doing so, they are probably generating a

A. rapid assessment instrument.

B. individualized rating scale.

C. goal attainment scale.

D. subjective rating scale.

100. In 2011, the average annual household income of the top 1 percent in the United States was approximately _____. By contrast, the average annual household income for the bottom 20 percent was about _____.

A. $250,000 .... $25,000

B. $1,500,000 .... $9,000

C. $500,000 .... $15,000

D. $750,000 .... $17,500

101. In the context of social work practice, professionalism involves: (1) sophisticated knowledge, competence, self-efficacy, and expertise in the provision of social work services; (2) respect for and adherence to the values of the social work profession and its code of ethics; and (3) personal and professional integrity, self-understanding and self-control, and social support. Among the remaining aspects of professionalism identified in *The Social Work Skills Workbook* are

A. critical thinking, scientific learning, and career-long learning.

B. confidence, hope, and optimism.

C. honesty, determination, and dedication.

D. appearance, style, and presentation.

102. When they encourage others to identify themselves by name and perhaps to share something about themselves, social workers are using the social work skill of

A. *engaging others.*

B. *seeking introductions.*

C. *preliminary exploration.*

D. *identifying others.*

103. Before meetings, contacts, and interviews with individuals, families, groups, organizations, and communities with whom they interact, social workers engage in _____. In doing so, social workers often address questions such as: "Why is this meeting occurring? What is its overall purpose? What do I hope to accomplish through this meeting? What is my tentative agenda? What might be the agenda of the people who will be involved or affected by the meeting? What might they hope to accomplish? What would I consider a successful meeting? What might they? What are my functions or roles in this meeting? How do I wish to begin? What things should I say? What questions should I ask? What might they want to ask of me? What kind of interactional process would I like to see? What kind might they? How would I like the meeting to conclude? How might they like to see it end?"

A. *agenda setting*

B. *clarification*

C. *preliminary planning*

D. *focusing*

104. After a client and social worker agree upon goals and plans for work, the social worker may appropriately engage in the skill of _____ if it becomes apparent that clients would probably benefit from a suggestion or recommendation that could contribute to the achievement of the agreed-upon goals for work.

A. *educating*

B. *advising*

C. *informing*

D. *interpreting*

105. Suppose a client (a high school senior) says, "I've been accepted to two universities. One offers the academic program that perfectly matches my career goals and interests. The other is located close to where my boyfriend will go to school. I'm hopelessly torn between the two options." The social worker responds to the client's statement by saying, "You're afraid that if you go to the school that you want to, the relationship with your boyfriend could end." In responding in this way, the social worker is probably using the skill of

A. *reflecting feeling.*

B. *going beyond what is said.*

C. *reflecting content.*

D. *reflecting feelings and meanings.*

106. Despite noble, idealistic, and altruistic motives, a social worker who lacks _____ might unwittingly act out unresolved personal issues or enact ideological, emotional, or behavioral patterns that harm the very people she or he hopes to help.

A. confidence and self-efficacy

B. knowledge and skill

C. integrity and commitment

D. self-awareness and self-control

107. According to the United States Census Bureau, the proportion of the nation's "working age" population (18–64 years) should _____ from 63 percent in 2008 to _____ in 2050.

A. increase . . . 65 percent

B. decrease . . . 61 percent

C. decrease . . . 49 percent

D. decrease . . . 57 percent

108. A major theme or trend in contemporary psychosocial services involves the assessment of motivation—particularly as it relates to the transtheoretical model (TTM) or the five "stages of change." The third of these five TTM stages is called

A. contemplation.

B. action.

C. maintenance.

D. preparation.

109. Suppose a client (a high school senior) says, "I've been accepted to two universities. One offers the academic program that perfectly matches my career goals and interests. The other is located close to where my boyfriend will go to school. I'm hopelessly torn between the two options." The social worker responds to the client's statement by saying, "You're feeling stuck because you don't know whether to pursue your academic goals or your relationship goals." In responding in this way, the social worker is probably using the skill of

A. *reflecting content.*

B. *focusing.*

C. *reflecting feelings and meanings.*

D. *reflecting feeling.*

110. When social workers suggest a possible focus or agenda for a meeting, they are using the social work skill of

A. *agenda setting.*

B. *focusing.*

C. *orienting others.*

D. *describing initial purpose.*

111. In advance of meetings, social workers seek to organize and manage their own personal thoughts, feelings, and physical sensations so that they do not interfere with their professionalism, performance, and delivery of social services. This skill is often referred to as

A. *calibrating.*

B. *focusing.*

C. *centering.*

D. *clarifying.*

112. The positive or negative treatment of people based on characteristics such as race, gender, religion, ethnicity, age, physical appearance or ability, or sexual orientation is best characterized as

A. ethnocentrism.

C. bias.

B. discrimination.

D. prejudice.

113. Individual or environmental markers associated with an increased likelihood that a negative outcome will occur are often called

A. negative probabilities.

C. risk factors.

B. negative effect factors.

D. effect sizes.

114. During the assessment phase of practice, social workers and clients attempt to make sense of the data gathered during the exploration phase. They identify issues, share hypotheses, and clarify issues for work. In addition, social workers also engage in the skills of

A. *organizing information* and *preparing a tentative assessment*.

C. *data analysis* and *interpretation*.

B. *proposing* and *finalizing*.

D. *exploring* and *reviewing*.

115. Although ethical decision making involves considerable challenges in all circumstances, those that involve _____ represent the greatest intellectual challenge of all and require the most advanced critical thinking skills.

A. subordinating one's personal views to those of the social work profession

C. issues that remind a social worker of his or her own personal problems

B. several relevant legal and ethical obligations that are inconsistent with each other

D. several relevant legal and ethical obligations that are consistent with each other

116. As conceptualized in the Educational Policy and Accreditation Standards (EPAS) of the Council on Social Work Education (2008), competencies are _____ that are comprised of knowledge, values, and skills.

A. helpful policy or practice interventions

C. culturally competent actions

B. measurable practice behaviors

D. professional judgments

117. In work with client systems of different size at various phases or stages of practice, social workers should consistently demonstrate the essential facilitative qualities of: (1) empathy, (2) respect, and (3) _____.

A. authenticity

C. support

B. understanding

D. compassion

118. Cross, et al.'s Cultural Competency Continuum (1989) contains several stages. In which stage do individuals, families, groups, organizations, and communities actively respect, affirm, and value the culture of diverse others through their beliefs, attitudes, policies, practices, words, and behaviors?

A. Stage 7

C. Stage 6

B. Stage 5

D. Stage 4

119. A _____ is a diagrammatic representation of a person, family, or household in social context—highlighting energy-enhancing and energy-depleting relationships

between members of a primary social system (for example, family or household) and the outside world.

A. a genogram

C. a famframe

B. an eco-map

D. a social systems map

120. Suppose a client who has been involved for several years with a violent and abusive man says, "I'm afraid to leave and I'm afraid to stay. If I stay, he'll beat me again. If I leave, he'll find me and beat me even more. He might even kill me." The social worker responds by saying, "You're terrified." In responding in this way, the social worker is probably using the skill of

A. *reflecting feelings.*

C. *responding with immediacy.*

B. *reflecting feelings and meanings.*

D. *focusing.*

121. Specific measures of various kinds may complement the assessment process and sometimes serve as indicators of goal attainment. One group of such measures are called RAIs—an acronym that stands for

A. *Rational Analysis Indices.*

C. *Readiness Assessment Indicators.*

B. *Readable Assessment Indicators.*

D. *Rapid Assessment Instruments.*

122. When people regularly make definitive assertions or claims based upon an assumption that the positions of authorities or the statements contained in authoritative texts represent absolute truth, they are probably engaged in

A. multiplistic thinking.

C. dualistic thinking.

B. magical thinking.

D. relativistic thinking.

123. Personal or situational safeguards that enhance a person's ability to resist stressful life events, risks or hazards and promote adaptation and competence are often called

A. effect sizes.

C. protective factors.

B. positive effect factors.

D. positive probabilities.

124. A social worker asks a client, "As we have talked about you and your situation, I've been wondering about the trouble you're having with sleep. It seems to me that you're only sleeping 2 or 3 hours each night." In this situation, the social worker is probably using the skill of

A. *identifying an issue.*

C. *advising.*

B. *confronting.*

D. *reflecting issues.*

125. In its Educational Policy and Accreditation Standards (EPAS), the Council on Social Work Education (CSWE) identifies _____ core competencies (the last of which contains four subordinate competencies that involve *engagement, assessment, intervention,* and *evaluation*).

A. 12

C. 6

B. 8

D. 10

126. In 2010, approximately _____ children lived in poverty in the United States.

A. 5.25 million

C. 15.75 million

B. 20 million

D. 10.5 million

127. During a meeting with a social worker, the client makes a commitment to undertake an action step during the next 7 days. In order to increase the probability of action, the social worker engages the client in
    A. *probability enhancement.*
    B. *rehearsing the action step.*
    C. *reviewing the action step.*
    D. *anticipatory evaluation.*

128. Based on their studies of happiness, Lyubomirsky and colleagues suggest that approximately _____ percent of a person's happiness results from voluntary, intentional activities.
    A. 60
    B. 80
    C. 40
    D. 20

129. According to the U.S. Bureau of Labor Statistics (BLS), in 2010, approximately _____ social workers were employed in the United States.
    A. 395,000
    B. 195,000
    C. 650,000
    D. 500,000

130. Of the various claims of ethical misconduct filed against social workers, the largest single category involves
    A. incompetence.
    B. poor quality practice.
    C. fraud or dishonesty of some kind.
    D. boundary violations.

131. DAC is an acronym that stands for *Description*, *Assessment*, and _____
    A. *Circumstances.*
    B. *Conditions.*
    C. *Contract.*
    D. *Conceptualization.*

132. As described in *The Social Work Skills Workbook*, a social work skill is a discrete set of _____ and _____ actions that are consistent and congruent with: (1) research-based knowledge; (2) social work values, ethics, and obligations; (3) the essential facilitative qualities or the core conditions; (4) the characteristics of professionalism; and (5) a legitimate social work purpose within the context of a phase or process of practice.
    A. cognitive .... behavioral
    B. professional .... interpersonal
    C. intrapersonal .... interpersonal
    D. psychological .... social

133. A social worker is meeting with Janna Olazavitz for the first time. The client says, "I'm Mrs. Olazavitz and I'd like your advice about how to help my 16-year-old son. He's gotten involved with the wrong crowd and his school grades have suffered. I'm worried he won't be able to get into college." Which of the following would be the best example of a social worker's optimum use of the talking and listening skills in responding to this client's statement?
    A. "So Janna, you'd like my help in helping your son."
    B. "Janna, you're terrified that your son is ruining his chances for a better life."
    C. "Mrs. Olazavitz, you're concerned about your son's new friends and his poor academic performance, and you'd like some guidance about how you might help him change things to improve his chances of going on to college."
    D. "Mrs. Olazavitz, you think your son's new friends have led him astray. His grades have dropped and you're worried that he might be drinking or using drugs."

134. Many clients readily offer ideas and explanations about "how" a problem might be resolved. We can refer to them as their

A. exploratory hypotheses.   C. change-oriented hypotheses.

B. theoretical hypotheses.   D. explanatory hypotheses.

135. In conducting a detailed exploration of a problem or issue, social workers often encourage clients to discuss its onset, evolution or development, and the situational contexts in which it occurs. In addition, we typically consider the frequency, intensity or severity, and _____ of each problematic episode.

A. prognosis   C. implication

B. duration   D. variability

136. The skill of _____ involves examining and considering information available to you and your agency before an initial contact with another person or persons

A. *preliminary assessing*   C. *preparatory reflection*

B. *preliminary preparation*   D. *preparatory reviewing*

137. Perhaps the most widely known and used measure of income inequality is the Gini index, also known as the Gini ratio or Gini Coefficient. Which of the following Gini scores would reflect the highest level of equality (or the lowest level of inequality)?

A. 0   C. 10

B. 1   D. 100

138. Currently, one of the most popular trait approaches to personality assessment involves attention to the "big five" personality factors. These five aspects or dimensions of personality are captured in the following acronym:

A. CEASE   C. OCEAN

B. FIVES   D. MULTI

139. Proficient use of the *preparing* skills contributes to a productive engagement between clients and social workers. Their use helps to reduce the high rates of premature discontinuation of needed services. Social workers who adequately prepare in advance of meetings are more likely to express accurate understanding of clients' views of the problem or issue that concerns them. Failure to do so _____ the probability of early dropout.

A. doubles   C. increases by half

B. triples   D. quadruples

140. According to the Council on Social Work Education (2008), pursuit of the social work profession's purpose is guided by a person and environment construct, a global perspective, respect for human diversity, and _____

A. knowledge based on scientific inquiry.   C. international law.

B. Judeo-Christian values.   D. basic humanitarian principles.

141. The skill of *active listening* involves three steps: The first is *inviting*. The other two are

A. *listening* and *reflecting*.   C. *mirroring* and *providing feedback*.

B. *hearing* and *talking*.   D. *receiving* and *registering*.

The Social Work Skills Test—Part 2[3]

Carefully read each of the following short-answer items. Then, use word-processing software to record your responses. Number each of your answers so that you may easily refer to the test items themselves. Label and date your document (for example, *Skills_Test_Pt2_08_26_2013*) for inclusion in your Social Work Skills Learning Portfolio and for later comparison with responses to subsequent test administrations.

After you have completed this part of the test, you may track the quality of your responses on a scale where *1= Unsatisfactory*, *2 = Inferior*, *3 = Satisfactory*, and *4 = Proficient*. An answer sheet for that purpose is available in Appendix 21.

After some time has passed, you might review your original answers and attempt to create better responses—especially for those in the *unsatisfactory* or *inferior* range.

1. The purpose of the social work profession is discussed in the Educational Policy and Accreditation Standards of the Council on Social Work Education, the International Federal of Social Workers' definition of social work, and the National Association of Social Workers' preamble to the Code of Ethics. In the context of mainstream North American society, which aspects of these statements of mission and purpose are "radical" in nature? What evidence would indicate to you that the social work profession is making genuine progress toward achievement of these radical aspirations?

2. Briefly explain how and why members of a dominant, majority group might be unaware of the privileges associated with their position in society.

3. In order to identify and refute common logical fallacies, recognize threats to internal and external validity, adopt the "universal intellectual standards," and demonstrate professionalism in practice, social workers must routinely engage in advanced critical thought, scientific inquiry, and career-long learning. Such high-level cognitive work is perhaps most characteristic of William Perry's "committed relativism" stage of intellectual development. Why do you think it is so difficult for social workers to avoid fallacious reasoning, adhere to the universal intellectual standards, engage in scientific inquiry, and consistently think critically in their personal and professional lives?

4. Culture exerts a powerful influence on the development and maintenance of human beliefs and human behavior. Because culture affects all humans, *cultural sensitivity* is a central element of professionalism in the context of social work practice. Culture-based values, traditions, and practices may not always promote human rights and social justice. Briefly identify a value or tradition from your own cultural background that impedes one or more of the rights identified in the United Nations Declaration of Human Rights. Then, identify a second cultural view or practice that supports at least one human right.

5. Use your own words to explain the meaning of the phrase "intersectionality of multiple factors" as it pertains to diversity.

6. Strong social support seems essential to human well-being. Like most things, however, there are favorable and unfavorable aspects of strong social support networks for people in general and for social workers in particular. In what ways might a strong social network sometimes contribute to a social worker's boundary violations with clients? How

---

[3] The items in Part 2 of the Social Work Skills Test are short-answer in nature. Although we can readily distinguish superior from inferior responses, various short answers could be "correct." Your professor may provide you with "model" responses for comparison with your own; or, after you have completed all items, you may compare your responses with those of your colleagues and discuss which ones are better or worse.

might a social worker who lacks a strong, positive social support network sometimes be susceptible to boundary violations?

7. In discussing social justice, John Rawls suggests that people adopt a "veil of ignorance" in thinking about, proposing, or considering potential policies and actions. What does this notion of "veil of ignorance" mean in the context of social justice?

8. In regard to human rights, what is meant by the terms *inherent*, *universal*, *inalienable*, and *indivisible*?

9. There are several aspects or characteristics of professionalism that social workers reflect throughout all aspects of their service with and on behalf of others. Which aspect or characteristic do you think social workers in general might find most difficult to demonstrate on a day-to-day basis over the course of a several-decade professional career?

10. In its *Code of Ethics*, the National Association of Social Workers (NASW) identifies a set of six core values. These core values serve as the foundation of social work's unique purpose and perspective. Service is listed first. In the context of professional social work practice, what does the value of service mean to you? Identify a situation in which a social worker might find it difficult to respect the service value? What are the other five NASW-identified core social work values?

11. As a social worker, you might periodically prepare plans to advance your own career learning in regard to a particular topic or area of expertise. Choose a subject area that interests you and then create a learning objective that corresponds to the fourth level of Bloom's taxonomy. Be sure to incorporate an appropriate action verb.

12. The concept of "personality" is widely used by many helping professionals in efforts to understand human behavior. Various personality tests, including those that address the "big five" personality factors, are frequently used as part of assessment processes. What does the term *personality* mean to you? How might the concept of personality be used and sometimes misused by social workers who emphasize the person-in-environment as a fundamental focus for attention?

13. Draw an abbreviated genogram of a family headed by a lesbian couple who have adopted a 7-year-old boy and a 6-year-old girl. Each of the adoptive parents had heterosexual parents. Their mothers are living. However, both of their fathers have died during the past 7 years.

14. Draw an abbreviated eco-map to illustrate positive, energy-enhancing relationships between a four-member nuclear family and their religious community, their neighborhood, and the workplaces of the parents. Also, depict conflicted, energy-depleting relationships between the parents and their respective in-laws and between the children and their school.

15. What are the common factors and essential facilitative qualities in relationships that account for much of the beneficial results of professional helping activities?

16. The social work skills are organized according to seven phases or processes of practice. What are the advantages and disadvantages of such a sequential phase-to-phase approach?

17. Several social work skills are associated with the preparing phase of practice. In what ways might active preparation before the first and all subsequent meetings enhance the quality of service and improve the rate of favorable outcomes? What risks might be associated with such preparation?

18. Yesterday, Mrs. Little telephoned the family service agency where you work to express concern that her husband of 6 months might be abusing her 7-year-old daughter, Shari. Although she loves her new husband, she's extremely worried about Shari—whose biological father abandoned the family several years earlier. In your agency, you serve as a social worker specializing in helping couples and families. You will be talking with Mrs. Little when she visits the agency later today.

    Demonstrate your knowledge of and ability to use the applicable preparing skills (*preparatory arranging*, *preparatory empathy*, *preliminary planning*, *preparatory self-exploration*, and *centering*) in advance of your first meeting with Mrs. Little. Label each of the skills with its relevant identification code. (See Appendix 16 for a list of skills and their associated codes. For example, PR001 through PR008 refer to the eight preparing skills.)

19. Assume that you are a social worker who has already prepared for an initial meeting with Mrs. Little (see previous item). The time for her appointment arrives. You walk up to her in the waiting room and then escort her to a private interview room.

    Write the words you would say in *beginning* with Mrs. Little. If applicable, use any or all of the beginning skills that would be relevant in this situation. When you've finished writing the words you would say, label each of the skills used with its relevant identification code. (See Appendix 16 for a list of skills and their associated codes. For example, BG001 through BG006 refer to the six beginning skills.) If you determine that a particular beginning skill would not be applicable as you begin in this situation, provide a brief rationale for its omission.

20. Why are the *beginning skills* so important to client satisfaction, professional integrity, legal duties and ethical obligations, and service outcomes?

21. A client who has been married for 1 year says, "We fight all the time about his teenage son—the one from his first marriage. My husband doesn't think I should discipline the boy at all. He doesn't want me to correct him or to punish him in any way. But, I'm around the boy much more than my husband is and I have to deal with the brat!"

    Write the words you would say in using two forms of the skill of *asking questions* in your attempt to encourage further client exploration following this client's statement. Make your first question *open-ended* and the second, *closed-ended*.

22. A 13-year-old female client in foster care says, "This family treats me like dirt. They call me names and don't let me do anything I want to do. Half the time they don't even feed me. I just hate it there!"

    Write the words you would say in using the skill of *seeking clarification* in your attempt to encourage further client exploration following this client's statement.

23. A 21-year-old male client says, "My father began to molest me when I was about 9 years old. When I think about it, I just shudder. It was so disgusting; so humiliating. Even today, whenever I think about it, I still feel dirty and damaged. My father kept doing it until I was 14. After that he'd try sometimes but I was too strong for him."

    First, write the words you would say in using the skill of *reflecting feelings* in response to the client's message. Then, write an alternate response in which you use the skill of *reflecting feelings and meanings*. Following that, write the words to use the skill of *going beyond what is said*. Next, compare the three responses. Which of the three would best communicate understanding and encourage the client to explore more fully and freely?

24. John, a 14-year-old male client says, "Sometimes I wonder whether there is something wrong with me. Girls just turn me off. But boys . . . when I'm close to a good-looking boy, I can feel myself becoming excited. Does that mean I'm gay?"

    Write the words you would say in using the skill of *reflecting content* in your attempt to encourage further client exploration following this client's statement.

25. John (see previous item) asks, "If I am gay, what will I do? If my mother finds out, she'll be crushed. She'll feel that it's her fault somehow. I'm so scared and so worried. If my friends learn that I'm gay, what will they do?"

    First, write the words you would say in using the skill of *reflecting feelings* in response to the client's message. Then, write an alternate response in which you use the skill of *reflecting feelings and meanings*. Following that, write the words to use the skill of *going beyond what is said*. Next, compare the three responses. Which of the three would best communicate understanding and encourage the client to explore more fully and freely?

26. An adult male client of African ancestry says, "Sometimes it seems so phony. I grew up hearing whites call me 'boy' and 'nigger.' I was poor as dirt and sometimes I was beaten just because of the color of my skin. But I fought on through it all. I kept my pride and made it to college. I did really well too. When I graduated, a lot of the big companies wanted to meet their minority quota so I was hired right away at a good salary. I've been at this company now for 5 years, and I have contributed a great deal. I've been promoted twice and received raises. But so far, not one white person in the company has ever asked me to his home. Now what does that say to you?"

    Write the words you would say in using the skill of *going beyond what is said* in your attempt to encourage further client exploration following this client's statement.

27. A 17-year-old male client says, "I don't know what's wrong with me. I can't get a date to save my life. Nobody will go out with me. Every girl I ask out says no. I don't have any real guy friends either. I am so lonely. Even my folks hate my guts! My mother and I fight all the time; and my stepdad will have nothing to do with me. I spend most of my time alone in my room listening to music. I know I'm real depressed, but I don't know what to do about it."

    Write the words you would say in using the skill of *partializing* in your attempt to focus the client's exploration following his statement.

28. What is a central distinction between the *exploring skills* and the *working and evaluating skills*?

29. Identify at least one way that researchers might intentionally or unintentionally increase the likelihood of erroneously obtaining significant findings in their studies.

30. What are the primary distinctions between the *assessing* and the *contracting skills*?

31. Suppose you serve as a social worker with a family with a teenage boy who has begun to engage in "cutting" behavior. That is, he uses a razorblade or other sharp instrument to cut his skin when he experiences strong emotions such as frustration, anger, sadness, or loneliness. He usually cuts his forearms but sometimes pierces his legs or abdomen. Write at least one *explanatory hypothesis* for the boy's cutting behavior. Then, write at least one *change-oriented hypothesis* about how the skin-cutting might be reduced or eliminated.

32. As a social worker, you are naturally interested in the social problems of poverty, oppression, and discrimination. Generate at least one *explanatory hypothesis* and one or two *change-oriented hypotheses* for each of these three major social problems.

33. Why is the systematic evaluation of both client satisfaction and progress toward goal achievement essential to professional social work practice?

34. You have been serving as a social worker in a counseling role with a voluntary client for about 6 months. The client has reached virtually all of the goals that you jointly identified during the contracting phase of work. You enjoy your visits with this client, and the client also appears to enjoy the meetings with you. You have extended the time frame for work once already, and as a professional you realize that it would be unwise to do so again. You therefore suggest to the client that you meet once more to conclude your working relationship.

When you make this suggestion, the client pauses for a moment and then says, "That sounds about right. You have helped me a great deal, and I think I am ready to try it on my own. In fact, you've become extremely important to me and I've come to like and respect you a great deal. I'd like it very much if we could become friends once I'm no longer a client. Instead of meeting one more time, I'd like to take you to dinner. What kind of food do you like?"

Identify and discuss the social work values, legal duties, and ethical principles, if any, that might apply in this situation. If applicable, develop a case-specific values hierarchy to help you resolve any conflicts. Then describe what you would do in this situation to behave in an ethical manner.

35. Why do you think that proficient use of the *ending skills* and a positive termination experience might be important to clients?

The remaining short-answer items are based upon the following case description.

Presume that you are a social worker in the Child Protective Services (CPS) unit of a Department of Child Welfare. Your job is to investigate allegations of child abuse and neglect and, if possible, determine if the child or children involved require protective service.

A county resident has telephoned CPS to report that she has observed severe bruises on the back and the legs of Paul K., an 8-year-old neighborhood child. The neighbor has heard loud arguments in the child's home and believes that the child has been beaten on several occasions. You are called to respond to the allegation. You drive to the neighborhood and go to the K. home, where the abuse is reported to have occurred. The door is answered by a woman who confirms that she is the child's mother, Mrs. K.

After you introduce yourself by name and profession, you describe your purpose and role and outline the relevant policy and ethical factors.

Mrs. K. says, "I know why you're here—it's that damn nosy neighbor down the street. She's always butting into other people's business. She called you, didn't she?"

You respond to Mrs. K.'s expression by saying, "I'm not allowed to reveal how information about possible child abuse or neglect comes to us. My job is to investigate reports whatever their source and determine whether a child is in danger. Is that clear?"

Mrs. K. says, "Yeah. Come on in. I guess you want to see Paul." She loudly calls for Paul (who has been playing in another room).

Paul enters the room with a quizzical look on his face. Using terms he can easily understand, you introduce yourself and outline your purpose and role. You take Paul to a quiet area, well away from his mother (who abruptly goes to the kitchen). Then you say, "I'm here to make sure that you are safe from harm and to find out whether anyone might have hurt you in any way. Paul, do you understand what I am saying? Yes? Okay, then, I'd like to ask you some questions. First, who lives in this house with you?"

Paul says, "Well, my mom lives with me. And, uh, uh, her boyfriend stays here a lot too."

You ask, "What is he like?"

Paul hesitates, looks questioningly toward the kitchen, and then looks back into your eyes. It looks to you that he's afraid to say anything more.

You respond by communicating your understanding about how difficult and frightening it is to be interviewed in this way.

Paul responds to your empathic communication by saying, "Yeah, it sure is."

You follow that by asking, "Paul, does anyone ever hurt you?"

Paul again hesitates, but then says, "Yeah. Charlie, that's my mom's boyfriend, sometimes hits me with his belt."

You reflect his statement. Paul responds to your empathic communication by saying, "Yeah. He and my mom get drunk and yell and hit each other. I get so scared. If I make any noise at all, Charlie starts yelling at me. Then he takes off his belt and beats me with it."

You communicate your understanding of the feeling and meaning inherent in his message. Then you ask an open-ended question concerning the nature of the beatings and the location of any bruises that might exist.

Paul responds to your question by saying, "I have bruises all over my legs and back and my bottom. It hurts real bad. Sometimes when Charlie beats me, I start to bleed. I hate him! I hate him! I wish he'd just leave and never come back."

You then ask Paul to elaborate further. He responds by saying, "Things were fine until Charlie showed up. Mom and I got along great! See, my real dad was killed in a car wreck before I was born and so it has always been just Mom and me—that is, until Charlie moved in."

---

36. Respond to Paul's statements by using the skill of *reflecting issues*.
37. After you reflect the issue, Paul says, "Yeah, that's it all right."

    Following that exchange, you excuse yourself from Paul and join Mrs. K. in the kitchen. You indicate that you have seen severe bruises on Paul's legs and back. You go on to say that you will take Paul into protective custody, obtain medical care, and place him in temporary foster care until a more complete investigation can be conducted. You indicate that the final decision about Paul's custody is in the hands of Judge Dixon, who will conduct the hearing. But before leaving with Paul, you add that you would like to share with her your view of the problem.

    Record the words you would say in using the skill of *identifying issues* with Mrs. K.
38. At this point, you provide Mrs. K. with a written summary of her rights and contact information so that she knows exactly who is responsible for Paul's care and safety during this time. Following a medical examination, you take Paul to the home of the temporary foster care family and introduce him to the parents.

    After saying goodbye to Paul and the foster-care family, you return to your office to prepare the case record. Outline the kinds of information that you might include in the *description section* of a case record as you consider organizing information concerning the K. case.
39. Outline, in general, what you might address in the *assessment section* of a case record that relates to the K. case.
40. Identify what you would include in the *contract section* of a case record as it relates to the K. case.
41. Based on your earlier description, formulate a goal that reasonably follows from the issue you identified with Mrs. K. Do so in two ways: First, write a *general goal statement*. Then, write a *specific goal statement* in SMART format.
42. Building on your view of the issue and the goal just described, identify at least two ways in which you could *evaluate progress* toward attainment of that particular goal.
43. Next, in a manner that is congruent with the issue, goal, and evaluation method, *formulate an action plan* by which you and the client in this case might work together toward goal achievement.

44. Several weeks have passed. Charlie has been charged with various crimes associated with child abuse and left the K. household. He may have fled the area. Mrs. K. has progressed from an initial state of confusion to a point where she has stopped drinking and is now actively engaged in counseling. Indeed, she seems to find the conversations interesting and stimulating as well as helpful. She has already successfully completed several between-session tasks and activities.

    Paul remains in temporary foster care, but he may be able to return home within this next week. Mrs. K. has visited him daily, and those visits have gone very well.

    During one of your meetings, Mrs. K. says to you (while tears stream down her cheeks), "You know, when I was a child, my stepfather used to beat me too. He made me pull down my pants and he beat me with a razor strap. I used to cry and cry but he kept doing it, and my mother could not or would not stop him. They never listened to me and nobody ever protected me. In fact, and it's strange to think about it this way, but when you came to this house to make sure that Paul was all right, that was the first time I had ever seen anybody try to protect a child from harm. And you are the first and only person who has ever seemed interested in me and in what I think and feel. Thank you so much for that."

    Write the words you would say in responding to Mrs. K.'s verbal and nonverbal expression with the skill of *responding with immediacy.*

45. During one of your conversations with Mrs. K., she says, "I knew Charlie was bad news from the moment I met him. I should have left the first time he hit me. Why do you think I stay with that guy?" Generate at least two *explanatory hypotheses* for her reluctance to leave Charlie when she realized he was dangerous to her and her son. Choose one of them and write the words you would use to respond to Mrs. K.'s question with the skill of *sharing hypotheses.*

46. Following that exchange, you continue to explore with Mrs. K. her history of relationships with alcoholic and abusive men. It's a pattern that seems remarkably similar to the relationship she observed between her own mother and her stepfather. In the midst of this discussion, she says, "I guess I must be masochistic. I must like to be beaten and degraded. Boy, am I ever sick!"

    Respond to Mrs. K.'s statement with the skill of *reframing a negative into a positive.*

47. Now, respond to Mrs. K.'s statement (above) with the form of *reframing* that *personalizes the meaning.*

48. This time, respond to Mrs. K.'s statement (above) with the form of *reframing* that *situationalizes the meaning.*

49. Now, respond to Mrs. K.'s statement (above) with the skill of *confronting.*

50. Following your *reframing* and *confronting* responses to Mrs. K.'s statements, it seems appropriate that you use the skill of *educating* in an attempt to help Mrs. K. understand how adults who were abused as children tend to think, feel, and behave. Write the words you might use in educating her about this topic.

51. Following your attempt to *educate* Mrs. K., it appears that she might benefit from some specific advice on how to be a better parent to her son Paul. Record the words you might use in *advising* her in this area.

52. Approximately 1 week goes by. Paul has returned home, and he and his mother are delighted. In a session with the two of them, you discuss one of the goals Mrs. K. has identified for herself: becoming a more loving parent and a better listener.

    You ask Paul, "How would you like your mother to show you she loves you?" Instead of answering the question, Paul grabs a ball and begins to bounce it.

    Respond to the situation just described by using the skill of *focusing.*

53. Later during the visit, Paul, Mrs. K., and you are "playing a game" of drawing on large pieces of paper. With crayons, each of you draws a picture of the K. family. Interestingly, Paul's drawing reflects a mother and a child who are both large in size—that is, the child (Paul) is every bit as tall and as large as is the mother (Mrs. K.).

Refer to the relative size of the mother and son as you generate at least one personal strength that might plausibly be reflected in Paul's drawing.

54. A few more weeks go by. Paul and Mrs. K. appear to be thriving. Paul is clearly no longer in danger and Mrs. K. is becoming an active and positive parent. You have been authorized by the court to provide up to four additional counseling sessions as you conclude your work together.

Write the words you might say to Paul and Mrs. K. in *pointing out endings*.

55. A month goes by. You, Paul, and Mrs. K. are meeting for the last time. Things are better than ever. They have achieved all of the identified goals and are extremely pleased with their progress. They are also grateful to you.

Write the words you might say in initiating a *review of the process* as part of ending your work with Paul and Mrs. K.

56. As you *review the process* as part of ending your work together, Mrs. K asks about the likelihood that she might at some point in the future become attracted to and involved with another abusive man. She asks, "I'm so afraid that, without your help, I'll simply repeat the pattern again and find another man just like Charlie or my father."

Respond to her statement by generating at least three risk factors and at least three protective factors that might plausibly be associated with the relationship pattern that Mrs. K. is so concerned about.

57. Write the words you might say in encouraging Paul and Mrs. K. to engage in a *final evaluation* as part of ending your work together.

58. Write the words you might say in *encouraging* Paul and Mrs. K. to *share their thoughts and feelings* as you conclude your work together.

59. Write the words you might say in *sharing your own ending feelings* before you, Paul, and Mrs. K. say your respective goodbyes.

60. Write the words you might say in *saying goodbye* to Paul and Mrs. K.

THE SOCIAL WORK SKILLS SELF-APPRAISAL QUESTIONNAIRE

Compiled from the exercises that conclude each chapter, this questionnaire yields an estimate of your self-appraised proficiency in the knowledge and skills addressed in the workbook. Read each statement carefully. Then, use the following 4-point rating scale to indicate the degree to which you agree or disagree with each statement. Record your numerical response in the space provided:

4 = Strongly agree

3 = Agree

2 = Disagree

1 = Strongly disagree

				Chapter 1 Self-Appraisal: Introduction
4	3	2	1	**Rating Statement**
				At this point in time, I can
☐	☐	☐	☐	1. Describe the mission and purposes of the social work profession.
☐	☐	☐	☐	2. Identify the characteristics of professionalism.
☐	☐	☐	☐	3. Define the concepts of social work skills and competencies.
☐	☐	☐	☐	4. Identify the phases or processes of social work practice.
☐	☐	☐	☐	5. Describe the essential facilitative qualities or conditions of empathy, respect, and authenticity.
☐	☐	☐	☐	6. Identify the nine aspects of professionalism addressed in *The Social Work Skills Workbook*.
☐	☐	☐	☐	7. Describe the five common factors associated with effective helping relationships.
☐	☐	☐	☐	8. Describe the purposes and functions of *The Social Work Skills Learning Portfolio*.
				Subtotal

				Chapter 2 Self-Appraisal: Professionalism
4	3	2	1	**Rating Statement**
				At this point in time, I can
☐	☐	☐	☐	1. Discuss the significance of professionalism for effective social work practice.
☐	☐	☐	☐	2. Discuss integrity as an integral aspect of professionalism.
☐	☐	☐	☐	3. Discuss the relationship of professional knowledge and self-efficacy, and self-understanding and self-control to effective social work practice.
☐	☐	☐	☐	4. Prepare a family genogram.
☐	☐	☐	☐	5. Prepare an eco-map.
☐	☐	☐	☐	6. Prepare a critical events timeline.
☐	☐	☐	☐	7. Discuss the dimensions of a personality assessment and recognize limitations in person-only forms of understanding and explanation.
☐	☐	☐	☐	8. Discuss the relationship of social support to effective social work practice.
☐	☐	☐	☐	9. Discuss the implications of selected aspects of professionalism for social work practice.
				Subtotal

				Chapter 3 Self-Appraisal: The Critical Thinking, Scientific Inquiry, and Career-Long Learning Skills
4	3	2	1	**Rating Statement**
				At this point in time, I can
☐	☐	☐	☐	1. Discuss critical thinking and scientific inquiry, and career-long learning and their implications for social work practice.
☐	☐	☐	☐	2. Use critical thinking skills to assess the credibility of a claim, conclusion, or argument; and to evaluate the quality of a research study.
☐	☐	☐	☐	3. Recognize logical fallacies in my own and in others' written and verbal communications.
☐	☐	☐	☐	4. Use scientific inquiry skills to formulate a precise question and search for, discover, and analyze one or more research studies related to a practice or policy-relevant topic.
☐	☐	☐	☐	5. Adopt universal intellectual standards in my scholarly and professional activities.
☐	☐	☐	☐	6. Assess my career-learning needs, establish learning goals, prepare learning plans, and document learning progress.
☐	☐	☐	☐	7. Assess proficiency in the skills of critical thinking and scientific inquiry, and career-long learning.
				Subtotal

4	3	2	1	Chapter 4 Self-Appraisal: Valuing Diversity; Advancing Human Rights and Social Justice; and Promoting Social Well-Being through Policy Practice
4	3	2	1	**Rating Statement**
				At this point in time, I can
☐	☐	☐	☐	1. Value diversity and difference in service to others.
☐	☐	☐	☐	2. Accept others and respect their autonomy.
☐	☐	☐	☐	3. Discuss the characteristics of human rights and concepts associated with social and economic justice.
☐	☐	☐	☐	4. Engage in activities to advance human rights and social and economic justice.
☐	☐	☐	☐	5. Discuss concepts and factors associated with social and economic well-being.
☐	☐	☐	☐	6. Engage in policy practice to promote social and economic well-being.
☐	☐	☐	☐	7. Assess proficiency in the knowledge and skills associated with valuing diversity and difference, advancing human rights and social and economic justice, and engaging in policy practice to promote social and economic well-being.
				Subtotal

Chapter 5 Self-Appraisal: The Ethical Decision-Making Skills

4	3	2	1	**Rating Statement**
				At this point in time, I can
☐	☐	☐	☐	1. Discuss the purposes and functions of ethical decision making.
☐	☐	☐	☐	2. Identify and discuss the legal duties that apply to helping professionals.
☐	☐	☐	☐	3. Access the laws that regulate the practice of social work in my locale.
☐	☐	☐	☐	4. Identify and discuss the fundamental values of the social work profession.
☐	☐	☐	☐	5. Discuss the ethical principles and standards that guide social work practice.
☐	☐	☐	☐	6. Identify the relevant legal duties and ethical principles that might apply in various professional contexts and situations.
☐	☐	☐	☐	7. Analyze and determine the relative priority of competing legal and ethical obligations through the development and use of a case-specific values hierarchy.
☐	☐	☐	☐	8. Use critical thinking skills to reach ethical decisions and plan appropriate action.
☐	☐	☐	☐	9. Assess proficiency in the ethical decision-making skills.
☐	☐	☐	☐	10. Assess my readiness for the profession of social work.
				Subtotal

				Chapter 6 Self-Appraisal: The Talking and Listening Skills
4	3	2	1		Rating Statement
					At this point in time, I can
☐	☐	☐	☐		1. Describe and discuss the talking, listening, and active-listening skills.
☐	☐	☐	☐		2. Engage diversity and difference through culturally sensitive communications.
☐	☐	☐	☐		3. Use nonverbal communications and body language in a professional manner.
☐	☐	☐	☐		4. Apply the talking skills—including written as well as verbal communication—in a professional manner.
☐	☐	☐	☐		5. Use the listening skills effectively.
☐	☐	☐	☐		6. Use the active-listening skills.
☐	☐	☐	☐		7. Assess my proficiency in the talking, listening, and active-listening skills.
					Subtotal

					Chapter 7 Self-Appraisal: The Preparing Skills
4	3	2	1		Rating Statement
					At this point in time, I can
☐	☐	☐	☐		1. Discuss the purposes and functions of preparing.
☐	☐	☐	☐		2. Engage in preparatory reviewing.
☐	☐	☐	☐		3. Engage in preparatory exploring.
☐	☐	☐	☐		4. Engage in preparatory consultation.
☐	☐	☐	☐		5. Engage in preparatory arranging.
☐	☐	☐	☐		6. Engage in preparatory empathy.
☐	☐	☐	☐		7. Engage in preparatory self-exploration.
☐	☐	☐	☐		8. Center myself.
☐	☐	☐	☐		9. Engage in preliminary planning and recording.
☐	☐	☐	☐		10. Assess my proficiency in the preparing skills.
					Subtotal

Chapter 8 Self-Appraisal: The Beginning Skills

4	3	2	1	Rating Statement
				At this point in time, I can
☐	☐	☐	☐	1. Discuss the purposes and functions of beginning.
☐	☐	☐	☐	2. Introduce myself.
☐	☐	☐	☐	3. Seek introductions.
☐	☐	☐	☐	4. Describe an initial purpose.
☐	☐	☐	☐	5. Orient clients to the process.
☐	☐	☐	☐	6. Discuss policy and ethical factors.
☐	☐	☐	☐	7. Seek feedback.
☐	☐	☐	☐	8. Assess my proficiency in the beginning skills.
				Subtotal

Chapter 9 Self-Appraisal: The Exploring Skills

4	3	2	1	Rating Statement
				At this point in time, I can
☐	☐	☐	☐	1. Discuss the purposes and functions of exploring.
☐	☐	☐	☐	2. Explore relevant aspects of the person-issue-situation and look for strengths.
☐	☐	☐	☐	3. Ask questions.
☐	☐	☐	☐	4. Seek clarification.
☐	☐	☐	☐	5. Reflect content.
☐	☐	☐	☐	6. Reflect feelings.
☐	☐	☐	☐	7. Reflect feelings and meanings.
☐	☐	☐	☐	8. Partialize.
☐	☐	☐	☐	9. Go beyond what is said.
☐	☐	☐	☐	10. Reflect issues.
☐	☐	☐	☐	11. Reflect hypotheses.
☐	☐	☐	☐	12. Assess proficiency in the exploring skills.
				Subtotal

4	3	2	1	Chapter 10 Self-Appraisal: The Assessing Skills
4	**3**	**2**	**1**	**Rating Statement**
				At this point in time, I can
☐	☐	☐	☐	1. Discuss the purposes and functions of assessment.
☐	☐	☐	☐	2. Identify issues.
☐	☐	☐	☐	3. Share hypotheses.
☐	☐	☐	☐	4. Clarify issues for work.
☐	☐	☐	☐	5. Organize descriptive information in the form of a written record.
☐	☐	☐	☐	6. Prepare an assessment and case formulation.
☐	☐	☐	☐	7. Assess proficiency in the assessing skills.
				Subtotal

4	3	2	1	Chapter 11 Self-Appraisal: The Contracting Skills
4	**3**	**2**	**1**	**Rating Statement**
				At this point in time, I can
☐	☐	☐	☐	1. Discuss the purposes and functions of contracting.
☐	☐	☐	☐	2. Establish goals.
☐	☐	☐	☐	3. Develop action plans.
☐	☐	☐	☐	4. Identify action steps.
☐	☐	☐	☐	5. Plan for evaluation.
☐	☐	☐	☐	6. Summarize the contract.
☐	☐	☐	☐	7. Assess proficiency in the contracting skills.
				Subtotal

4	3	2	1	Chapter 12 Self-Appraisal: The Working and Evaluating Skills
4	3	2	1	**Rating Statement**
				At this point in time, I can
☐	☐	☐	☐	1. Discuss the purposes and functions of working and evaluating.
☐	☐	☐	☐	2. Rehearse action steps.
☐	☐	☐	☐	3. Review action steps.
☐	☐	☐	☐	4. Evaluate progress.
☐	☐	☐	☐	5. Provide focus during meetings.
☐	☐	☐	☐	6. Educate others.
☐	☐	☐	☐	7. Advise others.
☐	☐	☐	☐	8. Represent clients.
☐	☐	☐	☐	9. Respond with immediacy.
☐	☐	☐	☐	10. Reframe messages.
☐	☐	☐	☐	11. Confront inconsistencies.
☐	☐	☐	☐	12. Point out endings.
☐	☐	☐	☐	13. Prepare written progress recordings.
☐	☐	☐	☐	14. Assess proficiency in the working and evaluating skills.
				Subtotal

4	3	2	1	Chapter 13 Self-Appraisal: The Ending Skills
4	3	2	1	**Rating Statement**
				At this point in time, I can
☐	☐	☐	☐	1. Discuss the purposes and functions of ending.
☐	☐	☐	☐	2. Review the process.
☐	☐	☐	☐	3. Engage clients in a process of final evaluation.
☐	☐	☐	☐	4. Share ending feelings and say goodbye.
☐	☐	☐	☐	5. Prepare a closing summary record.
☐	☐	☐	☐	6. Assess proficiency in the ending skills.
				Subtotal
				TOTAL

This questionnaire provides you with an indication of your self-appraised proficiency in the social work skills. Because it is based on your own beliefs about your proficiency, absolute scores are relatively unimportant. Rather, use the results as a stimulus both to ask yourself further questions concerning your competency with various skills and to develop plans by which to improve your proficiency in those skill areas that need additional study and practice. You may complete the questionnaire at various points throughout the learning process. Increased proficiency may be reflected in changing scores over time. In considering your results, please remember that a higher rating suggests a higher level of appraised proficiency.

To score the Social Work Skills Self-Appraisal Questionnaire, simply sum the total of your ratings to the 112 items. Your score should range somewhere between 112 and 448. A higher score suggests a higher level of appraised proficiency. In theory, a score of 336 (or an average of 3 on each of the 112 items) would indicate that, on average, you "agree" with statements suggesting that you are proficient in the 112 items. Please note, however, that such an average score does not necessarily indicate that you are proficient in all of the skills. You might obtain such a score by rating several items at the "4" or "strongly agree" level and an equal number at the "2" or "disagree level." Therefore, you should look carefully at your rating for each item, as well as the subtotals for each skill area.

Finally, you should recognize that this questionnaire reflects your own subjective opinions. You may consciously or unconsciously overestimate or perhaps underestimate your proficiency in these skills. Therefore, please use the results in conjunction with other evidence about your actual proficiency in the skills.

THE GENERAL SELF-EFFICACY SCALE

Instructions: The General Self-Efficacy (GSE) Scale[1] includes a series of statements about your personal attitudes, traits, and behaviors. Carefully read each statement and decide to what extent it reflects you. You will probably find that you agree with some statements and disagree with others. The answers are neither right nor wrong. Please describe yourself as you really are, not as you would like to be.

Rate the degree of agreement or disagreement by checking the box below the number that most closely reflects your view about each statement. Please use the following rating system:

1 = Not at all true
2 = Hardly true
3 = Moderately true
4 = Exactly true

The General Self-Efficacy Scale	
1 2 3 4	Rating Statement
☐ ☐ ☐ ☐	1. I can always manage to solve difficult problems if I try hard enough.
☐ ☐ ☐ ☐	2. If someone opposes me, I can find the means and ways to get what I want.
☐ ☐ ☐ ☐	3. It is easy for me to stick to my aims and accomplish my goals.
☐ ☐ ☐ ☐	4. I am confident that I could deal efficiently with unexpected events.

---

[1] From Schwarzer & Jerusalem (1995). Originally developed in 1985, the GSE Scale was slightly revised in 2000. Reproduced with permission.

The General Self-Efficacy Scale	
1 2 3 4	**Rating Statement**
☐ ☐ ☐ ☐	5. Thanks to my resourcefulness, I know how to handle unforeseen situations.
☐ ☐ ☐ ☐	6. I can solve most problems if I invest the necessary effort.
☐ ☐ ☐ ☐	7. I can remain calm when facing difficulties because I can rely on my coping abilities.
☐ ☐ ☐ ☐	8. When I am confronted with a problem, I can usually find several solutions.
☐ ☐ ☐ ☐	9. If I am in trouble, I can usually think of a solution.
☐ ☐ ☐ ☐	10. I can usually handle whatever comes my way.
	The General Self-Efficacy (GSE) Scale Score

To score the General Self-Efficacy Scale, sum your ratings for all items. Total GSE scale scores may range from 10 to 40. If, for example, you assigned a '3' (moderately true) rating to each of the 10 items, your total GSE Scale score would be 30. Alternately, you may use the mean or average score of the items. In that case, a total score of 30 on the 10 items could be reported as a 3.0 average.

As you review your results on the scale, remember that a "generalized sense of self-efficacy ... refers to a broad and stable sense of personal competence to deal effectively with a variety of stressful situations" (Luszczynska, Scholz, & Schwarzer, 2005, p. 440). Recognize that the scale does not assess specific skills or competencies that people might apply in specific circumstances. The General Self-Efficacy Scale is widely used throughout the world and much normative data are available. A higher score tends to indicate a stronger sense of generalized self-efficacy.

Based upon a study of nearly 9,000 men and women from five countries, average total scores on the 10 item GSE Scale ranged from 27.60 to 34.44. In the sample from the United States, 248 male high school students reflected average GSE Scale scores of 31.52 (SD=4.48) while 290 female students scored 30.64 (SD=4.45) (Luszczynska, Gutiérez-Doña & Schwarzer, 2005). Another United States sample of 1,594 adults (50.9% male; 49.1% female) reflected a total mean GSE Scale score of 29.48 (SD=5.13) (Schwarzer, 2011).

Consider your scores in light of these averages and view the results as indicative but not definitive of your general self-efficacy. Be sure to consider information from other sources as well. Our general sense of self-efficacy can change over time. As social workers in the contemporary world, most of us need a well-developed sense of self-efficacy to provide competent service in often highly stressful and frequently demanding circumstances. If your self-efficacy score is substantially below the average scores reflected by adults in the United States and other nations, you may wish to consider the possible implications for your performance as a social worker and perhaps take steps to strengthen your sense of generalized self-efficacy.

APPENDIX 5

SELF-CONTROL SCHEDULE

Please read carefully each of the statements contained in the following instrument.[1] Indicate how characteristic or descriptive each of the following statements is by using the rating code provided below:

+3 = Very characteristic of me
+2 = Rather characteristic of me
+1 = Somewhat characteristic of me
−1 = Somewhat uncharacteristic of me
−2 = Rather uncharacteristic of me
−3 = Very uncharacteristic of me

						Self-Control Schedule
+3	+2	+1	−1	−2	−3	**Rating Statement**
☐	☐	☐	☐	☐	☐	1. When I do a boring job, I think about the less boring parts of the job and about the reward I will receive when I finish.
☐	☐	☐	☐	☐	☐	2. When I have to do something that makes me anxious, I try to visualize how I will overcome my anxiety while doing it.
☐	☐	☐	☐	☐	☐	3. By changing my way of thinking, I am often able to change my feelings about almost anything.
☐	☐	☐	☐	☐	☐	4. I often find it difficult to overcome my feelings of nervousness and tension without outside help.
☐	☐	☐	☐	☐	☐	5. When I am feeling depressed, I try to think about pleasant events.
☐	☐	☐	☐	☐	☐	6. I cannot help thinking about mistakes I made.
☐	☐	☐	☐	☐	☐	7. When I am faced with a difficult problem, I try to approach it in a systematic way.
☐	☐	☐	☐	☐	☐	8. I usually do what I am supposed to do more quickly when someone is pressuring me.

---

[1] Copyright © 1998 by the Association for Behavioral and Cognitive Therapies. Reprinted by permission of the publisher.

Self-Control Schedule

+3	+2	+1	−1	−2	−3	Rating Statement
☐	☐	☐	☐	☐	☐	9. When I am faced with a difficult decision, I prefer to postpone it even if I have all the facts.
☐	☐	☐	☐	☐	☐	10. When I have difficulty concentrating on my reading, I look for ways to increase my concentration.
☐	☐	☐	☐	☐	☐	11. When I plan to work, I remove everything that is not relevant to my work.
☐	☐	☐	☐	☐	☐	12. When I try to get rid of a bad habit, I first try to find out all the reasons why I have the habit.
☐	☐	☐	☐	☐	☐	13. When an unpleasant thought is bothering me, I try to think about something pleasant.
☐	☐	☐	☐	☐	☐	14. If I smoked two packs of cigarettes a day, I would need outside help to stop smoking.
☐	☐	☐	☐	☐	☐	15. When I feel down, I try to act cheerful so that my mood will change.
☐	☐	☐	☐	☐	☐	16. If I had tranquilizers with me, I would take one whenever I felt tense and nervous.
☐	☐	☐	☐	☐	☐	17. When I am depressed, I try to keep myself busy with things I like.
☐	☐	☐	☐	☐	☐	18. I tend to postpone unpleasant tasks even if I could perform them immediately.
☐	☐	☐	☐	☐	☐	19. I need outside help to get rid of some of my bad habits.
☐	☐	☐	☐	☐	☐	20. When I find it difficult to settle down and do a task, I look for ways to help me settle down.
☐	☐	☐	☐	☐	☐	21. Although it makes me feel bad, I cannot help thinking about all sorts of possible catastrophes.
☐	☐	☐	☐	☐	☐	22. I prefer to finish a job that I have to do before I start doing things I really like.
☐	☐	☐	☐	☐	☐	23. When I feel physical pain, I try not to think about it.
☐	☐	☐	☐	☐	☐	24. My self-esteem increases when I am able to overcome a bad habit.
☐	☐	☐	☐	☐	☐	25. To overcome bad feelings that accompany failure, I often tell myself that it is not catastrophic and I can do anything.
☐	☐	☐	☐	☐	☐	26. When I feel that I am too impulsive, I tell myself to stop and think before I do something about it.
☐	☐	☐	☐	☐	☐	27. Even when I am terribly angry with someone, I consider my actions very carefully.

Self-Control Schedule

+3	+2	+1	−1	−2	−3	Rating Statement
☐	☐	☐	☐	☐	☐	28. Facing the need to make a decision, I usually look for different alternatives instead of deciding quickly and spontaneously.
☐	☐	☐	☐	☐	☐	29. Usually, I first do the thing I really like to do even if there are more urgent things to do.
☐	☐	☐	☐	☐	☐	30. When I realize that I am going to be unavoidably late for an important meeting, I tell myself to keep calm.
☐	☐	☐	☐	☐	☐	31. When I feel pain in my body, I try to divert my thoughts from it.
☐	☐	☐	☐	☐	☐	32. When I am faced with a number of things to do, I usually plan my work.
☐	☐	☐	☐	☐	☐	33. When I am short of money, I decide to record all my expenses in order to budget more carefully in the future.
☐	☐	☐	☐	☐	☐	34. If I find it difficult to concentrate on a task, I divide it into small segments.
☐	☐	☐	☐	☐	☐	35. Quite often, I cannot overcome unpleasant thoughts that bother me.
☐	☐	☐	☐	☐	☐	36. When I am hungry and I have no opportunity to eat, I try to divert my thoughts from my stomach or try to imagine that I am satisfied.
						Self-Control Score

Score the Self-Control Schedule in the following manner. First, reverse-score items 4, 6, 8, 9, 14, 16, 18, 19, 21, 29, and 35. On this scale, reverse-score means to change a positive number to its negative or a negative number to its positive (for example, a +3 would become −3; +2 would become −2; +1 would become −1). Then, sum the ratings for the 36 items. The total represents your self-control score.

As with other self-report measures, view the results of this inventory with a degree of caution. In assessing your capacity for self-control, consider information from other sources as well. In reviewing your score on the Self-Control Schedule, recognize that the scores could possibly range from −108 to +108. Average scores of most respondent samples tend to range from 23 to 27. The mean score of nonclinical populations tends to be approximately 25 ($SD = 20$) (Rosenbaum, 1980). A sample (Cournoyer, 1994) of 24 beginning MSW students scored an average of 36.46 ($SD = 20.60$) on the Self-Control Schedule. A higher score represents a greater degree or level of self-control. If your score is substantially less than these average scores, it may be helpful to institute a program designed to increase your level of self-control. If your score is +5 or lower, you should probably consult a professional concerning development of a program to enhance your self-control. If the score is reasonably accurate, such a low level of self-control could be problematic in your role as a professional social worker.

THE SOCIAL SUPPORT APPRAISALS SCALE

Please carefully read each of the items in the instrument[1] presented below. Respond to each item as carefully and accurately as you can by choosing the response that best reflects your opinion. Please use the following 4-point rating system to record your responses. Notice that a *lower* number indicates a greater degree of agreement.

1 = Strongly agree
2 = Agree
3 = Disagree
4 = Strongly disagree

The Social Support Appraisals Scale				
1	2	3	4	**Rating Statement**
☐	☐	☐	☐	1. My friends respect me.
☐	☐	☐	☐	2. My family cares for me very much.
☐	☐	☐	☐	3. I am not important to others.
☐	☐	☐	☐	4. My family holds me in high esteem.
☐	☐	☐	☐	5. I am well liked.
☐	☐	☐	☐	6. I can rely on my friends.
☐	☐	☐	☐	7. I am really admired by my family.
☐	☐	☐	☐	8. I am respected by other people.
☐	☐	☐	☐	9. I am loved dearly by my family.
☐	☐	☐	☐	10. My friends don't care about my welfare.

---

[1] *Springer and American Journal of Community Psychology, 14,* 1986, p. 195–219, © 1986 by Springer Science and Business Media; with kind permission from Springer Science+Business Media B.V.

The Social Support Appraisals Scale				
1	2	3	4	Rating Statement
☐	☐	☐	☐	11. Members of my family rely on me.
☐	☐	☐	☐	12. I am held in high esteem.
☐	☐	☐	☐	13. I can't rely on my family for support.
☐	☐	☐	☐	14. People admire me.
☐	☐	☐	☐	15. I feel a strong bond with my friends.
☐	☐	☐	☐	16. My friends look out for me.
☐	☐	☐	☐	17. I feel valued by other people.
☐	☐	☐	☐	18. My family really respects me.
☐	☐	☐	☐	19. My friends and I are really important to each other.
☐	☐	☐	☐	20. I feel like I belong.
☐	☐	☐	☐	21. If I died tomorrow, very few people would miss me.
☐	☐	☐	☐	22. I don't feel close to members of my family.
☐	☐	☐	☐	23. My friends and I have done a lot for one another.
				Overall Social Support Score
				SS-A Family Subscale Score
				SS-A Friends Subscale Score

To calculate your overall score on the Social Support Appraisals Scale, first reverse-score items 3, 10, 13, 21, and 22. Then add the ratings for the 23 items. Your overall SS-A score should range somewhere between 23 and 92.

This instrument also contains family and friends subscales. To determine your family subscale score, sum the ratings for items 2, 4, 7, 9, 11, 13, 18, and 22. Find your friends subscale score by adding the ratings for items 1, 6, 10, 15, 16, 19, and 23. The Family Social Support Appraisal Subscale score should range between 8 and 32. The Friends Social Support Appraisal Subscale score should range between 7 and 28.

As you reflect on the significance of these scores, please recognize that a lower score indicates a greater level of appraised social support. Researchers have used the SS-A Scale in numerous studies. The instrument appears to have acceptable validity and reliability characteristics. Various studies have yielded average overall SS-A Scale scores that range from the mid- to high-60s; average family subscale scores in the low- to mid-20s; and average friends subscale scores in the low 20s (Miller & Lago, 1990; O'Reilly, 1995). Consider your results in light of these average ranges.

THE CRITICAL THINKING QUESTIONNAIRE

Please read each of the statements contained in the following questionnaire.[1] Rate the degree of agreement or disagreement by checking the box below the number that most closely reflects your view. Notice that a *lower* number indicates a greater degree of agreement. Please use the following rating system:

1 = Strongly agree
2 = Agree
3 = Disagree
4 = Strongly disagree

Critical Thinking Questionnaire				
1	2	3	4	**Rating Statement**
☐	☐	☐	☐	1. I rarely make judgments based solely upon intuition or emotion.
☐	☐	☐	☐	2. I almost always think before I speak or act.
☐	☐	☐	☐	3. I almost never express opinions as if they were facts.
☐	☐	☐	☐	4. I always identify the assumptions underlying an argument.
☐	☐	☐	☐	5. I carefully consider the source of information in determining validity.
☐	☐	☐	☐	6. I rarely reach conclusions without considering the evidence.
☐	☐	☐	☐	7. I regularly think in terms of probabilities.
☐	☐	☐	☐	8. I rarely think in terms of absolutes.
☐	☐	☐	☐	9. I always question the validity of arguments and conclusions.
☐	☐	☐	☐	10. I rarely assume that something is valid or true.
☐	☐	☐	☐	11. I regularly identify my own biases and preferences.

---

[1] The Evidence-Based Social Work Questionnaire (EBSWQ). Copyright © 2000 by Barry R. Cournoyer.

Critical Thinking Questionnaire				
1	2	3	4	**Rating Statement**
☐	☐	☐	☐	12. I regularly think about issues of reliability.
☐	☐	☐	☐	13. I routinely identify my own logical fallacies.
☐	☐	☐	☐	14. I rarely say that something is true unless I have supporting evidence.
☐	☐	☐	☐	15. I regularly use a thinking process routine to reach decisions.
				Total CT Questionnaire Score (Sum ratings of items 1–15)

To score the questionnaire, simply sum the total of your ratings for all 15 items. Your overall score should range somewhere between 15 and 60. Lower scores suggest greater levels of critical thinking. Remember, however, that the questionnaire is still under development and its psychometric properties have not yet been determined. View the instrument and your results with caution. As a tentative indicator, however, you might compare your score with those of a convenience sample of 21 members of a foundation-year, MSW-level social work practice class. That sample yielded an average score of 32.38 (range 20–42; *SD* 6.26) on the critical thinking questionnaire (Cournoyer, 1999). Another sample of more than 90 foundation- and concentration-year MSW students combined reflected an average score of 31.79 ($n = 95$; range 20–51; *SD* 4.51) (Cournoyer, 2003).

THE LIFELONG LEARNING QUESTIONNAIRE

Please read each of the statements contained in the following questionnaire.[1] Rate the degree of agreement or disagreement by checking the box below the number that most closely reflects your view. Notice that a *lower* number indicates a greater degree of agreement. Please use the following rating system:

1 = Strongly agree

2 = Agree

3 = Disagree

4 = Strongly disagree

				Lifelong Learning Questionnaire
1	2	3	4	Rating Statement
☐	☐	☐	☐	1. I regularly read professional journals in my field.
☐	☐	☐	☐	2. I genuinely enjoy learning.
☐	☐	☐	☐	3. I always do more than the minimum requirements in courses, seminars, or workshops.
☐	☐	☐	☐	4. I regularly pursue opportunities to advance my knowledge and expertise.
☐	☐	☐	☐	5. I never become defensive when someone offers feedback that could improve my skill.
☐	☐	☐	☐	6. I like to study.
☐	☐	☐	☐	7. I know my personal learning style.
☐	☐	☐	☐	8. I am actively involved in learning experiences.
☐	☐	☐	☐	9. I take personal responsibility for my own learning.
☐	☐	☐	☐	10. I view examinations as a way to learn.

---

[1] The Lifelong Learning Questionnaire (LLQ). Copyright © 2000 by Barry R. Cournoyer.

Lifelong Learning Questionnaire				
1	**2**	**3**	**4**	**Rating Statement**
☐	☐	☐	☐	11. I know how to conduct a professional literature review.
☐	☐	☐	☐	12. I sometimes contact national and international experts in my learning efforts.
☐	☐	☐	☐	13. I have a list of learning goals.
☐	☐	☐	☐	14. I have specific plans to advance my learning.
☐	☐	☐	☐	15. I enjoy teaching others.
				Total LLL Questionnaire Score (Sum ratings of items 1–15)

To score the questionnaire, simply sum the total of your ratings for all 15 items. Your overall score should range somewhere between 15 and 60. Lower scores suggest greater levels of lifelong learning. Remember, however, that the questionnaire is still under development and its psychometric properties have not yet been determined. View the instruments and your results with caution. As a tentative indicator, however, you might compare your score with those of a convenience sample of 21 members of a foundation-year, MSW-level social work practice class. That sample yielded an average score of 33.10 (range 20–43; SD 7.44) on the lifelong learning questionnaire (Cournoyer, 1999). Another sample of more than 90 foundation- and concentration-year MSW students combined reflected an average score of 29.12 (n = 97; range 16–41; SD 5.44) (Cournoyer, 2003).

THE ACCEPTANCE OF OTHERS SCALE

This questionnaire[1] helps you assess your relative acceptance of others. It is not a test; right or wrong answers do not exist. Please use the following 5-point rating system to record your responses to each item.

1 = Almost always true

2 = Usually true

3 = True half of the time

4 = Only occasionally true

5 = Very rarely true

					Acceptance of Others Scale
1	**2**	**3**	**4**	**5**	**Rating Statement of Present Condition or Action**
☐	☐	☐	☐	☐	1. People are too easily led.
☐	☐	☐	☐	☐	2. I like people I get to know.
☐	☐	☐	☐	☐	3. People these days have pretty low moral standards.
☐	☐	☐	☐	☐	4. Most people are pretty smug about themselves, never really facing their bad points.
☐	☐	☐	☐	☐	5. I can be comfortable with nearly all kinds of people.
☐	☐	☐	☐	☐	6. All people can talk about these days, it seems, is movies, TV, and foolishness like that.
☐	☐	☐	☐	☐	7. People get ahead by using "pull" and not because of what they know.
☐	☐	☐	☐	☐	8. Once you start doing favors for people, they'll just walk all over you.
☐	☐	☐	☐	☐	9. People are too self-centered.

---

[1] From Fey (1955).

					Acceptance of Others Scale
1	**2**	**3**	**4**	**5**	**Rating Statement of Present Condition or Action**
☐	☐	☐	☐	☐	10. People are always dissatisfied and hunting for something new.
☐	☐	☐	☐	☐	11. With many people you don't know how you stand.
☐	☐	☐	☐	☐	12. You've probably got to hurt someone if you're going to make something out of yourself.
☐	☐	☐	☐	☐	13. People really need a strong, smart leader.
☐	☐	☐	☐	☐	14. I enjoy myself most when I am alone, away from people.
☐	☐	☐	☐	☐	15. I wish people would be more honest with me.
☐	☐	☐	☐	☐	16. I enjoy going with a crowd.
☐	☐	☐	☐	☐	17. In my experience, people are pretty stubborn and unreasonable.
☐	☐	☐	☐	☐	18. I can enjoy being with people whose values are very different from mine.
☐	☐	☐	☐	☐	19. Everybody tries to be nice.
☐	☐	☐	☐	☐	20. The average person is not very well satisfied with himself (or herself).
					Total Acceptance of Others Score

Score the Acceptance of Others Scale in the following manner: First, reverse-score items 2, 5, 16, 18, and 19. To reverse-score means to change an answer of 1 to 5, 2 to 4, 4 to 2, and 5 to 1. Ratings of 3 remain 3. Now add the answers for all 20 items to find your total score. Scores may range from a low of 20 to a high of 100. A higher score indicates a greater level of acceptance of others. As with other scales, however, interpret the results of this questionnaire with some caution. Use the results to formulate hypotheses to test by examining evidence from other sources. The guidelines that follow will help you evaluate your results (Fey, 1955).

People who score in the range of 85 to 100 generally tend to accept other people, to experience others as accepting of them, and to be accepted by others. The range from 66 to 84 includes the average scores of the majority of people. Approximately two-thirds of all people taking the scale score in this medium range. A sample (Cournoyer, 1994) of 20 beginning MSW students reflected an average score of 78.4 (SD = 7.61) on the Acceptance of Others Scale. Such midrange scores show a mixture of caution about and acceptance of people. Although less accepting of certain persons, individuals scoring in this range clearly have the capacity to accept others fully. People scoring in the range of 0 to 65 may be very cautious about and intolerant of others. This hesitancy about other people could be a consequence of significant social, emotional, or physical pain caused by others at some point in the past.

THE SATISFACTION WITH LIFE SCALE

Below are five statements with which you may agree or disagree. Using the following 7-point Satisfaction With Life Scale (SWLS), indicate the degree of your agreement with each item by checking the appropriate box adjacent to that item.

7 = Strongly agree

6 = Agree

5 = Slightly agree

4 = Neither agree nor disagree

3 = Slightly disagree

2 = Disagree

1 = Strongly disagree

Satisfaction With Life Scale							
7	6	5	4	3	2	1	Rating Statement
☐	☐	☐	☐	☐	☐	☐	1. In most ways my life is close to my ideal.
☐	☐	☐	☐	☐	☐	☐	2. The conditions of my life are excellent.
☐	☐	☐	☐	☐	☐	☐	3. I am satisfied with my life.
☐	☐	☐	☐	☐	☐	☐	4. So far I have gotten the important things I want in life.
☐	☐	☐	☐	☐	☐	☐	5. If I could live my life over, I would change almost nothing.
							Total

Score the SWLS (Diener, Emmons, Larsen, & Griffin, 1985) in the following manner. After you respond to each item, add the ratings to obtain a total score. Your score should range between 5 and 35. Interpret your scores according to the following guidelines as prepared by Dr. Ed Diener (2006, February 13):

Satisfaction With Life Scale: Interpretation Guidelines[1]

Dr. Ed Diener, author of the SWLS offers the following guidelines for interpreting scores (Diener, 2006, February 13):

30–35 Very High Score; Highly Satisfied: Respondents who score in this range love their lives and feel that things are going very well. Their lives are not perfect, but they feel that things are about as good as lives get. Furthermore, just because the person is satisfied does not mean she or he is complacent. In fact, growth and challenge might be part of the reason the respondent is satisfied. For most people in this high-scoring range, life is enjoyable, and the major domains of life are going well—work or school, family, friends, leisure, and personal development.

25–29 High Score: Individuals who score in this range like their lives and feel that things are going well. Of course their lives are not perfect, but they feel that things are mostly good. Furthermore, just because the person is satisfied does not mean she or he is complacent. In fact, growth and challenge might be part of the reason the respondent is satisfied. For most people in this high-scoring range, life is enjoyable, and the major domains of life are going well—work or school, family, friends, leisure, and personal development. The person may draw motivation from the areas of dissatisfaction.

20–24 Average Score: The average of life satisfaction in economically developed nations is in this range—the majority of people are generally satisfied, but have some areas where they very much would like some improvement. Some individuals score in this range because they are mostly satisfied with most areas of their lives but see the need for some improvement in each area. Other respondents score in this range because they are satisfied with most domains of their lives but have one or two areas where they would like to see large improvements. A person scoring in this range is normal in that they have areas of their lives that need improvement. However, an individual in this range would usually like to move to a higher level by making some life changes.

15–19 Slightly Below Average in Life Satisfaction: People who score in this range usually have small but significant problems in several areas of their lives, or have many areas that are doing fine but one area that represents a substantial problem for them. If a person has moved temporarily into this level of life satisfaction from a higher level because of some recent event, things will usually improve over time and satisfaction will generally move back up. On the other hand, if a person is chronically slightly dissatisfied with many areas of life, some changes might be in order. Sometimes the person is simply expecting too much, and sometimes life changes are needed. Thus, although temporary dissatisfaction is common and normal, a chronic level of dissatisfaction across a number of areas of life calls for reflection. Some people can gain motivation from a small level of dissatisfaction, but often dissatisfaction across a number of life domains is a distraction, and unpleasant as well.

10–14 Dissatisfied: People who score in this range are substantially dissatisfied with their lives. People in this range may have a number of domains that are not going well, or one or two domains that are going very badly. If life dissatisfaction is a response to a recent event such as bereavement, divorce, or a significant problem at work, the person will probably return over

---

[1] Copyright © by Ed Diener, February 13, 2006. Use is free of charge and granted by permission.

time to his or her former level of higher satisfaction. However, if low levels of life satisfaction have been chronic for the person, some changes are in order—in both attitudes and patterns of thinking, and probably in life activities as well. Low levels of life satisfaction in this range, if they persist, can indicate that things are going badly and life alterations are needed. Furthermore, a person with low life satisfaction in this range is sometimes not functioning well because their unhappiness serves as a distraction. Talking to a friend, member of the clergy, counselor, or other specialist can often help the person get moving in the right direction, although positive change will be up to the person.

5–9 Extremely Dissatisfied: Individuals who score in this range are usually extremely unhappy with their current life. In some cases this is in reaction to some recent bad event such as widowhood or unemployment. In other cases, it is a response to a chronic problem such as alcoholism or addiction. In yet other cases, the extreme dissatisfaction is a reaction due to something bad in life such as recently having lost a loved one. However, dissatisfaction at this level is often due to dissatisfaction in multiple areas of life. Whatever the reason for the low level of life satisfaction, it may be that the help of others is needed—a friend or family member, counseling with a member of the clergy, or help from a psychologist or other counselor. If the dissatisfaction is chronic, the person needs to change, and often others can help. (Diener, 2006, February 13, pp. 1–2)

Part That Is Common to Each Category To understand life satisfaction scores, it is helpful to understand some of the components that go into most people's experience of satisfaction. One of the most important influences on happiness is social relationships. People who score high on life satisfaction tend to have close and supportive family and friends, whereas those who do not have close friends and family are more likely to be dissatisfied. Of course the loss of a close friend or family member can cause dissatisfaction with life, and it may take quite a time for the person to bounce back from the loss.

Another factor that influences the life satisfaction of most people is work or school, or performance in an important role such as homemaker or grandparent. When the person enjoys his or her work, whether it is paid or unpaid work, and feels that it is meaningful and important, this contributes to life satisfaction. When work is going poorly because of bad circumstances or a poor fit with the person's strengths, this can lower life satisfaction. When a person has important goals, and is failing to make adequate progress toward them, this too can lead to life dissatisfaction.

A third factor that influences the life satisfaction of most people is personal—satisfaction with the self, religious or spiritual life, learning and growth, and leisure. For many people these are sources of satisfaction. However, when these sources of personal worth are frustrated, they can be powerful sources of dissatisfaction. Of course there are additional sources of satisfaction and dissatisfaction— some that are common to most people such as health, and others that are unique to each individual. Most people know the factors that lead to their satisfaction or dissatisfaction, although a person's temperament—a general tendency to be happy or unhappy—can color their responses.

There is no one key to life satisfaction, but rather a recipe that includes a number of ingredients. With time and persistent work, people's life satisfaction usually goes up when they are dissatisfied. People who have had a loss recover over time. People who have a dissatisfying relationship or work often make changes over time that will increase their satisfaction. One key ingredient to happiness, as mentioned above, is social relationships, and another key ingredient is to have important goals that derive from one's values, and to make progress toward those goals. For many people it is important to feel a connection to something larger than oneself. When a person tends to be chronically dissatisfied, they should look within themselves and ask whether they need to develop more positive attitudes to life and the world. (Diener, 2006, February 13, pp. 1–2)

APPENDIX 11

THE INTERVIEW RATING FORMS—CLIENT VERSION

The following rating form allows clients to provide constructive feedback about their social workers' professional skills. Social workers use these ratings to improve the quality of their service to you and other clients. You can be most helpful in this process by thinking carefully about each statement and providing the most accurate rating possible. Use the five-point scale to rate the degree of your agreement with each item. Notice that a *higher* number indicates a greater degree of agreement. Place a check mark in the box below the number that most closely reflects your view.

5 = Strongly Agree
4 = Agree
3 = Undecided
2 = Disagree
1 = Strongly Disagree

Talking and Listening Skills Rating Form					
5	4	3	2	1	Statement
☐	☐	☐	☐	☐	S6.1 The interviewer was sensitive to and respected my cultural beliefs and practices even when they differed from her or his own.
☐	☐	☐	☐	☐	S6.2 The interviewer's facial expressions, head movements, tone of voice, body positions, and physical gestures indicated that she or he was truly interested in me and everything I had to say.
☐	☐	☐	☐	☐	S6.3 The interviewer spoke clearly and audibly so that I easily heard everything she or he expressed during the conversation.
☐	☐	☐	☐	☐	S6.4 The interviewer used familiar words and language so that I understood everything she or he expressed during the conversation.
☐	☐	☐	☐	☐	S6.5 During the conversation, the interviewer listened attentively, respectfully, and nonjudgmentally to everything I expressed

Talking and Listening Skills Rating Form					
5	4	3	2	1	Statement
☐	☐	☐	☐	☐	S6.6 The interviewer remembered what I said during the interview so that she or he sometimes made reference to things I mentioned earlier.
☐	☐	☐	☐	☐	S6.7 The interviewer periodically summarized my messages in her or his own words so that I knew she or he accurately understood what I was trying to say.
☐	☐	☐	☐	☐	S6.8 Overall, I felt accepted, respected, valued, heard, and understood during this interview.
					TOTAL

Following a meeting in which the interviewer consistently demonstrates proficient use of the talking and listening skills, interviewees would usually assign ratings of 4 or 5 on each item. Possible total scores for the eight items range from 8 to 40. Scores between 32 and 40 indicate overall proficiency. However, make note of any items that receive ratings of less than 4. You may benefit from additional practice to strengthen skills in those areas.

The following rating form allows clients to provide constructive feedback about their social workers' professional skills. Social workers use these ratings to improve the quality of their service to you and other clients. You can be most helpful in this process by thinking carefully about each statement and providing the most accurate rating possible. Use the five-point scale to rate the degree of your agreement with each item. Notice that a *higher* number indicates a greater degree of agreement. Place a check mark in the box below the number that most closely reflects your view.

5 = Strongly Agree
4 = Agree
3 = Undecided
2 = Disagree
1 = Strongly Disagree

Preparing and Beginning Skills Rating Form					
5	4	3	2	1	Statement
☐	☐	☐	☐	☐	S7.1 The interviewer was well acquainted with information that had previously been provided.
☐	☐	☐	☐	☐	S7.2 The interviewer conveyed a sense of professionalism.
☐	☐	☐	☐	☐	S7.3 The interviewer was calm and confident.
☐	☐	☐	☐	☐	S7.4 The interviewer made arrangements in advance so the room, materials, and equipment were all ready for use.
☐	☐	☐	☐	☐	S7.5 The interviewer was eager to hear what I had to say.
☐	☐	☐	☐	☐	S7.6 The interviewer was open-minded and nonjudgmental.
☐	☐	☐	☐	☐	S7.7 The interviewer was well prepared for the meeting.
☐	☐	☐	☐	☐	S7.8 The interview was conducted in a competent manner.
☐	☐	☐	☐	☐	S8.1 The interviewer introduced herself or himself by name and profession.
☐	☐	☐	☐	☐	S8.2 The interviewer learned my name, pronounced it correctly, and used my name at several times during the meeting.
☐	☐	☐	☐	☐	S8.3 The interviewer suggested a general purpose or agenda for this meeting.
☐	☐	☐	☐	☐	S8.4 The interviewer asked me for feedback about the proposed agenda.
☐	☐	☐	☐	☐	S8.5 The interviewer suggested how I could actively participate in this process.
☐	☐	☐	☐	☐	S8.6 The interviewer informed me about relevant laws, ethics, and policies that might affect our work together.

Preparing and Beginning Skills Rating Form					
5	4	3	2	1	Statement
☐	☐	☐	☐	☐	S8.7 The interviewer asked me if I was unclear about anything or had any questions about anything discussed thus far.
☐	☐	☐	☐	☐	S8.8 Through tone of voice, facial expressions, nonverbal communications, and spoken words the interviewer conveyed a clear message that I am a valued and respected person who can contribute as an equal partner in our work together.
					TOTAL

Following a meeting in which the interviewer was prepared and consistently demonstrates proficient use of the beginning skills, interviewees would usually assign ratings of 4 or 5 on each item. Possible total scores for the 16 items range from 16 to 80. Scores of between 64 and 80 indicate overall proficiency. However, make note of any items that receive ratings of less than 4. You may benefit from additional practice to strengthen skills in those areas.

The following rating form allows clients to provide constructive feedback about their social workers' professional skills. Social workers use these ratings to improve the quality of their service to you and other clients. You can be most helpful in this process by thinking carefully about each statement and providing the most accurate rating possible. Use the five-point scale to rate the degree of your agreement with each item. Notice that a *higher* number indicates a greater degree of agreement. Place a check mark in the box below the number that most closely reflects your view.

5 = Strongly Agree
4 = Agree
3 = Undecided
2 = Disagree
1 = Strongly Disagree

Exploring Skills Rating Form	
5 4 3 2 1	Statement
☐ ☐ ☐ ☐ ☐	S10.1 The interviewer encouraged me to discuss in considerable detail the issues that most concern me.
☐ ☐ ☐ ☐ ☐	S10.2 The interviewer encouraged me to discuss aspects of myself that relate to the issues that concern me.
☐ ☐ ☐ ☐ ☐	S10.3 The interviewer encouraged me to discuss aspects of my situation that relate to the issues that concern me.
☐ ☐ ☐ ☐ ☐	S10.4 The interviewer recognized some of my positive abilities, successes, and wisdom.
☐ ☐ ☐ ☐ ☐	S10.5 The interviewer recognized some of the assets, resources, and sources of social support in my life.
☐ ☐ ☐ ☐ ☐	S10.6 The interviewer asked relevant questions that helped me to express myself more fully.
☐ ☐ ☐ ☐ ☐	S10.7 The interviewer periodically summarized my words in her or his own words so that I knew she or he accurately understood what I was trying to say.
☐ ☐ ☐ ☐ ☐	S10.8 The interviewer communicated understanding of my feelings.
☐ ☐ ☐ ☐ ☐	S10.9 The interviewer communicated understanding of the reasons behind my feelings.

Exploring Skills Rating Form					
5	4	3	2	1	Statement
☐	☐	☐	☐	☐	S10.10 The interviewer communicated understanding of something I truly thought or felt but had not yet actually said.
☐	☐	☐	☐	☐	S10.11 In her or his own words, the interviewer summarized the issues that I am most concerned about.
☐	☐	☐	☐	☐	S10.12 In her or his own words, the interviewer summarized my ideas about how or why these issues occur.
☐	☐	☐	☐	☐	S10.13 In her or his own words, the interviewer summarized my ideas about how these issues could be resolved.
					TOTAL

Following a meeting in which the interviewer was prepared and consistently demonstrates proficient use of the exploring skills, interviewees would usually assign ratings of 4 or 5 on each item. Possible total scores for the 13 items range from 13 to 65. Scores of between 52 and 65 indicate overall proficiency. However, make note of any items that receive ratings of less than 4. You may benefit from additional practice to strengthen skills in those areas.

The following rating form allows clients to provide constructive feedback about their social workers' professional skills. Social workers use these ratings to improve the quality of their service to you and other clients. You can be most helpful in this process by thinking carefully about each statement and providing the most accurate rating possible. Use the five-point scale to rate the degree of your agreement with each item. Notice that a *higher* number indicates a greater degree of agreement. Place a check mark in the box below the number that most closely reflects your view.

5 = Strongly Agree
4 = Agree
3 = Undecided
2 = Disagree
1 = Strongly Disagree

Assessing Skills Rating Form	
5 4 3 2 1	**Statement**
☐ ☐ ☐ ☐ ☐	S10.1 The interviewer introduced a possible problem or issue that I had not previously considered.
☐ ☐ ☐ ☐ ☐	S10.2 The interviewer introduced a possible way of thinking about how or why these issues occur.
☐ ☐ ☐ ☐ ☐	S10.3 The interviewer introduced a possible way of thinking about how these issues could be resolved.
☐ ☐ ☐ ☐ ☐	S10.4 The interviewer and I clearly identified and agreed upon the issues that we would work together to resolve.
	TOTAL

Following a meeting in which the interviewer was prepared and consistently demonstrates proficient use of the assessing skills, interviewees would usually assign ratings of 4 or 5 on each item. Possible total scores for the 4 items range from 4 to 20. Scores of between 16 and 20 indicate overall proficiency. However, make note of any items that receive ratings of less than 4. You may benefit from additional practice to strengthen skills in those areas.

The following rating form allows clients to provide constructive feedback about their social workers' professional skills. Social workers use these ratings to improve the quality of their service to you and other clients. You can be most helpful in this process by thinking carefully about each statement and providing the most accurate rating possible. Use the five-point scale to rate the degree of your agreement with each item. Notice that a *higher* number indicates a greater degree of agreement. Place a check mark in the box below the number that most closely reflects your view.

5 = Strongly Agree
4 = Agree
3 = Undecided
2 = Disagree
1 = Strongly Disagree

	Contracting Skills Rating Form
5 4 3 2 1	Statement
☐ ☐ ☐ ☐ ☐	S11.1 The interviewer and I clearly identified and agreed upon the goals that we would work together to achieve.
☐ ☐ ☐ ☐ ☐	S11.2 The interviewer and I agreed upon action plans to pursue our agreed-upon goals.
☐ ☐ ☐ ☐ ☐	S11.3 The interviewer and I identified one or more action steps that I plan to take.
☐ ☐ ☐ ☐ ☐	S11.4 The interviewer and I identified one or more action steps that she or he plans to take.
☐ ☐ ☐ ☐ ☐	S11.5 The interviewer and I agreed upon one or more ways to measure or evaluate progress toward our goals.
☐ ☐ ☐ ☐ ☐	S11.6 The interviewer summarized our agreement so that we both understand our goals and how we plan to accomplish them.
	TOTAL

Following a meeting in which the interviewer was prepared and consistently demonstrates proficient use of the contracting skills, interviewees would usually assign ratings of 4 or 5 on each item. Possible total scores for the 6 items range from 6 to 30. Scores of between 24 and 30 indicate overall proficiency. However, make note of any items that receive ratings of less than 4. You may benefit from additional practice to strengthen skills in those areas.

The following rating form allows clients to provide constructive feedback about their social workers' professional skills. Social workers use these ratings to improve the quality of their service to you and other clients. You can be most helpful in this process by thinking carefully about each statement and providing the most accurate rating possible. Use the five-point scale to rate the degree of your agreement with each item. Notice that a *higher* number indicates a greater degree of agreement. Place a check mark in the box below the number that most closely reflects your view.

5 = Strongly Agree
4 = Agree
3 = Undecided
2 = Disagree
1 = Strongly Disagree

Working and Evaluating Skills Rating Form	
5 4 3 2 1	Statement
☐ ☐ ☐ ☐ ☐	S12.1 The interviewer helped me get ready to take an action step by practicing it with me in a kind of rehearsal.
☐ ☐ ☐ ☐ ☐	S12.2 The interviewer encouraged me to discuss in detail each action step I had agreed to undertake so that I could learn from the experience and improve in the future.
☐ ☐ ☐ ☐ ☐	S12.3 The interviewer and I measured, reviewed, and evaluated progress toward goals so that we both know how things stand.
☐ ☐ ☐ ☐ ☐	S12.4 When I wandered, the interviewer sometimes got us back on track so that we focused on what I really wanted to address.
☐ ☐ ☐ ☐ ☐	S12.5 When I didn't know about something, the interviewer shared information that helped me understand.
☐ ☐ ☐ ☐ ☐	S12.6 The interviewer sometimes offered advice but did so in a way that left me free to accept or reject it.
☐ ☐ ☐ ☐ ☐	S12.7 The interviewer sometimes served as my representative or advocate.
☐ ☐ ☐ ☐ ☐	S12.8 The interviewer sometimes made tentative observations about what was happening in our relationship (that is, between him or her and me) at the very moment it occurred.
☐ ☐ ☐ ☐ ☐	S12.9 The interviewer sometimes took what I said and changed it so that I might think about something in a new or different way.

	Working and Evaluating Skills Rating Form
☐ ☐ ☐ ☐ ☐	S12.10 The interviewer sometimes gently pointed out inconsistencies in my thoughts, words, feelings, or actions so that I could consider the implications of those inconsistencies.
☐ ☐ ☐ ☐ ☐	S12.11 The interviewer reminded me about how many more meetings we would have together.
	TOTAL

Following a meeting in which the interviewer was prepared and consistently demonstrates proficient use of the working and evaluating skills, interviewees would usually assign ratings of 4 or 5 on each item. Possible total scores for the 11 items range from 11 to 55. Scores of between 44 and 55 indicate overall proficiency. However, make note of any items that receive ratings of less than 4. You may benefit from additional practice to strengthen skills in those areas.

The following rating form allows clients to provide constructive feedback about their social workers' professional skills. Social workers use these ratings to improve the quality of their service to you and other clients. You can be most helpful in this process by thinking carefully about each statement and providing the most accurate rating possible. Use the five-point scale to rate the degree of your agreement with each item. Notice that a *higher* number indicates a greater degree of agreement. Place a check mark in the box below the number that most closely reflects your view.

5 = Strongly Agree
4 = Agree
3 = Undecided
2 = Disagree
1 = Strongly Disagree

					Ending Skills Rating Form
5	4	3	2	1	Statement
☐	☐	☐	☐	☐	S13.1 In our final meeting, the interviewer helped me to review what we had done during our time together.
☐	☐	☐	☐	☐	S13.2 In our final meeting, the interviewer helped me to evaluate overall progress.
☐	☐	☐	☐	☐	S13.3 In our final meeting, the interviewer helped me to anticipate how I might apply what I've learned to other actual issues or to those that might possibly emerge sometime in the future.
☐	☐	☐	☐	☐	S13.4 The interviewer sincerely shared her or his thoughts and feelings about concluding our work together.
☐	☐	☐	☐	☐	S13.5 The interviewer helped me to share my thoughts and feelings about concluding our work together.
☐	☐	☐	☐	☐	S13.6 The interviewer said goodbye to me in a way that conveyed respect and appreciation for me.
☐	☐	☐	☐	☐	S13.7 The interviewer let me say goodbye in a way that felt real and sincere to me.
					TOTAL

Following a meeting in which the interviewer was prepared and consistently demonstrates proficient use of the ending skills, interviewees would usually assign ratings of 4 or 5 on each item. Possible total scores for the 7 items range from 7 to 35. Scores of between 28 and 35 indicate overall proficiency. However, make note of any items that receive ratings of less than 4. You may benefit from additional practice to strengthen skills in those areas.

EXPERIENTIAL INTERVIEW EXERCISE—GUIDELINES AND FORMS

EXPERIENTIAL INTERVIEWING EXERCISE: GUIDELINES FOR INTERVIEWING A PRACTICE CLIENT

You are about to embark upon a series of 30-minute interview sessions with a "practice client." You will serve in the role of "social worker" with a classmate or colleague who agrees to assume the role of practice client. The course or practicum instructor, or another professional social worker, must agree to serve the dual roles of: (1) your supervisor and (2) advocate for the practice client.

Social workers always benefit from constructive feedback about their performance, and dedicated learners usually want to maximize the impact of educational experiences. Contact with an instructor during the course of the experiential interviewing exercise makes good sense. His or her ideas and suggestions might increase your learning, enhance your social work skills proficiency, improve the quality of your performance, and perhaps heighten the practice client's satisfaction with the experience. Sometimes, however, practice clients also want or need to discuss the experience with someone other than the person assuming the role of social worker. For instance, during the exercise, a practice client might realize something about her or himself that warrants consideration of a referral to a social worker or other professional helper. At other times, a practice client might feel adversely affected by the experience and want advice from an advocate to help reduce or eliminate the damage. The supervisor/client advocate fulfills those functions and helps ensure the safety and well-being of the people involved—those in the role of practice client as well as those in the role of social worker.

Whoever serves in the role of practice client should understand that the learning exercise will require about 45 minutes of time for each of five meetings spread over the course of several weeks. Each formal interview is scheduled for 30 minutes. Immediately after that, you step out of your respective roles of social worker and practice client and, for 10–15 minutes, you become an active learner who seeks evaluative feedback from your colleague about the nature and quality of the interview, your performance, and her or his thoughts and feelings about the interview. Take notes during the post-interview feedback session so that you can reflect upon them at a later time.

The practice client should also realize that she or he must choose an actual issue to address during the five-session process. However, the issue should be one that is relatively modest and manageable. The practice client should not choose a serious problem, one that is of an urgent nature, or one that is especially tender. Colleagues who are currently dealing with severe issues, those in an especially fragile state, and those in highly vulnerable circumstances probably should not participate as practice clients.

To enhance learning, approach the experiential exercise as if you really are a social worker and your practice client really is your client. Recognize, however, the primary purpose for the learning experience is to help you gain proficiency in the social work skills. Although your colleague may benefit from the experience of assuming the role of practice client, any such benefits would be incidental. The primary purpose for this activity is educational in nature; it is not intended nor should it be interpreted as a therapeutic or professional service. Nonetheless, social work values and ethics apply before, during, and following the learning exercise. Adopt a professional attitude and approach throughout the experience. Maintain your role as social worker and encourage your practice client to do the same. Be sure to maintain confidentiality in verbal discussions with others; and adopt a fictitious name for the practice client to help disguise his or her identity when you take notes and prepare your case record.

Each meeting requires that you engage in the social work skills associated with one or more phases of practice. For example, you would use the preparing skills before you first contact and attempt to recruit a colleague. Such preparation enhances your readiness to engage a prospective practice client from the moment of first contact. Secure the formal consent of your colleague to serve in the role of practice client and maintain the signed document in a safe place. Also, keep audio- or video-recordings in a private, locked location. As you word-process documents for use during the exercise, ensure that they are accurate and carefully prepared at a professional level of quality; however, disguise information that might reveal the identity of the practice client. Create one or two electronic folders to keep your preliminary plans for meeting as well as any notes and documents you prepare throughout the course of the exercise. Ensure that all exercise-related materials are stored in secure locations.

Engage in preparation before the first and all subsequent meetings. During the first meeting, use the beginning skills as well as the basic skills of talking and listening; and do so in a culturally sensitive manner. Several exploring skills might be applicable as well. As part of your planning, anticipate how you might begin and how you might conclude each session. Use relevant exploring and assessing skills during the second meeting; and exploring, assessing, and contracting skills in the third. Use the working and evaluating skills in the fourth meeting; and the ending skills in the fifth. Seeking feedback and most of the exploring skills may be applicable in all interviews.

Keep professional quality records throughout. Following the third meeting, you should be able to prepare a Description, Assessment, and Contract (DAC) or its equivalent to guide the goal-directed efforts of both the practice client and you as the social worker. Following the fourth meeting, word-process a progress record; and after the final interview, prepare a closing summary. When combined, these documents along with additional materials such as a genogram, ecomap, or timeline; your planning notes; and client satisfaction and outcome-related measurement data constitute a Practice Client Case Record.

In summary, the specific tasks and activities for the Experiential Interviewing Exercise are as follows:

◆ **Enlist a Professor or Professional Social Worker to Serve as Supervisor and Client Advocate**
   If you are completing *The Social Work Skills Workbook* as part of a course or a practicum experience, the Experiential Interviewing Exercise may be a required assignment. If so, double check to ensure that your professor or field practicum instructor will indeed serve as your supervisor during the experience and as an advocate for the

practice client as well. If you are undertaking the Experiential Interviewing Exercise as part of your own career-learning, locate a professional social worker and secure his or her consent to fulfill those functions. Do not begin the learning exercise until a professional social worker formally agrees to serve as your supervisor and as an advocate for the practice client.

◆ **Prepare for a Recruitment Contact**
Before contacting a classmate or colleague in an effort to enlist him or her as a participant in the experiential interviewing exercise, use applicable preparing skills—including developing preliminary plans and preparing appropriate documents (such as a description of the exercise, guidelines for the practice client, and a consent to participate form). Word-process the preliminary plans and label the document "Practice Client Recruitment Contact." Deposit it in an electronic folder in a private and secure location to keep all notes and documents related to the Experiential Interviewing Exercise. In preparing for a recruitment contact, you might use some or all of the following preparing skills: (1) preparatory reviewing, (2) preparatory exploring, (3) preparatory consultation, (4) preparatory arranging, (5) preparatory empathy, (6) preparatory self-exploration, (7) centering, and (8) preliminary planning and recording.

◆ **Contact and Recruit a Practice Client**
If your professor or practicum instructor has not assigned a practice client to you, contact a classmate or colleague and use applicable beginning skills to describe the experiential interviewing learning exercise. Obtain his or her informed consent to participate as a practice client over the course of several weeks. In the recruitment contact, you might use some or all of the following beginning skills: (1) introducing yourself, (2) seeking introductions, (3) describing initial purpose, (4) orienting clients or others, (5) discussing policy and ethical factors, and (6) seeking feedback.

◆ **Prepare for the First Meeting with a Practice Client**
Before the first meeting with your practice client (a colleague or classmate who has been introduced to the learning exercise and provided informed consent), use applicable preparing skills. In the process of preparing for the first meeting, you might use some or all of the following skills: (1) preparatory reviewing, (2) preparatory exploring, (3) preparatory consultation, (4) preparatory arranging, (5) preparatory empathy, (6) preparatory self-exploration, (7) centering, and (8) preliminary planning and recording. Word-process your preliminary plans and deposit them in the "Practice Client Case Record Folder." Be sure to disguise the identity of the practice client.

• • • • • • • • • • • •

1. **First Meeting with a Practice Client: Beginning and Exploring**
During the first meeting with your practice client, use applicable beginning and exploring skills. You might use some or all of the following beginning skills: (1) introducing yourself, (2) seeking introductions, (3) describing initial purpose, (4) orienting clients, (5) discussing policy and ethical factors, and (6) seeking feedback. You may find that seeking feedback is useful at many points throughout all interviews. Many of the exploring skills are also almost universally applicable. These include: (1) asking questions, (2) seeking clarification, (3) reflecting content, (4) reflecting feelings, (5) reflecting feelings and meanings, (6) partializing, (7) going beyond what is said, (8) reflecting issues, and (9) reflecting hypotheses.

2. **Second Meeting with a Practice Client: Exploring and Assessing**

   During the second meeting with your practice client, use applicable assessing skills. These skills include: (1) identifying issues, (2) sharing hypotheses, and (3) clarifying issues for work. Some or all of the exploring skills may also be useful. Following the meeting, use the skills of (4) organizing descriptive information and (5) preparing an assessment and case formulation as you prepare word-processed case records.

3. **The Third Meeting: Exploring, Assessing, and Contracting**

   During the third meeting with your practice client, use applicable contracting skills. These include: (1) establishing goals, (2) developing action plans, (3) identifying action steps, (4) planning for evaluation, and (5) summarizing the contract. Several of the assessing and exploring skills may also be useful. Following the meeting, prepare a written summary of the service contract and integrate the description, assessment, and contract sections into a coherent whole.

4. **The Fourth Meeting: Working and Evaluating**

   During the fourth meeting with your practice client, use applicable working and evaluating skills. These include: (1) rehearsing action steps, (2) reviewing action steps, (3) evaluating, (4) focusing, (5) educating, (6) advising, (7) representing, (8) responding with immediacy, (9) reframing, (10) confronting inconsistencies, and (11) pointing out endings. Several of the exploring skills and perhaps some of the assessing and contracting skills may also be useful. Following the meeting, use the skill of (12) recording progress as you prepare a word-processed progress note about the meeting.

5. **The Fifth Meeting: Ending**

   During the fifth and final meeting with your practice client, use applicable ending skills. These include: (1) reviewing the process, (2) final evaluating, and (3) sharing ending feelings and saying goodbye. Several of the exploring and perhaps other phase-related skills may also be useful. Following the meeting, use the skill of (4) recording the closing summary as you prepare a word-processed progress note about the final meeting and the series as a whole.

STUDENT SOCIAL WORKER SIGNATURE SECTION

I _____ (insert your name as the student social worker) understand the requirements of the multiweek experiential interviewing exercise—including the ethical obligation to ensure the practice client's personal safety and well-being and to safeguard his/her privacy, confidentiality, and personal identity in any and all verbal and written communications.

_____   _____

(Signature of Student Social Worker)   (Date)

Summary of the Multiweek Experiential Interviewing Exercise		
Meeting Number	**Phase/Assignment**	**Tasks and Activities**
	Preparing for a Recruitment Contact Chapter 7: Experiential Interviewing Exercise	Before contacting a classmate or colleague in an effort to enlist him or her as a participant in the experiential interviewing exercise, use applicable preparing skills—including developing a preliminary plan, preparing appropriate documents (such as a description of the exercise, guidelines for the practice client, and an agreement to participate form)—and create an electronic folder in a private and secure location to keep all notes and documents related to the Experiential Interviewing Exercise.
	Contact and Recruit a Practice Client Chapter 8: Experiential Interviewing Exercise	Conduct a practice client recruitment contact with a colleague. If she or he genuinely understands the nature of the assignment and agrees to participate, provide a consent form that includes your signature as well as your colleague's. Store the consent form in a secure location.
1	Preparing for the First Meeting and Beginning with the Practice Client Chapter 9: Experiential Interviewing Exercise	Before the first contact with your practice client, use applicable preparing skills—including developing a preliminary plan—and create an electronic case record in a private and secure location to keep all notes and documents related to the Experiential Interviewing Exercise. Disguise the identity of your practice client. Use applicable beginning skills and exploring skills during the first 30-minute interview. Begin to prepare the description section of a DAC or its equivalent. Step out of roles and engage in a 10- to 15-minute post-interview feedback session.
2	Exploring and Assessing Chapter 10: Experiential Interviewing Exercises	Use applicable exploring skills and assessing skills during a 30-minute interview. Begin to prepare the assessment section of a DAC or its equivalent. Step out of roles and engage in a 10- to 15-minute post-interview feedback session.
3	Assessing and Contracting Chapter 11: Experiential Interviewing Exercise	Use applicable assessing skills and contracting skills during a 30-minute interview. Several exploring skills may be useful as well. Begin to prepare the contract section of a DAC or its equivalent. Step out of roles and engage in a 10- to 15-minute post-interview feedback session.

Summary of the Multiweek Experiential Interviewing Exercise		
Meeting Number	**Phase/Assignment**	**Tasks and Activities**
4	Working & Evaluating Chapter 12: Experiential Interviewing Exercise	Use applicable working and evaluating skills during a 30-minute interview. Several exploring skills may be useful as may skills from other phases. Prepare a progress note in SOAIGP or equivalent form. Step out of roles and engage in a 10- to 15-minute post-interview feedback session.
5	Ending Chapter 13: Experiential Interviewing Exercise	Use applicable ending skills during a 30-minute interview. Several exploring skills and working and evaluating skills may be useful as well. Prepare a closing summary. Step out of roles and engage in a 10- to 15-minute post-interview feedback session.

SOCIAL WORK SUPERVISOR & PRACTICE CLIENT ADVOCATE
AGREEMENT FORM

As a _____ (insert title; for example, social work professor, practicum instructor, professional social worker), I agree to serve as both a **social work supervisor** for you _____ (insert student's name) in your role of student social worker and as a **client advocate** for the person serving in the role of your role of practice client. Questions, concerns, complications, and grievances that you as the student social worker or that your colleague as the practice client have at any point before, during, or after the multiweek experiential interviewing exercise should be addressed to me. In this learning exercise, the safety and well-being of the participants take precedence over the educational objectives.

_____   _____

(Signature of Supervisor/Advocate)   (Date)

_____   _____

(Phone Numbers)   (E-mail Address)

_____   _____

(Signature of Student Social Worker)   (Date)

_____   _____

(Phone Numbers)   (E-mail Address)

GUIDELINES AND CONSENT FORM FOR THE PRACTICE CLIENT:

EXPERIENTIAL INTERVIEWING EXPERIENCE

1. Choose one or two real but relatively modest issues, problems, or concerns that you can personally manage. Do not choose any that have the potential to overwhelm your coping capacities. Be prepared to discuss in considerable detail the identified issues as well as personal and situational aspects that relate to them. Because social workers adopt a person-in-environment perspective, it is quite likely that the interviews could be broad in scope and quite in-depth—especially when it comes to the origin, development, duration, and severity of the issues themselves.

2. Create a fictitious name (pseudonym) that you and the student social worker can use throughout the process. Although the student social worker is ethically committed to maintaining your privacy and confidentially throughout the process, please adopt pseudonyms for yourself as well as for family members, friends, colleagues, and other people that you might discuss during the interviews. That provides some added protection. Also, disguise those characteristics that might readily identify you. For example, if you mention that your mother is the city's mayor, your identity might be compromised, as it would be if you provided your actual home address during a recorded interview.

3. Being honest about aspects of the identified issues, yourself, your history, and your life circumstances helps to add realism to the learning experience. Remember, however, to disguise information that might obviously compromise your privacy and reveal your true identity.

4. Realize that the exercise is educational in nature and is intended to provide the student social worker with opportunities to practice the social work skills. Do not expect that the social worker will actually be of any service whatsoever! She or he may be; but the primary purpose is not therapeutic or service oriented. Rather it is fundamentally educational in nature.

5. Understand that the experiential interviewing exercise will require you to meet five times with a student social worker over the course of several weeks. Each meeting is 30 minutes in length. At the end of that time, you and the student social worker will step out of your roles to engage in a 10- to 15-minute discussion about the interview. Be prepared to provide constructive evaluative feedback to the student social worker. In these post-interview processing sessions. As a practice rather than an actual client, you are in a valuable position to provide extraordinarily helpful feedback to a colleague who is learning to serve as a social worker. Maximize the learning potential by frankly sharing your thoughts and feelings about each meeting and about the student social worker's performance.

6. Learn how to contact your client advocate and feel free to do so if you have questions about the multiweek learning exercise; about either the practice client or social worker roles; about any excessive personal distress that arises during the exercise; or about anything about the experience that concerns you. Make note of the client advocate's name and contact information.

7. Learn how to contact your practice social worker and feel free to do so if you have questions or need to reschedule a meeting. Make note of his or her name and contact information.

Client Advocate's Name: _____

Office Address: _____

_____

Phones: _____

E-mails: _____

Student Social Worker's Name: _____

Phones: _____

E-mails: _____

    I understand the requirements of this multiweek experiential interviewing exercise and agree to participate as a practice client for five meetings—each of which is scheduled to last no longer than 1 hour. I also understand that this is an educational activity intended to help the student social worker practice and develop proficiency in essential social work skills.

_____   _____

(Signature of Practice Client)   (Date)

ALPHABETIZED LIST OF FEELING WORDS

abandoned
abased
abashed
abdicated
abducted
abhor
abominable
abrasive
abrupt
accepted
acclaimed
accused
accustomed
achieved
acknowledged
acquiesced
acrimonious
adamant
adapted
adept
adjusted
admired
admonished
adored
adrift
adventurous
adverse
advocated
affected
affectionate
affinity
afraid

aggravated
aggressive
aggrieved
aghast
agile
agitated
aglow
agonized
agony
agreeable
aimless
alarmed
alarming
alienated
alive
alleviate
alluring
alone
aloof
altruistic
amazed
ambiguous
ambitious
ambivalent
ameliorate
amicable
amused
anemic
angelic
angry
angst
anguish

animosity
annoyed
anomie
anonymous
antagonistic
antagonized
anticipation
antsy
anxious
apathetic
apocalyptic
apologetic
appalling
appetizing
apprehensive
approachable
approving
arbitrary
arcane
archaic
ardent
ardor
arduous
argumentative
arresting
arrogant
artificial
ashamed
assailed
assaulted
assertive
assuaged

assured
astonished
astounding
attuned
attached
attentive
attracted
audacious
auspicious
aversive
awarded
awful
back-sided
backstabbed
bad
balanced
balked
bamboozled
banking
barrage
bashful
basic
battered
bawdy
beaming
beaten
beautiful
beckoning
becoming
bedazzled
bedeviled
bedraggled

befuddled
begrudging
beguiling
beholden
belittled
bellicose
belligerent
belonging
bemoan
beneficent
benign
berated
bereaved
bereft
bested
betrayed
beware
bewildered
bewitched
biased
bidden
bigoted
bitter
blah
blamed
bleary
blessed
blissful
blocked
blue
blunted
blushed
bogged-down
boggled
bolstered
bonded
bored
botched
bothered
boundless
bountiful
boxed-in
braced
branded
brave
brazen
breached
bright

brilliant
brisk
broached
broken
browbeaten
bruised
brushed-off
brutalized
bucking
buck-passing
bugged
bulldozed
bullied
buoyant
burdened
burned
burned-out
busted
butchered
cakewalk
calculating
calling
callous
callow
calm
cancerous
candid
canned
capitulated
capricious
capsulated
captivated
captive
care
carefree
careful
careless
caretaking
caring
caroused
carping
cast-off
cataclysmic
catalyst
catapulted
catastrophic
catharsis
caught

caustic
cautious
celibate
cemented
censored
censured
certain
challenged
chancy
changeable
charismatic
charitable
charmed
charming
chased
chaste
cheap
cheapened
cheeky
cheered
cheerful
cheesy
cherished
chivalrous
chummy
chump
civil
clammy
clandestine
clean
cocksure
coherent
cohesive
coincidental
cold
cold-blooded
cold-shouldered
collared
collusive
combative
combustible
comfortable
come-on
coming-out
commanded
committed
compartmentalized
compassionate

compelling
compensated
competent
complacent
complementary
complete
compliant
complicated
complimented
composed
comprehensible
comprehensive
compressed
compromised
concentrating
concerned
conciliatory
conclusive
concocted
condemned
condescending
condoned
conducive
confident
confined
conflicted
congenial
congratulated
congruent
connected
conquered
conscientious
considerate
considered
consoled
consoling
conspiratorial
constant
consternation
constrained
constricted
constructive
contaminated
contemplative
contented
contentious
contributory
convenient

convinced
convincing
cool
corrected
corroborate
corrosive
cosmetic
counted
countered
courageous
courteous
covered
cowardly
cozy
crabby
crafty
craggy
crappy
credible
creepy
crestfallen
cried
cringe
critical
criticize
crooked
cross
crossed
crucified
cruddy
crummy
crushed
crystallized
curative
curious
cursed
cutoff
dangerous
debased
dejected
demeaned
demure
denigrated
depressed
detached
determined
devoted
disappointed

disapproval
disbelief
disgust
dismal
dismayed
displeased
distant
distasteful
distrust
disturbed
doubtful
dubious
ecstatic
elated
elevated
embarrassed
empty
enamored
energetic
enervated
enraged
enriched
enthusiastic
entrusted
envious
euphoric
exasperated
excited
exhausted
fantastic
fearful
fearless
ferocious
flighty
flustered
fondness
forgiveness
forgotten
forsaken
frazzled
friendly
frightened
frustrated
gagged
galvanized
gamy
garrulous
gawky

generous
genial
gentle
genuine
glad
glee
glib
gloomy
glow
glum
golden
good
graceful
graceless
gracious
grand
great
greedy
green
gregarious
grief
grim
gross
gruesome
grubby
gruff
grumpy
grungy
guarded
guiltless
guilty
gullible
gutsy
gutted
haggard
hammered
hamstrung
handcuffed
handicapped
handy
hang-dogged
hapless
happy
harassed
hard
hard-boiled
hard-edged
hardheaded

hardy
harmful
harmless
harried
hate
hated
haunting
hazardous
hazy
healthful
healthy
heartache
heartbroken
heartless
heartsick
heartwarming
helpful
helpless
hesitant
high-spirited
hoggish
hog-tied
homesick
honorable
hope
hopeful
hopeless
horny
horrendous
horrible
horrified
hostile
hot
hotblooded
hotheaded
huffy
humble
hungry
hung up
hurried
hurt
hyped
hysterical
ice-cold
idiotic
idyllic
ignominious
ill-at-ease

impatient	jerky	manipulative	nostalgic
impersonal	jolly	martyred	nosy
impetuous	joyful	masterful	noteworthy
impotent	joyless	mature	notorious
impressive	joyous	mean	oafish
impulsive	jubilant	meaningful	obdurate
inadequate	judged	meaningless	obedient
incoherent	judgmental	mean-spirited	object
incompetent	just	mediocre	obligated
incomplete	keen	meditative	obnoxious
inconsiderate	kind	melancholy	obscene
indebted	kindhearted	mellow	obstinate
indecisive	kinky	melodramatic	obstructionist
independent	kooky	mercurial	odd
indestructible	laborious	methodical	odious
indifferent	lenient	mind-boggling	offensive
indignant	light-headed	mindful	onerous
indiscreet	lighthearted	mindless	optimistic
indispensable	limited	mischievous	ornery
indulgent	lonely	miserable	outrage
inept	lonesome	mistrust	outrageous
infantile	loss	misty	pained
infatuated	lost	misunderstood	panic
inferior	lousy	monotonous	panic-stricken
inhibited	lovable	monstrous	paranoid
injurious	love	monumental	passionate
innocent	lovely	moody	passive
insane	lovesick	mortified	patchy
insatiable	love-struck	motivated	patient
insolent	low	mournful	peaceful
inspirational	loyal	muddled	penalized
intense	luckless	murky	permissive
interested	lucky	mushy	perplexed
intimate	ludicrous	mysterious	persecuted
intolerable	lukewarm	nasty	persistent
intolerant	mad	natural	personable
intoxicated	maddening	naughty	pessimistic
intrusive	magical	nauseous	petty
invincible	magnanimous	necessary	petulant
irate	magnetic	needful	phobic
irritable	magnificent	needy	phony
irritated	majestic	negative	picky
itchy	maladjusted	neglected	pitiful
jaded	malaise	neglectful	pivotal
jagged	malicious	nervous	pleasing
jaundiced	malignant	nice	pleasurable
jaunty	manic	noble	plentiful
jealous	manipulated	normal	poetic

poignant
poisonous
polluted
pout
praised
praiseworthy
prejudicial
pressure
presumptuous
prickly
pride
prideful
protective
proud
prudish
pulled
pushed
put-off
puzzled
quake
qualified
qualm
quandary
quarrelsome
queasy
quizzical
radiant
radiate
radical
rage
ragged
rancor
raped
rapture
rash
raucous
raunchy
rebellious
rebuffed
recalcitrant
reckless
reclusive
refreshed
regretful
reinvigorate
rejected
rejoice
rejuvenated

relaxed
released
relentless
relieved
relish
reluctant
remorse
remorseful
remorseless
remote
renewed
repellent
repentant
reprehensible
reprimanded
reproached
repugnant
repulsive
resentful
resentment
reserved
resigned
resilient
resistant
resolute
resolved
resourceful
respectful
responsible
responsive
restful
restless
restricted
reticent
retiring
revolting
revulsion
rewarding
ridiculed
risky
rosy
rotten
rough
rude
rueful
rugged
ruined
rundown

rush
rushed
sacked
sacred
sacrificial
sacrilegious
sacrosanct
sad
saddled
safe
sanctified
sanctimonious
sanguine
satisfied
scandalized
scandalous
scapegoated
scarce
scared
scarred
scattered
scrambled
scrapped
scrawny
searching
seasoned
secure
sedated
seductive
seedy
seeking
sensational
sensitive
sensual
sentimental
serious
settled
severe
sexual
shady
shaggy
shaken
shaky
shame
shameful
shameless
sheepish
shifty

shocked
shortchanged
shunned
sick
sickening
sincere
sinful
singled-out
sinister
skeptical
sleazy
sleepless
sleepy
slick
smug
soiled
solemn
solid
sordid
sorrow
spacey
spellbound
spiritual
spiteful
splendid
split
spoiled
spooky
squeamish
stable
stalked
steady
stern
stilted
stodgy
stressed
stretched
strong
strung-out
stuck
stumped
stunned
sullen
sunk
super
supported
supportive
surly

surprised
suspicious
sympathetic
taboo
taciturn
tacky
tactful
tactless
tainted
taken
taken-in
tangled
tattered
teased
tedious
teed-off
tempted
tempting
tenacious
tender
tension
tenuous
terminal
terrible
terrific
terrified
terrorized
testy
thankful
therapeutic
thick-skinned
thin-skinned
thoughtful
thoughtless
thrashed
threatened
threatening
thrifty
thrilled
thrilling
thunderstruck
ticked
ticked-off
timid
tingle
tingling

tired
tireless
tiresome
tolerate
torment
torpid
touched
tough
toxic
tragic
tranquil
transcendent
transformed
trapped
trashed
traumatic
treacherous
tricked
tricky
triggered
tripped
triumphant
trivial
troubled
troubling
trust
tuckered
turbulent
turned-off
turned-on
twinkling
tyrannized
ubiquitous
ugly
umbrage
unabashed
unaccepted
unaccustomed
unacknowledged
unappealing
unappreciated
unashamed
unbearable
uncared-for
uncertain
unclean

uncomfortable
undaunted
undecided
understood
undesirable
undisturbed
unequal
unfaithful
unfavorable
unglued
unified
unimportant
united
unjust
unkind
unlucky
unpleasant
unproductive
unreasonable
unrelenting
unrepentant
unresponsive
unsafe
unselfconscious
unselfish
unstable
upbeat
uprooted
upstaged
uptight
urgent
vacant
vain
valiant
valued
vandalized
vengeful
victimized
victorious
vigilant
vigorous
vindicated
virtuous
violated
violent
vital

vitriolic
vituperative
vulnerable
wacky
wane
wanted
wanting
washed-out
washed-up
wasted
weak
weakened
well-adjusted
well-balanced
well-intentioned
well-meaning
well-rounded
wicked
wide-awake
wide-eyed
wild
wild-eyed
wily
winced
winded
wiped-out
wired
wishful
withdrawn
wobbly
wonderful
wondrous
worried
worthless
worthwhile
worthy
wounded
wretched
wrought-up
xenophobic
yielded
yielding
zealous
zestful

DESCRIPTION, ASSESSMENT, AND CONTRACT (DAC): LYNN B. CHASE

I. Description

  A. Client Identification

    1. Date/Time of Interview: January 13/3:30–5:00 P.M.; Interviewed by Susan Holder, LSW

    2. Person Interviewed: Lynn B. Chase, Date of Birth: October 5, Age: 34

    3. Residence: 1212 Clearview Drive, Central City

    4. Home phone: 223-1234

    5. Employment: Assembler at Fox Manufacturing Co.

    6. Business phone: 567-5678

      a. Household Composition: Lynn Chase is married to Richard S. Chase, 35-year-old carpenter with Crass Construction Company—work phone 789-7890. They have a 12-year-old son, Robert L. Chase, sixth-grade student at Hope Middle School.

      b. Referral Source: Sandra Fowles (friend of Lynn Chase)

  B. Person, Family and Household, and Community Systems

    1. Person System

    Lynn Chase prefers to be addressed as "Lynn." She described herself as "Irish-American" and said she was "raised as a Roman Catholic." She indicated that her maiden name was Shaughnessy. She looked to me to be approximately 5 feet 6 inches tall and of medium build. On the date of this interview, I noticed that she wore contemporary slacks and blouse. I observed what appeared to be dark circles under her eyes, and the small muscles in her forehead looked tense. She seemed to walk slowly and expressed an audible sigh as she sat down. She spoke in an accent common to this area—although in a slow and apparently deliberate fashion. I noticed that she occasionally interrupted her speech to pause for several seconds, then sighed before resuming her speech.

2. Family and Household System

As reflected in the attached intergenerational family genogram [see Figure 2.1 in Chapter 2] that Mrs. Chase and I prepared during the initial interview, the household is composed of Lynn, Richard, Robert, and a mongrel dog, "Sly." They have lived on Clearview Drive for 5 years and "like it there." Their family life is "busy." During the week, Monday through Friday, both Lynn and Richard work from 8:00 A.M. to 5:00 P.M. One parent, usually Lynn, helps Robert ready himself for school and waits with him until the school bus stops at a nearby street corner at about 7:15 A.M. Then she drives herself to work. After school, Robert takes the bus home, arriving at about 3:45 P.M. He stays alone at home until his parents arrive at about 5:45 P.M. Mrs. Chase indicated that Robert and his father have a very positive relationship. They go to sporting events together and both enjoy fishing. Robert was a member of a Little League baseball team this past summer. His dad went to every game. She described her own relationship with Robert as "currently strained." She also indicated that although she "loves her husband, there is not much joy and romance in the relationship at this time."

3. Community System

As reflected in the attached eco-map (see Figure 2.3 in Chapter 2), Mrs. Chase indicated that the Chase family is involved with several other social systems. Mrs. Chase reported that the family regularly attends the First Methodist Church, although "not every week." She said that she occasionally helps with bake sales and other church activities. She indicated that Robert goes to Sunday school almost every week. Mrs. Chase said that her husband Richard does not engage in many social activities. "He doesn't really have close friends. Robert and I are his friends." She said that Richard attends Robert's sporting events and goes fishing with him. Outside of work and those activities with Robert, Richard spends most of his time working on the house or in the yard. She said that Richard has a workshop in the basement and constructs furniture for the home.

Mrs. Chase reported that Robert has generally been a good student. She said that his teachers tell her that he is shy. When called upon in class, they said, he speaks in a quiet and hesitant voice but usually has thoughtful answers to questions. Mrs. Chase indicated that Robert had played very well on his Little League baseball team this past summer. She said that his coach thought highly of him and believed that he would make the high school team in a few years. Mrs. Chase said that her son has two or three close friends in the neighborhood.

Mrs. Chase reported that the family lives in a middle-class neighborhood. She indicates that, racially, it is minimally integrated and that the rate of crime is low and the neighbors friendly. She indicated that most of the home owners tend to maintain their property carefully. Mrs. Chase said that her family is friendly with several families in the neighborhood, and perhaps once every month or so, two or three of the families get together for dinner or a cookout.

Mrs. Chase reported that her job is "okay" and she likes the people there. She indicated that her husband truly loves his work: "Being a carpenter is what he's made for."

C. Presenting Problems/Issues of Concern

Mrs. Chase said that she has been concerned lately because she and her son have been getting into arguments "all the time." She said that she does not know what causes the trouble. She reported that she becomes critical and angry toward Robert at the slightest provocation. She said that Robert is "not misbehaving" and that "it's really my own problem." She indicated that about 6 months ago she began to become more irritable with Robert and, to some extent, with Richard as well. She reported that she hasn't slept well and has lost about 10 pounds during that 6-month period. She indicated that she took up smoking again after quitting some 5 years ago and has begun to have terrible headaches several times each week. Mrs. Chase reported that these issues began about the time that she took the job at Fox Manufacturing 6 months ago. "Before that I stayed at home to care for Robert and the household."

When asked what led her to take the job, she said, "We don't have any real savings and we'll need money for Robert's college education. I thought I'd better start saving while we have a few years before he leaves. Also, one of my friends said there was an opening at Fox and that she'd love me to work there with her." Mrs. Chase indicated that she hoped these services would help her to feel less irritable, sleep better, have fewer headaches, discontinue smoking, and have fewer arguments with her son and husband.

D. Assets, Resources, and Strengths
Mrs. Chase acknowledged that she has an above-average intellect and a capacity to consider thoughtfully various aspects and dimensions of needs and problems/issues. She reported that she is extremely responsible: "At times, too much so." She said that she is dependable in fulfilling her various roles. Mrs. Chase said that the family has sufficient financial resources and that her job has provided them with a "little bit more than we actually need." She indicated that the family lives in a "nice home in a safe and pleasant neighborhood." She said that her job is secure. She indicated that even though she has worked there for only 6 months, her employer values her work highly and her colleagues enjoy her company. Mrs. Chase reported that she has several close women friends who provide her with support and understanding. She mentioned, however, that "most of the time I am the one who provides support to them." She said that she feels loved by her husband and indicated that both her husband and son would be willing to do anything for her.

E. Referral Source and Process; Collateral Information
Ms. Sandra Fowles, friend and neighbor, referred Mrs. Chase to this agency. Ms. Fowles is a former client of this agency. In talking about Mrs. Chase, Ms. Fowles said that she is "an incredibly kind and thoughtful woman who would give you the shirt off her back. She may be too kind for her own good." Ms. Fowles made preliminary contact with the agency on behalf of Mrs. Chase and asked whether agency personnel had time to meet with her. Subsequently, agency staff made a telephone contact with Mrs. Chase and scheduled an appointment for this date and time.

F. Social History
1. Developmental
   Mrs. Chase reported that she believed that her mother's pregnancy and her own birth and infancy were "normal." She described her childhood as "unhappy" (see personal and familial section below).

2. Personal, Familial, and Cultural
   As reflected in the attached intergenerational genogram (see Figure 2.2 in Chapter 2), Mrs. Chase reported the following about her personal and family history. She comes from a family of five. Her mother and father married while in their late teens. Her mother became pregnant with Lynn right away. Mrs. Chase is the eldest sibling. She has a brother 1 year younger and a sister 5 years her junior. Her parents are alive

and, she said, "Somehow, they are still married." Mrs. Chase reported that during her childhood her father "was, and still is, a workaholic" who was rarely home. She described her mother as an "unstable, angry, and critical woman who never praised me for anything and always put me down." Mrs. Chase said that she "raised her younger sister" because her mother was then drinking all the time. Mrs. Chase indicated that her mother has refrained from drinking alcohol for the past 3 years and now goes to Alcoholics Anonymous meetings. She described the relationship between her mother and father as "awful—they have hated each other for years." She said, "They don't divorce because they're Catholic." Mrs. Chase said that her mother disapproved of her marriage to Richard because he had been married once before. She said that her mother would not attend her wedding. She said that her mother continues to berate Richard and "frequently criticizes the way I am raising Robert too."

Mrs. Chase reported that she rarely sees her mother, who lives 200 miles away, but does visit her sister about once a month. She said that her sister frequently needs emotional support, advice, and sometimes financial assistance as well. Mrs. Chase said that her sister had formerly abused alcohol and drugs, but the problem is "now under control."

Mrs. Chase said that her husband's family was "even more messed up than mine—if that's possible." She indicated that Richard came from a family of five. She reported that his father abandoned the family when Richard was 9 and his sisters were 10 and 7. Mrs. Chase said that Richard's father had a serious drinking problem and that Richard remembered his father frequently beating both his mother and himself. Mrs. Chase indicated that Richard grew up in very destitute circumstances and learned to value money. She reported that even today he closely watches how the family's money is spent and worries that "we'll end up broke."

Mrs. Chase reported that her childhood was an unhappy one. She said that she remembers feeling "different" from other children. She indicated that as a child she was very shy, often afraid, and easily intimidated by other children. She reported that she often felt guilty and ashamed when parents or teachers criticized or corrected her. She indicated that she always tried to be "good" and, she continued, "for the most part—at least until my teenage years—I was." She said that she received excellent grades in school, although she remembered that other children sometimes taunted her by calling her a "teacher's pet." She said that she was slightly overweight during her childhood years and always thought of herself as "fat." She indicated that she had only a few friends during her younger years. She remembered one or two close childhood friends and described them as "shy and unattractive too." She recalled occasions when other children she had hoped would become friends "rejected" her. She remembered feeling sad and depressed on many occasions throughout her childhood.

3. Critical Events

As reflected in the attached critical events timeline (see Figure 2.4 in Chapter 2), Mrs. Chase described an incident that occurred when she was about 12 years old. She said that a boy she had liked said she was "fat" in front of a group of her peers. She said that she felt humiliated and "stayed at home and cried for days." She also recalled a time when she was about 14 or 15. She said she had begun to explore her body and to experiment with masturbation. She indicated that she found it pleasurable but believed that such behavior was sinful. She said that she discussed it with a priest during a regular confession. Mrs. Chase said that the priest became "very angry" at her and told her in a "loud and judgmental voice" to "stop abusing herself in that disgusting way."

She said that she felt horribly guilty and ashamed. She reported that this experience in particular led her to leave the Catholic Church a few years later. Mrs. Chase indicated that she has never been the victim of rape or any other violent crime. She did recall, however, several occasions when a male relative (maternal uncle) attempted to kiss her and fondle her breasts. She said that each time, she pushed him away but she remembered that she felt dirty and disgusted anyway. She said she was approximately 12 or 13 years old at the time and never told anyone about what had happened.

4. Sexual
Mrs. Chase reported that she did not date until her senior year in high school, when she went out with one boy a few times. She said that she "lost her virginity" in this relationship. She reported that she had sex with "lots of boys" after that but that she "never really enjoyed it." She indicated that she met her future husband Richard about 2 years after graduation from high school and that, she was "pleased to say," has since found sex to be pleasurable and satisfying. She said that her sex life has been "great throughout our marriage" but that she has not had much interest during the last several months.

5. Alcohol and Drug Use
Mrs. Chase stated that she does not now have an alcohol or drug use problem but recalled drinking heavily as an 18-year-old. She said that after she graduated from high school, she ran around with a crowd that "partied all the time." She said that she drank a lot of alcohol at that time. She indicated that at that time she sometimes drank in order to "belong" and to feel comfortable in sexual relations with boys.

6. Medical/Physical/Biological
Mrs. Chase reported that she has not had any major medical or physical problems except for an enlarged cyst in her uterus. She had that surgically removed approximately 8 years ago. She said that since that time she has been "unable to get pregnant again," although "both Richard and I wished we could have another child." She said that she has concluded that "it's not going to happen," and "I guess that's what's meant to be."

Mrs. Chase said that she "gained control of the weight problem" during the early years of her marriage by going to Weight Watchers. She indicated that she had recently spoken with her medical doctor about her occasional feelings of extreme fatigue, her change in sleep patterns, the unwanted loss of weight, and the periodic headaches. Her doctor could find nothing physically wrong and raised the question of "stress-related symptoms."

7. Legal
Mrs. Chase indicated that she and her family have not had any difficulties with the legal or criminal justice systems.

8. Educational
Mrs. Chase reported that she has a high school education and has taken approximately 2 years of college courses. She said that she had taken a course each semester until about 6 months ago, when she discontinued an evening course to "be at home more."

9. Employment
Mrs. Chase reported that she had worked in both secretarial and administrative positions following graduation from high school. She said that when Robert was born, she quit working outside the home to care for him. When he went to grammar school, she went back to work part-time. She said that she was laid off from that job about 3 years ago and was unable to find another part-time job that would enable her to be home at the end of Robert's school day. She indicated that a little more than

6 months ago, she and Richard decided that Robert was old enough to be at home alone for a couple of hours each day. She therefore applied for and secured the full-time position at Fox Manufacturing.

10. Recreational

Mrs. Chase reported that over the years she has found great pleasure in gardening. She also said, however, that during the last year or so she has discontinued that activity. She indicated that she thought she could rekindle that sense of satisfaction if she were to resume gardening again at some point in the future.

11. Religious/Spiritual

Mrs. Chase reported that she quit going to the Catholic Church at the age of 18 when she graduated from high school. She said she did not attend any church until the birth of her child. She indicated that she and her husband then decided that they wanted their children to have some religious involvement. She remembered joining the neighborhood Methodist Church because "it was nearby."

12. Prior Psychological, Social, or Medical Service

Mrs. Chase reported that she had not sought or received social or psychological services before and has not taken medication for depression. She reported that her mother has been in "therapy" for approximately 4 years.

II. Tentative Assessment of the Person-Issue-Situation

A. Problems/Issues

1. Nature, Duration, Frequency, Severity, and Urgency

The issues of irritability and argumentativeness toward her son and husband, shame and guilt following expressions of anger or arguments, sleeplessness, weight loss, headaches, and resumption of cigarette smoking appeared to emerge at about the time Mrs. Chase accepted full-time employment outside the home. She indicated that she had not experienced these symptoms previously, although she did say that her adolescent years were painful. At this point, it is not certain that her job is or will be as satisfying to her as child rearing and homemaking have been. There may be role strain or conflict between the family and work roles. As we attempted to analyze this issue, Mrs. Chase and I wondered if the symptoms might be indicative of increased stress associated with expanded demands on her time and energy and changes in roles and role identities. Although she now works at least 40 hours per week at her paid job, she also continues to perform all of the family and household duties she fulfilled before taking the outside job. Mrs. Chase appears to assume a protective, hard-working, caretaker role with her husband and son, siblings, and friends. Indeed, she seems to hold herself responsible for the thoughts, feelings, and behaviors of all members of her family.

2. Risk and Protective Factors; Exceptions

In a general sense, assumption of the full-time job seems to have precipitated the onset of the issues of concern. Mrs. Chase and I wondered if the symptoms may represent an indirect attempt to secure greater attention, appreciation, gratitude, and support from her husband and son or, if they worsen, to provide reasonable cause to quit the job and return to her previous family and household roles. The immediate precursors to the symptoms appear related to Mrs. Chase's beliefs and expectations about herself and perhaps others. She reports that she frequently worries about various things she "should" or "ought" to be doing and feels guilty that she is not fulfilling her parental, spousal, and household (homemaker) roles as well as she previously did.

According to Mrs. Chase, there were two occasions during the past 6 months when she felt a sense of contentment and happiness. The first occurred when Richard, Robert, and she went on a weekend trip to another city. They stayed in a hotel, ate in restaurants, went to a baseball game, and spent time talking and joking with each other. On the other occasion, Richard and she went on an overnight trip to attend a family friend's wedding.

The issues of concern have existed for about 6 months. Mrs. Chase and I estimated the severity of the problems and symptoms to be in the moderate range. She continues to fulfill all of her responsibilities in a competent manner. Mrs. Chase herself seems to experience the greatest discomfort from the issues—although Robert and to some extent, Richard, are also affected by the irritability and argumentativeness. Mrs. Chase and I concur that the issues are not life threatening and do not require immediate, emergency, or intensive intervention.

B. Person-in-Environment

1. Personal Factors

Mrs. Chase reflects a strong ethic of obligation and responsibility, especially toward her son and husband, but to most other people as well. She holds herself to extremely high standards and often feels guilty or worried that she's not doing well enough. She feels ashamed when she makes mistakes or believes she has hurt someone's feelings. She rarely engages in free and spontaneous play, relaxation, or recreation, and often feels quite uncomfortable when she does so. She previously enjoyed gardening, but since she took the full-time job at Fox Manufacturing, she has become reluctant to allow herself time for "unproductive" leisure and relaxation. Shortly after we began to explore the nature and scope of her expectations and caretaking activities, she wondered aloud if she might be doing too much for others. We wondered if she might feel stressed and guilty about the possibility that she might be unable to fulfill her responsibilities in the superior manner that she expects of herself. Indeed, she may feel guilty that she now spends less time with her son Robert and worried she may be unable to protect him from potentially dangerous circumstances. We wondered if this idea about protecting Robert might relate to her recollections of her own childhood, when she had not felt loved and protected. We also wondered if she might worry that Robert was approaching the age at which she, as a senior in high school, first had sex and began to drink—sometimes heavily. We wondered if she might be, in a sense, overprotecting her adolescent son at a time when he might be dealing with issues related to identity and the development of autonomy. Mrs. Chase, directly or indirectly, may be uneasy and unclear concerning her parenting role during this time. Her own adolescent experiences and the shame she felt may continue to affect her today in relation to her son Robert. She may wonder about his unfolding sexuality and be concerned about how he will deal with adolescent changes.

Mrs. Chase seems to view herself primarily as a wife and mother and as a hard-working, responsible member of the community. She appears to assume the role of a parent-like big sister with her siblings. She seems open to input from others and from me and has a well-established sense of personal identity in relation to family roles such as wife, mother, daughter, and eldest sibling. She and her husband had wanted more children, but a medical condition (the cyst or the surgery to remove it) prevented that. She seems less clear and secure, however, when it comes to other, more playful or recreational roles. In these areas, she appears more uncertain and less inner-directed. She has yet to formulate personal life goals that are distinct from those of her family.

Application of the *DSM-IV-TR* (American Psychiatric Association, 2000a) criteria might suggest a "V-Code" classification. V-Codes are issues of concern but do not necessarily indicate or relate to a psychiatric disorder or mental illness. The V-Codes that seem applicable to the person-issue-situation seem to be "Parent–Child Relational Problem," in recognition of the current strain between Mrs. Chase and her son, or perhaps "Phase of Life Problem," to reflect the stress associated with the change in role identity from primarily homemaker to homemaker plus full-time paid worker outside the home. The changing nature of the relationship with her teenage son may contribute as well.

The *DSM-IV-TR* diagnosis "Adjustment Disorder with Mixed Anxiety and Depressed Mood" might also be considered, although it is less applicable because the apparent stressor—assumption of the full-time job outside the home—occurred 6 months earlier. According to the *DSM*, most adjustment disorders are resolved—with or without professional aid—within 6 months of onset.

Application of the PIE Manual criteria (Karls & O'Keefe, 2008a) to Mrs. Chase and her situation might yield the following classification:

Factor I: Homemaker Role—Home, mixed type (ambivalence, responsibility, dependency), moderate severity, duration of 6 months to 1 year, adequate coping skills. Also consider parental role or perhaps spousal role problems.

Factor II: Other Affectional Support System Problem, low severity, more than 5 years' duration.

Might the fact that Robert is alone, unsupervised, and unprotected during 2 hours after school each weekday represent an important trigger to Mrs. Chase's feelings of stress, irritability, and guilt? Might she feel a conflict between earning money for her son's college education and being unavailable to him when he returns from school? Might she be afraid that he could be in some danger? Might Mrs. Chase believe that she is less able to protect Robert from the influence of the neighborhood boys now that she works outside the home? Does she feel an obligation to keep Robert entirely away from all potentially negative or risky phenomena? Does she suspect that Robert might be especially susceptible to negative peer pressure and that he might be unable to make responsible decisions or to resist temptations? Might she be associating Robert's adolescence with her own teenage experience? Could she be worried that Robert might indeed be fully capable of making mature decisions and might not need her as much anymore? What would Mrs. Chase need to conclude that Robert is reasonably safe during the 2-hour "latchkey" period?

How much does she really want to work outside the home? Does she truly enjoy the work? How does her husband feel about her job? How similar is Mrs. Chase to her father in terms of a workaholic, or compulsive, approach to life? Might her reactions to working outside the home be in some way related to her view of her father as "a workaholic who was never at home"? Might she feel guilty that "she's like her father"? Have the symptoms of irritability and argumentativeness led to a comparison with her mother—whom she views as angry, critical, and unstable? Might Mrs. Chase worry that if she does not do for others, they might not love or approve of her?

Based on information from the initial interview, Mrs. Chase and her family have a lengthy history of competent functioning. Individually and as a system, the family members appear to be coherent and stable. However, Mr. Chase, Robert, and especially Mrs. Chase have begun to experience strain associated with changing demands. It appears that Mrs. Chase has tried to continue to "do it all" and may feel worried and guilty that she is not as available to her son as he might need or want her to be.

Several factors may have relevance to the identified issues. First, Mrs. Chase comes from a family of origin where she assumed adult responsibilities from an early age. She reported that her mother abused alcohol and her father was a workaholic. It is possible that Mrs. Chase tends to assume substantial responsibility for others—perhaps especially family members. She apparently learned to do so from an early age. Working full-time outside the home may represent a major psychological conflict for her. One part of her, perhaps like her father, may be strongly tempted to invest a great deal of time and energy in her employment. Another part may feel much anxiety and uncertainty when she is away from the home. She is so familiar with the role of caretaker for her husband and son that she may sometimes feel anxious when she is away from home and unable to meet their needs. Second, Mrs. Chase wanted to have more children, but a medical condition has prevented that. She may have yet to explore fully and grieve for the loss of her dream for additional children. She may also invest even greater emotional energy in her son Robert, because "he's my only child; and the only one I'll ever have." Third, as an early adolescent, Robert is probably experiencing numerous physical, psychological, and social changes. Along with Mrs. Chase's employment, these changes may also add considerable stress to the family system. As a person emotionally attuned to the family, Mrs. Chase is understandably affected during this transition period. She may soon become aware of the limitations associated with an exclusively, family-centered role identification.

The current issues of concern may represent a kind of positive signal to Mrs. Chase to make some personal changes that could both liberate her from inhibitions that originated in childhood, and prepare her for a more peaceful and enjoyable second half of life. Although assumption of the full-time paid job outside the home seems associated with the onset of the issues of concern, it is plausible that the family system needed something to help her, her husband, and her son to proceed to the next stage of individual and family development. Application of Erikson's psychosocial theory of life cycle stages (Erikson, 1963, 1968) might suggest that Mrs. Chase could be engaged in "generativity versus stagnation" issues as she begins to pursue greater meaning in life and a more coherent sense of personal identity. Some issues related to certain earlier life cycle stages may require exploration (for example, autonomy versus shame and doubt, initiative versus guilt, identity versus role confusion). Application of Gilligan's theoretical approach to women's development might suggest that Mrs. Chase could be seeking enhanced intimacy and greater attachment to the most important people in her life (Gilligan, 1979, 1982). Although her commitment to and relationship with others have been strong, the degree of intimacy and closeness may have been inhibited by the dominance of the parent-like, caretaking role.

Mrs. Chase seems to reflect a high level of competence and possesses well-developed coping skills and defense mechanisms, which have served her well over the years. She has coped well with numerous life challenges, transitions, and issues. At present, however, her usual coping capacities appear less functional as she experiences atypical irritation and anger. At some level, she may fear that she is becoming more like her mother, whom she described as "unstable, angry, and critical."

In spite of the current concerns, however, she continues to function well in most social roles. She appears to possess a coherent and integrated personality. She reflects superior thinking capacities, probably possesses above-average intelligence, and is insightful and articulate. Since the time of her marriage to Richard, her lifestyle has been stable and congruent. In addition, she seems highly motivated to function well in the role of client and agent of change in her life.

Mrs. Chase and I wondered if certain cognitive beliefs could contribute to the identified problems. She commonly makes statements to herself (self-talk) such as "Think about others before oneself," "Do for others before doing for yourself," "Don't make mistakes," "Don't be a burden to others," "Don't think about yourself," and "Don't be selfish." These may be related to the gender-related role expectations of her family of origin, her religious training and experiences, and her cultural background. During the first interview, she concluded that there was a relationship between such beliefs and the current issues. This hypothesis seemed to heighten her motivation to reconsider what she believes and how she talks to herself.

2. Situational and Systemic Factors

Based on information gained in the first interview, the Chase family system appears organized in such a way that Mrs. Chase serves as the primary executive or manager, or perhaps "parent figure." She seems to have responsibility for the bulk of the household and family chores, functions, and activities. Mr. Chase apparently assumes few household duties with the exception of yard work, as well as home and auto repairs. She is the primary housekeeper and parent. She prepares the meals, does the shopping and cleaning, coordinates transportation for Robert, and pays the bills. Until Mrs. Chase began full-time work outside the home, the family rules and role boundaries were clear. Mrs. Chase sought ideas and input from Richard and Robert, but she made and implemented most family decisions. Now that she is home less often and there are increased demands on her, some of the rules and roles may be in flux. At this point, it seems that Mrs. Chase is trying to maintain her previous family and community duties while adding additional occupational responsibilities. She also appears concerned about certain "troubled teenage boys" in the neighborhood and worries that Robert might be negatively influenced by them. We wondered if she might especially be worried that Robert might begin to use alcohol or drugs.

It appears that communication and relational patterns within the Chase family are relatively open but inhibited and constrained. The family members are mutually affectionate and seem to like each other. According to Mrs. Chase, however, the male family members sometimes appear to "hint at" rather than clearly state their preferences. Mrs. Chase seems to respond to such indirect expressions by guessing what they really want. She cited an example where, at a recent family dinner, Robert "made a face" when he was served his meal. Mrs. Chase then asked, "What's the matter?" Robert said, "Nothing." Mrs. Chase asked, "Don't you like the meal? I'll get you something else." Robert said, "Don't bother, this is okay." Mrs. Chase said, "No, I'll get you something else to eat." Robert said, "Oh, okay. Thanks." At this point, Mrs. Chase interrupted her own meal, got up, and prepared something Robert wanted to eat.

When we considered the communication patterns in the family, we wondered if Richard and Robert realized that they sometimes express themselves indirectly through facial expressions and nonverbal gestures. Do they understand that Mrs. Chase often tries to "read their minds"—which may, indirectly, serve to encourage and maintain their patterns of indirect communication? What might be the consequence of more direct and full verbal expression within the family system? What would each family member stand to gain or lose?

Members of the Chase family appear to have adopted many of the stereotypic rules and roles of men, women, and children projected by the dominant North American culture. Robert's adolescence and Mrs. Chase's full-time outside employment probably represent the most significant stressors the family system now faces.

As a system, the Chase family may be approaching a phase when an adolescent child often stimulates a number of issues and decisions for all the family members and the family system as a whole. According to Mrs. Chase, Robert has begun to experience bodily changes and has become more self-conscious and self-centered. These changes may be affecting the nature of the relationship between Robert and Mrs. Chase and perhaps that with his father as well.

We wondered what might happen if Richard and Robert began to demonstrate a capacity to care for themselves and assume responsibility for some of the household chores. Might the frequency and intensity of Mrs. Chase's symptoms decrease if she had fewer family and household demands? Or might they increase if she concluded that she was not as "needed" by Robert and Richard? I wondered if Mrs. Chase would be willing to let her husband and son assume greater responsibility for household and family chores. Would they be willing to take on these duties? If they did shift the family structure and roles in such a manner, how would the family members respond?

What specific issues and dilemmas, if any, is Robert confronting during his adolescent years? How comfortable is Mrs. Chase with her son's desire for increasing freedom and personal responsibility? If she is not, might she reconsider her views about adolescent development? How does Mr. Chase relate to his son during this time? What hopes and dreams do Mr. and Mrs. Chase have for Robert's future? What doubts and fears do they have about him?

There seem to be sufficient resources to meet basic and urgent needs of the Chase family. They have adequate assets and opportunities to pursue their aspirations. They have not been subject to overt oppression or discrimination. Mrs. Chase appears to have the affection and support of her husband and son. Although her mother, father, and siblings do not appear to provide much in the way of interest, understanding, or support, she has several friends who care about her a great deal. In these relationships as in most others, she seems to "give more than she receives" and "knows more about others than others know about her." She also believes strongly that her husband and son, as well as numerous friends, would be willing to do anything they could to help her.

3. Motivation and Readiness; Stage of Change
Before the end of our first meeting together, Mrs. Chase concluded that throughout most of her life she has adopted a protective, parent-like, caretaking, and

people-pleasing role toward people in general and the members of her family in particular. She also said that "not only has this pattern left me feeling guilty and stressed, it may have interfered to some extent with Richard and Robert's ability to care for themselves." She smiled as she said, "I might have to become more selfish—for the sake of my husband and son."

By the end of our first meeting, Mrs. Chase appeared highly motivated to make personal changes to allow her to lighten her burdens of responsibility and permit others to assume more control over their own lives. She looked forward to feeling more relaxed and playful and more able to experience joy and pleasure. She indicated that this is very important to her, as it could help her overcome her "family legacy" of anger, criticism, shame, guilt, and workaholism. Mrs. Chase seemed comfortable with and confident in my ability to help her address these issues and willing to work collaboratively with me in the process.

In regard to Prochaska's transtheoretical scheme (Prochaska, Norcross, & DiClemente, 1994), Mrs. Chase probably fits within the latter portions of the contemplation and the early parts of the preparation stages of change. She appeared motivated by the idea that she might change patterns of thinking, feeling, and behaving that had their origins during her childhood. She also seemed encouraged by the idea that making those changes could not only make her life easier and more enjoyable, but also be of help to her husband and son.

Mrs. Chase believed that Richard and Robert would be enthusiastic about any efforts to help her. She felt secure and confident in their love and affection for her and thought they would place a high priority on helping to address the issues of irritability, argumentativeness, shame and guilt, sleeplessness, smoking behavior, and excessive weight loss. She also believed that they would join in an attempt to alter the family structure so that she could become less the "mommy" for both of them. She anticipated, however, that there might be times when all of them might be tempted to slip back into old familiar patterns.

She was less optimistic about her parents' and siblings' willingness to acknowledge problems or help to address them. She also seemed worried about the reactions of people at her job and friends within the church and community. She wondered if they might become confused and perhaps annoyed if she began suddenly to do less for them. However, she smiled when she said, "I'll talk with them about my issues, and we'll see what happens when I start to change."

4. Challenges and Obstacles

One aspect that may represent a personal challenge involves control. Mrs. Chase and I have not yet discussed the possible relationship between taking care of others and feelings of control. I wondered about the possibility that as she worries less about others and reduces her caretaking behavior, she may experience increased anxiety associated with a decreased sense of control. Indeed, she sometimes feels quite uncomfortable when she engages in playful or recreational activities.

In addition, some elements of her primary and secondary social systems may resist the changes she hopes to make. Despite their love and support, Richard and Robert might experience some resentment if they were expected to do more for themselves and take on additional household chores. Mrs. Chase's parents and siblings might also respond in a similar fashion, as might some of her work colleagues and church and community friends.

5. Risk Assessment

Despite the indications of distress and perhaps depression, Mrs. Chase and I concur that she does not represent a danger to herself or others. In response to a question concerning suicidal thoughts and actions, she indicated that she has never taken any self-destructive action and does not have suicidal thoughts. Similarly, she reported that she has never experienced thoughts about or taken actions intended to hurt another person. She also confirmed that she does not use drugs of any kind—only rarely takes an aspirin—and drinks at most one glass of wine per week.

C. Case Formulation

Based upon our assessment, Mrs. Chase and I hypothesized that changes in certain aspects of her personal and family life might resolve the identified issues. We thought that:

1. If Mrs. Chase logically examined the beliefs she developed during her childhood, she might decide to change some in a way that would enable her to feel less excessively responsible for the safety, well-being, and happiness of her son, her husband, and most other people she knows. We predicted that changes in her thinking would probably lead to changes to her feelings, emotions, and bodily sensations and would probably help her to sleep better as well.

2. If Mrs. Chase assumed somewhat less responsibility for the family and household work and her son Robert and husband Richard assumed somewhat more, Mrs. Chase would probably feel less stressed—if she simultaneously changed some of her beliefs and self-statements.

3. If Mrs. Chase encouraged Robert to assume more responsibility for his thoughts and actions and granted him somewhat greater freedom and autonomy, he would probably find it easier to address his adolescent development needs and the two of them would probably argue less and find their encounters more enjoyable.

Mrs. Chase's intelligence, maturity, insight, and motivation—along with the affection and support of her husband and son—suggest a high likelihood that the family will be able to address the identified issues effectively. I estimate that the probability of full and successful resolution is greater than 85 percent. I also anticipate a satisfactory outcome in 1 to 2 months of weekly meetings with Mrs. Chase and her immediate family.

III. Service Contract
  A. Issues
    1. Client-Identified Issues
    Mrs. Chase identified the following issues:
      a. Frequent arguments with her son, Robert, and, less often, with her husband, Richard
      b. Increased irritability, criticism, and anger toward Robert and, to a lesser degree, toward Richard
      c. Shame and guilt following arguments with her son
      d. Unplanned weight loss (10 pounds) over the past 6 months
      e. Sleep disturbance
      f. Resumption of cigarette smoking after 5 years' abstinence
      g. Fatigue
      h. Headaches

2. Worker-Identified Issues

Following the first interview, I tentatively identified the following as potential issues:

a. Ambivalence about job at Fox Manufacturing

b. Feelings of depression

c. Ambivalence about Robert's adolescence

d. Feelings of loss, disappointment, and grief because client probably cannot have another child

e. Stress and tension; anxiety

f. Thoughts and feelings of excessive responsibility and possibly of control

g. Role strain and possibly role conflict among roles of mother, wife, homemaker, and employee

h. Issues related to childhood experiences (that is, growing up in a family system with a parent who reportedly abused alcohol; largely absent and possibly work-aholic father; unhappy incidents with childhood peers; feeling overweight and unattractive; church-related issues; reported episodes of attempted molestation by maternal uncle)

i. Interactional styles that may be classified as predominantly nonassertive with occasional periods of aggressive verbal expression

3. Agreed-Upon Issues for Work

Mrs. Chase and I agreed on the following issues for work. These will provide us with a focus for our work together:

a. Frequent arguments with her son Robert and, less often, with her husband Richard

b. Irritability, criticism, and anger toward Robert and, to a lesser degree, toward Richard

c. Disproportionate feelings of shame and guilt

d. Sleep disturbance

e. Ambivalence regarding job at Fox Manufacturing

f. Stress and tension; anxiety

g. Thoughts and feelings of excessive responsibility and possibly of control

h. Role strain and possibly role conflict among roles of mother, wife, homemaker, and employee

B. Service Goals

Mrs. Chase and I agreed to work toward accomplishment of the following goals:

1. Within 6 weeks, decrease by 50 percent the frequency of unwarranted arguments with Robert and Richard and increase the frequency of satisfying interactions with them by 50 percent.

2. Within 6 weeks, decrease by 50 percent the frequency and intensity of inappro-priate feelings of irritability, criticism, and anger toward Robert and Richard and increase appropriate feelings of comfort and acceptance of them by 50 percent.

3. Within 6 weeks, decrease by 50 percent the frequency and intensity of dispropor-tionate feelings of shame and guilt, and increase feelings of self-acceptance and self-forgiveness by 50 percent.

4. Within 6 weeks, sleep 8 full hours per night and awaken feeling refreshed at least four of seven mornings a week.

5. Within 6 weeks, decrease the ambivalence about the job at Fox Manufacturing by deciding whether client really wants to keep the job.

6. Within 6 weeks, decrease the stress, tension, and anxiety and increase feelings of personal comfort and calmness by 50 percent.

7. Within 2 weeks, complete an in-depth exploration of the issue of excessive responsibility and control; by the end of that time, decide whether maintaining or lessening the current level of responsibility and control is desirable.

C. Plans

1. Action Plans/Service Approach

To achieve the final goals, Mrs. Chase and I agreed on the following action plans: Mrs. Lynn Chase and I (Susan Holder, social worker) will meet for eight 1-hour sessions during the next 2 months. Our purpose is to work together toward achievement of the final goals identified above. We will approach this work as a cooperative effort, with each party contributing ideas and suggestions. I will serve as counselor and facilitator and approach our work together from an integrated combination of cognitive-behavioral, problem-solving, family-systems, and task-centered approaches. On at least some occasions, we will ask Mrs. Chase's husband and son to join us. Throughout the 2-month period, we will monitor the rate and degree of progress. At the end of that time, we will determine whether to conclude our work, consult with or refer to someone else, or contract with each other for further work together.

a. Client Tasks/Action Steps

Mrs. Chase and I agreed that she would undertake the following steps during the first week of our work together. Other tasks will be identified and implemented later in the program.

◆ As a first step toward decreasing her stress, tension, and anxiety and increasing feelings of personal comfort and calmness, Mrs. Chase agreed to spend 15 minutes each day during the next week planning for or working in her garden.

◆ As a first step toward decreasing the frequency of her inappropriate feelings of irritability, criticism, and anger toward Robert and Richard and increasing appropriate feelings of comfort, understanding, and acceptance of them by 50 percent, Mrs. Chase agreed to do two things during the course of the next week. First, she agreed to resist temptations to "stuff" her feelings. Whether by writing them down on paper, verbally expressing them in a place where no one can hear, or expressing them directly to the relevant person or people, she agreed to express whatever feelings she experiences within a few minutes of the time that she first becomes aware of them. Second, she agreed to take 5 minutes every day to engage Robert and Richard pleasantly by inquiring about their thoughts, feelings, and activities.

◆ As a first step toward addressing the goal of determining whether a lessening of responsibility and control in some areas might be helpful, Mrs. Chase agreed to identify and write down as many reasons as she could why she should continue to maintain her current level of responsibility and control. Following that, Mrs. Chase agreed to identify as many reasons as she could why a lessening of her responsibility and control might be beneficial to her, her husband, and her son at this time. We agreed to review the two lists of reasons in our next meeting.

b. Worker Tasks

- ◆ I, Susan Holder, agreed to prepare this service agreement in written form and provide a copy to Mrs. Chase.
- ◆ I agreed to assume responsibility for planning tentative agendas for our meetings together and to consult with Mrs. Chase concerning the implementation of the action steps and their effects.
- ◆ I agreed to provide Mrs. Chase with a notebook and related materials for completing written tasks and monitoring progress.

c. In-Session Tasks

Mrs. Chase and I agreed that during our meetings together, we would undertake some or all the following activities (additional in-session tasks are to be identified and implemented later in the program):

- ◆ Value-clarification exercises intended to aid Mrs. Chase in addressing various issues about which she experiences ambivalence
- ◆ Self-talk analysis to help Mrs. Chase identify the "things she says to herself" that appear associated with attitudes of excessive responsibility and with the feelings of irritability, criticism, anger, depression, stress, and tension
- ◆ Strength-oriented, "bragging" exercises to help Mrs. Chase develop a stronger sense of individuality and autonomy—separate from her identity as wife, mother, and friend

d. Maintenance Tasks

Mrs. Chase and I agreed that the goals involve long-term change and require ongoing attention. Mrs. Chase indicated that she would recite the serenity prayer at least once per day for the next 365 days.

2. Plans to Evaluate Progress

We will evaluate progress toward goal achievement in several ways. First, Mrs. Chase agreed to keep a daily log in her notebook, where she intends to record the time and date of all "arguments" and all "satisfying interactions." Second, Mrs. Chase also agreed to log the time and date of all inappropriate feelings of "irritability, anger, and criticism" toward Richard or Robert, as well as all feelings of "comfort, understanding, and acceptance" of them. Third, Mrs. Chase agreed to use the logbook to record the number of hours slept each night and to rate, on a subjective scale of 1 to 10, how refreshed she feels upon awakening. Fourth, Mrs. Chase agreed to register completion of her daily 15 minutes of "gardening." Evaluation of progress toward other goals will occur by asking Mrs. Chase for self-reports. In regard to the issues of excessive responsibility and ambivalence about her job at Fox Manufacturing, progress will be indicated when Mrs. Chase reports that she has decided whether to lessen responsibility and control and whether she wants to keep her job. We concluded that a decision in either direction would represent progress. Finally, Mrs. Chase agreed to complete brief client satisfaction and session rating scales during each meeting to help improve service quality.

THE SOCIAL WORK SKILLS INTERVIEW RATING FORM

You may use this rating form[1] as part of the process of evaluating your own or others' performance of the social work skills during interviews with clients. You may use it, for example, in rating your performance during an interview with an individual, a couple, a family, or a small group. You may also use the form to provide evaluative feedback to a colleague who is attempting to improve the quality of his or her performance.

In using the rating form, please use the following coding system:

N/A During the course of the interview, the skill in question was not appropriate or necessary and was therefore not used, having no effect on the interview.

−4 During the course of the interview, the skill in question was attempted at an inappropriate time and in an unsuitable context, and was performed in an incompetent manner. Its use represent a major problem in the interview.

−3 During the course of the interview, the skill in question was used at an inappropriate time or in an unsuitable context, seriously detracting from the interview.

−2 During the course of the interview, the skill in question was attempted at an appropriate time and in a suitable context, but was done so in an incompetent manner, significantly detracting from the interview.

−1 During the course of the interview, the skill in question was not used at times or in contexts when it should have been, detracting from the interview.

0 During the course of the interview, the skill in question was used and demonstrated at a minimal level of competence. Its use did not detract from nor contribute to the interview.

+1 During the course of the interview, the skill in question was attempted at an appropriate time and in a suitable context, and was generally demonstrated at a fair level of competence. Its use represented a small contribution to the interview.

+2 During the course of the interview, the skill in question was attempted at an appropriate time and in a suitable context, and was generally demonstrated at a moderate level of competence. Its use represented a significant contribution to the interview.

---

[1] Because this rating form is intended for the purpose of evaluating social work skills used during face-to-face interviews, some skills related to professionalism, ethical decision making, assessing, and recording are not included.

+3 During the course of the interview, the skill in question was attempted at an appropriate time and in a suitable context, and was generally demonstrated at a good level of competence. Its use represented a substantial contribution to the interview.

+4 During the course of the interview, the skill in question was attempted at an appropriate time and in a suitable context, and was demonstrated at a superior level of performance. Its use represented a major contribution to the interview.

THE SOCIAL WORK SKILLS INTERVIEW RATING FORM	
Skill	**Rating**
Talking and Listening: The Basic Interpersonal Skills	
1. Culturally Sensitive Communications	+4 +3 +2 +1 0 −1 −2 −3 −4 N/A
Comments:	
2. Nonverbal Communications (Attending)	+4 +3 +2 +1 0 −1 −2 −3 −4 N/A
Comments:	
3. Talking (Speech and Language)	+4 +3 +2 +1 0 −1 −2 −3 −4 N/A
Comments:	
4. Hearing (Receiving Messages)	+4 +3 +2 +1 0 −1 −2 −3 −4 N/A
Comments:	
5. Observing	+4 +3 +2 +1 0 −1 −2 −3 −4 N/A
Comments:	

6. Encouraging	+4 +3 +2 +1 0 −1 −2 −3 −4 N/A
Comments:	

7. Remembering	+4 +3 +2 +1 0 −1 −2 −3 −4 N/A
Comments:	

8. Active Listening	+4 +3 +2 +1 0 −1 −2 −3 −4 N/A
Comments:	

Beginning

1. Introducing Yourself	+4 +3 +2 +1 0 −1 −2 −3 −4 N/A
Comments:	

2. Seeking Introductions	+4 +3 +2 +1 0 −1 −2 −3 −4 N/A
Comments:	

3. Describing Initial Purpose	+4 +3 +2 +1 0 −1 −2 −3 −4 N/A
Comments:	

4. Orienting Clients	+4 +3 +2 +1 0 −1 −2 −3 −4 N/A
Comments:	

5. Discussing Policy and Ethical Factors	+4 +3 +2 +1 0 −1 −2 −3 −4 N/A
Comments:	

6. Seeking Feedback	+4 +3 +2 +1 0 −1 −2 −3 −4 N/A
Comments:	

Exploring

1. Asking (Open- and Closed-Ended) Questions	+4 +3 +2 +1 0 −1 −2 −3 −4 N/A
Comments:	

2. Seeking Clarification	+4 +3 +2 +1 0 −1 −2 −3 −4 N/A
Comments:	

3. Reflecting Content	+4 +3 +2 +1 0 −1 −2 −3 −4 N/A
Comments:	

4. Reflecting Feelings	+4 +3 +2 +1 0 −1 −2 −3 −4 N/A
Comments:	

5. Reflecting Feelings and Meanings	+4 +3 +2 +1 0 −1 −2 −3 −4 N/A
Comments:	

6. Partializing	+4 +3 +2 +1 0 −1 −2 −3 −4 N/A
Comments:	

7. Going Beyond What Is Said	+4 +3 +2 +1 0 −1 −2 −3 −4 N/A
Comments:	

8. Reflecting Issues	+4 +3 +2 +1 0 −1 −2 −3 −4 N/A
Comments:	

9. Reflecting Hypotheses	+4 +3 +2 +1 0 −1 −2 −3 −4 N/A
Comments:	

Assessing

1. Identifying Issues	+4 +3 +2 +1 0 −1 −2 −3 −4 N/A
Comments:	

2. Sharing Hypotheses	+4 +3 +2 +1 0 −1 −2 −3 −4 N/A
Comments:	

3. Clarifying Issues for Work	+4 +3 +2 +1 0 −1 −2 −3 −4 N/A
Comments:	

Contracting	
1. Establishing Goals	+4 +3 +2 +1 0 −1 −2 −3 −4 N/A
Comments:	

2. Developing Action Plans	+4 +3 +2 +1 0 −1 −2 −3 −4 N/A
Comments:	

3. Identifying Action Steps	+4 +3 +2 +1 0 −1 −2 −3 −4 N/A
Comments:	

4. Planning for Evaluation	+4 +3 +2 +1 0 −1 −2 −3 −4 N/A
Comments:	

Working and Evaluating	
1. Rehearsing Action Steps	+4 +3 +2 +1 0 −1 −2 −3 −4 N/A
Comments:	

2. Reviewing Action Steps	+4 +3 +2 +1 0 −1 −2 −3 −4 N/A
Comments:	

3. Evaluating	+4 +3 +2 +1 0 −1 −2 −3 −4 N/A
Comments:	

4. Focusing	+4 +3 +2 +1 0 −1 −2 −3 −4 N/A
Comments:	

5. Educating	+4 +3 +2 +1 0 −1 −2 −3 −4 N/A
Comments:	

6. Advising	+4 +3 +2 +1 0 −1 −2 −3 −4 N/A
Comments:	

7. Representing	+4 +3 +2 +1 0 −1 −2 −3 −4 N/A
Comments:	

8. Responding with Immediacy	+4 +3 +2 +1 0 −1 −2 −3 −4 N/A
Comments:	

9. Reframing	+4 +3 +2 +1 0 −1 −2 −3 −4 N/A
Comments:	

10. Confronting Inconsistencies	+4 +3 +2 +1 0 −1 −2 −3 −4 N/A
Comments:	

11. Pointing Out Endings	+4 +3 +2 +1 0 −1 −2 −3 −4 N/A
Comments:	

Ending

1. Reviewing the Process	+4 +3 +2 +1 0 −1 −2 −3 −4 N/A
Comments:	

2. Final Evaluating	+4 +3 +2 +1 0 −1 −2 −3 −4 N/A
Comments:	

3. Sharing Ending Feelings and Saying Goodbye	+4 +3 +2 +1 0 −1 −2 −3 −4 N/A
Comments:	

TABLE OF SOCIAL WORK SKILLS

The skills addressed in this edition of *The Social Work Skills Workbook* are identified in the table below. Each skill may be classified according to the dimension or phase of practice. Such a system enables assessors and learners to "code" the use of a particular skill during observed or recorded interviews, or in transcripts of meetings.

	The Social Work Skills	ID
Common Conditions (CC)	CC001 Demonstrating empathy	CC001
	CC002 Demonstrating respect	CC002
	CC003 Demonstrating authenticity	CC003
Professionalism (PF)	PF001 Demonstrating integrity	PF001
	PF002 Applying professional knowledge and exhibiting self-efficacy	PF002
	PF003 Demonstrating self-understanding and maintaining self-control	PF003
	PF004 Giving and receiving social support	PF004
	PF005 Thinking critically and inquiring scientifically	PF005
	PF006 Engaging in career-long learning	PF006
	PF007 Valuing diversity and difference	PF007
	PF008 Advancing human rights and social justice	PF008
	PF009 Promoting social well-being and engaging in policy practice	PF009
Ethical Decision Making (ED)	ED001 Recognizing legal duties	ED001
	ED002 Applying the fundamental values and ethics of social work	ED002
	ED003 Identifying ethical and legal implications	ED003
	ED004 Resolving ethical dilemmas and taking appropriate action	ED004

The Social Work Skills		ID
Talking and Listening Skills (TL)	TL001 Engaging diversity and difference through culturally sensitive communications	TL001
	TL002 Communicating nonverbally and using body language	TL002
	TL003 Talking: using speech and language	TL003
	TL004 Listening: hearing, observing, encouraging, and remembering	TL004
	TL005 Active listening: combining talking and listening to promote understanding	TL005
Preparing Skills (PR)	PR001 Preparatory reviewing	PR001
	PR002 Preparatory exploring	PR002
	PR003 Preparatory consultation	PR003
	PR004 Preparatory arranging	PR004
	PR005 Preparatory empathy	PR005
	PR006 Preparatory self-exploration	PR006
	PR007 Centering	PR007
	PR008 Preliminary planning and recording	PR008
Beginning Skills (BG)	BG001 Introducing yourself	BG001
	BG002 Seeking introductions	BG002
	BG003 Describing an initial purpose	BG003
	BG004 Orienting clients	BG004
	BG005 Discussing policy and ethical factors	BG005
	BG006 Seeking feedback	BG006
Exploring Skills (EX)	EX001 Asking questions	EX001
	EX002 Seeking clarification	EX002
	EX003 Reflecting content	EX003
	EX004 Reflecting feelings	EX004
	EX005 Reflecting feelings and meanings	EX005
	EX006 Partializing	EX006
	EX007 Going beyond what is said	EX007
	EX008 Reflecting issues	EX008
	EX009 Reflecting hypotheses	EX009

	The Social Work Skills	ID
Assessing Skills (AS)	AS001 Identifying issues	AS001
	AS002 Sharing hypotheses	AS002
	AS003 Clarifying issues for work	AS003
	AS004 Organizing descriptive information	AS004
	AS005 Preparing an assessment and case formulation	AS005
Contracting Skills (CN)	CN001 Establishing goals	CN001
	CN002 Developing action plans	CN002
	CN003 Identifying action steps	CN003
	CN004 Planning for evaluation	CN004
	CN005 Summarizing the contract	CN005
Working and Evaluating Skills (WE)	WE001 Rehearsing action steps	WE001
	WE002 Reviewing action steps	WE002
	WE003 Evaluating	WE003
	WE004 Focusing	WE004
	WE005 Educating	WE005
	WE006 Advising	WE006
	WE007 Representing	WE007
	WE008 Responding with immediacy	WE008
	WE009 Reframing	WE009
	WE010 Confronting inconsistencies	WE010
	WE011 Pointing out endings	WE011
	WE012 Recording progress (documenting)	WE012
Ending Skills (EN)	EN001 Reviewing the process	EN001
	EN002 Final evaluating	EN002
	EN003 Sharing ending feelings and saying goodbye	EN003
	EN004 Recording the closing summary	EN004

TABLE OF SOCIAL WORK SKILLS SUPPORTING THE EPAS CORE COMPETENCIES, PRACTICE KNOWLEDGE, AND PRACTICE BEHAVIORS

The following table illustrates the relationships of the social work skills to the 10 core EPAS competencies (EP), the 28 practice knowledge dimensions (PK), and the 41 practice behaviors (PB) identified in the Educational Policies and Accreditation Standards (EPAS) of the Council on Social Work Education (CSWE) (2008). Each social work skill supports one or more of the core competencies and the practice knowledge and practice behaviors reflected within them. As students reflect proficiency in the social work skills, they simultaneously reflect proficiency in the competencies, practice knowledge, and practice behaviors associated with them.

Social Work Skills Supporting the 10 Core Competencies, the 28 Practice Knowledge Areas, and the 41 Practice Behaviors Specified in the EPAS

EP2.1.1: Identify with the social work profession and behave professionally	Supporting Social Work Skills
PK2.1.1 (1) Social workers serve as representatives of the profession, its mission, and its core values.	CC001 Demonstrating empathy
PK2.1.1 (2) Social workers know the profession's history.	CC002 Demonstrating respect
PK2.1.1 (3) Social workers commit themselves to the profession's enhancement and to their own professional conduct and growth.	CC003 Demonstrating authenticity
PB2.1.1 (1) Social workers advocate for client access to the services of social work.	PF001 Demonstrating integrity
	PF002 Applying professional knowledge and exhibiting self-efficacy
PB2.1.1 (2) Social workers practice personal reflection and self-correction to assure continual professional development.	PF003 Demonstrating self-understanding and maintaining self-control
PB2.1.1 (3) Social workers attend to professional roles and boundaries.	PF004 Giving and receiving social support
PB2.1.1 (4) Social workers demonstrate professional demeanor in behavior, appearance, and communication.	PF005 Thinking critically and inquiring scientifically
PB2.1.1 (5) Social workers engage in career-long learning.	PF006 Engaging in career-long learning
PB2.1.1 (6) Social workers use supervision and consultation.	PF007 Valuing diversity and difference
	PF008 Advancing human rights and social justice
	PF009 Promoting social well-being and engaging in policy practice
	ED002 Applying the fundamental values and ethics of social work
	TL001 Engaging diversity and difference through culturally sensitive communications
	TL002 Communicating nonverbally and using body language
	TL003 Talking: using speech and language
	TL004 Listening: hearing, observing, encouraging, and remembering
	PR003 Preparatory consultation
	PR006 Preparatory self-exploration
	PR007 Centering
	BG001 Introducing yourself
	BG006 Seeking feedback
	WE007 Representing
	EN001 Reviewing the process
	EN002 Final evaluating

EP2.1.2: Apply social work ethical principles to guide professional practice	Supporting Social Work Skills
PK2.1.2 (1) Social workers have an obligation to conduct themselves ethically and to engage in ethical decision making.	PF001 Demonstrating integrity
PK2.1.2 (2) Social workers are knowledgeable about the value base of the profession, its ethical standards, and relevant law.	PF002 Applying professional knowledge and exhibiting self-efficacy
PB2.1.2 (1) Social workers recognize and manage personal values in a way that allows professional values to guide practice.	PF003 Demonstrating self-understanding and maintaining self-control
PB2.1.2 (2) Social workers make ethical decisions by applying standards of the NASW Code of Ethics and, as applicable, of the IFSW/International Association of Schools of Social Work Ethics in Social Work Statement of Principles.	PF005 Thinking critically and inquiring scientifically
PB2.1.2 (3) Social workers tolerate ambiguity in resolving ethical conflicts.	PF006 Engaging in career-long learning
PB2.1.2 (4) Social workers apply strategies of ethical reasoning to arrive at principled decisions.	PF007 Valuing diversity and difference
	ED001 Recognizing legal duties
	ED002 Applying the fundamental values and ethics of social work
	ED003 Identifying ethical and legal implications
	ED004 Resolving ethical dilemmas and taking appropriate action
	BG005 Discussing policy and ethical factors

EP2.1.3: Apply critical thinking to inform and communicate professional judgments	Supporting Social Work Skills
PK2.1.3 (1) Social workers are knowledgeable about the principles of logic, scientific inquiry, and reasoned discernment.	PF001 Demonstrating integrity
PK2.1.3 (2) Social workers use critical thinking augmented by creativity and curiosity. Critical thinking also requires the synthesis and communication of relevant information.	PF002 Applying professional knowledge and exhibiting self-efficacy
PB2.1.3 (1) Social workers distinguish, appraise, and integrate multiple sources of knowledge, including research-based knowledge, and practice wisdom.	PF003 Demonstrating self-understanding and maintaining self-control
PB2.1.3 (2) Social workers analyze models of assessment, prevention, intervention, and evaluation.	PF005 Thinking critically and inquiring scientifically
	PF006 Engaging in career-long learning
	PF007 Valuing diversity and difference
	TL001 Engaging diversity and difference through culturally sensitive communications
	TL002 Communicating nonverbally and using body language
	TL003 Talking: using speech and language

(Continued)

EP2.1.3: Apply critical thinking to inform and communicate professional judgments	Supporting Social Work Skills
PB2.1.3 (3) Social workers demonstrate effective oral and written communication in working with individuals, families, groups, organizations, communities, and colleagues.	TL004 Listening: hearing, observing, encouraging, and remembering
	TL005 Active listening: combining talking and listening to promote understanding
	PR008 Preliminary planning and recording
	BG001 Introducing yourself
	BG002 Seeking introductions
	BG003 Describing an initial purpose
	BG004 Orienting clients
	BG005 Discussing policy and ethical factors
	BG006 Seeking feedback
	EX001 Asking questions
	EX002 Seeking clarification
	EX003 Reflecting content
	EX004 Reflecting feelings
	EX005 Reflecting feelings and meanings
	EX006 Partializing
	EX007 Going beyond what is said
	EX008 Reflecting issues
	EX009 Reflecting hypotheses
	AS001 Identifying issues
	AS002 Sharing hypotheses
	AS003 Clarifying issues for work
	AS004 Organizing descriptive information
	AS005 Preparing an assessment and case formulation
	CN001 Establishing goals
	CN002 Developing action plans
	CN003 Identifying action steps
	CN004 Planning for evaluation
	CN005 Summarizing the contract

WE001 Rehearsing action steps
WE002 Reviewing action steps
WE003 Evaluating
WE004 Focusing
WE005 Educating
WE006 Advising
WE007 Representing
WE008 Responding with immediacy
WE009 Reframing
WE010 Confronting inconsistencies
WE011 Pointing out endings
WE012 Recording progress (documenting)
EN001 Reviewing the process
EN002 Final evaluating
EN003 Sharing ending feelings and saying goodbye
EN004 Recording the closing summary

EP2.1.4: Engage diversity and difference in practice	Supporting Social Work Skills
PK2.1.4 (1) Social workers understand how diversity characterizes and shapes the human experience and is critical to the formation of identity. PK2.1.4 (2) Social workers understand diversity as intersection of multiple factors (age, class, color, culture, disability, ethnicity, gender, gender identity and expression, immigration status, political ideology, race, religion, and sexual orientation). PK2.1.4 (3) Social workers understand that, as a consequence of difference, a person's life experiences may include oppression, poverty, marginalization, and alienation as well as privilege, power, and acclaim.	CC001 Demonstrating empathy CC002 Demonstrating respect CC003 Demonstrating authenticity PF001 Demonstrating integrity PF002 Applying professional knowledge and exhibiting self-efficacy PF003 Demonstrating self-understanding and maintaining self-control PF004 Giving and receiving social support PF005 Thinking critically and inquiring scientifically PF006 Engaging in career-long learning PF007 Valuing diversity and difference PF008 Advancing human rights and social justice PF009 Promoting social well-being and engaging in policy practice

(Continued)

EP2.1.4: Engage diversity and difference in practice	Supporting Social Work Skills
PB2.1.4 (1) Social workers recognize the extent to which a culture's structures and values may oppress, marginalize, alienate, or create or enhance privilege and power. PB2.1.4 (2) Social workers gain sufficient self-awareness to eliminate the influence of personal biases and values in working with diverse groups. PB2.1.4 (3) Social workers recognize and communicate their under-standing of the importance of difference in shaping life experiences. PB2.1.4 (4) Social workers view themselves as learners and engage those with whom they work as informants.	ED002 Applying the fundamental values and ethics of social work ED004 Resolving ethical dilemmas and taking appropriate action TL001 Engaging diversity and difference through culturally sensitive communications TL002 Communicating nonverbally and using body language TL003 Talking: using speech and language TL004 Listening: hearing, observing, encouraging, and remembering TL005 Active listening: combining talking and listening to promote understanding PR005 Preparatory empathy PR006 Preparatory self-exploration PR007 Centering BG002 Seeking introductions BG004 Orienting clients BG006 Seeking feedback EX002 Seeking clarification EX007 Going beyond what is said AS001 Identifying issues AS002 Sharing hypotheses WE008 Responding with immediacy EN001 Reviewing the process EN002 Final evaluating EN003 Sharing ending feelings and saying goodbye
EP2.1.5: Advance human rights and social and economic justice	Supporting Social Work Skills
K2.1.5 (1) Social workers understand that each person, regardless of position in society, has basic human rights, such as freedom, safety, privacy, an adequate standard of living, health care, and education. PK2.1.5 (2) Social workers recognize the global interconnections of oppression and are knowledgeable about theories of justice and strategies to promote human and civil rights.	CC001 Demonstrating empathy CC002 Demonstrating respect CC003 Demonstrating authenticity PF001 Demonstrating integrity PF002 Applying professional knowledge and exhibiting self-efficacy

PK2.1.5 (3) Social work incorporates social justice practices in organizations, institutions, and society to ensure that these basic human rights are distributed equitably and without prejudice. PB2.1.5 (1) Social workers understand the forms and mechanisms of oppression and discrimination. PB2.1.5 (2) Social workers advocate for human rights and social and economic justice. PB2.1.5 (3) Social workers engage in practices that advance social and economic justice.	PF007 Valuing diversity and difference PF008 Advancing human rights and social justice PF009 Promoting social well-being and engaging in policy practice ED002 Applying the fundamental values and ethics of social work ED004 Resolving ethical dilemmas and taking appropriate action TL001 Engaging diversity and difference through culturally sensitive communications EX001 Asking questions EX002 Seeking clarification EX007 Going beyond what is said EX008 Reflecting issues EX009 Reflecting hypotheses AS001 Identifying issues AS002 Sharing hypotheses CN001 Establishing goals CN002 Developing action plans CN003 Identifying action steps WE005 Educating WE006 Advising WE007 Representing WE009 Reframing
EP2.1.6: Engage in research-informed practice and practice-informed research	**Supporting Social Work Skills**
PK2.1.6 (1) Social workers use practice experience to inform research, employ evidence-based interventions, evaluate their own practice, and use research findings to improve practice, policy, and social service delivery. PK2.1.6 (2) Social workers comprehend quantitative and qualitative research and understand scientific and ethical approaches to building knowledge.	PF001 Demonstrating integrity PF002 Applying professional knowledge and exhibiting self-efficacy PF005 Thinking critically and inquiring scientifically PF006 Engaging in career-long learning ED002 Applying the fundamental values and ethics of social work ED003 Identifying ethical and legal implications PR003 Preparatory consultation

(Continued)

EP2.1.6: Engage in research-informed practice and practice-informed research		Supporting Social Work Skills
PB2.1.6 (1) Social workers use practice experience to inform scientific inquiry. PB2.1.6 (2) Social workers use research evidence to inform practice.		PR008 Preliminary planning and recording BG006 Seeking feedback AS001 Identifying issues AS002 Sharing hypotheses AS003 Clarifying issues for work AS004 Organizing descriptive information AS005 Preparing an assessment and case formulation CN001 Establishing goals CN002 Developing action plans CN003 Identifying action steps CN004 Planning for evaluation WE003 Evaluating WE005 Educating WE006 Advising WE012 Recording progress (documenting) EN001 Reviewing the process EN002 Final evaluating EN004 Recording the closing summary
EP2.1.7: Apply knowledge of human behavior and the social environment		Supporting Social Work Skills
PK2.1.7 (1) Social workers are knowledgeable about human behavior across the life course; the range of social systems in which people live; and the ways social systems promote or deter people in maintaining or achieving health and well-being. PK2.1.7 (2) Social workers apply theories and knowledge from the liberal arts to understand biological, social, cultural, psychological, and spiritual development.		PF001 Demonstrating integrity PF002 Applying professional knowledge and exhibiting self-efficacy PF005 Thinking critically and inquiring scientifically PF006 Engaging in career-long learning PF007 Valuing diversity and difference PF008 Advancing human rights and social justice PF009 Promoting social well-being and engaging in policy practice ED002 Applying the fundamental values and ethics of social work TL001 Engaging diversity and difference through culturally sensitive communications EX001 Asking questions

PB2.1.7 (1) Social workers utilize conceptual frameworks to guide the processes of assessment, intervention, and evaluation. PB2.1.7 (2) Social workers critique and apply knowledge to understand person and environment.	AS001 Identifying issues AS002 Sharing hypotheses AS005 Preparing an assessment and case formulation CN002 Developing action plans CN003 Identifying action steps CN004 Planning for evaluation WE001 Rehearsing action steps WE002 Reviewing action steps WE003 Evaluating WE004 Focusing WE005 Educating WE006 Advising WE007 Representing WE008 Responding with immediacy WE009 Reframing WE010 Confronting inconsistencies WE011 Pointing out endings WE012 Recording progress (documenting) EN002 Final evaluating EN004 Recording the closing summary
EP2.1.8: Engage in policy practice to deliver effective social work services	**Supporting Social Work Skills**
PK2.1.8 (1) Social workers understand that policy affects service delivery, and actively engage in policy practice. PK2.1.8 (2) Social workers know the history and current structures of social policies and services; the role of policy in service delivery; and the role of practice in policy development.	PF001 Demonstrating integrity PF002 Applying professional knowledge and exhibiting self-efficacy PF005 Thinking critically and inquiring scientifically PF006 Engaging in career-long learning PF007 Valuing diversity and difference PF008 Advancing human rights and social justice PF009 Promoting social well-being and engaging in policy practice ED002 Applying the fundamental values and ethics of social work

(Continued)

EP2.1.8: Engage in policy practice to deliver effective social work services	Supporting Social Work Skills
PB2.1.8 (1) Social workers analyze, formulate, and advocate for policies that advance social well-being. PB2.1.8 (2) Social workers collaborate with colleagues and clients for effective policy action.	TL001 Engaging diversity and difference through culturally sensitive communications TL002 Communicating nonverbally and using body language TL003 Talking: Using speech and language TL004 Listening: hearing, observing, encouraging, and remembering TL005 Active listening: combining talking and listening to promote understanding PR001 Preparatory reviewing PR002 Preparatory exploring PR003 Preparatory consultation PR004 Preparatory arranging PR005 Preparatory empathy PR006 Preparatory self-exploration PR007 Centering PR008 Preliminary planning and recording BG003 Describing an initial purpose BG004 Orienting clients BG005 Discussing policy and ethical factors BG006 Seeking feedback EX001 Asking questions EX002 Seeking clarification EX003 Reflecting content EX004 Reflecting feelings EX005 Reflecting feelings and meanings EX006 Partializing EX007 Going beyond what is said EX008 Reflecting issues EX009 Reflecting hypotheses

AS001 Identifying issues
AS002 Sharing hypotheses
AS003 Clarifying issues for work
AS004 Organizing descriptive information
AS005 Preparing an assessment and case formulation
CN001 Establishing goals
CN002 Developing action plans
CN003 Identifying action steps
CN004 Planning for evaluation
WE001 Rehearsing action steps
WE002 Reviewing action steps
WE003 Evaluating
WE004 Focusing
WE005 Educating
WE006 Advising
WE007 Representing
WE008 Responding with immediacy
WE009 Reframing
WE010 Confronting inconsistencies
WE011 Pointing out endings
WE012 Recording progress (documenting)
EN001 Reviewing the process
EN002 Final evaluating
EN004 Recording the closing summary

Supporting Social Work Skills
PF002 Applying professional knowledge and exhibiting self-efficacy
PF005 Thinking critically and inquiring scientifically
PF006 Engaging in career-long learning
PF009 Promoting social well-being and engaging in policy practice

EP2.1.9: Respond to contexts that shape practice
PK2.1.9 (1) Social workers are informed, resourceful, and proactive in responding to evolving organizational, community, and societal contexts at all levels of practice.

(Continued)

EP2.1.9: Respond to contexts that shape practice	Supporting Social Work Skills		
PK2.1.9 (2) Social workers recognize that the context of practice is dynamic, and use knowledge and skill to respond proactively. PB2.1.9 (1) Social workers continuously discover, appraise, and attend to changing locales, populations, scientific and technological developments, and emerging societal trends to provide relevant services. PB2.1.9 (2) Social workers provide leadership in promoting sustainable changes in service delivery and practice to improve the quality of social services.	TL004 Listening: hearing, observing, encouraging, and remembering PR001 Preparatory reviewing PR002 Preparatory exploring PR003 Preparatory consultation PR008 Preliminary planning and recording BG003 Describing an initial purpose EX001 Asking questions EX002 Seeking clarification EX007 Going beyond what is said AS001 Identifying issues AS002 Sharing hypotheses AS005 Preparing an assessment and case formulation CN001 Establishing goals CN002 Developing action plans CN003 Identifying action steps CN004 Planning for evaluation WE005 Educating WE006 Advising WE007 Representing EN001 Reviewing the process EN002 Final evaluating		
EP2.1.10 (a–d) Engage, assess, intervene, and evaluate with individuals, families, groups, organizations, and communities	Supporting Social Work Skills		
PK2.1.10 (a–d) (1) Professional practice involves the dynamic and interactive processes of engagement, assessment, intervention, and evaluation at multiple levels. PK2.1.10 (a–d) (2) Social workers have the knowledge and skills to practice with individuals, families, groups, organizations, and communities.	Common Conditions (CC) CC001 Demonstrating empathy CC002 Demonstrating respect CC003 Demonstrating authenticity		

	Professionalism (PF)
PK2.1.10 (a–d) (3) Practice knowledge includes identifying, analyzing, and implementing evidence-based interventions designed to achieve client goals.	PF001 Demonstrating integrity
PK2.1.10 (a–d) (4) Practice knowledge includes using research and technological advances.	PF002 Applying professional knowledge and exhibiting self-efficacy
PK2.1.10 (a–d) (5) Practice knowledge includes evaluating program outcomes and practice effectiveness.	PF003 Demonstrating self-understanding and maintaining self-control
PK2.1.10 (a–d) (6) Practice knowledge includes developing, analyzing, advocating, and providing leadership for policies and services.	PF004 Giving and receiving social support
PK2.1.10 (a–d) (7) Practice knowledge includes promoting social and economic justice.	PF005 Thinking critically and inquiring scientifically
PB2.1.10 (a) (1) Social workers substantively and affectively prepare for action with individuals, families, groups, organizations, and communities.	PF006 Engaging in career-long learning
PB2.1.10 (a) (2) Social workers use empathy and other interpersonal skills.	PF007 Valuing diversity and difference
PB2.1.10 (a) (3) Social workers develop a mutually agreed-on focus of work and desired outcomes.	PF008 Advancing human rights and social justice
PB2.1.10 (b) (1) Social workers collect, organize, and interpret client data.	PF009 Promoting social well-being and engaging in policy practice
	Ethical Decision Making (ED)
PB2.1.10 (b) (2) Social workers assess client strengths and limitations.	ED001 Recognizing legal duties
PB2.1.10 (b) (3) Social workers develop mutually agreed-on intervention goals and objectives.	ED002 Applying the fundamental values and ethics of social work
PB2.1.10 (b) (4) Social workers select appropriate intervention strategies.	ED003 Identifying ethical and legal implications
PB2.1.10 (c) (1) Social workers initiate actions to achieve organizational goals.	ED004 Resolving ethical dilemmas and taking appropriate action
PB2.1.10 (c) (2) Social workers implement prevention interventions that enhance client capacities.	TL001 Engaging diversity and difference through culturally sensitive communications
PB2.1.10 (c) (3) Social workers help clients resolve problems.	**Talking and Listening Skills (TL)**
	TL002 Communicating nonverbally and using body language
	TL003 Talking: using speech and language
	TL004 Listening: hearing, observing, encouraging, and remembering
	TL005 Active listening: combining talking and listening to promote understanding
	Preparing Skills (PR)
	PR001 Preparatory reviewing
	PR002 Preparatory exploring
	PR003 Preparatory consultation
	PR004 Preparatory arranging
	PR005 Preparatory empathy

(Continued)

EP2.1.10 (a-d) Engage, assess, intervene, and evaluate with individuals, families, groups, organizations, and communities	Supporting Social Work Skills
PB2.1.10 (c) (4) Social workers negotiate, mediate, and advocate for clients. PB2.1.10 (c) (5) Social workers facilitate transitions and endings. PB2.1.10 (d) (1) Social workers critically analyze, monitor, and evaluate interventions.	PR006 Preparatory self-exploration PR007 Centering **PR008** Preliminary planning and recording **Beginning Skills (BG)** BG001 Introducing yourself BG002 Seeking introductions BG003 Describing an initial purpose BG004 Orienting clients BG005 Discussing policy and ethical factors BG006 Seeking feedback **Exploring Skills (EX)** EX001 Asking questions EX002 Seeking clarification EX003 Reflecting content EX004 Reflecting feelings EX005 Reflecting feelings and meanings EX006 Partializing EX007 Going beyond what is said EX008 Reflecting issues EX009 Reflecting hypotheses **Assessing Skills (AS)** AS001 Identifying issues AS002 Sharing hypotheses AS003 Clarifying issues for work AS004 Organizing descriptive information AS005 Preparing an assessment and case formulation

Contracting Skills (CN)
CN001 Establishing goals
CN002 Developing action plans
CN003 Identifying action steps
CN004 Planning for evaluation
CN005 Summarizing the contract

Working and Evaluating Skills (WE)
WE001 Rehearsing action steps
WE002 Reviewing action steps
WE003 Evaluating
WE004 Focusing
WE005 Educating
WE006 Advising
WE007 Representing
WE008 Responding with immediacy
WE009 Reframing
WE010 Confronting inconsistencies
WE011 Pointing out endings
WE012 Recording progress (documenting)

Ending Skills (EN)
EN001 Reviewing the process
EN002 Final evaluating
EN003 Sharing ending feelings and saying goodbye
EN004 Recording the closing summary

SELF-APPRAISAL OF PROFICIENCY IN THE EPAS CORE COMPETENCIES, PRACTICE KNOWLEDGE, AND PRACTICE BEHAVIORS

Derived from the Educational Policy and Accreditation Standards (EPAS) of the Council on Social Work Education (CSWE) (2008), this self-appraisal instrument helps you to an estimate of your self-appraised proficiency in the knowledge and practice abilities currently required of social work graduates of accredited educational programs. Read each item[1] carefully. Then, use the following 4-point rating scale to indicate the degree to which you agree or disagree with each statement. Mark a check in the box below the number that best reflections your opinion.

4 = Strongly agree

2 = Disagree

3 = Agree

1 = Strongly disagree

				Self-Appraisal of Proficiency in the EPAS Core Competencies, Practice Knowledge, and Practice Behaviors
4	3	2	1	**Rating Statement**
				At this point in time, I can or do
☐	☐	☐	☐	1. Identify with the social work profession and behave professionally. EP2.1.1
☐	☐	☐	☐	2. Serve as a representative of the profession, its mission, and its core values. PK2.1.1 (1)
☐	☐	☐	☐	3. Know the profession's history. PK2.1.1 (2)

---

[1] Items adapted from the Council on Social Work Education's "Educational Policy and Accreditation Standards" (2008) available at www.cswe.org.

4	3	2	1	Rating Statement
☐	☐	☐	☐	4. Demonstrate commitment to the profession's enhancement and to my own professional conduct and growth. PK2.1.1 (3)
☐	☐	☐	☐	5. Advocate for client access to the services of social work. PB2.1.1 (1)
☐	☐	☐	☐	6. Practice personal reflection and self-correction to assure continual professional development. PB2.1.1 (2)
☐	☐	☐	☐	7. Attend to professional roles and boundaries. PB2.1.1 (3)
☐	☐	☐	☐	8. Demonstrate professional demeanor in behavior, appearance, and communication. PB2.1.1 (4)
☐	☐	☐	☐	9. Engage in career-long learning. PB2.1.1 (5)
☐	☐	☐	☐	10. Use supervision and consultation. PB2.1.1 (6)
☐	☐	☐	☐	11. Apply social work ethical principles to guide professional practice. EP2.1.2
☐	☐	☐	☐	12. Conduct myself ethically and engage in ethical decision making. PK2.1.2 (1)
☐	☐	☐	☐	13. Know the value base of the profession, its ethical standards, and relevant law. PK2.1.2 (2)
☐	☐	☐	☐	14. Recognize and manage personal values in a way that allows professional values to guide practice. PB2.1.2 (1)
☐	☐	☐	☐	15. Make ethical decisions by applying standards of the NASW Code of Ethics and, as applicable, of the IFSW/International Association of Schools of Social Work Ethics in Social Work Statement of Principles. PB2.1.2 (2)
☐	☐	☐	☐	16. Tolerate ambiguity in resolving ethical conflicts. PB2.1.2 (3)
☐	☐	☐	☐	17. Apply strategies of ethical reasoning to arrive at principled decisions. PB2.1.2 (4)
☐	☐	☐	☐	18. Apply critical thinking to inform and communicate professional judgments. EP2.1.3
☐	☐	☐	☐	19. Know about the principles of logic, scientific inquiry, and reasoned discernment. PK2.1.3 (1)
☐	☐	☐	☐	20. Engage in critical thinking augmented by creativity and curiosity, and synthesize and communicate relevant information. PK2.1.3 (2)
☐	☐	☐	☐	21. Distinguish, appraise, and integrate multiple sources of knowledge, including research-based knowledge, and practice wisdom. PB2.1.3 (1)
☐	☐	☐	☐	22. Analyze models of assessment, prevention, intervention, and evaluation. PB2.1.3 (2)
☐	☐	☐	☐	23. Demonstrate effective oral and written communication in working with individuals, families, groups, organizations, communities, and colleagues. PB2.1.3 (3)

Self-Appraisal of Proficiency in the EPAS Core Competencies, Practice Knowledge, and Practice Behaviors				
4	**3**	**2**	**1**	**Rating Statement**
☐	☐	☐	☐	24. Engage diversity and difference in practice. EP2.1.4
☐	☐	☐	☐	25. Understand how diversity characterizes and shapes the human experience and is critical to the formation of identity. PK2.1.4 (1)
☐	☐	☐	☐	26. Understand diversity as intersection of multiple factors (age, class, color, culture, disability, ethnicity, gender, gender identity and expression, immigration status, political ideology, race, religion, and sexual orientation). PK2.1.4 (2)
☐	☐	☐	☐	27. Understand that, as a consequence of difference, a person's life experiences may include oppression, poverty, marginalization, and alienation as well as privilege, power, and acclaim. PK2.1.4 (3)
☐	☐	☐	☐	28. Recognize the extent to which a culture's structures and values may oppress, marginalize, alienate, or create or enhance privilege and power. PB2.1.4 (1)
☐	☐	☐	☐	29. Gain sufficient self-awareness to eliminate the influence of personal biases and values in working with diverse groups. PB2.1.4 (2)
☐	☐	☐	☐	30. Recognize and communicate my understanding of the importance of difference in shaping life experiences. PB2.1.4 (3)
☐	☐	☐	☐	31. View myself as a learner and engage those with whom I work as informants. PB2.1.4 (4)
☐	☐	☐	☐	32. Promote human rights and social justice. EP2.1.5
☐	☐	☐	☐	33. Understand that each person, regardless of position in society, has basic human rights, such as freedom, safety, privacy, an adequate standard of living, health care, and education. PK2.1.5 (1)
☐	☐	☐	☐	34. Recognize the global interconnections of oppression and am knowledgeable about theories of justice and strategies to promote human and civil rights. PK2.1.5 (2)
☐	☐	☐	☐	35. Incorporate social justice practices in organizations, institutions, and society to ensure that basic human rights are distributed equitably and without prejudice. PK2.1.5 (3)
☐	☐	☐	☐	36. Understand the forms and mechanisms of oppression and discrimination. PB2.1.5 (1)
☐	☐	☐	☐	37. Advocate for human rights and social and economic justice. PB2.1.5 (2)
☐	☐	☐	☐	38. Engage in practices that advance social and economic justice. PB2.1.5 (3)
☐	☐	☐	☐	39. Engage in research-informed practice and practice-informed research. EP2.1.6

4	3	2	1	Rating Statement
☐	☐	☐	☐	40. Use practice experience to inform research, employ evidence-based interventions, evaluate their own practice, and use research findings to improve practice, policy, and social service delivery. PK2.1.6 (1)
☐	☐	☐	☐	41. Comprehend quantitative and qualitative research and understand scientific and ethical approaches to building knowledge. PK2.1.6 (2)
☐	☐	☐	☐	42. Use practice experience to inform scientific inquiry. PB2.1.6 (1)
☐	☐	☐	☐	43. Use research evidence to inform practice. PB2.1.6 (2)
☐	☐	☐	☐	44. Apply knowledge of human behavior and the social environment. EP2.1.7
☐	☐	☐	☐	45. Know about human behavior across the life course; the range of social systems in which people live; and the ways social systems promote or deter people in maintaining or achieving health and well-being. PK2.1.7 (1)
☐	☐	☐	☐	46. Apply theories and knowledge from the liberal arts to understand biological, social, cultural, psychological, and spiritual development. PK2.1.7 (2)
☐	☐	☐	☐	47. Utilize conceptual frameworks to guide the processes of assessment, intervention, and evaluation. PB2.1.7 (1)
☐	☐	☐	☐	48. Critique and apply knowledge to understand person and environment. PB2.1.7 (2)
☐	☐	☐	☐	49. Engage in policy practice to deliver effective social work services. EP2.1.8
☐	☐	☐	☐	50. Understand that policy affects service delivery, and I actively engage in policy practice. PK2.1.8 (1)
☐	☐	☐	☐	51. Know the history and current structures of social policies and services; the role of policy in service delivery; and the role of practice in policy development. PK2.1.8 (2)
☐	☐	☐	☐	52. Analyze, formulate, and advocate for policies that advance social well-being. PB2.1.8 (1)
☐	☐	☐	☐	53. Collaborate with colleagues and clients for effective policy action. PB2.1.8 (2)
☐	☐	☐	☐	54. Respond to and shape an ever-changing professional context. EP2.1.9
☐	☐	☐	☐	55. Am informed, resourceful, and proactive in responding to evolving organizational, community, and societal contexts at all levels of practice. PK2.1.9 (1)
☐	☐	☐	☐	56. Understand that the context of practice is dynamic, and use knowledge and skill to respond proactively. PK2.1.9 (2)
☐	☐	☐	☐	57. Continuously discover, appraise, and attend to changing locales, populations, scientific and technological developments, and emerging societal trends to provide relevant services. PB2.1.9 (1)

				Self-Appraisal of Proficiency in the EPAS Core Competencies, Practice Knowledge, and Practice Behaviors
4	**3**	**2**	**1**		**Rating Statement**
☐	☐	☐	☐		58. Provide leadership in promoting sustainable changes in service delivery and practice to improve the quality of social services. PB2.1.9 (2)
☐	☐	☐	☐		59. Engage, assess, intervene, and evaluate with individuals, families, groups, organizations, and communities. EP2.1.10(a–d)
☐	☐	☐	☐		60. Understand the dynamic and interactive processes of engagement, assessment, intervention, and evaluation at multiple levels. PK2.1.10(a–d) (1)
☐	☐	☐	☐		61. Have the knowledge and skills to practice with individuals, families, groups, organizations, and communities. PK2.1.10(a–d) (2)
☐	☐	☐	☐		62. Identify, analyze, and implement evidence-based interventions designed to achieve client goals. PK2.1.10(a–d) (3)
☐	☐	☐	☐		63. Understand how to use research and technological advances. PK2.1.10(a–d) (4)
☐	☐	☐	☐		64. Understand how to evaluate program outcomes and practice effectiveness. PK2.1.10(a–d) (5)
☐	☐	☐	☐		65. Understand how to develop, analyze, advocate, and provide leadership for policies and services. PK2.1.10(a–d) (6)
☐	☐	☐	☐		66. Understand how to promote social and economic justice. PK2.1.10(a–d) (7)
☐	☐	☐	☐		67. Substantively and affectively prepare for action with individuals, families, groups, organizations, and communities. PB2.1.10 (a) (1)
☐	☐	☐	☐		68. Use empathy and other interpersonal skills. PB2.1.10 (a) (2)
☐	☐	☐	☐		69. Develop mutually agreed-on focuses of work and desired outcomes. PB2.1.10 (a) (3)
☐	☐	☐	☐		70. Collect, organize, and interpret client data. PB2.1.10 (b) (1)
☐	☐	☐	☐		71. Assess client strengths and limitations. PB2.1.10 (b) (2)
☐	☐	☐	☐		72. Develop mutually agreed-on intervention goals and objectives. PB2.1.10 (b) (3)
☐	☐	☐	☐		73. Select appropriate intervention strategies. PB2.1.10 (b) (4)
☐	☐	☐	☐		74. Initiate actions to achieve organizational goals; PB2.1.10 (c) (1)
☐	☐	☐	☐		75. Implement prevention interventions that enhance client capacities. PB2.1.10 (c) (2)

4	3	2	1	Rating Statement
☐	☐	☐	☐	76. Help clients resolve problems. PB2.1.10 (c) (3)
☐	☐	☐	☐	77. Negotiate, mediate, and advocate for clients. PB2.1.10 (c) (4)
☐	☐	☐	☐	78. Facilitate transitions and endings. PB2.1.10 (c) (5)
☐	☐	☐	☐	79. Critically analyze, monitor, and evaluate interventions. PB2.1.10 (d) (1)
				Total

This instrument can help you estimate your self-appraised proficiency in the core competencies, practice knowledge, and practice behaviors reflected in the Educational Policy and Accreditation Standards (EPAS) of the Council on Social Work Education (CSWE) (2008). Because it is based on your own appraisal, absolute scores are relatively unimportant. Rather, use the results as a stimulus to ask yourself further questions concerning your knowledge, skills, and abilities; and to develop plans by which to improve your proficiency. You may complete the instrument at various points throughout the learning process. Increased proficiency may be reflected in changing scores over time. In considering your results, please remember that a higher rating suggests a higher level of appraised proficiency.

To score the Self-Appraisal of Proficiency in the EPAS Core Competencies, Practice Knowledge, and Practice Behaviors instrument, simply sum the total of your ratings to the 79 items. Your score should range somewhere between 79 and 316. In theory, a score of 237 (or an average of 3 on each of the 79 items) would indicate that, on average, you "agree" with statements suggesting that you are quite proficient. Please note, however, that such an average score does not necessarily indicate that you are proficient in all dimensions. You might obtain such a score by rating several items at the "4" or "strongly agree" level and an equal number at the "2" or "disagree level." Therefore, you should look carefully at your rating for each item, as well as the total score.

If all learners in your program share their item ratings and total scores, perhaps anonymously, with a professor or program administrator, responses can be aggregated. When analyzed, they may reveal areas where students believe they are proficient and areas that require additional study or practice. Comparison of pre- and post-test scores of individual students or those of student cohorts represents another way to use this self-appraisal to assess progress and promote learning.

Finally, you should recognize that this instrument reflects your own subjective opinions. You may consciously or unconsciously overestimate or perhaps underestimate your proficiency. Therefore, please use these results in conjunction with other evidence to establish a more balanced appraisal.

SELF-APPRAISAL OF PROFICIENCY IN THE ASWB KNOWLEDGE, SKILLS, AND ABILITIES (BACHELOR'S LEVEL)

Derived from the content addressed in the Bachelor's level licensing examination of the Association of Social Work Board (ASWB) (2011), this self-appraisal instrument helps you to an estimate of your self-appraised proficiency in the knowledge, skills, and abilities currently reflected in social work practice. Read each item[1] carefully. Then, use the following 4-point rating scale to indicate the degree to which you agree or disagree with each statement. Mark a check in the box below the number that best reflections your opinion.

4 = Strongly agree

3 = Agree

2 = Disagree

1 = Strongly disagree

				Self-Appraisal of Proficiency in the ASWB Bachelor's Level Social Work Licensing Exam Knowledge, Skills, and Abilities
4	**3**	**2**	**1**	**Rating Statement**
				In my functioning as a social worker, I can or do apply a genuine understanding of
☐	☐	☐	☐	1. Typical and atypical physical growth and development
☐	☐	☐	☐	2. Typical and atypical cognitive growth and development
☐	☐	☐	☐	3. Typical and atypical social growth, development, and the socialization process

---

[1] Items adapted from "Content Outlines and KSAs: Social Work Licensing Examinations" (2011) available at www.aswb.org.

4	3	2	1	Rating Statement
☐	☐	☐	☐	4. Typical and atypical emotional growth and development
☐	☐	☐	☐	5. Typical and atypical sexual growth and development
☐	☐	☐	☐	6. Spiritual growth and development
☐	☐	☐	☐	7. Child behavior and development
☐	☐	☐	☐	8. Adolescent behavior and development
☐	☐	☐	☐	9. Young adult behavior and development
☐	☐	☐	☐	10. Middle adult behavior and development
☐	☐	☐	☐	11. Older adult behavior and development
☐	☐	☐	☐	12. The impact of physical, mental, and cognitive impairment on human development
☐	☐	☐	☐	13. The interplay of biological, psychological, social, and spiritual factors
☐	☐	☐	☐	14. Attachment and bonding
☐	☐	☐	☐	15. Basic human needs
☐	☐	☐	☐	16. Strengths-based and resilience theories
☐	☐	☐	☐	17. Defense mechanisms and human behavior
☐	☐	☐	☐	18. The psychosocial model
☐	☐	☐	☐	19. Group theories
☐	☐	☐	☐	20. Family theories and dynamics
☐	☐	☐	☐	21. Systems and ecological perspectives
☐	☐	☐	☐	22. Social change and community development theories
☐	☐	☐	☐	23. The influence of social context on behavior
☐	☐	☐	☐	24. Role theories
☐	☐	☐	☐	25. Gender roles
☐	☐	☐	☐	26. The interaction of culture, race, and/or ethnicity with behaviors, attitudes, and identity
☐	☐	☐	☐	27. The interaction of sexual orientation and/or gender with behaviors, attitudes, and identity
☐	☐	☐	☐	28. The interaction of age and/or disability with behaviors, attitudes, and identity
☐	☐	☐	☐	29. The interaction of spirituality and religion with behaviors, attitudes, and identity
☐	☐	☐	☐	30. The interaction of socioeconomic status with behaviors, attitudes, and identity
☐	☐	☐	☐	31. The dynamics and effects of stereotypes and discrimination

Self-Appraisal of Proficiency in the ASWB Bachelor's Level Social Work Licensing Exam Knowledge, Skills, and Abilities				
4	**3**	**2**	**1**	**Rating Statement**
☐	☐	☐	☐	32. The relationship of diversity and communication styles
☐	☐	☐	☐	33. The impact of the physical environment on client systems
☐	☐	☐	☐	34. The impact of the political environment on policy making and client systems
☐	☐	☐	☐	35. The impact of the social environment on client systems
☐	☐	☐	☐	36. The impact of the cultural environment on client systems
☐	☐	☐	☐	37. How to gather a biological, psychological, social, and spiritual history
☐	☐	☐	☐	38. How to gather and evaluate collateral information
☐	☐	☐	☐	39. Types of information available from employment, medical, psychological, psychiatric, and educational records
☐	☐	☐	☐	40. The components of a sexual history
☐	☐	☐	☐	41. The components of a family history
☐	☐	☐	☐	42. The process used in problem formulation
☐	☐	☐	☐	43. The methods of involving the client system in identifying the problem
☐	☐	☐	☐	44. The process of identifying the client system needs
☐	☐	☐	☐	45. The process of referring the client for additional evaluations (for example, medical, psychological, educational, and so on)
☐	☐	☐	☐	46. The use of assessment instruments in practice
☐	☐	☐	☐	47. Assessment of the client system's communication skills
☐	☐	☐	☐	48. Assessment of the client system's strengths, resources, and challenges
☐	☐	☐	☐	49. Assessment of the client system's ability and motivation to engage in the intervention process
☐	☐	☐	☐	50. Assessment of the client system's coping abilities
☐	☐	☐	☐	51. Assessment of the client's needed level of care (for example, supportive services, residential placement, continuum of care, and so on)
☐	☐	☐	☐	52. Assessment of group functioning
☐	☐	☐	☐	53. Assessment of community functioning
☐	☐	☐	☐	54. Assessment of the functioning of organizations
☐	☐	☐	☐	55. The differentiation of the use of, abuse of, and dependency on substances
☐	☐	☐	☐	56. The effects of addiction on the client
☐	☐	☐	☐	57. The effects of addiction on the family system and other relationships

4	3	2	1	Rating Statement
☐	☐	☐	☐	58. The indicators of addictions to gambling, sex, food, media, and so on
☐	☐	☐	☐	59. The co-occurrence of addiction and other disorders
☐	☐	☐	☐	60. The symptoms of mental and emotional illness across the lifespan
☐	☐	☐	☐	61. The symptoms of neurologic and organic conditions
☐	☐	☐	☐	62. The indicators of behavioral dysfunction
☐	☐	☐	☐	63. Prescription medications and other substances
☐	☐	☐	☐	64. The indicators, dynamics, and impact of sexual abuse across the lifespan
☐	☐	☐	☐	65. The indicators, dynamics, and impact of emotional abuse and neglect across the lifespan
☐	☐	☐	☐	66. The indicators, dynamics, and impact of physical abuse and neglect across the lifespan
☐	☐	☐	☐	67. The indicators, dynamics, and impact of intimate partner violence
☐	☐	☐	☐	68. The indicators, dynamics, and impact of other forms of exploitation across the lifespan (for example, financial, immigration status, sexual trafficking, and so on)
☐	☐	☐	☐	69. The dynamics and effects of life stage and life-cycle crises
☐	☐	☐	☐	70. The impact of physical and mental illness
☐	☐	☐	☐	71. The dynamics and effects of trauma
☐	☐	☐	☐	72. The dynamics and effects of loss, separation, and grief
☐	☐	☐	☐	73. The impact of care giving on families
☐	☐	☐	☐	74. Indicators of and response to client danger to self and others
☐	☐	☐	☐	75. Stages of crises
☐	☐	☐	☐	76. The development and maintenance of a helping relationship
☐	☐	☐	☐	77. The development, evaluation, and establishment of a measurable intervention plan
☐	☐	☐	☐	78. Techniques used to engage and motivate client systems
☐	☐	☐	☐	79. Work with involuntary client systems
☐	☐	☐	☐	80. How to contract with client systems
☐	☐	☐	☐	81. Clarification of the roles and responsibilities of the client system
☐	☐	☐	☐	82. Termination and follow-up in social work practice
☐	☐	☐	☐	83. The effect of caseload management on client systems
☐	☐	☐	☐	84. The crisis intervention approach
☐	☐	☐	☐	85. Cognitive and/or behavioral interventions

Self-Appraisal of Proficiency in the ASWB Bachelor's Level Social Work Licensing Exam Knowledge, Skills, and Abilities				
4	**3**	**2**	**1**	**Rating Statement**
☐	☐	☐	☐	86. Strengths-based and empowerment practice
☐	☐	☐	☐	87. Problem-solving approaches
☐	☐	☐	☐	88. Techniques used to teach skills to client systems (for example, role play, modeling, and so on)
☐	☐	☐	☐	89. Provision of education and information to client systems (for example, parenting, psychosocial aspects of health and illness, and so on)
☐	☐	☐	☐	90. How to teach coping strategies to client systems (for example, assertiveness, conflict resolution, stress management, and so on)
☐	☐	☐	☐	91. Group work approaches
☐	☐	☐	☐	92. Family practice approaches
☐	☐	☐	☐	93. Community practice approaches
☐	☐	☐	☐	94. Social policy development and analysis
☐	☐	☐	☐	95. Advocacy for micro-, mezzo-, and macro-client systems
☐	☐	☐	☐	96. Intervention with organizations (for example, organizational policy development, hierarchy, formal and informal power structures, and so on)
☐	☐	☐	☐	97. Determination of which individual, family, group, or combined modality meets the needs of client systems
☐	☐	☐	☐	98. Determination of which community or organizational approach meets the needs of client systems
☐	☐	☐	☐	99. The effect of the client system's abilities on the selection of an intervention (for example, literacy, employability, developmental level, cognitive ability, physical ability, and so on)
☐	☐	☐	☐	100. The effect of the client system's culture on the selection of an intervention
☐	☐	☐	☐	101. The effect of the client system's life stage on the selection of an intervention
☐	☐	☐	☐	102. Provision of case management services
☐	☐	☐	☐	103. How to refer client systems for services
☐	☐	☐	☐	104. Determination of the client's eligibility for services
☐	☐	☐	☐	105. Scope of practice and basic terminology of professions other than social work
☐	☐	☐	☐	106. The use of consultation and case conferences
☐	☐	☐	☐	107. Interdisciplinary and intradisciplinary team approaches

4	3	2	1	Rating Statement
☐	☐	☐	☐	108. Establishment, maintenance, and utilization of formal and informal service networks or community resources and supports
☐	☐	☐	☐	109. The use of objective and subjective data in written assessments and case notes
☐	☐	☐	☐	110. How to write and maintain client records (for example, client progress notes, and so on)
☐	☐	☐	☐	111. Development of reports for external organizations (for example, the courts, and so on)
☐	☐	☐	☐	112. Development of administrative reports (for example, grant reports, outcomes and evaluations, program proposals, accreditation reports, and so on)
☐	☐	☐	☐	113. How to record and monitor assessments and service plans
☐	☐	☐	☐	114. How to obtain and record service-related forms (for example, informed consent for services, consent for release of information, advanced directives, Do Not Resuscitate [DNR] and so on)
☐	☐	☐	☐	115. Legal and ethical issues regarding documentation
☐	☐	☐	☐	116. How to obtain information relevant to a given situation
☐	☐	☐	☐	117. The use of verbal and nonverbal communication techniques
☐	☐	☐	☐	118. Identification of the underlying meaning of communication
☐	☐	☐	☐	119. The use of active listening and observation
☐	☐	☐	☐	120. Interview techniques (for example, supporting, clarifying, confronting, validating, feedback, reflecting, and so on)
☐	☐	☐	☐	121. Elicitation of sensitive information (for example, substance abuse, sexual abuse, and so on)
☐	☐	☐	☐	122. How to interview clients with communication barriers (for example, language differences, use of interpreters, and so on)
☐	☐	☐	☐	123. Use of bias-free language in interviewing
☐	☐	☐	☐	124. How to respond to clients' resistant behaviors
☐	☐	☐	☐	125. Evaluation of one's own practice (for example, single-subject designs, goal-attainment scaling, task-achievement scaling, use of scales and instruments, and so on)
☐	☐	☐	☐	126. Critical evaluation of relevant research and statistical data (that is, understanding basic research design and methods)
☐	☐	☐	☐	127. Selection of interventions based on research
☐	☐	☐	☐	128. The use of data to inform and influence organizational and social policy

4	3	2	1	Self-Appraisal of Proficiency in the ASWB Bachelor's Level Social Work Licensing Exam Knowledge, Skills, and Abilities
				Rating Statement
☐	☐	☐	☐	129. The use of program evaluation (for example, needs assessment, formative and summative, cost-effectiveness, cost–benefit analysis, outcomes assessment, and so on)
☐	☐	☐	☐	130. Ethical issues and boundaries in the social worker–client relationship (for example, dual relationships, power differences, conflicts of interest, and so on)
☐	☐	☐	☐	131. The influence of the social worker's own values on the social worker–client system relationship
☐	☐	☐	☐	132. Ethical and legal issues regarding termination
☐	☐	☐	☐	133. Identification and resolution of ethical dilemmas
☐	☐	☐	☐	134. Ethical and legal issues regarding mandatory reporting (for example, abuse, threat of harm, impaired professionals, and so on)
☐	☐	☐	☐	135. Professional values and ethics (for example, competence, social justice, integrity, worth of the individual, and so on)
☐	☐	☐	☐	136. Legal and ethical issues regarding confidentiality
☐	☐	☐	☐	137. The secure use of client records, including electronic information
☐	☐	☐	☐	138. Legal and ethical issues regarding confidentiality and the competency of the client
☐	☐	☐	☐	139. Legal and ethical issues regarding confidentiality and minors
☐	☐	☐	☐	140. Protection and enhancement of client system self-determination
☐	☐	☐	☐	141. The client's right to refuse services (for example, medication, medical treatment, counseling, placement, and so on)
☐	☐	☐	☐	142. Minors and self-determination (for example, emancipation, age of consent, permanency planning and so on)
☐	☐	☐	☐	143. Competence and self-determination (for example, financial decisions, treatment decisions, and so on)
☐	☐	☐	☐	144. How to balance self-determination and client risk (for example, suicidal, homicidal, grave danger, and so on)
☐	☐	☐	☐	145. The use of empathy in the social worker–client relationship
☐	☐	☐	☐	146. The concepts of transference and countertransference
☐	☐	☐	☐	147. The use of acceptance in the social worker–client relationship
☐	☐	☐	☐	148. The appropriate use of self-disclosure

4	3	2	1	Rating Statement
☐	☐	☐	☐	149. Recognition and management of burnout, secondary trauma, and compassion fatigue
☐	☐	☐	☐	150. Transference and countertransference within supervisory relationships
☐	☐	☐	☐	151. Supervisee's role in supervision (for example, identifying learning needs, self-assessment, prioritizing, and so on)
☐	☐	☐	☐	152. The use of ongoing professional development to improve practice and stay current (for example, in-service training, licensing requirements, reviews of literature, workshops, and so on)
☐	☐	☐	☐	153. Differential use of consultation, peer support, and supervision
				Total

This instrument can help you estimate your self-appraised proficiency in the knowledge, skills, and abilities addressed in the ASWB-sponsored Bachelor's-level social work licensing examination. Because it is based on your own appraisal, absolute scores are relatively unimportant. Rather, use the results as a stimulus to ask yourself further questions concerning your knowledge, skills, and abilities; and to develop plans by which to improve your proficiency. You may complete the instrument at various points throughout the learning process. Increased proficiency may be reflected in changing scores over time. In considering your results, please remember that a higher rating suggests a higher level of appraised proficiency.

To score the Self-Appraisal of Proficiency in the ASWB Knowledge, Skills, and Abilities instrument, simply sum the total of your ratings to the 153 items. Your score should range somewhere between 153 and 612. In theory, a score of 459 (or an average of 3 on each of the 153 items) would indicate that, on average, you "agree" with statements suggesting that you are quite proficient. Please note, however, that such an average score does not necessarily indicate that you are proficient in all dimensions. You might obtain such a score by rating several items at the "4" or "strongly agree" level and an equal number at the "2" or "disagree level." Therefore, you should look carefully at your rating for each item, as well as the total score.

If all learners in your program share their item ratings and total scores, perhaps anonymously, with a professor or program administrator, responses can be aggregated. When analyzed, they may reveal areas where students believe they are proficient and areas that require additional study or practice. Comparison of pre- and post-test scores of individual students or those of student cohorts represents another way to use this self-appraisal to assess progress and promote learning.

Finally, you should recognize that this instrument reflects your own subjective opinions. You may consciously or unconsciously overestimate or perhaps underestimate your proficiency. Therefore, please use these results in conjunction with other evidence to establish a more balanced approximation of your current knowledge, skills, and abilities.

SELF-APPRAISAL OF PROFICIENCY IN THE ASWB KNOWLEDGE, SKILLS, AND ABILITIES (MASTER'S LEVEL)

Derived from content addressed in the Master's level licensing examination of the Association of Social Work Board (ASWB) (2011), this self-appraisal instrument helps you to an estimate of your self-appraised proficiency in the knowledge, skills, and abilities currently reflected in social work practice. Read each item[1] carefully. Then, use the following 4-point rating scale to indicate the degree to which you agree or disagree with each statement. Mark a check in the box below the number that best reflections your opinion.

4 = Strongly agree

3 = Agree

2 = Disagree

1 = Strongly disagree

				Self-Appraisal of Proficiency in the ASWB Master's Level Social Work Licensing Exam Knowledge, Skills, and Abilities
4	3	2	1	**Rating Statement**
				In my functioning as a social worker, I can or do apply a genuine understanding of
☐	☐	☐	☐	1. Developmental theories
☐	☐	☐	☐	2. Systems theories
☐	☐	☐	☐	3. Family theories
☐	☐	☐	☐	4. Group theories

---

[1] Items adapted from "Content Outlines and KSAs: Social Work Licensing Examinations" (2011) available at www.aswb.org.

4	3	2	1	Rating Statement
☐	☐	☐	☐	5. Psychodynamic theories
☐	☐	☐	☐	6. Behavioral, cognitive, and learning theories
☐	☐	☐	☐	7. Community development theories
☐	☐	☐	☐	8. Person in environment
☐	☐	☐	☐	9. Addiction theories and concepts
☐	☐	☐	☐	10. Communication theories
☐	☐	☐	☐	11. Defense mechanisms
☐	☐	☐	☐	12. Normal and abnormal behavior
☐	☐	☐	☐	13. Indicators of normal physical growth and development
☐	☐	☐	☐	14. Adult development
☐	☐	☐	☐	15. Effects of life crises
☐	☐	☐	☐	16. Impact of stress, trauma, and violence
☐	☐	☐	☐	17. Emotional development
☐	☐	☐	☐	18. Sexual development
☐	☐	☐	☐	19. Aging processes
☐	☐	☐	☐	20. Family life cycle
☐	☐	☐	☐	21. Family dynamics and functioning
☐	☐	☐	☐	22. Cognitive development
☐	☐	☐	☐	23. Social development
☐	☐	☐	☐	24. Child development
☐	☐	☐	☐	25. Basic human needs
☐	☐	☐	☐	26. Adolescent development
☐	☐	☐	☐	27. Human genetics
☐	☐	☐	☐	28. Gender roles
☐	☐	☐	☐	29. The impact of environment on individuals
☐	☐	☐	☐	30. The impact of physical, mental, and cognitive disabilities on human development
☐	☐	☐	☐	31. The interplay of biological, psychological, and social factors
☐	☐	☐	☐	32. The effects of family dynamics on individuals
☐	☐	☐	☐	33. The dynamics of grief and loss
☐	☐	☐	☐	34. The impact of economic changes on client systems

4	3	2	1	Self-Appraisal of Proficiency in the ASWB Master's Level Social Work Licensing Exam Knowledge, Skills, and Abilities
				Rating Statement
☐	☐	☐	☐	35. The effects of body image on self and relationships
☐	☐	☐	☐	36. Cultural, racial, and ethnic identity development
☐	☐	☐	☐	37. The strengths perspective
☐	☐	☐	☐	38. Abuse and neglect concepts
☐	☐	☐	☐	39. Indicators and dynamics of sexual abuse
☐	☐	☐	☐	40. Indicators and dynamics of psychological abuse and neglect
☐	☐	☐	☐	41. Indicators and dynamics of physical abuse and neglect
☐	☐	☐	☐	42. Characteristics of abuse perpetrators
☐	☐	☐	☐	43. Indicators and dynamics of exploitation
☐	☐	☐	☐	44. The influence of culture, race, and/or ethnicity on behaviors and attitudes
☐	☐	☐	☐	45. The influence of sexual orientation and/or gender identity on behavior and attitudes
☐	☐	☐	☐	46. The influence of disability on behaviors and attitudes
☐	☐	☐	☐	47. The effects of differences in values
☐	☐	☐	☐	48. The impact of cultural heritage on self-image
☐	☐	☐	☐	49. The impact of spirituality and/or religious beliefs on behaviors and attitudes
☐	☐	☐	☐	50. The effects of discrimination
☐	☐	☐	☐	51. Systemic (institutionalized) discrimination
☐	☐	☐	☐	52. Professional commitment to promoting justice
☐	☐	☐	☐	53. The impact of social institutions on society
☐	☐	☐	☐	54. The impact of diversity in styles of communicating
☐	☐	☐	☐	55. The influence of age on behaviors and attitudes
☐	☐	☐	☐	56. Psychopharmacology
☐	☐	☐	☐	57. The components of a biopsychosocial history
☐	☐	☐	☐	58. The components of a sexual history
☐	☐	☐	☐	59. Common prescription medications
☐	☐	☐	☐	60. The components of a family history
☐	☐	☐	☐	61. Basic medical terminology
☐	☐	☐	☐	62. Symptoms of mental and emotional illness

4	3	2	1	Rating Statement
☐	☐	☐	☐	63. Symptoms of neurologic and organic processes
☐	☐	☐	☐	64. Indicators of sexual dysfunction
☐	☐	☐	☐	65. Indicators of psychosocial stress
☐	☐	☐	☐	66. Indicators of traumatic stress and violence
☐	☐	☐	☐	67. Indicators of substance abuse and other addictions
☐	☐	☐	☐	68. The use of collateral sources to obtain relevant information
☐	☐	☐	☐	69. Methods used to evaluate collateral information
☐	☐	☐	☐	70. The process used in problem identification
☐	☐	☐	☐	71. Methods used to assess the client's communication skills
☐	☐	☐	☐	72. The use of observation
☐	☐	☐	☐	73. Methods of involving clients in identifying problems
☐	☐	☐	☐	74. Indicators of client's strengths and challenges
☐	☐	☐	☐	75. The use of assessment/diagnostic instruments in practice
☐	☐	☐	☐	76. Methods used to organize information
☐	☐	☐	☐	77. Current Diagnostic and Statistical Manual diagnostic framework and criteria
☐	☐	☐	☐	78. The components and function of the mental status examination
☐	☐	☐	☐	79. The process of social work assessment/diagnosis
☐	☐	☐	☐	80. Methods used in assessing ego strengths
☐	☐	☐	☐	81. Methods used to assess community strengths and challenges
☐	☐	☐	☐	82. Methods used in risk assessment
☐	☐	☐	☐	83. Indicators of client danger to self and others
☐	☐	☐	☐	84. Indicators of motivation and resistance
☐	☐	☐	☐	85. Methods used to identify service needs of clients
☐	☐	☐	☐	86. The use of interviewing techniques
☐	☐	☐	☐	87. The process of assessing the client's needed level of care
☐	☐	☐	☐	88. Factors used in determining the client's readiness/ability to participate in services
☐	☐	☐	☐	89. Criteria used in selecting intervention modalities
☐	☐	☐	☐	90. The components of an intervention or service plan
☐	☐	☐	☐	91. Human development considerations in the creation of an intervention plan
☐	☐	☐	☐	92. Methods used to develop an intervention plan

	Self-Appraisal of Proficiency in the ASWB Master's Level Social Work Licensing Exam Knowledge, Skills, and Abilities			
4 3 2 1	**Rating Statement**			
☐ ☐ ☐ ☐	93. Techniques used to establish measurable intervention or service plans			
☐ ☐ ☐ ☐	94. Methods used to involve clients in intervention planning			
☐ ☐ ☐ ☐	95. Methods for planning interventions with groups			
☐ ☐ ☐ ☐	96. Methods for planning interventions with organizations and communities			
☐ ☐ ☐ ☐	97. Cultural considerations in the creation of an intervention plan			
☐ ☐ ☐ ☐	98. Client advocacy			
☐ ☐ ☐ ☐	99. Empowerment process			
☐ ☐ ☐ ☐	100. Methods used in working with involuntary clients			
☐ ☐ ☐ ☐	101. Psychosocial approach			
☐ ☐ ☐ ☐	102. Components of the problem-solving process			
☐ ☐ ☐ ☐	103. Crisis intervention approach			
☐ ☐ ☐ ☐	104. Task-centered practice			
☐ ☐ ☐ ☐	105. Short-term interventions			
☐ ☐ ☐ ☐	106. Methods used to provide educational services to clients			
☐ ☐ ☐ ☐	107. Methods of conflict resolution			
☐ ☐ ☐ ☐	108. The use of case management			
☐ ☐ ☐ ☐	109. Techniques used to evaluate a client's progress			
☐ ☐ ☐ ☐	110. The use of contracting and goal setting with client systems			
☐ ☐ ☐ ☐	111. The use of timing in intervention			
☐ ☐ ☐ ☐	112. Phases of intervention			
☐ ☐ ☐ ☐	113. Indicators of client readiness for termination			
☐ ☐ ☐ ☐	114. Techniques used for follow-up in social work practice			
☐ ☐ ☐ ☐	115. The use of active-listening skills			
☐ ☐ ☐ ☐	116. Techniques used to motivate clients			
☐ ☐ ☐ ☐	117. Techniques used to teach skills to clients			
☐ ☐ ☐ ☐	118. The use and effects of out-of-home placement			
☐ ☐ ☐ ☐	119. Methods used to develop behavioral objectives			
☐ ☐ ☐ ☐	120. Client self-monitoring techniques			
☐ ☐ ☐ ☐	121. Technique of role play			
☐ ☐ ☐ ☐	122. Assertiveness training			

4	3	2	1	Rating Statement
☐	☐	☐	☐	123. Role modeling techniques
☐	☐	☐	☐	124. Limit setting
☐	☐	☐	☐	125. Methods used to develop learning objectives with clients
☐	☐	☐	☐	126. Models of intervention with families
☐	☐	☐	☐	127. Couples intervention/treatment approaches
☐	☐	☐	☐	128. Interventions with groups
☐	☐	☐	☐	129. Techniques for working with individuals within the group context
☐	☐	☐	☐	130. The use of expertise from other disciplines
☐	☐	☐	☐	131. Approaches used in consultation
☐	☐	☐	☐	132. Processes of interdisciplinary collaboration
☐	☐	☐	☐	133. Methods used to coordinate services among service providers
☐	☐	☐	☐	134. A multidisciplinary team approach
☐	☐	☐	☐	135. Case recording and record keeping
☐	☐	☐	☐	136. Methods used to facilitate communication
☐	☐	☐	☐	137. Verbal and nonverbal communication techniques
☐	☐	☐	☐	138. Techniques that explore underlying meanings of communication
☐	☐	☐	☐	139. Methods used to obtain/provide feedback
☐	☐	☐	☐	140. Methods used to interpret and communicate policies and procedures
☐	☐	☐	☐	141. Methods used to clarify the benefits and limitations of resources with clients
☐	☐	☐	☐	142. The use of case recording for practice evaluation or supervision
☐	☐	☐	☐	143. The use of single-subject designs in practice
☐	☐	☐	☐	144. Evaluation of practice
☐	☐	☐	☐	145. Interpretation and application of research findings to practice
☐	☐	☐	☐	146. Process used to refer clients for services
☐	☐	☐	☐	147. The use of cognitive-behavioral techniques
☐	☐	☐	☐	148. Culturally competent social work practice
☐	☐	☐	☐	149. Concepts of organizational theories
☐	☐	☐	☐	150. The impact of social welfare legislation on social work practice
☐	☐	☐	☐	151. Methods used to establish service networks or community resources
☐	☐	☐	☐	152. Techniques for mobilizing community participation
☐	☐	☐	☐	153. Techniques of social planning methods

4	3	2	1	Self-Appraisal of Proficiency in the ASWB Master's Level Social Work Licensing Exam Knowledge, Skills, and Abilities
				Rating Statement
☐	☐	☐	☐	154. Techniques of social policy analysis
☐	☐	☐	☐	155. Techniques to influence social policy
☐	☐	☐	☐	156. Techniques of working with large groups
☐	☐	☐	☐	157. The use of networking
☐	☐	☐	☐	158. Approaches to culturally competent practice with organizations and communities
☐	☐	☐	☐	159. Advocacy with communities and organizations
☐	☐	☐	☐	160. The impact of agency policy and function on service delivery
☐	☐	☐	☐	161. Professional values and ethics
☐	☐	☐	☐	162. Client self-determination
☐	☐	☐	☐	163. The intrinsic worth and value of the individual
☐	☐	☐	☐	164. The client's right to refuse service
☐	☐	☐	☐	165. Ethical issues regarding termination
☐	☐	☐	☐	166. Bioethical issues
☐	☐	☐	☐	167. The identification and resolution of ethical dilemmas
☐	☐	☐	☐	168. Ethics to practice issues
☐	☐	☐	☐	169. The responsibility to seek supervision
☐	☐	☐	☐	170. The use of professional development to improve practice
☐	☐	☐	☐	171. Professional boundaries
☐	☐	☐	☐	172. Legal and ethical issues regarding confidentiality, including electronic communication
☐	☐	☐	☐	173. The use of client records
☐	☐	☐	☐	174. Ethical and legal issues regarding mandatory reporting
☐	☐	☐	☐	175. How to obtain informed consent
☐	☐	☐	☐	176. Social worker–client relationship patterns
☐	☐	☐	☐	177. The concept of empathy
☐	☐	☐	☐	178. The process of engagement in social work practice
☐	☐	☐	☐	179. The concept of a helping relationship
☐	☐	☐	☐	180. The principles of relationship building
☐	☐	☐	☐	181. Professional objectivity in the social worker–client relationship
☐	☐	☐	☐	182. The concepts of transference and countertransference

4	3	2	1	Rating Statement
☐	☐	☐	☐	183. The use of the social worker–client relationship as an intervention tool
☐	☐	☐	☐	184. Social worker–client relationships in work with communities and organizations
☐	☐	☐	☐	185. Social worker–client relationships in work with small groups
☐	☐	☐	☐	186. Methods used to clarify roles of the social worker
☐	☐	☐	☐	187. The social worker's roles in the problem-solving process
☐	☐	☐	☐	188. The client's roles in the problem-solving process
☐	☐	☐	☐	189. The influence of the social worker's values on the social worker–client relationship
☐	☐	☐	☐	190. Dual relationships
☐	☐	☐	☐	191. The influence of cultural diversity on the social worker–client relationship
				Total

This instrument can help you estimate your self-appraised proficiency in the knowledge, skills, and abilities addressed in the ASWB-sponsored Bachelor's-level social work licensing examination. Because it is based on your own appraisal, absolute scores are relatively unimportant. Rather, use the results as a stimulus to ask yourself further questions concerning your knowledge, skills, and abilities; and to develop plans by which to improve your proficiency. You may complete the instrument at various points throughout the learning process. Increased proficiency may be reflected in changing scores over time. In considering your results, please remember that a higher rating suggests a higher level of appraised proficiency.

To score the Self-Appraisal of Proficiency in the ASWB Knowledge, Skills, and Abilities instrument, simply sum the total of your ratings to the 191 items. Your score should range somewhere between 191 and 764. In theory, a score of 573 (or an average of 3 on each of the 191 items) would indicate that, on average, you "agree" with statements suggesting that you are quite proficient. Please note, however, that such an average score does not necessarily indicate that you are proficient in all dimensions. You might obtain such a score by rating several items at the "4" or "strongly agree" level and an equal number at the "2" or "disagree level." Therefore, you should look carefully at your rating for each item, as well as the total score.

If all learners in your program share their item ratings and total scores, perhaps anonymously, with a professor or program administrator, responses can be aggregated. When analyzed, they may reveal areas where students believe they are proficient and areas that require additional study or practice. Comparison of pre- and post-test scores of individual students or those of student cohorts represents another way to use this self-appraisal to assess progress and promote learning.

Finally, you should recognize that this instrument reflects your own subjective opinions. You may consciously or unconsciously overestimate or perhaps underestimate your proficiency. Therefore, please use these results in conjunction with other evidence to establish a more balanced approximation of your current knowledge, skills, and abilities.

ANSWER SHEETS FOR THE SOCIAL WORK SKILLS TEST

The Social Work Skills Test—Part 1

Name: _____ Date: _____ Administration: 1 2 3

Use a #2 pencil to record your answers to the True-False and Multiple-Choice items contained in Part 1 of The Social Work Skills Test by filling in the bubble below the letter that reflects the best answer.

1.	A B C D ○ ○ ○ ○	2.	A B C D ○ ○ ○ ○	3.	A B C D ○ ○ ○ ○
4.	A B C D ○ ○ ○ ○	5.	A B C D ○ ○ ○ ○	6.	A B C D ○ ○ ○ ○
7.	A B C D ○ ○ ○ ○	8.	A B C D ○ ○ ○ ○	9.	A B C D ○ ○ ○ ○
10.	A B C D ○ ○ ○ ○	11.	A B C D ○ ○ ○ ○	12.	A B C D ○ ○ ○ ○
13.	A B C D ○ ○ ○ ○	14.	A B C D ○ ○ ○ ○	15.	A B C D ○ ○ ○ ○
16.	A B C D ○ ○ ○ ○	17.	A B C D ○ ○ ○ ○	18.	A B C D ○ ○ ○ ○
19.	A B C D ○ ○ ○ ○	20.	A B C D ○ ○ ○ ○	21.	A B C D ○ ○ ○ ○
22.	A B C D ○ ○ ○ ○	23.	A B C D ○ ○ ○ ○	24.	A B C D ○ ○ ○ ○
25.	A B C D ○ ○ ○ ○	26.	A B C D ○ ○ ○ ○	27.	A B C D ○ ○ ○ ○
28.	A B C D ○ ○ ○ ○	29.	A B C D ○ ○ ○ ○	30.	A B C D ○ ○ ○ ○

	A	B	C	D			A	B	C	D			A	B	C	D
31.	○	○	○	○		32.	○	○	○	○		33.	○	○	○	○
34.	○	○	○	○		35.	○	○	○	○		36.	○	○	○	○
37.	○	○	○	○		38.	○	○	○	○		39.	○	○	○	○
40.	○	○	○	○		41.	○	○	○	○		42.	○	○	○	○
43.	○	○	○	○		44.	○	○	○	○		45.	○	○	○	○
46.	○	○	○	○		47.	○	○	○	○		48.	○	○	○	○
49.	○	○	○	○		50.	○	○	○	○		51.	○	○	○	○
52.	○	○	○	○		53.	○	○	○	○		54.	○	○	○	○
55.	○	○	○	○		56.	○	○	○	○		57.	○	○	○	○
58.	○	○	○	○		59.	○	○	○	○		60.	○	○	○	○
61.	○	○	○	○		62.	○	○	○	○		63.	○	○	○	○
64.	○	○	○	○		65.	○	○	○	○		66.	○	○	○	○
67.	○	○	○	○		68.	○	○	○	○		69.	○	○	○	○
70.	○	○	○	○		71.	○	○	○	○		72.	○	○	○	○
73.	○	○	○	○		74.	○	○	○	○		75.	○	○	○	○
76.	○	○	○	○		77.	○	○	○	○		78.	○	○	○	○
79.	○	○	○	○		80.	○	○	○	○		81.	○	○	○	○
82.	○	○	○	○		83.	○	○	○	○		84.	○	○	○	○
85.	○	○	○	○		86.	○	○	○	○		87.	○	○	○	○

88. A B C D ○ ○ ○ ○	89. A B C D ○ ○ ○ ○	90. A B C D ○ ○ ○ ○
91. A B C D ○ ○ ○ ○	92. A B C D ○ ○ ○ ○	93. A B C D ○ ○ ○ ○
94. A B C D ○ ○ ○ ○	95. A B C D ○ ○ ○ ○	96. A B C D ○ ○ ○ ○
97. A B C D ○ ○ ○ ○	98. A B C D ○ ○ ○ ○	99. A B C D ○ ○ ○ ○
100. A B C D ○ ○ ○ ○	101. A B C D ○ ○ ○ ○	102. A B C D ○ ○ ○ ○
103. A B C D ○ ○ ○ ○	104. A B C D ○ ○ ○ ○	105. A B C D ○ ○ ○ ○
106. A B C D ○ ○ ○ ○	107. A B C D ○ ○ ○ ○	108. A B C D ○ ○ ○ ○
109. A B C D ○ ○ ○ ○	110. A B C D ○ ○ ○ ○	111. A B C D ○ ○ ○ ○
112. A B C D ○ ○ ○ ○	113. A B C D ○ ○ ○ ○	114. A B C D ○ ○ ○ ○
115. A B C D ○ ○ ○ ○	116. A B C D ○ ○ ○ ○	117. A B C D ○ ○ ○ ○
118. A B C D ○ ○ ○ ○	119. A B C D ○ ○ ○ ○	120. A B C D ○ ○ ○ ○
121. A B C D ○ ○ ○ ○	122. A B C D ○ ○ ○ ○	123. A B C D ○ ○ ○ ○
124. A B C D ○ ○ ○ ○	125. A B C D ○ ○ ○ ○	126. A B C D ○ ○ ○ ○
127. A B C D ○ ○ ○ ○	128. A B C D ○ ○ ○ ○	129. A B C D ○ ○ ○ ○
127. A B C D ○ ○ ○ ○	128. A B C D ○ ○ ○ ○	129. A B C D ○ ○ ○ ○
130. A B C D ○ ○ ○ ○	131. A B C D ○ ○ ○ ○	132. A B C D ○ ○ ○ ○
133. A B C D ○ ○ ○ ○	134. A B C D ○ ○ ○ ○	135. A B C D ○ ○ ○ ○
136. A B C D ○ ○ ○ ○	137. A B C D ○ ○ ○ ○	138. A B C D ○ ○ ○ ○
139. A B C D ○ ○ ○ ○	140. A B C D ○ ○ ○ ○	141. A B C D ○ ○ ○ ○

The Social Work Skills Test—Part 2

Name: _____ Date: _____ Administration: 1 2 3

After you have completed word-processing your short answers to items contained in Part 2 of The Social Work Skills Test, reflect upon them or engage other learners in discussions to establish more proficient from less proficient responses. Some professors may provide "model responses" that you may compare to your own. Please track the quality of your responses to the short-answer items by using a #2 pencil to fill in the bubble below the letter that corresponds to the following scale: *A = Proficient, B = Satisfactory, C = Inferior, D = Unsatisfactory*. In a week or so, you might reconsider your short answers and attempt to create better responses.

1. A B C D ○ ○ ○ ○	2. A B C D ○ ○ ○ ○	3. A B C D ○ ○ ○ ○
4. A B C D ○ ○ ○ ○	5. A B C D ○ ○ ○ ○	6. A B C D ○ ○ ○ ○
7. A B C D ○ ○ ○ ○	8. A B C D ○ ○ ○ ○	9. A B C D ○ ○ ○ ○
10. A B C D ○ ○ ○ ○	11. A B C D ○ ○ ○ ○	12. A B C D ○ ○ ○ ○
13. A B C D ○ ○ ○ ○	14. A B C D ○ ○ ○ ○	15. A B C D ○ ○ ○ ○
16. A B C D ○ ○ ○ ○	17. A B C D ○ ○ ○ ○	18. A B C D ○ ○ ○ ○
19. A B C D ○ ○ ○ ○	20. A B C D ○ ○ ○ ○	21. A B C D ○ ○ ○ ○
22. A B C D ○ ○ ○ ○	23. A B C D ○ ○ ○ ○	24. A B C D ○ ○ ○ ○
25. A B C D ○ ○ ○ ○	26. A B C D ○ ○ ○ ○	27. A B C D ○ ○ ○ ○
28. A B C D ○ ○ ○ ○	29. A B C D ○ ○ ○ ○	30. A B C D ○ ○ ○ ○
31. A B C D ○ ○ ○ ○	32. A B C D ○ ○ ○ ○	33. A B C D ○ ○ ○ ○
34. A B C D ○ ○ ○ ○	35. A B C D ○ ○ ○ ○	36. A B C D ○ ○ ○ ○
37. A B C D ○ ○ ○ ○	38. A B C D ○ ○ ○ ○	39. A B C D ○ ○ ○ ○
40. A B C D ○ ○ ○ ○	41. A B C D ○ ○ ○ ○	42. A B C D ○ ○ ○ ○
43. A B C D ○ ○ ○ ○	44. A B C D ○ ○ ○ ○	45. A B C D ○ ○ ○ ○

46.	A ○	B ○	C ○	D ○		47.	A ○	B ○	C ○	D ○		48.	A ○	B ○	C ○	D ○
49.	A ○	B ○	C ○	D ○		50.	A ○	B ○	C ○	D ○		51.	A ○	B ○	C ○	D ○
52.	A ○	B ○	C ○	D ○		53.	A ○	B ○	C ○	D ○		54.	A ○	B ○	C ○	D ○
55.	A ○	B ○	C ○	D ○		56.	A ○	B ○	C ○	D ○		57.	A ○	B ○	C ○	D ○
58.	A ○	B ○	C ○	D ○		59.	A ○	B ○	C ○	D ○		60.	A ○	B ○	C ○	D ○

REFERENCES

"cultural sensitivity." (2007). *A Dictionary of Public Health.* Oxford Reference Online. Retrieved June 1, 2012, from http://www.oxfordreference .com.proxy2.ulib.iupui.edu/views/ENTRY .html?subview=Main&entry=t235.e974>

"privilege." (2010). *New Oxford American Dictionary.* Oxford Reference Online. Retrieved April 25, 2012, from www.oxfordreference.com

"profession." (1999). *The Oxford American Dictionary of Current English.* Oxford Reference Online. Retrieved March 9, 2012, from www.oxfordreference.com

"professional." (2009). *The Oxford English Dictionary [OED] Online.* Retrieved September 6, 2009, from www.oxfordreference.com

Ajzen, I. (1991). The theory of planned behavior. *Organizational Behavior and Human Decision Processes, 50,* 179–211.

Ajzen, I., & Fishbein, M. (1980). *Understanding attitudes and predicting social behavior.* Upper Saddle River, NJ: Prentice Hall.

Akobeng, A.K. (2005). Understanding systematic reviews and meta-analysis. *Archives of Disease in Childhood, 90*(8), 845–848.

Albarracin, D., Johnson, B.T., Fishbein, M., & Muellerleile, P.A. (2001). Theories of reasoned action and planned behavior as models of condom use: a meta-analysis. *Psychological Bulletin, 127*(1), 142–161.

Alexander, M. (2010). *The new Jim Crow: Mass incarceration in the age of colorblindness.* New York: New Press.

Alpert, J.L., Brown, L.S., Ceci, S.J., Courtois, C.A., Loftus, E.F., & Ornstein, P.A. (1996). *American Psychological Association: Working group on investigation of memories of childhood sexual abuse.* Final Report. Washington, DC: American Psychological Association.

Alter, C., & Egan, M. (1997). Logic modeling: A tool for teaching critical thinking in social work practice. *Journal of Social Work Education, 33*(1), 85–102.

Alter, C., & Murty, S. (1997). Logic modeling: A tool for teaching practice evaluation. *Journal of Social Work Education, 33*(1), 103–117.

Altmann, H. (1973). Effects of empathy, warmth and genuineness in the initial counseling interview. *Counselor Education and Supervision, 12,* 225–229.

Altshuler, S.J. (1999). Constructing genograms with children in care: Implications for casework practice. *Child Welfare, 78*(6), 777–790.

Amaro, H., Raj, A., Vega, R.R., Mangione, T.W., & Perez, L.N. (2001). Racial/ethnic disparities in the HIV and substance abuse epidemics: Communities responding to the need. *Public Health Reports, 116*(5), 434–448.

American Psychiatric Association. (2000a). *Diagnostic and statistical manual* (4th ed. text rev.) [Electronic version]. Washington, DC: American Psychiatric Association.

American Psychiatric Association. (2000b). *Position statement: Therapies focused on memories of childhood physical and sexual abuse.* Washington, DC: American Psychiatric Association.

American Psychiatric Association. (2003). American Psychiatric Association practice guideline for the assessment and treatment of patients with suicidal behaviors. Retrieved June 22, 2006, from http://www.psych.org/psych_pract/treatg/pg /SuicidalBehavior_05-15-06.pdf

American Psychiatric Association. (in press). *Diagnostic and statistical manual* (5th ed.). Washington, DC: American Psychiatric Association.

American Psychological Association. (2009a). Children with positive outlooks are better learners. *ScienceDaily.* Retrieved August 10, 2009, from http://www.sciencedaily.com/releases/2009 /08/090807135054.htm

American Psychological Association. (2009b). *Publication manual of the American Psychological Association* (6th ed.). Washington, DC: American Psychological Association.

Amnesty International. (1997). First steps: A manual for starting human rights education. Retrieved from http://www.hrea.org/erc/Library/display _doc.php?url=http%3A%2F%2Fwww.hrea .org%2Ferc%2FLibrary%2FFirst_Steps%2Findex _eng.html&external=N

Anderson, L.W., & Krathwohl, D.R. (Eds.). (2001). *A taxonomy for learning, teaching, and assessing: A revision of Bloom's taxonomy of educational objectives.* New York: Longman.

Anker, M., Duncan, B., & Sparks, J. (2009). Using client feedback to improve couple therapy outcomes: A randomized clinical trial in a naturalistic setting. *Journal of Consulting and Clinical Psychology, 77,* 693–704.

Anker, M., Owen, J., Duncan, B., & Sparks, J. (2010). The alliance in couple therapy: Partner influence, early change, and alliance patterns in a naturalistic sample. *Journal of Consulting and Clinical Psychology, 78,* 635–645.

Antman, E.M., Lau, J., Kupelnick, B., Mosteller, F., & Chalmers, T.C. (1992). A comparison of results of meta-analyses of randomized control trials and recommendations of clinical experts: Treatments for myocardial infarction. *Journal of the American Medical Association, 268,* 240–248.

Applewhite, S.L. (1996). Curanderismo: Demystifying the health beliefs and practices of elderly Mexican Americans. In P.L. Ewalt, E.M. Freeman, S.A. Kirk, & D.L. Poole (Eds.), *Multicultural issues in social work* (pp. 455–468). Washington DC: NASW Press.

Armstrong, K. (2010). *Twelve steps to a compassionate life.* New York: Alfred A. Knopf.

Aronson, E., & Aronson, J. (2012). *The social animal* (11th ed.). New York: Worth Publishing.

Arum, R., & Roksa, J. (2011). *Academically adrift: Limited learning on college campuses.* Chicago: University of Chicago Press.

Asay, T.P., & Lambert, M.J. (1999). The empirical case for the common factors in therapy: Quantitative factors. In M.A. Hubble, B.L. Duncan, & S.D. Miller (Eds.), *The heart and soul of change: What works in therapy* (pp. 23–55). Washington, DC: American Psychological Association.

Associated Press. (2009, June 9). Social worker pleads guilty in case linked to Danieal Kelly. Retrieved July 29, 2009, from http://abclocal.go.com/wpvi/story?section=news/local&id=6856954&rss=rss-wpvi-article-6856954

Association for Women's Rights in Development. (2004, August). Intersectionality: A tool for gender and economic justice. *Women's Rights and Economic Change, 9,* 1–8. Retrieved from http://www.awid.org/Library/Intersectionality-A-Tool-for-Gender-and-Economic-Justice2

Association of Social Work Boards. (2011). Content outlines and KSAs: Social work licensing examinations. Retrieved April 22, 2012, from http://www.aswb.org/pdfs/2011KSAs.pdf

Association of Social Work Boards. (2012). Links to social work statutes and regulations. Retrieved July 10, 2012, from http://www.aswb.org/SWL/statutesregulations.asp#

Astatke, H., Black, M.M., & Serpell, R. (2000). Use of Jessor's theoretical framework of adolescent risk behavior in Ethiopia: Implications for HIV/AIDS prevention. *Northeast African Studies, 7*(1), 63–84.

Atkins, D.M., & Patenaude, A.F. (1987). Psychosocial preparation and follow-up for pediatric bone marrow transplant patients. *American Journal of Orthopsychiatry, 57*(2), 246–252.

Austin, D.M. (1997). The profession of social work: In the second century. In M. Reisch & E. Gambrill (Eds.), *Social work in the 21st century* (pp. 376–386). Thousand Oaks, CA: Pine Forge Press.

Axtell, R.E. (1998). *Gestures: The do's and taboos of body language around the world* (2nd ed.). New York: John Wiley & Sons.

Axtell, R.E. (2007). *Essential do's and taboos: The complete guide to international business and leisure travel.* New York: John Wiley & Sons.

Baker, M.R., & Steiner, J.R. (1996). Solution-focused social work: Metamessages to students in higher education opportunity programs. In P.L. Ewalt, E.M. Freeman, S.A. Kirk, & D.L. Poole (Eds.), *Multicultural issues in social work* (pp. 295–309). Washington DC: NASW Press.

Balgopal, P.R., Fong, R., Lu, Y.E., Park, Y., Choi, Y., Mohan, B., & DuongTran, P. (2008). Asian Americans. In T. Mizrahi & L.E. Davis (Eds.), *Encylopedia of social work* (20th, e-reference ed.). New York: National Association of Social Workers and Oxford University Press.

Bandler, R., & Grinder, J. (1979). *Frogs into princes: Neuro-linguistic programming.* Moab, UT: Real People.

Bandler, R., & Grinder, J. (1982). *Reframing: Neuro-linguistic programing and the transformation of meaning.* Moab, UT: Real People.

Bandura, A. (1977). Self-efficacy: Toward a unifying theory of behavior change. *Psychological Review, 84,* 191–215.

Bandura, A. (1992). Exercise of personal agency through the self-efficacy mechanism. In R. Schwarzer (Ed.), *Self-efficacy: Thought control of action* (pp. 355–394). Washington, DC: Hemisphere.

Bandura, A. (1995a). Exercise of personal and collective efficacy in changing societies. In A. Bandura (Ed.), *Self-efficacy in changing societies* (pp. 1–45). New York: Cambridge University Press.

Bandura, A. (Ed.). (1995b). *Self-efficacy in changing societies.* New York: Cambridge University Press.

Bandura, A. (1997). *Self-efficacy: The exercise of control.* New York: W. H. Freeman and Company.

Barker, R.L. (2003). *The social work dictionary* (5th ed.). Washington, DC: National Association of Social Workers.

Barrett, S., & Jarvis, W.T. (Eds.). (1993). *Health robbers: A close look at quackery in America.* Buffalo, NY: Prometheus Books.

Barth, R.P., Lee, B.R., Lindsey, M.A., Collins, K.S., Strieder, F., Chorpita, B.F., . . . Sparks, J.A. (2012). Evidence-based practice at a crossroads: The timely emergence of common elements and common factors. *Research on Social Work Practice, 22,* 108–119. doi: 10.1177/1049731511408440

Bartlett, H. (1958). The working definition of social work practice. *Social Work, 3*(2), 1028–1030.

Bartlett, H. (1970). *The common base of social work practice*. New York: National Association of Social Workers.

Basow, S.A., & Rubenfeld, K. (2003). "Troubles talk": Effects of gender and gender-typing. *Sex Roles: A Journal of Research, 48*, 183–187.

Batson, C.D. (2009). These things called empathy: Eight related but distinct phenomena. In J. Decety & W. Ickes (Eds.), *The social neuroscience of empathy* (pp. 3–15). Cambridge, MA: The MIT Press.

Battaglini, D.J., & Schenkat, R.J. (1987). Fostering cognitive development in college students—The Perry and Toulmin models. *ERIC Clearinghouse on Reading and Communication Skills*. Retrieved June 21, 2006, from http://www.ericdigests.org/pre-925/perry.htm

Beauchamp, T.L., & Childress, J.F. (1983). *Principles of biomedical ethics* (2nd ed.). New York: Oxford University Press.

Becker, M.H. (1974). The health belief model and personal health behavior. *Health Education Monographs, 2*, 324–508.

Belenky, M., Clinchy, B., Goldberger, N., & Tarule, J. (1986). *Women's ways of knowing: The development of self, voice, and mind*. New York: Basic Books.

Belsky, G., & Gilovich, T. (2000). *Why smart people make big money mistakes—and how to correct them: Lessons from the new science of behavioral economics*. New York: Simon & Schuster.

Benet-Martinez, V., & John, O.P. (1998). *Los Cinco Grandes* across cultures and ethnic groups: Multitrait multimethod analyses of the Big Five in Spanish and English. *Journal of Personality and Social Psychology, 75*, 729–750.

Benjamin, R. (2009). *Searching for Whitopia: An improbable journey to the heart of White America*. New York: Hyperion.

Berg, I.K. (1994). *Family-based services: A solution-focused approach*. New York: W.W. Norton.

Berg, I.K., & De Jong, P. (1996). Solution-building conversations: Co-constructing a sense of competence with clients. *Families in Society: The Journal of Contemporary Human Services, 77*, 376–391.

Berg, I.K., & Reuss, N.H. (1998). *Solutions step by step: A substance abuse treatment manual*. New York: Norton.

Berkman, C.S., Turner, S.G., Cooper, M., Polnerow, D., & Swartz, M. (2000). Sexual contact with clients: Assessment of social workers' attitudes and educational preparation. *Social Work, 45*(3), 223–235.

Berlin, S.B. (1990). Dichotomous and complex thinking. *Social Service Review, 64*(1), 46–59.

Berlin, S.B. (2005). The value of acceptance in social work direct practice: A historical and contemporary view. *Social Service Review, 79*(3), 482–510.

Berman, A.L., Jobes, D.A., & Silverman, M.M. (2006). *Adolescent suicide: Assessment and intervention* (2nd ed.). Washington, DC: American Psychological Association.

Bernhardt, B., & Rauch, J.B. (1993). Genetic family histories: An aid to social work assessment. *Families in Society: The Journal of Contemporary Human Services, 74*(4), 195–205.

Besharov, D.J., & Besharov, S.H. (1987). Teaching about liability. *Social Work, 32*(6), 517–522.

Bey, J. (2012, March 2). She the people (blog): The world as women see it: Rush Limbaugh's attack on Sandra Fluke was hate speech. *The Washington Post: PostPolitics*. Retrieved March 3, 2012, from http://www.washingtonpost.com/blogs/she-the-people/post/rush-limbaughs-attack-on-sandra-fluke-was-hate-speech/2012/03/02/gIQAZVxrmR_blog.html

Beyer, B.K. (1988). *Developing a thinking skills program*. Boston: Allyn & Bacon.

Biagi, E. (1977). The social work stake in problem-oriented recording. *Social Work in Health Care, 3*(2), 211–222.

Biswas-Diener, R. (2012). *The courage quotient: How science can make you braver*. San Francisco, CA: Jossey-Bass.

Blackburn, S. (1996). *The Oxford Dictionary of Philosophy*. Oxford Reference Online. Retrieved from http://www.oxfordreference.com/views/ENTRY.html?subview=Main&entry=t98.e173

Bloom, B.S., & Krathwohl, D.R. (1956). *Taxonomy of educational objectives: The classification of educational goals, by a committee of college and university examiners: Handbook I: Cognitive Domain*. New York: Longmans, Green.

Blount, M., Thyer, B.A., & Frye, T. (1992). Social work practice with Native Americans. In D.F. Harrison, J.S. Wodarski, & B.A. Thyer (Eds.), *Cultural diversity and social work practice* (pp. 107–134). Springfield, IL: Charles C. Thomas.

Bogie, M.A., & Coleman, M. (2002). Facing a malpractice claim. *NASW Assurance Services Practice Pointers, 3*(2), 1. Retrieved from http://www.naswinsurancetrust.org/facing_malpractice_claim.php

Bogo, M. (2010). *Achieving competence in social work through field education*. Buffalo; Toronto: University of Toronto Press.

Bohart, A.C., & Greenberg, L.S. (1997a). Empathy and psychotherapy: An introductory overview. In A.C. Bohart & L.S. Greenberg (Eds.), *Empathy reconsidered: New directions in psychotherapy* (pp. 3–31). Washington, DC: American Psychological Association.

Bohart, A.C., & Greenberg, L.S. (Eds.). (1997b). *Empathy reconsidered: New directions in psychotherapy*. Washington, DC: American Psychological Association.

Bohart, A.C., & Tallman, K. (2010). Clients: The neglected common factor in psychotherapy. In B.L. Duncan, S.D. Miller, B.E. Wampold, & M.A. Hubble (Eds.), *The heart and soul of change: Delivering what works in therapy* (2nd ed., pp. 83–111). Washington, DC: American Psychological Association.

Borchard, E.M. (1932). *Convicting the innocent: Errors of criminal justice*. New Haven, CT: Yale University Press.

Bozarth, J.D. (1997). Empathy from the framework of client-centered theory and the Rogerian hypothesis. In A.C. Bohart & L.S. Greenberg (Eds.),

Empathy reconsidered: New directions in psychotherapy (pp. 81–102). Washington, DC: American Psychological Association.

Brainerd, C.J., & Reyna, V.F. (2005). *The science of false memory*. New York: Oxford University Press.

Brammer, R. (2004). *Diversity in counseling*. Pacific Grove, CA: Brooks/Cole.

Branch Jr., W.T., & Gordon, G.H. (2004). Making the most of challenging patient interviews: Staying attuned to patients' emotions and personality styles–and your own reactions to them–enhances the efficacy of the medical interview. *Patient Care, 38*(7), 26–31.

Breggin, P.R. (1997). *The heart of being helpful: Empathy and the creation of a healing presence*. New York: Springer.

Bricker, J., Kennickell, A.B., Moore, K.B., & Sabelhaus, J. (2012). Changes in U.S. family finances from 2007 to 2010: Evidence from the Survey of Consumer Finances. *Federal Reserve Bulletin, 98*(2), 1–80. Retrieved from http://www.federalreserve .gov/pubs/bulletin/2012/PDF/scf12.pdf

Brickman, P., & Campbell, D.T. (1971). Hedonic relativism and planning the good society. In M.H. Appley (Ed.), *Adaptation level theory: A symposium* (pp. 287–302). New York: Academic Press.

Brissett-Chapman, S. (1995). Child abuse and neglect: Direct practice. In R.L. Edwards (Ed.), *Encyclopedia of social work* (19th ed., Vol. 1, pp. 353–366). Washington, DC: NASW Press.

Brockman, J. (Ed.). (2009). *What have you changed your mind about? Today's leading minds rethink everything*. New York: HarperCollins.

Brody, H., & Brody, D. (2000). Three perspectives on the placebo response: Expectancy, conditioning, and meaning. *Advances in Mind-Body Medicine, 16*(3), 216–232.

Bronson, D.E., & Davis, T.S. (2012). *Finding and evaluating evidence: Systematic reviews and evidence-based practice*. Oxford; New York: Oxford University Press.

Brooks, D. (2011). *The social animal: The hidden sources of love, character, and achievement*. New York: Random House.

Burchum, J.L.R. (2002). Cultural competence: An evolutionary perspective. *Nursing Forum, 37*(4), 5–15.

Burke, P., & Parker, J. (2007). *Social work and disadvantage: Addressing the roots of stigma through association*. London; Philadelphia: Jessica Kingsley Publishers.

Burrill, G. (1976). The problem-oriented log in social casework. *Social Work, 21*(1), 67–68.

Bush, G.W. (2002). Address before a joint session of the congress on the state of the union. Retrieved July 2, 2006, from http://www.presidency.ucsb.edu/ws /index.php?pid=29644

Cabral, R.R., & Smith, T.B. (2011). Racial/ethnic matching of clients and therapists in mental health services: A meta-analytic review of preferences, perceptions, and outcomes. *Journal of Counseling Psychology, 58*(4), 537–554. doi: 10.1037/a0025266

Callahan, D. (2004). *The cheating culture: Why more Americans are doing wrong to get ahead*. New York: Houghton Mifflin Harcourt.

Cameron, K.S., & Quinn, R.E. (1999). *Diagnosing and changing organizational culture*. Upper Saddle River, NJ: Prentice Hall.

Cameron, W.B. (1963). *Informal sociology: A casual introduction to sociological thinking*. New York: Random House.

Campbell, A., & Hemsley, S. (2009). Outcome Rating Scale and Session Rating Scale in psychological practice: Clinical utility of ultra-brief measures. *Clinical Psychologist, 13*(1), 1–9.

Campbell, D. (1974). *If you don't know where you're going you'll probably end up somewhere else*. Niles, IL: Argus Communications.

Campbell, D.T., Cook, T.D., & Cook, T.H. (1979). *Quasi-experimentation*. Chicago, IL: Rand McNally.

Campbell, D.T., & Stanley, J.C. (1966). *Experimental and quasi-experimental designs for research*. Chicago, IL: Rand McNally.

Campbell, J. (1972). *The hero with a thousand faces* (2nd ed.). Princeton, NJ: Princeton University Press.

Campbell, J., & Moyers, B. (1988). *The power of myth* (2nd ed.). New York: Doubleday.

Campbell, W., Bush, C., Brunell, A., & Shelton, J. (2005). Understanding the social costs of narcissism: The case of the tragedy of the commons. *Personality and Social Psychology Bulletin, 31*(10), 1358–1368.

Canli, T., Omura, K., Haas, B., Fallgatter, A., Constable, R.T., & Lesch, K.P. (2005). Beyond affect: A role for genetic variation of the serotonin transporter in neural activation during a cognitive attention task. *Proceedings of the National Academy of Sciences, U.S.A., 102*(34), 12224–12229.

Cantle, F. (2000). What is a "learning organization" in general practice? A case study. *Health Services Management Research, 13*(3), 152–155.

Caplan, P.J. (2012, April 27). Psychiatry's bible, the DSM, is doing more harm than good. *The Washington Post*. Retrieved from http://www.washingtonpost.com /opinions/psychiatrys-bible-the-dsm-is-doing-more- harm-than-good/2012/04/27/gIQAqy0WlT_print .html

Caplan, R.B., & Caplan, G. (2001). *Helping the helpers not to harm: Iatrogenic damage and community mental health*. New York: Brunner-Routledge.

CareerJournal.com editors. (2006a, July 11). 2006 best careers: The results are in. Retrieved July 15, 2006, from http://www.careerjournal.com/reports /bestcareers/20060711-intro.html

CareerJournal.com editors. (2006b, July 11). Best careers methodology: How we got our results. Retrieved July 15, 2006, from http://www.careerjournal. com/reports/bestcareers/20060711-method.html

Carkhuff, R.R. (1987). *The art of helping VI*. Amherst, MA: Human Resource Development Press.

Carkhuff, R.R., & Anthony, W.A. (1979). *The skills of helping*. Amherst, MA: Human Resource Development.

Carkhuff, R.R., & Truax, C.B. (1965). Training in counseling and psychotherapy. *Journal of Consulting Psychology, 29*, 333–336.

Carr, A. (2003). *Positive psychology*. New York: Brunner-Routledge.

Carter, C.S., Harris, J., & Porges, S.W. (2009). Neural and evolutionary perspectives on empathy. In J. Decety & W. Ickes (Eds.), *The social neuroscience of empathy* (pp. 169–182). Cambridge, MA: The MIT Press.

Caspar, F., Del Re, A.C., Fluckiger, C., Jorg, U., Wampold, B.E., & Znoj, H. (2012). Valuing clients' perspective and the effects on the therapeutic alliance: A randomized controlled study of an adjunctive instruction. *Journal of Counseling Psychology, 59*(1), 18–26.

Castex, G.M. (1996). Providing services to Hispanic/Latino populations: Profiles in diversity. In P.L. Ewalt, E.M. Freeman, S.A. Kirk, & D.L. Poole (Eds.), *Multicultural issues in social work* (pp. 523–538). Washington DC: NASW Press.

Catalano, R.F., Hawkins, J. D., Berglund, M. L., Pollard, J. A., & Arthur, M. W. (2002). Prevention science and positive youth development: Competitive or cooperative frameworks. *Journal of Adolescent Health, 31*, 230–239.

Center for Substance Abuse Prevention. (2001). 2001 annual report on science-based prevention programs. Retrieved July 23, 2006, from http://www.samhsa.gov/centers/csap/modelprograms/pdfs/2001Annual.pdf

Centers for Disease Control and Prevention. (2012). Behavioral Risk Factor Surveillance System. Retrieved August 13, 2012, from http://www.cdc.gov/brfss/

Central Intelligence Agency. (2012). World Factbook: Field Listing: Ethnic Groups. Retrieved January 18, 2012, from https://www.cia.gov/library/publications/the-world-factbook/fields/2075.html?countryName=&countryCode=&regionCode=5

Chapin, R.K. (2007). *Social policy for effective practice: A strengths approach*. Boston: McGraw-Hill.

Chin, W.W., Salisbury, W.D., Pearson, A.W., & Stollak, M.J. (1999). Perceived cohesion in small groups: Adapting and testing the Perceived Cohesion Scale in a small-group setting. *Small Group Research, 30*(6), 751–766. doi: 10.1177/104649649903000605

Christ, W.R., Clarkin, J.F., & Hull, J.W. (1994). A high-risk screen for psychiatric discharge planning. *Health and Social Work, 19*(4), 261–270.

Christakis, N.A., & Fowler, J.H. (2009). *Connected: The surprising power of our social networks and how they shape our lives*. New York: Little, Brown, and Company.

Clarridge, C. (2009, May 9). Seattle Times: Former social worker sentenced to jail for indecent liberties. Retrieved July 29, 2009, from http://seattletimes.nwsource.com/html/localnews/2009198734_webgill08m.html

Claus, R.E., & Kindleberger, L.R. (2002). Engaging substance abusers after centralized assessment: Predictors of treatment entry and dropout. *Journal of Psychoactive Drugs, 34*, 25–31.

Cohen, J.A. (1988). *Statistical power analysis for the behavioral sciences* (2nd ed.). Hillsdale, NJ: Lawrence Erlbaum Associates.

Coker, R. (2001). Distinguishing science and pseudoscience. Retrieved September 10, 2009, from http://www.quackwatch.org/01QuackeryRelatedTopics/pseudo.html

Coleman, J.S. (1988). Social capital in the creation of human capital. *The American Journal of Sociology, 94*, S95–S120. doi: 10.2307/2780243

Collaboration for Environmental Evidence. (2012). The CEE library of completed systematic reviews. Retrieved August 3, 2012, from http://www.environmentalevidence.org/Reviews.html

Compton, B.R., Galaway, B., & Cournoyer, B.R. (2005). *Social work processes* (7th ed.). Pacific Grove, CA: Brooks/Cole.

Compton, W.C. (2004). *Introduction to positive psychology*. Belmont, CA: Wadsworth.

Cone, J.D. (1997). Issues in functional analysis in behavioral assessment. *Behaviour Research and Therapy, 35*(3), 259–275.

Congress, E.P. (1994). The use of culturalgrams to assess and empower culturally diverse families. *Families in Society: The Journal of Contemporary Human Services, 75*, 531–540.

Congress, E.P. (1999). *Social work values and ethics: Identifying and resolving ethical dilemmas*. Belmont, CA: Wadsworth.

Congress, E.P. (2000). What social workers should know about ethics: Understanding and resolving ethical dilemmas. *Advances in Social Work, 1*(1), 1–25.

Congressional Budget Office. (2011). *Trends in the distribution of household income between 1979 and 2007*. Washington, DC: Author. Retrieved from http://cbo.gov/publication/42729

Cook, D.J., Greengold, N.L., Ellrodt, A.G., & Weingarten, S.R. (1997). The relation between systematic reviews and clinical guidelines. *Annals of Internal Medicine, 127*, 210–216.

Cook, T.D., & Campbell, D.T. (Eds.). (1979). *Quasi-experimentation: Design and analysis issues for field settings*. Chicago, IL: Rand-McNally.

Cook, T.D., Cooper, H., Cordray, D.S., Hartmann, H., Hedges, L., Light, R.J., . . . Mosteller, F. (1992). *Meta-Analysis for explanation: A casebook*. New York: Russell Sage Foundation.

Corak, M. (2006). Do poor children become poor adults? Lessons from a cross country comparison of generational earnings mobility: Discussion paper no. 1993. Retrieved from http://ftp.iza.org/dp1993.pdf

Corcoran, J. (2011). *Helping skills for social work direct practice*. New York: Oxford University Press.

Corey, G., Corey, M.S., & Callanan, P. (2003). *Issues and ethics in the helping professions* (6th ed.). Pacific Grove, CA: Brooks/Cole.

Cosgrove, L. (2011). The DSM, Big Pharma, and Clinical Practice Guidelines: Protecting patient autonomy and informed consent. *International Journal of Feminist Approaches to Bioethics, 4*(1), 11–25.

Cosgrove, L., & Krimsky, S. (2012). A comparison of DSM-IV and DSM-5 panel members' financial associations with industry: A pernicious problem persists. *PLoS Medicine, 9*(3), 1–4. doi: 10.1371/journal.pmed.1001190

Cosgrove, L., Krimsky, S., Vijayaraghavan, M., & Schneider, L. (2006). Financial ties between DSM-IV panel members and the pharmaceutical industry. *Psychotherapy and Psychosomatics, 75*(3), 154–160.

Council on Social Work Education. (2008). Educational policy and accreditation standards. Retrieved August 9, 2009, from http://www.cswe.org/NR/rdonlyres/2A81732E-1776-4175-AC42-65974E96BE66/0/2008EducationalPolicyandAccreditationStandards.pdf

Cournoyer, B.R. (1994). *Unpublished data regarding self-esteem, acceptance of others, and assertiveness among beginning MSW students.* Indiana University School of Social Work, Indianapolis, Indiana.

Cournoyer, B.R. (1999). *Unpublished data regarding foundation year MSW students' critical thinking and lifelong learning.* Indiana University School of Social Work, Indianapolis, Indiana.

Cournoyer, B.R. (2003). *Unpublished data regarding foundation and concentration year MSW students' critical thinking and lifelong learning.* Indiana University School of Social Work, Indianapolis, Indiana.

Cournoyer, B.R. (2004). *The evidence-based social work skills book.* Boston: Allyn & Bacon.

Cournoyer, B.R., & Powers, G.T. (2002). Evidence-based social work: The quiet revolution continues. In A.R. Roberts & G.J. Greene (Eds.), *Social workers' desk reference* (pp. 798–807). New York: Oxford University Press.

Cournoyer, B.R., & Stanley, M.J. (2002). *The social work portfolio: Planning, assessing and documenting lifelong learning in a dynamic profession.* Pacific Grove, CA: Brooks/Cole.

Cowger, C.D. (1994). Assessing client strengths: Clinical assessment for client empowerment. *Social Work, 39*(3), 262–268.

Cowger, C.D. (1996). Assessment of client strengths. In D. Saleebey (Ed.), *The strengths perspective in social work practice* (2nd ed., pp. 59–73). New York: Longman.

Cox, C.B. (1996). Discharge planning for dementia patients: factors influencing caregiver decisions and satisfaction. *Health and Social Work, 21*(2), 97–106.

Cox, R.J., & Amsters, D.A. (2002). Goal Attainment Scaling: An effective outcome measure for rural and remote health services. *Australian Journal of Rural Health, 10,* 256–261.

Crits-Christoph, P., Ring-Kurtz, S., Hamilton, J.L., Lambert, M.J., Gallop, R., McClure, B., . . . Rotrosen, J. (2012). A preliminary study of the effects of individual patient-level feedback in outpatient substance abuse treatment programs. *Journal of Substance Abuse Treatment, 42*(3), 301–309. doi: 10.1016/j.jsat.2011.09.003

Cross, T., Bazron, B., Dennis, K., & Isaacs, M. (1989). *Toward a culturally competent system of care* (Vol. 1). Washington, DC: Georgetown University.

Csikszentmihalyi, M., & Csikszentmihalyi, I.S. (Eds.). (2006). *Life worth living: Contributions to positive psychology.* New York: Oxford University Press.

Cummins, L.K., Sevel, J.A., & Pedrick, L.E. (2006). *Social work skills demonstrated: Beginning direct practice* (2nd ed.). Boston: Pearson/Allyn and Bacon.

Dalal PK, S.T. (2009). Moving towards ICD-11 and DSM-5: Concept and evolution of psychiatric classification. *Indian Journal of Psychiatry, 51*(4), 310–319.

Dalton, A.N., & Spiller, S.A. (2012). Too much of a good thing: The benefits of implementation intentions depend on the number of goals. *Journal of Consumer Research, 39*(3), 600–614. doi: 10.1086/664500

Danieal Kelly. (2009). *Philadelphia Inquirer.* Retrieved from http://www.philly.com/inquirer/hot_topics/26375979.html

Davis, K., Schoen, C., & Stremikis, K. (2010, June). Mirror, mirror on the wall: How the performance of the U.S. Health Care System Compares Internationally: 2010 update. Retrieved July 10, 2012, from http://www.commonwealthfund.org/Publications/Fund-Reports/2010/Jun/Mirror-Mirror-Update.aspx?page=all

Davis, S., & Botkin, J. (1994). The coming of knowledge-based businesses. *Harvard Business Review, 72*(5), 165–170.

De Jong, P., & Berg, I.K. (2002). *Interviewing for solutions.* Pacific Grove, CA: Brooks/Cole.

de la Llama, V.A., Trueba, I., Voges, C., Barreto, C., & Park, D.J. (2012). At Face(book) value: Uses of Facebook in hiring processes and the role of identity in social networks. *International Journal of Work Innovation, 1*(1), 114–136. doi: 10.1504/12.47984

de Shazer, S. (1988). *Clues: Investigating solutions in brief therapy.* New York: W. W. Norton.

de Shazer, S., Berg, I.K., Lipchick, E., Nunnally, E., Molnar, A., Gingerich, W., & Weiner-Davis, M. (1986). Brief therapy: Focused solution development. *Family Process, 25,* 207–221.

de Waal, F.B.M. (2009). *The age of empathy: Nature's lessons for a kinder society.* New York: Harmony Books.

Dean, R.G. (2001). The myth of cross-cultural competence. *Families in Society: The Journal of Contemporary Human Services, 82*(6), 623–630.

Deardorff, D.K. (Ed.). (2009). *The Sage handbook of intercultural competence.* Thousand Oaks, CA: Sage Publications.

Delgado, M. (2007). *Social work with Latinos: A cultural assets paradigm.* Oxford; New York: Oxford University Press.

DeNavas-Walt, C., Proctor, B.D., & Smith, J.C. (2011). *Income, Poverty, and Health Insurance Coverage in the United States: 2010.* U.S. Census Bureau, Current Population Reports, P60–239. Retrieved from http://www.census.gov/prod/2011pubs/p60-239.pdf

Department for International Development. (2012). Research for Development (R4D) database: Systematic reviews. Retrieved August 3, 2012, from http://www.dfid.gov.uk/R4D/SystematicReviews.aspx

DeRienzo-DeVivio, S. (1992). Childhood lead poisoning: Shifting to primary prevention. *Pediatric Nursing, 18*(6), 565–567.

DeSteno, D., & Valdesolo, P. (2011). *Out of character: Surprising truths about the liar, cheat, sinner (and saint) lurking in all of us.* New York: Crown Publishing.

Devine, T., & Maassarani, T.F. (2011). *The corporate whistle-blower's survival guide: A handbook for committing the truth.* San Francisco, CA: Berrett-Koehler Publishers.

Diamandis, P.H., & Kotler, S. (2012). *Abundance: The future is better than you think.* New York: Free Press.

Dickinson, E. (1924/2000). The complete poems of Emily Dickinson. Retrieved from www.bartleby.com/113/

Diener, E. (2006, February 13). Understanding Scores on the Satisfaction with Life Scale. Retrieved August 8, 2009, from http://www.psych.uiuc.edu/~ediener/Understanding%20SWLS%20Scores.pdf

Diener, E., Emmons, R.A., Larsen, R.J., & Griffin, S. (1985). The Satisfaction With Life Scale. *Journal of Personality Assessment, 49,* 71–75.

Diener, E., Lucas, R.E., & Scollon, C.N. (2006). Beyond the hedonic treadmill: Revising the adaptation theory of well-being. *American Psychologist, 61*(4), 305–314. doi: 10.1037/0003-066x.61.4.305

Digman, J.M. (1990). Personality structure: Emergence of the five-factor model. *Annual Review of Psychology, 41,* 417–440.

Dolgoff, R., Loewenberg, F.M., & Harrington, D. (2009). *Ethical decisions for social work practice* (8th ed.). Belmont, CA: Brooks/Cole.

Drisko, J.W., & Grady, M.D. (2012). *Evidence-based practice in clinical social work.* New York: Springer.

Duncan, B.L., Miller, S.D., Sparks, J., Claud, D., L., R., Brown, J., & Johnson, L. (2003). The Session Rating Scale: Preliminary psychometric properties of a "working" alliance measure. *Journal of Brief Therapy, 3,* 3–12.

Duncan, B.L., Miller, S.D., Wampold, B.E., & Hubble, M.A. (Eds.). (2010). *The heart and soul of change: Delivering what works in therapy* (2nd ed.). Washington, DC: American Psychological Association.

Dybicz, P. (2011). Interpreting the strengths perspective through narrative theory. *Families in Society: The Journal of Contemporary Human Services, 92*(3), 247–253.

Dziegielewski, S.F. (2008). Problem identification, contracting, and case planning. In W. Rowe & L.A. Rapp-Paglicci (Eds.), *Comprehensive handbook of social work and social welfare: Social work practice* (Vol. 3, pp. 78–97). Hoboken, NJ: John Wiley & Sons, Inc.

Ebstein, R.B., Novick, O., Umansky, R., Priel, B., & Osher, Y. (1996). Dopamine D4 receptor (D4DR) exon III polymorphism associated with the human personality trait of novelty seeking. *Nature Genetics, 12,* 78–80.

Edelman, P. (2012). *So rich, so poor: Why it's so hard to end poverty in America.* New York: The New Press.

Edmundson, W.A. (2004). *An introduction to rights.* Cambridge: Cambridge University Press.

Egan, G. (1982). *Exercises in helping skills: A training manual to accompany The Skilled Helper* (2nd ed.). Monterey, CA: Brooks/Cole.

Egan, G. (2010a). *The skilled helper* (9th ed.). Belmont, CA: Brooks/Cole.

Egan, M. (2010b). *Evidence-based interventions for social work in health care.* New York: Routledge.

Ekman, P. (1982). *Emotion in the human face* (2nd ed.). New York: Cambridge University Press.

Ekman, P. (1999). Basic emotions. In T. Dalgleish & T. Power (Eds.), *The handbook of cognition and emotion* (pp. 45–60). Sussex, UK: John Wiley & Sons, Ltd.

Ekman, P., & Friesen, W.V. (1975). *Unmasking the face: A guide to recognizing emotions from facial clues.* New York: Prentice Hall.

Elder, L., & Paul, R. (1996). Critical thinking development: A stage theory with implications for instruction. Retrieved June 16, 2008, from http://www.criticalthinking.org/resources/articles/ct-development-a-stage-theory.shtml

Epperson, D.L., Bushway, D.J., & Warman, R.E. (1983). Client self-terminations after one counseling session: Effects of problem recognition, counselor gender, and counselor experience. *Journal of Counseling Psychology, 30,* 307–315.

EPPI-Centre. (2012). What is the EPPI-Centre? Online Evidence Library. Retrieved August 3, 2012, from http://eppi.ioe.ac.uk/cms/Default.aspx?tabid=63

Epstein, J.A., & Botvin, G.J. (2002). The moderating role of risk-taking tendency and refusal assertiveness on social influences in alcohol use among inner-city adolescents. *Journal of Studies on Alcohol, 63*(4), 456–459.

Erikson, E.H. (1963). *Childhood and society* (2nd ed.). New York: W. W. Norton.

Erikson, E.H. (1968). *Identity, youth and crisis* (2nd ed.). New York: W. W. Norton.

Escudero, V., Heatherington, L., & Friedlander, M.L. (2010). Therapeutic alliances and alliance building in family therapy. In J.C. Muran & J.P. Barber (Eds.), *The therapeutic alliance: An evidence-based guide to practice* (pp. 240–262). New York: The Guilford Press.

Etzioni, A. (1999). *The limits of privacy.* New York: Basic Books.

Evans, D.R., Hearn, M.T., Uhlemann, M.R., & Ivey, A.E. (2008). *Essential interviewing: A programmed approach to effective communication* (7th ed.). Belmont, CA: Brooks/Cole.

Evans, N.J., & Jarvis, P.A. (1986). The Group Attitude Scale: A measure of attraction to group. *Small Group Research, 17*(2), 203–216. doi: 10.1177/104649648601700205

Evans, T., & Hardy, M. (2010). *Evidence and knowledge for practice.* Cambridge, MA: Polity.

Everstine, D.S., & Everstine, L. (1983). *People in crisis: Strategic therapeutic interventions.* New York: Brunner/Mazel.

Everstine, L., Everstine, D.S., Heymann, G.M., True, D.H., Johnson, H.G., & Seiden, R.H. (1980). Privacy and confidentiality in psychotherapy. *American Psychologist, 35,* 828–840.

Ewing, C.P., & McCann, J.T. (2006). *Minds on trial: Great cases in law and psychology.* New York: Oxford University Press.

Ewing, J.A. (1984). Detecting Alcoholism: The CAGE questionnaire. *JAMA: The Journal of the American Medical Association, 252*(14), 1905–1907. doi: 10.1001/jama.1984.03350140051025

Fessenden, F., & McLean, A. (2011, October 28). Where the 1 percent fit in the hierarchy of income, *New York Times*. Retrieved from http://www.nytimes.com/interactive/2011/10/30/nyregion/where-the-one-percent-fit-in-the-hierarchy-of-income.html

Fey, W.F. (1955). Acceptance by others and its relation to acceptance of self and others: A revaluation. *Journal of Abnormal and Social Psychology, 30*, 274–276.

Fieldhouse, P., & Bunkowsky, L. (2002). Asphalt artisans: Creating a community eco-map on the playground. *Green Teacher, 67*, 16–19.

Fischer, J., & Corcoran, K. (2007a). *Measures for clinical practice: A sourcebook, Vol. 1: Couples, families, and children* (4th ed.). New York: Oxford University Press.

Fischer, J., & Corcoran, K. (2007b). *Measures for clinical practice: A sourcebook, Vol. 2: Adults* (4th ed.). New York: Oxford University Press.

Fishbein, M., & Middlestadt, S.E. (1989). Using the theory of reasoned action as a framework for understanding and changing AIDS-related behaviors. In V.M. Mays, G.W. Albee, & S.F. Schneider (Eds.), *Primary prevention of AIDS: Psychological approaches* (pp. 93–110). London: Sage.

Fishbein, M., Middlestadt, S.E., & Hitchcock, P.J. (1994). Using information to change sexually transmitted disease-related behaviors. In R.J. DiClemente & J.L. Peterson (Eds.), *Preventing AIDS: Theories and methods of behavioral interventions* (pp. 61–78). New York: Plenum Press.

Fletcher, J.F. (1966). *Situational ethics: The new morality*. Louisville, KY: Westminster John Knox Press.

Fleuridas, C., Leigh, G.K., Rosenthal, D.M., & Leigh, T.E. (1990). Family goal recording: An adaptation of goal attainment scaling for enhancing family therapy and assessment. *Journal of Marital and Family Therapy, 16*, 389–406.

Fong, R. (2003). Cultural competence with Asian Americans. In D. Lum (Ed.), *Culturally competent practice: A framework for understanding diverse groups and justice issues* (2nd ed., pp. 261–281). Pacific Grove, CA: Brooks/Cole.

Fontes, L.A. (2008). *Interviewing clients across cultures: A practitioner's guide*. New York: Guilford Press.

Fortune, A.E., McCallion, P., & Briar-Lawson, K. (2010). *Social work practice research for the twenty-first century*. New York: Columbia University Press.

Fox, E., Ridgewell, A., & Ashwin, C. (2009). Looking on the bright side: Biased attention and the human serotonin transporter gene. *Proceedings of the Royal Society B: Biological Sciences, 276*(1663), 1747–1751. doi: 10.1098/rspb.2008.1788

Frame, M.W. (2000). The spiritual genogram in family therapy. *Journal of Marital & Family Therapy, 26*(2), 211–216.

Franks, C., & Riedel, M. (2008). Privilege. In T. Mizrahi & L.E. Davis (Eds.), *Encyclopedia of social work* (20th, e-reference ed.). New York: Oxford University Press.

Fraser, M.W., Richman, J.M., & Galinsky, M.J. (1999). Risk, protection, and resilience: Toward a conceptual framework for social work practice. *Social Work Research*, 23(3), 131–143.

Frisch, M.B. (2005). *Quality of life therapy: Applying a life satisfaction approach to positive psychology and cognitive therapy*. New York: John Wiley & Sons.

Fujita, F., & Diener, E. (2005). Life satisfaction set point: Stability and change. *Journal of Personality and Social Psychology, 88*(1), 158–164. doi: 10.1037/0022-3514.88.1.158

Fuller, R.W. (2002). *Somebodies and nobodies: Overcoming the abuse of rank*. Gabriola Island, BC, Canada: New Society Publishers.

Galbraith, J.K. (2012). *Inequality and instability: A study of the world economy just before the Great Crisis*. New York: Oxford University Press.

Gambrill, E.D. (1999). Evidence-based practice: An alternative to authority-based practice. *Families in Society: The Journal of Contemporary Human Services, 80*(4), 341–350.

Gambrill, E.D. (2001). Social work: An authority-based profession. *Research on Social Work Practice, 11*(2), 166–176.

Gardner, D.L., Huber, C.H., Steiner, R., Vazquez, L.A., & Savage, T.A. (2008). The development and validation of the inventory of family protective factors: A brief assessment for family counseling. *The Family Journal, 16*(2), 107–117. doi: 10.1177/1066480708314259

Garmezy, N. (1985). The NIMH-Israeli high-risk study: Commendation, comments, and cautions. *Schizophrenia Bulletin, 11*(3), 349–353.

Garmezy, N. (1986). *Risk and protective factors in the major mental disorders*. Chicago, IL: John D. and Catherine T. MacArthur Foundation.

Garvin, C. (1987). *Contemporary group work* (2nd ed.). Englewood Cliffs, NJ: Prentice Hall.

Garvin, C. (1997). *Contemporary group work* (3rd ed.). Boston: Allyn & Bacon.

Garvin, C., & Seabury, B. (1997). *Interpersonal practice in social work: Promoting competence and social justice* (2nd ed.). Boston: Allyn & Bacon.

General Assembly of the United Nations. (1948). *Universal declaration of human rights*. New York: Author.

General Assembly of the United Nations. (1966a). International convenant on civil and political rights. Retrieved July 1, 2009, from http://www.un.org/millennium/law/iv-4.htm

General Assembly of the United Nations. (1966b). International convenant on economic, social, and cultural rights. Retrieved July 1, 2009, from http://www.unhchr.ch/html/menu3/b/a_cescr.htm

Gibbs, L., & Gambrill, E. (1996). *Critical thinking for social workers: A workbook*. Thousand Oaks, CA: Pine Forge Press.

Gilbert, D.J., & Franklin, C. (2001). Developing culturally sensitive practice evaluation skills with Native American individuals and families. In R. Fong & S. Furuto (Eds.), *Culturally competent practice* (pp. 396–411). Boston: Allyn & Bacon.

Gilgun, J.F. (1998). Clinical instruments for assessing client assets and risks. *The Medical Journal of Allina, 7*, 31–33.

Gilgun, J.F. (2004a). The 4-D: Strengths-based assessments for youth who've experienced adversities. *Journal of Human Behavior in the Social Environment, 10*(4), 51–73.

Gilgun, J.F. (2004b). A strengths-based approach to child and family assessment. In D. Catheral (Ed.), *Handbook of stress, trauma and the family* (pp. 307–324). New York: Taylor Francis.

Gilgun, J.F. (2005). Evidence-based practice, descriptive research, and the Resilience-Schema-Gender Brain Functioning (RSGB) assessment. *British Journal of Social Work, 35*(6), 843–862.

Gilligan, C. (1979). Woman's place in man's life cycle. *Harvard Educational Review, 49*(4), 431–446.

Gilligan, C. (1982). *In a different voice: Psychological theory and women's development.* Cambridge, MA: Harvard University Press.

Gini, C. (1921). Measurement of inequality of incomes. *The Economic Journal, 31*(121), 124–126.

Glaser, S.R., Zamanou, S., & Hacker, K. (1987). Measuring and interpreting organizational culture: The Organizational Culture Survey. *Management Communication Quarterly, 1*(2), 173–198.

Glass, G.V. (1976). Primary, secondary and meta-analysis of research. *Educational Research, 5*, 3–8.

Gleeson, J.P., & Philbin, C.M. (1996). Preparing caseworkers for practice in kinship foster care: The supervisor's dilemma. *The Clinical Supervisor, 14*(1), 19–34.

Gleick, J. (2011). *The information: A history, a theory, a flood.* New York: Pantheon Books.

Glisson, C., Dulmus, C.N., & Sowers, K.M. (2012). *Social work practice with groups, communities, and organizations: Evidence-based assessments and interventions.* Hoboken, NJ: Wiley.

Gokhale, J., & Kotlikoff, L.J. (2000, October 1). The baby boomers' mega-inheritance—Myth or reality? *Economic Commentary.* Retrieved from http://www.clevelandfed.org/research/commentary/2000/1001.pdf

Goldstein, H. (1987). The neglected moral link in social work practice. *Social Work, 32*, 181–186.

Good Tracks, J. (1973). Native American noninterference. *Social Work, 18*, 30–34.

Goode, T.D., Dunne, M.C., & Bronheim, S.M. (2006). The evidence base for cultural and linguistic competency in health care. *The Commonwealth Fund, 37.* Retrieved from http://www.commonwealthfund.org/~/media/Files/Publications/Fund%20Report/2006/Oct/The%20Evidence%20Base%20for%20Cultural%20and%20Linguistic%20Competency%20in%20Health%20Care/Goode_evidencebasecultlinguisticcomp_962%20pdf.pdf

Goodman, G., & Esterly, G. (1988). *The talk book: The intimate science of communicating in close relationships.* Emmaus, PA: Rodale.

Gould, N., & Baldwin, M. (Eds.). (2004). *Social work, critical reflection, and the learning organization.* Aldershot, UK: Ashgate.

Gray, P. (2007). *Psychology* (5th ed.). New York: Worth Publishers.

Greene, G.J., & Lee, M.Y. (2011). *Solution-oriented social work practice: An integrative approach to working with client strengths.* New York: Oxford University Press.

Greenhalgh, T. (1997a). How to read a paper: Papers that summarise other papers (systematic reviews and meta-analyses). *British Medical Journal, 315*, 672–675.

Greenhalgh, T. (1997b). *How to read a paper: The basics of evidence based medicine.* London: BMJ Publishing.

Greenhalgh, T. (2001). *How to read a paper: The basics of evidence based medicine* (2nd ed.). London: BMJ Publishing. Retrieved from http://www.journalclub.co.uk/resources/Greenhalgh%20-%20How%20to%20read%20a%20paper.pdf

Grimshaw, J.M., Shirran, L., Thomas, R., Mowatt, G., Fraser, C., Bero, L., . . . O'Brien, M.A. (2001). Changing provider behavior: An overview of systematic reviews of interventions. *Med Care, 39*(8), II-2–II-45.

Grinnell, R.M. (1997). *Social work research & evaluation: Quantitative and qualitative approaches* (5th ed.). Itasca, IL: F.E. Peacock.

Grinnell, R.M. (2011). *Social work research and evaluation: Foundations of evidence-based practice.* New York: Oxford University Press.

Grinnell, R.M., Gabor, P., Unrau, Y.A., & Gabor, P. (2010). *Program evaluation for social workers: Foundations of evidence-based programs.* Oxford; New York: Oxford University Press.

Grinnell, R.M., & Unrau, Y.A. (2008). *Social work research and evaluation: Foundations of evidence-based practice* (8th ed.). New York: Oxford University Press.

Gross, S.R., Jacoby, K., Matheson, D.J., Montgomery, N., & Patil, S. (2004). Exonerations in the United States, 1989-2003. Retrieved from http://www.soros.org/initiatives/usprograms/focus/justice/articles_publications/publications/exonerations_20040419

Gudykunst, W.B., & Kim, Y.Y. (2003). *Communicating with strangers: An approach to intercultural communication* (4th ed.). Boston: McGraw-Hill.

Guerino, P., Harrison, P.M., & Sabo, W.J. (2012, February 9). *Prisoners in 2010.* Washington, DC: U.S. Department of Justice Bureau of Justice Statistics. Retrieved from http://bjs.ojp.usdoj.gov/content/pub/pdf/p10.pdf

Guyatt, G.H., Sackett, D.L., & Sinclair, J.C. (1995). Users' guide to the medical literature IX. A method for grading health care recommendations. *Journal of the American Medical Association, 274*, 1800–1804.

Haidt, J. (2012). *The righteous mind: Why good people are divided by politics and religion.* New York: Pantheon Books.

Haidt, J., Seder, J.P., & Kesebir, S. (2008). Hive psychology, happiness, and public policy. *The Journal of Legal Studies, 37*(S2), 133S–S156.

Halley, J., Eshleman, A., & Vijaya, R.M. (2011). *Seeing white: An introduction to white privilege and race.* Lanham, MD: Rowman & Littlefield Publishers.

Hammond, D., Hepworth, D., & Smith, V. (1977). *Improving therapeutic communication.* San Francisco, CA: Jossey-Bass.

Hansenfeld, Y. (1985). The organizational context of group work. In M. Sundel, P.H. Glaser, R. Sarri, & R. Vinter (Eds.), *Individual change through small groups* (2nd ed., pp. 294–309). New York: The Free Press.

Hanson, R.K., & Morton-Bourgon, K.E. (2009). The accuracy of recidivism risk assessments for sexual offenders: A meta-analysis of 118 prediction studies. *Psychological Assessment, 21*(1), 1–21.

Hanvey, C.P., & Philpot, T. (1994). *Practising social work.* New York: Routledge.

Hardy, K.V., & Laszloffy, T.A. (1995). The cultural genogram: Key to training culturally competent family therapists. *Journal of Marital and Family Therapy, 21*(3), 227–237.

Harrison, J.A., Mullen, P.D., & Green, L.W. (1992). A meta-analysis of studies of the Health Belief Model with adults. *Health Education Research, 7*(1), 107–116. doi: 10.1093/her/7.1.107

Hartman, A. (1978). Diagrammatic assessment of family relationships. *Social Casework, 59*, 465–476.

Hartman, A., & Laird, J. (1983). *Family-centered social work practice.* New York: The Free Press.

Hawkins, E.J., Lambert, M.J., Vermeersch, D.A., Slade, K., & Tuttle, K. (2004). The effects of providing patient progress information to therapists and patients. *Psychotherapy Research, 14(3)*, 308–327.

Hawkins, J.D., Catalano, R. F., & Miller, J. Y. (1992). Risk and protective factors for alcohol and other drug problems in adolescence and early adulthood: Implications for substance abuse prevention. *Psychological Bulletin, 112*(1), 64–105.

Hayes, D., Humphries, B., & Cohen, S. (2004). *Social work, immigration and asylum debates, dilemmas and ethical issues for social work and social care practice.* London; New York: Jessica Kingsley Publishers.

Haynes, S.N. (1998). The assessment-treatment relationship and functional analysis in behavior therapy. *European Journal of Psychological Assessment* [Special Issue: Assessment for treatment], *14*(1), 26–35.

Haynes, S.N., Leisen, M.B., & Blaine, D.D. (1997). Design of individualized behavioral treatment programs using functional analytic clinical case models. *Psychological Assessment, 9*(4), 334–348.

Helmer, D., Savoie, I., Green, C., & Kazanjian, A. (2001). Evidence-based practice: Extending the search to find material for the systematic review. *Bulletin of the Medical Library Association, 89*(4), 346–352.

Hennessey, R. (2011). *Relationship skills in social work.* London: Sage.

Henrichson, C., & Delaney, R. (2012, January). *The price of prisons: What incarcerations costs taxpayers.* New York: VERA Institute of Justice Center on Sentencing and Corrections.

Henry, S. (1981). *Group skills in social work.* Itasca, IL: F. E. Peacock.

Henry, S. (1992). *Group skills in social work* (2nd ed.). Pacific Grove, CA: Brooks/Cole.

Hepworth, D.H., Rooney, R. H., Rooney, G. D., Strom-Gottfried, K., & Larsen, J. A. (2006). *Direct social work practice: Theory and skills* (7th ed.). Pacific Grove, CA: Brooks/Cole-Thomson Learning.

Herring, R.H. (1996). *Decision making with child abuse victims and their families in a pediatric setting: The use of the Hood Herring Risk Assessment Matrix (HHRAM).* Unpublished doctoral dissertation. Howard University, Washington, DC.

Hess, H., & Hess, P.M. (1999). Termination in context. In B. Compton & B. Galaway (Eds.), *Social work processes* (6th ed., pp. 489–495). Pacific Grove, CA: Brooks/Cole.

Higgins, J.P.T., & Green, S. (Eds.). (2011). *Cochrane handbook for systematic reviews of interventions* [Version 5.1.0]. Oxford, UK: The Cochrane Collaboration. Retrieved from http://www.cochrane-handbook.org/

Hill, C.E., & Gormally, J. (1977). Effect of reflection, restatement, probe, and nonverbal behaviors on client affect. *Journal of Counseling Psychology, 24*, 92–97.

Hill, C.E., & Gormally, J. (2001). Effects of reflection, restatement, probe, and nonverbal behaviors on client affect. In C.E. Hill (Ed.), *Helping skills: The empirical foundation* (pp. 229–242). Washington, DC: American Psychological Association.

Hinnells, J.R. (2010). *The Routledge companion to the study of religion.* London; New York: Routledge.

Hodge, D.R. (2000). Spiritual ecomaps: A new diagrammatic tool for assessing marital and family spirituality. *Journal of Marital and Family Therapy, 26*(2), 217–228.

Hodge, D.R. (2001a). Spiritual assessment: A review of major qualitative methods and a new framework for assessing spirituality. *Social Work, 46*(3), 203–214.

Hodge, D.R. (2001b). Spiritual genograms: A generational approach to assessing spirituality. *Families in Society: The Journal of Contemporary Human Services, 82*(1), 35–48.

Hodge, D.R. (2005). Spiritual ecograms: A new assessment instrument for identifying clients' strengths in space and across time. *Families in Society: The Journal of Contemporary Human Services, 86*(2), 287–296.

Hoffart, A., Borge, F.-M., Sexton, H., & Clark, D.M. (2008). The role of common factors in residential cognitive and interpersonal therapy for social phobia: A process-outcome study. *Psychotherapy Research, 19*(1), 1–14.

Hoffer, E. (1973). *Reflections on the human condition.* New York: Harper & Row.

Hofstede, G.H., & Hofstede, G.J. (2005). *Cultures and organizations: Software of the mind* (Rev. and expanded 2nd ed.). New York: McGraw-Hill.

Hogan, M. (2012). *The four skills of cultural diversity competence: A process for understanding and practice* (4th ed.). Belmont, CA: Brooks/Cole.

Holden, G. (1991). The relationship of self-efficacy appraisals to subsequent health related outcomes: A meta-analysis. *Social Work in Health Care, 16*(1), 53–93.

Holden, G., Barker, K., Rosenberg, G., & Onghena, P. (2008). The Evaluation Self-Efficacy Scale for assessing progress toward CSWE accreditation related objectives: A replication. *Research on Social Work Practice, 18*(1), 42–46. doi: 10.1177/1049731507303954

Holden, G., Cuzzi, L., Rutter, S., Chernack, P., & Rosenberg, G. (1997). The Hospital Social Work Self-Efficacy Scale: A replication. *Research on Social Work Practice, 7*(4), 490–499.

Holden, G., Cuzzi, L., Rutter, S., Rosenberg, G., & Chernack, P. (1996). The Hospital Social Work Self-Efficacy Scale: Initial development. *Research on Social Work Practice, 6*(3), 353–365.

Holden, G., Cuzzi, L., Spitzer, W., Rutter, S., Chernack, P., & Rosenberg, G. (1997). The Hospital Social Work Self-Efficacy Scale: A partial replication and extension. *Health and Social Work, 22*(4), 256–263.

Holden, G., Meenaghan, T., & Anastas, J. (2003). Determining attainment of the EPAS Foundation Program objectives: Evidence for the use of self-efficacy as a outcome. *Journal of Social Work Education, 39*(3), 425–440.

Holden, G., Meenaghan, T., Anastas, J., & Metrey, G. (2001). Outcomes of social work education: The case for social work self-efficacy. *Journal of Social Work Education, 38*(1), 115–134.

Holmes, R.L. (2003). *Basic moral philosophy* (3rd. ed.). Belmont, CA: Wadsworth.

Homelessness Research Institute. (2012, January). The State of Homelessness in America 2012. Washington, DC: National Alliance to End Homelessness.

Hönisch, B., Ridgwell, A., Schmidt, D.N., Thomas, E., Gibbs, S.J., Sluijs, A., . . . Williams, B. (2012). The geological record of ocean acidification. *Science, 335*(6072), 1058–1063. doi: 10.1126/science.1208277

Horvath, A.O., & Bedi, R.P. (2002). The alliance. In J.C. Norcross (Ed.), *Psychotherapy relationships that work* (pp. 37–69). New York: Oxford University Press.

Horvath, A.O., Symonds, D., & Tapia, L. (2010). Therapeutic alliances in couple therapy. In J.C. Muran & J.P. Barber (Eds.), *The therapeutic alliance: An evidence-based guide to practice* (pp. 210–239). New York: The Guilford Press.

Hubble, M.A., Duncan, B.L., & Miller, S.D. (1999). Introduction. In M.A. Hubble, B.L. Duncan, & S.D. Miller (Eds.), *The heart and soul of change: What works in therapy* (pp. 1–19). Washington, DC: American Psychological Association.

Hudson, W.W. (1982). *The clinical measurement package: A field manual.* Homewood, IL: Dorsey.

Hulko, W. (2009). The time- and context-contingent nature of intersectionality and interlocking oppressions. *AFFILIA: Journal of Women and Social Work, 24*(1), 44–55.

Human Genome Project Information. (2008). Genetic anthropology, ancestry, and ancient human migration. Retrieved August 18, 2009, from http://www.ornl.gov/sci/techresources/Human_Genome/elsi/humanmigration.shtml

Human Rights Watch. (2012). "I had to run away"—The imprisonment of women and girls for "moral crimes" in Afghanistan. Retrieved June 11, 2012, from http://www.hrw.org/sites/default/files/reports/afghanistan0312webwcover_0.pdf

Humes, K.R., Jones, N.A., & Ramirez, R.R. (2011, March). *Overview of Race and Hispanic Origin: 2010.* Washington, DC: U.S. Census Bureau. Retrieved from http://www.census.gov/prod/cen2010/briefs/c2010br-02.pdf

Hunt, D.L., & McKibbon, K.A. (1997). Locating and appraising systematic reviews. *Annals of Internal Medicine, 126*, 532–538.

Hunt, M. (1997). *How science takes stock: The story of meta-analysis.* New York: Russell Sage Foundation.

Iacoboni, M. (2008). *Mirroring people: The new science of how we connect with others.* New York: Farrar, Straus and Giroux.

Iatridis, D.S. (2008). Policy practice. In T. Mizrahi & L.E. Davis (Eds.), *Encylopedia of social work* (20th, e-reference ed.). New York: National Association of Social Workers and Oxford University Press.

Ickes, W. (2003). *Everyday mind reading: Understanding what other people think and feel.* Amherst, NY: Prometheus Books.

Indiana General Assembly. (2012). Indiana Code Title 25 Article 23.6, Chapters 1–11. Retrieved July 10, 2012, from http://www.in.gov/legislative/ic/code/title25/ar23.6/

Inglehart, R. (2004). Subjective well-being rankings of 82 societies (based on combined Happiness and Life Satisfaction scores). Retrieved August 4, 2009, from http://margaux.grandvinum.se/SebTest/wvs/articles/folder_published/publication_488

Inglehart, R. (2006). Inglehart-Welzel cultural map of the world. Retrieved August 4, 2009, from http://margaux.grandvinum.se/SebTest/wvs/SebTest/wvs/articles/folder_published/article_base_54

Inglehart, R., Foa, R., Peterson, C., & Welzel, C. (2008). Development, freedom, and rising happiness: A global perspective (1981–2007). *Perspectives on Psychological Science, 3*(4), 264–285. doi: 10.1111/j.1745-6924.2008.00078.x

Inglehart, R., & Welzel, C. (2005). *Modernization, cultural change and democracy.* New York: Cambridge University Press.

International Federation of Social Workers. (2000, October 4, 2005). Definition of social work. Retrieved May 13, 2009, from http://www.ifsw.org/en/p38000208.html

International Initiative for Impact Evaluation. (2012). Systematic reviews. Retrieved August 3, 2012, from http://www.3ieimpact.org/en/evidence/systematic-reviews/

Internet Public Library. (2009). IPL Kidspace: Say hello to the world. Retrieved August 27, 2009, from http://www.ipl.org/div/hello

Isaac, S., & Michael, W.B. (1971). *Handbook in research and evaluation.* San Diego, CA: EdITS publishers.

Ivey, A.E. (1988). *Intentional interviewing and counseling: Facilitating client development* (2nd ed.). Pacific Grove, CA: Brooks/Cole.

Ivey, A.E., Ivey, M.B., & Zalaquett, C.P. (2010). *Intentional interviewing and counseling: Facilitating client development in a multicultural society* (7th ed.). Belmont, CA: Wadsworth, Cengage Learning.

Ivey, A.E., Ivey, M.B., Zalaquett, C.P., & Quirk, K. (2012). *Essentials of intentional interviewing: Counseling in a multicultural world* (2nd ed.). Belmont, CA: Brooks/Cole, Cengage Learning.

Jacoby, S. (2008). *The age of American unreason.* New York: Pantheon.

Jaramillo, P.A. (2010). Building a theory, measuring a concept: Exploring intersectionality and Latina activism at the individual level. *Journal of Women, Politics & Policy, 31*(3), 193–216.

Jessor, R. (1991). Risk behavior in adolescence: A psychosocial framework for understanding and action. *Journal of Adolescent Health, 12,* 507–605.

Jessor, R., Bos, J.V.D., Vanderyn, F.M., & Turbin, M.S. (1995). Protective factors in adolescent problem behavior: Moderator effects and developmental change. *Developmental Psychology, 31,* 923–933.

John, O.P. (2007–2009). Berkeley personality lab. Retrieved July 27, 2009, from http://www.ocf.berkeley.edu/~johnlab/index.htm

John, O.P., Donahue, E.M., & Kentle, R.L. (1991). *The Big Five Inventory—Versions 4a and 5b.* University of California, Berkeley, Institute of Personality and Social Research. Berkeley, CA.

John, O.P., Naumann, L.P., & Soto, C.J. (2008). Paradigm shift to the integrative big-five trait taxonomy: History, measurement, and conceptual Issues. In O.P. John, W.R. Robins, & L.A. Pervin (Ed.), *Handbook of personality: Theory and research* (pp. 114–158). New York, NY: Guilford Press.

John, O.P., & Srivastava, S. (1999). The big-five trait taxonomy: History, measurement, and theoretical perspectives (final draft). Retrieved July 27, 2009, from http://www.uoregon.edu/~sanjay/pubs/bigfive.pdf

Johnson, D. (2011, September 15). Income gap: Is it widening? *Random Samplings: The Official Blog of the U.S. Census Bureau.* Retrieved from http://blogs.census.gov/2011/09/15/income-gap-is-it-widening/

Johnson, H.C. (1978). Integrating the problem-oriented record with a systems approach to case assessment. *Journal of Education for Social Work, 14*(3), 71–77.

Johnson, L.C. (1995). *Social work practice: A generalist approach* (5th ed.). Newton, MA: Allyn and Bacon.

Johnston, M. (1997). *Spectral evidence. The Ramona case: Incest, memory, and truth on trial in Napa Valley.* Boston: Houghton Mifflin.

Jones, T., & Evans, D. (2000). Conducting a systematic review. *Australian Critical Care May, 13*(2), 66–71.

Jonsen, A.R., & Toulmin, S. (1988). *The abuse of casuistry: A history of moral reasoning.* Berkeley: University of California Press.

Jordan, C. (2008). Assessment. In T. Mizrahi & L.E. Davis (Eds.), *Encyclopedia of social work* (20th, e-reference ed.). New York: National Association of Social Workers and Oxford University Press.

Julian, D.A. (1997). The utilization of the logic model as a system level planning and evaluation device. *Evaluation and Program Planning, 20*(3), 251–257.

Julian, D.A., Jones, A., & Deyo, D. (1995). Open systems evaluation and the logic model: Program planning and evaluation tools. *Evaluation and Program Planning, 18*(4), 333–341.

Kadushin, A. (1983). *The social work interview* (2nd ed.). New York: Columbia University Press.

Kadushin, A., & Kadushin, G. (1997). *The social work interview: A guide for human service professionals* (4th ed.). New York: Columbia University Press.

Kagle, J.D. (2002). Record-keeping. In A.R. Roberts & G.J. Greene (Eds.), *Social workers' desk reference* (pp. 28–33). New York: Oxford University Press.

Kagle, J.D., & Kopels, S. (1994). Confidentiality after Tarasoff. *Health and Social Work, 19*(3), 217–223.

Kagle, J.D., & Kopels, S.L. (2008). *Social work records* (3rd ed.). Long Grove, IL: Waveland Press.

Kahneman, D. (2011). *Thinking, fast and slow.* New York: Farrar, Straus and Giroux.

Kamya, H.A. (2000). Hardiness and spiritual well-being among social work students: Implications for social work education. *Journal of Social Work Education, 36*(2), 231–240.

Karls, J.M., & O'Keefe, M.E. (Eds.). (2008). *Person-in-environment system manual* (2nd ed.). Washington, DC: NASW Press.

Karls, J.M., & Wandrei, K.E. (1994). *PIE manual: Person-in-environment system: The PIE classification system for social functioning problems.* Washington, DC: NASW Press.

Karpman, S.B. (1968). Fairy tales and script drama analysis. *Transactional Analysis Bulletin, 7*(26), 39–43.

Karpman, S.B. (1971). Options. *Transactional Analysis Journal, 1*(1), 79–87.

Karstin Slade, M.J.L., S. Cory Harmon, David W. Smart, Russ Bailey. (2008). Improving psychotherapy outcome: The use of immediate electronic feedback and revised clinical support tools. *Clinical Psychology & Psychotherapy, 15*(5), 287–303.

Kaufman, L., & Jones, R.L. (2003, May 23). Report finds flaws in inquiries on foster abuse in New Jersey, *The New York Times.*

Keefe, T. (1976). Empathy: The critical skill. *Social Work, 21,* 10–14.

Keiley, M.K., Dolbin, M., Hill, J., Karuppaswamy, N., Liu, T., Natrajan, R., … Robinson, P. (2002). The cultural genogram: Experiences from within a marriage and family therapy training program. *Journal of Marital & Family Therapy, 28*(2), 165–178.

Keith-Lucas, A. (1972). *The giving and taking of help.* Chapel Hill: University of North Carolina Press.

Kellogg, N., & The American Academy of Pediatrics Committee on Child Abuse and Neglect. (2005). The evaluation of sexual abuse in children. *Pediatrics, 116*(2), 506–512. doi: 10.1542/peds.2005-1336

Kelly, M.S. (2010). *School social work: An evidence-informed framework for practice.* Oxford; New York: Oxford University Press.

Kenrick, D.T., Griskevicius, V., Neuberg, S. L., & Schaller, M. (2010). Renovating the pyramid of needs: Contemporary extensions built upon ancient foundations. *Perspectives on Psychological Science, 5,* 292–314.

Keshav, S. (2007). How to read a paper. *Computer Communication Review, 37*(3), 83–84. Retrieved from http://ccr.sigcomm.org/online/files/p83-keshavA.pdf

Khimm, S. (2011, October 6). Who are the 1 percent? (updated). *The Washington Post.* Retrieved from http://www.washingtonpost.com/blogs/ezra-klein/post/who-are-the-1-percenters/2011/10/06/gIQAn4JDQL_blog.html

Kiresuk, T.J., & Sherman, R.E. (1968). Goal attainment scaling: A general method for evaluating comprehensive community health programs. *Community Mental Health Journal, 4,* 443–453.

Kiresuk, T.J., Smith, A., & Cardillo, J.E. (Eds.). (1994). *Goal attainment scaling: Applications, theory & measurement.* Mahwah, NJ: Lawrence Erlbaum Associates.

Kirk, S.A., & Kutchins, H. (1992). *The selling of DSM: The rhetoric of science in psychiatry.* New York: Aldine de Gruyter.

Kirk, S.A., & Kutchins, H. (1994). The myth of the reliability of DSM. *The Journal of Mind and Behavior, 15*(1/2), 71–86.

Kitchener, K.S. (2000). *Foundations of ethical practice, research, and teaching in psychology.* Mahwah, NJ: Lawrence Erlbaum.

Kivel, P. (2002). *Uprooting racism: How white people can work for racial justice.* Gabriola Island, BC, Canada: New Society Publishers.

Klein, E. (2012, March 2). High health-care costs: It's all in the pricing. *The Washington Post.* Retrieved from http://www.washingtonpost.com/business/high-health-care-costs-its-all-in-the-pricing/2012/02/28/gIQAtbhimR_story.html?wprss=rss_homepage

Kohn, S.M. (2011). *The whistleblower's handbook: A step-by-step guide to doing what's right and protecting yourself* (2nd ed.). Guilford, CT: Lyons Press.

Kondrat, M.E. (1999). Who is the "self" in self-aware: Professional self-awareness from a critical theory perspective. *Social Service Review, 73*(4), 451–477.

Konigsberg, R.D. (2011). *The truth about grief: The myth of its five stages and the new science of loss.* New York: Simon and Schuster.

Koocher, G.P., & Keith-Spiegel, P. (1990). *Children, ethics, and the law: Professional issues and cases.* Lincoln: University of Nebraska Press.

Kovacs, P.J., & Bronstein, L.R. (1999). Preparation for oncology settings: What hospice social workers say they need. *Health and Social Work, 24*(1), 57–64.

Krill, D.F. (1986). *The beat worker: Humanizing social work & psychotherapy practice.* Lanham, MD: University Press of America.

Krznaric, R. (2012). Outrospection: Roman Krznaric's blog on empathy and the art of living. Retrieved March 23, 2012, from http://www.romankrznaric.com/outrospection

Kubetin, S.K. (2003). 20% dropout rate hinders prolonged therapy. *Clinical Psychiatry News, 31*(1), 54.

Kubler-Ross, E. (1969). *On death and dying.* New York: Macmillan.

Kutchins, H. (1991). The fiduciary relationship: The legal basis for social workers' responsibilities to clients. *Social Work, 36*(2), 106–114.

Kutchins, H. (1998). Does the fiduciary relationship guarantee a right to effective treatment? *Research on Social Work Practice, 8*(5), 615–622.

Kutchins, H., & Kirk, S.A. (1997). *Making us crazy: DSM: The psychiatric bible and the creation of mental disorders.* New York: Free Press.

Lambert, M.J. (1992). Implications of outcome research for psychotherapy integration. In J.C. Norcross & M.R. Goldfried (Eds.), *Handbook of psychotherapy integration* (pp. 94–129). New York: Basic Books.

Lambert, M.J. (2010a). *Prevention of treatment failure: The use of measuring, monitoring, and feedback in clinical practice.* Washington, DC: American Psychological Association.

Lambert, M.J. (2010b). "Yes, it is time for clinicians to routinely monitor treatment outcome." In B.L. Duncan, S.D. Miller, B.E. Wampold, & M.A. Hubble (Eds.), *The heart and soul of change: Delivering what works in therapy* (2nd ed., pp. 239–266). Washington, DC: American Psychological Association.

Lambert, M.J., & Bergin, A.E. (1994). The effectiveness of psychotherapy. In A.E. Bergin & S.L. Garfield (Eds.), *Handbook of psychotherapy and behavior change* (4th ed., pp. 143–189). New York: Wiley.

Lambert, M.J., & Cattani-Thompson, K. (1996). Current findings regarding the effectiveness of counseling: Implications for practice. *Journal of Counseling and Development, 74,* 601–608.

Lambert, M.J., & Shimokawa, K. (2011). Collecting client feedback. *Psychotherapy, 48*(1), 72–79. doi: 10.1037/a0022238

Lambert, M.J., Whipple, J.L., Vermeersch, D.A., Smart, D.W., & Hawkins, E.J. (2002). Enhancing psychotherapy outcomes via providing feedback on patient progress: a replication. *Clinical Psychology & Psychotherapy, 9(2),* 91–103.

Lambert, R.G., & Lambert, M.J. (1984). The effects of role preparation for psychotherapy on immigrant clients seeking mental health services in Hawaii. *Journal of Community Psychology, 12*(3), 263–275.

Lang, S.S. (2002). Social support networks trump number of parents. *Human Ecology, 30*(4), 24.

Langer, L.M., Warheit, G.J., & McDonald, L.P. (2001). Correlates and predictors of risky sexual practices among a multi-racial/ethnic sample of university students. *Social Behavior and Personality, 29*(2), 133–144.

Larsen, E. (2006). *A nation gone blind: America in an age of simplification and deceit.* Emeryville, CA: Shoemaker and Hoard.

Lawsuit seeks discharge treatment-planning at NYC jails. (1999). *Mental Health Weekly, 9*(34), 1–2.

Lazarus, A. (1984). *In the mind's eye: The power of imagery for personal enrichment.* New York: Guilford.

Lee, M.Y. (1997). A study of solution-focused brief family therapy: Outcomes and issues. *The American Journal of Family Therapy, 25,* 3–17.

LeGault, M.R. (2006). *Think: Why crucial decisions can't be made in the blink of an eye.* New York: Threshold Editions.

Levenson, J.S., & Morin, J.W. (2006). Risk assessment in child sexual abuse cases. *Child Welfare, 85*(1), 59–82.

Levinson, D. (1998). *Ethnic groups worldwide: A ready reference handbook.* Santa Barbara, CA: Greenwood Publishing Group.

Lewis, R., & Ho, M. (1975). Social work with Native Americans. *Social Work, 20,* 379–382.

Lie, G.-Y., & Lowery, C.T. (2003). Cultural competence with women of color. In D. Lum (Ed.), *Culturally competent practice: A framework for understanding diverse groups and justice issues* (2nd ed., pp. 282–308). Pacific Grove, CA: Brooks/Cole.

Lin, N. (2001). *Social capital: A theory of social structure and action.* New York: Cambridge University Press.

Lincoln, K.D. (2000). Social support, negative social interactions, and psychological well-being. *Social Service Review, 74*(2), 231–252.

Lindsay, D.S., Hagen, L., Read, J.D., Wade, K.A., & Garry, M. (2004). True photographs and false memories. *Psychological Science, 15*(3), 149–154.

Linley, P.A., Joseph, S., & Seligman, M.E.P. (Eds.). (2004). *Positive psychology in practice.* New York: John Wiley & Sons.

Lipchik, E. (2002). *Beyond technique in solution-focused therapy.* New York: Guilford Press.

Loftus, E.F. (1997). Creating false memories. *Scientific American, 277*(3), 70–75.

Loftus, E.F. (2003). Make-believe memories. *American Psychologist, 58*(11), 864–873.

Longres, J.F. (1995). Hispanics overview. In R.L. Edwards (Ed.), *Encyclopedia of social work* (19th ed., Vol. 2, pp. 1214–1222). Washington, DC: NASW Press.

Luborsky, L. (1996). The Helping Alliance Questionnaire: Patient version. In B. Ogles, M. Lambert, & K. Masters (Eds.), *Assessing outcome in clinical practice* (pp. 150–151). Boston: Allyn and Bacon.

Lum, D. (2008). Culturally competent practice. In T. Mizrahi & L.E. Davis (Eds.), *Encyclopedia of social work* (20th, e-reference ed.). New York: National Association of Social Workers and Oxford University Press.

Lum, D. (Ed.). (2003). *Culturally competent practice: A framework for understanding diverse groups and justice issues* (2nd ed.). Pacific Grove, CA: Brooks/Cole.

Lumsden, C.J., & Wilson, E.O. (1981). *Genes, mind, and culture: The coevolutionary process.* Cambridge, MA: Harvard University Press.

Luszczynska, A., Gutiérez-Doña, B., & Schwarzer, R. (2005). General self-efficacy in various domains of human functioning: Evidence from five countries. *International Journal of Psychology, 40*(2), 80–89.

Luszczynska, A., Scholz, U, & Schwarzer, R. (2005). The General Self-Efficacy Scale: Multicultural validation studies. *Journal of Psychology, 139*(5), 439–457.

Lykken, D., & Tellegen, A. (1996). Happiness is a stochastic phenomenon. *Psychological Science, 7,* 186–189.

Lyubomirsky, S. (2006). Is it possible to become lastingly happier? Answers from the modern science of well-being. *The Vancouver Dialogues* (pp. 53–56). Vancouver, BC: Truffle Tree Publishing.

Lyubomirsky, S., Sheldon, K., & Schkade, D. (2005). Pursuing happiness: The architecture of sustainable change. *Review of General Psychology, 9*(2), 111–131.

Macartney, S. (2011, Nov.). *Child Poverty in the United States 2009 and 2010: Selected Race Groups and Hispanic Origin.* Washington, DC: U.S. Census Bureau. Retrieved from http://www.census.gov/prod/2011pubs/acsbr10-05.pdf

Maddi, S.R., Wadhwa, P., & Haier, R.J. (1996). Relationship of hardiness to alcohol and drug use in adolescents. *American Journal of Drug and Alcohol Abuse, 22*(2), 247–258.

Magill, F.N. (Ed.). (1998). *Psychology basics.* Pasadena, CA: Salem Press.

Maluccio, A. (1979). *Learning from clients: Interpersonal helping as viewed by clients and social workers.* New York: The Free Press.

Maluccio, A., & Marlow, W. (1974). The case for contract. *Social Work, 19,* 28–36.

Mapp, S.C. (2008). *Human rights and social justice in a global perspective: An introduction to international social work.* New York: Oxford University Press.

Markman, A. (2012, July 27). Why do Americans accept wealth inequality? *Huffington Post.* Retrieved July 28, 2012, from http://www.huffingtonpost.com/art-markman-phd/why-do-americans-accept-w_b_1709753.html?view=screen

Markward, M.J., & Yegidis, B.L. (2011). *Evidence-based practice with women: Toward effective social work practice with low-income women.* Thousand Oaks, CA: SAGE Publications.

Marson, S.M., & Dran, D. (2006). Goal attainment scaling. Retrieved July 10, 2006, from http://www.marson-and-associates.com/GAS/GAS_index.html

Martens, W.M., & Holmstrup, E. (1974). Problem-oriented recording. *Social Casework, 55*(9), 554–561.

Martin, D.J., Garske, J.P., & Davis, M.K. (2000). Relation of the therapeutic alliance with outcome and other variables: A meta-analytic review. *Journal of Consulting and Clinical Psychology, 68*(3), 438–450. doi: IO.I037//0022-006X.68.3.438

Martin, R. (1994). *The philosopher's dictionary* [electronic version] (2nd ed.). Orchard Park, NY: Broadview Press.

Maslow, A.H. (1943). A theory of human motivation. *Psychological Review, 50*(4), 370–396.

Maslow, A.H. (1968). *Toward a psychology of being* (2nd revised ed.). New York: Reinhold.

Masten, A.S. (1994). Resilience in individual development: Successful adaptation despite risk and adversity. In M.C. Wang & E.W. Gordon (Eds.), *Education resilience in inner-city America: Challenges and prospects* (pp. 3–25). Hillsdale, NJ: Lawrence Erlbaum.

Mathews, I., & Crawford, K. (2011). *Evidence-based practice in social work*. Exeter, UK: Learning Matters.

Mattaini, M.A. (1990). Contextual behavior analysis in the assessment process. *Families in Society: The Journal of Contemporary Human Services, 2*, 425–444.

Mattaini, M.A. (1993a). *More than a thousand words: Graphics for clinical practice*. Washington, DC: NASW Press.

Mattaini, M.A. (1993b). *Visual EcoScan for clinical practice* (Version 1.0.). Washington, DC: NASW Press.

Mattaini, M.A. (1995). Visualizing practice with children and families. *Early Child Development and Care, 106*, 59–74.

Mattaini, M.A., & Thyer, B.A. (Eds.). (1996). *Finding solutions to social problems: Behavioral strategies for change*. Washington, DC: American Psychological Association Press.

Mattison, M. (2000). Ethical decision making: The person in the process. *Social Work, 45*(3), 201–212.

McGoldrick, M., & Gerson, R. (1985). *Genograms in family assessment*. New York: W. W. Norton.

McGoldrick, M., Gerson, R., & Shellenberger, S. (1999). *Genograms: Assessment and interventions* (2nd ed.). New York: W. W. Norton.

McLaren, N. (2008). *Humanizing madness: Psychiatry and the cognitive neurosciences*. Ann Arbor, MI: Loving Healing Press.

McMillen, J.C., & Groze, V. (1994). Using placement genograms in child welfare practice. *Child Welfare, 73*(4), 307–318.

McMillen, J.C., & Rideout, G.B. (1996). Breaking intergenerational cycles: Theoretical tools for social workers. *The Social Service Review, 70*(3), 378–399.

McPeck, J.E. (1990). *Teaching critical thinking: Dialogue and dialectic*. New York: Routledge.

McTaggart, L. (2011). *The bond: Connecting through the space between us*. New York: Free Press.

McWhirter, D.A., & Bible, J.D. (1992). *Privacy as a constitutional right: Sex, drugs, and the right to life*. New York: Quorum Books.

Medlin, J. (2004). Sweet candy, bitter poison. *Environmental Health Perspectives, 112*(14), A803.

Mehrotra, G. (2010). Toward a continuum of intersectionality theorizing for feminist social work scholarship. *AFFILIA: Journal of Women and Social Work, 25*(4), 417–430.

Meier, P.S., Barrowclough, C., & Donmall, M.C. (2005). The role of the therapeutic alliance in the treatment of substance misuse: a critical review of the literature. *Addiction, 100*(3), 304–316. doi: 10.1111/j.1360-0443.2004.00935.x

Meyer, C.H. (1993). *Assessment in social work practice*. New York: Columbia University Press.

Meyer, R.G., & Weaver, C.M. (2006). *Law and mental health: A case-based approach*. New York: Guilford.

Middleman, R.R., & Goldberg, G.G. (1990). *Skills for direct practice in social work*. New York: Columbia University Press.

Miller, M., & Lago, D. (1990). The well-being of older women: The importance of pet and human relations. *Anthrozooes, 3*(4), 245–252.

Miller, S.D., Duncan, B.L., Sorrell, R., & Brown, G.S. (2005). The partners for change outcome management system. *Journal of Clinical Psychology, 61*(2), 199–208.

Miller, S.D., Duncan, Barry L., Brown, J., Sorrell, R., & Chalk, B. (2006). Using outcome to inform and improve treatment outcomes. *Journal of Brief Therapy, 5*, 5–22.

Miller, S.D., Hubble, M.A., & Duncan, B.L. (Eds.). (1996). *Handbook of solution-focused brief therapy*. San Francisco, CA: Jossey-Bass.

Miller, S.D., Wampold, B., & Varhely, K. (2008). Direct comparisons of treatment modalities for youth disorders: A meta-analysis. *Psychotherapy Research, 18*(1), 5–14.

Miller, W.R. (1995). *Motivational enhancement therapy manual: A clinical research guide for therapists treating individuals with alcohol abuse and dependence*. Washington, DC: U.S. Government Printing Office.

Miller, W.R., & Rollnick, S. (1991). *Motivational interviewing: Preparing people to change addictive behavior*. New York: Guilford Press.

Miller, W.R., & Rollnick, S. (2002). *Motivational interviewing: Preparing people for change* (2nd ed.). New York: Guilford Press.

Minahan, A. (1981). Purpose and objectives of social work revisited. *Social Work, 26*(1), 5–6.

Miranda v. Arizona, 384 U.S. 436 (1966).

Monahan, S.C., Mirola, W.A., & Emerson, M.O. (2011). *Sociology of religion: A reader*. Boston: Allyn & Bacon.

Montagu, A., & Matson, F. (1979). *The human connection*. New York: McGraw-Hill.

Moore, B.N., & Parker, R. (1995). *Critical thinking* (4th ed.). Mountain View, CA: Mayfield.

Moore, W.S. (2003, October). The Perry Network & the Center for the Study of Intellectual Development. Retrieved June 21, 2006, from http://www.perrynetwork.org

Moos, R., & Otto, J. (1972). The Community-Oriented Programs Environment Scale: A methodology for the facilitation and evaluation of social change. *Community Mental Health Journal, 8*(1), 28–37.

Moos, R.H., & Moos, B.S. (2009). *Family environment scale manual: Development, applications, and research* (4th ed.). Palo Alto, CA: Center for Health Care Evaluation, Deptartment of Veterans Affairs, Stanford University Medical Centers, Mind Garden.

Morello, C., & Mellnik, T. (2012, May 17). Census: Minority babies are now majority in United States. *The Washington Post*. Retrieved from http://www.washingtonpost.com/local/census-minority-babies-are-now-majority-in-united-states/2012/05/16/gIQA1WY8UU_story.html

Morone, J.A. (2003). *Hellfire nation: The politics of sin in American history*. New Haven, CT: Yale University Press.

Morrow-Howell, N., Chadiha, L.A., Proctor, E.K., Hourd-Bryant, M., & Dore, P. (1996). Racial differences in discharge planning. *Health and Social Work, 21*(2), 131–139.

Mueller, J., Polansky, D., Foltin, C., Polivaev, D., & Other Contributers. (2010). FreeMind: A program for creating and viewing mindmaps (Version 0.9.0). Retrieved January 18, 2012, from http://freemind.sourceforge.net/

Mulac, A., Erlandson, K.T., Farrar, W.J., Hallett, J.S., Molloy, J.L., & Prescott, M.E. (1998). "Uh-huh. What's that all about?" Differing interpretations of conversational backchannels and questions as sources of miscommunication across gender boundaries. *Communication Research, 25*, 641–668.

Mullen, P.D., Ramirez, G., Strouse, D., Hedges, L.V., & Sogolow, E. (2002). Meta-analysis of the effects of behavioral HIV prevention interventions on the sexual risk behavior of sexually experienced adolescents in controlled studies in the United States. *Journal of Acquired Immune Deficiency Syndromes, 30*, S94–S105.

Muran, J.C., & Barber, J.P. (Eds.). (2010). *The therapeutic alliance: An evidence-based guide to practice.* New York: The Guilford Press.

Murphy, J.J. (1999). Common factors of school based change. In M.A. Hubble, B.L. Duncan, & S.D. Miller (Eds.), *The heart and soul of change: What works in therapy* (pp. 361–386). Washington, DC: American Psychological Association.

Myers, J.E.B. (1992). *Legal issues in child abuse and neglect.* Newbury Park, CA: Sage Publications.

Narayan, D., & Cassidy, M.F. (2001). A dimensional approach to measuring social capital: Development and validation of a Social Capital Inventory. *Current Sociology, 49*(2), 59–102.

Narcotics Anonymous. (2008). *Narcotics anonymous* (6th ed.). Chatsworth, CA: Narcotics Anonymous World Services.

NASW Assurance Services. (2012). Social Worker Professional Liability. Retrieved July 10, 2012, from http://www.naswinsurancetrust.org/social_worker_professional_liability.php?page_id=11

Nathan, P.E., & Gorman, J.M. (Eds.). (2007). *A guide to treatments that work* (3rd revised ed.). New York: Oxford University Press.

National Association of Colleges and Employers. (2011). Job Outlook 2012. Bethlehem, PA: National Association of Colleges and Employers.

National Association of Social Workers. (1981). *Standards for the classification of social work practice.* Silver Spring, MD: Author.

National Association of Social Workers. (1996, June). Evaluation and treatment of adults with the possibility of recovered memories of childhood sexual abuse. Retrieved June 12, 2006, from https://www.socialworkers.org/practice/clinical/recvrmem.asp

National Association of Social Workers. (1998, June). Evaluation and treatment of adults with the possibility of recovered memories of childhood sexual abuse. Retrieved July 12, 2009, from https://www.socialworkers.org/practice/clinical/recvrmem.asp

National Association of Social Workers. (2001). NASW standards for cultural competence in social work practice. Retrieved May 15, 2009, from http://www.socialworkers.org/practice/standards/NASWCulturalStandards.pdf

National Association of Social Workers. (2005). *NASW procedures for professional review* (Revised 4th ed.). Retrieved from http://www.socialworkers.org/nasw/ethics/ProceduresManual2006.pdf

National Association of Social Workers. (2008). Code of ethics of the National Association of Social Workers. Retrieved June 15, 2009, from http://www.socialworkers.org/pubs/code/default.asp

National Association of Social Workers. (2012a). NASW Practice Standards. Retrieved July 16, 2012, from http://www.socialworkers.org/practice/default.asp?topic=standards#swtopics

National Association of Social Workers. (2012b). *Social work speaks: NASW Policy Statements, 2012–2014* (9th ed.). Washington, DC: NASW Press.

National Center for Cultural Competence. (2004). Cultural Competence Continuum. Retrieved September 10, 2009, from www.nccccurricula.info/documents/TheContinuumRevised.doc

National Research Council. (1996). *National science education standards.* Washington, DC: National Academy Press.

National Science Teachers Association Board of Directors. (2000, July). NSTA position statement: The nature of science. Retrieved May 13, 2009, from http://www.nsta.org/about/positions/natureofscience.aspx

National Science Teachers Association Board of Directors. (2004, October). NSTA position statement: Scientific inquiry. Retrieved May 13, 2009, from http://www.nsta.org/pdfs/PositionStatement_ScientificInquiry.pdf

Neff, K. (2011). *Self-compassion: Stop beating yourself up and leave insecurity behind.* New York: HarperCollins.

Neuliep, J.W. (2012). *Intercultural communication: A contextual approach.* Thousand Oaks, CA: Sage.

Ngo-Metzger, Q., Telfair, J., Sorkin, D.H., Beverly Weidmer, Weech-Maldonado, R., Hurtado, M., & Hays, R.D. (2006). Cultural competency and quality of care: Obtaining the patient's perspective. *The Commonwealth Fund, 39.* Retrieved from http://www.commonwealthfund.org/~/media/Files/Publications/Fund%20Report/2006/Oct/Cultural%20Competency%20and%20Quality%20of%20Care%20%20Obtaining%20the%20Patients%20Perspective/Ngo%20Metzger_cultcompqualitycareobtainpatientperspect_963%20pdf.pdf

Nieuwsma, J.A., Trivedi, R.B., McDuffie, J., Kronish, I., Benjamin, D., & Williams, J.W. (2012). Brief psychotherapy for depression: A systematic review and meta-analysis. *International Journal of Psychiatry in Medicine, 43*(2), 129–151.

O'Connell, B. (2005). *Solution-focused therapy* (2nd ed.). Thousand Oaks, CA: Sage Publications.

O'Neill, P. (1998). *Negotiating consent in psychotherapy.* New York: New York University Press.

O'Neill, R.E., Horner, R.H., Albin, R.W., Sprague, J.R., Storey, K., & Newton, J.S. (1997). *Functional assessment and program development for problem behavior: A practical handbook* (2nd ed.). Pacific Grove, CA: Brooks/Cole.

O'Reilly, B.K. (1995). The Social Support Appraisals scale: Construct validation for psychiatric patients. *Journal of Clinical Psychology, 51*(1), 37–42.

OECD. (2011). Divided We Stand: Why Inequality Keeps Rising—An Overview of Growing Income Inequalities in OECD Countries: Main Findings: Organisation for Economic Co-operation and Development (OECD). Retrieved from http://www.oecd.org/els/socialpoliciesanddata/dividedwestandwhyinequalitykeepsrising.htm

Office for Civil Rights. (2003). *HIPAA. Final modifications to privacy rule.* Washington, DC: United States Department of Health and Human Services.

Ong, A.D., & Dulmen, M.V. (Eds.). (2006). *The Oxford handbook of methods in positive psychology.* New York: Oxford University Press.

Organisation for Economic Co-operation and Development. (2011). *Divided we stand: Why inequality keeps rising.* Paris: OECD Publishing.

Owen, J.J., Rhoades, G.K., Stanley, S.M., & Markman, H.J. (2011). The role of leaders' working alliance in premarital education. *Journal of Family Psychology, 25*(1), 49–57. doi: 10.1037/a0022084

Oxman, A.D., & Guyatt, G.H. (1993). The science of reviewing research. *Annals of the New York Academy of Sciences, 703,* 125–133.

Pai, M., Mcculloch, M., Gorman, J.D., Pai, N., Enanoria, W., Kennedy, G., . . . John M. Colford, J. (2004). Systematic reviews and meta-analyses: An illustrated, step-by-step guide. *The National Medical Journal of India, 17*(2), 86–95. Retrieved from http://ssrc.tums.ac.ir/SystematicReview/Assets/Pai_NMJI_2004_Systematic_reviews_illustra.pdf

Paine, T. (1791). The rights of man: Answer to Mr. Burke's attack on the French Revolution (3rd ed.). Boston: I. Thomas and E.T. Andrews.

Palinkas, L.A., & Soydan, H. (2012). *Translation and implementation of evidence-based practice.* New York: Oxford University Press.

Patterson, C.H. (1984). Empathy, warmth and genuineness in psychotherapy: A review of reviews. *Psychotherapy, 21,* 431–438.

Paul, R. (1993). *Critical thinking: What every person needs to survive in a rapidly changing world* (3rd ed.). Santa Rosa, CA: Foundation for Critical Thinking.

Paul, R., & Elder, L. (1996). Universal intellectual standards. Retrieved May 13, 2009, from http://www.criticalthinking.org/page.cfm?PageID=527&CategoryID=68

Paul, R., & Elder, L. (1997). The elements of reasoning and the intellectual standards: Helping students assess their thinking. Retrieved June 18, 2008, from http://www.criticalthinking.org/resources/articles/content-thinking.shtml

Paul, R., & Elder, L. (2002). *Critical thinking: Tools for taking charge of your professional and personal life.* New York: Financial Times Prentice Hall.

Peck, D. (2011). *Pinched: How the great recession has narrowed our futures and what we can do about it.* New York: Crown Publishing.

Pedersen, P.B., Crethar, H., & Carlson, J. (2008). *Inclusive cultural empathy: Making relationships central in counseling and psychotherapy.* Washington, DC: American Psychological Association.

Pedersen, P.B., Draguns, J.G., Lonner, W.J., & Trimble, J.E. (Eds.). (2008). *Counseling across cultures* (6th ed.). Thousand Oaks, CA: Sage Publications.

Pekarik, G. (1988). The relationship of counselor identification of client problem description to continuance in a behavioral weight loss program. *Journal of Counseling Psychology, 35,* 66–70.

Pekarik, G. (1991). Relationship of expected and actual treatment duration for child and adult clients. *Journal of Child Clinical Psychology, 20,* 121–125.

Pelkonen, M., Marttunen, M., Laippala, P., & Lonnqvist, J. (2000). Factors associated with early dropout from adolescent psychiatric outpatient treatment. *Journal of the American Academy of Child and Adolescent Psychiatry, 39*(3), 329–336.

Perlman, H.H. (1957). *Social casework: A problem-solving process.* Chicago: University of Chicago Press.

Perlman, H.H. (Ed.). (1969). *Helping: Charlotte Towle on social work and social casework.* Chicago: University of Chicago Press.

Perlman, H.H. (1979). *Relationship: The heart of helping people.* Chicago: University of Chicago Press.

Perry, W.G. (1970). *Forms of intellectual and ethical development in the college years: A scheme.* New York: Holt Rinehart & Winston.

Perry, W.G. (1981). Cognitive and ethical growth: The making of meaning. In A.W. Chickering (Ed.), *The modern American college: Responding to the new realities of diverse students and a changing society* (pp. 76–116). San Francisco, CA: Jossey-Bass.

Perry, W.G. (1982). *How to develop competency-based vocational education.* Ann Arbor, MI: Prakken Publications.

Peters, R.D., Leadbeater, B.J.R., & McMahon, R.J. (2005). *Resilience in children, families, and communities: Linking context to practice and policy.* New York: Kluwer Academic/Plenum Publishers.

Peterson, C. (2006). *A primer in positive psychology.* New York: Oxford University Press.

Peterson, C., & Seligman, M.E.P. (2004). *Character strengths and virtues: A handbook and classification.* New York: Oxford University Press.

Petraitis, J., Flay, B. R., Miller, T. Q., Torpy, E. J., & Greiner, B. (1998). Illicit substance use among adolescents: A matrix of prospective predictors. *Substance Use and Misuse, 33,* 2561–2604.

Phillips, H. (1957). *Essentials of social group work skill.* New York: Association Press.

Pinderhughes, E. (1979). Teaching empathy in cross-cultural social work. *Social Work, 24,* 312–316.

Pine, R.C. (1996). *Essential logic: Basic reasoning skills for the Twenty-First Century.* New York: Oxford University Press.

Pinker, S. (2011). *The better angels of our nature: Why violence has declined.* New York: Viking Penguin.

Piper, W.E., & Ogrodniczuk, J.S. (2010). The therapeutic alliance in group therapy. In J.C. Muran & J.P. Barber (Eds.), *The therapeutic alliance: An evidence-based guide to practice* (pp. 263–282). New York: The Guilford Press.

Pizzigati, S. (1992). *The maximum wage: A common-sense perscription for revitilizing America—By taxing the very rich.* New York: Apex.

Pizzigati, S. (2004). *Greed and good: Understanding and overcoming the inequality that limits our lives.* Lanham, MD: Rowman & Littlefield/Apex Press.

Pollio, D.E., & Macgowan, M.J. (2011). *Evidence-based group work in community settings.* London; New York: Routledge.

Pope-Davis, D.B., Coleman, H.L.K., Liu, W.M., & Toporek, R.L. (Eds.). (2003). *Handbook of multicultural competencies in counseling and psychology.* Thousand Oaks, CA: Sage.

Postman, N. (1985). *Amusing ourselves to death: Public discourse in the age of show business.* New York: Penguin Books.

Potapchuk, M., Leiderman, S., Bivens, D., & Major, B. (Eds.). (2005). *Flipping the script: White privilege and community building* (Updated ed.). United States: MP Associates, Inc. and the Center for Assessment and Policy Development.

Potter, J. (1996–2009). Big Five Personality Test. Retrieved July 27, 2009, from http://www .outofservice.com/bigfive/

Press, E. (2012). *Beautiful souls: Saying no, breaking ranks, and heeding the voice of conscience in dark.* New York: Farrar, Straus and Giroux.

Prochaska, J.O. (1999). How do people change, and how can we change to help many more people? In M.A. Hubble, B.L. Duncan, & S.D. Miller (Eds.), *The heart and soul of change: What works in therapy* (pp. 227–255). Washington, DC: American Psychological Association.

Prochaska, J.O., & Norcross, J.C. (2007). *Systems of psychotherapy: A transtheoretical analysis* (6th ed.). Belmont, CA: Thomson Brooks/Cole.

Prochaska, J.O., Norcross, J.C., & DiClemente, C.C. (1994). *Changing for good: A revolutionary six-stage program for overcoming bad habits and moving your life positively forward.* New York: Avon.

Prochaska, J.O., & Velicera, W.F. (1998). Behavior change: The transtheoretical model of health behavior change. *American Journal of Health Promotion, 12*(1), 38–48.

Proctor, E.K., Morrow-Howell, N., & Kaplan, S.J. (1996). Implementation of discharge plans for chronically ill elders discharged home. *Health and Social Work, 21*(1), 30–40.

Putnam, R.D. (1995). Bowling alone: America's declining social capital. *Journal of Democracy, 6*(1), 65–78.

Putnam, R.D. (2001). Social capital: Measurement and consequences. *ISUMA: Canadian Journal of Policy Research, 2,* 41–51.

Putnam, R.D. (Ed.). (2002). *Democracies in flux: The evolution of social capital in contemporary society.* Oxford; New York: Oxford University Press.

Putnam, R.D., & Campbell, D.E. (2010). *American grace: How religion divides and unites us.* New York: Simon & Schuster.

Putnam, R.D., Feldstein, L.M., & Cohen, D. (2003). *Better together: Restoring the American community.* New York: Simon & Schuster.

Quann, V., & Wien, C.A. (2006, July). The visible empathy of infants and toddlers. *Beyond the Journal: Young Children on the Web.* Retrieved March 23, 2012, from http://www.naeyc.org/files /yc/file/200607/Quann709BTJ.pdf

Ragg, D.M. (2011). *Developing practice competencies: A foundation for generalist practice.* Hoboken, NJ: Wiley.

Ramirez-Valles, J. (2002). The protective effects of community involvement for HIV risk behavior: A conceptual framework. *Health Education Research, 17*(4), 389–403.

Rapp, C.A., & Goscha, R.J. (2006). *The strengths model: Case management with people with psychiatric disabilities* (2nd ed.). New York: Oxford University Press.

Rawls, J. (1958). *Justice as fairness.* New York: Irvington.

Rawls, J. (1971). *A theory of justice.* Cambridge, MA: Belknap Press of Harvard University Press.

Rawls, J. (1999). *A theory of justice* (Rev. ed.). Cambridge, MA: Belknap Press of Harvard University Press.

Rawls, J., & Kelly, E. (2001). *Justice as fairness: A restatement.* Cambridge, MA: Belknap Press of Harvard University Press.

Reamer, F.G. (1994). *Social work malpractice and liability.* New York: Columbia University Press.

Reamer, F.G. (1995a). Ethics and values. In R.L. Edwards (Ed.), *Encyclopedia of social work* (19th ed., Vol. 1, pp. 893–902). Washington, DC: NASW Press.

Reamer, F.G. (1995b). Malpractice claims against social workers: First facts. *Social Work, 40*(5), 595–601.

Reamer, F.G. (1997). Ethical standards in social work: The NASW Code of Ethics. In R.L. Edwards (Ed.), *Encyclopedia of social work, 1997 Supplement* (19th revised ed., Vol. Supplement). Washington, DC: NASW Press.

Reamer, F.G. (1998). *Ethical standards in social work: A critical review of the NASW Code of Ethics.* Washington, DC: NASW Press.

Reamer, F.G. (2000). The social work ethics audit: A risk-management strategy. *Social Work in Health Care, 45*(4), 355–366.

Reamer, F.G. (2008). Eye on Ethics: Deception in Social Work. *Social Work Today, 8*(6), 12–13.

Reamer, F.G., & Conrad, S.A.P. (1995). Professional choices: Ethics at work [Video]. Washington, DC: NASW Press.

Recent cases. (2001). Recent cases: Evidence-Sixth Circuit holds that Tarasoff disclosures do not vitiate psychotherapist-patient privilege-*United States v. Hayes*, 227 F.3d 578 (6th Cir. 2000). *Harvard Law Review, 114*(7), 2194–2200.

Reid, W.J. (1992). *Task strategies: An empirical approach to clinical social work.* New York: Columbia University Press.

Renard, J. (2002). *The handy religion answer book.* Detroit, MI: Visible Ink Press.

Reuters News Service. (2009, April 21). Social worker surrenders license after admitting guilt in judicial fraud case. Retrieved July 29, 2009, from http://www.reuters.com/article/pressRelease /idUS156370+21-Apr-2009+PRN2009042

Rhodes, M. (1986). Ethical dilemmas in social work practice. London: Routledge & Kegan Paul.

Rhodes, M. (1998). Ethical challenges in social work. *Families in Society: The Journal of Contemporary Human Services, 79*(3), 231–233.

Richmond, M.E. (1944). *Social diagnosis.* New York: The Free Press. First published in 1917.

Ripple, L. (1955). Motivation, capacity, and opportunity as related to the use of casework service: Plan of study. *Social Service Review, 29,* 172–193.

Ripple, L., & Alexander, E. (1956). Motivation, capacity, and opportunity as related to the use of casework service: Nature of client's problem. *Social Service Review, 30,* 38–54.

Ripple, L., Alexander, E., & Polemis, B.W. (1964). *Motivation, capacity, and opportunity: Studies in casework theory and practice.* Chicago: University of Chicago School of Social Service Administration.

Rocha, C.J. (2007). *Essentials of social work policy practice.* Hoboken, NJ: John Wiley & Sons.

Roeckelein, J.E. (1998). *Dictionary of theories, laws, and concepts in psychology.* Westport, CT: Greenwood Publishing.

Rogers, C.R. (1951). *Client centered therapy.* New York: Houghton Mifflin.

Rogers, C.R. (1957). The necessary and sufficient conditions of psychotherapeutic personality change. *Journal of Consulting Psychology, 21,* 95–103.

Rogers, C.R. (1961). *On becoming a person.* Boston: Houghton Mifflin.

Rogers, C.R. (1975). Empathic: An unappreciated way of being. *Counseling Psychologist, 5,* 2–10.

Rogers, J.R., Lewis, M.M., & Subich, L.M. (2002). Validity of the Suicide Assessment Checklist in an emergency crisis center. *Journal of Counseling and Development, 80*(4), 493–502.

Rollnick, S., & Miller, W.R. (1995). What is motivational interviewing? *Behavioural and Cognitive Psychotherapy, 23,* 325–334.

Rosenbaum, M. (1980). A schedule for assessing self-control behaviors: Preliminary findings. *Behavior Therapy,* 11, 109–121.

Rosenstock, I.M. (1990). The health belief model: Explaining health behavior through experiences. In K. Glanz, F. M. Lewis, & B. K. Rimer (Eds.), *Health behavior and health education: Theory, research and practice* (pp. 39–62). San Francisco, CA: Jossey-Bass.

Rosenstock, I.M., Strecher, V., & Becker, M. (1994). The Health Belief Model and HIV risk behavior change. In R.J. DiClemente & J.L. Peterson (Eds.), *Preventing AIDS: Theories and methods of behavioral interventions* (pp. 5–24). New York: Plenum Press.

Rosenstock, I.M., Strecher, V.J., & Becker, M.H. (1988). Social learning theory and the health belief model. *Health Education Quarterly, 15*(2), 175–193.

Rosenzweig, S. (1936). Some implicit common factors in diverse methods of psychotherapy. *American Journal of Orthopsychiatry, 6,* 412–415.

Ross, L.D. (1977). The intuitive psychologist and his shortcomings: Distortions in the attribution process. In L. Berkowitz (Ed.), *Advances in experimental social psychology* (Vol. 10, pp. 173–220). New York: Academic Press.

Roth, A., & Fonagy, P. (Eds.). (1996). *What works for whom? A critical review of psychotherapy research.* New York: The Guilford Press.

Rothenberg, P.S. (2002). *White privilege: Essential readings on the other side of racism.* New York: Worth Publishers.

Royse, D. (1995). *Research methods in social work* (2nd ed.). Chicago, IL: Nelson-Hall.

Roysircar, G. (2003). *Multicultural counseling competencies 2003: Association for Multicultural Counseling and Development.* Alexandria, VA: American Counseling Association.

Roysircar, G., Sandhu, D.S., & Bibbins, V.E. (Eds.). (2003). *Multicultural competencies: A guidebook of practices.* Alexandria, VA: American Counseling Association.

Rubin, A., & Babbie, E. (2001). *Research methods for social work* (4th ed.). Belmont, CA: Wadsworth.

Rubin, A., & Babbie, E.R. (2007). *Essential research methods for social work.* Belmont, CA: Thomson Brooks/Cole.

Rudner, L., Glass, G.V., Evartt, D.L., & Emery, P.J. (2000). *A user's guide to the meta-analysis of research studies.* College Park, MD: ERIC Clearinghouse on Assessment and Evaluation, University of Maryland.

Rush Jr., A.J., First, M.B., & Blacker, D. (Eds.). (2008). *Handbook of psychiatric measures* (2nd ed.). Washington, DC: American Psychiatric Publishing, Inc.

Rutter, M. (1979). Protective factors in children's responses to stress and disadvantage. *Annals of the Academy of Medicine Singapore, 8*(3), 324–338.

Rutter, M. (1985). Resilience in the face of adversity. Protective factors and resistance to psychiatric disorder. *British Journal of Psychiatry, 147,* 598–611.

Rutter, M. (1987). Psychosocial resilience and protective mechanisms. *American Journal of Orthopsychiatry, 57*(3), 316–331.

Rutter, P.A., & Behrendt, A.E. (2004). Adolescent suicide risk: Four psychosocial factors. *Adolescence, 39*(154), 295–302.

Rzepnicki, T.L., McCracken, S.G., & Briggs, H.E. (2012). *From task-centered social work to evidence-based and integrative practice: Reflections on history and implementation.* Chicago, IL: Lyceum Books.

Safran, J.D., & Muran, J.C. (2000). *Negotiating the therapeutic alliance: A relational treatment guide.* New York: Gulford.

Sagan, C. (1995). *The demon-haunted world: Science as a candle in the dark*. New York: Random House.

Saguaro Seminar of the Harvard University Kennedy School of Government. (2000). Social Capital Community Benchmark Survey. Retrieved September 4, 2009, from http://www.hks.harvard.edu/saguaro/communitysurvey/index.html

Saguaro Seminar of the Harvard University Kennedy School of Government. (2002, September). The Social Capital Community Benchmark Survey: Short Form. Retrieved September 4, 2009, from http://www.hks.harvard.edu/saguaro/pdfs/socialcapitalshortform.pdf

Saguaro Seminar of the Harvard University Kennedy School of Government. (2006). Social Capital Community Survey. Retrieved September 4, 2009, from http://www.hks.harvard.edu/saguaro/2006sccs.htm

Saleebey, D. (2001). The Diagnostic Strengths Manual? *Social Work, 46*(2), 183–187.

Saleebey, D. (Ed.). (2009). *The strengths perspective in social work practice* (5th ed.). Boston: Pearson.

Saltzman, A., & Proch, K. (1990). *Law in social work practice*. Chicago, IL: Nelson-Hall.

Samantrai, K. (2004). *Culturally competent public child welfare practice*. Pacific Grove, CA: Brooks/Cole.

Sánchez-Meca, J., Rosa-Alcázar, A.I., Marín-Martínez, F., & Gómez-Conesa, A. (2010a). Corrigendum to "Psychological treatment of panic disorder with or without agoraphobia: A meta-analysis". *Clinical Psychology Review, 30*(6), 815–817. doi: 10.1016/j.cpr.2010.05.005

Sánchez-Meca, J., Rosa-Alcázar, A.I., Marín-Martínez, F., & Gómez-Conesa, A. (2010b). Psychological treatment of panic disorder with or without agoraphobia: A meta-analysis. *Clinical Psychology Review, 30*(1), 37–50. doi: 10.1016/j.cpr.2009.08.011

Sandel, M.J. (1982). *Liberalism and the limits of justice*. New York: Cambridge University Press.

Sandel, M.J. (2009). *Justice: What's the right thing to do?* New York: Farrar, Straus and Giroux.

Sands, R.G., & Gellis, Z.D. (2012). *Clinical social work practice in behavioral mental health: Toward evidence-based practice*. Boston: Allyn & Bacon.

Sar, B.K. (2000). Preparation for adoptive parenthood with a special-needs child: Role of agency preparation tasks. *Adoption Quarterly, 3*(4), 63–80.

Satir, V. (1972). *Peoplemaking*. Palo Alto, CA: Science and Behavior Books.

Saucier, D.A., Miller, C. T., & Doucet, N. (2005). Differences in helping Whites and Blacks: A meta-analysis. *Personality and Social Psychology Review, 9*, 2–16.

Savani, K., & Rattan, A. (2012). A choice mind-set increases the acceptance and maintenance of wealth inequality. *Psychological Science, 23*(7), 796–804. doi: 10.1177/0956797611434540

Savani, K., Stephens, N.M., & Markus, H.R. (2011). The unanticipated interpersonal and societal consequences of choice: Victim blaming and reduced support for the public good. *Psychological Science, 22*(6), 795–802. doi: 10.1177/0956797611407928

Scanlon, P.M., & Neumann, D.R. (2002). Internet plagiarism among college students. *Journal of College Student Development, 43*(3), 374–385.

Schneider, R.L., & Lester, L. (2001). *Social work advocacy: A new framework for action*. Belmont, CA: Wadsworth/Thomson Learning.

Schon, D.A. (1990). *Educating the reflective practitioner: Toward a new design for teaching and learning in the professions*. New York: John Wiley & Sons.

Schutte, N.S., & Malouff, J.M. (1995). *Sourcebook of adult assessment strategies*. New York: Plenum Press.

Schwartz, W. (1971). On the use of groups in social work practice. In W. Schwartz & S. Zalba (Eds.), *The practice of group work* (pp. 3–24). New York: Columbia University Press.

Schwartz, W. (1976). Between client and system: The mediating function. In R.R. Roberts & H. Northen (Eds.), *Theories of social work with groups* (pp. 188–190). New York: Columbia University Press.

Schwarzer, R. (2011). Everything you wanted to know about the General Self-Efficacy Scale but were afraid to ask. Retrieved June 13, 2012, from http://userpage.fu-berlin.de/~health/faq_gse.pdf

Schwarzer, R. (Ed.). (1992). *Self-efficacy: Thought control of action*. Washington, DC: Hemisphere.

Schwarzer, R., & Fuchs, R. (1995). Changing risk behaviors and adopting health behaviors: The role of self-efficacy beliefs. In A. Bandura (Ed.), *Self-efficacy in changing societies* (pp. 259–288). New York: Cambridge University Press.

Schwarzer, R., & Jerusalem, M. (1995). Generalized Self-Efficacy Scale. In J. Weinman, S. Wright, and M. Johnston, *Measures in health psychology: A user's portfolio. Causal and control beliefs* (pp. 35–37). Windsor, UK: NFER-NELSON.

Scovern, A.W. (1999). From placebo to alliance: The role of common factors in medicine. In M.A. Hubble, B.L. Duncan, & S.D. Miller (Eds.), *The heart and soul of change: What works in therapy* (pp. 259–295). Washington, DC: American Psychological Association.

Seabury, B. (1975). Negotiating sound contracts with clients. *Public Welfare, 37*, 33–39.

Seabury, B. (1976). The contract: Uses, abuses and limitations. *Social Work, 21*, 16–21.

Seligman, M.E.P. (2002). *Authentic happiness: Using the new positive psychology to realize your potential for lasting fulfillment*. New York: Free Press.

Seligman, M.E.P. (2011). *Flourish: a visionary new understanding of happiness and well-being*. New York: Free Press.

Seligman, M.E.P., & Csikszentmihalyi, M. (2000). Positive psychology: An introduction. *American Psychologist, 55*, 5–14.

Selzer, M.L. (1971). The Michigan Alcoholism Screening Test: The question for a new diagnostic instrument. *American Journal of Psychiatry, 127*, 1653–1658.

Selzer, M.L., Vinokur, A., & van Rooijen, L. (1975). A self-administered Short Michigan Alcoholism Screening Test (SMAST). *Journal of Studies on Alcohol and Drugs, 36*(1), 117–126.

Senge, P.M. (1992). Building learning organizations. *Journal of Quality and Participation, 15*(2), 30–38.

Shermer, M. (1997). *Why people believe weird things: Pseudoscience, superstition, and other confusions of our time.* New York: W. H. Freeman Company.

Shermer, M. (2001, December). More baloney detection: How to draw boundaries between science and pseudoscience, Part II. *Scientific American, 285,* 34. doi: 10.1038/scientificamerican1201-34

Shermer, M. (2001, November). Baloney detection: How to draw boundaries between science and pseudoscience, Part I. *Scientific American, 285,* 36–36. doi: 10.1038/scientificamerican1101-36

Shermer, M. (2009). The Baloney Detection Kit. Retrieved September 10, 2009, from http://www.michaelshermer.com/2009/06/baloney-detection-kit

Shierholz, H. (2012, February 3). U.S. labor market starts 2012 with solid positive signs but fewer jobs than it had 11 years ago. Retrieved March 3, 2012, from http://www.epi.org/publication/labor-market-starts-2012-solid-positive/

Shifrel, S. (2009, June 25). New York Daily News: Bar mitzvah tutor guilty in molests. Retrieved July 29, 2009, from http://www.nydailynews.com/news/ny_crime/2009/06/25/2009-06-25_bar_mitzvah_tutor_guilty_in_molests.html

Shulman, L. (1992). *The skills of helping individuals, families, and groups* (3rd ed.). Itasca, IL: F. E. Peacock.

Shulman, L. (2009). *The skills of helping individuals, families, groups, and communities* (6th ed.). Belmont, CA: Wadsworth.

Shuman, A.L., & Shapiro, J.P. (2002). The effects of preparing parents for child psychotherapy on accuracy of expectations and treatment attendance. *Community Mental Health Journal, 38*(1), 3–16.

Sidell, N., & Smiley, D. (2008). *Professional communication skills in social work.* Boston: Allyn & Bacon/Pearson.

Siegel, D.J. (2012a). *The developing mind: How relationships and the brain interact to shape who we are* (2nd ed.). New York: Guilford Press.

Siegel, D.J. (2012b). *Pocket guide to interpersonal neurobiology: An integrative handbook of the mind.* New York: W.W. Norton.

Simkin, M.G., & McLeod, A. (2010). Why do college students cheat? *Journal of Business Ethics, 94*(3), 441–453. doi: 10.1007/s10551-009-0275-x

Sinha, S.P., Nayyar, P., & Sinha, S.P. (2002). Social support and self-control as variables in attitude toward life and perceived control among older people in India. *Journal of Social Psychology, 42*(4), 527–541.

Skinner, H.A. (1982). The Drug Abuse Screening Test. *Addictive Behaviors, 7*(4), 363–371. doi: 10.1016/0306-4603(82)90005-3

Small, S. (2000). Introduction to prevention. Retrieved July 25, 2006, from http://wch.uhs.wisc.edu/01-Prevention/01-Prev-Intro.html

Smalley, R.E. (1967). *Theory for social work practice.* New York: Columbia University Press.

Smiley, T., & West, C. (2012). *The rich and the rest of us: A poverty manifesto.* New York: SmileyBooks.

Smokowski, P.R. (1998). Prevention and intervention strategies for promoting resilience in disadvantaged children. *Social Service Review, 72*(3), 337–365.

Smokowski, P.R., Mann, E.A., Reynolds, A.J., & Fraser, M.W. (2004). Childhood risk and protective factors and late adolescent adjustment in inner city minority youth. *Children and Youth Services Review, 26*(1), 63–91.

Smuts, B. (1995). The evolutionary origins of patriarchy. *Human Nature, 6*(1), 1–32. doi: 10.1007/bf02734133

Snider, L. (2012, April 19). Jury finds Karen Stevens, Boulder-area social worker, guilty of Medicare fraud. *Daily Camera.* Retrieved from http://www.dailycamera.com/boulder-county-news/ci_20435916/jury-finds-karen-stevens-boulder-area-social-worker

Snyder, C.R., & Lopez, S.J. (Eds.). (2005). *Handbook of positive psychology.* New York: Oxford University Press.

Sommers, S. (2011). *Situations matter: Understanding how context transforms your world.* New York: Riverhead.

Sorrells, K. (2013). *Intercultural communication: Globalization and social justice.* Thousand Oaks, CA: Sage.

Sowers, K.M., & Dulmus, C.N. (Eds.). (2008). *Comprehensive handbook of social work and social welfare.* Hoboken, N.J.: John Wiley & Sons.

Sparks, J.A., & Duncan, B.L. (2010). Common factors and family therapy: Must all have prizes? In B.L. Duncan, S.D. Miller, B.E. Wampold, & M.A. Hubble (Eds.), *The heart and soul of change: Delivering what works in therapy* (2nd ed., pp. 357–391). Washington, DC: American Psychological Association.

Spears, V.H. (2012, July 24). Ex-state social worker sentenced to five years for falsifying child-abuse reports. *Lexington Herald-Leader.* Retrieved from http://www.kentucky.com/2012/07/24/2268971/ex-state-social-worker-sentenced.html

Specter, M. (2011, December 12). The power of nothing. *The New Yorker, 87*(40), 30–36.

Spence, T. (1775). The real rights of man: A lecture to the Philosophical Society of Newcastle. Retrieved June 30, 2009, from http://www.ditext.com/spence/rights.html

Spitzer, R.L., Williams, J.B.W., & Endicott, J. (2012). Standards for DSM-5 Reliability. *The American Journal of Psychiatry, 169*(5), 537–538.

Sprenkle, D.H., Blow, A.J., & Dickey, M.H. (1999). Common factors and other nontechnique variables in marriage and family therapy. In M.A. Hubble, B.L. Duncan, & S.D. Miller (Eds.), *The heart and soul of change: What works in therapy* (pp. 329–359). Washington, DC: American Psychological Association.

Srivastava, S. (2006). Measuring the Big Five Personality Factors. Retrieved June 24, 2006, from http://www.uoregon.edu/~sanjay/bigfive.html

Srivastava, S., John, O.P., Gosling, S.D., & Potter, J. (2003). Development of personality in early and middle adulthood: Set like plaster or persistent change? *Journal of Personality and Social Psychology, 84*, 1041–1053.

Stanovich, K.E. (1999). *Who is rational? Studies of individual differences in reasoning*. Mahweh, NJ: Lawrence Erlbaum.

Stiglitz, J.E. (2012). *The price of inequality: How today's divided society endangers our future*. New York: W.W. Norton.

Stotland, E. (2001). Empathy. In W.E. Craighead & C.B. Nemeroff (Eds.), *The Corsini encyclopedia of psychology and behavioral science* (3rd ed.). New York: Wiley.

Strom-Gottfried, K.J. (1999). Professional boundaries: An analysis of violations by social workers. *Families in Society: The Journal of Contemporary Human Services, 80*(5), 439–450.

Strom-Gottfried, K.J. (2000a). Ensuring ethical practice: An examination of NASW code violations, 1986-97. *Social Work in Health Care, 45*(3), 251–261.

Strom-Gottfried, K.J. (2000b). Ethical vulnerability in social work education: An analysis of NASW complaints. *Journal of Social Work Education, 36*(2), 241–252.

Strom-Gottfried, K.J. (2003). Understanding adjudication: Origins, targets, and outcomes of ethics complaints. *Social Work in Health Care, 48*(1), 85–95.

Substance Abuse and Mental Health Services Administration. (2012a). National Registry of Evidence-based Programs and Practices (NREPP). Retrieved July 16, 2012, from http://www.nrepp.samhsa.gov/Index.aspx

Substance Abuse and Mental Health Services Administration. (2012b). Practice guidelines. Retrieved July 16, 2012, from http://store.samhsa.gov/facet/Professional-Research-Topics/term/Practice-Guidelines

Sue, D.W. (1977). Counseling the culturally different: A conceptual analysis. *Personnel and Guidance Journal, 55*, 422–425.

Sue, D.W. (2006). *Multicultural social work practice*. Hoboken, NJ: Wiley.

Sue, D.W., & Sue, D. (2008). *Counseling the culturally diverse: Theory and practice* (5th ed.). New York: Wiley.

Sundman, P. (1997). Solution-focused ideas in social work. *Journal of Family Therapy, 19*(2), 159–172.

Sutton, A.J., Abrams, K.R., Jones, D.R., Sheldon, T.A., & Song, F. (2000). *Methods for meta-analysis in medical research*. New York: John Wiley and Sons.

Swift, J.K., & Greenberg, R.P. (2012). Premature discontinuation in adult psychotherapy: A meta-analysis. *Journal of Consulting and Clinical Psychology*. doi: 10.1037/a0028226

Swift, J.K., Greenberg, R.P., Whipple, J.L., & Kominiak, N. (2012). Practice recommendations for reducing premature termination in therapy. *Professional Psychology: Research and Practice, 43*(4), 379–387. doi: 10.1037/a0028291

Szasz, T.S. (2007). *The medicalization of everyday life: Selected essays*. Syracuse, NY: Syracuse University Press.

Szumal, J.L. (2003). *Organizational Culture Inventory interpretation and development guide*. Plymouth, MI: Human Synergistics International.

Tallman, K., & Bohart, A.C. (1999). The client as a common factor: Clients as self-healers. In M.A. Hubble, B.L. Duncan, & S.D. Miller (Eds.), *The heart and soul of change: What works in therapy* (pp. 91–131). Washington, DC: American Psychological Association.

Tannen, D. (1990). *You just don't understand: Women and men in conversation*. New York: Morrow.

Tannen, D. (1994). *Talking from 9 to 5: How women's and men's conversational styles affect who gets heard, who gets credit, and what gets done at work*. New York: Morrow.

Tannen, D. (2001). The power of talk: Who gets heard and why. In I. Asherman & S. Asherman (Eds.), *The Negotiation Sourcebook* (2nd ed., pp. 245–257). Amherst, MA: HRD Press.

The Associated Press. (2000). Former state social worker admits he stole $1,900 from foster child. *The Seattle Times*. Retrieved from http://community.seattletimes.nwsource.com/archive/?date=20000331&slug=4012840

The British Psychological Society. (2008). *Guidelines on memory and the law: Recommendations from the scientific study of human memory, A report from the Research Board*. Leicester, UK: Author.

The Campbell Collaboration. (2012a). The Campbell Library of Systematic Reviews. Retrieved August 3, 2012, from http://www.campbellcollaboration.org/library.php/

The Campbell Collaboration. (2012b). What helps? What harms? Based on what evidence? Retrieved July 16, 2012, from http://www.campbellcollaboration.org/

The Cochrane Collaboration. (2002). What is a meta-analysis? Retrieved August 1, 2012, from http://www.cochrane-net.org/openlearning/HTML/mod12-2.htm

The Cochrane Collaboration. (2012a). Cochrane reviews. Retrieved August 3, 2012, from http://www.cochrane.org/cochrane-reviews

The Cochrane Collaboration. (2012b). Working together to provide the best evidence for health care. Retrieved July 16, 2012, from http://www.cochrane.org/

The New York Times staff. (2003a, May 11). Correcting the record: Times reporter who resigned leaves long trail of deception, *New York Times*, p. A1.

The New York Times staff. (2003b, May 11). Witnesses and documents unveil deceptions in a reporter's work, *New York Times*, p. A26.

The World Bank Social Capital Thematic Group. (2009). Measurement tools-social capital. Retrieved September 3, 2009, from http://go.worldbank.org/KO0QFVW770

Tingley, J.C. (2001). *The power of indirect influence*. New York: AMACOM Books.

Toffler, A. (1983). *The third wave*. New York: Bantam.

Tolson, E.R., Reid, W.J., & Garvin, C.D. (1994). *Generalist practice: A task-centered approach*. New York: Columbia University Press.

Toulmin, S. (1981). The tyranny of principles. *Hastings Center Report, 11*(6), 31–39.

Trout, J.D. (2009). *Why empathy matters: The science and psychology of better judgment*. New York: Penguin.

Truax, D.B., & Carkhuff, R.R. (1967). *Toward effective counseling and pyschotherapy: Training and practice*. Chicago; New York: Aldine Atherton.

Turner, R.J., & Marino, F. (1994). Social support and social structure: A descriptive epidemiology. *Journal of Health of Social Behavior, 35*, 193–212.

Tuzman, L., & Cohen, A. (1992). Clinical decision making for discharge planning in a changing psychiatric environment. *Health and Social Work, 17*(4), 299–307.

Twenge, J.M. (2006). *Generation me: Why today's young Americans are more confident, assertive, entitled—And more miserable than ever before*. New York: Free Press.

Twenge, J.M., & Campbell, K. (2009). *The narcissism epidemic: Living in the age of entitlement*. New York: Free Press.

Twenge, J.M., Konrath, S., Foster, J.D., Campbell, W.K., & Bushman, B.J. (2008). Egos inflating over time: A cross-temporal meta-analysis of the Narcissistic Personality Inventory. *Journal of Personality, 76*(4), 875–902. doi: 10.1111/j.1467-6494.2008.00507.x

U.S. Census Bureau. (2008). U.S. Census Bureau News: An older and more diverse nation by midcentury. Retrieved July 17, 2009, from http://www.census.gov/Press-Release/www/releases/archives/population/012496.html

U.S. Census Bureau. (2009). U.S. POPClock projection. Retrieved July 19, 2009, from http://www.census.gov/population/www/popclockus.html

U.S. Census Bureau. (2012). 2010 American Community Survey. Retrieved July 9, 2012, from http://www.census.gov/acs/www/

U.S. Census Bureau Current Population Survey. (2008). Annual Social and Economic Supplement, POV 46, *Poverty Status by State: 2007*. Retrieved August 4, 2009, from http://www.census.gov/hhes/www/macro/032008/pov/new46_100125_01.htm

U.S. Citizen and Immigration Services. (2009). Lawful Permanent residence ("Green Card"). Retrieved August 27, 2009, from http://www.uscis.gov/greencard

U.S. Department of Agriculture Food and Nutrition Services. (2012, April 11). Supplemental Nutrition Assistance Program (SNAP). Retrieved July 7, 2012, from http://www.fns.usda.gov/snap/applicant_recipients/eligibility.htm#income

U.S. Department of Education National Center for Education Statistics. (1997). A brochure: protecting the privacy of student education. Retrieved July 11, 2009, from http://nces.ed.gov/pubs97/P97527/Appdx_a.asp

U.S. Department of Education National Center for Education Statistics. (1998). FERPA fact sheet. Retrieved July 11, 2009, from http://nces.ed.gov/pubs98/safetech/appendix-b.asp

U.S. Department of Health and Human Services. (2001). Standards for privacy of individually identifiable health information. Retrieved August 10, 2009, from http://aspe.hhs.gov/admnsimp/final/pvcguide1.htm

U.S. Department of Health and Human Services. (2005). 42CFR2-Part 2: Confidentiality of alcohol and drug abuse patient records. Retrieved August 10, 2009, from http://www.access.gpo.gov/nara/cfr/waisidx_06/42cfr2_06.html

U.S. Department of Health and Human Services. (2009). Health information privacy. Retrieved August 10, 2009, from http://www.hhs.gov/ocr/privacy/index.html

U.S. Department of Health and Human Services. (2012). National guideline clearinghouse. Retrieved July 16, 2012, from http://www.guideline.gov

U.S. Department of Health and Human Services Office of Minority Health. (2009a). Health care language services implementation guide. Retrieved August 13, 2009, from https://www.thinkculturalhealth.org

U.S. Department of Health and Human Services Office of Minority Health. (2009b). Think cultural health: Bridging the health care gap through cultural competency continuing education programs. Retrieved August 13, 2009, from https://www.thinkculturalhealth.org

U.S. Department of Health and Human Services' Office on Women's Health, & General Services Administration's Federal Citizen Information Center. (2012). Breastfeeding Resources Action Kit. Retrieved August 5, 2012, from http://promotions.usa.gov/breastfeeding.html

U.S. Department of Justice. (2009). Americans with Disabilities Act (ADA) homepage: Information and Technical assistance. Retrieved August 10, 2009, from http://www.ada.gov

U.S. Department of Labor. (2012, January 1). Wage and Hour Division (WHD): minimum wage laws in the states. Retrieved July 6, 2012, from http://www.dol.gov/whd/minwage/america.htm

U.S. Department of Labor. (2012, March 29). Bureau of Labor Statistics Occupational Outlook Handbook, 2012-13 Edition, Social Workers. Retrieved April 12, 2012, from http://www.bls.gov/ooh/community-and-social-service/social-workers.htm

Ujifusa, A. (2008, July 30). Gazette.net: Chevy Chase social worker sentenced for fraud. Retrieved July 29, 2009, from http://www.gazette.net/stories/073008/bethnew215338_32592.shtml

UNICEF. (2009). Breastfeeding initiatives exchange: Why breastfeed? Retrieved August 8, 2009, from http://www.unicef.org/programme/breastfeeding

United Nations. (1979). Convention on the elimination of all forms of discrimination against women (CEDAW). Retrieved July 31, 2009, from http://www.un.org/womenwatch/daw/cedaw

United Nations. (1989, December 12). Convention on the rights of the child. Retrieved July 31, 2009, from http://www.unicef.org/crc

United Nations. (2006, December 13). Convention on the rights of persons with disabilities. Retrieved

July 31, 2009, from http://www.un.org/disabilities /default.asp?navid=12&pid=150

United Nations. (2012). The future we want: Outcome of Rio+20: United Nations Conference on Sustainable Development. Retrieved July 7, 2012, from http://daccess-dds-ny.un.org/doc /UNDOC/GEN/N12/381/64/PDF/N1238164 .pdf?OpenElement

United Nations Conference on Environment and Development. (1992). Convention on biological diversity. Retrieved September 10, 2009, from http://www.cbd.int/history

United Nations Development Programme. (2011a). Human development index. Retrieved July 10, 2012, from http://hdr.undp.org/en/statistics/hdi/

United Nations Development Programme. (2011b). *Human Development Report 2011: Sustainability and Equity: A Better Future for All*. New York: Palgrave Macmillan. Retrieved from http:// hdr.undp.org/en/media/HDR_2011_EN_ Complete.pdf

United Nations Human Development Programme. (2011). Gender Inequality Index (GII): Frequently asked questions. Retrieved July 10, 2012, from http://hdr.undp.org/en/statistics/gii/

United Nations Office of the High Commissioner for Human Rights. (1996). Fact Sheet No.2 (Rev.1), The International Bill of Human Rights. Retrieved July 1, 2009, from http://www.unhchr.ch /html/menu6/2/fs2.htm

United States v. Hayes, 227 F. 3d 578 (6th Cir. 2000).

Valor-Segura, I., Exposito, F., & Moya, M. (2011). Victim blaming and exoneration of the perpetrator in domestic violence: The role of beliefs in a just world and ambivalent sexism. *The Spanish Journal of Psychology, 14*(1), 195–206.

Van Prooijen, J.-W., & Van den Bos, K. (2009). We blame innocent victims more than I do: Self-construal level moderates responses to just-world threats. *Personality and Social Psychology Bulletin, 35*(11), 1528–1539. doi: 10.1177/0146167209344728

Van Soest, D., & Garcia, B. (2003). *Diversity education for social justice: Mastering teaching skills*. Alexandria, VA: Counseling on Social Work Education.

VandeCreek, L., & Knapp, S. (1993). *Tarasoff and beyond: Legal and clinical considerations in the treatment of life-endangering patients* (Rev. ed.). Sarasota, FL: Professional Resource Press.

VandeCreek, L., & Knapp, S. (2001). *Tarasoff and beyond: Legal and clinical considerations in the treatment of life-endangering patients* (3rd ed.). Sarasota, FL: Professional Resource Press.

Vaux, A., Phillips, J., Holly, L., Thompson, B., Williams, D., & Stewart, D. (1986). The Social Support Appraisals (SSA) Scale: Studies of reliability and validity. *American Journal of Community Psychology, 14*(2), 195–219.

Verwey, B., van Waarde, J., Bozdag, M., van Rooij, I., De Beurs, E., & Zitman, F. (2010). Reassessment of suicide attempters at home, shortly after discharge from hospital. *Crisis, 31*(6), 303–310.

Videka-Sherman, L. (1988). Meta-analysis of research on social work practice in mental health. *Social Work, 33*, 325–338.

Videka-Sherman, L. (1995). Meta-analysis. In R.L. Edwards (Ed.), *Encylopedia of social work* (19th ed., Vol. 2, pp. 1711–1720). Washington, DC: NASW Press.

Vinter, R.D. (1963). Analysis of treatment organizations. *Social Work, 8*, 3–15.

Virués-Ortega, J., & Haynes, S.N. (2005). Functional analysis in behavior therapy: Behavioral foundations and clinical application. *International Journal of Clinical and Health Psychology, 5*(3), 567–587.

Wakefield, H., & Underwager, R. (1992). Recovered memories of alleged sexual abuse: Lawsuits against parents. *Behavioral Sciences & the Law, 10*(4), 483–507.

Wakefield, J.C. (2012). Should prolonged grief be reclassified as a mental disorder in DSM-5? Reconsidering the empirical and conceptual arguments for complicated grief disorder. *The Journal of Nervous and Mental Disorders, 200*(6), 499–511. doi: 10.1097/NMD.0b013e3182482155

Walmsley, R. (2009). *World prison population list* (8th ed.). London: King's College London International Centre for Prison Studies.

Walsh, F. (2006). *Strengthening family resilience [electronic resource]* (2nd ed.). New York: Guilford Press.

Wampold, B.E. (2001). *The great psychotherapy debate: Models, methods, and findings*. Mahwah, NJ: Lawrence Erlbaum.

Wampold, B.E. (2010). The research evidence for common factors models: A historically situated perspective. In B.L. Duncan, S.D. Miller, B.E. Wampold, & M.A. Hubble (Eds.), *The heart and soul of change: Delivering what works in therapy* (2nd ed., pp. 49–81). Washington, DC: American Psychological Association.

Watson, J.C., & Kalogerakos, F. (2010). The therapeutic alliance in humanistic psychotherapy. In J.C. Muran & J.P. Barber (Eds.), *The therapeutic alliance: An evidence-based guide to practice* (pp. 191–209). New York: The Guilford Press.

Wattendorf, D.J., & Hadley, D.W. (2005). Family history: The three-generation pedigree. *American Family Physician, 72*, 441–448.

Weaver, H.N. (2004). The elements of cultural competence: Applications with Native American clients. *Journal of Ethnic & Cultural Diversity in Social Work, 13*(1), 19–35.

Weaver, H.N., & Bearse, M.L. (2008). Native Americans. In T. Mizrahi & L.E. Davis (Eds.), *Encyclopedia of social work* (20th, e-reference ed.). New York: National Association of Social Workers and Oxford University Press.

Wegscheider-Cruse, S. (1985). *Choice-making*. Pompano Beach, FL: Health Communications.

Weinberger, J. (1993). Common factors in psychotherapy. In G. Stricker & J.R. Gold (Eds.), *Comprehensive handbook of psychotherapy integration* (pp. 43–58). New York: Plenum.

Weinberger, J. (1995). Common factors aren't so common: The common factors dilemma. *Clinical Psychology: Science and Practice, 2*, 45–69.

Weinberger, J. (2003). Common factors. In W.E. Craighead & C.B. Nemeroff (Eds.), *The Corsini encyclopedia of psychology and behavioral science*. New York: John Wiley & Sons.

Werner, E.E. (1986). Resilient offspring of alcoholics: A longitudinal study from birth to age 18. *Journal of Studies on Alcohol and Drugs, 47*(1), 34–40.

Werner, E.E. (1989). High-risk children in young adulthood: A longitudinal study from birth to 32 years. *American Journal of Orthopsychiatry, 59*(1), 72–81.

West, R. (2005). Time for a change: putting the Transtheoretical (Stages of Change) Model to rest. *Addiction, 100*(8), 1036–1039. doi: 10.1111/j.1360-0443.2005.01139.x

Western, B. (2006). *Punishment and inequality in America*. New York: Russell Sage.

Whipple, J.L., & Lambert, M.J. (2011). Outcome measures for practice. *Annual Review of Clinical Psychology, 7*(1), 87–111. doi: 10.1146/annurev-clinpsy-040510-143938

Whitaker, R. (2010). *Anatomy of an epidemic: Magic bullets, psychiatric drugs, and the astonishing rise of mental illness in America*. New York: Crown Publishing.

Whitfield, C.L., Whitfield, B.H., Park, R., & Prevatt, J. (2006). *The power of humility: Choosing peace over conflict in relationships*. Deerfield Beach, FL: Health Communications.

Whitfield, K.E., & Wiggins, S. (2003). The influence of social support and health on everyday problem solving in adult African Americans. *Experimental Aging Research, 29*(1), 1–13.

Whittaker, J.K. (2001). The context of youth violence: Resilience, risk and protection. *Social Service Review, 75*(4), 682–684.

Wierzbicki, M., & Pekarik, G. (1993). A meta-analysis of psychotherapy dropout. *Professional Psychology Research and Practice, 24*, 190–195.

Wikipedia. (2012). Lists of ethnic groups. Retrieved July 20, 2012, from http://en.wikipedia.org/wiki/Lists_of_ethnic_groups

Williams, J.B. (1994). PIE research issues. In J.M. Karls & K.E. Wandrei (Eds.), *Person-In-Environment (PIE) System: The PIE classification system for social functioning problems* (pp. 197–202). Washington, DC: NASW Press.

Williams, J.B. (2008). Diagnostic and statistical manual of mental disorders. In T. Mizrahi & L.E. Davis (Eds.), *Encyclopedia of social work* (20th, e-reference ed.). New York: National Association of Social Workers and Oxford University Press.

Williams, J.B., Karls, J.M., & Wandrei, K.E. (1989). The Person-in-Environment (PIE) system for describing problems of social functioning. *Hospital and Community Psychiatry, 40*(11), 1125–1127.

Wilson, D.B. (2012). Practical Meta-Analysis Effect Size Calculator. Retrieved August 1, 2012, from http://www.campbellcollaboration.org/resources/effect_size_input.php

Wilson, S.J. (1980). *Recording: Guidelines for social workers*. New York: The Free Press.

Witte, J., & Green, M.C. (2012). *Religion and human rights: An introduction*. New York: Oxford University Press.

Wodarski, J.S. (1992). Social work practice with Hispanic Americans. In D.F. Harrison, J.S. Wodarski, & B.A. Thyer (Eds.), *Cultural diversity and social work practice* (pp. 71–106). Springfield, IL: Charles C. Thomas.

Wodarski, J.S., & Hopson, L.M. (2012). *Research methods for evidence-based practice*. Los Angeles, CA: Sage.

Woititz, J.G. (1983). *Adult children of alcoholics*. Pompano Beach, FL: Health Communications.

Wolman, B.B. (Ed.). (1973). *Dictionary of behavioral science*. New York: Van Nostrand Reinhold.

Womack, T.J.C. (2001). Placebo response in clinical trials [Article]. *Applied Clinical Trials, 10*(2), 32.

Woodruff, P. (2001). *Reverence: Renewing a forgotten virtue*. New York: Oxford University Press.

Woody, R.H. (1997). *Legally safe mental health practice: Psycholegal questions and answers*. Madison, CT: Psychosocial Press.

World Bank. (2011, July). Gross national income per capita 2010, Atlas method and PPP. Retrieved July 2, 2012, from http://siteresources.worldbank.org/DATASTATISTICS/Resources/GNIPC.pdf

World Health Organization. (2007). International classification of diseases-10th revision. Retrieved September 25, 2009, from http://apps.who.int/classifications/apps/icd/icd10online

World Health Organization. (2009). Infant and young child feeding: Model chapter for textbooks for medical students and allied health professionals. Retrieved from http://whqlibdoc.who.int/publications/2009/9789241597494_eng.pdf

World People's Conference on Climate Change and the Rights of Mother Earth. (2010a). People's agreement. Retrieved from http://pwccc.wordpress.com/support/

World People's Conference on Climate Change and the Rights of Mother Earth. (2010b). Universal declaration of the rights of mother earth. Retrieved from http://pwccc.wordpress.com/programa/

World Values Survey. (2009). The world's most comprehensive investigation of political and sociocultural change. Retrieved August 3, 2009, from http://www.worldvaluessurvey.org

Wright, D.A. (2004). Risk and protective factors for adolescent drug use: Findings from the 1999 National Household Survey on Drug Abuse. Retrieved July 23, 2006, from http://www.oas.samhsa.gov/1999Prevention/HTML/toc.htm

Wright, R. (1995). *The moral animal: The new science of evolutionary psychology*. New York: Vintage.

WSLS-TV Staff Reports. (2010, October 27). Former Grayson Co. social worker admits to stealing from elderly. Retrieved July 24, 2012, from http://www2.wsls.com/news/2010/oct/27/2/former-grayson-co-social-worker-admits-stealing-el-ar-590532/

Wynn, M. (2012, May 23). Ex-social worker pleads guilty in records tampering. *Louisville Courier-Journal*. Retrieved from http://www.courier-journal .com/article/20120522/NEWS01/305210091/ Ex-social-worker-pleads-guilty-records-tampering

Yale Center for Environmental Law and Policy. (2012). Environmental performance index 2012. Retrieved July 10, 2012, from http://epi.yale.edu/epi2012 /rankings

Yalom, I.D., Houts, P.S., Newell, G., & Rand, K.H. (1967). Preparation of patients for group therapy. A controlled study. *Archives of General Psychiatry, 17*(4), 416–427.

Yegidis, B.L., & Weinbach, R.W. (2002). *Research methods for social workers* (4th ed.). Boston: Allyn & Bacon.

Yegidis, B.L., Weinbach, R.W., & Morrison-Rodriquez, B. (1999). *Research methods for social workers* (3rd ed.). Boston: Allyn and Bacon.

Zimbardo, P.G. (2007). *The Lucifer effect: Understanding how good people turn evil*. New York: Random House.

Zuniga, M.E. (2001). Latinos: Cultural competence and ethics. In R. Fong & S. Furuto (Eds.), *Culturally competent practice* (pp. 47–60). Boston: Allyn & Bacon.

Zuniga, M.E. (2003). Cultural competence with Latino Americans. In D. Lum (Ed.), *Culturally competent practice: A framework for understanding diverse groups and justice issues* (2nd ed., pp. 238–260). Pacific Grove, CA: Brooks/Cole.

INDEX